CAREER COUNSELING

Foundations, Perspectives, and Applications

200l01

DAVID CAPUZZI

Johns Hopkins University
Professor Emeritus, Portland State University

MARK D. STAUFFER

Oregon State University

Boston ■ New York ■ San Francisco ■ Mexico City ■ Montreal
Toronto ■ London ■ Madrid ■ Munich ■ Paris ■ Hong Kong
Singapore ■ Tokyo ■ Cape Town ■ Sydney

Executive Editor: *Virginia Lanigan*
Series Editorial Assistant: *Scott Blaszak*
Marketing Manager: *Kris Ellis-Levy*
Composition and Prepress Buyer: *Andrew Turso*
Manufacturing Buyer: *Andrew Turso*
Cover Coordinator: *Joel Gendron*
Editorial-Production Coordinator: *Mary Beth Finch*
Editorial-Production Service: *Stratford Publishing Services*
Electronic Composition: *Stratford Publishing Services*

For related titles and support materials, visit our online catalog at www.ablongman.com

Between the time Web site information is gathered and then published, it is not unusual for some sites to have closed. Also, the transcription of URLs can result in unintended typographical errors. The publisher would appreciate notification where these errors occur so that they may be corrected in subsequent editions.

Library of Congress Cataloging-in-Publication Data

Career counseling : foundations, perspectives, and applications / David Capuzzi and Mark D. Stauffer [editors].
    p. cm.
  Includes bibliographical references and index.
  ISBN 0-205-43108-9
    1. Vocational guidance.   I. Capuzzi, David.   II. Stauffer, Mark D.

HF5381.C265233 2005
331.702—dc22

2005045228

CONTENTS

PART III CONTEXTUAL PERSPECTIVES ON CAREER AND LIFESTYLE PLANNING 255

PART IV CAREER AND LIFESTYLE PLANNING WITH SPECIFIC POPULATIONS 361

PREFACE

The profession of counseling has been described as one in which counselors interact with clients to assist them in learning about themselves, their families, and their styles of interacting with others at home, at work, and in their communities for the purpose of discovering the most meaningful way to view themselves, and those they interact with, on a daily basis. Counselors in school, mental health, rehabilitation, hospital, private practice, and a variety of other settings must be thoroughly prepared to support clients in their quest to develop their identities, capacities, and abilities to cope with the rapid social/cultural, technological, and economic changes that are occurring in the twenty-first century. Professional organizations, accrediting bodies, licensure boards, and graduate preparation programs and departments now stress the importance of developing standards for the education and supervision of counselors with both the knowledge and the skills base needed to support clients in a discovery process that affects their future and their lifestyle planning. As the profession has matured, more and more emphasis has been placed on the importance of preparing counselors to work holistically with clients as they search for meaning in their lives.

One of the primary ways individuals develop a sense of identity and meaning is through their careers and the relationship that career choices and pathways have to personality traits, values, interests, communication styles, preferred living and working environments, and uses of leisure time. Viewing "career" in this manner is certainly holistic and demands that the counselor approach career and lifestyle planning with clients in a most comprehensive, personal, and developmental way. Counselors engaged in career and lifestyle planning with clients must be thoroughly prepared conceptually and able to translate concepts that will be helpful to clients through the use of relevant skills and techniques. They must also develop the contextual perspectives needed for competent practice and learn the unique requirements of clients who are representative of specific populations.

The content of this textbook is derived from the standards and competencies developed by professional associations and groups such as the National Career Development Association, the Association for Counselor Education and Supervision, the National Occupational Information Coordinating Committee, and the Council for the Accreditation of Counseling and Related Educational Programs. Reviews of the most current journal and textbook information on career and lifestyle planning have also been used in the process of identifying the content areas included in the 18 chapters of the book. This book also reflects the view of the editors that counselors must be prepared in a holistic manner since career and lifestyle planning with clients is inherently related to the search for identity and meaning for their lives.

The book is unique in both format and content. The contributing authors' format provides state-of-the-art information by experts who are nationally and internationally recognized for their expertise, research, and publications related to career and lifestyle planning. The content provides readers with areas not always addressed in introductory texts. Examples include chapters on career and lifestyle planning with clients in mental health, rehabilitation, and couples and family counseling settings, as well as discussion of gender issues in career and lifestyle planning. Chapters focused on career and lifestyle planning with gay, lesbian, bisexual, and transgender clients; ethnic and minority clients; and clients with addictive behaviors provide perspectives often overlooked in texts of this kind. The book ends with a very unique chapter focused on how a career counselor can increase his or her personal and professional effectiveness. Both the format and the content enhance the readability and interest for the reader and should engage and motivate graduate students in counseling and aligned professions.

The book is designed for graduate students who are taking a preliminary course in career and lifestyle planning in a CACREP or CACREP-equivalent graduate program. It presents a comprehensive overview of the foundations of career counseling, the skills and techniques needed for career counseling, contextual perspectives on career and lifestyle planning, and a discussion of career and lifestyle planning with specific populations. We, as editors, know that one text cannot adequately address all the factors that comprise the complex and holistic aspects of career and lifestyle planning with clients. We have, however, attempted to provide our readers with a broad perspective based on current professional literature and the rapidly changing world we live in while at this juncture with the new millennium. The following overview highlights the major features of the text.

OVERVIEW

The format for the coedited textbook is based on the contributions of authors who are recognized, nationally and internationally, for their expertise, research, and publications. With few exceptions, each chapter contains case studies that illustrate the practical applications of the concepts presented. Most chapters refer the reader to websites containing information that supplements the information already presented. Students will find it helpful to use the study material contained in the Companion Website: www.ablongman.com/capuzzi1e. Professors may want to make use of the Power Point presentation developed for each of the chapters as well as the test manual, which can be used to develop quizzes and exams on the book's content. (Please contact your Allyn & Bacon representative to obtain.)

The text is divided into the following five parts: Part I, Foundations of Career Counseling; Part II, Skills and Techniques; Part III, Contextual Perspectives on Career and Lifestyle Planning; Part IV, Career and Lifestyle Planning with Specific Populations; and, Part V, Epilogue.

Part I, Foundations of Career Counseling (Chapters 1–4), begins with information dealing with the historical perspectives that serve as the foundation for current approaches to career and lifestyle planning with clients. Key players, legislation, theories, institutions and professional organizations, licensure and accreditation issues, and world events are all chronicled and discussed to provide the reader with the contextual background needed to assimilate subsequent chapters. Chapters focused on theoretical perspectives, holistic views of career and lifestyle planning, and ethical and legal issues in career counseling are also included in this first section of the book.

Part II, Skills and Techniques (Chapters 5–9), presents information on the skills and techniques counselors must acquire to do competent work with clients requesting assistance with career and lifestyle planning. Individual and group assessment and appraisal; using technology, information, and other resources; developing comprehensive plans of action for clients; program promotion, management, and implementation; and supervision, coaching, and consultation provide the content for the five chapters in this part of the text. All of these chapters provide overviews and introduce readers to the skills and techniques that can be used in the career-counseling process in a variety of settings.

Part III, Contextual Perspectives on Career and Lifestyle Planning (Chapters 10–13), presents information relative to career and lifestyle planning with clients in school, mental health, vocational rehabilitation, and couples, marriage, and family settings. These chapters highlight information that has relevance and application to these diverse contexts.

Part IV, Career and Lifestyle Planning with Specific Populations (Chapters 14–17), covers the wide spectrum of clients who "present" for the services of the career counselor. Topics in this section of the text include gender issues in career and lifestyle planning; career and lifestyle planning with gay, lesbian, bisexual, and transgender clients; pertinent issues faced by ethnic and racial minorities; and the challenges faced by clients dealing with addictive behaviors.

Part V, Epilogue (Chapter 18), includes a concluding chapter written to address the career and lifestyle planning issues faced by counselors and other members of the helping professions as they strive to increase their personal and professional effectiveness.

Every attempt has been made by the editors and contributors to provide the reader with current information in each of the 18 areas of focus. It is our hope that this first edition of *Career Counseling: Foundations, Perspectives, and Applications* will provide the beginning graduate student counselor with the foundation needed for supervised practice in the arena of career and lifestyle planning with clients.

ACKNOWLEDGMENTS

We would like to thank the authors who contributed their time, expertise, and experience to the development of this textbook. They have done a superb job of addressing the basics of career and lifestyle planning with clients. We would also like to thank those who provided the external reviews of the first draft of the manuscript for this text: Andrew Daire, University of Central Florida; Andrew V. Beale, Virginia Commonwealth University; and John Baughman, Baylor University. Their critiques and suggestions were invaluable in the process of bringing this textbook to its current stage of development. Our thanks are also extended to our families and our colleagues who supported our efforts. Special thanks go to Virginia Lanigan and the other staff at Allyn & Bacon for their encouragement, creativity, and diligent efforts, which culminated in the publication of our book.

David Capuzzi and Mark D. Stauffer

MEET THE EDITORS

David Capuzzi, Ph.D., N.C.C., L.P.C., is a past president of the American Counseling Association (ACA) and is a counselor educator at Johns Hopkins University. He is professor emeritus and former coordinator of counselor education in the Graduate School of Education at Portland State University in Portland, Oregon.

From 1980 to 1984, Dr. Capuzzi was editor of *The School Counselor*. He has authored a number of textbook chapters and monographs on the topic of preventing adolescent suicide and is coeditor and author, with Dr. Larry Golden, of *Helping Families Help Children: Family Interventions with School-Related Problems* (1986) and *Preventing Adolescent Suicide* (1988). In 1989, 1996, 2000, and 2004, he coauthored and edited *Youth at Risk: A Prevention Resource for Counselors, Teachers, and Parents;* in 1991, 1997, 2001, and 2005, *Introduction to the Counseling Profession;* in 1992, 1998, 2002, and 2006, *Introduction to Group Counseling* (retitled *Introduction to Group Work* in 2006); and in 1995, 1999, and 2003, *Counseling and Psychotherapy: Theories and Interventions* with Douglas R. Gross. *Approaches to Group Work: A Handbook for Practitioners* (2003) and *Sexuality Counseling* (2002), the latter coauthored and edited with Larry Burlew, and *Suicide Across the Life Span* (2004) are his three most recently conceptualized texts. He has authored or coauthored articles in a number of ACA-related journals.

A frequent speaker and keynoter at professional conferences and institutes, Dr. Capuzzi has also consulted with a variety of school districts and community agencies interested in initiating prevention and intervention strategies for adolescents at risk for suicide. He has facilitated the development of suicide prevention, crisis management, and postvention programs in communities throughout the United States; provides training on the topics of youth at risk and grief and loss; and serves as an invited adjunct faculty member at other universities as time permits. He is the first recipient of ACA's Kitty Cole Human Rights Award and also a recipient of the Leona Tyler Award in Oregon.

Mark D. Stauffer, M.S., is a doctoral student in the Counselor Education and Supervision program at Oregon State University where he serves as a doctoral teaching staff member. He specialized in couples, marriage, and family counseling during his graduate work in the Counselor Education program at Portland State University where he worked as a research assistant.

Mark enjoys scholarly writing and authored a chapter in *Suicide Across the Life Span* (2004) and coauthored chapters in *Introduction to the Counseling Profession* (2005) and *Introduction to Group Work* (2006). This textbook, and the 2006 edition of *Introduction to Group Work*, are his first two coedited works.

Mark was a 2003 Chi Sigma Iota international fellow and Chi Sigma chapter president at Portland State University. He remains active on local and national levels with the counseling honor society.

Mark has worked in the Portland Metro Area in Oregon at crisis centers and other nonprofit organizations providing counseling to individuals, couples, and families. He has studied and trained in the Zen tradition, is vitally interested in spirituality issues in counseling and the use of meditation and mindfulness in the counseling process, and aspires to a career as a counselor educator, writer, and part-time private practitioner.

MEET THE AUTHORS

Deborah P. Bloch, Ph.D., has focused her work on the career development of individuals and the organizational structures that promote a healthy work environment. She is the author of the *Salient Beliefs Review: Connecting Spirit and Work*, coauthor of *SoulWork: Finding the Work You Love, Loving the Work You Have*, and the coeditor of *Connections between Spirit and Work in Career Development: New Perspectives and Practical Approaches*. Four of her books, which are designed to help people find the jobs that are right for them, have sold more than 150,000 copies. They include: *How to Write a Winning Resume (4th ed.)*; *How to Have a Winning Job Interview (3rd ed.)*; *How to Make the Right Career Moves*; and *How to Get a Good Job and Keep It (2nd ed.)*. Bloch is Professor of Organization and Leadership at the University of San Francisco. Previously, she taught at Baruch College of the City University of New York. In addition to her university work, Bloch has worked as a consultant in the United States and abroad. Bloch has paid particular attention to the career development of high school students. Her work in this area included the development and implementation of New York City's first computer-based career information system. She has served as president of the National Career Development Association and of the Association of Computer-Based Systems for Career Information. Bloch received the Distinguished Service Award of the Association of Computer-Based systems for Career Information, the Resource Award of the Career Planning and Adult Development Network, and the Merit Award of the National Career Development Association. In 2003, she was named a Fellow of the National Career Development Association. Bloch received her Ph.D. in organizational studies from New York University, an M.S. in Counselor Education from St. John's University, and a B.A. cum laude, in English, from Brooklyn College.

Sharon L. Bowman, Ph.D., is Professor and Chair of the Department of Counseling Psychology and Guidance Services at Ball State University in Muncie, Indiana, where she has taught for the past fifteen years. She is also a private practitioner. She earned her master's in counseling psychology from the University of Akron, and her doctorate in Counseling Psychology from Southern Illinois University at Carbondale. She has written chapters and articles on vocational counseling and development with minority clients and a wide variety of multicultural counseling issues.

Rebecca M. Dedmond, Ph.D., Assistant Professor at George Washington University and Director of the Alexandria School Counseling program, has spent the past five years as adjunct faculty member for the University of the Virgin Islands and Executive Director of the Virgin Islands Resource Center for the Disabled. A private practice counselor and consultant, Dedmond is the president and cofounder of the Agere Foundation, an educational foundation that promotes business and education partnerships for career development. Dedmond has served as a consultant for the World Bank in Ghana,

West Africa, and held various counseling positions at the elementary, high school, and university levels. She received her M.S. in counseling from the University of North Carolina at Greensboro and a Ph.D. in education leadership from the Virginia Commonwealth University, Richmond.

Dennis W. Engels, Ph.D., has served as a Regents' Professor at the University of North Texas, Denton, since 1976. He is Past President of the Texas Counseling Association, a Past President and a Charter Fellow of the National Career Development Association; editor of *Counseling and Values*, the journal of the Association for Spiritual, Ethical, and Religious Values in Counseling; and Past Chair of the American Counseling Association's Council of Journal Editors. He has held numerous offices and chairs in state and national professional organizations, served as a consulting editor on several nationally refereed journals, and consults with public- and private-sector organizations and agencies throughout the United States. He is a Licensed Professional Counselor, a National Certified Counselor, a National Certified Career Counselor, and a Master Career Counselor. He holds degrees in English from St. Norbert College and the University of Wisconsin and a doctorate in counseling from Wisconsin University.

Gina L. Evans, M.A., is a third-year doctoral student in the Counseling Psychology program at Ball State University. She plans to pursue a career as an academician and practitioner upon completing her doctoral degree. Her primary research interests include multicultural counseling with an emphasis on career development, disordered eating behaviors, and identity development.

Kathy M. Evans, Ph.D., Associate Professor at the University of South Carolina, received her Ph.D. from Pennsylvania State University. Evans has written 30 publications and made over 50 national, regional, and local presentations. Her research, writing, and teaching focus on culture, career, family, and women's issues in counseling and in training counselors.

Rich W. Feller, Ph.D., is Professor of Counseling and Career Development and University Distinguished Teaching Scholar at Colorado State University. Recent work includes coauthorship of *Career Transitions in Turbulent Times;* the CDM video series, *Tour of Your Tomorrow;* and contributing authorship of ACT's DISCOVER program. A trustee of the National Career Development Association, he consults and speaks internationally.

Jane Goodman, Ph.D., is a Professor of Counseling and Director of the Adult Career Counseling Center at Oakland University in Rochester, Michigan. Previously, she was a career counselor and organizational consultant at a counseling/consulting center. She received her bachelor's degree in sociology from the University of Chicago and her doctoral and master's degrees in counseling from Wayne State University. She has been active in professional associations for over twenty-five years and was the

2001–2002 President of the American Counseling Association. Her published works include three books, several guides or monographs, and many book chapters and journal articles, primarily in the area of career development.

Mary H. Guindon, Ph.D., is an Associate Professor and Chair of the Department of Counseling and Human Services at Johns Hopkins University. She also coordinates the master's and postmaster's programs in Organizational Counseling, an innovative and unique specialty area combining counseling skills and expertise with organizational development and behavior principles. She holds a Ph.D. from the University of Virginia. She has over twenty years of private practice experience with individuals and groups, and has provided various workshops and consultation services in educational, corporate, governmental, hospital, and community settings. Guindon specializes in counselor accountability, career development and mental health, and issues of self-esteem. She has published many journal articles and book chapters and made numerous presentations at national and international professional conferences. She is a Licensed Clinical Professional Counselor (LCPC-MD), a Licensed Psychologist (PA), a National Certified Counselor (NCC), and a Global Career Development Facilitator Instructor (GCDF-I). She is Past President of the New Jersey Mental Health Counselors Association, Past President of the New Jersey Association of Counselor Education and Supervision, Past Mid-Atlantic Regional Advisor for the American Mental Health Counselors Association, and a Fellow in the Pennsylvania Psychological Association.

Henry L. Harris, Ph.D., is an associate professor at the University of North Carolina at Charlotte. He has held offices and leadership positions in state and national professional organizations. He earned his M.Ed. from the University of North Carolina at Chapel Hill and his Ph.D. from the University of Virgina. He is also a Licensed Professional Counselor.

Barbara Richter Herlihy, Ph.D., is a professor in the Counselor Education program at the University of New Orleans. She has worked as a counselor and supervisor in schools, agencies, and private practice. Her primary focus in research and teaching is counselor ethics. Her books include *Ethical, Legal, and Professional Issues in Counseling*, with Ted Remley, and *Boundary Issues in Counseling* and the *ACA Ethical Standards Casebook* (5th ed.), both with Gerald Corey. She has presented workshops and seminars on ethics across the United States and internationally. She combines her work in ethics with other research interests in feminist therapy, multicultural counseling, and counselor supervision.

Ellen Hawley McWhirter, Ph.D., is an Associate professor in the Counseling Psychology program at the University of Oregon. She received her B.A. from the University of Notre Dame and her master of counseling and Ph.D. in counseling psychology from Arizona State University. Dr. McWhirter is the author of Counseling for Empowerment (1994, American Counseling Association) and co-author of Youth at Risk: A Comprehensive Response, 3rd ed. (2004, Brooks/Cole). Her teaching interests include career counseling, research seminar, and clinical practica, and her scholarly interests focus on ethnic minority and female adolescent career development and on promoting empowerment through counseling and counselor training.

David S. Miller, M.S.W., is a doctoral student in counseling psychology at the University of Oregon. He holds bachelor's degrees in anthropology and in social thought and political economy from the University of Massachusetts at Amherst. David also holds a master's degree in clinical social work from the University of Texas at Austin. His research interests include the history of psychology, vocational psychology, men's issues, and in particular, the influence of masculine socialization and gender role conflict on career decision making and career satisfaction. A charter member of the University of Oregon Men's Center (UOMC), David is currently serving as its Director. From 2003–2004 he served as the graduate student representative to the Advisory Council for the American Psychological Association's Committee on Accreditation, and since 2002 he has been working as a junior faculty member of a master's program in Family and Human Services at the University of Oregon.

Jerry A. Olsheski, Ph.D., is an Associate Professor of Counselor Education and Coordinator of the Rehabilitation Counseling Program at Ohio University. He has worked as a rehabilitation counselor, director of vocational services, and rehabilitation administrator. Prior to his appointment at Ohio University, Olsheski served as the Director of Disability Management Services at the University of Cincinnati Center for Occupational Health. He also has developed several disability management and transitional work programs for employers and labor organizations.

Scott D. Rasmus, Ph.D., received his doctorate in Counselor Education from the University of Central Florida. He holds two licenses in Florida, one in Marriage and Family Therapy (LMFT) and the other in Mental Health Counseling (LMHC), as well as a license in Mississippi as a Licensed Professional Counselor (LPC). His areas of professional interest are marriage and family therapy, testing and assessment techniques, school counseling, research, and outcome measurement. His clinical and administrative experiences include working as coordinator for a community counselor clinic, counseling in an alternative high school setting, and facilitating anger management groups for perpetrators of domestic violence. He currently serves as Research Chairperson for the American College Counseling Association (ACCA) and is a National Certified Counselor (NCC) with the National Board of Certified Counselors (NBCC).

Donald A. Schutt, Jr., Ph.D., has been the Director of Human Resource Development in the Office of Human Resources at the University of Wisconsin–Madison since January 1998. In his current position, he manages the development and delivery of centralized professional and career development workshops for over 18,000 employees at the university. Formerly, Schutt was a Career Development Specialist at the Center on Education and Work in the School of Education at the University of Wisconsin–Madison. He has presented over 150 workshops and seminars focusing on a variety of topics, including leadership development, management strategies, employee relations, and professional and career development concepts; he also teaches an undergraduate

Leadership Seminar at the university. In addition, he has written three books focusing on career centers and implementing career development systems in organizations. Schutt is a National Certified Counselor, a Licensed Professional Counselor in the state of Wisconsin, and a Master Career Development Professional. His educational background includes a Ph.D. and M.A. in Counselor Education from the University of Iowa and a B.A. in Journalism and Economics from the University of Wisconsin–Madison.

Pat Schwallie-Giddis, Ph.D., is a national leader in school counseling and a recognized expert in career counseling and career development. Currently she is an Assistant Professor at George Washington university and the Director of Graduate Programs in the university's Department of Counseling and Human and Organizational Studies. In October 1995 she was honored by the university as the Distinguished Educator of the Year. Pat has been recognized many times for her untiring service to education and counseling, including receiving the American Counseling Association's Carl D. Perkins Legislative Award and the Spirit of America Award from the AVA/Guidance Division and the United States Air Force for Outstanding Service in Career Guidance. Pat has coauthored, with her husband, Dr. James Giddis (Professor Emeritus, Florida State University), a definitive guidebook for use by counselors in developing and implementing successful school-to-work efforts. Most recently she coauthored a book titled *Counseling Activities for Life Skills and Career Development*, with activities including team building, self-management, and goal setting.

Marie F. Shoffner, Ph.D., is an Associate Professor of Counselor Education at the University of Virginia, where she coordinates the School Counseling program. Previously, she taught at the University of North Carolina at Greensboro for eight years. Dr. Shoffner received her Ph.D. in Counselor Education from the University of Virginia, her M.Ed. in Counselor Education from the University of Virginia, an M.E. in Electrical Engineering from the University of Virginia, and a B.S. in Mathematics from the College of William and Mary. She has primarily focused her research on the early career development of individuals underrepresented in careers such as mathematics, science, and technology. She has written chapters and articles on career development and career counseling, collaboration among school personnel, the career development of girls, school counselors and mathematics, and school counseling. She has made presentations at national, regional, and state conferences; has held several offices and chairs in state and national professional organizations; and has served, and continues to serve, as an editorial board member on several nationally refereed journals. Shoffner is a National Certified Counselor and a National Certified School Counselor.

Suzanne Simon, M.Ed., is a doctoral student in Educational Leadership (Special Education and Counselor Education Specialization) in the Graduate School of Education at Portland State University. She has a master's degree in adult education with a concentration in gerontology from San Francisco State University. She has teaching and research interests in the areas of lifelong learning, memory, meta-cognition, dementia, and social change and justice issues related to long-term care of the elderly. Suzanne authored a chapter in *Suicide across the Life Span* (2004), as well as the one in this text.

Laura R. Simpson, M.Ed., is a Licensed Professional Counselor who has practiced as a mental health clinician for the past fifteen years. She is the Adult/DD Services Coordinator for a Regional Mental Health Center in Clarksdale, Mississippi. Additionally, she serves as an adjunct professor for the Counselor Education department at Delta State University. She recently completed her Ph.D. in Counselor Education at the University of Mississippi. Her special interests include secondary traumatic stress, spirituality, and supervision.

Donna S. Starkey, M.Ed., is a Licensed Professional Counselor, National Certified Counselor, and Approved Clinical Supervisor. She is currently employed with the Counselor Education Program at Delta State University as the Clinical Lab Director, providing supervision to practicum and intern students in a variety of settings. Her career experiences include providing vocational preparation for individuals with developmental disabilities and serving as the Adult Outpatient Services Coordinator in a community mental health setting. She recently completed a Ph.D. in Counselor Education and Supervision at the University of Mississippi.

Cheryl L. Stolz, B.A., completed three years of her psychology degree at the University of Saskatchewan in Saskatoon, Saskatchewan, Canada. She received her B.A. at the University of North Dakota in 2003, and is currently enrolled in the Ph.D. program in Counseling Psychology at the University of North Dakota. Her main area of interest is in relation to lesbian, gay, bisexual, and transgender (LGBT) issues in counseling, particularly with aging LGBT clients.

Zarus E. Watson, Ph.D., is an associate professor in the Counselor Education Program at the University of New Orleans (UNO). He is the cofounder, research director, and principal investigator of the UNO Research Center for Multiculturalism and Counseling. He has served as a Research Coordinator and Counselor for the Student Support Services Project at Our Lady of Holy Cross College and as a Pediatric Researcher for the Louisiana State University Health Sciences Center. He conducts organizational workshops and consults with K–12 schools as well as business and industry. His teaching and research interests include macrosystemic conditioning, cultural competence issues in counseling and consultation, and sociorace, class, and gender identity development within and between groups.

Kara Brita Wettersten, Ph.D., is an Assistant Professor of Counseling Psychology at the University of North Dakota. A graduate of the University of Kansas, Wettersten specializes in vocational research and practice related to underserved and underresourced populations. Her current vocational research interests include the impact of domestic violence on women's working lives and the development of a measure of work hope.

David A. Whitcomb, Ph.D., is an Assistant Professor in the Department of Counseling at the University of North Dakota. After earning a bachelor's degree in psychology, Whitcomb worked for six years as a Vocational Instructor and then Vocational Counselor while pursuing a master's degree and then a Ph.D. in Counseling Psychology.

He has published and presented on the following topics: lesbian, gay, bisexual, and transgender (LGBT) identity development; gender roles; the sociopolitical context of coming out as LGBT; social justice in counseling psychology; and HIV prevention. Currently Whitcomb is the Chair of the Section for Lesbian, Gay, and Bisexual Awareness, Society of Counseling Psychology (www.div17.org/lgba) and the Chair of the Greater Grand Forks HIV/AIDS Network. He also coordinates grant-funded outreach programs on campus and within the community for HIV prevention and LGBT-safe-school initiatives.

Chris Wood, Ph.D., is currently an Assistant Professor at The Ohio State University, in their nationally ranked Counselor Education program. He previously taught career development at the University of Arizona and at Oregon State University. He is a nationally and internationally respected counselor educator and currently serves on the editorial review board of the ASCA journal, *Professional School Counseling*. A Nationally Certified Counselor (NCC) and a Nationally Certified School Counselor (NCSC), he has previous experience as a high school counselor, a guidance department chair, a counselor/group leader at a residential youth facility for troubled teens, and a career counselor/assessment coordinator at an alternative school serving grades 7–12. Wood has published articles and book chapters on career development, school counseling, and counseling supervision. His research interests focus on career development interventions in schools and school counseling programs.

PART I

FOUNDATIONS OF CAREER COUNSELING

Career and lifestyle planning with clients has an interesting history and encompasses a number of basic premises and foundational perspectives about which the counselor needs to be educated. This part of the text provides the beginning counselor education student with an overview of both the historical context of career counseling and the philosophical basis on which the counselor must practice. History, theoretical perspectives, holistic approaches, and ethical and legal issues are presented as foundational to the material included in subsequent parts of the text.

Historical influences on the evolution of career counseling are outlined in Chapter 1, "The History of Career Counseling: From Frank Parsons to 21st Century Challenges." The chapter traces the emergence and development of career and lifestyle planning with clients through nine historical stages derived from the work of Mark Pope and Roger Aubrey. The reader will find that this chapter provides a fascinating, thorough, and interesting chronology of events, legislation, and educational and vocational trends that have contributed to the emergence of the holistic approach to assisting clients with career and lifestyle planning.

Chapter 2, "Career Development: Theoretical Perspectives," examines theories of career development that have emerged during the last century. Trait and factor, developmental, sociological, learning theory, values and needs based, and cognitive are a few examples of the approaches that are discussed in the chapter. Examples of applications for practitioners are also included.

Existential and spiritual aspects of how an individual's search for meaning affects career and lifestyle planning are pertinent to the role of the career counselor and a holistic approach to working with clients. Chapter 3, "Toward a Holistic View," discusses the way spirituality, hope, and optimism enter into the career decision-making process. In addition, the concepts of planned happenstance, positive uncertainty, and the postmodern approaches of narrative, integrative life planning, and constructivism are presented to provide the reader with a tapestry, woven with philosophical/spiritual threading, that can be used to enrich the career counseling process for both the counselor and the client.

In every counseling specialization, pertinent legal and ethical issues exist: some are shared and some are unique to a particular specialization. Chapter 4, "Ethical and Legal Issues, Principles, and Standards in Career Counseling," addresses the ethical and legal issues related to career counseling. The content reflects the ethical/legal parameters outlined by a number of professional organizations such as the National Career Development Association and the American Counseling Association. Dilemmas faced by career counselors hired in business and industry settings and created by the use of computers and the Internet are also included.

CHAPTER 1

THE HISTORY OF CAREER COUNSELING

From Frank Parsons to Twenty-first-Century Challenges

DAVID S. MILLER

ELLEN HAWLEY MCWHIRTER
University of Oregon

All career and vocational theories develop within a particular historical context. Examining the historical roots and development of different theories provides a basis for understanding their lineages, a context for how career theories have developed over time, and a sense of their connection to the history of the United States and prevailing culture. In this chapter, we examine major influences on U.S. vocational counseling theory in an effort to present a contextual portrait of the field and its growth. This will include key players, legislation, theorists, institutions and professional organizations, licensure and accreditation issues, and world events. We hope that this context will assist readers in evaluating and critiquing contemporary career theory and practice.

It is crucial to begin with definitions. Based on Richardson (1993) and Blustein, McWhirter, and Perry (2005), we find it useful to define *work* as a central human activity that may be paid or unpaid and that is designed to fulfill the tasks of daily living and ensure survival. *Career* is a subset of work characterized by volition, pay, and hierarchical and thematic relationships among the various jobs that constitute a career, and *vocation* is a more general term, subsuming both work and career. However, these contemporary definitions are sometimes at odds with the language utilized in the history of vocational counseling. In recognition of changing terminology over time, we adopt within this chapter the broader definition of *career* offered by the National Vocational Guidance Association (1973): "a time-extended working out of a purposeful life pattern through work undertaken by the individual." We also incorporate Sharf's (2002) notion that a career incorporates "how individuals see themselves in relationship to what they do" over the course of the life-span, which highlights the relationship between work and identity (p. 3).

Gysbers, Heppner, Johnston, and Neville (2003) identify five tenets on which career counseling research and practice have historically been based. They are (1) individualism and autonomy, (2) affluence, (3) an open structure of opportunity based on assumptions of merit, (4) work as the central role in people's lives, and (5) the logical, linear, and progressive development of work and career (pp. 53–57). These tenets reflect the values of mainstream U.S. culture: the focus is on the individual, individuation is seen as progress and development, volition and unconstrained choices guide occupational decisions, cultural values of individual loyalty (vs. family or collectivist decision making) are presumed, the world of work operates as a meritocracy free from biases (e.g., racism, sexism, etc.), and work is the most important aspect of people's lives. These assumptions rely on a static work culture and environment that no longer exist, even for those who once enjoyed their benefits, and completely ignore the realities of many other people (Gysbers et al., 2003).

The analysis by Gysbers and his colleagues provides an excellent example of the extent to which the aims and beliefs of career counseling have been influenced by larger social forces. It also illustrates why career counseling has failed to benefit many people who have sought its services, and why many others have viewed career counseling as not useful or relevant to them. In fact, "cultural encapsulation continues to characterize much of our current theory and practice in career development. This universal application of Eurocentric constructs must be overcome if all counselors, regardless of race or ethnicity, are to provide ethical and effective career counseling to all clients" (Gysbers et al., 2003, p. 60). Throughout the history of vocational counseling, and today, there have been strong proponents of the position that identifying and transforming the structures and practices that perpetuate occupational stratification, inequality, and workplace injustices is a critical dimension of career counseling practice (Blustein, Juntunen, & Worthington, 2000; Blustein et al., 2005; O'Ryan, 2003).

This chapter traces the emergence and development of vocational and career guidance over nine historical stages. We derived these stages primarily from the works of Mark Pope (2000) and Roger Aubrey (1977). Within each stage, we present a sampling of historical events, legislation, and educational and vocational trends that contributed to the development of career guidance. These events should be viewed as a launching point for further inquiry rather than a definitive catalogue of the influences on this field. We begin with the Industrial Revolution.

STAGE ONE: THE BEGINNING (1890–1914)

> the mid- and late 1800s . . . [were] . . . marked by a devastating civil war, periods of economic depression, the closing of the American frontier, unbridled growth of large metropolitan areas, large waves of uneducated and unskilled immigrants, a war with the fading Spanish empire, unchecked expansion of

family fortunes through business and industry, abrupt and unforeseen modes of communication and transportation, legal freeing of millions of former slaves without concomitant economic and social autonomy, the challenge to established religions by social and biological Darwinism, the rapid spread of compulsory school attendance laws, concentration of job opportunities in large cities, growth of state and federal government to cope with the earlier enlargement of corporate and industrial complexes, the struggle of women for basic human rights, and the increased exploitation of many segments of the United States population by unscrupulous hucksters and entrepreneurs. (Aubrey, 1977, pp. 288–289)

As the preceding paragraph indicates, the years in which vocational guidance emerged in the United States were marked by the large-scale economic and demographic changes that followed the Industrial Revolution. The second major immigration wave in the United States was marked by mass movement into the cities and urban areas from rural parts of the United States and abroad, including people from many nations, members of ethnic minority groups, farmers, Southerners, and youth (DeBell, 2001; McLemore, Romo, & Baker, 2001; Pope, 2000). Some writers have attributed the xenophobia that accompanied this immigration to restrictive immigration legislation following World War I and continuing through the Depression and World War II (McLemore et al., 2001), though it would perhaps be more likely to suggest that xenophobia and restrictive legislation acted interdependently. There was little sympathy for the plight of new arrivals, many of whom found work only in the most abysmal conditions (Bettman, 1974; Gourley, 1999; Sinclair, 1905). Labor unions, which began in the middle of the previous century, and mass actions that emerged with the Great Upheaval in 1877 grew in strength to become important political forces by the turn of the century (Brecher, 1997; DeBell, 2001).

The turn-of-the-century job market was characterized by changes in required job skills (DeBell, 2001). Though most opportunities for employment consisted of unskilled labor in the major industries of mining, railroads, factories, and mills (Baker, 2002; Pope, 2000; Sharf, 2002), rising industrialization offered a number of new occupations and opportunities (Watkins, 1992). Engineer Frederick Taylor published a theory of scientific management in 1911; implementation of his principles radically increased worker productivity but was criticized as dehumanizing to workers (Harris, 2000). The emergence of large organizations and subsequent prohibition against individuality and self-expression affected a shift in the relationship between identity and work. No longer would Romantic-era sentiments about expressing one's core identity through a "vocational passion" apply; such sentiments were replaced by a more pragmatic definition of identity based on one's place within an organization (Savickas, 1993, p. 206). This shifted the locus of work identity from "a calling from God" (internal) to "what your neighbors call you" (external), which Savickas (1993, p. 206) linked with the emergence of the "career ladder."

The Triangle Shirtwaist fire of 1911 and Upton Sinclair's *The Jungle* (1905) were among events that brought the extreme conditions of the workplace to the attention of the general public (e.g., Scott, 1911). Although middle- and upper-class white women did not enter the labor force in large numbers until World War II, many other women of this era engaged in paid labor in an effort to stave off extreme poverty and compensate for widespread male un- and underemployment (Bettman, 1974; Gourley, 1999; Peterson & Gonzales, 2000). Children were present in the labor force in great numbers and were subjected to terrible working conditions, due in part to the absence of child labor laws (Aubrey, 1977; Baker, 2002). The first child labor law was not passed nationally until 1908 (DeBell, 2001). Today, while labor laws protect the majority of U.S. children, other children are still exposed to abysmal working conditions, including migrant farmworker children (Tucker, 2000) and those who are forced into the child sex industry (Estes & Weiner, 2002).

The Protestant work ethic and social Darwinism were dominant sociocultural influences of the time (Peterson & Gonzales, 2000), conveying, respectively, that hard work leads (inevitably) to success and that only the strongest and hardest-working could, and should, survive. The Protestant work ethic has been critiqued for its limited multicultural relevance and "disrespect for immigrant work habits" (Peterson & Gonzales, 2000, p. 51). For example, it ignores social and political restrictions on individual occupational success, sustaining the myth of "a structure of opportunity open to all who strive" (Gysbers et al., 2003, p. 55). Despite the diverse nature of the U.S. workforce and accompanying work ethics, the Protestant work ethic remains the most frequently cited work ethic of the time (see Peterson & Gonzales, 2000, for an extended discussion).

Two Movements

> [The] injustice and suffering wrought by massive technological change . . .
> shape[d] the early destiny of guidance. . . . [T]he single greatest support for
> vocational guidance in the early 1900s came from the social reform movement. (Aubrey, 1977, pp. 289–290)

The social, political, and economic changes in which the nation was embroiled gave rise to two movements that were to prove very important to the history of vocational guidance: the Progressive movement and the educational reform movement. The Progressive moment arose from the idea that science and technology should be used to benefit the common good and move people toward human perfection (Baker, 2002). Comprised of reformists who worked to alleviate negative social conditions through universally applied action, the movement was rooted in the belief that the government should help the individual and the community (Pope, 2000). Progressives lobbied for women's suffrage, regulation of industry, educational reform, and the enactment of child labor laws (Baker, 2002).

The educational reform movement emerged in response to vast increases in school enrollments. Mass immigration into the cities, changes in child labor laws as a result of the "child-saving" movement, and the need for more highly educated workers all swelled the ranks of school classrooms (Aubrey, 1977; Baker, 2002). Student diversity increased in terms of language, background, education, and aptitude (Aubrey, 1977; Baker, 2002). Changes in student composition meant that old methods of teaching were no longer as effective and that greater flexibility was needed, leading to a call for widespread educational reform in academic content and teaching methodology

(Baker, 2002). Factory and corporate schools of large industrial corporations emerged to meet the increasing need to train workers (Harris, 2000). Although focused on skill-specific training, many corporate schools, such as those of General Electric or Westinghouse, "taught everything from basic English to specific, production-related technical skills" (Harris, 2000, p. 5). These corporate schools may have served a larger acculturative function as well.

The Beginnings of Vocational Guidance

The ideals of the Progressive and educational reform movements were perhaps best reflected in the work of Frank Parsons, a Boston-based attorney whose emergence as the leader of vocational guidance has been described as a historical inevitability (Brewer, 1942; O'Brien, 2001; Seligman, 1994). Observing Parsons's vocational journey from engineer to lawyer, professor, mayoral candidate, and, finally, guidance godfather, Watkins (1992) joked that Parsons was a man desperately in need of career counseling. Parsons's work through the Civic Service House's Vocation Bureau in Boston responded to changing needs in industry and the workforce by focusing on the school-to-work (STW) transition of children (Blustein et al., 2000; Super, 1955). The Civic Service House had been providing a forum for self-governing clubs of immigrants and socialites interested in civic action and justice, who hoped to better the circumstances of those individuals who formerly had had little or no hope of rising above their social and economic status (Brewer, 1942; Hartung & Blustein, 2002; Pope, 2000; Zytowski, 2001). Sensing that some members of the Civic Service House wanted more education, the first two directors (Meyer Bloomfield and Philip Davis) created the Breadwinner's College (soon to become the Breadwinner's Institute) to provide primary and continuing education (Brewer, 1942; Zytowski, 2001). One of the college's first instructors was the civic-minded Parsons, who had already been active as a professor and dean of liberal arts (Brewer, 1942). In 1906, Parsons delivered "The Ideal City," a lecture detailing the need to counsel young people about vocational decisions (Brewer, 1942) as a means of empowering them and working toward social justice (O'Brien, 2001). This lecture generated tremendous interest and led to the formation of the Vocation Bureau to realize its message (see Brewer, 1942; Zytowski, 2001).

The Vocation Bureau of Boston is generally considered the original site of the vocational guidance movement in the United States (Hartung & Blustein, 2002). In a location separate from the Civic Service House, the bureau provided assistance to students, trained the first vocational counselors, facilitated the school-to-work transition (Zytowski, 2001), and promoted the idea of "vocational choice as a form of individual and social efficiency, a part of the progressive ideal" (Baker, 2002, p. 377). Parsons's (1909) *Choosing a Vocation* served as a foundation for much vocational guidance thought throughout the remainder of the century (Baker, 2002; Hartung & Blustein, 2002; Watkins, 1992). Parsons (1909) recommended a three-step model: (1) evaluating the individual's interests, abilities, values, and skills, (2) identifying the requirements of various occupations, and (3) matching individuals to suitable occupations via true reasoning. All three steps were designed to achieve a harmonious result and establish efficiency in labor. Over time, this approach has become known as *trait and factor theory*.

Although Parsons intended to address the social problems of his day scientifically (Hartung & Blustein, 2002; Savickas, 1993), by contemporary standards, his techniques for career guidance would be considered commonsense pragmatics rather than the result of empirical inquiry (Aubrey, 1977). Methods of testing and assessment now associated with Parsons's theory were not available in his lifetime, but his emphasis on assessment had a major influence on the subsequent development of vocational assessment tools (Watkins, 1992).

A year after Parsons died in 1908, he was honored at the first vocational conference in Boston. This conference initiated steps toward the creation of a guidance counselors' organization (Aubrey, 1977), resulting in the 1913 formation of the National Vocational Guidance Association (NVGA) in Grand Rapids, Michigan (Gibson & Mitchell, 1999; Pope, 2000). In the same year, the U.S. Department of Labor was formed and began to gather workforce statistics (Pope, 2000). For the founders of NVGA, it was a time "of growth and high hopes for vocational guidance" (Pope, 2000, p. 197).

At the same time that Parsons was promoting vocational guidance in Boston, a school administrator by the name of Jesse Davis was making the first city-wide efforts to incorporate guidance into the schools in Grand Rapids, Michigan. Davis began teaching vocational guidance during one English composition class period per week (Aubrey, 1977; Brewer, 1942). He advocated a study of the self and of occupations that was similar to the approach espoused by Parsons. Believing that properly moral youth would choose civic-minded careers, Davis focused on the development of moral consciousness, character, and ethical behavior as they affected career choices (Aubrey, 1977). He conceived of vocational guidance in the somewhat religious terms of finding one's "calling" (Gibson & Mitchell, 1999). A Progressive who was instrumental in the formation of the NVGA, Davis also served as its second president (Pope, 2000).

There were two distinct tracks of training to prepare high school students for graduation: college preparatory and vocational education. John Dewey (1916) has been described as a farsighted advocate for integrating the two tracks so as to discourage replication of class distinctions (Blustein et al., 2000) and discrimination based on an individual's job (the discriminatory "occupationism" described by Krumboltz, 1991, p. 310). Today the two-track system still exists, as does the debate over its logic and consequences (Blustein et al., 2000; Hartung & Blustein, 2002). Awareness of both potential discrimination and the need for counselors to exercise sensitivity and advocacy has formed the basis for the "fundamental conundrum" (Blustein et al., 2000, p. 443) of the field through the present day: how to conduct research and focus on non-college-bound students without increasing current levels of stigmatization or discrimination (Blustein et al., 2000). Consequently, Baker (2002) and others (Hawks & Muha, 1991; O'Brien, 2001) have suggested that vocational guidance has moved away from its social justice goals over time.

Other vocational theorists of the time included Anna Reed, Eli Weaver, and David Hill. Only Hill (writing in New Orleans) articulated a need for diversity in education and vocational guidance (Gibson & Mitchell, 1999). Anna Y. Reed's work developed along lines similar to those of Parsons, though she was more concerned with the job system than the individual. As a result, she focused on the employability of the youth as his or her worth and worked to match youth to existing jobs (Gibson & Mitchell, 1999). Across the country, cities and schools were forming departments and courses on vocational guidance, ranging from voluntary bureaus, like the one headed by Reed in Seattle, to the efforts of Eli Weaver, who incorporated vocational guidance into the public school system of New York City (Brewer, 1942). By 1910, some form of vocational guidance was being offered in schools (though not yet systemwide) in over 35 cities, and the first university course in the subject was taught at Harvard in 1911 (Aubrey, 1977). As quickly as it had begun, vocational guidance was about to gain even more momentum. World War I, greater entry of vocational guidance into the schools, and a drive for empirical testing would increase awareness and the perceived legitimacy of the field.

STAGE TWO: CALLS FOR MEASUREMENT; VOCATIONAL GUIDANCE IN THE SCHOOLS (1914–1929)

This stage opened with World War I, which involved the mobilization of 4.355 million men from the United States. Of this group, 126,000 died and 234,300 were wounded (see Iavarone, 2001), presenting vast economic and vocational challenges for surviving family members and for those who returned home wounded. The war and its aftermath were the dominant contextual influences in this time period. Also during this era, women gained the right to vote (1919), Henry Ford was selling cars for $290, Frank Lloyd Wright was designing homes in California and Japan, the first skyscrapers were going up, and James Langston Hughes published his first book of poetry.

The postwar period saw a surge in testing in public education and in private institutions (Super, 1955). Student diversity continued to increase in schools, and the increasing importance of literacy skills in the workplace translated into greater attention to vocational guidance (Pope, 2000). Ongoing, large-scale immigration as well as World War I fueled an eruption of legislative action, including the Immigration Act of 1917, the Emergency Quota Act of 1921, and the Immigration Act (Johnson-Reid) of 1924 (McLemore et al., 2001). Based on the "national origins principle," which promoted the immigration of only certain, "superior and preferable," groups, the quota-based restrictions enacted in 1917–1924 continued through the third wave of immigration in the United States, during the Depression and World War II (DeBell, 2001; McLemore et al., 2001, p. 97).

Vocational Instruments

The early years of the vocational guidance movement were characterized by a split between those who advocated for continuing experiential self-assessment ("What kinds of things are you skilled at doing?") and those who argued for empirical testing to increase the reliability and validity of early objective assessment methods (American Psychological Association [APA], 1956; Aubrey, 1977; Super, 1955). Calls for the scientific evaluation of assessment tools began as early as 1911 and were soon echoed in government (Baker, 2002). This paralleled a shift from knowledge via individual experience (i.e., subjectivity) to an emphasis on science and objectivity (Savickas, 1993). *Psychometrics* (the field concerned with design and analysis of the measurement of human characteristics) took on great significance at this time because (1) its principles were useful in developing vocational and intellectual assessments, and (2) use of psychometrics helped to establish the credibility of vocational guidance as a profession and justified its presence in the schools (Aubrey, 1977; Watkins, 1992). The move toward credibility was also supported at this time by publication of the NVGA's "Principles and Practices of Vocational Guidance" (Borow, 1974, as cited in Pope, 2000. Information about the history of credentialing of career counselors can be found in Engels et al., 1995, and the Website www.ncda.org under *information for consumers*.)

The debate over experiential self-assessment versus increased empirical testing was ultimately and (perhaps) prematurely resolved by the onset of World War I. The army needed a means to quickly place thousands of men into positions for which they had the skills or aptitude (Super, 1983). Standardized objective tests suitable for group administration, such as the Army Alpha and Army Beta tests, were developed based on pioneering work in intelligence testing by Alfred Binet and Lewis Terman, among others (Super, 1983). The predecessors of today's Army General Classification Test (the Armed Services Vocational Aptitude Battery, or ASVAB) were administered to over 2 million men during World War I (Baker, 2002; Seligman, 1994; Walsh & Betz, 1995). In 1927, E. K. Strong published the Strong Vocational Interest Blank for Men (Strong, 1927; Walsh & Betz, 1995), a standardized assessment measure that remains one of the most widely used interest assessment measures (Seligman, 1994). The use of standardized tests for admissions and placement decisions spread into higher education as army psychologists obtained postwar employment in colleges and universities (Gibson & Mitchell, 1999; Williamson, 1965). Testing continued despite controversy over the accuracy and validity of intelligence measurement (Williamson, 1965), which continues today. Such testing has not always been used in a way that is beneficial to humanity, as results have been used to justify the inequitable treatment of ethnic minorities and immigrants in the education system (McLemore et al., 2001).

Legislation

As veterans began returning home, many wounded in body, mind, or both, the United States was faced with the challenge of how to provide them with a means of self-support, or, if employment was not an option, some other form of assistance; this situation inspired the vocational rehabilitation movement (Heppner, Casas, Carter, & Stone, 2000). The Vocational Rehabilitation Act of 1918 provided job training for returning veterans. Part of the Veteran's Administration (VA), the Veterans' Bureau was created in 1921 and provided vocational rehabilitation and education programming for disabled veterans of World War I (Gibson & Mitchell, 1999). The Smith-Hughes Act of 1917 provided further funding for vocational education and organized guidance programs in elementary and secondary schools (Pope, 2000). In 1921, the Workers' Education Bureau and the first Labor Extension Program at the University of California–Berkeley were initiated in response to the need for vocational education. Workman's compensation, begun in 1910 in New York, had spread to 45 states by 1921 (Danek et al., 1996).

Vocational Education

Throughout the decade, vocational guidance became even more entrenched in the school systems, resulting in permanent organizations in school systems in cities such as Boston and Philadelphia (1915), Chicago (1916), South Bend, Indiana, Berkeley, California (1919), and Detroit (1920) (Brewer, 1942). During this time, the organization of vocational guidance programs remained inconsistent. Efforts to systematize the field within school systems and cities were slowed due to a lack of understanding of vocational guidance as a comprehensive experience that included research, practice trials, choices, readjustment, and counseling (Brewer, 1942). As a result, some individuals wanted to focus on placement, while others favored gathering information and safeguarding children's rights (Brewer, 1942).

In industry, corporate schools continued to operate, such as the Carnegie Corporation's American Association for Adult Education (AAAE; Harris, 2000). Organized labor continued trying to meet the needs of both workers and employers, walking the fine line between advocating for training versus education and determining how aggressive to make its demands and actions (Brecher, 1997; Harris, 2000). Corporate schools continued a similar struggle with regard to the level of education to provide for their workers. The Carnegie AAAE's idea, that adult education should create informed citizens, yet also citizens who would "maintain social stability" (Harris, 2000, p. 32), parallels the debate of whether to use education to challenge class distinctions, as articulated in the works of Dewey (Blustein et al., 2000).

This period also marked the beginnings of greater organization in the vocational guidance profession; the NVGA produced *Vocational Guidance*, its first journal, in 1915. In 1924, the National Civilian Rehabilitation Association (NCRA) convened for the first time. Three years later it underwent a name change to become the National Rehabilitation Association (Heppner et al., 2000). As the use of, and reliance on, standardized testing increased, some have noted that attention to contextual factors as important in selecting an occupation decreased, as did the "counseling" dimension of vocational guidance (Aubrey, 1977). Aubrey also notes that this paralleled American reliance on authority and rigidity. The emphasis on testing increased over the course of the next decade, as Americans looked to vocational guidance to help ease the crises created by mass unemployment caused by the Great Depression (Super, 1955).

STAGE 3: THE GREAT DEPRESSION AND THE EXPECTATIONS OF A NATION (1929–1939)

During this era, Europe was undergoing a widespread economic depression. Abysmal working and living conditions as well as civil and social unrest across the world did nothing to abate mass levels of immigration into the United States. This wave of immigrants did not find the conditions of which they had dreamed. On October 24, 1929, the U.S. stock market crashed, precipitating the Great Depression. Unemployment and underemployment were rampant (Terkel, 1986). To address this crisis, the Franklin D. Roosevelt (FDR) administration's New Deal created public programs for employment through the Civilian Conservation Corps of 1933 and the Works Progress Administration (WPA) of 1935 (Pope, 2000).

During this time period, unions became much more organized. The Knights of Labor was among the first unions to appear. Aspiring for social justice, this order emphasized rallying people around their identities as workers first: "the Order tried to teach the American wage-earner that he was a wage-earner first and a bricklayer, carpenter, miner, shoemaker . . . a Catholic, Protestant, Jew, white, black, Democrat, Republican after" (Ware, 1964, as quoted in Brecher, 1997, p. 43). Although women are not mentioned in this quote, they also held jobs, were subjected to terrible conditions, and were active in organized action (Brecher, 1997). While the Knights of Labor aspired to goals that were congruent with those of the common worker, not all unions were so fair-minded; for example, such inclusive and justice-oriented goals were not emulated by the emerging unions affiliated with the American Federation of Labor (AFL). These unions "generally included only highly skilled craft workers, excluding—in practice and often by deliberate intent—African Americans, women, many immigrants, and non-craft workers" (Brecher, 1997, p. 69). Thirty years later, the site of craft unions and construction industry in Philadelphia would catch President Richard Nixon's eye as a stronghold against affirmative action and would be targeted in his Philadelphia Order (Bruner, n.d.), a plan to guarantee fair hiring practices.

Organized labor was by no means a cure-all for worker problems. Disaffection with the slow and careful progress of the unions combined with fears of collaboration between union leaders and owners to lead to dramatic changes in mass action for social justice (Brecher, 1997). Citizen self-help organizations, such as the Unemployed Council in Chicago and the Unemployed Citizens League in Seattle, began to form (Brecher, 1997). Seen in this light, the New Deal may have been motivated as much by widespread fear of mass uprisings as by humanitarian concern over the loss of jobs: "it was widely felt that . . . spontaneous mass action would become a revolutionary movement if conditions continued to worsen" (Brecher, 1997, p. 164; Pope, 2000).

Legislation

Vocational guidance had established its utility during the testing and placement successes of World War I. Now the nation looked to vocational guidance to help with the employment crises of the Depression (Herr & Shahnasarian, 2001; Super, 1955). Vocational education legislation continued with the George-Reed Act in 1929 and the George-Ellzey Act of 1934 (Pope, 2000). The George-Deen Act of 1936 continued the financial support for vocational guidance works that had begun with the Smith-Hughes Act of 1917 (Herr & Shahnasarian, 2001; Pope, 2000). The new act led to the creation of the Occupational and Informational Guidance Branch of the U.S. Office of Education and provided money to states to create positions for education supervisors and guidance in the schools (Hoyt, 2001). Greater numbers of supervisors and guidance counselors in the schools meant greater entrenchment, and consequently more guidance accomplished, in the schools at this time. The "child study" movement of the 1930s continued to raise expectations of teacher accountability and responsibility (Gibson & Mitchell, 1999). The efforts of the Progressives finally came to fruition with the passage of the Fair Labor Standards Act of 1938, which explicitly outlawed exploitative child labor (Pope, 2000).

Under Roosevelt's New Deal legislation, the Department of Labor's Employment Security program developed offices for job placement and counseling for unemployed Americans in 1933 (Gibson & Mitchell, 1999), as did the U.S. Employment Service, the National Employment Counseling Association, and numerous employee assistance programs. The Social Security Act became law in 1935, providing a guaranteed source of retirement income to all Americans who qualified. In 1938, the B'nai Brith organization founded Jewish Vocational Services to provide counseling, placement, and service for Jewish individuals and families (Pope, 2000; Seligman, 1994).

Vocational Instruments

The psychometrics movement continued to gather momentum during this period through the Minnesota Employment Stabilization Research Institute (MESRI; Super, 1955; Watkins, 1992). Led by a number of vocational giants, including E. G. Williamson, John Darley, and Donald Paterson, the institute began responding to the educational and vocational needs of unemployed Americans as it developed psychometric tests (Watkins, 1992). The institute's work sparked great interest in public and private vocational guidance centers, and the U.S. Employment Service soon became involved, joining with public and private enterprise to expand the research and applications of the institute into the larger society (Super, 1955, p. 4). This strengthened the connections between education, psychometrics, social work, and vocational guidance, as well as the organizational power of the NVGA (Super, 1955).

This era was also marked by the publication of E. G. Williamson's (1939) trait and factor manual, *How to Counsel Students*, which focused on the importance of testing and measurement in the tradition of Parsons (Gibson & Mitchell, 1999). In 1939, the U.S. Department of Labor produced what was the inevitable result of the scientific credibility movement: the *Dictionary of Occupational Titles* (*DOT*; U.S. Department of Labor, 1940). An encyclopedic listing of vocational fields, the *DOT* was a highly organized classification system for occupations and provided extensive information about the nature of occupational activities, worker traits, work settings, and educational and training requirements for a large group of occupations (Sharf, 2002). The *DOT* provided, for the first time, a common organizational framework for occupations. This came just in time, as the United States was about to enter another world war, with masses of new people entering (and leaving) the workforce, and as the field of vocational guidance was beginning to critique its own models (e.g., Armor, 1969). The *DOT* was updated continuously until 1991 when it was replaced by the online database O*Net (http://online.onetcenter.org/).

STAGE 4: WORLD WAR II, MORE TESTING, AND MAJOR THEORETICAL INFLUENCES (1940–1957)

The entry of the United States into World War II coincided with the end of the Depression. Preparation and engagement in the war, as well as its aftereffects, resulted in labor and population booms, increased access to free public education, and the entry of middle-class white women into the labor force in greater numbers than ever before (Aubrey, 1977; Seligman, 1994). Most women found jobs in heavy industry associated with the war effort, while the government provided some day care and household assistance as incentives (Faludi, 1991). Following the war, most of those same women were rushed out of heavy industry. Many decided to remain in the job market, although due to political realities of the time, women were often forced to accept lower-paying, lower-status clerical and administrative positions. Despite this, their participation in the labor market continued to grow (Faludi, 1991).

Personal freedom and autonomy were dominant national themes (Aubrey, 1977). Counseling psychology emerged as a new specialty in this time period. It was a combination of vocational guidance, psychometrics, and counseling that emphasized a holistic perception of the individual (Gelso & Fretz, 2001; Super, 1955). The vocational needs of women of color and working-class women, who had long been part of the workforce, continued to be ignored in research and practice literatures, even as they continued to enter the workforce in large numbers (Seligman, 1994). The power of organized labor continued to grow, and approximately one-third of the labor force was unionized in 1955 (DeBell, 2001).

Vocational Instruments

As with World War I, the U.S. role in World War II prompted attention to the continued development and refinement of psychometric tools to assist in placing large numbers of personnel into appropriate jobs (Super, 1983). Following the war, the mental health and vocational needs of returning veterans—and the workers they inadvertently displaced— became evident. Such needs expanded the demand for counseling and guidance and testing, just as they had following World War I (Baker, 2002; Pope, 2000). The Armed Services Vocational Aptitudes Battery (ASVAB) was developed at this time by the U.S. Department of Defense (Sharf, 2002). Major tools developed during this time included the Army General Classification Test (replacing the Alpha Test), the General Aptitude Test Battery (GATB; Dvorak, 1947), and the *Occupational Outlook Handbook* (*OOH*; U.S. Department of Labor, 1949; see Super, 1983). The early stages of development of the Myers-Briggs Type Indicator (MBTI), a popular personality indicator based on Carl Jung's theory, commenced during this time period. Refinement and revision of the Strong Interest Inventory continued, with separate scales for women having been added in 1933 (Sharf, 2002; Strong, 1943, 1955; Walsh & Betz, 1995).

Vocational Legislation

Following World War II, major legislation addressed the needs of veterans. The GI Bill of 1946 allocated funding for college, job training, and home ownership (Faludi, 1999), and the George-Barden Act of the same year provided funding to train school counselors in higher education settings (Hoyt, 2001), as well as money for related travel expenses. This funding increased certification and the professionalization of career guidance (Herr & Shahnasarian, 2001). Both pieces of legislation promoted occupational training and education for veterans, with funding for VA counseling centers coming from the

George-Barden Act (Gibson & Mitchell, 1999). In 1947, the Feingold Report recommended that guidance be more than a focus on education and that it be applicable to other areas of life. It should include all students, including those with behavioral and emotional problems, and not just those whose educational careers seemed promising. Feingold's call for "guidance of the whole child" was reminiscent of the child study movement of the 1930s, which called for the educational system to attend to the overall development of the child (e.g., mastery of developmental tasks, style of learning, etc.; Gibson & Mitchell, 1999, p. 10).

Vocational Theory

Vocational guidance theory was also changing. The growing dominant culture themes of increased personal autonomy and self-determination were incongruent with the assumptions of unalterable personal qualities on which trait and factor counseling was based (Aubrey, 1977). Theoretical writings on vocational guidance were losing ground to counseling in the professional and practice literature, and during the 1950s vocational guidance shifted to include a more developmental focus (Aubrey, 1977). Even the nomenclature changed, as the descriptor *vocational guidance* began to be replaced by terms like *career counseling* and *career development* (Pope, 2000).

Stage theories of development from related disciplines sparked changes in vocational guidance (Gibson & Mitchell, 1999). For example, Erikson's *Childhood and Society* (1950) articulated eight stages of psychosocial development and focused on the domains of ideology, family, and vocation (Peterson & Gonzales, 2000). His influence can be seen in theories such as those of Ginzberg, Ginsburg, Axelrad, and Herma (1951), Super (1953, 1957, 1990), and Gottfredson (1981, 1996). Ginzberg and colleagues (1951) combined trait and factor theory with Erikson's work to describe decision making as a developmental process involving personal-environmental factors (Peterson & Gonzales, 2000).

Erikson's work also influenced a young Donald Super (Peterson & Gonzales, 2000). Super, a vocational psychologist whose work spanned six decades, created a highly integrative model of vocational development across the life-span that focused on the ideas of self-concept and career maturity (Sharf, 2002; Super, 1990). Later revisions emphasized identity development and the adoption of roles as linked with occupation and both self-concept and vocational self-concept development, including variables such as parental influence (Gibson & Mitchell, 1999). These adaptations paralleled the later phases and revisions of Ginzberg et al.'s (e.g., Ginzberg, 1984) model, and eventually led to the Person by Environment (PxE) Theory (Gibson & Mitchell, 1999).

Erikson's work was followed in 1954 by another landmark: Maslow's (1954) Hierarchy of Needs, in which he stated that human needs were satisfied in a hierarchical progression. This theory influenced Anne Roe (1956, 1957), whose developmental theory of occupational classification and selection included a strong emphasis on the parent-child interaction (1957; see also Peterson & Gonzales, 2000; Sharf, 2002). Roe's system for categorizing occupations was followed by Holland's (1959) theory of personality types and occupational classification. Holland would continue working on variations of his model and become a giant in vocational counseling, as his work spanned more than four decades. Holland's theory had a strong trait and factor influence, with later revisions that included concepts of consistency, congruence, and differentiation, with a focus on matching internal qualities and the environment of the workplace (e.g., Holland, 1992, 1997).

Alongside developmental influences, the growth of interpersonal counseling and psychotherapy had an enormous impact on vocational guidance (Aubrey, 1977). Carl Rogers's (1939, 1951) groundbreaking focus on genuineness, empathic responses, and unconditional positive regard for clients reflected the national *zeitgeist* (spirit of the time) of self-determination, personal autonomy, and empowerment (Aubrey, 1977). His techniques were incorporated into vocational counseling and have been credited with changing its primary focus (Super, 1955). Specifically, the importance of psychometrics and testing was changed to a greater emphasis on the client's personal experience (Gibson & Mitchell, 1999; Super, 1955). Whereas career counselors in the past had focused on the vocational problems of their clients and worked to find solutions, the influence of Rogers (alongside Erikson, Maslow, and others) led to a greater focus on counseling the *person* and on understanding the individual problem as just one aspect of living. In other words, vocational counseling became contextualized (rooted in the context of client's lives; Super, 1955).

Vocational Organization

The changes in theory and techniques resulted in political and organizational realignments within vocational guidance (Super, 1955). The American Psychological Association's Division of Counseling and Guidance (Division 17) was established in 1946 by E. G. Williamson and John Darley (of MESRI fame), though it officially changed its name to the Division of Counseling Psychology in 1952 (APA, 1956; Super, 1955) and subsumed vocational guidance into psychology (Super, 1955). Many academic departments were restructured to include a greater focus on counseling psychology doctoral programs than on master's programs in vocational guidance and counseling. More intensive training of counseling psychologists led to rapid supplanting of vocational counselors in some circles (Super, 1955). For example, in 1952 the VA rewrote job descriptions to include a more holistic focus, replacing the job title of *vocational counselor* with that of *counseling psychologist* (APA, 1956).

Due in part to the desire to project a stronger identity, the NVGA, the flagship organization of vocational guidance, merged with the Guidance Supervisors and Counselor Trainers and the American College Personnel Association to form the American Personnel and Guidance Association (APGA) in 1952 (Super, 1955). The consolidation into APGA resulted in more than a 50 percent decline in membership in the NVGA (Pope, 2000). Super (1955) attributed this decline to the heterogeneous membership of NVGA, which included many members "whose primary affiliation is elsewhere" (p. 6). Although vocational counseling was struggling to maintain its identity within psychology, the field continued to grow, with greater emphasis on training, educational requirements, and interdisciplinary influences. As this stage closed, the threat of war with the Soviet Union emerged, strongly shaping the next stage.

STAGE 5: THE SPACE RACE, CIVIL RIGHTS, AND THE GREAT SOCIETY (1958–1970)

The launching of *Sputnik I* in the Soviet Union demonstrated advances in technology that caught the immediate attention of the United States. Concerned that the country was lagging behind the Soviets in science and technology, a series of legislative actions were initiated that intended to increase the quality and quantity of U.S. scientists (Borow, 1974). The National Defense Education Act (NDEA) of 1958 provided mass funding for vocational guidance in the schools, in hopes that the new school personnel would greatly increase the numbers of talented young men—and women—interested in pursuing higher education in math and science (Pope, 2000).

Following President John F. Kennedy's assassination, President Lyndon B. Johnson (LBJ) carried forward elements of Kennedy's vision by initiating the War on Poverty and working to create a "Great Society." Scholarship from other disciplines continued to enhance the relevance and efficacy of vocational guidance (Aubrey, 1977). For example, von Bertalanffy's (1968) "systems theory" enriched vocational psychology through its later application to family therapy by Gregory Bateson and others (Peterson & Gonzales, 2000). This period also increased the emphasis on finding *meaning* in work, as "many young people wanted jobs that were meaningful and . . . would allow them to change the world for the better" (Borow, 1974; Pope, 2000, p. 200).

The striving for meaning developed alongside a resurging commitment to social justice. The 1960s saw a rising national awareness of the major social, educational, and economic inequalities that existed across ethnic, racial, and gendered domains; this was accompanied by growing mistrust and unease with the major social institutions of the United States, including the government and the military (Borow, 1974; Dixon, 1987). Throughout the decade, various civil rights movements emerged, with focus growing from an original concentration on African Americans to the broader sector of people challenged by inequity and injustice, including gays and lesbians, people with disabilities, all racial and ethnic minorities, and women (Heppner et al., 2000). Mass action for these causes ranged from sit-ins to mass riots, such as the Watts riots of 1965 (Borow, 1974). In addition, the conflict in Southeast Asia and very high levels of unemployment in the United States contributed to mass action and civil unrest in the nation (Pope, 2000). It did not take long for the government to connect civil unrest with increasing numbers of out-of-school and out-of-work youth and a lack of employment opportunities (Herr, 1974).

Legislation

As with the social climate during FDR's administration, civil disorder and crises prompted the presidential administrations of the 1960s to use vocational legislation to maintain homeostasis (Herr, 1974; Pope, 2000) and respond to great forces for social change. Legislation in this time period was significant in three ways: (1) minority groups and women began to be directly addressed and involved in vocational legislation, along with the emergence of affirmative action, (2) ecological factors such as educational, social, or cultural barriers to vocational success were overtly considered for the first time, and (3) vocational guidance itself became even more integral to legislation aimed at reducing economic or occupational woes. Pope (2000) has described the years from 1960 to 1979 as being a "boom for counseling" (p. 208). As it addressed the social and economic inequalities, vocational guidance received its largest support to date: "To a degree unparalleled in . . . American history, vocational guidance and counseling became identified consistently in federal or in state legislation as a vital part of the manpower [*sic*] policies designed to respond to human needs in the occupational and economic arenas. Program after program, regardless of its target population . . . included an emphasis on providing vocational counseling or guidance" (Herr, 1974, p. 33).

The Area Redevelopment Act of 1961 focused on attracting jobs to impoverished areas, followed by the provisions for assistance and job skills to workers of the Manpower Development and Training Act (MDTA) of 1962 (Herr, 1974). Beginning with this act, legislative efforts addressed the impact of occupational change on the other areas of an individuals' life and acknowledged the existence of social and political barriers to occupational success (Herr, 1974). Further, instead of simply waiting for eligible recipients to request services, active recruitment strategies for the MDTA were initiated (Herr, 1974). Also in 1962, a presidential panel of vocational education consultants delivered a report that resulted in the Vocational Education Act of 1963 (Pope, 2000). In 1963, the Community Mental Health Centers Act initiated rehabilitative services for the mentally ill (Gibson & Mitchell, 1999).

Under Title VII of the Civil Rights Act of 1964, discrimination in employment based on race, color, religion, sex, and national origin was outlawed. This applied to both direct treatment in the workplace and to indirect methods, such as discriminatory practices or procedures either in hiring or in the workplace (Peterson & Gonzales, 2000). On September 24, 1965, President Johnson issued Executive Order 11246, enforcing equality in hiring and employment of people of color, also known as *affirmative action*. Just prior to enacting the order, President Johnson echoed the affirmative action sentiments of former President Kennedy in a commencement address to graduates at Howard University:

> You do not wipe away the scars of centuries by . . . taking a man who for years has been hobbled by chains, liberate him, bring him to the starting line of a race, saying, "you are free to compete with all the others," and still justly believe you have been completely fair. . . . This is the next and more profound stage of the battle for civil rights. We seek not just freedom but opportunity. (Bruner, n.d.)

This order was amended two years later to include discrimination based on gender (Bruner, n.d.). In 1967, the Age Discrimination in Employment Act guaranteed similar protections.

In 1965, new legislation increased the funding for the Vocational Rehabilitation Administration, acknowledging the influence that social and environmental factors could have on vocational development and opportunity (Herr, 1974). The Economic Opportunity Act of 1964 created a wealth of programs, including Job Corps, Neighborhood Youth Corps, Volunteers in Service to America (VISTA), Youth Opportunity Centers, the U.S. Employment Service Human Resource Development Program,

Head Start, and the New Careers Program (Herr, 1974; Pope, 2000). The Social Security Act of 1967 contained a Work Incentive Program (WIN) for education, training, and support to help welfare recipients find work (Herr, 1974; Pope, 2000). The Elementary and Secondary Education Act of 1969 provided aid for children in impoverished areas (Pope, 2000).

The National Defense Education Act of 1958

The NDEA "had a greater influence on the career counseling movement than any other single event" (Hoyt, 2001, p. 376). The NDEA was drafted and passed in 1958. It provided educators and counselors with funds and training to scout and encourage young people (mostly males) to enroll in science and math classes (Pope, 2000). Specifically, the act provided grant money to develop local guidance programs and for the training of counselors to staff them; it also became somewhat involved in accreditation and licensure consolidations for school counselors (Gibson & Mitchell, 1999). Combined with other legislative acts, the NDEA helped spark a 400 percent increase in the number of school counselors, greatly improving counselor-to-student ratios from 1958 to 1967 (Aubrey, 1977). This "acknowledgment of the vital link among our national well-being, personnel needs, and education" (Gibson & Mitchell, 1999, p. 12) normalized the presence of the guidance counselor and of testing in the schools and provided governmental legitimacy to the profession in the eyes of the country (Gibson & Mitchell, 1999). The NDEA funded an entire generation of counselors, counselor educators, and counseling psychologists.

Vocational Theory

During the 1960s, the APGA literature strongly advocated bringing guidance to every student rather than focusing only on college-bound students, similar to the critique presented in the 1947 Feingold report (Aubrey, 1977). The developmental focus continued in counseling and guidance literature, including Wrenn's (1962) *The Counselor in a Changing World*, Tiedeman and O'Hara's (1963) model of self-development, cognitive development and career decision making, and the trait and factor–based Work Adjustment theory of Lofquist and Dawis (1969; see also Gibson & Mitchell, 1999). This decade was the first in which any attention was paid to the career development of persons with disabilities who were not veterans (Szymanski, Hershenson, Enright, & Ettinger, 1996); simultaneously, vocational researchers began to examine populations other than men. Terman and Oden (1959) published a landmark follow-up study of a sample of gifted students, finding that while the gifted men were largely physicists, physicians, and lawyers, the majority of gifted women were housewives or, if they worked outside of their homes, secretaries.

Vocational Instruments

Instruments based on personality and development continued to develop; the Myers-Briggs Type Indicator test was published in 1962 (Sharf, 2002), and the Kuder

Occupational Interest Scale (KOIS) was developed in 1966 (Walsh & Betz, 1995). In the late 1960s, career counselors began using computer technology, beginning with the System of Interactive Guidance and Information (SIGI) and the Computerized Vocation Information System (CVIS; Harris-Bowlsbey, 2003). In the 1970s, CVIS became DISCOVER and SIGI became SIGI Plus (Harris-Bowlsbey, 2003).

Vocational Organizations

The increased inclusion of vocational counseling in legislative initiatives led to increased visibility and prominence in aspects of everyday life, including school, community, and public and private organizations (Herr, 1974; Pope, 2000). As part of this increased focus, the U.S. Employment Services began to develop subprofessional career counselors, a movement that reached its apex in the mid-1960s (Hoyt, 2001). Also in the mid-1960s, school counselors joined together to form a Guidance Division of the American Vocational Association (AVA), indicating a resurgence of interest in career counseling among school counselors (Hoyt, 2001). The National Vocational Guidance Association celebrated its fiftieth anniversary as an organization, and its membership began to recover from the losses sustained in the merger with APGA (Pope, 2000). In 1964, the American School Counselor Association clarified the roles and functions of school counselors in its Policy for Secondary School Counselors (Gibson & Mitchell, 1999).

Aubrey (1977) suggests that the consolidation and expansion of vocational guidance led to more opportunities and possibilities in the field. This, in turn, led to a critical need for self-examination and clarity regarding future directions, such as the nature of the clientele served and methodologies used.

STAGE 6: THE BOOM YEARS CONTINUE (1970–1979)

The 1970s witnessed the decline of the Great Society of LBJ. Disaffection and mistrust of the government that had begun with the rising social conscience of the 1960s continued following Watergate and the end of the Vietnam War. Rising unemployment, an unstable economy, and increasing attention to ways in which the vocational needs of women and ethnic minorities had been ignored all contributed to a "growing apathy towards established institutions" (Aubrey, 1977, p. 294). The identification of vocational services as essential elements of social change legislation continued to spark interest in (and funding for) infusing career development and occupational information into career education, in an attempt "to provide a career-based emphasis in the educational curriculum at all levels, not solely for the work-bound" (Blustein et al., 2000, p. 438).

Vocational Legislation

In 1971, the U.S. Office of Education granted $9 million toward developing career education models (Gibson & Mitchell, 1999). Career education incorporated career development (i.e., career decision-making and planning) and occupational skills and work-based training into the regular school curriculum, to be included as a necessary part of everyday life and hence less divisive of the college- and work-bound youth (Blustein et al., 2000). Commissioner of Education Sidney Marland ushered in a new age for vocational counseling, which gained "widespread acceptance in the educational establishment in the United States. . . . In less than a decade, more than ten major national associations endorsed career education, hundreds of publications on career education were published and distributed, and an astounding array of proponents and interpreters of the career education concept emerged" (Gibson & Mitchell, 1999, p. 312). The surge in popularity of vocational counseling extended from 1974 to 1982, as over $10 million was made available for career education. During this period, "school counselor interest in career counseling seemed to grow markedly," and vocational counseling made "small but significant efforts" to focus on the needs of women, ethnic minorities, and people with disabilities, Nonetheless, as late as 2001, Hoyt remarked that the "career counseling needs of both women and minorities continue to be inadequately addressed" (2001, p. 378). Although research on the vocational development and career needs of women and minorities had begun earlier (Fitzgerald & Betz, 1983), such areas would not receive significant attention until the 1980s and 1990s.

Emerging legislation was more inclusive of those groups traditionally ignored by vocational counseling. In 1974, the Women's Educational Equity Act "provided career-related grants for special populations of girls and women" (Hansen, 2003, p. 45). The Higher Education Act of 1965 was amended and updated in 1972 to ensure the continuation of community services and educational opportunities, as well as extending support for desegregation in the schools (Herr, 1974). These amendments also created a Bureau of Occupation and Adult Education within the U.S. Office of Education and extended funding for underrepresented and underserved populations of the Vocational Education Act of 1968 (Herr, 1974). The Equal Employment Opportunities Commission, which had been criticized for its lack of enforcement authority, was granted expanded legislative authority and was joined by the Departments of Justice and Labor, the Civil Service Commission, and the Civil Rights Commission to form the Equal Employment Opportunity Coordinating Council in an attempt to maximize its power, reach and effect (U.S. Equal Employment Opportunity Commission, n.d.).

In 1973 the Rehabilitation Act for people with disabilities was passed as part of a legislative focus on empowerment of individuals with disabilities, as was the Education for All Handicapped Children Act of 1977 (Danek et al., 1996). In 1976, educational amendments were passed to the Vocational Education Act of 1963 and 1968, formally creating the National and State Occupational Information Coordinating Committees (NOICC and SOICC, respectively). Both committees consolidated service delivery across (federal or state) agencies, thus generating a boom in the availability of information about the world of work (Pope, 2000). Throughout the 1970s, vocational legislation continued to focus on job placement (versus career counseling), emphasizing a return to work with a minimum of lost wages (Danek et al., 1996). The military influence on vocational counseling continued with the Vietnam Veterans Readjustment Act of 1974, which extended services to veterans with less severe injuries; the major focus of this act and its ensuing amendments has been to provide veterans with job skills suitable to gain stable employment (Danek et al., 1996).

Vocational Instruments

Computerized assessment development continued with SIGI Plus, DISCOVER, Career Information System (CIS), and Guidance Information System (GIS; Harris-Bowlsbey, 2003). The profession began to critique (Betz & Fitzgerald, 1995) and test its vocational assessments for cross-cultural relevance (Fouad, 1993). Some of the issues raised included levels of comfort across different cultures with the items on an individual test, generalizability concerns, data interpretation, language problems, and cultural differences in the willingness to disclose information (Fouad, 1993). In addition, theories of vocational behavior and/or development were critiqued for failing to address how people differ across different domains of identity, such as gender (Fouad, 1993), sexual orientation, race/ethnicity, or level of physical ability. At the same time, researchers began to examine differences and similarities in vocational development and concerns of racial and ethnic minorities and of women (Fitzgerald & Betz, 1983; Smith, 1983).

Vocational Theory

Bandura's (1969) *Principles of Behavior Modification* introduced social learning theory as a promising new direction for vocational counseling (Sharf, 2002). His subsequent work on potent constructs such as self-efficacy expectations (Barndura, 1977, 1986) promoted additional research and theoretical developments that eventually became the foundation for social cognitive theory (Sharf, 2002). In 1975, Krumboltz, Mitchell, and Gelatt (1975) applied social learning theory to career counseling; Krumboltz later extended it to career decision making (e.g., 1979, 1996). Krumboltz conceived of learning as an interaction between genetic and environmental factors. This model represented a convergence of Bandura's model (itself part of a larger body of literature that includes von Bertalanffy's work on family systems and Bronfenbrenner's work on ecological development) and work by other career theorists that increasingly acknowledged the complex role of the environment.

While Krumboltz and colleagues focused on the individual process of social learning, other theorists were beginning to think more broadly. The stage theories of career development of the 1940s through 1970s made way for a broader conceptualization of careers across the life-span (Gibson & Mitchell, 1999). Gysbers and Moore (1973) produced Life Career Development Theory with a focus on the interaction of all aspects of an individual's life (Gysbers, Heppner, & Johnston, 2003). Their theory fused environmental and developmental concepts, including Super's concepts of the roles, settings, and events in which a person is engaged over the life-span. Life Career Development Theory suggested that counselors think about career and work as the intersection of the roles, settings, and events that occur over a person's life. As such, counselors should consider the different life stages, personal factors, and individual differences (e.g., race, ethnicity, socioeconomic status, sexual orientation, level of physical ability, etc.) as they influence the settings in which people operate (Gysbers, Heppner, & Johnston, 2003). Gysbers and colleagues also recommended a focus on the bidirectional influence of work and life events: just as work influences an individual's external world, so does the external world influence the work environment. Life Career Development theory became even more inclusive with its 1992 revision, incorporating larger, societal-level factors (Gysbers, et al., 2003). At the end of the decade, Edwin Herr (1979) published *Guidance and Counseling in the Schools* and Urie Bronfenbrenner (1979) proposed his ecological model of human development.

Vocational Organization

In the 1970s, guidance counselors began self-examination about public perception of their function, such as carrying the responsibility for the direction, academic success, and occupational choices of their students (Gibson & Mitchell, 1999). This examination continued during the 1970s and 1980s and was manifested through trends toward greater accountability, more data-based programs, and objective assessments (Gibson & Mitchell, 1999). The focus on self-assessment and the continued search for credibility as a profession resulted in proposals for standard competencies (Engels, Minor, Sampson, & Splete, 1995; Pope, 2000). A series of position papers in the 1970s by the American Vocational Association and APGA, the Association for Counselor Education and Supervision and Career Education Project of APGA resulted in a competency list published by the National Vocational Guidance Association in 1982. This, in turn, led to the first specialty recognized by the National Board of Certified Counselors: National Certified Career Counselor (Engels et al., 1995; Pope, 2000) and the first National Career Counselor Exam in 1983 (Pope, 2000). However, even as the field continued to respond to demands for accountability and credibility, an infrastructure that had traditionally excluded groups of people was struggling to come to terms with diverse clients and members.

STAGE 7: INCLUSION OF A WIDER CULTURE (1980–1989)

The interest in, and growing recognition of, the diverse composition of U.S. society continued into the 1980s amid the second largest wave of immigration in U.S. history (DeBell, 2001). Legislation, research money, grants, new theories, critiques, and adaptations to existing theories increasingly included discussions or foci on the needs of diverse populations (Heppner et al., 2000). At the same time, the field was still overwhelmingly comprised of, and governed by, white counselors and psychologists.

A decline in the power of organized labor occurred alongside increased needs for technological skills and contract labor, both of which were beginning to emerge as transformational factors (Brecher, 1997; DeBell, 2001). Very high rates of unemployment, calls for educational reform in standards and in teaching, and an increased focus on schools as the arenas for improvement (Blustein et al., 2000) recapitulated the expectations placed on teachers and schools during Parsons's time. Socially, this time period was marked by a backlash against changes in social norms that accompanied women's entry into the workplace in greater numbers, as many in the media fought against this progress (Faludi, 1991).

Legislation

The legislative focus on connecting youth with vocational training continued. Hoyt (1974) has suggested the focus on education to be a simple matter of mathematics: vocational education occurs most frequently in the schools, as the site where individuals who are at their most malleable stages of life are most accessible. The Comprehensive Employment and Training Act of 1982 provided federal assistance to state and local governments for developing relevant job-training programs for youth and adults of lower incomes (Gibson & Mitchell, 1999). In 1984, the Carl D. Perkins Vocational Education Act supported the development of programs that would facilitate "self-assessment, career planning, career decision making and employability skills" for underserved populations (Gibson & Mitchell, 1999, p. 313). Because of the strong emphasis on schooling, efforts to reconnect homeless youth with schools were supported via the Homeless Assistance Act of 1987 (Gibson & Mitchell, 1999). Support for education and training in high-tech occupations followed in 1988 via the Omnibus Trade and Competitiveness Act (Pope, 2000). During this time period the Department of Labor and the National Occupational Information Coordinating Committee (NOICC) awarded grant money for the development of career information systems and guidance information systems, which led to computer-based career services and guidance systems (Gibson & Mitchell, 1999).

Vocational Theory

Vocational theorists continued to increase attention to family influences on work and the growing diversity of the workforce, and overall they continued to develop more holistic and inclusive models. Hackett and Betz (1981) applied Bandura's self-efficacy theory to understanding both women and men's math-related confidence and performance, and Mitchell and Krumboltz (1984) applied it to career decision making (Peterson & Gonzales, 2000). Isaacson (1985) described learning theory as the basis for vocational identity and focused on genetic and environmental factors (Gibson & Mitchell, 1999). Miller-Tiedeman and Tiedeman (1990) developed Life Career Theory, a holistic and integrative understanding of life and career decision-making development (Peterson & Gonzales, 2000).

Critiques that theories did not address the vocational development of individuals with disabilities began to emerge during the 1980s (Szymanski et al., 1996), just as increased attention to special populations began to bear results. Publications addressing the needs of women and minorities appeared in greater numbers, for example, Betz and Fitzgerald's *Career Psychology of Women* (1987). Gottfredson's (1981, 1996, 2002) theory of circumscription and compromise combined developmental progression, awareness of the exterior world, self-concept, and women's issues; later scholars (e.g., Bowman, 1995) applied this theory to ethnic minority women. Astin (1984) presented a model of career choices and behavior depicting an interaction of psychological, cultural, and environmental factors that produce career choice and work behavior. In her model, Astin incorporated the constructs of motivation, expectations, sex-role socialization, and the structure of opportunity. Farmer (1985) examined the career choices and aspirations of girls and ethnic minority adolescents. Brown-Collins and Sussewell (1986) created the developmental Multiple Self-Referent Model for African American women, a model that was later adapted by Gainor and Forrest (1991) to conceptualize the different types of self-identity that may influence and/or be instigated by workplace experiences of African American women.

Vocational Organization

The new golden age of career counseling was accompanied by a number of important conferences (Gibson & Mitchell, 1999). Notable among them were the 20/20 Conference: Building Strong School Counseling Programs in 1987, the National Career Development Association (NCDA) Diamond Jubilee Conference, and the First Conference of the Association for Counselor Education and Supervision in 1988, which established task forces to study national world-of-work concerns (Gibson & Mitchell, 1999). Kenneth Hoyt addressed the annual meeting of NCDA in 1988 to review the vocational progress made by women and minorities since the end of the 1960s (Pope, 2000). Finally, in 1984 the NVGA officially changed its name to the National Career Development Association (NCDA), "completing [the] process [of change] began by Donald Super in the 1950s" (Pope, 2000, p. 204).

STAGE 8: MAKING SOME PROGRESS TOWARD DIVERSITY AND COLLABORATION (1990–PRESENT)

Steady declines in wages for skilled and semiskilled labor began in the 1970s and continued into the 1990s. The ensuing crisis precipitated increased attention to the school-to-work (STW) transition, yielding a wealth of writings on the topic (Blustein et al., 2000). Politicians were not oblivious to this; Presidential hopeful Bill Clinton included STW issues in his platform in 1992 (Blustein et al., 2000). Increasing diversity in the workplace began to create different kinds of job-related stress; as environments began to change, different skills were needed and changes in the very nature of how work was constructed began to accelerate (Savickas, 1993). Discrimination and sexual harassment in the workplace received media attention on a national level. The appointment of Justice Clarence Thomas to the U.S. Supreme Court despite allegations of sexual harassment of a co-worker and investigations of allegations at the U.S. Navy Convention at the Tailhook Hotel in 1991 called broader attention to the seriousness and prevalence of sexual harassment, as well as the need for prevention and protective measures.

Legislation

The Americans with Disabilities Act (ADA) of 1990 was hailed as the most comprehensive civil rights legislation passed for individuals with disabilities (Danek et al., 1996). Reworking the Rehabilitation Act of 1973, the ADA extended federal funding to private, public, and nonprofit agencies to focus on employment skills and end discrimination

(Danek et al., 1996). In the same year, the Higher Education Act, the Elementary and Secondary Education Act, and the Carl D. Perkins Act were all reauthorized (Pope, 2000). The Education for All Handicapped Children Act of 1975 was restructured into the Individuals with Disabilities Education Act of 1990, which focused on the STW transition (Danek et al., 1996). An emphasis on lifetime learning coursed through these pieces of legislation; for example, the Task Force on Education's report issued a call for reform including a need for transferable skills and lifetime learning habits (Blustein et al., 2000). This led to the creation of the Secretary's Commission for Achieving Necessary Skills (SCANS) to identify competencies and foundations of learning to prepare youth for competition in a global market (Blustein et al., 2000). Although this represented a change in focus for educational reform (Blustein et al., 2000), governmental programs (at least in theory) had been considering multiple aspects of the vocational ecology for many years.

The Job Training Partnerships Act (JTPA) of 1992 established local, state, and federal agencies to foster collaboration among schools, employers, and communities in the process of facilitating youths' entry into the world of work (Gibson & Mitchell, 1999). Like its predecessor, the Manpower Development and Training Act of 1962, the JTPA focused on job training as a means of overcoming economic and social barriers to employment (Danek et al., 1996). The School-to-Work Opportunity Act (STWOA) and the One-Stop Career Centers Act of 1994 also provided opportunities for improving the ecology surrounding a student's movement from school to work (Herr & Niles, 1998; Pope, 2000). The latter act provided funding for partnerships for students, to include their parents, schools, government agencies, and local businesses (Blustein et al., 2000). The STWOA focused on career counseling and exploration in schools to provide students with accurate and realistic knowledge and skills (Gibson & Mitchell, 1999), which afforded counselors an opportunity to intervene at multiple levels of an individuals' ecology (Herr & Niles, 1998). An alliance between the U.S. Departments of Labor and Education (Gibson & Mitchell, 1999), the STWOA prefaced a larger restructuring of welfare, the Personal Responsibility and Work Opportunity Reconciliation Act (PRWORA) of 1996. The PRWORA changed the face of government assistance by restructuring work, establishing time limits for receiving government aid, and mandating that recipients of aid find jobs; often the jobs they found were those of displaced state workers (Anelauskas, 1999). A summary of findings on STW published by the American Psychological Association can be found at http://www.apa.org/pubinfo/school/homepage1.html.

The PRWORA replaced the governmental programs of Aid to Families with Dependent Children and the Job Opportunities and Basic Skills (JOBS) training program (Peterson & Gonzales, 2000). The PRWORA included the Workforce Initiative Act and the Welfare to Work Act; the latter set a five-year limit on Temporary Aid to Needy Families (TANF; Pope, 2000). The Workforce Initiative Act focused on finding work for individuals and training them on the job, regardless of the match; this had dramatic implications for the career counselor, as it was a complete departure from the historical foundations on which the profession was based (Blustein et al., 2000; Pope, 2000). Numerous scholars and researchers have documented the negative impact of these acts on mothers who use welfare and women affected by domestic violence (Anelauskas, 1999; Faludi, 1991; Kaplan, 1997).

Vocational Theory

Research on women and career development continued during this period, as vocational counseling continued its overall focus on understanding the effects of discrimination on work behavior, performance, experiences, and satisfaction (Heppner et al., 2000). During the 1990s, vocational texts emerged for ethnic minorities (e.g., Fouad & Bingham, 1995; Leong, 1995) and for individuals who identified as gay or lesbian. Critiques that career counseling was not inclusive of the diverse range of life experiences of people in the United States continued (Betz & Fitzgerald, 1995), forming the basis for the revision of many theories, including Blustein and Spengler's (1995) Domain-Sensitive approach (Gysbers et al., 2003). Gysbers and Moore's (1973) Life Career Development Theory was revised in 1992 to include ecological theory and the influence of personal identity factors such as race, religion, gender, social class, and sexual orientation as they shaped the experiences of the individual (Gysbers et al., 2003). The Person by Environment (PxE) approach emerged as a new incarnation of trait and factor theory (Peterson & Gonzales, 2000). Lent, Brown, and Hackett (1994) applied Bandura's social cognitive theory (1969, 1977) to the development of career-related interests, goals, and attainments, stimulating a great deal of subsequent research.

The validity of contemporary career development theories for African Americans, Latinos, Native Americans, and Asian Americans, as well as gay, lesbian, and bisexual people and other groups not considered in initial theory development, was continuously called into question. Osipow and Littlejohn (1995) stated that the changing workplace required a modification of the theories, even for the white males on which they had been developed, as the world of work had begun to change drastically. The authors suggested that career counselors strive to create a more inclusive environment, valuing multicultural contributions of the diverse workforce rather than promoting assimilation (Osipow & Littlejohn, 1995). During the mid-1990s, calls were issued for a theory that integrated aspects of racial/ethnic identity development, self-identity development, and career development (e.g., Bowman, 1995; Osipow & Littlejohn, 1995); Bingham and Ward (1997) provided one promising step in that direction. The late 1990s and turn of the century represented a culmination of the drive toward contextual understanding of career choice and development. For example, a special edition of the *Career Development Quarterly* addressed context and service delivery in terms of socioeconomic status (Lent, 2001), sexual orientation (Chung, 2001), and sociopolitical context and issues of power (Santos, Ferreira, & Chaves, 2001).

Unlike some other areas of psychology (e.g., Stricker et al., 1990; Sue, Bingham, Porche-Burke, & Vasquez, 1999), there was, and continues to be, a dearth of literature concerning the need for recruitment and retention of ethnic minority students and faculty in the area of vocational counseling and psychology. Increasingly diverse work environments sparked the needs for greater representation, visibility, and expansion of techniques to address issues for diverse populations and the changing workplaces (Thomas, 1990). Nor is this limited to theory. Betz and Fitzgerald (1995) noted a great disparity between the percentage of people of color in the workplace and their representation in research samples.

Vocational Organization

In 1996, the Vocational Behavior and Career Intervention Special Interest Group became the Society for Vocational Psychology, a section of the Division of Counseling Psychology (Heppner et al., 2000). Through the decade, the NCDA and NOICC funded studies through the Gallup Organization about attitudes toward work and schools on the part of ethnic and racial minorities. The 1990s included a greater focus on women and minorities, the rise of career services available in different forms (e.g., Internet), and international expansion of theory and service delivery (Pope, 2000). The year 1995 marked the adoption of a comprehensive nondiscriminatory policy by the NCDA to include sexual orientation as a "protected category"; in the same year the NCDA changed the composition of its board of directors to include more applied workers (Pope, 2000). This was followed in 1997 by competency and performance indicators as well as ethical considerations for career counseling on the Internet (Hampson & Lumsden, 2000). Looking to the future, in 1998 the NCDA and ACES formed a joint Commission on Preparing Counselors for Career Development in the 21st Century to address the lack of interest and excitement in teaching career counseling (Hansen, 2003; Savickas, 2003). Although these trends in the world of work had been developing over time, the increasing rapidity of available information worked to accelerate the strains they would put on existing career counseling services and models, leading to new challenges for workers and career counselors in the next millennium.

STAGE 9: THE FUTURE

> The old notion of "choosing a vocation," based on the assumption that one does this only once, must be discarded. (Hoyt, 2001, p. 379)

Structure and Characteristics of the Work Environment

The changes wrought in the U.S. economy and world of work by the Information Age have been as profound as those wrought by the Industrial Revolution over a century ago; they call to mind the embryonic cultural context that preceded the initial emergence of career counseling (DeBell, 2001; Savickas, 2003). The workplace is rapidly transforming, with increasing numbers of minorities, women, youth, and workers over 45 years of age (Gysbers, Heppner, & Johnston, 2003). There are widespread assertions that the international restructuring of the workplace has changed every aspect of work, making some jobs obsolete, decreasing the security and longevity of others, and increasing the importance of adaptability, creative activities, teamwork, technological aptitude and literacy, and the ability to work at a faster pace without traditional boundaries (Gysbers et al., 2003; Harris, 2000; Peterson & Gonzales, 2000). Education has assumed even greater importance, it has become more difficult to predict job futures, and the utility and reliability of the "rugged individual" model is being supplanted by a more interdependent model that includes market forces, an international economy, and the realization of more individual powerlessness (Savickas, 1993). Hansen (2003) notes that in conjunction with these changes, the attacks of September 11, 2001, increasing exposure of corporate corruption, sniper attacks in the U.S. capital, the passage of the "Patriot Act," economic recession, and a continued lack of universal health care have resulted in demoralization and decreased sense of security among U.S. workers, who suffer increasing amounts of anxiety, depression, and existential crises.

Downsizing, specialization and outsourcing, and increased use of temporary labor and employees have led to fewer benefits for a majority of workers and the valuing of skill and performance over loyalty and tenure (Gysbers et al., 2003; Harris, 2000). Increasing job mobility often translates into decreased investment in other workers and in any particular company. In addition, disengagement from the work site contributes to a decreasing power base of organized labor and alienation from co-workers. Brecher (1997) contends that government actions of the past twenty years, such as President Ronald Reagan's aggressive action in the air traffic controllers' strike of the 1980s, have sent a powerful message about the federal stance on the importance and power of unions. Current decreases in participation in organized labor may signal a return to conditions at the turn of the twentieth century (DeBell, 2001).

Existential and Life-Span Challenges

Historically, the social construction of race and gender has been subject to the needs of the work world (Brodkin, 1998). Changes in the workplace have contributed to, and been influenced by, new social definitions and expectations concerning gender roles and cultural identity (Gysbers et al., 2003). Increases toward equality in the workplace have led to more sharing of roles and functions in the household, which in turn has led to changes in family composition and increased work-family conflicts (Gibson & Mitchell, 1999; Gysbers et al., 2003). The changing world of work also presents new challenges for career counselors as they attempt to address concerns of aging clients who are working longer, the interruption of careers for child rearing, and more unemployment, underemployment, and midlife career changes (Gibson & Mitchell, 1999). Multiple careers across the life-span are now the norm. Workers are increasingly expected to self-manage their careers and are turning to career counselors for assistance in negotiating the complexity of this task (DeBell, 2001; Herr, 2003). In addition, there is growing awareness of the extent to which those workers who are not engaged in "careers" are on the margins of contemporary vocational theories, research, and practice (Blustein et al., 2005). Vocational and career professionals are challenged to continue efforts to make career education and counseling services beneficial to this very large segment of the population.

International expansion of the world of work has been accompanied by existential issues such as "anger management, stress management . . . cross cultural and transnational mobility skills . . . assimilation stress, culture shock [and] confusion about work norms and behavioral expectations"; increasing the likelihood that career counselors will be called upon to utilize skills in stress reduction, conflict resolution, and cultural adaptation and requiring additional training to address these needs (Herr, 2003, p. 13; see also Niles, 2003; Parmer & Rush, 2003). The increasingly globalized work world has additional implications for international career counseling, as counselors must both support clients who have international agendas and work collaboratively with international colleagues for service delivery and research (Hansen, 2003).

Tools

Current vocational and career counselors are striving to meet the new challenges in step; recent special issues of the *Journal of Career Assessment*, for example, have addressed career-counseling assessment issues in the next millennium (*Career assessment for a new millenium*, 2000) and the current fervor created by the Internet-counseling phenomenon (*Career assessment on the Internet*, 2000). Recent authors have also recommended that counselors' knowledge of the world of work include changes in job markets; counselors should expand their knowledge to areas that affect that world, such as by reading national periodicals like the *Wall Street Journal* (DeBell, 2001; Herr & Niles, 1998). Counselors should be competent to address additional concerns such as discrimination and should gather a realistic appraisal of the barriers facing some clients in order to develop strategies "at all points in the career cycle from career development, to choice, through adjustment, to retirement" (Fouad, 1993, p. 4). This includes ongoing examination of the biases inherent in current and emerging assessment tools, familiarity with such tools, and work to develop more culturally sensitive tools and processes (Fouad, 1993; Gysbers et al., 2003). The *Career Development Quarterly* recently focused a special issue on career-counseling assessment issues of women of color and white women (*Career development of women of color and white women*, 2002). Career counselors should be aware that extreme poverty still exists in the United States, that clients may be moving from—or toward—conditions of poverty, and that socioeconomic status (SES) plays a complex role in shaping a person's life trajectory, perceived opportunities, and so on (e.g. Liu, 2001, 2003; Peterson & Gonzales, 2000).

Training New Counselors, the World Wide Web and Ethics for the New Age

Technological capacity and capability have outpaced vocational counseling competency, and the training of career counselors must reflect these changes (Hansen, 2003; Harris, 2000; Herr, 2003). The establishment of career centers on college campuses, specialized career counseling centers for different populations, and Internet career coaches and entrepreneurs are but a few examples of developments relevant to career counselors (Harris-Bowlesby, 2003; Whiston, 2003). According to Hansen (2003), the marginalization of career counseling in training programs, decreased passion for teaching career counseling coursework, and the advent of Internet career-coaching entrepreneurs are all leading to the "deprofessionalization" of career counseling (Hansen, 2003, p. 47). Hansen has called for counselors to continue to use technology in their work and to develop further ethical guidelines for computer-assisted counseling. Tang (2003) suggests that using computers to match clients with potential jobs could free up more time for career counselors to focus on the more complex aspects of each client's situation. In addition, promising trends that we hope to see furthered in the coming years include international collaboration (e.g., the 2003 Society for Vocational Psychology meeting was held in Coimbra, Portugal), advocacy for greater diversity in education, and greater recruitment and retention of career counselors from underrepresented populations; such trends reflect the social justice roots of the field (Hansen, 2003; O'Brien, 2001; Pope, 2003; Tang, 2003).

Advocacy

Legislative efforts over the previous century have consistently relied upon vocational counseling to ease social, political, and economic transitions and remediate social injustices. As a result, career counseling has become institutionalized as a part of governmental initiatives for change (Herr, 2003). Because of this relationship, Herr (2003) and others (e.g., Blustein et al., 2005; Hansen, 2003; Pope, 2003) have argued that career counselors have a responsibility to become actively involved in legislative efforts, making legislators aware of career counseling's needs, theories, practices, and research, and giving legislators "facts, trends, results and costs—not opinions" (Herr, 2003, p. 12). For example, despite major moves in theory and practice toward holistic career counseling, most government programs are still focused on simply matching people to jobs (Hansen, 2003). The fact that career counselors are often in a variety of settings yet isolated from each other and from existing research only contributes to this lack of communication in government: the problem is that "voids in legislation" have led to unfocused, uninformed efforts, duplication of services, and incoherent services (Herr, 2003, p. 14).

Research

Vocational research has focused more on understanding career development and decision making rather than on specific intervention techniques, thus resulting in a gap between theory and practice that is duplicated in legislative efforts (Niles, 2003; Whiston, 2003). Research that emerges from, and informs, practice is clearly needed (Savickas, 2003). Brown and Krane's (2000) meta-analysis of career counseling interventions provided an important heuristic for vocational research. They found that career interventions are likely to produce the greatest effects if the interventions (a) include written exercises (b) provide individualized assessment interpretation and feedback, (c) give current information on the world of work, (d) include role models that demonstrate effective strategies, and (e) attend to building support. This work represents an important advance in career counseling research; nonetheless, Whiston contends that "career counselors do not know what works with which clients under what conditions" (2003, p. 37). The dearth of research with women and minorities noted since the 1970s has continued (Savickas, 2003; Tang, 2003; Whiston, 2003), making it difficult to apply research findings to the diverse work world. Parmer and Rush (2003) suggest additional research should be undertaken with understudied client populations such as the non-college-bound students, nonnative English speakers, and people with HIV/AIDS, while Tang (2003) calls for more research with working adults and Harris-Bowlsbey (2003) recommends research on Web-based interventions, quality assurance, triaging client needs, and the use of computers to ameliorate the counselor workloads.

New Models

Integrative career development models combining occupational development with racial identity development are needed (Bowman, 1995; Gysbers, Heppner, Johnston, et al., 2003; Osipow & Littlejohn, 1995); the work of Bingham and Ward (1997) is one example of such integration. Blustein and his colleagues have been active in articulating various dimensions of the need for integrative models. For example, Hartung and Blustein (2002) argue that newer thinking about contextual factors such as social, political, and economic elements must be incorporated into vocational counseling. They propose the integration of the rational models that evolved from Parsons's work with postmodern models that are culturally relevant and pluralistic. They offer the example of the School-to-Career program, a collaboration between the counseling psychology program at Boston College and the Boston Public Schools (Hartung & Blustein, 2002). Blustein, McWhirter, and Perry (2005) propose an emancipatory communitarian approach to vocational theory development that attends to social inequities, structural injustice, and the working lives of marginalized people. Blustein et al. (2000) suggest that interdisciplinary convergence of thought will have the greatest power to influence policy development as well as research and practice. New interdisciplinary alliances, such as those described Brabeck, Walsh, Kenny, and Comilang (1997), are also important models. Recently there has been a resurgence in the literature about forging links between career counseling, advocacy, and social justice, such as through involvement with legislative action (Fassinger, 2001) or through combining teaching, research, and service delivery to serve high-risk populations (Blustein, 2001; Chronister et al., 2003; O'Brien, 2001). These and other trends suggest that the work of career counselors is likely to be varied, dynamic, and highly valuable to society in the coming decades.

SUMMARY

Career counseling has changed significantly since its inception, while preserving many fundamental elements. The field originated to assist youth in the process of identifying work for which they were suited. As the value of this assistance became more widely recognized, vocational guidance units were added to school curricula. Vocational guidance served both the work bound and the college bound, though in fact the two groups quite often received very different types of training, and distinctions between the two groups have never been adequately addressed within the field. Early calls for measurement in vocational guidance were amplified with World War I, which created a need to quickly and efficiently match large numbers of soldiers to suitable positions. The war coincided with greater expansion of school-based vocational guidance.

Legislative efforts over time demonstrate recognition of the positive effects of vocational guidance, and guidance was increasingly seen as a means to alleviate social problems. This was particularly apparent during the Great Depression and LBJ's Great Society and following the 1957 launch of *Sputnik I* by the Soviet Union. During World War II, vocational guidance again played an important role in the placement of soldiers into appropriate positions. The writings and theories of Carl Rogers,

Erik Erikson, and Abraham Maslow emerged to influence vocational guidance theory. For example, counselors began to understand vocational problems contextually and began working more holistically with clients.

Beginning in the 1960s and continuing through today, critiques of vocational psychology have identified the lack of attention to the vocational needs and development of major groups such as women, ethnic and racial minorities, homosexuals, and individuals with disabilities. While attention to cultural, linguistic, and other types of diversity has certainly increased, there remains a great deal more to do in the areas of theory development, assessment, research, and practice in order to increase the relevance and utility of vocational psychology to a broader segment of the population.

Toward the end of the twentieth century, career theories continued to develop contextually and holistically. The beginning of the twenty-first century has witnessed changes in the job marketplace, such as rapid expansion of required skills, changing work environments, and the transformation of work from one format to another. These changes parallel some of the changes in motion one hundred years ago, when vocational guidance began.

CONCLUDING REMARKS

In this chapter we have presented an overview of some of the primary influences that have shaped the evolution of vocational guidance and career counseling. In the process, we discovered that writing a book might have been an easier task, because of the complexity and density of the historical and contextual information available. We are awed by the extent to which our unique interests, backgrounds, oversights, and values shaped the development of this work, a process quite parallel to how vocational guidance and career counseling itself was shaped. We hope that readers will continue to critically reflect on the influences and factors identified here, as well as the many other influences that also could have been included—just as we will. Finally, we hope that the material included has provided the reader with a useful background for learning in greater detail about the theory and practice of career counseling.

REFERENCES

American Psychological Association, Division of Counseling Psychology, Committee on Definition. (1956). Counseling psychology as a specialty. *American Psychologist, 11,* 282–285.

Anelauskas, V. (1999). *Discovering America as it is.* Atlanta: Clarity Press.

Armor, D. J. (1969). *The American school counselor.* New York: Russell Sage Foundation.

Astin, H. S. (1984). The meaning of work in women's lives: A sociopsychological model of career choice and work behavior. *The Counseling Psychologist, 12,* 117–126.

Aubrey, R. F. (1977). Historical development of guidance and counseling and implications for the future. *Personnel and Guidance Journal, 55,* 288–295.

Baker, D. B. (2002). Child saving and the emergence of vocational psychology. *Journal of Vocational Behavior, 60,* 374–381.

Bandura, A. (1969). *Principles of behavior modification*. New York: Holt, Rinehart & Winston.

Bandura, A. (1977). *Social learning theory*. Englewood Cliffs, NJ: Prentice Hall.

Bandura, A. (1986). *Social foundations of thoughts and action: A social cognitive theory*. Englewood Cliffs, NJ: Prentice Hall.

Bettman, O. (1974). *The good old days: They were terrible!* New York: Random House.

Betz, N. E., & Fitzgerald, L. F. (1995). Career assessment and intervention with racial and ethnic minorities. In F. T. L. Leong (Ed.), *Career development and vocational behavior of racial and ethnic minorities* (pp. 263–280). Mahwah, NJ: Erlbaum.

Bingham, R. P., & Ward, C. M. (1997). Theory into assessment: A model of women of color. *Journal of Career Assessment, 5*, 383–402.

Blustein, D. L. (2001). Extending the reach of vocational psychology: Toward an integrative and inclusive psychology of work. *Journal of Vocational Behavior, 59*, 171–182.

Blustein, D. L., Juntunen, C. L., & Worthington, R. L. (2000). The school-to-work transition: Adjustment challenges of the forgotten half. In S. D. Brown & R. W. Lent (Eds.), *Handbook of counseling psychology* (pp. 435–470). New York: Wiley.

Blustein, D. L., McWhirter, E. H., & Perry, J. C. (2005). Toward an emancipatory communitarian approach to vocational development theory. *The Counseling Psychologist, 33*, 141–179.

Blustein, D. L., & Spengler, P. M. (1995). Personal adjustment: Career counseling and psychotherapy. In W. B. Walsh & S. H. Osipow (Eds.), *Handbook of vocational psychology* (2nd ed., pp. 295–329). Mahwah, NJ: Erlbaum.

Borow, H. (1974). Apathy, unrest and change: The psychology of the 1960s. In E. Herr (Ed.), *Vocational guidance and human development* (pp. 3–31). Boston: Houghton Mifflin.

Bowman, S. (1995). Career intervention strategies and assessment issues for African Americans. In F. T. L. Leong (Ed.), *Career development and vocational behavior of racial and ethnic minorities* (pp. 137–164). Mahwah, NJ: Erlbaum.

Brabeck, M., Walsh, M. E., Kenny, M., & Comilang, K. (1997). Interprofessional collaboration for children and families: Opportunities for counseling psychology in the 21st century. *The Counseling Psychologist, 25*, 615–636.

Brecher, J. (1997). *Strike!* Boston: South End Press.

Brewer, J. M. (1942). *History of vocational guidance*. New York: Harper.

Brodkin, K. (1998). *How Jews became white folks and what that says about race in America*. New Brunswick, NJ: Rutgers University Press.

Bronfenbrenner, U. (1979). *The ecology of human development: Experiments by nature and design*. Cambridge, MA: Harvard University Press.

Brown, S. D., & Krane, N. E. R. (2000). Four (or five) sessions and a cloud of dust: Old assumptions and new observations about career counseling. In S. D. Brown & R. W. Lent (Eds.), *Handbook of counseling psychology* (pp. 740–766). New York: Wiley.

Brown-Collins, A. R., & Sussewell, D. R. (1986). The Afro-American woman's emerging selves. *Journal of Black Psychology, 13*, 1–11.

Bruner, B. (n.d.). Timeline of affirmative action milestones. Retrieved August 13, 2004, from http://www.infoplease.com/spot/affirmativetimeline1.html

Career assessment for a new millennium. (2000). Special section of the *Journal of Career Assessment, 8*(4).

Career assessment on the Internet. (2000). Special issue of the *Journal of Career Assessment, 8*(1).

Career development of women of color and white women. (2002). Special issue of *Career Development Quarterly, 50*(4).

Chronister, K. M., Wettersten, K., & Brown, C. (2003). *Vocational psychology research for the liberation of battered women*. Manuscript submitted for publication.

Chung, Y. B. (2001). Work discrimination and coping strategies: Conceptual frameworks for counseling lesbian, gay, and bisexual clients. *Career Development Quarterly, 50,* 33–44.

Danek, M. M., Conyers, L. M., Enright, M. S., Munson, M., Brodwin, M., Hanley-Maxwell, C., & Gugerty, J. (1996). Legislation concerning career counseling and job placement for people with disabilities. In E. M. Szymanski & R. M. Parker (Eds.), *Work and disability: Issues and strategies in career development and job placement* (pp. 39–78). Austin, TX: PRO-ED.

DeBell, C. (2001). Ninety years in the world of work in America. *Career Development Quarterly, 50,* 77–88.

Dewey, J. (1916). *Democracy and education: An introduction to the philosophy of education.* New York: Macmillan.

Dixon, D. N. (1987). From Parsons to profession: The history of guidance and counseling psychology. In J. Glover & R. Ronning (Eds.), *Historical foundations of educational psychology* (pp. 107–120). New York: Plenum Press.

Dvorak, B. J. (1947). The new U.S.E.S. General Aptitude Test Battery. *Journal of Applied Psychology, 31,* 372–376.

Engels, D. W., Minor, C. W., Sampson, J. P., & Splete, H. H. (1995, November/December). Career counseling specialty: History, development and prospect. *Journal of Counseling and Development, 74,* 134–138.

Erikson, E. H. (1950). *Childhood and society.* New York: Norton.

Estes, R. J., & Weiner, N. (2002). *The commercial sexual exploitation of children in the U. S., Canada, and Mexico.* Retrieved October 18, 2003, from http://caster.ssw.upenn.edu/~restes/CSEC.htm.

Faludi, S. (1991). *Backlash: The undeclared war against American women.* New York: Crown Publishers.

Faludi, S. (1999). *Stiffed: The betrayal of the American man.* New York: William Morrow.

Farmer, H. S. (1985). Model of career and achievement motivation for women and men. *Journal of Counseling Psychology, 32,* 363–390.

Fassinger, R. (2001). *Using the master's tools: Social advocacy at the national level.* Paper presented at the Fourth National Conference on Counseling Psychology, Houston, TX.

Fitzgerald, L. F., & Betz, N. E. (1983). Issues in the vocational psychology of women. In W. B. Walsh & S. H. Osipow (Eds.), *Handbook of vocational psychology* (Vol. 1, pp. 83–160). Hillsdale, NJ: Erlbaum.

Fouad, N. A. (1993). Cross cultural vocational assessment. *Career Development Quarterly, 42,* 4–13.

Fouad, N. A., & Bingham, R. P. (1995). Career counseling with racial and ethnic minorities. In W. B. Walsh & S. H. Osipow (Eds.), *Handbook of vocational psychology: Theory, research and practice,* 2nd ed. (pp. 331–365). Mahwah, NJ: Erlbaum.

Gainor, K., & Forrest, L. (1991). African American women's self-concept: Implications for career decisions and career counseling. *Career Development Quarterly, 39,* 261–373.

Gelso, C. J., & Fretz, B. R. (2001). *Counseling psychology* (2nd ed.). Fort Worth, TX: Harcourt Brace.

Gibson, R. L., & Mitchell, M. H. (1999). *Introduction to counseling and guidance.* Upper Saddle River, NJ: Merrill.

Ginzberg, E. (1984). Career development. In D. Brown & L. Brooks (Eds.), *Career choice and development: Applying contemporary theories to practice* (pp. 169–191). San Francisco: Jossey-Bass.

Ginzberg, E., Ginsburg, S., Axelrad, S., & Herma, J. (1951). *Occupational choice: An approach to a general theory.* New York: Columbia University Press.

Gottfredson, L. (1981). Circumscription and compromise: A developmental theory of occupational aspiration. *Journal of Counseling Psychology, 28,* 545–579.

Gottfredson, L. S. (1996). Gottfredson's theory of circumscription and compromise. In D. Brown, L. Brooks, & Associates (Eds.), *Career choice and development,* 3rd ed. (pp. 179–232). San Francisco: Jossey-Bass.

Gottfredson, L. S. (2002). Gottfredson's theory of circumscription, compromise, and self-creation. In D. Brown & Associates (Eds.), *Career choice and development*, 4th ed. (pp. 85–148). San Francisco: Jossey-Bass.

Gourley, C. (1999). *Good girl work: Factories, sweatshops, and how women changed their role in the American workforce*. Brookfield, CT: Millbrook Press.

Gysbers, N. C., Heppner, M. J., & Johnston, J. A. (2003). *Career counseling: Process, issues and techniques.* Boston, MA: Allyn & Bacon.

Gysbers, N. C., Heppner, M. J., Johnston, J. A., & Neville, H. A. (2003). Empowering life choices: Career counseling in cultural contexts. In N. Gysbers, M. Heppner, & J. Johnston, (Eds.), *Career counseling: Process, issues and techniques* (pp. 50–76). Boston, MA: Allyn & Bacon.

Gysbers, N. C., & Moore, E. J. (1973). *Life Career Development Theory: A model.* Columbia: University of Missouri Press.

Hackett, G., & Betz, N. E. (1981). Self-efficacy approach to the career development of women. *Journal of Vocational Behavior, 18,* 326–339.

Hansen, S. S. (2003). Career counselors as advocates and change agents for equality. *Career Development Quarterly, 52,* 43–53.

Harris, H. (2000). Defining the future or reliving the past? Unions, employers, and the challenge of workplace learning (Information Series No. 380). *ERIC Clearinghouse on Adult, Career, and Vocational Education.* Retrieved August 1, 2003, from http://ericave.org/mp_harris_01.asp

Harris-Bowlsbey, J. (2003). A rich past and a future vision. *Career Development Quarterly, 52,* 18–25.

Hartung, P. J. & Blustein, D. L. (2002, Winter). Reason, intuition, and social justice: Elaborating on Parsons's career decision making model. *Journal of Counseling and Development, 80,* 41–47.

Hawks, B. K., & Muha, D. (1991). Facilitating the career development of minorities: Doing it differently this time. *Career Development Quarterly, 39,* 251–260.

Heppner, P. P., Casas, J. M., Carter, J., & Stone, G. L. (2000). The maturation of counseling psychology: Multifaceted perspectives, 1978–1998. In S. D. Brown & R. W. Lent (Eds.), *Handbook of counseling psychology* (3rd ed., pp. 3–49). New York: Wiley.

Herr, E. L. (1974). Manpower policies, vocational guidance, and career development. In E. Herr (Ed.), *Vocational guidance and human development* (pp. 32–62). Boston: Houghton Mifflin.

Herr, E. L. (1979). *Guidance and counseling in the schools: The past, present, and future.* Falls Church, VA: American Personnel and Guidance Association.

Herr, E. L. (2003). The future of career counseling as an instrument of public policy. *Career Development Quarterly, 52,* 8–17.

Herr, E. L., & Niles, S. G. (1998). Career: Social action in behalf of purpose, productivity and hope. In Courtland C. Lee & Garry R. Walz (Eds.), *Social action: A mandate for counselors.* Alexandria, VA: American Counseling Association.

Herr, E. L., & Shahnasarian, M. (2001). Selected milestones in the evolution of career development practices in the 20th century. *Career Development Quarterly, 49,* 225–237.

Holland, J. L. (1959). Theory of vocational choice. *Journal of Counseling Psychology, 6,* 35–45.

Holland, J. L. (1992). *Making vocational choices: A theory of vocational personalities and work environments.* Odessa, FL: Psychological Assessment Resources.

Holland, J. L. (1997). *Making vocational choices: A theory of vocational personalities and work environments.* Odessa, FL: Psychological Assessment Resources.

Hoyt, K. B. (2001). A reaction to Mark Pope's (2000) "A brief history of career counseling in the United States." *Career Development Quarterly, 49,* 374–379.

Iavarone, M. (2001). Trenches on the web. Retrieved March 23, 2005, from http://www.worldwar1.com/hcrates.htm.

Isaacson, L. E. (1985). *Basics of career counseling.* Boston: Allyn & Bacon.

Kaplan, A. (1997). Domestic violence and welfare reform. *Welfare Reform News, Issue Notes, 1*(8). Retrieved November 12, 2003, from http://www.welfareinfo.org/domesticissue.htm.

Krumboltz, J. D. (1979). A social learning theory of career decision making. In A. M. Mitchell, G. B. Jones, & J. D. Krumboltz (Eds.), *Social learning and career decision making* (pp. 19–49). Cranston, RI: Carroll Press.

Krumboltz, J. D. (1991). The 1990 Leona Tyler Award Address: Brilliant insights—Platitudes that bear repeating. *The Counseling Psychologist, 19,* 298–315.

Krumboltz, J. D. (1996). A learning theory of career counseling. In M. L. Savickas & W. B. Walsh (Eds.), *Handbook of career counseling theory and practice* (pp. 55–80). Palo Alto, CA: Consulting Psychologists Press.

Krumboltz, J. D., Mitchell, A., & Gelatt, H. G. (1975). Applications of social learning theory of career selection. *Focus on Guidance, 8,* 1–16.

Lent, E. B. (2001). Welfare-to-work services: A person centered perspective. *Career Development Quarterly, 50,* 22–32.

Lent, R. W., Brown, S. D., & Hackett, G. (1994). Toward a unified social cognitive theory of career and academic interest, choice and performance. *Journal of Vocational Behavior, 45,* 79–122.

Leong, F. T. L. (Ed.). (1995). *Career development and vocational behavior of racial and ethnic minorities.* Mahwah, NJ: Erlbaum.

Liu, W. M. (2001). Expanding our understanding of multiculturalism: Developing a social class worldview model. In D. B. Pope-Davis and H. L. K. Coleman (Eds.), *The intersection of race, class, and gender in counseling psychology* (pp. 127–170). Thousand Oaks, CA: Sage Publications.

Liu, W. M. (2003). The social class-related experiences of men: Integrating theory and practice. *Professional Psychology: Research and Practice, 33,* pp. 355–360.

Lofquist, L. H., & Dawis, R. V. (1969). *Adjustment to work.* New York: Appleton-Century-Crofts.

Maslow, A. H. (1954). *Motivation and personality.* New York: Harper & Row.

McLemore, S. D., Romo, H. D., & Baker, S. G. (2001). *Racial and ethnic relations in America.* Needham Heights, MA: Allyn & Bacon.

Miller-Tiedeman, A., & Tiedeman, D. (1990). Career decision-making: An individualistic perspective. In D. Brown, L. Brooks & Associates (Eds.), *Career choice and development: Applying contemporary theories to practice* (pp. 308–337). San Francisco: Jossey-Bass.

Mitchell, L., & Krumboltz, J. D. (1984). Research of human decision making: Implications for career decision makers and counselors. In D. Brown & R. Lent (Eds.), *Handbook of counseling psychology* (pp. 238–280). New York: Wiley.

National Vocational Guidance Association (NVGA), American Vocational Association (AVA). (1973). *Position paper on career development.* Washington, DC: Authors.

National Vocational Guidance Association, Board of Directors. (1982, June). Vocational/career counseling competencies. *NVGA Newsletter, 22,* 6.

Niles, S. G. (2003). Career counselors confront a critical crossroad: A vision of the future. *Career Development Quarterly, 52,* 70–77.

O'Brien, K. M. (2001). The legacy of Parsons: Career counselors and vocational psychologists as agents of social change. *Career Development Quarterly, 50,* 66–77.

O'Ryan, L. (2003). Career counseling and social justice. *Counselors for Social Justice Newsletter, 4,* 1, 3.

Osipow, S. H., & Littlejohn, E. M. (1995). Toward a multicultural theory of career development: Prospects and dilemmas. In F. T. L. Leong (Ed.), *Career development and vocational behavior of racial and ethnic minorities* (pp. 251–262). Mahwah, NJ: Lawrence Erlbaum Associates.

Parmer, T., & Rush, L. C. (2003). The next decade in career counseling: Cocoon maintenance or metamorphosis? *Career Development Quarterly, 52,* 26–34.

Parsons, F. (1909). *Choosing a vocation.* Boston: Houghton-Mifflin.

Peterson, N., & Gonzales, R. C. (2000). *The role of work in people's lives: Applied career counseling and vocational psychology.* Belmont, CA: Brooks/Cole.

Pope, M. (2000). A brief history of career counseling in the United States. *Career Development Quarterly, 48,* 194–211.

Pope, M. (2003). Career counseling in the twenty-first century: Beyond cultural encapsulation. *Career Development Quarterly, 52,* 54–60.

Richardson, M. S. (1993). Work in people's lives: A location for counseling psychologists. *Journal of Counseling Psychology, 40,* 425–433.

Roe, A. (1956). *The psychology of occupations.* New York: Wiley.

Roe, A. (1957). Early determinants of vocational choice. *Journal of Counseling Psychology, 4,* 212–217.

Rogers, C. R. (1939). *Counseling and psychotherapy.* Boston: Houghton Mifflin.

Rogers, C. R. (1951). *Client-centered therapy.* Boston: Houghton Mifflin.

Sampson, J. P. & Lumsden, J. A. (2000). Ethical issues in the design and use of Internet-based career assessment. *Journal of Career Assessment, 8,* 21–35.

Santos, E. J. R., Ferreira, J. A., & Chaves, A. (2001). Implications of sociopolitical context for career services delivery. *Career Development Quarterly, 50,* 45–55.

Savickas, M. L. (1993). Career counseling in the postmodern era. *Journal of Cognitive Psychotherapy: An International Quarterly, 7,* 205–215.

Savickas, M. L. (2003). Advancing the career counseling profession: Objectives and strategies for the next decade. *Career Development Quarterly, 52,* 87–96.

Scott, M. F. (1911, April 15). The factory girl's danger. *The Outlook.* Retrieved November 1, 2003, from http://www.ilr.cornell.edu/trianglefire/texts/newspaper/outlook_041511.html

Seligman, L. (1994). *Developmental career counseling and assessment.* Thousand Oaks, CA: Sage Publications.

Sharf, R. S. (2002). *Applying career development theory to counseling.* Pacific Grove, CA: Brooks/Cole.

Sinclair, U. (1905). *The jungle.* New York: Signet.

Smith, E. J. (1983). Issues in racial minorities' career behavior. In W. B. Walsh & S. H. Osipow (Eds.), *Handbook of vocational psychology* (Vol. 1, pp. 83–160). Hillsdale, NJ: Erlbaum.

Stricker, G., Davis-Russell, E., Bourg, E., Duran, E., Hammond, R., McHollan, S., Polite, K., & Vaughan, B. E. (Eds.). (1990). *Toward ethnic diversification in psychology education and training.* Washington, DC: American Psychological Association.

Strong, E. K. (1927). *Vocational interest blank.* Palo Alto, CA: Stanford University Press.

Strong, E. K. (1943). *Vocational interests of men and women.* Stanford, CA: Stanford University Press.

Strong, E. K. (1955). *Vocational interests 18 years after college.* Minneapolis: University of Minnesota Press.

Sue, D. W., Bingham, R. P., Porche-Burke, L., & Vasquez, M. (1999). The diversification of psychology: A multicultural revolution. *American Psychologist, 54,* 1061–1069.

Super, D. (1983). The history and development of vocational psychology: A personal perspective. In W. B. Walsh & S. H. Osipow (Eds.), *Handbook of vocational psychology: Volume 1. Foundations* (pp. 5–38). Hillsdale, NJ: Erlbaum.

Super, D. E. (1953). A theory of vocational development. *American Psychologist, 8,* 185–190.

Super, D. E. (1955). Transition: From vocational guidance to counseling psychology. *Journal of Counseling Psychology, 2,* 3–9.

Super, D. E. (1957). *The psychology of careers.* New York: Harper.

Super, D. E. (1990). A lifespan-lifespace approach to career development. In D. Brown, L. Brooks, & Associates. (Eds.). *Career choice and development: Applying contemporary theories to practice* (2nd ed., pp. 197–261). San Francisco: Jossey-Bass.

Szymanski, E. M., Hershenson, D. B., Enright, M. S., & Ettinger, J. M. (1996). Career development theories, constructs, and research: Implications for people with disabilities. In E. M. Szymanski & R. M. Parker (Eds.), *Work and disability: Issues and strategies in career development and job placement* (pp. 79–126). Austin, TX: PRO-ED.

Tang, M. (2003). Career counseling in the future: Constructing, collaborating, advocating. *Career Development Quarterly, 52,* 61–69.

Terkel, S. (1986). *Hard times: An oral history of the Great Depression.* New York: Pantheon Books.

Terman, L. M., & Oden, M. H. (1959). *Genetic studies of genius: Vol. 5. The gifted group at midlife.* Stanford, CA: Stanford University Press.

Thomas, R. R. (1990, March–April). From affirmative action to affirming diversity. *Harvard Business Review, 68,* 107–117.

Tiedeman, D. V., & O'Hara, R. P. (1963). *Career development: Choice and adjustment.* New York: College Entrance Examination Board.

Tucker, L. (2000). *Fingers to the bone: United States' failure to protect child farmworkers.* New York: Human Rights Watch.

U.S. Department of Labor. (1940). *Dictionary of occupational titles.* Washington, DC: U.S. Government Printing Office.

U.S. Department of Labor. (1949). *Occupational outlook handbook.* Washington, DC: U.S. Government Printing Office.

U.S. Equal Employment Opportunity Commission (EEOC). (n.d.). Home page. Retrieved August 13, 2004, from http://www.eeoc.gov/

Von Bertalanffy, L. (1968). *General systems theory: Foundation, development, application.* New York: Braziller.

Walsh, W. B., & Betz, N. E. (1995). *Tests and assessment.* Englewood Cliffs, NJ: Prentice Hall.

Ware, N. J. (1964). *The labor movement in the United States, 1860–1895: A study in democracy.* New York: Vintage.

Watkins, C. E. (1992). Historical influences on the use of assessment methods in counseling psychology. *Counseling Psychology Quarterly, 5,* 177–188.

Whiston, S. C. (2003). Career counseling: 90 years old yet still healthy and vital. *Career Development Quarterly, 52,* 35–42.

Williamson, E. G. (1939). *How to counsel students.* New York: McGraw-Hill.

Williamson, E. G. (1965). *Vocational counseling.* New York: McGraw-Hill.

Wrenn, C. G. (1962). *The counselor in a changing world.* Washington, DC: American Personnel and Guidance Association.

Zytowski, D. G. (2001). Frank Parsons and the progressive movement. *Career Development Quarterly, 50,* 57–65.

CHAPTER 2

CAREER COUNSELING
Theoretical Perspectives

MARIE F. SHOFFNER
University of Virginia

Our world is quickly changing, and has changed considerably over the last half-century. The world of work is very different from our parents' and grandparents' world of work. Our current reality includes downsizing and subsequent job loss, rapid technological advancements, with changes in jobs and in industries; changes in occupational structure; decreases in job benefits; an interdependent global economy and international labor competition; changing demographics; increased self-employment; and fewer low-wage jobs (Herr, Cramer, & Niles, 2004; Liptak, 2001). The career counselor must be able to understand the utility of various theories to be able to apply them to client career development and career choice. Before being able to effectively and efficiently provide career services appropriate to our times, the counselor must understand well-established and emerging career theories, their strengths and weaknesses, how to apply them to practice, and how research has supported or failed to support the various tenets of the theories for diverse populations and a rapidly changing vocational terrain.

The various career theories that guide career counseling practice can be classified as trait and factor theories, developmental theories, cognitive/learning theories and approaches, psychodynamic approaches, contextual, ecological and sociological theories, and several additional theories such as values-based theory and chance or accident theories. Before describing each of these types and the various theories, I would like to first present an analogy developed by a career theorist-practitioner as a helpful tool in understanding the utility of various theories of career development and counseling.

WHAT GOOD IS A THEORY?

A useful theory provides a framework for understanding complex phenomena; a career theory is a way of summarizing what we see and what we know by constructing explanations for career development and behavior. According to a useful metaphor presented by

John Krumboltz, a theory is "an attempt to represent some aspect of behavior, much in the same way that a map is an attempt to represent some geographic territory" (1994, p. 9) or facts about that territory (e.g., rainfall, topology, etc.). Maps vary in purpose, over-simplify facts, may distort certain features (e.g., a large city is not really a black dot ringed by a black circle), often represent things we cannot see, differ in scale, vary in usefulness (e.g., a map of average rainfall in Virginia has a different use than a map of the streets of New York City), and, because they are based on current knowledge, may contain errors that are corrected as more knowledge is accumulated (Krumboltz, 1994). In short, "a good theory is a simplified representation of some domain constructed so that users can ask questions about that domain with an increased probability of receiving valuable answers" (Krumboltz, 1994, p. 12). As you read about the various career theories presented in this chapter, keep in mind the specific map to career development and choice that each of the theories offers. Some theories will be better at addressing specific choice points in the career process, others will be better at explaining the development of career interests or the adjustment process to the world of work, and still others will be better at explaining the external factors that impact choice and persistence in the realm of careers.

TRAIT AND FACTOR APPROACHES

In 1909, Frank Parsons developed a way of helping young people to become success-fully employed. His three-pronged approach has become known as the trait and factor approach and consists of (1) individual knowledge, including interests, abilities, and skills; (2) knowledge of the job; and (3) logical or reasoned matching of the individual's traits to the job that best "fits" him or her. (See Figure 2.1.) This approach is the general approach used in all of the career theories that are based on matching individuals to

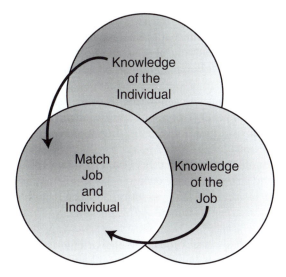

**FIGURE 2.1   Parsons'
Trait and Factor Theory**

work environments so that they will be successful in, and satisfied with, their work. In this section, I will present two of the most well-known and well-established matching theories, Holland's typological theory and Dawis and Lofquist's theory of work adjustment (currently person-environment correspondence).

Holland's Theory of Personality Types

Theoretical Concepts.   John Holland is generally acknowledged as among the most influential people in the field of career counseling and practice. There exist more empirical studies regarding Holland's theory than any other, and more articles have been written about his theory of personality orientations or types than any other in vocational psychology (Spokane, 1996). In a special edition of the *Journal of Vocational Behavior* dedicated to 40 years of Holland's work, Savickas and Gottfredson (1999) stated, "In addition to prompting a tremendous amount of empirical research in vocational and I/O psychology, the theory has provided major breakthroughs in conceptualizing vocational interests and career decision making, constructing interest inventories, organizing occupational information, counseling for career development, and structuring career education curricula" (p. 2).

In 1959, Holland presented his theory of career choice, in which the underlying premise was that individuals choose situations and environments that satisfy their personality orientations (Holland, 1959). In 1969, he introduced the circular and hexagonal structure of his six personality orientations (Holland, Whitney, Cole, & Richards, 1969). The focus of Holland's theory has been on why career choice occurs and the outcome of that choice, rather than on how or why personality orientations develop. Like other trait and factor approaches, the theory attempts to match individual stable traits with the characteristics of complex work environments (Liptak, 2001; Spokane, 1996).

According to Holland's theoretical view of career choice, occupations are not merely a set of work skills, but instead represent a "way of life." Holland's theory of personality types explicitly addresses the influence of behavioral style and personality type on choice of career. In fact, style and type, which are relatively unchanging traits, are considered the major influence on career choice. Personal interests are a manifestation of one's personality, and one's personality leads one to seek satisfaction in work that "fits" it.

Holland's theory is based on the following four major assumptions:

1. In our culture, most persons can be categorized as one of six types: Realistic, Investigative, Artistic, Social, Enterprising, or Conventional;
2. There are six kinds of environments: Realistic, Investigative, Artistic, Social, Enterprising, or Conventional;
3. People search for environments that will let them exercise their skills and abilities, express their attitudes and values, and take on agreeable problems and roles; and
4. A person's behavior is determined by an interaction between personality and the characteristics of the environment (Holland, 1973, pp. 2–4).

Holland further defines these six basic modal personal orientations and six modal occupation orientations, based on the belief that people will enter, and stay in, work that is similar to (or congruent with) their personality type. These types are part of a personal orientation that is based on life experiences and heredity, reflects interests and personality, and is fairly stable. Thus, choice of career is an extension of one's personality type into the world of work—a choice made to satisfy an individual's preferred personal orientation. People are categorized as predominant in one of six types: Realistic (those who do things; includes skilled trades, many technical occupations, and several service occupations), Investigative (those who think about things; includes scientific occupations and several technical occupations), Artistic (those who create things; includes artistic, literary, and musical occupations), Social (those who help others; includes social welfare occupations and education), Enterprising (those who persuade others; includes sales and managerial occupations), and Conventional (those who organize; includes clerical occupations). The combination and pattern of all six orientations are used to describe a person's personality. However, the first three are the dominant combinations and the most often used in matching individuals to an occupation. Holland, in his later work (1992), states that members in a vocation have similar personalities, similar histories of personal development, and similar responses to situations. Therefore, these groups of individuals create work environments characteristic of their vocation (Holland, 1992).

In Holland's later work, he presents his circular structure and hexagonal description of vocational types (see Figure 2.2). In his circular structure, he posits that the six types can be envisioned as arranged in a circular form, with those types that are more similar to each other placed closer to each other on this circle and those least similar placed farthest away from each other. Thus, the Realistic and Investigative types are adjacent to each other, while the Realistic and Social types are far from each other. The order of the six types is, therefore, *R*ealistic, *I*nvestigative, *A*rtistic, *S*ocial, *E*nterprising, and *C*onventional (RIASEC).

The hexagonal description further structures this ordering by arranging those types that are similar to be equidistant from each other in the circular arrangement, thus forming a hexagon within the circle. For example, Investigative is adjacent to both Realistic and Artistic. According to the hexagonal limitation, then, Investigative is as far from Realistic as it is from Artistic. Two types are the most different if they are at opposite ends of the hexagon and most similar if they are adjacent to each other on the hexagon. Notice that Realistic and Social are further from each other than Realistic is from any other type. This indicates that Realistic is most dissimilar to Social. Likewise, Investigative is further from Enterprising than any other. If you examine the brief definitions of each of the types as given previously, you may be able to develop some hypotheses about the differences between two people of very different (opposite) Holland personality types.

Holland's theory posits four basic theoretical constructs that provide additional information when examining an individual's typology. The most widely used is the construct of congruence. Congruence is the level of closeness between an individual's type code and a particular work environment and is calculated using various mathematical formulas to estimate "fit" (Brown & Gore, 1994). There is congruence between a person's type and a particular occupation when the occupation type matches the person's type; when there is congruence, a person is more likely to be satisfied with his or her

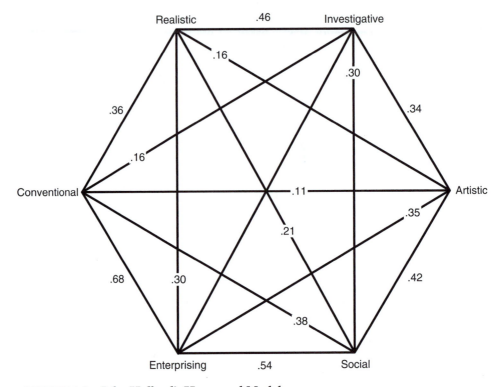

FIGURE 2.2   John Holland's Hexagonal Model

occupation. For example, if a person's three primary types are IAR and the Investigative type is very dominant, then there would be congruence between that person's type and a scientific research position, but little congruence between this person's type and a clerical position. In fact, job stability and success, in addition to satisfaction, are influenced by the congruence between personality type and the work environment (Liptak, 2001; Niles & Harris-Bowlsbey, 2002).

Consistency is the relatedness of a person's top types, or the degree to which the first two primary types are similar. The closer the top two types are on the hexagonal model, the more consistency there is in the person's style and behavior. For example, in the hexagonal model, someone with a RIA typology would have a consistent profile because R, I, and A are close on the model and R and I are contiguous. On the other hand someone with an RSA typology would have a profile that is not consistent.

Differentiation indicates a crystallization of interests; it is the extent to which the levels of the type codes differ. In using the first three letters of someone's type, this difference would be most important between the first and second orientation. For instance, if a person's type is RIA but the levels of all three types are the same, that person's type would not have clear differentiation. A flat profile on all six types would exhibit the lowest differentiation. On the other hand, if a person's type is RIA and the assessment indicates high levels of R and much lower levels of I and A, then that person has a differentiated type.

Finally, Holland defined identity as the "possession of a stable and clear picture of one's own goals, interests and talents" (Holland, 1985, p. 5). Identity can be assessed through Holland's Vocational Identity Scale, which will be discussed in Chapter 5. Likewise, work environments that have clarity, stability, and consistency have a clear work identity.

Strengths and Weaknesses.   Research results support a limited number of occupational personality types, thus supporting the validity of the use of unique types in career choice and career counseling. Research on the circular and hexagonal nature of the six types suggests that there is a structure underlying the Holland Code, as based on interest inventories. The ordering of the types (RIASEC) also is consistently supported (Day & Rounds, 1998; Rounds, McKenna, Hubert, & Day, 2000; Rounds & Tracey, 1993, 1996; Tracey & Rounds, 1992, 1993, 1996), although the actual model may be more oval than circular and perhaps may even best be described as spherical. Researchers investigating the theory underlying the hexagonal shape, or equal distances between adjacent types, have found mixed results. This may be due more to methodological issues than to an actual insufficiency of the theory (Tracey, Darcey, & Kovalski, 2000). The relationship between congruence and job satisfaction has been shown to be relatively small (Chartrand & Walsh, 1999; Meir, Esformes, & Friedland, 1994; Meir & Navon, 1992; Tokar, Fischer, & Subich, 1998), although the difficulties of operationalizing satisfaction (Prediger, 2000) and congruence indices (Camp & Chartrand, 1992) may be limiting factors in these studies.

Holland's theory has been criticized in the past for potential racial and gender bias in the measurement and assumptions of the typology model, yet research results from studies of these factors have been mostly supportive (Anderson, Tracey, & Rounds, 1997; Day, Rounds, & Swaney, 1998; Fouad, Harmon, & Borgen, 1997; Havercamp, Collins, & Hansen, 1994; Rounds & Tracey, 1996; Ryan, Tracey, & Rounds, 1996; Tang, Fouad, & Smith, 1999). The ordering of the types has been confirmed, although not always in a circular shape (Tracey, 1997). The more restricted hexagonal model, which assumes equal distances between adjacent personality types, has been supported in some of the studies mentioned previously (Prediger, 2000). However, in other research, attempts to show invariance of the circular model (a circular RIASEC order) and hexagonal model (equidistance of adjacent types) across gender or culture have failed (Hansen, Collins, Swanson, & Fouad, 1993; Tinsley, 2000). In other words, even when a circular structure may have been supported, the distances between adjacent types have differed by gender, race, or culture.

Holland's theory also has been criticized for not addressing the role of culture and oppression in creating and sustaining work environments. For example, according to

Holland (1997), men score higher on R, I, and E, and women score higher on S, A, and C. Historically, careers that tend to be Realistic, Investigative, and Enterprising tend to pay higher salaries and provide more upward career development than those careers that are primarily Social, Artistic, or Conventional. This persistent criticism cannot be addressed by a theory that focuses on the personality types that exist and the current realities of work environments. This differential scoring is a direct reflection of current gender differences in these careers, not a reflection of the theory. (For further discussion of Holland's theory, culture, and diverse populations, see Chapters 14, 15, and 16.)

The major strengths of this theory are that it is easy for both counselor and client to understand, it is a practical way of organizing information, it is supported by a considerable body of research, and there are a number of valid, reliable instruments based on the theory that can be used by career counselors. It is conceivable that the greatest weakness of Holland's theory is the simplicity of its application, which can lead to possible misuse of the results. In other words, there may be a tendency for an unaware or less experienced counselor to allow the test results to lead to recommendations of a limited number of career choice possibilities. Because trait and factor models are often presented as rigid, Holland's current model is sometimes seen as similar to earlier matching approaches. In fact, however, Holland presents a complex theory of the relationships and interactions between individuals and work environments (Spokane, 1994, 1996). Perceived model inflexibility may be due more to practitioners' lack of understanding of the model and lack of knowledge regarding the research on occupational disparities.

Theory of Work Adjustment

Theoretical Concepts.   The theory of work adjustment (TWA) (Dawis, England, & Lofquist, 1964) also developed from the trait and factor approach to career counseling. Like Holland's theory, TWA advocates the importance of person-environment fit in the career choice process, and like various learning theories, acknowledges the important role of reinforcement and skill (Dawis, 1994; Rounds & Hesketh, 1994). Although the name of the theory was changed to person-environment correspondence (PEC) in 1991 (Dawis & Lofquist, 1993; Lofquist & Dawis, 1991), the theory is very similar to its original presentation in 1964 (Dawis et al.,). TWA focuses primarily on the adjustment to work, while PEC focuses on the "fit" of a person for a particular work environment. The theory posits that the career development process is the unfolding of the individual's abilities and requirements, in interaction with the individual's various environments, including home, school, play, and work. Correspondence between the person and the environment is optimal and will lead to success and satisfaction. A primary premise of the theory is that "person and environment attempt to achieve and maintain correspondence with each other" (Dawis, 1996, p. 81).

TWA is founded on the psychological traits and concepts of abilities and skills, reinforcement values (needs and values), satisfaction (and satisfactoriness as determined by the employer), and person-environment correspondence. Abilities and values provide the basis or structure of the personality, while skills and needs, which are surface traits, are changeable. In TWA (and in PEC), an individual has many observable skills and a few inferred abilities; an individual also has a set of needs, which can be grouped by inferred values (Sharf, 2002). For example, Dawis and Lofquist (1984) define Status (a reinforcement value) as including the needs of Advancement, Recognition, Authority, and Social Status. A client with a high need for advancement in his or her career (with increasing responsibility and authority) can be inferred to place a high value on Status. In addition to skills, abilities, needs, and values, individuals have a personality style and various adjustment behaviors. One's personality style is composed of celerity (speed of initiating environmental interaction), pace (activity level of interaction), rhythm (pattern of interaction), and endurance (sustainability of interaction), while one's adjustment behaviors include individual levels of flexibility, activeness, reactiveness, and perseverance (Dawis, 1994, 1996). Similar to the individual's structure of personality, the work environment structure is based on the abilities and values of the people who work in that environment.

This leads to a work "culture" that influences the individual and is also influenced by the individual. This relationship of mutual responsiveness (Dawis & Lofquist, 1984) implies that the person and the work environment attempt to achieve and maintain correspondence with each other. This interactive process then provides a perspective of work adjustment as ongoing and ever-changing. Work adjustment happens when an individual improves or maintains his or her fit or correspondence with the work environment. This may happen through change in the individual, change in the environment, or both. The individual's needs are primary in their influence on fit; job fit involves matching the individual's traits with the requirements of the work environment. Work adjustment is indicated by an individual's overall job satisfaction, satisfaction with the various aspects of the work environment, satisfaction of needs, and fulfillment of aspirations and expectations. Work adjustment is also indicated by the perceptions of the individual's productivity and efficiency as held by the supervisor and others in the work environment (i.e., the individual's satisfactoriness). In summary, satisfaction drives the system and the satisfaction-dissatisfaction continuum influences the individual's behaviors on the job, as well as the work environment's organizational behavior. Satisfaction is related to work adjustment, which leads to job tenure and better job performance (Dawis, 1996).

In applying the theory of work adjustment or person-environment correspondence to career choice, one is basically applying a trait and factor model, first assessing the individual and various work environments, as in Figure 2.1, and then determining person-environment match (or correspondence). The important difference is that this model assumes that both the individual and the work environment are subject to change and will influence each other. In applying the theory to work adjustment, one is going beyond trait and factor and is instead attempting to help clients understand what adjustments are needed, which ones are potential individual changes, and which may be changes needed in the work environment or organization.

Hershenson's TWA approach (Hershenson, 1981, 1996) is somewhat different from Dawis and Lofquist's conceptualization. Hershenson uses a developmental approach to explain the interaction among domains within a person and in the work environment. (For further information on this theory, see Chapter 12).

Strengths and Weaknesses. Research on TWA in general is supportive of the primary propositions. For example, Bizot and Goldman (1993), in a longitudinal study, found that the correspondence between personal aptitudes and job predicted satisfac-toriness, with work satisfaction providing an additional amount of explanation for satisfactoriness. They also found that satisfactoriness predicted satisfaction, as did correspondence between current interests and job. These relationships did not hold when original interests (at the beginning of the study) were used, rather than current interests as measured eight years later. In another study, Hesketh, McLachlan, and Gardner (1992) found that the correspondence between work preferences and job perception was correlated with satisfaction and that both satisfaction and performance (satisfactoriness) were related to tenure intentions. Other studies also have supported the predictive influence of person-environment fit on tenure and satisfaction (e.g., Bretz & Judge, 1994). Despite primarily supportive research findings, however, TWA research faces similar operationalization issues as other "fit" theories, which may account for the mixed results and the low predictive power that researchers sometime find. Determining how best to measure correspondence continues to be a challenge (Hesketh et al., 1992; Rounds, Dawis, & Lofquist, 1987).

The strength of TWA lies in a solid research foundation, which led to the original formulation of the theoretical propositions, operationalized constructs (Brown, 2003), and a continued focus on empirical results to support the theory. Another strength is its applicability to work adjustment issues for various populations (Degges-White & Shoffner, 2002; Harper & Shoffner, 2004; also see Chapter 15 in this book). One chal-lenge in using this theory with clients in an exploratory phase of career development centers on its complex theoretical formulations, which are often difficult for high school and college students to grasp. When thinking about person-environment correspon-dence, it is easier for clients (and sometimes practitioners) to conceptualize types (as in Holland's theory) than to conceptualize the various dimensions delineated in TWA.

In discussing the relevance of their theory to women and members of racial minorities, Dawis (1996) states that these variables are important background informa-tion that may account for structures and styles of personality and adjustment. However, he contends that this does not limit the relevance of TWA, but rather the societal restrictions and socialization that influence the early opportunities of those who histor-ically have been oppressed.

Values-based Career Counseling

The values-based approach to career counseling (Brown, 1996; Brown & Crace, 1996) posits that values are the primary salient characteristic of career decision making, more so than individual interests. These values are formed and influenced by external sources and are prioritized by individuals. In this approach, individual-work congruence is a value-based fit that is reached when the structure of an individual's values matches the value structure of the work environment. In some ways, then, values-based career coun-seling is a form of trait and factor theory. However, rather than looking at the dimen-sions of congruence as related to interests or aptitudes, this approach suggests that counselors examine the values that may drive an individual to be drawn to one type of career rather than another. Clients can then explore their potential fit to occupational "cultures," or work environments composed of other individuals with similar values.

Because of its relative newness to the career-counseling literature, there is little research on outcomes associated with this approach. (For further discussion of cultural and individual values, see Chapter 16.)

DEVELOPMENTAL THEORIES

Unlike trait and factor approaches, developmental theories provide a framework for understanding the unfolding process of career and career choice over the life-span. In this section, I present Donald Super's theory of vocational development and Linda Gottfredson's theory of circumscription and compromise. (For further discussion of developmental issues with diverse populations, see Chapters 14, 15, and 16.)

Theory of Vocational Development

Theoretical Concepts.   In the mid-1950s, Donald Super published works that were to greatly influence the way we envision the career. These early works presented a multifaceted developmental career theory built on the tenets of several areas of psychology and the work of Ginzberg and colleagues (Ginzberg, Ginsburg, Axelrad, & Herma, 1951). Super described his theory as a differential-developmental-social-phenomenological approach. In a set of propositions, he posited a strong relationship between an individual's personal growth and his or her career development. He did not focus on choice points (e.g., career choice), as did previous theorists and researchers, but rather on the developmental process of vocational behavior and the relationship of this unfolding process to various life roles (Super, Savickas, & Super, 1996). In addition to supporting the importance of individual abilities and interests, Super contributed to our understanding of the salience of values as providing meaning and purpose. The latest rendition of Super's theory (Super, Savickas, & Super, 1996) contains the final set of propositions for this theory.

Super assumed that an individual's career choice was not merely the result of matching his or her abilities and interests to the world of work, but an expression of his or her self-concept. Thus, people are satisfied to the degree that they can "implement self-concept" through their work choice, thereby connecting with the personal meaning of their abilities, interests, values, and choices (Super et al., 1996).

Another major concept in Super's theory of career development was that of the Life-Space (Table 2.1), which includes the constructs of Lifestyle, Life Roles, Life Role Salience, Life Structure, and Values. Super's Life Career Rainbow (Super, 1980) represents an individual's life career from birth to death and includes the nine major Life Roles of child, student, leisurite, citizen, worker, homemaker, spouse (or partner), parent, and pensioner, across the four arenas of home, school, work, and community (see Figure 2.3). Over the life-span, the role of work is connected to these other roles and to the importance of each role in an individual's life at any particular time (Life Role Salience). These Life Roles together constitute the Lifestyle; the sequence of various Life Roles over time is the Life Cycle and provides structure to the Life Space. The overall structure is the Career Pattern, a central aspect of Super's theory.

TABLE 2.1 Super's Life-Space, Life-Span

Primary Life Roles	Child Student Leasurite Citizen Worker Homemaker Partner Parent Pensioner Life role relates to behaviors, motives, and sentiments more than merely position.
Life Arenas	Home School Work Community Life roles are exercised in four arenas. One role can be played out in several theatres.
Life Space	The constellation of life roles played out by individuals in life stages. Life-spaces differ between individuals because of personal factors (e.g. interests, needs, values,) and situational factors (e.g. family, culture, gender, societal forces)
Life Role Salience	The importance of a role. Awareness of which life roles are more or less important.
Lifestyle	The simultaneous combination of life roles
Life Cycle	Sequence of life roles
Major Life Stages	GROWTH EXPLORATION ESTABLISHMENT MAINTENANCE DISENGAGEMENT Recycling of stages throughout life, "minicycles," or a cycling through stages across the lifespan "maxicycle."
Lifespan	The course of life or "maxicycle" of stages
Life Structure	The "career pattern" that results from role salience and structuring of various life roles

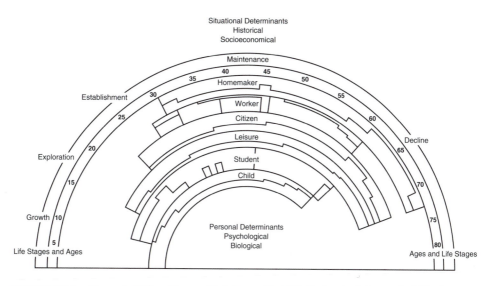

FIGURE 2.3   Super's Life—Career Rainbow: Six Life Roles in Schematic Life-Space

Source: From Super, D. E. (1990). A lifespan, life-space approach to career development. In D. Brown, L. Brooks, & Associates (Eds.), *Career choice and development: Applying contemporary theories to practice* (2nd ed., p. 212). Hoboken, NJ: Wiley. Reprinted with permission of John Wiley & Sons, Inc.

In his developmental approach to career, Super posited a stage model of vocational choice and development in which he envisioned career choice as a continuous, lifelong progression of stages and substages. Although these stages were initially considered primarily linear and predictable, the revised theory (Super, 1990) included cyclical aspects of the stages and showed how similar developmental challenges with variations are met at each stage. Each of these five stages will be briefly discussed.

The Growth Stage, typically occurring from birth through age 14, includes the substages of curiosity, fantasy, interest, and capacity. Tasks consist of the formation of a self-concept through interaction with adult figures (e.g., parent, guardian, coach, etc.), and an orientation to work through chores and responsibilities at school and home. During this stage, children begin to get a sense of what they are able to do and what interests them. The Exploration Stage (ages 15–24) includes crystallizing, specifying, and implementing. During this time, the individual begins to connect the self-concept to the world of work and to identify types of work through part-time jobs, summer work, and job shadowing. The individual makes the transition from school to work or to further education. There is often a tentative commitment to some beginning jobs, and much learning about potentially satisfying occupations occurs through trial and error. The Establishment Stage (ages 25–44) includes stabilizing, consolidating, and advancing. The individual works to make their place in their chosen field of work. This tends to be a productive time; the individual pursues advancement (e.g., promotion, additional responsibility) and economic stability. The Maintenance Stage (ages 45–64) includes the substages of holding, updating, and innovating. The individual maintains his or her level of achievement despite the challenges of competition, rapid changes in technology, and family. Often this is a stage of considerable professional activity, although it may also become a time of stagnation for some. The final stage, Disengagement or Decline (from 65 to death) involves decelerating, retirement planning, and retirement living. During this time, there is a clear change in level of work activity and often greater activity in roles involving family, volunteering, and leisure (Super, 1980, see Table 2.2.)

In addition to the concepts already mentioned, Super is credited with inventing the construct of career maturity (Super et al., Savickas, & Super, 1996). Career maturity refers to a person's readiness to handle the challenges involved in exploring and identifying a career choice. The construct of career maturity includes decision-making ability, career exploration, career planning, and an understanding of the world of work and of specific occupations. Successfully navigating any of the five stages or the transitions between stages depends on an individual's career maturity. In determining a client's level of career maturity, the counselor may assess planfulness, exploratory attitudes, decision-making skills, realistic self-appraisal, and the client's knowledge of

TABLE 2.2   The Cycling and Recycling of Developmental Tasks through the Life-Span

	AGE			
LIFE STAGE	**Adolescence 14-25**	**Early Adulthood 25-45**	**Middle Adulthood 45-65**	**Late Adulthood Over 65**
Decline	Giving less time to hobbies	Reducing sports participation	Focusing on essential activities	Reducing work hours
Maintenance	Verifying current occupational choice	Making occupational position secure	Holding own against competition	Keeping up what is enjoyed
Establishment	Getting started in a chosen field	Settling down in a permanent position	Developing new skills	Doing things one has always wanted to do
Exploration	Learning more about more opportunities	Finding opportunity to do desired work	Identifying new problems to work	Finding a good retirement spot
Growth	Developing a realistic self-concept	Learning to relate to others	Accepting one's limitations	Developing non-occupational roles

Source: From Super D. E. (1990) A life-span, life-space approach to career development. In D. Brown, L. Brooks, & Associates, (Eds.), *Career Choice and Development: Applying contemporary theories to practice.* 2nd ed., (p. 212). Hoboken, NJ: John Wiley and Sons, Inc.

developmental tasks and of occupations. Career maturity is a psychosocial aspect of adolescence, while career adaptability is the equivalent construct for most adults (Super et al., 1996).

Strengths and Weaknesses.   Super's developmental theory forms a "segmented," rather than a comprehensive, theory. This means that there are many parts of the theory that can stand alone and should be researched separately from the other aspects. This makes Super's work difficult to research as a whole. However, various segments of the theory have been tested and the findings generally support various aspects of Super's model.

Although Super's early theory did not explicitly address the context in which the roles exist, there are clearly contextual factors that affect the career pattern, in particular, life-role salience (Niles & Goodnough, 1996). These factors include the effects of the dominant culture (racial, age, and gender stereotypes and traditional gender and age expectations) and the individual's culture (career beliefs and life themes).

Theory of Circumscription and Compromise

Theoretical Concepts.   Linda Gottfredson (1981, 1996) is one of the few theoreticians who has presented a theory on how childhood influences career development and career choice. In her original monograph, published in 1981, Gottfredson states that vocational self-concept begins early in childhood and is defined through four orientations to work (Figure 2.4). She proposes the way in which children organize their learning about the world of work (Krumboltz, 1994).

The first orientation is formed during the ages of 3 to 5 and is focused on size and power. During this stage, children begin to show interest in certain types of careers based on the perceived power that those in that career have. This is often in the form of physical power (e.g., fireman, athlete) or social power and fame (e.g., rock star, movie star). During the next period, ages 6 through 8, children further delineate their

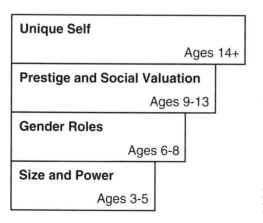

FIGURE 2.4   Gottfredson's Development Stages

occupational "space" based on sex role. Girls begin to rule out careers that they see as male dominated (e.g., doctor, scientist), and boys rule out careers that they see as female oriented (e.g., nurse, office secretary). From ages 9 through 13, children circumscribe their options based on the prestige and perceived social valuation of occupations. Children now talk about being doctors, lawyers, or crime scene investigators, with the previously delineated sex role restrictions still in place. The final stage begins at about age 14 (early adolescence) and is focused on the unique self, consisting of interests, abilities, and other traits specific to the individual. As children proceed through these orientations, they limit, or "circumscribe," an occupational space, which is referred to as a region or zone of acceptable alternatives. Occupations and careers that fall out of this region are no longer considered as options (Gottfredson, 1981). This is often an unconscious process, in that these possibilities are often not even readily accessible to the individual as possible self-schemas.

If, as these children become adolescents and adults and begin to examine options, a particular career or career path that was retained in the zone of acceptable alternatives is no longer an available option, individuals become willing to compromise their acceptable alternatives. Gottfredson believed that this would happen in the opposite order from the circumscription process. In other words, individuals would first be willing to compromise occupational choices based on their individual interests and abilities (the self), before they would consider compromising occupational prestige and value (Gottfredson, 1981).

Further development of this theory has posited the idea that one can use schema, especially gender schema, to understand some of these complex processes. In addition, individuals may use an individualized weighting process for each schema (Vandiver & Bowman, 1996).

Strengths and Weaknesses. Research has shown that these orientations are important in the development of vocational self-concept (Henderson, Hesketh, & Tuffin, 1988; Hesketh, Elmslie, & Kaldor, 1990) and that children circumscribe their options based on these orientations. However, research on the order of compromise has produced mixed results. The circumscription and compromise processes appear to be much more complex than Gottfredson had envisioned in her theory. More research is needed on the theoretical propositions, as well as on interventions designed to address issues of circumscription and compromise.

LEARNING AND COGNITIVE THEORIES

Learning and cognitive approaches to career development and career counseling are based on various learning theories. They focus on the impact of cognition and the effects of learning on the career choice and development process. Some of these theories also consider the factors that affect an individual's learning, and thus indirectly affect his or her choices. In this section, I will present Krumboltz's theory, social cognitive career theory, and the cognitive information processing approach.

Social Learning Theory

Theoretical Concepts.   The social learning theory of career development was first introduced in the 1970s (Krumboltz, 1979; Krumboltz, Mitchell, & Jones, 1976) as the social learning theory of career decision making (SLTCDM). This theory recognized the importance of cognitive processes and behavior in career decision making and explicitly addressed the influence of reinforcement and learning on the career development and choice processes. In 1996, Krumboltz (Krumboltz, 1996; Mitchell & Krumboltz, 1996) refined aspects of this theory into the learning theory of career counseling (LTCC), which focuses more specifically on cognitive-behavioral interventions and the goals and outcomes of counseling.

The four primary factors in both SLTCDM and LTCC are genetics (gender, race, physical characteristics, and specific talents such as music), environment (social, cultural, political, economic, geographic, and climate), learning experiences (both instrumental and associative), and task-approach skills (including work habits, performance abilities, and thought processes). Krumboltz believed that the last two of these four factors are learned, and thus can be addressed by counselors. In fact, learning through experiences (both instrumental and associative) and human interaction is the primary focus of career development and decision making, according to this theory. An individual will choose an occupation or field of work if he or she has success in tasks believed to be required for that occupation has observed or been made aware of a role model reinforced for such tasks, others (especially family and friends) speak of the advantages of this profession, or he or she observes the positive aspects (in words or in images) associated with the occupation (Krumboltz, 1994).

Krumboltz (1996) further identifies four important and current needs for today's changing work world. First of all, people need to expand their knowledge, skills, and interests if they are to remain useful employees. Second, people should assume that change will happen and prepare for it, rather than assume work stability; they often will need help in learning how to do so. Third, people need to be empowered and encouraged to expand and change. Last, counselors need to play a primary role in dealing with all career problems, not just the choice of an occupation or career (Krumboltz, 1996). The most useful and effective career counselor today, according to Krumboltz, will be the professional who promotes and encourages client learning. (For an example of the use of LTCC with college athletes, see Shurts & Shoffner, 2004.)

Strengths and Weaknesses.   Because learning theories, especially LTCC, are most concerned with counselor-facilitated client learning and view clients as dynamic, changing, learning individuals, the theory has wide applicability to diverse populations. LTCC, like social cognitive career theory (described next), is grounded in Bandura's well-tested general social learning theory, and therefore, many of its foundational premises have been supported. However, more research studies, particularly outcome studies, should be conducted on LTCC.

Because of the focus on learning and client "adaptability," counselors using LTCC may ignore critical contextual factors. In particular, it is important that counselors understand and acknowledge clients' restricted opportunity structure, which may have provided differential learning experiences, with possible long-term consequences and restricted options. Some of these experiences cannot be undone or redone. For example, placement in lower-level math classes in middle school and early high school will restrict future options at the postsecondary level. Similarly, a counselor working with a client within an LTCC framework might choose to facilitate the development of coping skills for dealing with institutional barriers, rather than attempting to change systemic oppression. Career counselors should not ignore their advocacy role of confronting and working to change systemic attitudes that perpetuate sexism, racism, or other "isms" in education and in the workplace.

Cognitive Information Processing

Theoretical Concepts.   The cognitive information processing (CIP) approach to decision making and to career problem solving is designed to "help persons make an appropriate current career choice and, while doing so, to learn improved problem-solving and decision-making skills that they will need for future choices" (Sampson, Reardon, Peterson, & Lenz, 2004, p. 2). The major assumptions of this approach are as follows: (1) Thoughts (cognitions) and emotions (affect) are inseparable in career decision making and problem solving, and emotions can motivate individuals in either positive or negative ways. (2) Career problems are addressed through knowledge (content) and thinking about that knowledge in order to make choices. (3) Career resources can help individuals organize the vast amount of constantly changing knowledge about the world and about themselves so that they can make informed choices. (4) Information-processing skills can be learned and improved so that individuals can become better at making decisions (Sampson et al., 2004).

The CIP approach involves two primary dimensions, the CASVE (for Communication, Analysis, Synthesis, Valving, Execution) cycle, which is used to help identify strategies for assessment, screening, counseling, and resource room design, and the Pyramid of Information Processing Domains. The Pyramid of Information Processing Domains (Figure 2.5) delineates the areas of cognition involved in career decision making. The base of the pyramid (or triangle) is formed by the two components of the Knowledge Domain: self-knowledge (who am I?) and occupational knowledge (what are my options?). The next domain, resting upon the knowledge domain, is the Decision-Making Skills Domain. This domain involves the information-processing skills used in the CASVE cycle (how do I make decisions?), which will be discussed below. Finally, the top of the pyramid consists of the Executive Processing Domain (metacognitions). This domain includes self-talk, self-awareness, and cognitive monitoring (Niles & Harris-Bowlsbey, 2002; Sampson et al., 2004).

The CASVE cycle is a sequential decision-making procedure involving the following: *c*ommunication (identifying a need, a problem, or a gap between what is and what would be ideal), *a*nalysis (identifying what is needed, especially in the way of information, and how to acquire what is needed), *s*ynthesis (identifying alternatives and narrowing the list to a set of likely and acceptable alternatives), *v*aluing (prioritizing the alternatives based on the individual's values, the effect on others, and the likelihood of success), and *e*xecution (developing strategies as a plan of action and implementing the

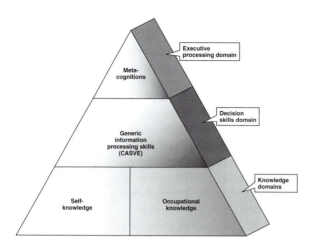

FIGURE 2.5   The Pyramid of Information Processing Domains

Source: Adapted from Peterson, G., Sampson, J., & Reardon, R. E. (1991). *Career development and services: A cognitive approach.* Brooks/Cole Publishing Company, a division of Thompson International Publishing, Inc.

chosen alternative) (Reardon, Lenz, Sampson, & Peterson, 2000; Sampson et al., 2004). The career counselor can help clients to learn the components of this cycle and how to use the steps for career choice and decision making. It is hoped that this approach to decision making will continue to be useful to clients in other areas of their lives.

Strengths and Weaknesses.   Cognitive information processing appears to be an excellent approach to use with clients who are motivated to use linear decision-making models. The theoretical propositions are laid out in such a manner that researchers will be able to test them. It is still early in the development and investigation of the theory, so there are few empirical findings to date.

Social Cognitive Career Theory

Theoretical Concepts.   SCCT, derived from Bandura's (1977, 1986) general social cognitive theory, focuses on the "(a) formation and elaboration of career-relevant interests, (b) the selection of academic and career choice options, and (c) performance and persistence in educational and occupational pursuits" (Lent, Brown, & Hackett, 1994, p. 79). The primary constructs of SCCT are self-efficacy beliefs, which are the subjective beliefs that one is able to perform particular tasks; outcome expectations, the beliefs that these behaviors will result in particular outcomes; and goal mechanisms. The framework further describes the influence of person factors, contextual factors, and experiential and learning factors (Bandura, 1977, 1986) on academic and career development and on choice. In fact, SCCT recognizes and addresses the critical importance of individuals' beliefs and perceptions about their skills, potential outcomes, perceived barriers and supports, and perceived ability to deal with barriers.

In SCCT, learning experiences shape self-efficacy beliefs and outcome expectations, and are influenced by factors such as educational opportunity and family context (Ferry, Fouad, & Smith, 2000; Lent et al., 1994; Lent, Brown, & Hackett, 2000).

Self-efficacy beliefs influence choice, actual performance, and persistence (Bandura, 1977; Lent et al., 1994), and act as moderators between experience and career interests (Lent et al., 1994). Goal aspirations, and ultimately goal choices, are influenced by interests and by relevant self-efficacy and outcome expectation beliefs. Self-efficacy is believed to have a direct influence on the development of outcome expectations, with both constructs influencing interests and aspirations. In addition, these aspirations are mediated and moderated by perceived barriers, perceived supports, and contextual factors (Lent et al., 2000). Career aspirations and choices, therefore, are not based on interests alone, but also are influenced by self-efficacy and outcome expectations, as well as perceived barriers, perceived supports, and other contextual influences. Beliefs about one's ability to cope with various perceived barriers (coping self-efficacy) may also influence an individual's perceived options. (For further discussion of real and perceived barriers, see Chapters 14, 15, and 16.)

Outcome expectations incorporate the concept of values. In other words, the salience of particular outcome expectations, as well as the strength of these as reinforcers, depends on the individual (Lent et al., 1994, 2000). Career-relevant outcome expectations include the anticipation of physical outcomes (e.g., financial gain, lifestyle), the gaining of social approval, and self-satisfaction outcomes (Bandura, 1986; Lent et al., 1994). Research has also indicated two additional categories of outcome expectations: relational outcomes and generativity outcomes (Shoffner, Newsome, & Barrio, 2004).

Prior to the development of SCCT, Hackett and Betz (1981) asserted that girls' and women's beliefs regarding specific careers, such as mathematics and science, were influenced by low self-efficacy due to gender socialization experiences. This low self-efficacy, in turn, limited their interest in, and exploration of, these topics. This implied that differential access to sources of self-efficacy and reinforcement limited potential options. Thus, although the constructs of the theory are internal and cognitive, they are highly influenced by socialization and institutional factors that may restrict options and the utilization of individual strengths and abilities. (See the next section, "Theories of Embedded Careers.")

Strengths and Weaknesses.   This theory has been used to successfully explain the career development of a number of diverse populations, including girls and women (Betz & Hackett, 1987), members of racial minority groups (Byars & Hackett, 1998; Hackett & Byars, 1996), and gay and lesbian individuals (Morrow, Gore, & Campbell, 1996). Research has consistently demonstrated the important influence of women's beliefs about their ability (self-efficacy) on their choice of nontraditional careers (Betz & Fitzgerald, 1987), in forecasting science- and mathematics-related interests (Lent, Lopez, & Bieschke, 1991), and on other career-related choices and performance (Hackett, 1985; Hackett & Lent, 1992). The impact of ability on self-efficacy, and its subsequent influence on outcome expectations and specific interests, has also been supported (Lopez, Lent, Brown, & Gore, 1997). Research by Betz and Voyten (1997) has supported the relationship between lower outcome expectations and decreased exploratory behavior. Fouad and Smith (1996) found that self-efficacy significantly, but indirectly, influenced career-related interests through its relationship to interests and outcome expectations. They also found strong pathways between outcome expectations and intentions.

Research on the influence of perceived barriers and supports has primarily lent support to the tenets of SCCT (Lent et al., 2001). Both high school and college populations perceive barriers to reaching their educational and career goals (McWhirter, 1997; McWhirter, Hackett, & Bandalos, 1998; Swanson & Tokar, 1991), although the impact of these perceptions on future career choices and goals is not clear. For high school youth, perceived barriers did not explain youth's academic plans or expectations regarding careers (McWhirter, 1997; McWhirter et al., 1998). The theory posits that it is the perception of barriers, and not their actual existence or strength, that influences career outcomes (Albert & Luzzo, 1999; Luzzo, 1996). The effect comes from the individual's subjective perception of, and response to, these barriers. Perceived support from both parents and teachers is instrumental in its effect on career-related outcomes (Lapan, Hinkelman, Adams, & Turner, 1999; McWhirter et al., 1996).

Clearly, there is much in the way of research support for SCCT, which is one of its primary strengths. In addition, it is a theory that can be directly and effectively applied to career counseling. A direct focus on perceptions and beliefs regarding self-efficacy, outcomes, barriers, and supports can lead to targeted interventions for providing structured activities for developing self-efficacy in specific areas, for countering erroneous outcome expectations, and for exploring perceived barriers and appropriate coping skills. (For an example of the use of SCCT with first-generation college students, see Gibbons & Shoffner, 2004.)

THEORIES OF EMBEDDED CAREER

Similar to Blustein's 1994 concept of the embedded self, or the self in relationship with others and the environment, career and career development can be viewed as embedded in the larger context of social and environmental interchange and relationship. Several career theories and approaches are focused on the influence of the environment on career development and the individual's internal (meaning-making) or external (behavior) outcomes of these relationships. Some of the theories that we have already discussed (e.g., SCCT) could conceivably fall into this category, but have not been put here because of their primary emphasis on some other aspect of career theory, such as cognition. Theories of "embedded career" include contextualism, the ecological approach, sociological theories, and additional theories that are similar in their focus on context or system. (See Chapter 6 for a description of complexity theory and Chapter 13 for a presentation of family systems theory.)

Contextualism

Theoretical Concepts.   Contextual approaches to career theory and career counseling are grounded in constructivist approaches, which state that there is an ongoing, dynamic, and reciprocal interaction between individuals and their environments (their context). This is in contrast to the approaches that depict individuals as passive recipients of input and subject to developmental stages and growth (Patton & McMahon, 1999). This ongoing reciprocal relationship, as delineated in contextualism, is based on individuals' perceptions and the personal meaning assigned to the events and experiences of which they are a part. Therefore, individuals' career development is based in their construction of personal meaning regarding their actions, their experiences, and "external" events (Zunker, 2002, p. 98). Two primary tenets of this theory, then, are that behavior is caused "by the social context in which the behavior occurs" and that "reality is a matter of perception" (Young, Valach, & Collin, 1996, p. x). Thus, the role of the career counselor is to explore the meaning that clients have created and are creating (their narrative) and to facilitate their continued construction of their career path by projecting their narratives into the future (Savickas, 1995). The focus of counseling can be on the three parts of action discussed by Young and colleagues (1996): unobservable behavior, unobservable internal processes, and the meaning associated with the results of action, from the point of view of both the client and other observers.

Strengths and Weaknesses.   As with psychodynamic approaches (see the next section), the strength of contextualism from a career-counseling perspective is its focus on the client's reality and perception. Its greatest weakness is inherent in most phenomenological approaches: it is difficult to research because the process is at least as important as the outcome, and much of the process is internal to the client. Nonetheless, investigations of its utility in career counseling through outcome research would be helpful in providing us with evidence that constructivist approaches have some relevance and efficacy. In addition, qualitative methodologies would be useful in helping practitioners know what approaches work best in facilitating and coconstructing clients' meaning making.

An Ecological Perspective

Similar to the contextual approach, the ecological approach to career counseling conceptualizes clients as within, and influenced by, their various environments (Cook, Heppner, & O'Brien, 2002). This perspective is based on Bronfenbrenner's 1979 ecological model and provides a lens through which to provide service to clients for whom the assumptions of more traditional approaches do not apply. The assumptions of many of the earlier career theories are that the roles of family and of work are separate in the lives of clients, that individualism is a driving force, that work is central in our clients' lives, that career development is linear and rational, and that the opportunity structure is the same for all individuals (Barrio & Shoffner, in press; Cook et al., 2002). Although these traditional theories may still be relevant, it is important for the career counselor to assess, with each individual (and unique) client, the relevance of any model for that person.

In the ecological approach, the counselor goes beyond the co-construction of meaning to address specific environmental factors that may be influencing the client's optimal career development (Cook et al., 2002). In other words, an ecological perspective uses interventions focused on changing the individual's interactions with the environment. In working with clients, the authors of this approach suggest the following main intervention themes: Clarifying and Affirming Life Options; Managing Multiple

Roles; Obtaining Needed Resources; Creating Healthy Work Environments; and Linking Individuals with Role Models and Mentors. (More information on the ecological approach is presented in Chapter 12.)

Strengths and Weaknesses.   The primary strength of the ecological approach is its recognition and focus on the ecological systems of which the client is a part. In addition, the approach provides some specific guidelines for working with clients. However, the approach is relatively new, so there is little research to support its premises or the effectiveness of its use in career counseling. However, given its focus on context, this approach offers some promise in addressing the career-counseling needs of diverse populations.

Sociological Theories of Career Development

Sociological theories of career development are founded in sociology and sociological research and center on the domains of status, stratification, and organizational behavior. These theories, more clearly than others, directly address the restrictive or enhancement influence of institutional factors, the influence of parental social status on individual capabilities and opportunity, and the restrictive impact of work-system dynamics on financial, social, and psychological choice and satisfaction (Hotchkiss & Borrow, 1990).

PSYCHODYNAMIC APPROACHES

There are several additional approaches to career development and career counseling that, although perhaps not as often utilized or researched, are important in understanding the various ways to approach career work with clients. Psychodynamic theories of career development focus on issues of ego identity, life scripts, and life themes and are often extensions of the theories of Alfred Adler (life themes) and Erik Erikson (ego identity development). They also may focus on the role of affect in career development, the role of the family of origin in shaping career development and career identity, the interaction between career identity and identity development, and work identity. In summary, these approaches are based on internal structures of motivation and the constructs of identity, lifestyle, the self, and family systems (Bordin, 1990, 1994). The foci of recent psychodynamic career theories have been: (1) ego identity in career development (Blustein, 1994) and the impact of relationships on career development (e.g., Blustein, Prezioso, Schultheiss, 1995; Blustein, Walbridge, Friedlander, & Palladino, 1991; Schultheiss, Kress, Manzi, & Glasscock, 2001), (2) life themes and how clients construct their identity and live out life scripts as extensions of this identity (e.g., Savickas, 1998), and (3) adult play and its implications for career counseling (e.g., Bordin, 1994). (For information regarding Roe's needs theory, another psychodynamic approach, see Chapter 5. Note that postmodern approaches also focus on clients' construction of story and the meaning assigned to various aspects of this story. For an example, see the presentation of narrative approaches in Chapter 3.)

Of the psychodynamic approaches, perhaps the most directly applicable to the work of a career counselor is the application of lifestyle as it influences adulthood and the developing career self. Here the primary idea is that early recollection can be used to help clients understand their lifestyle. This understanding, then, can help them explore and identify career options that seem to be most appropriate to their lifestyle.

Strengths and Weaknesses.   There is relatively little research on psychodynamic approaches to career counseling. The research that does exist tends to focus on the development of career identity as part of the development of a healthy identity during adolescence and early adulthood or the role of parental influence on early career identity.

Psychodynamic career counseling is best used with verbal clients, and is appropriate in addressing gender and cultural issues. The approach tends to be strength based and includes an emphasis on the subjective world of the client; thus, it may be one of the more culturally responsive approaches to career counseling work with clients from diverse populations.

The major strength of this approach to career counseling is its focus on clients' constructed understanding of their identity and their past in relation to career exploration and adjustment. This strength, however, is also a major weakness, in that it does not lend itself to quantitative methods of research in order to support its claims. However, the use of qualitative methodologies may be very useful in exploring how individuals construct their identities and develop their life scripts, and how these, in turn, influence their career exploration, decision making, and ultimately, their work adjustment.

CONCLUSION

All of the types of theories discussed in this chapter provide us with different categories of maps: trait and factor, developmental, learning and cognitive, embedded careers, and psychodynamic. Within each of these types, each theory or approach provides the career theorist, researcher, or practitioner with a guide to particular aspects of the career development process. Not all these theories will be equally applicable across the needs and stages of various career clients, and not all will be equally applicable to all populations. This is no different from counseling in general. Each counseling intervention should be geared to what will best optimize the client's career and work growth.

REFERENCES

Albert, K. A., & Luzzo, D. A. (1999). The role of perceived barriers in career development: A social cognitive perspective. *The Journal of Counseling and Development, 77,* 431–437.

Anderson, M. Z., Tracey, T. J. G., & Rounds, J. (1997). Examining the invariance of Holland's vocational interest model across gender. *Journal of Vocational Behavior, 50,* 349–364.

Bandura, A. (1977). Self-efficacy: Toward a unifying theory of behavioral change. *Psychological Review, 84,* 191–215.

Bandura, A. (1986). *Social foundations of thought and action.* Englewood Cliffs, NJ: Prentice Hall.

Barrio, C. A., & Shoffner, M. F. (in press). Career counseling with persons living with HIV: An ecological approach. *Career Development Quarterly*.

Betz, N. E., & Fitzgerald, L. F. (1987). *The career psychology of women*. San Diego, CA: Academic Press.

Betz, N. E., & Hackett, G. (1987). Concept of agency in educational and career development. *Journal of Counseling Psychology, 34*, 299–308.

Betz, N. E., & Voyten, K. K. (1997). Efficacy and outcome expectations influence career exploration and decidedness. *Career Development Quarterly, 46*, 179–189.

Bizot, E. B., & Goldman, S. H. (1993). Prediction of satisfactoriness and satisfaction: An 8-year follow up. *Journal of Vocational Behavior, 43*, 19–29.

Blustein, D. L. (1994). Who am I?: The question of self and identify in career development. In M. L. Savickas & R. W. Lent (Eds.), *Convergence in career development theories: Implications for science and practice* (pp. 139–154). Palo Alto, CA: CPP Books.

Blustein, D. L., Prezioso, M. S., & Schultheiss, D. P. (1995). Attachment theory and career development: Current status and future directions. *Counseling Psychologist, 23*, 416–432.

Blustein, D. L., Walbridge, M. M., Friedlander, M. L., & Palladino, D. E. (1991). Contributions of psychological separation and parental attachment to the career development process. *Journal of Counseling Psychology, 38*, 39–50.

Bordin, E. S. (1990). Psychodynamic models of career choice and satisfaction. In D. Brown & L. Brooks (Eds.), *Career choice and development: Applying contemporary theories to practice* (2nd ed., pp. 102–144). San Francisco: Jossey-Bass.

Bordin, E. S. (1994). Work and play. In M. L. Savickas & R. W. Lent (Eds.), *Convergence in career development theories: Implications for science and practice* (pp. 53–61). Palo Alto, CA: CPP Books.

Bretz, R. D., Jr., & Judge, T. A. (1994). Person-organization fit and the theory of work adjustment: Implications for satisfaction, tenure and career success. *Journal of Vocational Behavior, 44*, 32–54.

Bronfenbrenner, U. (1979). *The ecology of human development*. Cambridge, MA: Harvard University Press.

Brown, D. (1996). A holistic, values-based model of career and life role choice and satisfaction. In D. Brown, L. Brooks, & Associates (Eds.), *Career choice and development* (3rd ed.). San Francisco: Jossey-Bass.

Brown, D. (2003). *Career information, career counseling, and career development* (8th ed.). Boston, MA: Allyn & Bacon.

Brown, D., Brooks, L., & Associates (Eds.). (1996). *Career choice and development* (3rd ed.). San Francisco: Jossey-Bass.

Brown, D., & Crace, R. K. (1996). Values in life role choices and outcomes: A conceptual model. *Career Development Quarterly, 44*, 211–224.

Brown, S. D., & Gore, P. A. (1994). An evaluation of interest congruence indices: Distribution characteristics and measurement properties. *Journal of Vocational Behavior, 45*, 310–327.

Byars, A. M., & Hackett, G. (1998). Applications of social cognitive theory to the career development of women of color. *Applied and Preventive Psychology, 7*, 255–267.

Camp, C. C., & Chartrand, J. M. (1992). A comparison and evaluation of interest congruence indices. *Journal of Vocational Behavior, 41*, 162–182.

Chartrand, J., & Walsh, W. B. (1999). What should we expect from congruence? *Journal of Vocational Behavior, 55*, 136–146.

Cook, E. P., Heppner, M. J., & O'Brien, K. M. (2002). Career development of women of color and white women: Assumptions, conceptualization, and interventions from an ecological perspective. *Career Development Quarterly, 50*, 291–305.

Dawis, R. V. (1994). The theory of work adjustment as convergent theory. In M. L. Savikas & R. W. Lent (Eds.), *Convergence in career development theories* (pp. 33–44). Palo Alto, CA: CPP Books.

Dawis, R. V. (1996). The theory of work adjustment and person-environment-correspondence counseling. In D. Brown, L. Brooks, et al. (Eds.), *Career choice and development: Applying contemporary theories to practice* (3rd ed., pp. 75–120). San Francisco: Jossey-Bass.

Dawis, R. V., England, G. W., & Lofquist, L. H. (1964). A theory of work adjustment. *Minnesota Studies in Vocational Rehabilitation, no. 15, 1–27.*

Dawis, R. V., & Lofquist, L. H. (1984). *A psychological theory of work adjustment: An individual-differences model and its applications.* Minneapolis, MN: University of Minnesota Press.

Dawis, R. V., & Lofquist, L. H. (1993). From TWA to PEC. *Journal of Vocational Behavior, 43,* 113–121.

Day, S. X., & Rounds, J. (1998). Universality of vocational interest structure among racial and ethnic minorities. *American Psychologist, 53,* 728–736.

Day, S. X., Rounds, J., & Swaney, K. (1998). The structure of vocational interests for diverse racial-ethnic groups. *Psychological Science, 9,* 40–44.

Degges-White, S. D., & Shoffner, M. F. (2002). Career counseling with lesbian clients: Using the theory of work adjustment as a framework. *Career Development Quarterly, 51,* 87–96.

Ferry, T. R., Fouad, N. A., & Smith, P. L. (2000). The role of family context in a social cognitive model for career-related choice behavior: A math and science perspective. *Journal of Vocational Behavior, 57,* 348–364.

Fouad, N., Harmon, L. W., & Borgen, F. H. (1997). Structure of interests in employed male and female members of U.S. racial-ethnic minority and non-minority groups. *Journal of Counseling Psychology, 44,* 339–345.

Fouad, N. A., & Smith, P. L. (1996). A test of a social cognitive model for middle school students: Math and science. *Journal of Counseling Psychology, 43,* 338–346.

Gibbons, M. M., & Shoffner, M. F. (2004). Prospective first-generation college students: Meeting their needs through social cognitive career theory. *Professional School Counseling, 8,* 91–97.

Ginzberg, E., Ginsburg, S. W., Axelrad, S., & Herma, J. (1951). *Occupational choice: An approach to a general theory.* New York: Columbia University Press.

Gottfredson, L. S. (1981). Circumscription and compromise: A developmental theory of occupational aspirations [Monograph]. *Journal of Counseling Psychology, 28,* 545–579.

Gottfredson, L. S. (1996). Circumscription and compromise: A developmental theory of occupational aspirations. In D. Brown, L. Brooks, & Associates (Eds.), *Career choice and development: Applying contemporary theories to practice* (3rd ed., pp. 170–232). San Francisco: Jossey-Bass.

Hackett, G. (1985). The role of mathematics self-efficacy in the choice of math-related majors of college women and men: A path model. *Journal of Counseling Psychology, 32,* 47–56.

Hackett, G., & Betz, N. E. (1981). A self-efficacy approach to the career development of women. *Journal of Vocational Behavior, 18,* 326–339.

Hackett G., & Byars, A. M. (1996). Social cognitive theory and the career development of African American women. *Career Development Quarterly, 44,* 322–340.

Hackett, G., & Lent, R. W. (1992). Theoretical advances and current inquiry in career psychology. In S. D. Brown & R. W. Lent (Eds.), *Handbook of counseling psychology* (2nd ed., pp. 419–451). New York: Wiley.

Hansen, J. I. C., Collins, R. C., Swanson, J. L., & Fouad, N. A. (1993). Gender differences in the structure of interests. *Journal of Vocational Behavior, 42,* 200–211.

Harper, M. C., & Shoffner, M. F. (2004). Counseling for continued career development after retirement: An application of the theory of work adjustment. *Career Development Quarterly, 52,* 272–284.

Haverkamp, B. E., Collins, R. C., & Hansen, J. I. (1994). Structure of interests of Asian-American college students. *Journal of Counseling Psychology, 41,* 256–264.

Henderson, S., Hesketh, B., & Tuffin, A. (1988). A test of Gottfredson's theory of circumscription. *Journal of Vocational Behavior, 32,* 37–48.

Herr, E. L., Cramer, S. H., & Niles, S. G. (2004). *Career guidance and counseling through the life span: Systematic approaches* (6th ed.). Boston, MA: Pearson Education.

Hershenson, D. B. (1981). Work adjustment, disability, and the three r's of vocational rehabilitation: A conceptual model. *Rehabilitation Counseling Bulletin, 25,* 91–97.

Hershenson, D. B. (1996). Work adjustment: A neglected area in career counseling. *Journal of Counseling and Development, 74,* 442–446.

Hesketh, B., Elmslie, S., & Kaldor, W. (1990). Career compromise: An alternative account to Gottfredson's theory. *Journal of Counseling Psychology, 37,* 49–56.

Hesketh, B., McLachlan, K., & Gardner, D. (1992). Work adjustment theory: An empirical test using a fuzzy rating scale. *Journal of Vocational Behavior, 40,* 318–337.

Holland, J. L. (1959). A theory of vocational choice. *Journal of Counseling Psychology, 6,* 35–45.

Holland, J. L. (1973). *Making vocational choices: A theory of careers.* Englewood Cliffs, NJ: Prentice-Hall.

Holland, J. L. (1985). *Making vocational choices: A theory of vocational personalities and work environments* (2nd ed.). Englewood Cliffs, NJ: Prentice-Hall.

Holland, J. L. (1992). *Making vocational choices* (2nd ed.). Odessa, FL: Psychological Assessment Resources.

Holland, J. L. (1997). *Making vocational choices: A theory of vocational personalities and work environments* (3rd ed.). Odessa, FL: Psychological Assessment Resources.

Holland, J. L., Whitney, D. R., Cole, N. S., & Richards, J. M. (1969). An empirical occupational classification derived from a theory of personality and intended for practice and research. *ACT Research Reports, 29*(22).

Hotchkiss, L., & Borow, H. (1990). Sociological perspectives on work and career development. In D. Brown & L. Brooks (Eds.), *Career choice and development: Applying contemporary theories to practice* (pp. 262–307). San Francisco: Jossey-Bass.

Krumboltz, J. D. (1979). A social learning theory of career decision making. Revised and reprinted in A. Mitchell, G. Jones, & J. Krumboltz (Eds.), *Social learning and career decision making* (pp. 19–49). Cranston, RI: Carroll Press.

Krumboltz, J. D. (1994). Improving career development theory from a social learning perspective. In M. L. Savickas & R. W. Lent (Eds.), *Convergence in career development theories: Implications for science and practice* (pp. 9–31). Palo Alto, CA: CPP Books.

Krumboltz, J. D. (1996). A learning theory of career counseling. In M. L. Savickas & W. B. Walsh (Eds.), *Handbook of career counseling theory and practice* (pp. 55–80). Palo Alto, CA: Davies-Black.

Krumboltz, J. D., Mitchell, A., & Jones, G. (1976). A social learning theory of career selection. *The Counseling Psychologist, 6,* 71–81.

Lapan, R. T., Hinkelman, J. M., Adams, A., & Turner, S. (1999). Understanding rural adolescents' interests, values, and efficacy expectations. *Journal of Career Development, 26,* 107–124.

Lent, R. W., Brown, S. D., Hackett, G. (1994). Toward a unifying social cognitive theory of career and academic interest, choice, and performance [Monograph]. *Journal of Vocational Behavior, 45,* 79–122.

Lent, R. W., Brown, S. D., & Hackett, G. (2000). Contextual supports and barriers to career choice: A social cognitive analysis. *Journal of Counseling Psychology, 47,* 36–49.

Lent, R. W., Brown, S. E., Brenner, B., Chopra, S. B., Davis, T., Talleyrand, R., & Suthakaran, V. (2001). The role of contextual supports and barriers in the choice of math/science educational options: A test of social cognitive hypotheses. *Journal of Counseling Psychology, 48,* 474–483.

Lent, R. W., Lopez, F. G., & Bieschke, K. J. (1991). Mathematics self-efficacy: Sources and relation to science-based career choice. *Journal of Counseling Psychology, 38,* 424–430.

Liptak, J. J. (2001). *Treatment planning in career counseling*. Belmont, CA: Brooks/Cole.

Lofquist, L. H., & Dawis, R. V. (1991). *Essentials of person environment correspondence counseling*. Minneapolis: University of Minneapolis Press.

Lopez, F. G., Lent, R. W., Brown, S. D., & Gore, P. A. (1997). Role of social-cognitive expectations in high school students' mathematics-related interest and performance. *Journal of Counseling Psychology, 44*, 44–52.

Luzzo, D. A. (1996). Exploring the relationship between the perception of occupational barriers and career development. *Journal of Career Development, 22*, 239–248.

McWhirter, E. H. (1997). Perceived barriers to education and career: Ethnic and gender differences. *Journal of Vocational Behavior, 50*, 124–140.

McWhirter, E. H., Hackett, G., & Bandalos, D. L. (1998). A causal model of the educational plans and career expectations of Mexican American high school girls. *Journal of Counseling Psychology, 45*, 166–181.

Meir, E. I., Esformes, Y., & Friedland, N. (1994). Congruence and differentiation as predictors of workers' occupational stability and job performance. *Journal of Career Assessment, 2*, 40–54.

Meir, E. I., & Navon, M. (1992). A longitudinal examination of congruence hypotheses. *Journal of Vocational Behavior, 41*, 35–47.

Mitchell, L. K., & Krumboltz, J. D. (1996). Krumboltz's learning theory of career choice counseling. In D. Brown, L. Brooks, & Associates (Eds.), *Career choice and development: Applying contemporary theories to practice* (3rd ed., pp. 233–276). San Francisco: Jossey-Bass.

Morrow, S. L., Gore, P. A., Jr., & Campbell, B. W. (1996). The application of a sociocognitive framework to the career development of lesbian women and gay men. *Journal of Vocational Behavior, 48*, 136–148.

Niles, S. G., & Goodnough, G. E. (1996). Life-role salience and values: A review of recent research. *Career Development Quarterly, 45*, 65–86.

Niles, S. G., & Harris-Bowlsbey, J. (2002). *Career development interventions in the 21st century*. Upper Saddle River, NJ: Pearson Education.

Parsons, F. (1909). *Choosing a vocation*. Boston, MA: Houghton Mifflin.

Patton, W., & McMahon, M. (1999). *Career development and systems theory: A new relationship*. Belmont, CA: Brooks/Cole.

Prediger, D. J. (2000). Holland's hexagon is alive and well—though somewhat out of shape: Response to Tinsley. *Journal of Vocational Behavior, 56*, 197–204.

Reardon, R. C., Lenz, J. G., Sampson, J. P., Jr., & Peterson, G. W. (2000). *Career development and planning: A comprehensive approach*. Pacific Grove, CA: Brooks/Cole.

Rounds, J., McKenna, M. C., Hubert, L., & Day, S. X. (2000). Tinsley on Holland: A misshapen argument. *Journal of Vocational Behavior, 56*, 205–215.

Rounds, J., & Tracey, T. J. (1996). Cross-cultural structural equivalence of RIASEC models and measures. *Journal of Counseling Psychology, 43*, 310–329.

Rounds, J. R., Dawis, R. V., & Lofquist, L. H. (1987). Measurement of person-environment fit and prediction of satisfaction in the theory of work adjustment. *Journal of Vocational Behavior, 31*, 297–318.

Rounds, J. R., & Hesketh, B. (1994). Theory of work adjustment: Unifying principles and concepts. In M. L. Savickas & R. W. Lent (Eds.), *Convergence in career development theories: Implications for science and practice* (pp. 177–186). Palo Alto, CA: CPP Books.

Rounds, J. R., & Tracey, T. J. (1993). Prediger's dimensional representation of Holland's RIASEC circumplex. *Journal of Applied Psychology, 78*, 875–890.

Ryan, J. M., Tracey, T. J. G., & Rounds, J. (1996). Generalizability of Holland's structure of vocational interests across ethnicity, gender and socioeconomic status. *Journal of Counseling Psychology, 43,* 330–337.

Sampson, J. P., Jr., Reardon, R. C., Peterson, G. W., & Lenz, J. G. (2004). *Career counseling and services: A cognitive information processing approach.* Belmont, CA: Brooks/Cole.

Savickas, M. L. (1995). Constructivist counseling for career indecision. *Career Development Quarterly, 43,* 363–373.

Savickas, M. L. (1998). Career style assessment and counseling. In T. J. Sweeney (Eds.), *Adlerian counseling: A practitioner's approach* (pp. 329–359). Philadelphia, PA: Accelerated Development.

Savickas, M. L., & Gottfredson, G. D. (1999). Introduction to Holland's theory (1959–1999): 40 years of research and application. *Journal of Vocational Behavior, 55,* 1–4.

Schultheiss, D. E. P., Kress, H. M., Manzi, A. J., & Glasscock, J. M. J. (2001). Relational influences in career development: A qualitative inquiry. *Counseling Psychologist, 29,* 214–239.

Sharf, R. S. (2002). *Applying career development theory to counseling* (3rd ed.). Pacific Grove, CA: Brooks/Cole.

Shoffner, M. F., Newsome, D. W., & Barrio, C. A. (2004). *Youth's outcome expectations: A qualitative study.* Manuscript submitted for publication.

Shurts, W. M., & Shoffner, M. F. (in press). Providing career counseling for collegiate student-athletes: A learning theory approach. *Journal of Career Development.*

Spokane, A. R. (1994). The resolution of incongruence and the dynamics of person-environment fit. In M. L. Savickas & R. W. Lent (Eds.), *Convergence in career development theories: Implications for science and practice* (pp. 119–137). Palo Alto, CA: CPP Books.

Spokane, A. R. (1996). Holland's theory. In D. Brooks & L. Brown (Eds.), *Career choice and development: Applying contemporary theories to practice* (2nd ed., pp. 33–74). San Francisco: Jossey-Bass.

Super, D. E. (1980). A lifespan, life space approach to career development. *Journal of Vocational Behavior, 16,* 282–298.

Super, D. E. (1990). A life-span, life-space approach to career development. In D. Brooks & L. Brown (Eds.), *Career choice and development: Applying contemporary theories to practice* (2nd ed., pp. 197–261). San Francisco: Jossey-Bass.

Super, D. E., Savickas, M. L., & Super, C, M. (1996). The life-span, life-space approach to careers. In D. Brooks & L. Brown (Eds.), *Career choice and development: Applying contemporary theories to practice* (3rd ed., pp. 121–178). San Francisco: Jossey-Bass.

Swanson, J. L., & Tokar, D. M. (1991). College students' perceptions of barriers to career development. *Journal of Vocational Behavior, 38,* 92–106.

Tang, M., Fouad, N. A., & Smith, P. L. (1999). Asian Americans career choices: A path model to examine factors influencing their career choices. *Journal of Vocational Behavior, 54,* 142–157.

Tinsley, H. F. A. (2000). The congruence myth: An analysis of the efficacy of the person-environment fit model. *Journal of Vocational Behavior, 56,* 147–179.

Tokar, D. M., Fischer, A. R., & Subich, L. M. (1998). Personality and vocational behavior: A selective review of the literature, 1993–1997. *Journal of Vocational Behavior, 53,* 115–153.

Tracey, T. J. G. (1997). The structure of interests and self-efficacy expectations: An expanded examination of the spherical model of interests. *Journal of Counseling Psychology, 44,* 32–43.

Tracey, T. J. G., Darcey, M., & Kovalski, T. M. (2000). A closer look at person-environment fit. *Journal of Vocational Behavior, 56,* 216–224.

Tracey, T. J. & Rounds, J. R. (1992). Evaluating the RIASEC circumplex using high point codes. *Journal of Vocational Behavior, 41,* 295–311.

Tracey, T. J., & Rounds, J. R. (1993). Evaluating Holland's and Gati's vocational-interest models: A structural meta-analysis. *Psychological Bulletin, 113*, 229–246.

Tracey, T. J., & Rounds, J. R. (1996). The spherical representation of vocational interests. *Journal of Vocational Behavior, 48*, 3–41.

Vandiver, B. J., & Bowman, S. L. (1996). A schematic reconceptualization and application of Gottfredson's model. In M. L. Savickas & W. B. Walsh (Eds.), *Handbook of career counseling theory and practice* (pp. 155–168). Palo Alto, CA: Davies-Black.

Young, R. A., Valach, L., & Collin, A. (1996). A contextual explanation of career. In D. Brown, L. Brooks, & Associates (Eds.), *Career choice and development* (3rd ed., pp. 477–512). San Francisco: Jossey-Bass.

Zunker, V. G. (2002). *Career counseling: Applied concepts of life planning* (6th ed.). Pacific Grove, CA: Brooks/Cole.

······ ▬▬▬▬▬▬▬▬▬▬▬▬▬▬▬▬▬

CHAPTER 3

TOWARD A HOLISTIC VIEW

JANE GOODMAN
Oakland University

In recent years a number of people have addressed the idea that career and personal counseling are inseparable (for example, Bloch & Richmond, 1997; Jepsen, 1992; Looby & Sandhu, 2002). The reader needs only to consider his or her own career to realize how personal it indeed is. Not only are our careers central to our identity, but they affect, and are affected by, all of the other areas of our lives. Making a career decision in a vacuum is worse than meaningless, it is counterproductive. Career counselors who ask clients to set aside all other areas of life as they consider their career choices are doing a serious disservice. It must be said here that clients often err in this regard as well. They may resist life planning as being more complex than they wish. The search for simple answers is a common one. Counselors have an obligation to explain the process and explain what makes effective decisions, as opposed to merely efficient decisions. In many cases there may be what can be called an unconscious conspiracy between counselor and client to avoid ambiguity, short-circuit the process, and "decide already!"

FOUR CASE EXAMPLES

Melissa Winters loved her work as a sommelier at a four star restaurant. She loved creating the wine list and helping customers select wines for what was, for many, a special occasion. Her work was primarily evenings and weekends. This had worked well for her as a young, single woman, but she had recently married and wanted to have her evenings free to spend with her new husband, who worked a standard "nine to five" day.

Diego Sanchez was a successful and satisfied pediatric surgeon until he developed Parkinson's disease in his early 50s. He could no longer perform surgery due to his tremors. He had worked many years to develop his surgical expertise, and was terrified that he would not be able again to find work that he loved.

Takesha Jones had always wanted to be an elementary school teacher, but she completed her training at a time when school districts were laying off, not hiring, teachers. Her friends are telling her to look for a job in business, where they think she would thrive. Should she abandon her dream?

James Green has just turned 30. He is beginning to question his wisdom in dropping out of high school at age 16, without a diploma. Although he has supported himself reasonably well as a roofer, he is tired of the seasonal uncertainty and the hard physical labor. He wonders, "Is this all there is for me?"

There are thousands, maybe hundreds of thousands, of people like Melissa Winter, Diego Sanchez, Takesha Jones, and James Green. They all hope to find work that meets their financial and physical needs. But they also hope to find work that helps to meet their need to find meaning in their lives. This chapter will discuss individuals' desire for "right work," the pathways to manage a satisfying career, and the barriers that may be placed in their way due to world and national economic conditions, poverty, and discrimination.

We will follow each of these individuals as we explore finding meaning in work and career, individual choice, the decision-making process, and the balance among work, family, leisure, and community life. Although we recognize that each of these elements overlaps considerably with others, we will describe them as if they were discrete. We will also look at some pathways and barriers to each individual's successful career development.

BARRIERS

Individuals face barriers from the environment as well as from their own expectations, beliefs, sense of self-efficacy, and general mental health. Identifying barriers and planning strategies to overcome, avoid, or change them is an important aspect of the counseling process. Although the focus of this chapter is on helping individuals find meaning in their work, it is important to remember that people lead lives in context. Evans, Rotter, and Gold (2002) focus on the intersection of these three aspects. As they put it:

> We are not as "individual" as we may think, or even hope, but rather present for counseling as a representative, or reflection of, our relational and sociological contexts. What we have learned about ourselves as a family member, son, or daughter, male or female, member of a specific religious group, racial or ethnic group, and so on are vital components of our self definition, in our career concerns as well as general life decisions (p. 23)

In other words, we are whole beings, which is why, in this chapter, we encourage a holistic view of career counseling. Our spirituality may provide a pathway that assists in coping with, and perhaps even transcending, barriers, but it does not, in and of itself, eliminate them.

External Barriers

Let us begin with external barriers. Many Americans do not have "liberty and justice for all," as promised in the Pledge of Allegiance. Many are condemned by poverty to poor educations, poor prenatal and childhood nutrition, and reduced access to the opportunity structure. Many have reduced intellectual abilities due to pollution and environmental hazards such as lead paint. Others face discrimination due to prejudice such as racism, sexism, ageism, prejudice against homosexuals, or a handicapping condition. Still others have limited access to jobs or education by virtue of living in rural areas or communities affected by the loss of a major industry. Unskilled or minimally skilled workers are harder hit by these circumstances. In 1950, 60 percent of jobs in the United States were unskilled, with a high school diploma optional. By 1991, however, unskilled jobs were 35 percent of the nation's workforce and a high school diploma had become expected. It is projected that in 2005, only 15 percent of the workforce will be unskilled (Ingham Intermediate School District, 1998). This enormous change has left many people unprepared to find work that provides an adequate income.

Melissa was fortunate to have no obvious external barriers. She was successful in what was traditionally a male province and was a middle-class member of the majority in all ways. However, Melissa had found her job as a sommelier by working first as a waitress and learning about wine through on-the-job training. She had no obvious training for other positions. She had no resume and no experience of serious job hunting.

Diego Sanchez had grown comfortable in his role as Doctor Sanchez. The third child in a large Mexican American family, Dr. Sanchez had had to work extremely hard to complete his education. A serious barrier for Dr. Sanchez is the fact that he is over 50. Workers over 40 are protected by federal regulations for a reason: age discrimination exists. If Dr. Sanchez is interested in retraining, this barrier may be even higher.

Takesha Jones is an African American woman in her early 20s. She attended private schools because her professional parents were not happy with the public schools in the urban area in which they lived. She has always felt confident about her abilities to succeed in anything she chose, so the circumstances she is now facing surprise her. She believed she could overcome any societal barrier, but does not know what to do with an economic one. Takesha loves the urban area where she lives and does not want to relocate. She is close to her family and would be unhappy living far away from them. Information that there are teaching jobs in distant states or in rural areas is not reassuring to her. Takesha has no memory of making a conscious decision to become a teacher. It is what she had "always known" she would do. She has no idea how she might decide on a different occupation.

James Green has created many of his own barriers. Dropping out of school was, he realizes in retrospect, a poor decision. He also fathered a child, whom he helps to support, although he is no longer married to the child's mother. He has another child, with the woman he lives with, and he is also a primary provider for her other two children, although their father does pay some child support. His partner works at a low-paying job, which barely covers the costs of day care for the younger two children. Her job does provide health insurance for her and the three children, but James is not covered, as they are not married. That is another decision facing him. If he leaves his job, should he get married just for health insurance? After his failed first marriage he is very uncertain about "taking the plunge" again. James's circumstances are a combination of external and internal barriers. His lack of confidence in his relationship complicates his decision making, as do some poor decisions from his past.

Internal Barriers

Identifying and finding ways of mastering external barriers is an important component of career counseling, but equally important, and sometimes harder to identify, are internal barriers. These may include a poor self-concept, lack of hope or optimism, fear of failure, or even fear of success. Mental or emotional disorders may make it difficult for an individual to make good decisions or to find and keep good jobs.

Melissa's lifestyle choices were creating a conflict for her concerning family time versus work she loved. We will discuss issues of finding life balance later in this chapter. In this case, her values and preferences were creating a barrier to the easy decision of continuing as a sommelier. However, they may also be used to point the way to a decision better fitted to her present life.

Dr. Sanchez's parents were supportive emotionally, but were not able to help him financially. His two older sisters and his two younger brothers were very proud of the doctor in the family. He was ashamed; although he knew it was unreasonable, he felt that he had let them down by becoming ill. He believed that his ethnicity would make it more difficult to make a career change, just as he felt when he originally pursued the surgical branch of medicine. Although this is an external barrier, his fear of the discrimination becomes an internal one. Dr. Sanchez had not considered career counseling for his problem. He had been raised in a family that believed that getting outside help was a sign of weakness, and although he frequently recommended counseling for his patients, he did not think this advice applied to him.

All the people in our case examples are faced with internal and external barriers. As we follow them through their career development, we will look at career-counseling approaches that might assist them in finding satisfying work and overcoming the barriers that they face. Although it is beyond the scope of this chapter, we believe it is also important for career counselors to advocate on behalf of clients, as well as to teach clients how to advocate on their own behalf. (For more information, see American Counseling Association 2003, Schlossberg, Waters, & Goodman, 1995, pp. 261–267.)

PATHWAYS

Helping individuals find the right path is the goal of most career counseling. For young people, the challenge is to identify first steps; for others, it is to determine where to proceed next. There may be forks in the road, unexpected obstacles, steep hills, or easy slopes. Although the goal may be to identify an occupation or field of study, it is important to remember that this is usually one in a series, not *the* occupation, nor even the last education and training that will be needed. The U.S. Bureau of Labor Statistics (2002) estimates that the average baby boomer in the United States held 9.6 different jobs from the ages of 18 to 36. Peterson (1995) states that "most people entering the workforce today will have three to five careers and eight to ten jobs" (p. xiv). The basic structure of the labor force has also changed. These changes are a result of the combination of changing birthrates, the entry of large numbers of women into the workforce—from 30 percent in 1950 up to an estimated 48 percent in 2050—the aging of the workforce, and its increased diversity (Toossi, 2002).

Today's world rarely provides individuals with a job for life. Most will need retraining and will need to make several changes during their working lives. For some clients this is a relief, as making a decision for life can be daunting. For others, it is an added pressure. They resist accepting that they will have to engage in the decision-making process again, probably more than once. In the sections that follow, we will discuss aspects of these decisions and present a variety of counseling tools that can be used to promote healthy transitions.

FINDING MEANING IN WORK AND CAREER

"Man's search for meaning" (Frankl, 1963) is not a new concept. Perhaps Frost (1930, p. 314) put it most eloquently in his poem "Two Tramps in Mud Time":

> *But yield who will to their separation,*
> *My object in living is to unite*
> *My avocation and my vocation*
> *As my two eyes make one in sight.*

People's search for meaning through career is also not a new concept, but it has had a resurgence in recent years. Frankl's (1963) proposition was that meaning is essential to survival. Drawing from his own concentration camp experience, he attempted to understand why some people survived that hell on earth emotionally intact while others did not. His observation was that those who were able to find even small amounts of meaning during the experience fared better than those who were not able to. This meaning might have come from helping another, from finding a way to practice one's art, or, for most, from a spiritual connection. Frankl's small book has been extremely influential to many individuals involved in helping others. Career counselors can learn much about the human heart and soul from its pages.

Career development was formerly called vocational guidance, and the word *vocation* finds its roots in the Latin *vocare*, which means "to call." A vocation was, therefore, a calling from God. Many people refer to their work as a calling, referring, perhaps unconsciously, to this meaning of the word *vocation*. The recent increased attention to meaning seems to touch a deep chord in individuals. For many others, however, paid work is only a means to an end—survival or paying for necessities in order for the individual to engage in what they consider their "real" work. The poet Wallace Stevens worked as an insurance executive. Another poet, e. e. cummings, sold tokens in the New York subways. Many artists, musicians, and actors have "day jobs" to pay the rent. Others find satisfaction in family, in community service, or in personal hobbies.

If we were to depend on fiction to form our views of work, we would be hard-pressed to find much. The dearth of fiction that focuses on, or even includes, people's working lives was addressed by Miller (2004). She suggested that novelists, who often have other jobs that they hate in order to support themselves while they write, do not see that it is possible for work to be enjoyable. She cites the work of several researchers who have found the opposite, that many people not only enjoy their work, but do not even take advantage of all of the time off they have available, preferring work life to home life. She concludes that the workplace is often an environment where "people find adventure, camaraderie, and even intimacy" (Miller, 2004, p. 23).

Career counselors must be sensitive, however, to the fact that not all clients are interested in finding meaningful paid jobs, or in finding work where the tasks themselves are meaningful. A landmark study by McClelland, Atkinson, Clark, and Lowell (1953) found that although many people are motivated by the need for achievement— that is, a need to accomplish something they believe is important. Many others are motivated by the need for affiliation. For these people, what they do is often less important than who they do it with. Career counselors, who themselves are usually in the "need achievement" category, need to be mindful of the needs of their clients who have different motivational structures. It is also important to pay attention to the variety of worldviews expressed by clients. This results not only from cultural diversity, but also from generational changes in belief systems. As Anderson (2003) puts it:

> There has been a basic shift in the realms of psychology and modern science away from the logical positivism that once shaped people's worldviews. The shift toward postmodernism and social constructionism is an important movement regarding how people view reality. Instead of fundamental and absolute truths, laws and principles, there is now a belief in multiple perspectives and a variety of ways of perceiving. Within the postmodern viewpoint, the context in which individuals live is emphasized and meaning emerges through human relationships, language, culture and personal meaning making (p. 14).

Sometimes we see this need for meaning more clearly when it is missing.

In researching the phenomenon of burnout through case studies, Malach-Pines and Yafe-Yanai (2001) concluded that career burnout resulted from a failure in the search for meaning through work. They assert that every person they interviewed who had experienced burnout had also experienced a lack of meaning in his or her work. They assert that the unconscious often plays a role in career decision making, and that taking a psychodynamic or psychoanalytic approach can be a fruitful way to help clients examine causes of burnout, or even career choice. Through cases studies, they present the idea, reminiscent of Savickas (1997), that one's symptoms can lead to one's solution, that one's preoccupation can become one's occupation, and that, quoting Satan in Milton's (1667/1940) *Paradise Lost*, "Our torments also may, in length of time, become our elements" (p. 33). The radio commentator and essayist David Sedaris (2000) provides a wonderful example of this. In his book *Me Talk Pretty One Day*, he describes his speech defect and embarrassing speech therapy in elementary school. One might wonder if his career as a speaker is a way of making his torment become his element.

Savickas (1997) deconstructs the word *spirituality* to remind us of its origin, which is "breath" or "wind." If we think about the word *inspire*, we can see that its original meaning was "to breathe into." We now use it to mean "to hearten, to give confidence to, to raise one's spirits." Moving beyond matching interests and skills, Savickas distinguishes traditional career counseling from "career counseling that attends to the individual's spirit, . . . [that] addresses how people can use occupations and work for personal and spiritual development" (p. 6).

It is easy to see how attention to spirituality can relate to an existential worldview in which the focus is on experiencing, living in the present, and finding meaning in living (see, for example, Adler, 1964; May, 1969). However, Gendlin (1973) takes us a step beyond existentialism to a theory he calls "experiential psychotherapy." This theory has four bases.

Described in a greatly oversimplified manner, they are: (a) experiencing, to mean all of the aspects of physical and emotional feelings; (b) interaction, "living in an infinite universe and in situations, a context of other people, of words and signs, of physical surroundings, of past, present, and future" (p. 324); (c) authenticity, by which he means a carrying forward, implying continuity and next steps, and (d) "focaling," which he later calls "focusing" (Gendlin, 1981), relating to purpose mediated by values. If career counselors follow Gendlin's ideas, they help their clients both experience the moment fully and plan for a future consistent with their values. It is particularly important for *career* counselors to help their clients maintain this dual focus on the present and the future.

In an article focusing on existentialism and career development, Cohen (2003) proposed a cyclical four stage model: responsibility, evaluation, action, and reevaluation. In each stage the existential question needs to be faced, that is, how does this relate to the freedom and responsibility to find or create a meaningful existence? Central to this model is the assertion that in order for people to obtain and maintain career satisfaction, they must be satisfied with the "meaning and opportunities for authentic existence that the occupation provides" (p. 195). Cohen (2003) asserts that because career decisions are so important, when people fully appreciate both their freedom and responsibility, the decision may evoke deep, existential angst. The unconscious conspiracy alluded to earlier can result when the counselor "buys into" this anxiety and provides solutions for the client. Drawing on the work of philosophers such as Tillich (1952), Heidegger (1949), and Kierkegaard (1950), along with Frankl (1963), Cohen argues that "Who am I?" becomes a question that supercedes "What can I do?" The role of the career counselor becomes, then, helping individuals identify what will make meaning for them in their life roles as well as in their work roles. The search for meaning as translated into career counseling includes discussing the role of an individual's spirituality, helping him or her find hope and optimism, and making decisions that enhance the possibilities of finding meaning in work. In the sections that follow, we will discuss these three major roles.

INTEGRATING SPIRITUALITY AND WORK

Looby and Sandhu (2002) suggest that the current interest in spirituality in the workplace is a result of the increasing levels of isolation and existential frustration during the 1990s (p. 17). They cite a study by Mitroff and Denton (1999), who interviewed senior executives and human resources professionals. Mitroff and Denton found that "most participants wished to express and develop their whole selves at work" (Looby & Sandhu, 2002, p. 23). Looby and Sandhu (2002) cite increasing workplace violence and other evidence of alienation that suggest that integrating spirituality in the workplace would be a positive step. They propose 12 standards for what we might call a spiritually competent workplace (pp. 27–28):

1. Creativity, encouraging individuals to find new ways of being and doing
2. Communication, fostering teamwork and honest expression
3. Respect, for self and others
4. Partnership, taking responsibility and working together
5. Vision, seeing the possible and desiring to grow
6. Flexibility, readiness to change and resilience
7. Energy, excitement stemming from creativity
8. Fun, enjoying, valuing, and revering each day
9. Finding self, helping individuals be "in harmony with themselves and the universe" (p. 28)
10. Values training, ensuring that employees share company values
11. Relational management, creating a trusting and honest environment
12. Stress management, helping employees to lead healthy lives, including balancing work and personal lives

Whether or not each aspect relates directly to spirituality, they are certainly components of a desirable workplace.

The extent to which the concept of a more spiritual—or, perhaps, humane— workplace is provided by Greider (2003) on his Website. Discussing his new book, *The Soul of Capitalism*, (2003), Greider states:

> Yes, we are fabulously wealthy as a nation, but are we truly free? How can people be considered free when their daily lives are so closely regimented by the confinements imposed upon them at work, rules that tell them to turn off their brains and take orders, no back talk? The content and conditions of work for most Americans—even in well-salaried positions—are determined from above by a steep pyramid of distant managers, who are often brutally indifferent to the human consequences or even to what the employees know about how the company functions (and malfunctions). These confining circumstances, once associated with the assembly line, have crept very far up the job ladder. Indeed, the satisfactions inherent in doing a good job—intangible qualities of human fulfillment enjoyed by conscientious workers at every level—have been steadily degraded in recent decades, even for many high-skilled professionals.

These writers speak about spirituality as if we have a common understanding of what that is, but actually, spirituality is difficult to define (McSherry & Cash, 2004; Tisdell, 1999). In attempting to define the concept, Tisdell pointed to connectedness of history, interconnectedness of life, and a sense of transcendence. Wuthnow (1998) proposed that spirituality includes (1) a sense of connectedness to place, "spirituality of dwelling"; (2) questing and finding one's path or journey through life, "spirituality of seeking"; and (3) carrying on a legacy of social action, "spirituality of moral responsibility." Jankowski (2002) discussed spiritual resilience, finding purpose and meaning by adhering to sets of larger beliefs, exercise of faith, and experience of a connection with God. Others have added that spirituality involves "a sense of awe" (Ellison, 1994) and peak experiences (Wilber, 2000). Still others speak of ritual and ceremony. The sum of these comments is that the term *spirituality* encompasses a variety of concepts, but that there is agreement that it is distinguishable from organized religion per se and includes a sense of transcendence that is beyond ordinary experience.

Attending to the connection between spirituality and work has both a long history and a recent resurgence. Counselors assisting clients with career-related issues and decisions are increasingly finding it important to include spirituality in their work. Bloch (1997, pp. 204–205) suggests that there are three implications for individuals of trying to find "right work," and that there are six implications for counselors. Individuals need to understand the "nature of meaning in lifework and its particular relationship to a sense of connectedness and absorbedness" (p. 204). They also need to practice meditation, visualization, or other form of "stillness" as a way to discover or uncover meaning and spirituality in their own lives. One morning as I was writing this chapter, I took my dog for a walk on a railroad right of way that passes a small woods. As we were returning I saw a small doe, daintily nibbling the vegetation at the edge of the trees. Quietly the dog sat and we both watched the deer as she first watched us, then returned to eating, and finally melted back into the woods. That "stillness" lasted for hours, as I wondered at my dog's ability to sense the preciousness of the moment and treasured the connectedness I had felt.

Finally, individuals need to practice intentionality, a way of using one's mind to influence events. Although this last leg of the client's tripod is counter to linear, scientific thinking, Bloch cites a body of literature to make a strong case for its inclusion in one's approach (1997, pp. 197–204). There are six guidelines for counselors: (a) accept that each individual is a work in progress; (b) be in harmony with oneself; (c) recognize the uniqueness of each individual; (d) practice intentionality oneself; (e) be open to learning from other's cultures and experiences; and (f) see yourself as a teacher. Young (1983), reflecting on her life in an introspective book called *Inscape: A Search for Meaning*, comments that she has experienced life, reflected deeply on it, and lived it. In the foreword, Lotus (1983) says, "I am grateful to her for reminding me of the need to deal with life's paradoxes, such as being both a participant in life and an observer of life; making sense of my life while at the same time accepting the mystery of it" (n.p.). People for whom spirituality is an important component of life decisions often reflect on death and the afterlife as they make decisions for this life. Others talk about living this life to the fullest. A career development activity that resonates with many is composing one's own obituary or imagining what would be on one's tombstone. The idea behind these kinds of activities is to focus on values and goals.

In discussing life after the biblical three score and ten, Heilbrun (1997) said: "I find it powerfully reassuring not to think of life as borrowed time. Each day one can say to oneself: I can always die; do I choose death or life? I daily choose life the more earnestly because it is a choice" (p. 10). Heilbrun committed suicide in October 2003, at the age of 77. Her son Robert was quoted as follows in her obituary. "She had not been ill. She wanted to control her destiny, and she felt her life was a journey that had concluded" http://www.nytimes.com/2003/10/11/obituaries/11HEIL.html (Retrieved, October 11,

2003.) Although most would probably disagree with Heilbrun's choice to commit suicide, her focus on *choosing* how to spend each day of life is one that resonates with many.

Others define spirituality more narrowly, as they look at the integration of religion into an organization. They describe such activities as breakfast prayer groups, Bible study, and allowing employees time off to celebrate religious holidays, even when they are not national holidays. Given the increased diversity of religious beliefs that comes with the increased diversity of the United States, this latter is becoming more important, while at the same time it is more challenging to managers.

According to Brewer (2001), the connection between work and spirituality relates to a personal sense of life's meaning, an unfolding sense of self, and purpose that is expressed and driven by action. She developed the concept of a "Vocational Souljourn Paradigm," defined as, "the ongoing interior process of discovering meaning, being, and doing and the expression of that discovery in the exterior world of work through four possible paths: job, occupation, career, and Vocation" (p. 84). She suggests that one find out during career counseling:

(a) What is the nature of this client's relationship to work with regard to a whole life? (b) What does this client find meaningful? (c) Who is this person, and how does the wish to implement self in work become expressed? (d) Is this client coming to counseling for change in work/life choices, acceptance of life as it is, or some discovery of life goals and purpose? (p. 84).

These questions could be very useful for Dr. Sanchez as he attempts to find new meaning in his life. He is currently in need of finding new life goals and purposes.

THE EFFECTS OF HOPE AND OPTIMISM ON CAREER DECISION MAKING

Hope has been defined as belief in the face of doubt. In order for persons to be willing to take action on their own behalf, it is essential that they have hope. Without hope, action seems futile, and it is hard to sustain energy when the desired outcome does not seem possible. Two elements of hope and optimism will be discussed in the following, self-efficacy beliefs and learned optimism.

Self-Efficacy Beliefs

The attitude that one can act on one's own behalf and that it will make a difference is the core of self-efficacy. Originally proposed by Bandura (1977), self-efficacy theory has become a widely used explanatory system for many behaviors. Career inaction may be attributed to lack of self-efficacy beliefs. It is logical not to act when one believes that it will make no difference. To intervene, therefore, we need to help clients develop a sense of efficacy, rather than simply exhorting them to "try harder!" A hallmark of self-efficacy theory, in contrast to self-esteem theory, is that it is situation dependent.

For example, a person may have a strong sense of efficacy about his or her ability to relate to people but poor efficacy beliefs concerning academic learning.

Brown (1992) asserted that self-efficacy expectations are learned, and that therefore new expectations can be learned. There are three keys to self-efficacy: action, effort, and persistency. Counselors can help clients develop a better sense of efficacy through empowering experiences, role models, messages, and emotions. For example, how might we help James develop a better sense of self-efficacy? We might guess that his school experiences have not left him with a strong sense of academic efficacy. We might also guess that he is unsure of his ability to do work greatly different from roofing. Brown would suggest that we help James identify empowering experiences from the past. We might also help him develop new empowering experiences that are related to his current challenges. For example, if he is indeed unsure of his scholastic ability, we might have him enroll in an adult education class in an area in which we suspect he will be comfortable, woodworking perhaps. The object is to be difficult enough to help him improve his expectations, but easy enough that we know he will succeed.

In order to help James identify empowering role models, we may need to enlist his assistance. Whom does he identify with who has been successful? Again, it is important that these people be close enough to how James sees himself, that he can see himself doing what they do. Group counseling is often an appropriate venue for finding role models; often someone else in the group either is an appropriate role model or knows someone who can fill that bill. It is well known that empowering messages are useful only when they are believed. The messenger needs to be someone believable, the message has to be close enough to James's ideas that he can accept its truth, and James has to want to absorb a new self-image. If all of these conditions are met, James may enhance his self-efficacy beliefs in a new arena. Finally, Brown (1992) suggests, emotions also need to be empowering. If James's stress is overpowering, he will not have the energy to change his beliefs; if he does not care enough, he may not be willing to do the work to change them. Brown says that one needs to have dreams—of what you want—and turn them into visions—of what you will attain. Sometimes the dream itself is an achievement.

Learned Optimism

Seligman (1998, pp. 217–220) has suggested that optimism is a critical life skill and that it can be learned. Seligman proposes teaching skills that transform pessimists into optimists. The first is *distraction*. This is a process of shifting focus away from distressing thoughts and toward more positive ones. The admonition, "Don't think about it!" does not seem to work. The admonition, "Think about something positive instead," actually does seem to work. Dr. Sanchez might, for example, change the thought, "I am worthless if I am no longer a surgeon" to "I have a renewed opportunity to contribute to developing new physicians through my teaching." We are reminded poignantly of the scientist in Levinson's (1978) *Season's of a Man's Life:*

> He had given up the image of himself as a youthful hero going out to save the world, but had not yielded to the threatening specter of the dried-up, dying old man. He accepted himself as a middle aged man of considerable achievement, experience and

integrity. . . . He was content to make a modest social contribution as parent, concerned citizen, scientist, teacher, and mentor to the younger generation. He had a sense
of well-being (p. 277).

We can only hope that Dr. Sanchez can reach such comfort. This kind of reframing, if not used punitively, can help clients learn to be more optimistic. It is punitive if
we try to gloss over the challenges, struggle, and grief that change can bring. It is
encouraging if we help people move on after a time of mourning for what is lost.

Reframing can help James Green change the belief: "Work is simply drudgery.
No one in my family likes their work. I don't expect to either," to "I would like to be
the first in my family to have a satisfying career. What can I do to increase the likelihood of that happening?"

Seligman's second technique is *disputation*. This is a process of actually arguing
with a thought—either internal self-talk or negative statements that have been made
by others. Three of Seligman's suggestions for disputation are discussed next:

1. Evidence: Encourage clients to ask themselves, "What is the actual evidence that
   this thought or accusation is true?" Find contrary evidence. For example, if they
   are thinking that because they performed poorly on a test they are terrible students, remind them of all of the tests they have done well on or remind them that
   they perform better in practical situations. Dr. Sanchez may need to remind
   himself of what he knows as a medical person: Parkinson's is not something he
   brought on himself.
2. Alternatives: Encourage clients to ask themselves, "What are the alternative
   explanations for this event?" James Green may need to consider that he was
   young when he dropped out of school and that he is now more mature.
3. Implications: Encourage clients to consider their catastrophic expectations and
   then examine whether they are really likely. Takesha Jones could find out if it is
   true that school districts are not hiring anyone at all. Perhaps certain fields like
   mathematics or special education are still good career avenues.

Approaching the Decision-Making Process

Many authors have described decision-making strategies. Some are logical and sequential; some draw more on feelings and intuition. Contrary adages abound: He who hesitates is lost; Look before you leap. Napoleon is supposed to have said, "Take time to
deliberate, but when the time for action has arrived, stop thinking and go in" (Safire &
Safir, 1982, p. 74). You have read elsewhere in this volume about several theories of
career development. In recent years several people have focused their attention instead
on strategies of career counseling. These are not atheoretical, but rather describe
processes that are guides for the practitioner. We will describe several of these
approaches here: planned happenstance, positive uncertainty, learned optimism, and
some of the so-called postmodern approaches.

Planned Happenstance

Originally developed by Mitchell, Levin, and Krumboltz (1999), planned happenstance proposes that "chance favors the prepared mind" (attributed to Louis Pasteur). Most schoolchildren have heard the story of Archimedes running naked through the streets of Greece shouting "Eureka," having "discovered" specific gravity while in the bath. Deriving inspiration from such stories and others, such as the development of Velcro®, Post-its®, Wite-Out®, and penicillin, Mitchell et al. encouraged counselors to teach their clients to develop their curiosity. Clients are helped to "generate, recognize, and incorporate chance events into their career development" (p. 117).

Mitchell et al. reframed indecision as open-mindedness. They suggested that counselors teach clients to embrace uncertainty, to see it as part of the process of discovery, and to resist premature foreclosure in decision making. The authors argued that the usual response to indecision is discomfort and that clients are urged by internal and external forces to have definite plans. We are reminded here of the unconscious conspiracy alluded to previously: the pressure felt by client and counselor to reduce ambiguity and seek a finite plan. Career counseling is seen as a step in making those plans. The perhaps paradoxical intervention of encouraging indecision can create discomfort and resistance from clients who want clarity and closure. It requires a leap of faith and trust in both the counselor and the process. Mitchell et al. (1999) proposed five skills to promote using chance events to increase career options:

1. Curiosity: exploring new learning opportunities
2. Persistence: exerting effort despite setbacks
3. Flexibility: changing attitudes and circumstances
4. Optimism: viewing new opportunities as possible and attainable
5. Risk Taking: taking action in the face of uncertain outcomes (p. 118)

Melissa Winter's career dilemma provides a good opportunity to demonstrate how one might operationalize these principles. Melissa's counselor can help her identify how chance has helped her in the past to find satisfying work, and she can be reassured that her anxiety is normal. Let us follow Melissa through the experience of implementing a planned happenstance approach to her decision. First she can be taught career exploration skills that include practicing *curiosity*. She might, for example, be asked to spend a week noting things she wonders about. She might then choose one of those things to explore more fully and actually research (K. E. Mitchell, personal communication, 1997). If any of these explorations have a career focus, that is wonderful; if not, they can be seen as training the curiosity muscles. Second, she can be asked to identify when in her past life she needed to be *persistent*, how she overcame frustration and disappointment, and how she maintained her efforts even in the face of difficulties. She may well need to call upon these strengths again, so it is important for her to identify and own them. Next, we will encourage Melissa to be flexible. She is motivated by her commitment to her new marriage to find day work. She will probably not be able to find a sommelier job without weekend and evening work, so she needs to look beyond her comfort level. There may be other wine-related jobs; there may be other jobs where she need work only some nights or weekends; there may be jobs that use her transferable skills of the ability to learn and understand complex ideas or to relate well to people. Melissa has many options if she will open her mind to them. We do not know if Melissa is willing to retrain, but this is another arena for flexibility.

To help Melissa learn and embrace *optimism*, we will follow Seligman's (1998) suggestions (described earlier). Finally, to help Melissa take advantage of her *risk taking* skills, we could have her list all the risks she has taken in the past—physical, emotional, intellectual—as well as the more specific career risks. She could then assess which have paid off for her, which have not, and why. We hope that this will give her a more confident sense of how and when she can take risks and will encourage her to use this confidence in her current situation.

It would certainly be a disservice to unemployed clients who need work immediately to refuse to help them make short-term plans. It is more appropriate to help them with both short- and long-term goals, that is, finding immediate work to satisfy life needs while continuing the career exploration process, which could lead to more satisfying work in the long run. Maslow's hierarchy (1954) suggests that one must meet physiological, safety, and belonging needs before one can look to satisfy the need for self-esteem and importance, let alone the needs for information, understanding, beauty, and self-actualization. To push clients to try to reach self-actualization when they are worried about their next meal is not only cruel, it is unlikely to achieve its aim.

Positive Uncertainty

In positive uncertainty, Gelatt (1991) influentially proposed a method of fostering career resilience with his series of paradoxes related to career decisions: (1) be focused and flexible about what you want, (2) be aware and wary about what you know, (3) be objective and optimistic about what you believe, and (4) be practical and "magical" about what you do (pp. 7–10). His approach is one of "Using *both* [emphasis added] rational and intuitive techniques" (n. p.) to make decisions. How do we implement these paradoxes in working with clients?

The world of today requires that people plan for a lifetime of self-managed careers. The mutual loyalty bonds that formerly tied employer and employee are much less strong than perhaps they once were. Individuals leave employment and employers let people go with great regularity. It is a rare day that the newspapers do not announce another round of layoffs.

Powers and Rothausen (2003) suggest that "the flexibility needed by employers has translated into insecurity, financial pressures, overwork, and increased risk to income and quality of work life for many middle class workers and especially for older workers, women, and minorities" (p. 160). In the twenty-first century, many people will need to learn:

> how to change with change, accept ambiguity and uncertainty, negotiate job or career changes, multiple times in their working lifetimes, be able to plan and act on shifting career opportunities . . . and have the motivation to be career resilient—to persist in the face of change and unplanned for problems and difficulties. (Herr, 2001, p. 208, quoted in Herr, Cramer, & Niles, 2004, p. 69)

Powers and Rothausen (2003) propose a new model for working with middle-class, mid-career workers. They state that this group, about 60 percent of American workers, is the most affected by these labor market changes (p. 158). The model presumes that people are satisfied in their jobs; for those who are not, they suggest that other career models are more appropriate. There are three core concepts: (a) *defining work* as a set of activities that can provide value for many employers and that provides meaning for one-self, as distinguished from a traditional definition that includes a specific function for a specific employer, that is, a position; (b) *identifying the future requirements* to do the work, a component assuming self-management of one's career, and therefore of the training and education necessary to maintain or update skills rather than depending on an employer for such training, as well as a commitment to keeping up with current information relating to trends in order to foresee the need for a career transition; (c) *choosing a developmental direction* that defines a phase of three to five years in the future. Powers and Rothausen (2003) provide a series of questions for use by career counselors for each of these tasks. For example, they would ask a person defining work stage, "With what activity or effort at work do you most identify? About what do you feel passionate to learn more? What activities fire your interest and imagination?" (p. 178). In the stage of identifying future requirements, they would ask: "What are the future challenges in doing this work? What are the performance benchmarks for this work? What technological changes will have a major impact on this work?" (p. 178). In determining developmental direction, they suggest determining if the person's development is job oriented, work-maintenance oriented, or work-growth oriented, and planning accordingly (p. 175).

Casto (2003, n. p.) states:

> My own concept of career is like a wardrobe, where you "try on" different outfits throughout your lifetime, and continue to check the mirror to see if it still fits and matches your current style and taste. In the modern world of work, you will need to find work that is "suited" to you. Think of your life's work as your wardrobe. It is ever-changing as you move through life, changing as your styles and interests change. Throughout the process, you will be tailoring yourself to fit different roles, and to meet changing work styles and expectations.

A number of catch phrases have sprung up to describe this phenomenon, for example "You, Inc." The idea is that individuals are responsible for their own career planning and career management. They are, in effect, their own corporation. It has been suggested, therefore, that individuals not wait for a crisis to engage in career development activities.

The concept of the preventive checkup, or dental model (Goodman, 1991, 1992) has been used as a way of describing ongoing career development activities. The premise behind much school-based career counseling is that once we become adults, we are prepared to become self-directed and independent in managing our lives. The dental model proposes that our need for career assistance does not end with completion of our formal education. It suggests that we need to see career counselors as we see dentists, throughout our lives, for regular checkups and routine maintenance, to navigate successfully in today's rapidly changing world. During checkups, individuals might get assistance in analyzing employment trends in their own or related industries or they might assess their own interests and values to determine if there is still a good fit with their current situation. Often individuals change as they mature, leading to a desire for different work. Lifestyle changes can also influence career satisfaction. An income, for example, that was satisfying for a young single person, may now be inadequate to support young children and defray the costs of child care or send older children to college. Furthermore, the long hours necessary to earn that kind of income may no longer be necessary when children are grown, and people may then wish to "trade" money for more leisure or more job flexibility. In addition, many career counselors find that intrapersonal needs have changed. Jung (1959) talked about the move to androgyny, a state in which men seek out and find their so-called feminine side, and women their so-called masculine side. Goodman and Waters (1985) termed this stage of development the time of "affective men and effective women."

This development can also lead to what as been termed the dromedary camel syndrome, or the "out of sync career commitment curve" (Goodman & Waters, 1985). The two-humped camel symbolizes traditional women's career commitment graph, where there is often a declining career commitment—though not always declining work hours—during the child-rearing years. Although this may be changing somewhat, anecdotal evidence still supports the thesis that many women stay home, work part time, or otherwise reduce their career investment during the years when their children are young. The one-humped dromedary symbolizes men's more predictable career trajectory. A problem may arise for dual-career couples when a traditional man's declining curve crosses his partner's second climb. Her enhanced career investment may come at the exact time as his is declining. Career counselors working with couples doing retirement planning may want to keep this potential conflict in mind.

Managing Change

In speaking about the difficulty of change, Bloch (2004) discusses how change often means separation from some aspect of one's past. However, she sees separation and connectedness as part of the complexity of life, like the yin and yang, which are complementary spiritual symbols. She concludes, "Perhaps the most important knowledge that the counselor can impart is how to accept and utilize change and how to understand and rely upon the connectedness of life" (p. 343). In defining spirituality as the embodiment of this connectedness, she encourages readers to find spirituality in work through seven "connectors" (2004, p. 347): (1) being open to change, (2) finding balance in life, (3) having enough energy to do what you want to do, (4) being a part of communities of work, companionship, culture, and "the cosmic community," (5) finding one's calling, (6) finding harmony or flow, and (7) achieving unity, defined as "believing that the work you do has a purpose beyond earning money and in some way serves others" (p. 347).

Gelatt's (1991) thesis is that, whatever approach you use, you must be both decisive *and* flexible about change. In the best-seller, *Who Moved My Cheese?* (1998), Johnson presented an allegory of mice that resist change to the point of starvation and compared them to mice that accept change and move on. The lessons learned by the "resilient" mouse are: (1) change happens, (2) anticipate change, (3) monitor change, (4) adapt to change quickly, (5) change, (6) enjoy change, and (7) be ready to quickly change again and again. The underlying message is that, not only is change constant, but also one must embrace change and see it as leading to more positive outcomes. In *Going to Plan B*, Schlossberg and Robinson (1996) discussed the resilience that is required when anticipated things do not happen—these are nonevents, in their terminology. They posited a series of responses—acknowledging, easing, refocusing, reshaping—that are necessary to cope with these nonevents.

Schlossberg (Schlossberg et al., 1995) proposed a so-called "4 S" system of looking at transitions that included four basic elements. They are (each beginning with "S") situation, self, available support, and strategies. This taxonomy is actually an assessment system, but it can be used to structure a counseling interview and it provides a broad enough base to encompass many of the aspects of career decision making discussed earlier. Let us discuss each of the elements in turn, using James Green as our client.

What is James's *situation*? He is working at a job that no longer satisfies his physical or financial needs. He is also unhappy about the insecurity of the seasonal nature of his work, so we can say that his emotional needs are also unsatisfied. James has several children he helps to support, and he is facing a decision about marriage. The timing of the possible transition is good, in that it is his choice, not a choice imposed on him. It is in his control and there does not seem to be a need for an immediate decision. James has the luxury, unlike someone who is unemployed, of making a more thoughtful decision than his first career decision, that of dropping out of high school.

What do we know about James's *self*? We know that he was probably impulsive in his decision to leave school and perhaps in his early marriage. We know that he seems to be more mature now and more thoughtful about his life course. He is responsible about paying child support and also helps support his partner's other two children. He is apparently in good physical health. We do not know anything about James's emotional or mental health, nor do we know much about his interests, skills, abilities, or other personal characteristics such as willingness to take risks, or values such as desire for autonomy or prestige. These are all aspects of James that we will need to find out in our interviews, perhaps by engaging him in a narrative and hearing his story. We may also try to ascertain if James left school because learning was difficult for him. If so, and if getting more education turns out to be a goal for James, we may need to look at some kind of learning support.

We know a little bit about James's *support* system. We know that he lives with a woman and their child, as well as her other children. We do not know anything else about James's life space. Does he have an extended family with whom he is close? Do they live nearby? What about his friendships? We might ask James to complete an extended Genogram, including, not only family, but also other important people in his life. We might also suggest that James look at his stress system. These are sometimes the same people as in a support system, and comparing the two can be helpful in understanding James's life space. We may suspect, as mentioned, that James's school experience implies that he does not find paper and pencil the best way to learn. If that is the case, we may want to ask James, instead of writing a Genogram, to create a family sculpture (Satir, 1964) or to find another kinesthetic way of assessing his support. One way that I have found useful would be to simply have James draw a circle, with himself in the middle, and list his supports as spokes in the wheel, identifying the role they play as he goes. It is important to encourage him to look also at nonpeople supports, such as exercise, faith, a pet, or happy memories. He might also list the more pragmatic support aspects, such as a working car, good health, and so forth. Such an activity may help him realize the amount of support he has or, alternatively, to recognize that he does not have the support he would like and must learn some support-access skills.

Finally, what *strategies* is James using to manage his anticipated transition? Schlossberg (Schlossberg et al., 1995) indicated that there are three categories of strategies. What can James do to change his situation? What can he do to change the meaning of the situation? Finally, how can he manage the concomitant stress? Let us address each category in turn. James wants a new job and a new line of work. He needs strategies for decision making and, most probably, for pursuing further education, at least as far as a high school diploma or a general education diploma (GED). He may need to learn job search techniques and the rest that a job search entails. Schlossberg's model would imply that we first find out what strategies James already knows and then develop a plan for filling in the gaps. Changing the meaning of a situation is a delicate task. We do not want to run the risk of trivializing his problems with a clichéd response such as, "When you have lemons, make lemonade." However, perhaps James can grow to see that he does have an opportunity to create a more satisfying and meaningful life. His visit to a career counselor in the first place indicates a readiness to look at change. His counselor needs to capitalize on that readiness. Discussion of his strengths, his support, and so forth from previous sections can be brought into this part of the model. Finally, James needs to either access or learn stress management techniques.

The vast amount of information available on the Internet has created a dilemma for many career decision makers. People who try to get "all the information" before deciding can become paralyzed by the amount available. Furthermore, the information is not always accurate. There are no fact checkers on the Internet. Gelatt's edict to be wary takes on particular significance in light of this explosion of (often inaccurate) information. Gelatt's (1991) final directive, to be practical and "magical" about what you do, encourages us to be creative, to "dream the impossible dream," while keeping our feet on the ground, to mix a metaphor. Although I do not believe the adage, "If you dream it, you can do it," I do believe that if you cannot dream something, you cannot do it. Sitting home and waiting for magic probably will not help someone to reach goals, but being in the right place at the right time is more likely to come about if one is in lots of places.

A similar worldview is expressed by Langer (1997) as she discusses *mindful learning*. She states that we must appreciate "both the conditional, or context-dependent nature of the world and the value of uncertainty" (p. 15). She describes three characteristics of her approach: "the continuous creation of new categories; openness to new information; and an implicit awareness of more than one perspective" (p. 4). Dependence on context is one of the hallmarks of the postmodern approaches that we will discuss next.

POSTMODERN APPROACHES

Narrative

Perhaps the most influential career-counseling approach to be brought forth in recent years is that of using narrative as a basis for the career-counseling interview. Because it can encompass any of the techniques described previously, it can be seen as a way of integrating many perspectives. Drawing its roots from the ancient tradition of storytelling, the narrative approach simply proposes that we have clients tell their stories. These stories can then be used to develop themes and to understand individuals at a deeper level. Savickas (2001) describes four levels of career theories. The first relates to vocational personality types. Chiefly associated with the RIASEC codes of John Holland (1959), types have been shown to have cross-cultural validity and a high amount of inheritability, to relate to an individual, and to be relatively context free. The second type identified by Savickas (2001) is defined as being connected to contextual factors such as historical context as well as relating to an individual's personal life space. These are usually called career concerns. The third type is identified as related to career narratives. Narratives, "compose a life. . . . They give a life meaningful continuity over time" (p. 310). Savickas warns us that narratives are particularly appropriate for middle-class people who probably have more career options, but recommends them nonetheless as a useful counseling approach. Savickas's fourth level, although beyond the scope of this discussion, is designed to describe the process of continuity and change in career development.

Several people have proposed techniques designed to elicit these stories. Savickas (2003) recommends asking the following questions:

1. Whom do you admire? Whom would you pattern your life after? Whom did you admire growing up? How are you like this person? How are you different from this person?
2. Do you read any magazines regularly? Which ones?
3. What do you like to do in your free time?
4. Do you have a favorite saying or motto?
5. What are (were) your three favorite subjects in school? What subjects do (did) you hate?
6. What is your earliest recollection?

From these questions counselors can help their clients construct a narrative, looking for themes, patterns, continuities, and discontinuities. Others have suggested having clients divide their lives into chapters or acts in a play. Jepsen (1992) suggests that the client then simultaneously becomes the play's star, playwright, director, and audience.

Integrative life planning

Another postmodern approach is suggested by Hansen (1997, 2002). Her holistic approach includes:

1. finding work that needs doing in changing global contexts
2. weaving our lives into a meaningful whole
3. connecting family and work (negotiating roles and relationships)
4. valuing pluralism and inclusivity
5. managing personal transitions and organizational change
6. exploring spirituality and life purpose (2002, p. 61)

Let us look at what applying these six points might look like for Takesha Jones. Takesha found work that needed doing, but it is also necessary to find someone to employ one to do the work. Just because many people live in substandard housing or drive on pothole-marred roads does not mean that there is money to solve these problems. If Takesha wants to work as a teacher, she will either have to find somewhere else to work, find another way to earn a living and teach on a voluntary basis during her leisure hours, or, as we suggested, specialize in an area where there are openings. Another way for Takesha to approach her dilemma is to look at the underlying values beneath her desire to teach. Is it because she loves the act of teaching, because she loves children, or perhaps because she sees teaching as a way of making a difference in a troubled world? Are there other reasons? The answers would help her apply Hansen's first principle. What about number two? We have only discussed Takesha's occupational decisions thus far. We would need to know more about the rest of her life. We might use Savickas's (2003) questions or Super's (1980) rainbow to help us explore other areas of her life. Hansen's (1997) third principle involves negotiating the balance of family and work. This is an issue of both time and emotional involvement. As we saw with Melissa, the work schedule can in itself conflict with family life. Total work hours are also an issue for many. There are only 168 hours in a week. Having clients construct a time "pie" can help them assess if they are content with the current distribution. As they plan future jobs, they can insert the time commitment for the work into their pie to assess the fit. As this assessment is made, it is important to include aspects such as time spent commuting, required overtime, and any work brought home. Many men and women choose jobs with less commitment during the time their children are small. Part of the dual-career negotiation process may be whether both members of the couple or either will make what may be seen as a sacrifice during these years. Both members of the couple will need to deal with reduced income if one works fewer hours or not at all. Single parents obviously have an even harder time balancing work and family needs. Many people later in their lives and careers find themselves trying to take care of aging or ill parents or other relatives. Career counselors must keep these and similar issues in mind when helping clients choose occupations to pursue. Takesha has none of these issues at present, but she hopes someday to marry and have children. Her desire to be a teacher is partly predicated on the understanding that she will have a work schedule similar to that of her children.

Hansen (1997) suggests that individuals express their values of pluralism and inclusivity in decision making about their life career. Following on the understanding that our world is more interconnected than ever before, she states that this globalism dictates "a new philosophy of career planning in which the focus is not so much on individual occupational choice for personal satisfaction and livelihood as on multiple choices over a lifetime not only for individual wholeness but for life with meaning, that is for work that benefits self and community" (p. 3). This same idea has been expressed as the development of nations, which parallels individual development, from dependence (childhood), to counterdependence (adolescence, sometimes called rebellion), to independence (young adulthood), to interdependence (maturity). This paradigm shift is reflected in the conflict often experienced by first-generation Americans, whose parents may hold to cultural beliefs of putting the family or the community first while the new generation is encouraged to be autonomous and individualistic in their decision making. Hansen, provocatively, is suggesting that we need to move to embrace the former cultural stance. For Takesha, this approach fits with her own belief system. Part of her reason for wanting to teach is to be part of her community, to make a difference for children who perhaps did not have her advantages of educated parents and private school.

Takesha's current transition is one of finishing school and seeking her first full-time career position. Although graduation is called commencement, underlining its place in the beginning of a new life stage, it is also an ending. For students like Takesha, who loved school, it is an ending faced with some sadness. Takesha's counselor needs to help her manage her feelings about her transition as well as the decisions about her future. (For more on managing transitions, see the section on Schlossberg's (Schlossberg et al., 1995) transition theory earlier in this chapter. Although Takesha is not yet in an organization, it would not be amiss for her counselor to help her be aware of the changes she will face, to arm her for the predictable upheaval in any organization in which she finds herself.

Finally, it is important that Takesha be given the opportunity to explore her own spirituality and life purpose. As we discussed earlier in the section on spirituality, the existential quest for meaning is an important one for many. We might guess, given Takesha's altruistic goals, that she would value finding meaning in work.

Constructivist Theories

The hallmark of constructionist approaches is their nonlinear nature. As eloquently described by Peavy (1998), a constructiveness counseling session is "a workshop where the counselor and the client jointly build understandings of the client's relations with significant aspects of his or her immediate milieu, [and] make plans and projects which the client can use to navigate and participate in social life successfully and with meaning" (p. 47). Peavy proposed that the counseling process is jointly constructed with the client and that the focus is on clients' understanding of themselves and their life space. He used the term *bricolage* to emphasize the construction process, that is, one that is made brick by brick, with the bricks being the clients' life experience and the counselor as the mason. Constructivism assumes a paradigm shift from looking at behavior to looking at action and meaning; from determining causation to assessing reciprocal influence; from believing in one reality to holding that there are multiple realities; and from seeing the self as determined to seeing it as a work in progress, that must be constructed (p. 45). Constructivist counselors use narrative approaches to enter the life space of their clients, develop mutual trust and respect, and explore possible career paths. The theory assumes that counselors are culturally competent, that is, that they have knowledge of, and respect for, cultural differences; they understand the sociopolitical context in which their clients live; and they allow for nonlinear emergent conversations.

Valach and Young (2004) proposed a contextual action theory of career counseling, based on "the notion that career is constructed through the intentional goal-directed actions of persons and that counseling is a process that involves both action and career" (p. 61). They maintained that we must diverge from seeing career decision making as solely an individualistic activity and see it rather as part of the social contract, the relationship among the counselor, the client, and the context in which they live and act. This redefinition of the career-counseling process includes paying attention to the emotional content of clients' lives, and their life situation as well as to the more traditional components of career counseling.

Schulthiess (2003) puts forth a passionate proposal for a relational approach to career counseling. She suggests that traditional career counseling can be enhanced by using a relational approach to assessment and intervention. Building on feminist and other early work suggesting that connectedness should be held as an equal value to autonomy, she argues that "the goal of integrating relational theory with career theory is to provide a more holistic integrative conceptual framework, or meta-perspective, that recognizes the value of relational connection and, quite simply, the realities of people's lives" (p. 304).

In the foregoing we have discussed the centrality of individuals' careers to their lives. We have talked about how counselors can help their clients find personal meaning in work and have identified a number of strategies to assist in that process. Barriers and pathways to succeeding in this quest were described, as were methods of integrating the ideas behind self-efficacy and learned optimism theories into the career-counseling process.

The concepts of spirituality, hope, and optimism and a variety of decision making processes were also presented. These included planned happenstance, positive uncertainty, and the postmodern approaches of narrative, integrative life planning, and constructivism. School-based career counseling and adult transitions were also briefly described. Through following four cases, we have attempted to demonstrate the application of several of these concepts and theories.

USEFUL WEBSITES

The following Websites provide additional information relating to the chapter topics:

http://www.unconventionalideas.com/values.html

http://www.spiritualityatwork.com

http://www.workplacespirituality.info

http://www.spirituality.com

http://www.yoursoulatwork.com

http://www.ericacve.org/docgen.asp?tbl+tia&D=116–17k

http://directory.google.com/Top/Society/Work/Workplace_Spirituality/

http://www.kl.oakland.edu/services/instruction/pathfinders/careers2.htm

http://www.bls.gov/oco/

http://www.careerkey.org/english/

http://www.ericacve.org/docgen.asp?tbl+tia&D=116–17k

REFERENCES

Adler, A. (1964). *Superiority and social interest.* Evanston, IL: Northwestern University Press.

American Counseling Association. (2003). Advocacy competencies. Retrieved October 18, 2003, from http://www.counseling.org/site/DocServer/advocacy_competencies1.pdf?

Anderson, M. L. (2003). *Spirituality and coping with work transitions.* Unpublished Dissertation, Oakland University.

Bandura, A. (1977). Self-efficacy: Toward a unifying theory of behavioral change. *Psychological Review, 84,* 191–215.

Bloch, D. P. (1997). Spirituality, intentionality and career success: The quest for meaning. In D. P. Bloch & L. J. Richmond (Eds.), *Connections between spirit and work in career development* (pp. 185–208). Palo Alto, CA: Davies Black.

Bloch, D. P. (2004). Spirituality, complexity, and career counseling. *Professional School Counseling, 7,* 343–350.

Bloch, D. P. & Richmond, L. J. (Eds.). (1997). *Connections between spirit and work in career development.* Palo Alto, CA: Davies Black.

Brewer, E. W. (2001). Vocational souljourn paradigm: A model of adult development to express spiritual wellness as meaning, being, and doing in work and life. *Counseling and Values, 45*(2), 83–92.

Brown, M. (1992, November). *Self-efficacy.* Paper presented to the Michigan Association of Counseling and Development.

Casto, M. L. (2003, October 16). What is a career anyway? *Career convergence.* Retrieved from http://ncda.org/

Cohen, B. N. (2003). Applying existential theory and interventions to career decision-making. *Journal of Career Development, 29,* 195–209.

Ellison, E. H. (1994). *Spiritual well-being scale.* Nyack, NY: Life Advance.

Evans, K. M., Rotter, J. C., & Gold, J. M. (Eds.). (2002). *Synthesizing family, career, and culture: A model for counseling in the twenty-first century.* Alexandria, VA: American Counseling Association.

Frankl, V. E. (1963). *Man's search for meaning: An introduction to logotherapy.* New York: Washington Square Press.

Frost, R. (1930). *The poems of Robert Frost.* New York: Random House.

Gelatt, H. B. (1991). *Creative decision making: Using positive uncertainty.* Los Altos, CA: Crisp.

Gendlin, E. T. (1973). Experiential psychotherapy. In R. Corsini (Ed.), *Current psychotherapies* (pp. 317–352). Itasca, IL: Peacock.

Gendlin, E. T. (1981). *Focusing.* New York: Bantam.

Goodman, J. (1991). Career development for adults in organizations and in the community. In National Occupational Information Coordinating Committee (Ed.), *The national career development guidelines: Progress and possibilities.* Washington, DC: Author.

Goodman, J. (1992). The key to pain prevention: The dental model for counseling. *American Counselor, 1*(2), 27–29.

Goodman, J., & Waters, E. B. (1985). Conflict or support: Work and family in middle and old age. *Journal of Career Development, 12,* 92–98.

Greider, W. (2003). *The question of power.* Retrieved October 16, 2003, from http://williamgreider.com/article.php?article_id=13

Hansen, L. S. (1997). *Integrative life planning: Critical tasks for career development and changing life patterns.* San Francisco: Jossey-Bass.

Hansen, L. S. (2002). Integrative life planning (ILP): A holistic theory for career counseling with adults. In S. Niles (Ed.), *Adult career development: Concepts, issues, and practices.* Tulsa, OK: National Career Development Association.

Heidegger, M. (1949). *Existence and being.* Chicago: Regency.

Heilbrun, C. G. (1997). *The last gift of time: Life beyond sixty.* New York: Dial.

Herr, E. L., Cramer, S. H., & Niles, S. G. (2004). *Career guidance and counseling through the lifespan: Systematic approaches* (6th ed.). Boston: Pearson.

Holland. J. L. (1959). A theory of vocational choice. *The Journal of Counseling Psychology, 6,* 35–45.

Ingham Intermediate School District. (1998). *Career preparation: Careers by choice, not by chance.* Mason, MI: author.

Jankowski, P. J. (2002). Postmodern spirituality: Implications for promoting change. *Counseling and Values, 47,* 69–80.

Jepsen, D. A. (1992). Understanding careers as stories. In M. Savickas (Chair), *Career as story.* Baltimore: American Association for Counseling and Development.

Johnson, S. (1998). *Who moved my cheese?* New York: G. P. Putnam's Sons.

Jung, C. G. (1959). *Basic writings.* New York: Random House.

Kierkegaard, S. (1950). *The point of view.* London: Oxford University Press.

Langer, E. J. (1997). *The power of mindful learning.* Reading, MA: Addison-Wesley.

Levinson, D. J. (1978). *The seasons of a man's life.* New York: Ballantine.

Looby, E. J., & Sandhu, D. S. (2002). Spirituality in the workplace: An overview. In D. S. Sandhu (Ed.), *Counseling employees: A multifaceted approach.* Alexandria, VA: American Counseling Association.

Lotus, A. (1983). Foreword. In C. I. Young, *Inscape: A search for meaning* (n.p.). Rochester, MI: Oakland University, Continuum Center.

Malach-Pines, A., & Yafe-Yanai, O. (2001). Unconscious determinants of career choice and burnout: Theoretical model and counseling strategy. *Journal of Employment Counseling, 38,* 170–184.

Maslow, A. H. (1954). *Motivation and personality.* New York: Harper & Row.

May, R. (1969). *Love and will.* New York: W. W. Norton.

McClelland, D. C., Atkinson, J. W., Clark, R. A., & Lowell, E. L. (1953). *The achievement motive.* Englewood Cliffs, NJ: Prentice-Hall.

McSherry, W., & Cash, K. (2004). The language of spirituality: An emerging taxonomy. *International Journal of Nursing Studies, 41,* 151–161.

Miller, L. (2004, August 8). Works for me. *The New York Times Book Review,* p. 23.

Milton, J. (1940). *Paradise lost.* New York: Heritage Press. (Original work published in 1667)

Mitchell, K. E., Levin, A. L., & Krumboltz, J. D. (1999). Planned happenstance: Constructing unexpected career opportunities. *Journal of Counseling and Development, 2,* 115–124.

Peavy, V. (1998). A new look at interpersonal relations in counseling. *Educational and Vocational Guidance Bulletin, 62,* 45–50.

Peterson, L. (1995). *Starting out, starting over.* Palo Alto, CA: Davies-Black.

Powers, S. J., & Rothausen, T. J. (2003). The work-oriented midcareer development model. *The Counseling Psychologist, 31,* 157–197.

Safire, W., & Safir, L. (1982). *Good advice.* New York: Wings Books.

Satir, V. (1964). *Conjoint family therapy.* Palo Alto, CA: Science and Behavior Books.

Savickas, M. L. (1997). The spirit in career counseling: Fostering self completion through work. In D. P. Bloch & L. J. Richmond (Eds.), *Connections between spirit and work in career development* (pp.185–208). Palo Alto, CA: Davies Black.

Savickas, M. L. (2001). In F. T. L. Leong & A. Barak (Eds.), *Contemporary models in vocational psychology: A volume in honor of Samuel Osipow.* (pp. 295–320). Mahwah, NJ: Erlbaum.

Savickas, M. L. (2003 September 4). *The career theme interview.* Paper presented to the International Association of Educational and Vocational Guidance, Berne, Switzerland.

Schlossberg, N. K., & Robinson, S. P. (1996). *Going to plan B.* New York: Simon & Schuster.

Schlossberg, N. K., Waters, E. B., & Goodman, J. (1995). *Counseling adults in transition.* New York: Springer.

Schultheiss, D. E. P. (2003). A relational approach to career counseling: Theoretical integration and practical application. *Journal of Counseling and Development, 81,* 301–310.

Sedaris, D. (2000). *Me talk pretty one day.* Boston: Little Brown.

Seligman, M. E. P. (1998). *Learned optimism* (2nd ed.). New York: Pocket Books.

Super, D. E. (1980). A life-span, life space approach to career development. *Journal of Vocational Behavior, 16,* 282–298.

Tillich, P. (1952). *The courage to be.* New Haven, CT: Yale University Press.

Tisdell, E. J. (1999). The spiritual dimension of adult development. In C. Clark & R. Caffarella (Eds.), *An update on adult development theory: New directions for adult and continuing education,* (pp. 84, 87–95). San Francisco: Jossey-Bass.

Toossi, M. (2002). A century of change: The U.S. labor force, 1950–2050. *Monthly Labor Review, 125,* 5, 15–28.

U. S. Bureau of Labor Statistics (2002). *News: United States Department of Labor* (U.S.D.L. Publication No. 02–497). Washington, DC: U.S. Government Printing Office.

Valach, L., & Young, R. A. (2004). Some cornerstones in the development of a contextual action theory of career development. *International Journal for Educational and Vocational Guidance, 4,* 61–81.

Wilber, K. (2000). *Integral psychology: Consciousness, spirit, psychology, therapy.* Boston: Shambhala.

Wuthnow, R. (1998). *After heaven: Spirituality in America since the 1950s.* Berkeley: University of California Press.

Young, C. I. (1983). *Inscape: A search for meaning.* Rochester, MI: Oakland University, Continuum Center.

CHAPTER 4

ETHICAL AND LEGAL ISSUES, PRINCIPLES, AND STANDARDS IN CAREER COUNSELING

DENNIS W. ENGELS
University of North Texas

HENRY L. HARRIS
University of North Carolina at Charlotte

Legal and ethical issues, principles, codes, and statutes govern and enhance the work of career counselors and others working in career development. This chapter addresses selected legal issues and ethical issues, standards, and principles for the purpose of reviewing and discerning implications for ethical career-counseling practice, career counselor preparation, and research. While ethics is typically discussed in terms of organizational codes and standards for professions, this chapter also looks at individual ethics and individual and collective aspects of a work ethic as means to address current and anticipated issues confronting career development professionals and their clients. Additionally, this chapter reviews selected ethical standards, principles, issues, and legal concerns related to career development and career counseling as means to discerning and discussing implications for work and life today, with special emphasis on how these considerations and implications affect the work of career counselors, career development workers, and their clients.

SOME GUIDING ETHICAL PRINCIPLES

While ethics discussions commonly generate questions, the authors start this chapter on career counseling by noting something of an ethical "answer" in the form of guiding principles, instead. As noted in the Preamble of the Ethical Standards of the American Counseling Association (ACA, 1995) and the National Career Development Association

(NCDA, 2001), counselors and career counselors are dedicated to promoting the worth, dignity, uniqueness, and potential of every person with whom they counsel. These noble and inspiring human principles and characteristics have been a longstanding positive traditional base for, and a consensus goal of, members of ACA; NCDA, all ACA Divisions, branches, and entities; and the National Board for Certified Counselors (1991). Worth and dignity are major points, as well, in Principle D of the 1992 American Psychological Association's *Ethical Principles of Psychologists and Code of Conduct* (1992).

Counselors can take great pride in, and empowerment from, this altruistic dedication to human worth, dignity, uniqueness, and potential. In all their courses, the authors remind their counseling students to always "keep their eyes on the prize" of promoting human worth, dignity, uniqueness, and potential, noting that such a focus affords something of an ethical barometer for what a counselor is doing and considering. If one can say that what one is doing is designed to promote and achieve these noble and empowering human principles and characteristics for one's clients, one can have some sense that what one is doing is ethical in spirit, motivation, intention, and focus. Hopefully, readers find a sense of inspiration in these principles and a sense of adherence to this focus throughout this chapter.

DEFINITIONS

Ethics

Ethics can be variously defined as "the study of standards of conduct and moral judgment; moral philosophy, . . . the system or code of morals of a particular person, religion, group, profession, etc." (*Webster's New World College Dictionary*, 1999, p. 488), or "a set of moral principles, . . . rules of conduct governing a particular group, . . . moral principles, as of an individual: *His (her) ethics forbade cheating* (Random House, 2000, p. 453). Philosophers also remind us that ethics is an area of philosophy that examines virtue, character, and the good life (Mann & Kreyche, 1966), while attending to a counselor's motives, activities, and goals. As noted, professional ethics are frequently discussed in terms of collective and consensus value sets and standards of conduct. This chapter also includes attention to the individual aspects cited in these definitions because, ultimately, individual counselors must make ethical decisions.

Beauchamp and Childress (1994), Welfel (2002), Urofsky and Engels (2003), and many others discuss the importance of counselors enhancing their ethical capacity by understanding ethical foundations, including philosophical origins in moral philosophy and related ethical theory. Freeman (2000) and Freeman, Engels, and Altekruse (2004) also articulate and advocate counselor commitment to wisdom, insight, good judgment, and morality in applying professional skill and knowledge. In addition to the fundamental importance of an individual professional's responsibility for ethical behavior, it should also be noted that standards, including ethical standards, are predicated on minima—on the least one must do (Council for Accreditation of Counseling and Related Educational Programs, 2001, p. 104), and counselors can and should stay mindful of ethical principles as means to go beyond minimal ethical requirements (Engels, 1981).

In summary, professional ethics for career counselors encompasses individual practitioner knowledge of, skill in, and commitment and adherence to professional organizational standards as a basis for wise moral decisions in professional practice. In attending to the vital importance of wisdom and the importance of philosophical bases for ethics and ethical behavior for individual professionals, Freeman and colleagues (2004) also point out that wisdom and principles could be lost by having too narrow a focus on situational details and specific counselor knowledge and skills. Hence, counselors need to focus on ethical principles, the most fundamental of which are nonmalificence and beneficence, "do no harm," and "do good."

Ethic

Ethic, a key word and concept for all professionals, can be defined as "the body of moral principles or values held by or governing a culture, group or individual," *a personal ethic* (Random House, 2000, p. 453), or " 1. a system of moral standards or values, *the humanist ethic,* 2. a particular moral standard or value, *the success ethic* (*Webster's New World College Dictionary,* 1999, p. 488). For a variety of reasons noted later in this chapter, this construct of an ethic, most notably an individual client's work ethic, has considerable value for helping career counselors and their clients address contemporary and future ethical and legal issues.

ETHICAL STANDARDS IN CAREER COUNSELING

In counseling and counseling specialties, a code of ethics is the foundation for a successful profession and for competent and successful professionals. Ethical standards are also one of the most crucial components of counseling practice, client trust, and client success. Following Parsons's pioneering social reform work in individual employment and rudimentary career planning, circa 1909, career development professionals have attended carefully to the best ways to serve clients well and ethically. Moreover, leaders in NCDA and the specialty area of career counseling continuously work to articulate, promulgate, and advocate for ethical standards in career development and career counseling.

Ethical standards can be seen as the central anchor in any profession and any professional specialty. In this regard, career counselors actually find more than one anchor or ethical base, in that NCDA has adopted the Code of Ethics of the National Board for Certified Counselors (NBCC; NCDA, 2001), while maintaining its membership in ACA and adherence to the ACA ethical standards. The standards were last revised by NCDA in 1991, and are reviewed annually (2001). Because counseling literature is not replete with articles on ethical issues in career development (Niles, 1997; Pate & Niles, 2002) and because the NCDA standards afford practitioners both breadth and depth of topical coverage, this chapter looks at highlights of the NCDA ethical standards to attend to, and review, some key ethical issues.

Selected aspects of NCDA's ethical standards (NCDA, 2001) are offered here to highlight the depth and breadth of the standards, while affording some practitioners a refresher. Section A of the NCDA Ethical Standards, titled "General," outlines responsibilities and expected behaviors of professionals (NCDA, 2001). This section says professionals must perform at the highest level of their ability, practice ethical behavior at all times, be accountable for professional behavior at all times, and refrain from falsifying or exaggerating professional qualifications or abilities. Additionally, career professionals must only pursue positions for which they are qualified and must recognize and address personal limits of skill and knowledge. Career counselors also must help clients who cannot afford the counselor's fee to find services at a more acceptable cost for the client. Career professionals must not bring their own issues into the counseling relationship and are directed to avoid meeting personal needs at the expense of their clients. Finally, career counselors must remain conscious of their potential impact on clients' lives. To highlight one aspect of the spirit of this section, the authors have heard of career counselors who concentrate their accountability and responsibility on another person or entity, such as an employer paying for the counseling service, rather than on the client of the service. This general section and the overall standards make it clear that career counselors are ethically obligated to serve their clients. Career counselors working in a human relations department are clearly responsible and accountable to the employees and dependents with whom they counsel, as well as to the employer.

Section B, "Counseling Relationship," details expected behaviors within the counselor-client dyad or group (NCDA, 2001), including the career professional's primary commitment and responsibility to respect client integrity and welfare. Confidentiality of all information obtained in the relationship must be a top priority, however, in the case of a client in imminent danger to him- or herself or others, the counselor has the responsibility of notifying appropriate authorities. When case notes are used for teaching, information should be general enough to ensure the client's identity is protected. Informed consent means counselors must inform the client of the goals, purpose, techniques, treatment methods, rules, procedures, and limitations of counseling (NCDA, 2001). Relationships with the client, other than the counseling relationship, must be avoided to prevent compromise, loss of professional objectivity, or client exploitation. A counselor must notify the client that the counselor may consult confidentially with other mental health professionals about the client, if appropriate. Counselors must develop cultural awareness of populations served and use culturally relevant techniques in their practice. Referrals should be made, as appropriate. Group-counseling participants should be screened to maintain group welfare.

When using computer applications in career counseling, the counselor must confirm that the information is appropriate and nondiscriminatory. The counselor must obtain knowledge, including hands-on use, search experience, and assurance that the information is current, accurate, and relevant within the computer-based system. Additionally, the counselor must determine if the client is capable (emotionally, intellectually, and physically) of using the application. Staying with the example of a counselor whose services are funded by an employer or source other than the client, the counselor's primary duty in relation to Section B (and all sections) is to the client, and the counselor must always attend to informed client consent for counseling, including apprizing the client of any and all reporting requirements and other factors that might jeopardize or compromise confidentiality.

Section C, "Measurement and Evaluation," emphasizes a very common area of career counseling practice and an area wherein career counselors have considerable expertise, for example, regarding core aspects of instrument validity and reliability. One example of areas where career counselors can help the public and policy makers might be in terms of the technical and human complexities one sees in assessment. Schultz and Schultz (2002, p. 121), in reminding psychologists to protect client worth, dignity, and welfare, note the importance of counselor competence and adherence to formal assessment protocols and compliance with a producer's guidelines for using career assessment instruments. In this regard, counselors only provide raw scores to professionals who are qualified to properly interpret results and to ensure an understandable interpretation of results to the client. Schultz and Schultz (2002) provide an excellent example of problems that can arise in career assessment as they address the need for respect of, and privacy regarding, intimate personal issues. They cite the *Soroka v. Dayton-Hudson* case, in which the California Court of Appeals held that, unless an employer could prove the direct relationship of an applicant's sexual habits and religious faith to the job sought, questions on an employment-screening instrument regarding sex and religion violated an applicant's privacy rights (Schultz & Schultz, 2002, pp. 121–122). Certainly, awareness of such ethical, legal, and moral complexities can help counselors see the need for formal preparation and continuing education in ethics. Better articulation of these issues could afford strong platforms for career counselors advocating credentialing and other public policy requirements aimed at protecting clients. Another example related to assessment might focus on the appearance of software-based assessment reports that appear to be highly personalized, when they are really prepackaged and software driven. Counselors certainly need to understand this categorical reality of software printouts and need to be vigilant regarding client deference to their seemingly highly personalized objectivity, lest clients or counselors put too much faith in these categorical assessments.

Additionally, counselors need to understand and clarify for clients that we use relatively few tests in counseling. While there are technical and semantic reasons for noting that most of the instruments counselors use are not tests, the important technical and ethical reason for clarifying this point for clients focuses on the test-like appearance of most of these instruments and the high likelihood that clients will regard assessment results as some objective and valid set of test results. For example, an interest inventory printout, while appearing highly personalized and highly objective, could be inferred by clients as a set of objective competency test results rather than a set of categorical statements related to interests. Additionally, clients might easily fail to appreciate that these instruments point out apparent commonality of client interest with interests of the norming occupational groups, rather than explicit client interest in any specific occupation. Additionally, counselors would do well to seek out an appropriate battery of assessment instruments, rather than relying on—and giving clients a sense of relying on—only one or two instruments.

Finally, counselors need to actively work with clients in interpreting client assessment data. The senior author recalls an instance early in his studies for the priesthood, when a priest-psychologist assigned an assessment battery to the seminarians and then simply returned the assessment results to the group, stating that they should be self-explanatory. When this author saw a very low interest inventory score in "clerical," his first impression related to the work of the cleric or clergy and gave him a sense that God had sent a computerized message that he was not a good candidate for the clergy. While this author quickly came to realize that "clerical" could relate to the work of a clerk, rather than a cleric, the example serves to highlight many of the points attended to in this section of the ethical standards.

Section D, "Research and Publication," outlines guidelines for research within the field of career counseling, including human subjects guidelines, informed consent, and the principal investigator's ethical competence and acknowledgment of responsibility. Results are reported in a manner that decreases the possibility that they are misleading, and original data are made available to others who want to replicate the study, while ensuring that the identity of subjects is protected. Investigators must demonstrate familiarity with, and citation of, previous research conducted in the area and must disseminate results that hold promise for improving the field.

One major concern related to research and publication can center on giving credit to all contributors to published works, in proportion with author or creator contribution. One hears of too many instances of confusion or worse in terms of crediting all contributors to published works or other scholarly products. One important means of attending to this issue of giving appropriate credit to contributors is to approach this matter in a manner similar to the informed consent with which counselors enter into counseling relationships with clients. The key ethical point is that the list of authors should reflect the sequence and level of contribution to the work.

Section E, "Consulting," outlines responsibilities of professionals serving as consultants. In adhering to NCDA's ethical standards, they must be self-aware, have the necessary competencies and resources, understand and agree on the goals of the selected interventions, and encourage clients to adapt and grow. Counselors serving as consultants need to be honest and straightforward in communicating counselor competencies and in entering into consulting agreements, again, with good attention to informed consent.

The final section of the NCDA Ethical Standards, "Private Practice," notes the importance of making services accessible in both private and public settings and of producing accurate advertisements and specific specialty credentialing of each member of a joint practice, along with the admonition to terminate if the counseling relationship ceases to be productive or violates the NCDA Ethical Standards (NCDA, 2001). Career coaching appears to be one area where much more attention to ethics is needed, and professional associations, perhaps most notably NCDA, need to continue attending to important ethical issues related to career coaching, such as most of the concerns noted in this section, for example, honesty regarding one's credentials and professional competence. Professional identity and credentials are also most important matters for career counselors and the career-counseling profession, as designations and credentials proliferate nationally and internationally. Career development facilitators (CDFs), for example, are expected to work under the immediate supervision of a career counselor, however, one can readily see the temptation for CDFs and their employers to disregard or overlook this fundamental aspect of the CDF-credentialing process, possibly at the expense of a client's health and career development or the reputation of the career-counseling profession. Suffice it to say, credentialing is a matter of utmost ethical concern and an important aspect of professional ethics for career counselors.

As one can see, many of these standards are general enough to be relative to any field of counseling, however, it is important to note how these standards are the foundation of this specialty and are vital to a successful career practice, with guidelines for providing the highest quality of services to clients, and, in turn, to society as a whole. Again, career counselors have a primary responsibility to their clients in addition to any other parties who might be involved in paying for the career counseling.

While the NCDA ethical standards are relatively clear and regularly reviewed by NCDA's ethics committee, ethical standards are likely to have some purposeful and principled ambiguity. It would be impossible and imprudent to try to cover every possible ethical issue, and trying to make the standards extremely prescriptive would likely risk missing general principles, while also risking a minimalization of the wondrous complexities of human development and behavior. Moreover, career counselors who hold professional credentials and membership in multiple professional organizations incur multiple ethical and legal obligations, which can add substantial complexity, contradictions, and dilemmas to ethical decision making and practice, especially when these different ethical codes conflict. Adding legal requirements adds yet more complexity, as do additional factors, such as stipulations by a counselor's employer, leading to important implications of ethically and legally serving one's employer. Central among these issues is the need for counselors to always stay committed to a counselor's primary responsibility to the client.

SOME PERSPECTIVES ON ETHICAL AND LEGAL ISSUES AND PRACTICE

While some ethical and legal decisions seem clear, straightforward, and intuitively clear in terms of appropriate professional counselor action requirements, ultimately, all ethical decisions require individual counselor judgment, and many decisions, situations, and actions lack clarity and call for more than simply looking at the literal standards or the law to arrive at wise professional judgment. To illustrate some of the complexity for counselors considering ethical and legal issues in career counseling and career development, Engels, Wilborn, and Schneider (1990) used a 2×2 table (shown here), to juxtapose the terms *ethical* and *legal*.

1. Ethical and Legal	2. Legal, not Ethical
3. Ethical, not Legal	4. Not Legal, not Ethical

As one can see in the compartmentalized illustration, counseling intentions and behaviors in quadrant 1 that are clearly both legal and ethical (e.g., providing professional counseling services consistent with one's expertise, experience, and credentials) tend to seem somewhat straightforward. Decisions and behaviors based in this quadrant of the diagram might not constitute the same level of problem or quandary for practitioners as the more nebulous choices and actions represented in quadrants 2 and 3.

Complexities

Nebulous ethical and legal issues in career development abound (as shown in quadrants 2 and 3), reflecting the complexity of human circumstances, issues and actions, while also appreciating even many gray areas of quadrants 1 and 4. Among many examples one could use to highlight the complexity of discerning issues and acting ethically, one could note a number of concerns.

As an example in the ethical/not legal quadrant, informing a potential victim that a client intends that person physical harm would comply with the majority decision in the *Tarasoff v. Regents of the University of California* (1974/1976), while violating a long-standing Texas statute based on the primacy of confidentiality and a client's right to privacy (Mappes, Robb, & Engels, 1985), a stance that was recently reaffirmed (*Thapar v. Zezulka*, 1999). A minority opinion in the *Tarassof* case agreed with the majority opinion of the Texas Supreme Court ruling in *Thapar v. Zezulka* (1999), stating that a mental health professional can be liable for violating a client's right to an assumption of privacy if the counselor warns a potential victim of the client's threats. In the face of two so completely different majority legal conclusions regarding a counselor's ethical duty to warn, counselors need to consider such a matter very carefully. In addressing such quandaries, knowledge of ethical or moral theory could help counselors find personal ethical peace and a basis for action (a matter attended to later in this chapter).

As an example in the legal/not ethical quadrant, engaging in consensual sexual relations with a current adult client could be legal but would not be ethical. Moreover, ethical standards may vary widely concerning when, if ever, one might engage in sexual relations with a former client. A prudent rule of thumb is to stay vigilant about the focus of counseling and one's professional obligation of valuing and enhancing client worth, dignity, uniqueness, and potential, as first steps to helping counselors stay focused and avoid such possible human temptations in this intensely personal work of career counseling, at times when clients are especially vulnerable. Clarity of focus and goals for career counseling, starting with informed consent, can help counselors and clients stay focused on productive counseling relationships.

In the not legal/not ethical quadrant, physically harming a client, sexually exploiting a juvenile client, falsely advertising one's credentials or expertise, or charging for services not performed are all examples of practices that are simultaneously unethical and illegal. Similar to quadrant 1, quadrant 4 may be illustrative of issues less complex than issues represented in quadrants 2 and 3. However, it is clear that one can see considerable gray and complexity across the entire chart and, by extension, across much of the work of career development professionals. Again, these examples only serve to highlight the myriad concerns, issues, and difficulties of professional ethical decision making and behavior involved in all counseling, including career counseling.

Further complicating the matter for career development practice is the existence of many career development practitioner competency bases, credentials, and designations, including paraprofessionals and some practitioners with no counseling credentials or formal preparation, who offer services similar to services offered by professional career counselors. These authors join Pate and Niles (2002) in delimiting the scope of this discussion to professional career counselors, career development professionals, and paraprofessionals, such as CDFs, who are working under the supervision of a professional career counselor. As noted in the earlier discussion of career coaching and CDFs, these are ongoing areas of major concern, with profound ethical issues, requiring career counselor vigilance and advocacy for ethical practice.

Pate and Niles (2002) discuss yet another important gray area in noting that many career counselors and career development professionals provide some professional services that may or may not be considered counseling, such as time management, educational advising, career placement, resume editing, and other services aimed at improving client employability skills. Pate and Niles (2002) wonder whether a career counselor at a university counseling center who edits a student's resume incurs the same level of ethical accountability as would be incurred in career or mental health counseling. Determining whether and which ethical standards pertain to these activities is a matter that merits considerable attention by practitioners and researchers.

Addressing Ethics and Ethical and Legal Career Issues

Seen in light of this array of complex issues, concerns, and activities, there is a strong need for career counselors to be aware of legal and ethical issues and to be familiar with laws and personal and organizational ethical standards and guidelines as bases for ethical decision making and legal and ethical behavior. By extension, counselor educators need cognizance of this complexity and knowledge and skill in helping aspiring career counselors explore, acquire, commit to, and comply with professional ethics. Professional organizations, such as NCDA, also need to continue working to educate policy makers, the public, NCDA members, and others on legal and ethical matters related to all facets of career counseling and career development.

While these implications may seem self-evident, and while counseling literature has an abundance of resources attending to ethics, in writing this chapter, these authors found relatively few recent articles, chapters, or other sources dedicated to ethical and legal issues in, and implications for, career counseling. In the *Career Development Quarterly's* annual review of 1996 research and practice in career counseling and career development (Niles, 1997), professional ethics was one of the few areas noted as needing attention from career professionals, and subsequent annual reviews have discovered little attention to ethics. Whiston and Brecheisen's (2002) review of 2001 career research, counseling, and development literature noted some attention to ethical issues regarding facets of assessment and electronic/technology-based career counseling and career development work, but made no mention of other attention to ethical aspects of career development.

Hansen (2003), Savickas (2003), and Whiston (2003) also alerted readers to works advocating the larger and higher moral plain in addressing sociopolitical issues, such as exposing and removing barriers to individual human and career growth for the economically disadvantaged and widening the scope of populations served by career counseling and career development professionals. These calls for greater attention to the less fortunate parallel yet another level of implications for professionals, such as pro bono service. Obviously, these large-scale issues will also require individual and organizational advocacy via public policy. Career professionals, NCDA, and other professional associations have much to offer in helping formulate and refine public policy related to all aspects and segments of the workforce. Arguably, the best mode of articulation of, and advocacy for, individual practitioners to impact policy is membership and participation in public policy initiatives of their professional associations.

Problems and issues of human disempowerment, such as sexual harassment, unethical supervisory behavior, unfair hiring, unfair promotion practices, workplace violence, exploitation, illegal treatment of nonresident workers, multicultural and diversity issues, and misuse of assessment, are among many social, personal, and personnel areas that could benefit from ethical career counselor attention in the form of counselor advocacy for workers at all levels and in the form of career counselor private and public policy initiatives. As noted, with the exception of ethical issues related to assessment and electronic or Web-based counseling, the authors found relatively few recent works on career-specific ethical issues, such as those listed here. Hence, it seems appropriate to recommend that career-counseling professionals, researchers, and professional organizations devote conscious attention to ethical and legal issues as a means to clearly articulate public policy needs and priorities.

Legal Issues

Typically, one incurs legal liability or accountability under the law as one increases one's expertise and competence. In our increasingly litigious society, all counselors are well advised to carry liability insurance and to become familiar with laws specific to the counselor's primary duties, such as, for example, career counselors serving as expert witnesses regarding worker disability or divorce and spousal support mediation, while always remembering the counselor's primary ethical obligation to the client. While some career counselors also have ethical and legal obligations to employers and third-party payers, responsibilities and obligations to the client must not be diminished or subordinated. These and other legal matters can constitute strong negative reinforcers in prompting counselors to avoid lawsuits or have a solid defense in the event of a lawsuit, and these issues could also serve as positive reinforcers to increase counselors' desire to behave ethically. Suffice it to say, one must be aware of, or have access to, someone knowledgeable of all pertinent legislation related to the area in the country or world in which one functions and relevant to the services one offers. Legal care and similar legal advice and access resources, available via some professional organizations, can be an excellent member service for professional organizations. Moreover, one's ability to note how one's behavior complies with official ethical standards and principles or legal guidance could afford a major basis for a plausible defense in a lawsuit.

ATTENTION TO CLIENT ETHICS: REVISITING THE WORK ETHIC IN THE UNITED STATES

In the horrific events of September 11, 2001, in New York City; Washington, D.C.; and rural Pennsylvania and in the aftermath felt around the world, citizens of the United States were simultaneously shocked into a new individual and societal state of heightened attention to physical security and personal safety and reassured in basic human decency in seeing the heroic efforts of people from all social and economic strata and all walks of life who rose to help victims and survivors. The bravery, unselfishness, kindnesses, and diligence of rescue workers and others certainly constitute an incredible modeling of human character and nobility, and of human ethics in action.

While the nation continues grieving and working to recover from this hideous assault, continuing revelations of an extensively harmful, yet far more subtle, oppression of another kind served to undermine many working Americans' trust of corporate leadership and sound an alarm for the breakdown of the social contract between employers and employees. In the massive and devastating corporate accounting scandals involving Enron, Tyco, Worldcom, Arthur Anderson, and many other major corporate and business entities came a clarion call for public scrutiny and for employee vigilance and self-care. The extent of this contractual breakdown is poignantly reflected in the words of Andrew Fastow, one of the self-confessed engineers of the Enron debacle.

"I and other members of Enron's senior management fraudulently manipulated Enron's publicly reported financial results." Furthermore, "Our purpose was to mislead investors and others about the true financial position of Enron and, consequently, to inflate artificially the price of Enron's stock and maintain fraudulently Enron's credit rating." Fastow said he "also enriched myself and others at the expense of Enron's shareholders and in violation of my duty of honest services to those shareholders" (Maxon, 2004, p. 7A). Deputy U.S. Attorney General James Comey's comments also seem especially poignant in describing the effects of this despicable behavior.

> The crime in Enron hurt tens of thousands of people. It took jobs, it took life savings, it broke spirits. We wish we could undo that harm, but we can't. What we can do is what the folks involved in this effort have been doing for the last two years, and that is to work like crazy to find those responsible and punish them in a way that is just and that also serves as a warning to other morally challenged executives. (Maxon, 2004, p. 7A)

As of January 2004, the Enron investigation brought charges against 26 defendants, as well as conviction of Enron's auditor, the Arthur Anderson accounting firm (Maxon, 2004, p. 7A).

Robin Zuckerman, editor-in-chief of *U.S. News & World Report*, was among the many who condemned these hideous betrayals of trust and called for ethical response in corporate boardrooms. In noting that "ethics has moved to the top of the agenda in many major companies" (Zuckerman, 2004, p. 72) and that corporate leaders and ethics officers must work vigorously to reverse the incredible ethical vacuum and moral bankruptcy of leaders of such major corporations, Zuckerman closed with hope for substantial reform.

Fastow's very words and those of a member of the prosecution also provide a powerful and immediate implication for all employees to be at least healthy skeptics regarding employee entitlements and other facets of the traditional social contract that held that employees who worked with due diligence and did good work could expect parallel and reciprocal effort, commitment, and loyalty from employers in providing for employee health and welfare (Hill, 1996; Macoby & Terzi, 1981; Schultz & Schultz, 2002). Fastow's attention to his responsibility to shareholders, with no mention of any responsibility to company employees, adds yet another dimension to the moral vacuum into which the social contract seems drawn today, portending yet another implication for workers. Beyond awareness of the hideous breach of trust and respect and heightened vigilance and skepticism, McCortney and Engels (2003) note that employees will likely need to reexamine and possibly recalibrate their individual and collective work ethic, as a means of self-preservation and good personal and career stewardship (Hansen et al., 2001). For the near term at least, these betrayals by corporate leaders amplify earlier calls by Kanter and Mirvis, (1989), Peterson and Gonzalez (2005), and Rifkin (1995) for employee vigilance and healthy skepticism or apprehension regarding employer-employee participation in the social contract. Additionally, career counselors may need to focus on helping clients attend to the stark realities of this substantial undermining of the basis for employee trust of employers by emphasizing this need for individuals to become able owners and stewards of their own careers. When added to the spector of multinational corporations with a sense of allegiance only to shareholders, these stark recent examples of corporate leaders' betrayal of employees seem to portend the need for substantial attention to employee safety, security, and welfare issues.

HISTORY AND PRECEDENTS FOR LOOKING FORWARD

Just as Frank Parsons, Jesse Davis, and other career practitioners led the way for founding the National Vocational Guidance Association (now NCDA) in 1913 as the first national counseling association, career practitioners have long addressed and anticipated many issues in counseling and counselor ethics. One poignant example of career counseling's early and longstanding attention to and leadership in major counseling advances and issues is manifest in software based interactive guidance systems, such as JoAnn Harris Bowlsbey's pioneering work developing and implementing Computerized Vocational Information System (CVIS) in the early 1970s. This long history of computer-based guidance systems affords a useful context of knowledge and experience to help counselors in other specialties assuage the perceptions of the 1990s and today of urgency regarding "unprecedented" ethical issues emerging in the face of extensive use of World Wide Web–based assessment, counseling, and other Internet services.

As many concerns regarding counseling via the Internet emerged in the 1990s, career counselors familiar with computer-based interactive guidance information systems, such as CVIS, CHOICES, DISCOVER, and SIGI-PLUS, among others, could afford other counselors a sense of context and perspective based on those earlier computer software-based career systems. In effect, there were numerous precedents for, and much experience in, affording clients counselor-originated service via software in an electronic platform, more than 20 years in advance of counselor use of the Internet for counseling, affording career counselors a more incremental perspective for Web-based and other electronic approaches to counseling. Suffice it to say, in our dynamic and sometimes turbulent world, career counseling's vanguard activities make it a most important specialty for clients and for counselors in other specialties, and ethics is a highly important element in this and all facets of career counseling.

Among pertinent historical counseling landmarks noted in any outline of the history of career counseling are the initial ideas of Frank Parsons that, arguably, started contemporary counseling by helping clients understand and find means for some influence and autonomy over their role in the world of work. Theories of career development, choice, and counseling have emerged to support and define this career counseling specialty, as have career-counseling competencies, credentialing, and standards for ethics, for career counselor preparation, and for respect for clients (Engels, 1994; Engels, Minor, Sampson, & Splete, 1995; Smith, Engels, & Bonk, 1985). Ironically, many counselor educators seem not to realize or appreciate the parallel centrality of work in the thinking of such mainstream counseling pioneers as Adler, Freud, and Jung, but each of those pioneers noted and attended to work and career because of the primal importance of work in life.

Moral and Other Philosophical Bases for Ethical Practice

Welfel and Lipsitz (1983), Welfel (2002), and Kitchener (1984a) among others, noted that counselors need to know themselves well and need some knowledge of moral principles to make personal sense of the ethical standards, while also addressing conflicts within, among, and between the codes of ethics or between ethics and law. Bersoff and Koeppl's (1993) attention to the consensus nature of a profession's ethical standards serves as another reminder that ethical standards represent the least one must do. Moreover, they also note the importance for career counselors of seeking insight into personal, societal, and client ethical and moral principles and values. Central among these principles are veracity, or truthfulness (Meara, Schmidt, & Day, 1996); core principles of autonomy, nonmaleficence, beneficence, and justice (Beauchamp & Childress, 1994); and fidelity (Kitchener, 1984b, 1991, 1996), as well as a counselor's personal integrity, good judgment, wisdom, and prudence.

CONCLUSION

Until career counselors can find means to the admittedly difficult learning tasks of acquiring fuller insight and empowerment in these and other moral bases for ethical motivation and practice, we might all benefit by close attention to models of those who delve more deeply into those philosohpical bases and those offering sound approaches to ethical practice (Neukrug, Lovell, & Parker, 1996; Savickas, 1995). Welfel (2002, p. 23f.), for example, affords counselors an insightful and comprehensive model and ten-step approach for ethical decision making, moving from ethical dedication and appreciation for underlying moral bases for counseling and ethical behavior through good scrutiny of current standards, pertinent laws, professional research, and advice to conscious deliberation and a decision, followed by substantial processing regarding the specific focus of this decision and case as well as implications for the future. Some more fundamental guidance also comes from the standards and these models. Emanating from the NCDA and ACA ethical standards is a clear message that career counselors should network. Having a most trusted local colleague or two for confidential consultation on vital ethical issues is fundamental. Through participation in local chapters of state counseling organizations, new career counselors can seek mentors, and veteran career counselors can mentor and also establish networks with peers. ACA's Website, ethics committee and professional staff services also include resources for members seeking ethical advice. NCDA's 2004 start of a national mentoring model, including participation of past presidents, eminent career award winners, NCDA Fellows and other career professionals, holds great promise as another excellent networking resource. Attention to models, resources, and approaches such as these might go far in helping career counselors promote client worth, dignity, uniqueness and potential.

REFERENCES

American Counseling Association. (1995). *ACA code of ethics and standards of practice*. Alexandria, VA: Author.

American Psychological Association. (1992). *Ethical principles of psychologists and code of conduct*. Washington, DC: Author.

Beauchamp, T. L., & Childress, J. F. (1994). *Principles of biomedical ethics* (4th ed.). New York: Oxford University Press.

Bersoff, D. N., & Koeppl, P. M. (1993). The relation between ethical codes and moral principles. *Ethics and Behavior, 3*, 345–357.

Council for the Accreditation of Counseling and Related Educational Programs. (2001). *CACREP manual*. Alexandria, VA: author.

Engels, D. W. (1981). Maximal ethics in counselor education. *Counseling and Values, 26*, 48–54.

Engels, D. W. (Ed.). (1994). *The professional practice of career counseling and consultation: A resource document*. Alexandria, VA: National Career Development Association.

Engels, D. W., Minor, C. W., Sampson, J. P., & Splete, H. H. (1995). Career counseling speciality: History, development, and prospect. *Journal of Counseling and Development, 74*, 134–138.

Engels, D. W., Wilborn, B. L., & Schnieder, L. J. (1990). Ethics curricula for counselor preparation programs. In B. Herlihy & L. Golden (Eds.), *Ethical standards casebook* (pp. 111–126). Alexandria: VA: American Association for Counseling and Development.

Freeman, S. J. (2000). *Ethics: An introduction to philosophy and practice*. Belmont, CA: Wadsworth/ Thomson Learning.

Freeman, S. J., Engels, D. W., & Altekruse, M. K. (2004). Foundations for ethical standards and codes: The role of moral philosophy and theory in ethics. *Counseling and Values, 48*, 163–173.

Hansen, L. S., Dagley, J. C., Engels, D. W., Goodman, J., Hayslip, J. B., Herr, E. H., Herring, R. D., Hhu, X., Jackson, A., Lopez-Baez, S., & Minor, C. W. (2001). *Preparing for career development in the new millennium*. (ACES/NCDA Position Paper). Alexandria, VA: Association for Counselor Education and Supervision.

Hansen, L. S. (2003). Career counselors as advocates and change agents for equality. *Career Development Quarterly, 52*, 43–53.

Hill, R. B. (1996). Historical context of the work ethic. Retrieved September 9, 2002, from http://www.coe.uga.edu/~rhill/workethic/hist/htm

Kanter, D. L., & Mirvis, P. H. (1989). *The cynical Americans: Living and working in an age of discontent and disillusion.* San Francisco: Jossey-Bass.

Kitchener, K. S. (1984a). Ethics and counseling psychology: Distinctions and directions. *The Counseling Psychologist, 12,* 15–18.

Kitchener, K. S. (1984b). Intuition, critical-evaluation and ethical principles: The foundation for ethical decisions in counseling psychology. *The Counseling Psychologist, 12,* 43–55.

Kitchener, K. S. (1991). The foundation of ethical practice. *Journal of Mental Health Counseling, 13,* 236–246.

Kitchener, K. S. (1996). There is more to ethics than principles. *The Counseling Psychologist, 24,* 92–97.

Macoby, M., & Terzi, K. (1981). What happened to the work ethic? In J. O'Toole, J. L. Scheiber, & L.C. Wood (Eds.), *Working, changes and choices* (pp. 162–171). New York: Human Sciences Press.

Mann, J. A., & Kreyche, G. F. (Eds.). (1966). *Reflections on man: Readings in philosophical psychology from classical philosophy to existentialism.* New York: Harcourt Brace & World.

Mappes, D., Robb, G., & Engels, D. (1985). Ethical and legal issures in counseling and psychotherapy. *Journal of Counseling and Development, 64,* 246–252.

Maxon, T. (2004, January 15). Two down, more to go at Enron? *Dallas Morning News,* 1A, 7A.

McCortney, A. L., & Engels, D.W. (2003). Revisiting the work ethic in America. *Career Development Quarterly, 52,* 132–140.

Meara, N. M., Schmidt, L. D., & Day, J. D. (1996). Principles and virtues: A foundation for ethical decisions, policies, and character. *The Counseling Psychologist, 24,* 4–77.

National Board for Cetified Counselors, Inc. (1991). *Ethical standards.* Greensboro, NC: Author.

National Career Development Association. (2001). *National career development association ethical standards.* Retrieved September 3, 2003, from http:// www.ncda.org/about/poles.html

Neukrug, E., Lovell, C., & Parker, R. J. (1996). Employing ethical codes and decision-making models: A developmental process. *Counseling and Values, 40,* 98–106.

Niles, S. G. (1997). Annual review: Practice and research in career counseling and development—1996. *Career Development Quarterly, 46,* 115–141.

Pate, R. H., & Niles, S. G. (2002). Ethical issues in career development interventions. In S. Niles & J. Harris-Bowlsbey (Eds.), *Career development interventions in the 21st century.* Columbus, OH: Merrill, Prentice-Hall.

Peterson, N., & Gonzalez, R. C. (2005). The role of work in people's lives: Applied career counseling and vocational counseling psychology (2nd ed.) Belmont, CA: Wadsworth/Thomson.

Random House. (2000). *Webster's college dictionary* (6th ed). New York: Author.

Rifkin, J. (1995). *End of work: Decline of the global labor force and the dawn of the post-market era.* New York: G. P. Putnam Sons.

Savickas, M. L. (1995). Constructivist counseling for career indecision. *Career Development Quarterly, 43,* 363–373.

Savickas, M. L. (2003). Advancing the career counseling profession: Objectives and strategies for the next decade. *Career Development Quarterly, 51,* 87–96.

Schultz, D., & Schultz, M. E. (2002). *Psychology and work today* (8th ed.). Upper Saddle River, NJ: Pearson Education.

Smith, R., Engels, D., & Bonk, E. (1985). The past and future of the National Vocational Guidance Association: History at the crossroads. *Journal of Counseling and Development, 63,* 420–424.

Tarasoff v. Regents of the University of California, 529 p.2d 553 118 Cal. Rptr. 129 (1974), vacated, 17 Cal. 3d 425, 551 p.2d 334, 131 Cal. Rptr. 14 (1976).

Thapar v. Zezulka, 994 S.W. 2d at 635, Texas Supreme Court (1999).

Urofsky, R. I., & Engels, D.W. (2003). Philosophy, moral philosophy, and counseling ethics: Not an abstraction. *Counseling and Values, 47,* 118–130.

Webster's New World College Dictionary (4th ed.). (1999). New York: Macmillan.

Welfel, E. R. (2002). *Ethics in counseling and psychotherapy: Standards, research, and emerging issues* (2nd ed.). Pacific Grove, CA: Brooks/Cole.

Welfel, E. R., & Lipsitz, N. E. (1983). Wanted: A comprehensive approach to ethics research and education. *Counselor Education and Supervision, 22,* 320–332.

Whiston, S. C. (2003). Career counseling: 90 years old yet still healthy and vital. *Career Development Quarterly, 52,* 35–42.

Whiston, S. C., & Brecheisen, B.K. (2002). Annual review: Practice and research in career counseling and development—2001. *Career Development Quarterly, 51,* 98–145.

Zuckerman, M. B. (2004, January 19). Editorial: Policing the corporate suites. *U.S. News & World Report,* 72.

PART II

SKILLS AND TECHNIQUES

The responsibilities of career counselors, regardless of the settings in which they implement their roles, require that they become competent to provide their clients with a variety of services. These services cannot be delivered unless a counselor has mastered a number of core knowledge and skills areas. This section of the textbook provides the reader with an overview and introduction to the career-counseling skills and associated knowledge base that become the focus of much of the counselor's educational and supervisory experience.

Chapter 5, "Individual and Group Assessment and Appraisal," is organized to provide the reader with a general understanding of a broad range of career appraisal methods. The psychometric concepts discussed provide the foundation from which to understand career appraisal. Instruments described in this chapter include those created in support of theories of career counseling as well as those developed to measure specific career-related constructs. Care has been taken to provide a description of each instrument and its uses as well as its availability. While not intended to be an exhaustive presentation of assessment and appraisal instruments, the information in the chapter includes the most commonly used tools.

Chapter 6, "Using Information and Technology in Career Counseling," explores the purposes and sources of career information. The sources of career information range from comprehensive career information delivery systems to specialized systems offering only occupational or educational information and uses of the Internet for job search success. Throughout the chapter the emphasis is on two aspects of the world in which we live—interconnectedness and change. Readers are challenged to stay abreast and informed of the changes and additions to the information base available for career and lifestyle planning with clients, which grows exponentially every day.

The competent career counselor will develop a strong working alliance with clients seeking assistance with career and lifestyle planning during the initial phase of the counseling relationship. It is during this initial phase that relevant appraisal and information, as addressed in Chapters 5 and 6, can be introduced and used for the benefit of clients. As the career-counseling process progresses, the counselor must assist clients with the articulation of concrete goals, along with action plans and timetables. Chapter 7, "Developing Comprehensive Career Development Plans for Your Clients," discusses comprehensive planning with clients.

Connecting job placements with clientele, promoting counseling among potential client populations, successfully managing a career center, developing liaisons with supervisors and referral sources in your and other work settings, and evaluating program effectiveness are all essential to the promotion, management, and implementation of a successful career-counseling program. Chapter 8, "Program Promotion, Management, and Implementation," addresses the competencies connected with creating and maintaining a viable program. . . .

Chapter 9, "Supervision, Coaching, and Consultation," addresses the fact that many career counselors find that they are soon expected to supervise employees and paraprofessionals in the context of their work settings. In addition, career counselors often coach clients so that they can succeed in a job interview, successfully negotiate for an advancement or pay raise, or appropriately approach and resolve a conflict with a colleague. The career counselor must also accommodate requests for consultation regarding implementation of the requirements of the Americans with Disabilities Act, stress in the workplace, program management, and case consultation. This chapter focuses on these aspects of the role of a career counselor.

CHAPTER 5

INDIVIDUAL AND GROUP ASSESSMENT AND APPRAISAL

DONNA S. STARKEY

SCOTT D. RASMUS
Delta State University

INTRODUCTION

Career assessment tools are appraisal methods specifically designed to enhance the career decision-making process. While some instruments serve more general purposes, this chapter focuses on their career-counseling applications. Career counselors use assessment methods to identify information salient to clients' career decisions. Additionally, many instruments serve as predictive indicators of potential occupational performance and clients' work-related satisfaction. Assessment tools are to be used as a component of the career-counseling process and never serve as a substitute for counseling.

This chapter is organized to provide counselors with a general understanding of a broad range of career appraisal methods. The psychometric concepts discussed provide the foundation from which to understand career appraisal. Instruments presented in this chapter include those created in direct support of theories of career counseling as well as those developed to measure specific career-related constructs. For each assessment, care has been taken to provide a description of the instrument and its uses as well as information regarding availability. While not intended as an exhaustive list, this chapter presents some of the more commonly used tools. It is hoped that career counselors will find these tools suitable to a wide variety of applications.

PSYCHOMETRIC CONCEPTS

Mental health professionals who utilize career assessments must have a general working knowledge of concepts like reliability, validity, and standard error of measurement if they are to employ these instruments competently. Each provides a layer of protection for test users to administer, score, and interpret results from various aptitude, achievement, interest, value, maturity, and personality tests in an appropriate manner and adhere to ethical practice.

Reliability is a measure of how repeatable and consistent the scores are when a test is administered to a group of individuals on two or more occasions, when similar forms of a test are used with the same group of examinees, or when one wants to investigate the consistency of how the test items were answered relative to each other on a given administration of the test. All reliability values represent correlation coefficients that range from 0 to 1. *Test-retest reliability* is a measure of a test's stability over time, as evidenced by a correlation coefficient called the stability coefficient, between an initial administration of a test and those occurring weeks or months later. A second type of reliability is called *equivalent forms reliability*. Equivalent forms reliability yields a measure of the relationship between two sets of scores derived from a group of individuals taking similar forms of a test at or about the same time. The result is defined as the coefficient of equivalence. Finally, a third form of reliability, termed *internal consistency*, offers a correlation coefficient that serves to give a measure of item consistency between one or more split halves of the test. For example, the odd and even questions on an inventory divide it into one possible split halves. Cronbach's alpha (Cronbach, 1951) and the Kuder-Richardson formula (Kuder & Richardson, 1937) are often mentioned as internal consistency coefficients, depending on what item format was employed for the test.

Another related concept to reliability, the standard error of measurement (SEM), provides a means for the practical implementation of reliability when interpreting scores from a particular test. This concept assists clients in understanding that their scores have some inherent variability associated with them. Classical test theory assumes that no score is perfect and that there is always some source of measurement error associated with the test setting, due to the test taker and the administrative conditions. For example, a test taker may misinterpret the meaning of a particular question on a test or find the test location unsatisfactory. This type of test variability causes an examinee's obtained score to be different from his or her true score on a test. As a matter of fact, test theory assumes that instances of a person's true score are normally distributed around the observed score, with the SEM serving as the standard deviation (SD) for a person's scoring distribution. Accordingly, one's true score falls within $+1$ and -1 SEM above and below one's observed score 68 percent of the time. For example, if Jim receives a 60 on the Career Resiliency Inventory and the manual states that the SEM for the test is 4, then Jim's true score will fall between 56 and 64 approximately 68 percent of the time. SEM is dependent on two factors: the SD for the test scores and the reliability coefficient associated with those scores. SEM values can range from 0 to the SD of scores for a given test. The size of the SEM and the reliability associated with it provide some support for the validity of the test.

The test's validity defines its accuracy and integrity by providing evidence that the test truly measures what it is supposed to measure. Most test manuals recognize three main types of validity: content, criterion, and construct. Content validity is evidence obtained from experts in the field of a particular content domain (e.g., career interest) that ensures the test measures the domain it was intended to assess. Content experts review and verify that all the items on a test adequately and appropriately represent the defined domain to be evaluated. Criterion validity is a second form of validity, which takes test scores on a domain to be measured, such as career readiness, and relates them to a practical criterion (e.g., frequency of career exploration activities), either in the present or in the future. For instance, aptitude test scores provide a means to predict future abilities or behaviors, perhaps in college or on the job.

A final major type of validity, known as construct validity, provides evidence that the personal trait or characteristic measured by a test or scale is homogenous (factorial validity), correlates highly with other tests purported to measure the same or similar constructs (convergent validity), correlates minimally with constructs deemed dissimilar (divergent validity), and supports theoretical assumptions deemed to be the natural implications of the construct (research validity). For example, a researcher may formulate a hypothesis that career maturity should increase with age, as defined by developmental theory. If a longitudinal study using a career maturity inventory supports this trend over time, this research could be used to provide evidence for the construct validity of the test.

NORMS AND SCORING

Test norms are descriptive statistical data derived from a representative group of scores to serve as a comparison for individuals taking the test. Norms provide crucial information for test interpretation purposes. Oftentimes raw scores of a test are transformed into percentiles or standard scores. Both types of transformed scores describe a means of relating where one's score falls in comparison to others who took the test. For instance, a person who scores at the 50th percentile scores higher than 50 percent of the people in the norming group who took the test. Similarly, standard scores are transformed raw scores that usually provide simple integer values for the means and SDs calculated from the scores of the norming group for ease of test interpretation. Typical standard scores on career inventories are z scores (fixed mean = 0, fixed SD = 1), T scores (fixed mean = 50, fixed SD = 10), stanines (fixed mean = 5, fixed SD = 2) and sten scores (fixed mean = 5.5, fixed SD = 2). Examinee scores are referenced to how many SDs a score falls above and below the mean (which, if the scores are normally distributed, can be referenced to the standard normal curve).

One question of primary importance for the test administrator is whether the examinee matches the norming group for the test in age, gender, race, socioeconomic status, geographical location, education level, job or career type, and other relevant demographic characteristics. Norms many times try to employ a national sample based on the proportions of the most recent national census demographic breakdown. Although this sounds like a good idea, in fact, it may not be representative of one's local population. For example, one would be cautious in using a U.S. nationally normed career interest inventory on college-bound Chinese students thinking of attending a university in the United States and of then returning to China to seek work opportunities. Another example would be using an aptitude inventory based on national norms with a group of 12th grade high school students in the southern United States to predict grade point average (GPA) at a particular university in their first semester.

It is important to realize that norms do not always represent mainstream groups in our society but rather may be representative of former substance abusers, high school dropouts, learning disabled children, nontraditional students, or another, similarly atypical, group in our society. Some norms may be typical of student abilities at particular grade levels (grade norms, as on achievement tests), while others are more representative of one's specific age (age norms, for maturity or developmental type of tests). The development of local norms for specific job placement issues may be more relevant than national or general norms, but most counselors do not have the resources or the time to create them. For this reason, counselors must be cautious in extrapolating results from career-related tests, especially if norms are inconsistent with a client's background.

ETHICAL CONSIDERATIONS

In addition to competence in the arena of psychometric properties for career instruments, counselors need to have awareness of the applicable ethical codes and standards related to assessment, scoring, interpretation, and test development. The American Psychological Association, in its ethical codes, offers 11 separate subcategories under the heading of assessment (American Psychological Association, 2002). The American Counseling Association has a similar section in its ethical codes dealing with evaluation, assessment, and interpretation, which identifies 12 standards of ethical competence (American Counseling Association, 1995). The National Board of Certified Counselors similarly has developed 15 standards in a section of its codes titled "Measurement and Evaluation" (National Board of Certified Counselors, 1997). Specific areas of appropriate test use covered by these three professional codes include informed consents/ orientations, obsolete data/testing materials, test security/copyright requirements, classification/diagnosing of examinees, qualifications/training requirements, and standards for appropriate test selection.

An additional set of standards, provided by the Joint Committee on Testing Practice, emphasizes test development to a greater degree than the codes already mentioned in this section. The Code of Fair Testing Practices in Education recognizes ethical competencies for developers and users of educational tests in the areas of development/selection, interpretation, fairness, and informed practice (Joint Committee on Fair Testing Practices, 1988).

THE USE OF ASSESSMENTS IN
CAREER COUNSELING

Career assessments are employed by counselors functioning in a variety of settings. Keeping this in mind, it is important for counselors to consider when and how such practices should occur, as well as how the results should be presented to the client. Oftentimes, one's career is viewed as a means to personal satisfaction and growth in addition to the fulfillment of material needs (Drummond & Ryan, 1995). As such, informal career assessments will take place in virtually every counseling relationship, as life concerns may be exacerbated or directly influenced by career-related issues.

To solicit pertinent information, a thorough intake assessment should include questions about work and work history. Responses to these items may lead the counselor to further investigate a client's employment status, either informally via interview or formally through the use of career inventories. Even if the counselor is not performing career counseling services per se, career assessments may prove beneficial to the therapeutic growth of the client. As in any counseling relationship, the practitioner must take care to focus on the whole person, including his or her career and lifestyle needs.

A counselor's particular work setting will probably dictate the degree to which career assessments are used in the counseling process. High school counselors most certainly will employ a battery of instruments to assess academic achievement and occupational interest at some point in a student's academic life. Counselors involved in human resource programs may find that much of their work involves career counseling and the assessments accompanying that effort. Finally, counselors in private practice or other settings may find that career assessment is a necessary part of their work.

In addition to competency in the administration and scoring of recommended instruments, the ethical provision of career assessment services includes the review of the assessment needs and outcomes with the client. The client must have an understanding of what the instrument is intended to assess and what it will and will not provide in terms of outcome information. An orientation session offered by the test administrator discussing the purpose and rationale for each instrument is suggested for all clients involved. Additionally, the counselor must provide informed consent regarding confidentiality and the storage of assessment records. Finally, the counselor must explain the rights and responsibilities held by the client in a testing situation (Joint Committee on Testing Practices, 1988).

Upon completion of the assessment or assessments, the counselor will likely conduct an interpretation session with the client. During this session, the counselor will thoroughly review test score ranges, including the SEM, prior to sharing the results. When presenting results, it is important that the counselor check in with the client frequently to determine how the information is being received. The counselor will help the client extract his or her individualized meaning from the instrument and frame it in the context of the client's experience. Client questions should be solicited and a thorough summary of the results provided. Finally, the counselor and client will want to work together to develop career goals based on the information gleaned from the assessment process.

ASSESSMENTS DEVELOPED TO SUPPORT THEORIES

A number of dominant theories have emerged in the field of career counseling, many of which have been discussed previously in this text. In the course of theory development, assessment tools have been created to aid in the application of such theories to the career-counseling process. The instruments in this section were developed specifically in support of particular career theories.

Holland's Theory

John Holland (1992) developed a typological approach to career choice, which identifies personality characteristics of individuals and characteristics of various environments. He believed that both traits and settings could be classified into just six categories, defined by the letters RIASEC, for Realistic, Investigative, Artistic, Social, Enterprising, and Conventional. Vocational and avocational settings were basically defined by the codings of the kinds of people that comprised them. Holland used a pictorial graphic of a hexagon to serve as a visual aid to emphasize the interrelationships between the RIASEC letters assigned to each of the points on it in a circular-type arrangement (Holland, 1992, 1994c). For example, adjacent points, like "R" and "C," on the hexagon indicate more compatibility in personality traits and work duties than, say, an "R" and "S" coding, which includes diametrical opposites on the hexagon. The more adjacent categories were considered to have more consistency and overlap in their characteristics than those that were not.

Holland (1992) also felt that individuals would actively seek out environments that matched their personality styles. For instance, individuals who are considered to be "S" (social) personality types tend to display an interest in helping others. These individuals typically search for social environments where their talents and abilities seem to have the best fit, and thus provide the most personal satisfaction. Holland, Fritzsche, and Powell (1997) looked at three-letter preference codes for each personality and environment to evaluate the degree of match between them; this was defined as their congruence. The goal of career counseling in this approach is to increase both self- and career knowledge to promote effective career decision making, leading to the best possible match between the person and the environment.

Counselors employing the Holland approach often utilize various inventories to assess individual and job characteristics for goodness-of-fit purposes to promote personal satisfaction and success. Some common inventories developed by Holland and others to assess personality characteristics and their relationship to career choice are the following.

Self-Directed Search (SDS).   The SDS was initially developed to deal with vocational problems but also provides a way for students and adults to have a career-counseling experience when they do not have access to a counselor, or through personal choice (Holland, Powell, & Fritzsche, 1997). As a self-administered and self-scored instrument, the SDS uses two booklets, an *Assessment Booklet* and *The Occupation Finder*, to determine one's summary code and to identify possible career options. For instance, in an SDS, a typical assessment booklet evaluates a person's activities, competencies, occupations, and self-estimates in 228 items (Holland, 1994b). Besides these sections, the booklet also provides a means for individuals to write down their future career aspirations ("Occupational Daydreams" section) prior to completing the assessment for comparison purposes. The associated *Occupation Finder* booklet has 1,309 occupations listed by three-letter summary codes (Holland, 1994a). See the case study provided in the box.

■ ■ ■ ■ ■ ■

CASE STUDY

John, a white 17-year-old high school junior, is considering options for college. He has been interested in meteorology since his middle school days. He purchased some weather instruments with his weekly allowance at that time so he could chart weather data and even provides weather information from time to time to a television station in a nearby major city. Besides tracking the weather, John's hobbies include computers, running, and reading self-help psychology books. John has been using a Web-authoring software program his father purchased for him last year to create Webpages for himself and a few of his friends. He appears to have a knack for doing this. In addition to this, running has always been an outlet he has enjoyed, especially since joining the cross-country team at his high school. John has also enjoyed reading self-help psychology books when time permits because he says it make him feel better when he reads them.

John's grades have been A' s in math and science but B's in English and history. Last marking period he received a C in English literature because he was bored with the class.

John also values helping others by volunteering in a local soup kitchen once a month with his family as an outreach program provided by his church. His parents have encouraged him to get more involved with a local peer group in the social service area. John's father has carved out a career in copper tubing sales for a regional distributor, while his mom has worked in the nursing field since his preschool years. Both his parents have attended college to obtain associates degrees in their respective fields. John has an older brother, Sam, age 19 years, who has already gone off to college at an aeronautical university, desiring a career as an airline pilot. His younger brother, Pete, age 15 years, has opted not to go to college because he wants to pursue a military career as a mechanic.

John's grandparents were first-generation immigrants from Austria who were factory workers and coal miners, with no formal education past the sixth grade. They have lived their entire lives in a coal mining town up in the northeastern part of the United States.

John has been troubled lately by his inability to commit to a career path since his senior year is just four months away, so he decides to make an appointment with his school guidance counselor, Mrs. Catwick. During the meeting, Mrs. Catwick discusses John's concerns with him and then encourages him to take the Self-Directed Search (SDS), Form R (Holland, 1994b), stating "This may help you to consider what occupations may be of interest to you and how strongly you feel about each of them." John sits down and fills the inventory out under her guidance.

John first lists his "Occupational Daydreams" (Holland, 1994b), or the occupations he's most thought about for the future, and then uses the SDS *Occupation Finder* (Holland, 1994a) to identify the most relevant three letter RIASEC codes for each one (see table).

Occupation	Code
Meteorologist	IRS
Counselor	SIA
Computer Programmer	IRC

(continued)

CONTINUED

At the request of Mrs. Catwick, John also looks up the occupation codes for his parents so he can understand the influence each has had on his career decision-making process. Mrs. Catwick discusses this with him.

Occupation	Code
Father—Sales Representative	ESR
Mother—Licensed Practical Nurse	SAC

John goes on to complete the SDS *Assessment Booklet*, identifying the activities that he likes or dislikes and feels competent in or not, and also recognizing the interest or disinterest he has in various occupations. He then rates his abilities and skills in 14 different areas, such as mechanical, teaching, managerial, sales, and clerical. His results pertaining to the six Holland RIASEC categories (Realistic, Investigative, Artistic, Social, Enterprising, and Conventional) are as follows:

	R	I	A	S	E	C
Activities	2	8	2	6	1	1
Competencies	5	7	3	4	1	4
Occupations	3	6	7	4	1	2
Self-Estimates1	4	5	2	4	2	2
Self-Estimates2	3	5	2	5	1	2
Total Scores	17	31	16	23	6	11
Summary Code	ISR					

Mrs. Catwick now has John look up in *The Occupational Finder* (Holland, 1994a) the jobs listed under his summary code, ISR, as well as any jobs that pique his interest under all of the three letter permutations of this code type: IRS, SIR, SRI, RIS, and RSI. She explains to John that investigative (I) types like himself find investigative jobs most satisfying, which include scientific occupations and some technical ones. Social (S) types enjoy social jobs and prefer education-oriented or social service positions. This second type was somewhat less important to John, as compared to the investigative type. Finally, realistic (R) types like realistic jobs and prefer skilled trades, service occupations, or technical positions. This third type was the one of the three, I-S-R, that least resembled John's personality characteristics but provided a better fit than any of the Artistic, Enterprising, and Conventional occupations

■ ■ ■ ■ ■

(Holland, 1994c). John developed the following listing of jobs that he would like to investigate further:

Code	Occupation	DOT	ED
ISR	Exercise Physiologist	076.121–018	5
IRS	Meteorologist	025.062–010	5
IRS	Internet/Intranet Administrator		4
RIS	Forester	040.167–010	5
RSI	Data Communications/ Telecommunications Analyst	031.262–010	5

DOT—Dictionary of Occupational Titles Codes

ED—Education Levels required.

Mrs. Catwick also helps John to recognize that the three occupations on his "Occupational Daydreams" list (Holland, 1994b) were pretty consistent with his results on the SDS because of his strong to moderate interest in investigative (I) and social (S) activities. She provides additional information on his list of preferred occupations indicating ED codes of "5," which implied a college education or an advanced degree were needed for those particular occupations. She also encourages him to go to the local library to read up on the job descriptions in the *Dictionary of Occupational Titles* (U.S. Department of Labor, 1991) for each of his identified occupations. Finally, she hands John a copy of *You and Your Career* (Holland, 1994c) to reinforce the material discussed in the counseling session and schedules a follow-up appointment with him.

QUESTIONS FOR DISCUSSION
1. What other experiences or sources of information would you consider for John when discussing his career options?
2. How would you process John's family vocational history with him? What kind of relevance does it have for him at this point?
3. What kind of strategy would you have to work with John in the follow-up session?
4. The SDS is one part of the career-counseling process for John. Describe, in a step-by-step manner, your own career-counseling approach to working with John.
5. Pick an ethical code that can be accessed online, either APA (www.apa.org), ACA (www.counseling.org), or NBCC (www.nbcc.org). What particular standards are most important for Mrs. Catwick to consider when administering, scoring and interpreting the SDS with John?

Other instruments related to Holland's theory include the Vocational Preference Inventory, Career Attitudes and Strategic Inventory, and Strong Interest Inventory. Each was either authored by John Holland himself or supports his RIASEC framework.

Vocational Preferences Inventory (VPI).   A forerunner to the SDS, the VPI was utilized to help develop Holland's theory and typology underlying his career choice classification system (Holland, Fritzsche, & Powell, 1997). The inventory assesses personality and interest on 11 scales, including Realistic, Investigative, Social, Conventional, Enterprising, Artistic, Self-Control, Masculinity-Femininity, Status, Infrequency, and Acquiescence (Holland, 1985).

Career Attitudes and Strategic Inventory (CASI).   The CASI is a 130-item inventory targeting employed and unemployed adults. It was developed to evaluate some general obstacles, attitudes, feelings, and experiences that might influence a person's career selection. Scores are charted on a profile sheet in nine areas of career adaptation: Job Satisfaction, Work Involvement, Skill Development, Dominant Style, Career Worries, Interpersonal Abuse, Family Commitment, Risk-Taking Style, and Geographical Barriers (Holland & Gottfredson, 1994). A supplemental checklist of 21 career obstacles (e.g., health and emotional difficulties) that many people worry about is provided as part of the test package also.

Author(s):   John Holland (SDS, VPI, CASI) and Gary Gottfredson (CASI)

Availability: Self-Directed Search (SDS), Vocational Preference Inventory (VPI), and Career Attitudes and Strategies Inventory (CASI) Psychological Assessment Resources, Inc.
P.O. Box 998
Odessa, FL 33556
(800) 889-8378
http://www.parinc.com

Strong Interest Inventory (SII).   A 317-item inventory evaluating an individual's interest in various occupations, school subjects, activities, types of people, and other preferences (Harmon, Hansen, Borgen & Hammer, 1994). Results yield information about a person's preferences in 6 General Occupational Themes (GOT), based on Holland's RIASEC classification, as well as 25 subthemes (e.g., artistic—culinary arts, investigative—science) on the Basic Interest Scales (BISs). Additional scales include the 211 occupational scales and 4 new personal style scales.

Author: E. K. Strong

Availability: Strong Interest Inventory
Consulting Psychologists Press Inc.
3803 E. Bayshore Road
P.O. Box 10096
Palo Alto, CA 94303
(800) 624-1765
http://cpp-db.com

Super's Life-Span Theory

Super's life-span theory is a developmental approach to career counseling. Maintaining that individuals go through various career stages established by internal and external forces rather than tied to chronological age, Super's theory offers clients the opportunity to identify and organize those factors that influence them. Assessment tools are important to this endeavor. Super and his colleagues developed many of the instruments associated with this theory. Super believes that interests and preferences are "to be viewed in the light of career maturity, the salience of life roles, and the values sought in life as moderator variables" (Super & Osborne, 1992, p. 74). Measures associated with this theory include appraisals of interest, values, and roles.

Interest.   Super recommends beginning an assessment battery with the Strong Interest Inventory (SII). Previously described (in the Holland section), this measure provides information related to the client's interest in multiple occupational themes. As such, it is an elemental measure of client's interests that functions well within Super's theory.

Values.   Two instruments are available through this theory to measure values. The Work Values Inventory and the Values Scale were developed to measure both intrinsic and extrinsic values related to motivation. Clients are affected by both their internal needs and the external means by which they satisfy those needs. For the client seeking a first job or considering changing jobs, exploration of these values can be a meaningful starting point for counseling.

Work Values Inventory.   The brief, 45-item Work Values Inventory (WVI) also measures both extrinsic and intrinsic values associated with work environment and satisfaction (Drummond, 2000). Intended for Grade 7 through adult, the WVI measures such constructs as altruism, creativity, intellectual stimulation, surroundings, and relations with supervisors and associates. Each scale contains three items to be considered on a 5-point Likert scale, ranging from unimportant (1) to very important (5; Hood & Johnson, 1991). Easily administered and hand-scored, this measure is a useful compliment to other career considerations.

> *Author:*   Donald Super
> *Availability:*   Houghton Mifflin Company
> 222 Berkley Street
> Boston, MA 02116
> (800) 225-3362
> http://www.hmco.com

The Values Scale.   The Values Scale (VS) measures 21 values intended to help clients discern the importance of work within other life roles. Focusing on both intrinsic and extrinsic values, the Values Scale measures ability utilization, advancement, authority, creativity, lifestyle, personal development, physical activity, risk, social interaction, social relations, working conditions, cultural identity, physical prowess, and economic security (Drummond, 2000). Developed for ages high school through adult, the accompanying normative data can facilitate discussion of client values and career options. Used in this manner, the VS is an effective tool to narrow the field of desirable positions (Schoenrade, 2002).

Author:	Donald E. Super and Dorothy D. Nevil
Availability:	Consulting Psychologists Press, Inc.
	3803 East Bayshore Road
	P.O. Box 10096
	Palo Alto, CA 94303
	(800) 624-1765
	http://cpp-db.com

Roles.   Super's theory also accounts for a variety of roles, work related and other. The Salience Inventory (SI) was developed to measure the importance of such roles, taking into account client levels of attraction to such jobs and the different responsibilities that go with them (Zytowski, 1988). The only widely used instrument to measure such a construct, the SI is easily administered to groups. A total of 170 items is presented, with a 4-point scale ranging from "never" to "always," and the scale can be hand- or machine-scored.

Author:	Dorothy D. Nevill and Donald E. Super
Availability:	Consulting Psychologists Press
	3803 E. Bayshore Road
	Palo Alto, CA 94303
	(800) 624-1765
	www.cpp-db.com

This battery of assessments created to support Super's Life-Span Theory of career development does not include information about aptitude. If needed, Super proposes that the Differential Aptitude Test, Armed Services Vocational Battery, or the Miller Analogies Test (discussed under the aptitude section of this chapter) would provide the necessary information (Super & Osborne, 1992).

Theory of Work Adjustment

The theory of work adjustment (TWA), an outgrowth of landmark research at the University of Minnesota, is concerned with the relationship between the individual and the work environment (Dawis, 1980). The individual brings a set of needs to the employment setting that are greater than the need for an income. According to this theory, clients come to understand the many and varied reasons they choose work, including such desires as status, sense of accomplishment, and a reputable employer. In turn, the employment setting has requirements of the individual that must be met. In the theory of work adjustment, the client's skills and needs interact with the workplace requirements and methods of reinforcement. The client's satisfaction with the work and the satisfactoriness of the client for the organization leads ultimately to the client's length of employment or tenure (Dawis, 1980). For example, a client with high satisfaction for the work who is not able to meet the needs of the workplace or is not satisfactory to the organization will have a briefer tenure than an employee who is a better match to the workplace. Within the structure of TWA, a number of assessment tools emerged.

Needs/Values.   The Minnesota Importance Questionnaire (MIQ) (1981) was designed to measure the client's work needs and values in order to determine worker satisfaction in adults, ages 16 and above. Additionally, the individual's preferred methods of reinforcement emerge in this instrument. Two forms are available, including a paired form, which allows the client to select one of two options, or a ranked form, which requires the client to order items based on values (Benson, 1988). Machine-scored and suitable for group administration, this instrument surveys 20 needs: Ability Utilization, Achievement, Activity, Advancement, Authority, Company Policies and Practices, Compensation, Co-workers, Creativity, Independence, Moral Values, Recognition, Responsibility, Security, Social Service, Social Status, Supervision–Human Relations, Supervision-Technical, Variety, and Working Conditions. Six values are appraised: Achievement, Altruism, Autonomy, Comfort, Safety, and Status. From this, a prediction of satisfaction with particular occupations can be made (Layton, 1992).

Job Satisfaction.   The Minnesota Satisfaction Questionnaire (MSQ, 1967) is a measure of client satisfaction with an occupation. Similar to the MIQ, the MSQ measures adults' satisfaction in their current employment setting on the same 20 needs subscales listed previously (Thompson & Blain, 1992).

Other.   The Minnesota Job Description Questionnaire (MJDQ, 1968) was developed to assess how well a particular work setting meets the 20 needs found on the MIQ and MSQ (Sharf, 2002). Additionally, the Minnesota Occupational Classification System delineates over 1,700 occupations in terms of Occupational Ability Patterns and Occupational Reinforcer Patterns to facilitate the client and counselor exploration of a suitable career path based on client preferences (Sharf, 2002).

Authors:	James B. Rounds, Jr., George A. Henly, Ren V. Dawis, Lloyd H. Lofquist, and David J. Weiss
Availability:	Minnesota Importance Questionnaire Vocational Psychology Research N620 Elliot Hall University of Minnesota-Twin Cities 75 East River Road Minneapolis, MN 55455-0344 (612) 625-1367 http://www.psych.umn.edu/psylabs/vpr/default.htm
Authors:	David J. Weiss, Ren V. Dawis, George W. England, and Lloyd H. Lofquist

Availability:	Minnesota Satisfaction Questionnaire Vocational Psychology Research N620 Elliot Hall University of Minnesota-Twin Cities 75 East River Road Minneapolis, MN 55455-0344 (612) 625-1367 http://www.psych.umn.edu/psylabs/vpr/default.htm
Authors:	Fred H. Borgen, David J. Weiss, Howard E. A. Tinsley, Ren V. Dawis, and Lloyd H. Lofquist
Availability:	Minnesota Job Description Questionnaire Vocational Psychology Research N620 Elliot Hall University of Minnesota-Twin Cities 75 East River Road Minneapolis, MN 55455-0344 (612) 625-1367 http://www.psych.umn.edu/psylabs/vpr/default.htm

Abilities: No aptitude scales were developed in support of this theory but the General Aptitude Test Battery, a widely used measure of abilities discussed later in this chapter, is often used to provide information about the client's aptitude for a particular work setting (Sharf, 2002).

Krumboltz

Krumboltz's Learning Theory of Career Counseling (LTCC) is a practical theory that focuses on the clients and the experiences that have shaped their career beliefs and choices. Initially developed by Krumboltz, Mitchell, and Gelatt in the mid-1970s, LTCC is built on factors influencing clients seeking career counseling. These factors include personal characteristics and environmental events outside of the clients' control and learning opportunities and skills acquired throughout their lives (Mitchell, Levin, & Krumboltz, 1999). LTCC holds that assumptions made by clients about these factors influence career choice (Krumboltz, 1994). Counselors working within this theory help clients to identify assumptions or beliefs and facilitate an understanding of their influence on career preference and choices.

Career choice in the LTCC is considered a continuous process influenced by ongoing learning experiences. As such, assessment is considered to be another learning experience. The theory suggests the utilization of aptitude tests to determine task-approach skills as well as interest inventories to serve as starting points for dialogue about career preference. LTCC considers the role of the counselor as that of an educator, or catalyst for awareness, rather than a "matchmaker" (Mitchell et al., 1999). The primary assessment tool in the learning theory of career counseling is the Career Beliefs Inventory.

Career Beliefs Inventory (CBI).   The CBI was developed by Krumboltz to help clients become aware of attitudes or beliefs that may be interfering with their attainment of career goals. It is best used at the beginning of the counseling process and has proved particularly useful for the high school and college populations as well as those clients considering mid-life career changes (Krumboltz, 1994). The 96-item instrument assesses client beliefs about the following five subscales:

1. My Current Career Situation
2. What Seems Necessary for My Happiness
3. Factors That Influence My Decisions
4. Changes I Am Willing to Make
5. Effort I Am Willing to Initiate

Rather than defining particular occupations suited to the client, the CBI outcomes integrate career and personal-counseling topics that will help define optimal career paths. The focus is on investigating assumptions or beliefs that may interfere with client career choices rather than merely pairing client interests with job codes. The test manual states, "What appears to be inappropriate or self-defeating behavior may become understandable when one discovers the assumptions and beliefs on which each person operates" (Krumboltz, 1991, p. 1). Success is defined in CBI as helping clients to develop the self-awareness needed to create satisfying career paths for themselves. In this theoretical model, such success includes ongoing learning and increased satisfaction in both their work and personal lives (Krumboltz, 1998).

The contention is that the CBI transcends traditional career assessment because of the multidimensional focus of engaging the client about the "why" along with the "what" of career choice (Krumboltz, 1994). Given that it measures different constructs than other instruments available to career counselors, the CBI may be most useful as a compliment to other traditional interest and ability assessments (Walsh, 1995).

Author: John D. Krumboltz

Availability: The Career Beliefs Inventory
Consulting Psychologists Press Inc.
3803 E. Bayshore Road
P.O. Box 10096
Palo Alto, CA 94303
(800) 624-1765
http://cpp-db.com

Cognitive Information Processing (CIP) Theory

The CIP model was developed to help adolescents and adults achieve an optimal level of career problem-solving and decision-making skills in support of their career choices (Peterson, Sampson, Reardon, & Lenz, 1996). Career choice is viewed as a problem-solving activity through new learning in the areas of Self-Knowledge, Occupational Knowledge, Information-Processing Abilities, and Metacognitive Awareness. Learning is also emphasized in a seven-step counseling sequence, including the initial interview, preliminary assessment, problem definition and analysis, goal formulation, individual learning plan creation, execution of the learning plan, and a review or generalization phase of treatment (Peterson et al., 1996). In this model, career-related problems are viewed as "gaps" between an existing situational state and an ideal one. For example, one common type of gap may be a client's struggle between knowing one has to make a job choice and then feeling one has, in fact, made an appropriate one. However, a preliminary assessment of client readiness is necessary before problem-related activities begin in the CIP approach. One of the instruments specifically developed to address readiness is the Career Thoughts Inventory (CTI).

Career Thoughts Inventory (CTI). The CTI is an instrument devised within the CIP framework measuring client mental readiness or dysfunction in the areas of Decision Making Confusion (DMC), Commitment-Anxiety (CA), and External Conflict (EC) (Sampson, Peterson, Lenz, Reardon, & Saunders, 1996a). The 48-item inventory targets high school and college students as well as general adult populations to explore their ability to cognitively focus on the career decision-making process, to understand how their anxiety contributes to career indecisiveness, and also to assess their ability to differentiate between their own perceptions of career options and the influences of significant others. A workbook serves as an adjunct to the test and provides exercises to assist individuals in identifying and working through dysfunctional thought patterns which get in the way of career choice (Sampson, Peterson, Lenz, Reardon, & Saunders, 1996b). The instrument is meant to be self-administered and self-scored, but professional assistance is recommended to double-check the scoring and to aid the client in interpretation (Fontaine, 1999).

Authors:	James Sampson, Gary Peterson, Janet Lenz, Robert Reardon, and Denise Saunders
Availability:	Career Thoughts Inventory (CTI)
	Psychological Assessment Resources, Inc.
	P.O. Box 998
	Odessa, FL 33556
	(800) 889-8378
	http://www.parinc.com

Another instrument, not specifically linked to the CIP model but utilized to help assess career decision-making status, is the My Vocational Situation (MVS) inventory.

My Vocational Situation (MVS). The MVS was developed for Grade 9 through adult to assess three potential problem areas in career decision making: vocational identity, personal or environmental barriers, and the need for information or training. The instrument is self-administered and self-scored (Kapes & Mastie, 2002).

Authors:	John Holland, Denise Daiger, and Paul Power
Availability:	My Vocational Situation
	Consulting Psychologists Press Inc.

3803 E. Bayshore Road
P.O. Box 10096
Palo Alto, CA 94303
(800) 624-1765
http://cpp-db.com

Roe's Theory

Anne Roe developed a psychoanalytic theory of career development and career choice based on human needs related to early childhood experiences (Roe, 1956). A person's attachment history with his or her parents was thought to shape his or her personal and relational preferences (e.g., attitudes, interests, abilities, and desire for closeness) in adulthood, especially in influencing one's vocational choice. An important theme of Roe's work was the assumption that as a result of upbringing, a person develops a relational life pattern, either toward other people or away from them. Occupations were then grouped according to these criteria, as either "person-orientated" or "non-person-orientated" (Roe, 1956). The former category highlighted occupational classifications, such as service, business contact, organization, general culture, and arts or entertainment. Non-person-oriented categories included positions in science, technology, and the outdoors (e.g., farming, forestry). Roe created a two-dimensional career classification system based on a person's affinity to connect with others (fields) and his or her motivation to achieve status in a particular occupational setting (levels). The levels' dimension evidenced more of a person's internal drive or motivation to find satisfaction, with life at higher levels of self-actualization similar to the process identified by Maslow's Hierarchy of Needs. Roe (1957) considered six occupational levels, ranging from unskilled through professional or managerial positions.

Roe's classification scheme has led to the development of a number of career assessment instruments based on her ideas. Three of them are the Vocational Interest Inventory, Occupational Preference Inventory (OPI), and Career Occupational Preference System (COPS-P) Professional Level Interest Inventory.

Vocational Interest Inventory (VII).   The Vocational Interest Inventory (VII) measures a person's interest intensity in the eight occupational fields already mentioned (e.g., service, business contact, organization) for Roe's classification system. Comprised of two 56-item sections, the VII evaluates the occupational and activity preferences of older high school students to assist them in choosing a college major. Although the inventory was intended to be self-administered and self-interpreted, computer-generated reports appear to offer extensive information identifying job listings related to the highest scores on the test, education levels needed to obtain them, and a ranking of 25 college majors related to the taker's mean profile (Herman, 1998; Law, 1998).

Author: Patricia Lunneborg

Availability: Vocational Interest Inventory
         Western Psychological Services
         12031 Wilshire Blvd.

Los Angeles, CA 90025
800-648-8857
http://www.wpspublish.com

A second inventory developed out of Roe's classification system was the Occupational Preference Inventory (OPI).

Occupational Preference Inventory (OPI).   The OPI serves as a computer-based assessment to assist individuals with career decision making in Grade 11 through adulthood (Kapes & Mastie, 2002). Results are presented in a profile format highlighting relevant personal information such as career preferences, interests, and predicted MBTI/aptitude scores.

Authors:	Brainard & Brainard
Availability:	PAQ Services, Inc.
	Data Processing Division
	1625 North 1000 East
	North Logan, UT 84321
	435-752-5698
	http://www.pag.com

Career Occupation Preference System Professional Level Interest Inventory (COPS-P).   The Career Occupational Preference System (COPS-P) Professional Level Interest Inventory was developed to measure career interest for those seeking professional career status (Albanese, 2001). College-bound high school students, college students, and adult professionals benefit from a set of inventories and resource materials that not only help them to identify career options related to their personal preferences, but also review a wealth of in-depth information about a number of career alternatives.

Author:	Lisa Knapp-Lee, Lila Knapp, and Robert Knapp
Availability:	Educational and Industrial Testing Service (EdIts)
	P. O. Box 7234
	San Diego, CA 92167
	800-416-1666
	http://www.edits.net/index2.htm

ASSESSMENTS BY TYPE

Not all career appraisal methods have been created to support theories of career counseling. The majority of instruments available to counselors were developed to measure specific constructs salient to the career decision-making process. The instruments in this section are presented by type, or the construct they were designed to measure.

Assessments of Aptitude, Ability, and Achievement

An aptitude is defined as an ability, tendency, or capacity that is inherited or is the result of environment and life experiences (Zunker & Osborn, 2002). Whether such traits are natural or acquired, a measure of aptitude has some ability to predict how well clients will do in a particular activity (Worthen, White, Fan, & Sudweeks, 1999). Aptitude tests are more sophisticated than intelligence tests in that they measure more specialized constructs and a broader array of experiences relevant to traditional achievement tests (Harrington & Schafer, 1996). Measures of aptitude and ability are cornerstones in career counseling assessment practices, as high school students frequently take one or more of these instruments prior to graduation to assist their vocational direction. Often, the appraisals are group administered and computer scored to aid the school counselor in mass administration and interpretation. Additionally, measures of skills and abilities serve clients beyond the high school population who are interested in determining suitability for a given occupation. As such, career counselors may consider using these appraisals as a supplement to other inventories.

In a survey of professionals using aptitude measures conducted by Kapes and Mastie (2002), the most commonly used instruments were the Differential Aptitude Test, the General Aptitude Test Battery, and the Armed Services Vocational Aptitude Battery. Those and other commonly employed aptitude tests are presented in this section.

Differential Aptitude Test: The Differential Aptitude Test (DAT) is actually a battery of aptitude tests providing scores for the subtests of Verbal Reasoning, Numerical Ability, Abstract Reasoning, Clerical Speed and Accuracy, Mechanical Reasoning, Space Relations, Spelling, and Language Usage. It is designed for group administration and use with students in Grades 8–12 or other young adult populations. The combined Verbal Reasoning and Numerical Ability score serves as the best indicator of academic and vocational interest and provides the basis for advising (Pennock-Román, 1988). Counselors will want to work with clients using the available DAT *Individual Report*, as the clear narrative interpretations provide the greatest impact to the client (Wang, 2002).

> *Authors:*   G. K. Bennet, H. G. Seashore, and A. G. Wesman
> *Availability:*   The Psychological Corporation
> 19500 Bulverde Rd.
> San Antonio, TX 78259
> 1-800-872-1726
> http://www.psychcorpcenter.com

General Aptitude Test Battery: The General Aptitude Test Battery (GATB) is a broad measure of nine occupational aptitudes such as general learning and manual dexterity. This test is intended for students in Grades 9–12 as well as adults and can be group-administered. Developed by the U.S. Employment Service primarily for administration through local state employment security agencies, qualified schools, and other organizations may obtain permission to administer this assessment. The GATB is designed to help clients make comparisons of their abilities with those of employed adults (Keesling & Healy, 1988). This awareness serves as a springboard for career counseling using the GATB.

> *Availability:*   Your local employment service agency, or
> U.S. Employment Service
> Western Assessment Research and Development Center
> 140 East Third Street
> Salt Lake City, UT 84111
> http://www.uses.doleta.gov

Armed Services Vocational Aptitude Battery.   Developed by the U.S. Department of Defense, the Armed Services Vocational Aptitude Battery (ASVAB) is designed for high school seniors and is provided at no cost to schools through a cooperative venture. Results of this widely used instrument yield students' abilities in three areas: Academic, Verbal, and Mathematical. Resultant ASVAB scores are used to compare test takers to other students nationally. The instrument is designed to facilitate self-awareness, career exploration, and career planning with suggestions for suitable occupations including military careers (U.S. Military Entrance Processing Command, 2002).

> *Availability:*   Your local high school, or
> U.S. Department of Defense
> Defense Manpower Data Center
> Personnel Testing Division
> 99 Pacific Street, Suite 155A
> Monterey, CA 93940
> (408) 583-2400
> http://www.dmdc.osd.mil/dmdc.html

Other aptitude tests include the Wonderlic Basic Skills Test, the Scholastic Aptitude Test and ACT Assessment, the Graduate Record Examination, and the Miller Analogies Test.

Wonderlic Basic Skills Test: The Wonderlic Basic Skills Test (WBST) is a measurement of verbal skills, including the subtests of Word Knowledge, Sentence Construction, and Information Retrieval, and quantitative skills, including the subtests of Explicit Problem Solving, Problem Solving, and Interpretive Problem Solving. Intended for group or individual administration, the WBST is suitable for assessing job readiness in teenage and young adult populations and has significant potential for providing clients information about their career decisions (Hanna & Hughey, 2002). Additionally, this instrument has been approved by the U.S. Department of Education as a means of qualifying students for Title 10 federal financial assistance. This instrument can be computer scored by the counselor with appropriate software. A desirable feature of this instrument is that falsified answer sheets are easily identified during scoring and the computer report will indicate to the administrator that the client should be retested (Donlon, 1998).

> *Availability:* Wonderlic, Inc.
> 1795 N. Butterfield Road
> Libertyville, IL 60048
> (800) 323-3742
> http://www.wonderlic.com

SAT/ACT Assessment. The SAT and ACT Assessment are measures of readiness for undergraduate school. Minimum scores on these instruments often serve colleges and universities as gatekeepers in the admission process.

> *Availability:* SAT
> Educational Testing Service
> College Board Programs
> P.O. Box 6200
> Princeton, NJ 08541
> http:// www.ets.org
>
> ACT National Office
> 2201 North Dodge Street
> PO. Box 168
> Iowa City, IA 52243-0168
> (319) 337-1000
> http://www.act.org

Graduate Record Examination: The Graduate Record Examination (GRE) is an assessment of readiness for graduate school. Used to help distinguish between students of similar backgrounds, the GRE General Test measures skills acquired throughout the educational process that are common to all fields of study. Analytical writing, verbal, and quantitative skills are also measured. Administered by Educational Testing Service (ETS), the GRE is provided in computer or paper form through local testing centers worldwide (ETS, n.d.).

> *Availability:* GRE
> Educational Testing Service
> P.O. Box 6000
> Princeton, NJ 08541-6000
> (800) 473-2255
> www.gre.org

Miller Analogies Test. The Miller Analogies Test (MAT) was developed over 70 years ago to assess readiness for graduate school, often as an alternative to the GRE. Its aim is to differentiate between high-functioning graduate applicants by serving as a test of cognitive complexity (Ivens, 1995). The test consists of 100 analogies, which are presented to the clients in a 50-minute time period, thus requiring swift responses. Its usefulness is limited to clients looking at the potential for graduate school in their career decisions and to the programs to which they apply.

> *Availability:* The Psychological Corporation
> 19500 Bulverde Rd.
> San Antonio, TX 78259
> 1-800-872-1726
> http://www.psychcorpcenter.com

Assessments of Interests

An important factor in career decision making is the concept of client interests. Generally defined as a set of beliefs or attitudes toward a given activity, interest is linked to motivation to engage in some form of that activity (Drummond, 2000). Career instruments that measure interest have long been a part of developmental, life-span theorists. Previously in this chapter we have discussed the use of the Strong Interest Inventory (SII) and the Self-Directed Search (SDS), which are often associated with Holland's typology theory, as well as the Vocation Interest Inventory (VII) and the California Occupational Preference Survey (COPS), which are often associated with Roe's psychoanalytic theory. Other measures of interest are available to career counselors for use in defining what clients are attracted to in their work and personal lives. Due to the idiosyncratic nature of the information being gathered, these instruments are typically in the form of a self-report questionnaire. They often serve as only one piece of information in the career decision-making puzzle. The following three interest inventories are widely used; the Kuder Occupational Interest Survey, the Kuder General Interest Survey, and the Career Assessment Inventory.

Kuder Occupational Interest Survey. The Kuder Occupational Interest Survey (KOIS), Form DD, relates client interests with interests typical of 126 occupational groups. Appropriate for clients from 10th grade through adult, the instrument requires clients to rate 100 activity triads in terms of which activity of each triad the client prefers. This method of rating preference is to elicit patterns of interest rather than intensity of that interest (Kelly, 2002). Validity of this instrument is strong, with over half of study participants winding up in a career field suggested by their outcomes on this measure (Worthen, White, Fan, & Sudweeks, 1999).

> *Author:* G. Frederic Kuder
> *Availability:* National Career Assessment Services, Inc.
> 601 Visions Parkway
> PO Box 277
> Adel, IA 50003
> (800) 314-8972
> http://www.kuder.com

Kuder General Interest Survey, Form E. The Kuder General Interest Survey (KGIS) was developed to measure the general interests of a younger population than the KOIS (Pope, 1995). The KGIS is written at a sixth-grade level and measures broad occupational themes in 10 areas, including Outdoor, Mechanical, Computational, Scientific, Persuasive, Artistic, Literary, Musical, Social Service, and Clerical. The instrument can be administered in small classroom settings or with larger groups and is self-scorable or machine scorable. Like the KOIS, clients select one of three activity choices they like the best, and the one they like the least, in an effort to elicit preferences. The KGIS is typically used by school counselors to stimulate general career discussion rather than focus on specific career decisions (Pope, 2002).

Author: G. Frederic Kuder

Availability: National Career Assessment Services, Inc.
                  601 Visions Parkway
                  PO Box 277
                  Adel, IA 50003
                  (800) 314-8972
                  http://www.kuder.com

Career Assessment Inventory.   The Career Assessment Inventory (CAI) was originally developed for use with clients interested in occupations that did not require a post–high school education (Kehoe, 1992). An enhanced version has broadened the measurement to include professional occupational interests but the CAI is targeted to non–baccalaureate degree seekers (Miner & Sellers, 2002). Using Holland's organizing themes as a foundation, this instrument is patterned after the Strong Interest Inventory and is intended for clients from high school through adult. The CAI is easily administered to groups, and machine-scoring service or local machine scoring are available.

Author: Charles B. Johansson

Availability: Pearson Assessments
                  5601 Green Valley Dr.
                  Bloomington, MN 55437
                  (800) 627-7271
                  (Fax) 800-632-9011
                  http://pearsonassessments.com

Assessments of Values

Closely related to interest and personality, values are integral components to client decision making. Values are generally defined as cognitive, emotional, and behavioral factors that manifest themselves as beliefs (Zunker & Osborn, 2002). Their role in career decision making can be highlighted through the use of a variety of established instruments in the field. These instruments may help counselors "stimulate discussions of values and their relationship to career decision-making" (Zunker & Osborn, 2002, p. 160). The previously discussed Values Scale and Salience Inventory from Super's life-span theory of career counseling, as well as the Minnesota Importance

Questionnaire from the theory of work adjustment, are excellent examples of values instruments available to career counselors. Other quality measures of values include:

Study of Values.   The Study of Values (SoV) is a broad inventory that measures the strength of preference in the areas of theoretical, economic, aesthetic, social, political, and religious values. This self-administered measure is intended for Grades 10 through adult, and comparative norms are provided by age and occupation. As such, assessing the Study of Values outcomes as they relate to clients' personal values can be a useful staring point for career discussion (Hood & Johnson, 1991).

Author: G. W. Allport, P. E. Vernon, and G. Lindzey
Availability: Riverside Publishing Company
                  425 Spring Lake Drive
                  Itasca, IL 60143-2079
                  (800) 323-9540
                  http://www.riverpub.com

Survey of Personal Values.   The Survey of Personal Values (SPV) is a measure of how individuals cope with daily life problems and stressors. Intended for high school and adult populations, this measure surveys values related to practical mindedness, achievement, variety, decisiveness, orderliness, and goal orientation. This self-administered instrument, which can be quickly hand scored, may be most useful in the area of personnel selection as well as career guidance (Erchul 1989). Its companion test, the Survey of Interpersonal Values, provides additional information related to the client's approach to interpersonal relationships.

Author: Leonard V. Gordon
Availability: Pearson Reid London House
                  Suite 1600
                  One North Dearborn
                  Chicago, IL 60602
                  (800) 922-7343
                  http://www.pearsonreidlondonhouse.com

Career Orientation Placement and Evaluation Survey.   The Career Orientation and Evaluation Survey (COPES) is an instrument intended for the junior high through community college population. One element of the larger Career Occupational Preference System (COPSystem), the COPES is designed to measure individual values that relate to occupational motivation (Wickwire, 2002). Seven work values are presented to clients using the following forced-choice options: investigative versus accepting, practical versus carefree, leadership versus supportive, orderliness versus flexibility, recognition versus privacy, aesthetic versus realistic, and social versus reserved. A self-interpretive scoring guide and profile relates scores to specific occupational clusters (Wickwire, 2002).

Author:	Lisa Knapp-Lee, Robert R. Knapp, and Lila F. Knapp
Availability:	Ed ITS
	P.O. Box 7234
	San Diego, California 92167
	(800) 416-1666
	http://www.edits.net/copes.html

Rokeach Values Survey.   The Rokeach Values Survey (RVS) is a two-part instrument that offers clients the opportunity to rank order lists of values to facilitate the discernment of important values for the client. "Terminal" or desired end-state values are ranked such as freedom, happiness, national security, and true friendship. Also ranked are "instrumental" values that indicate a client's beliefs about conduct such as ambition, cheerfulness, and courage. Through these rankings, the Rokeach Values Survey provides information useful for exploration of the client's value system as well as changes within the values system (Sanford, 1995).

Author:	Milton Rokeach
Availability:	Consulting Psychologists Press Inc.
	3803 E. Bayshore Road
	P.O. Box 10096
	Palo Alto, CA 94303
	(800) 624-1765
	http://cpp-db.com

Chronicle Career Quest.   The Chronicle Career Quest (CCQ) was developed to help students assess career opportunities. Structured in concert with the U.S. Employment Service *Guide for Occupational Exploration* (*GOE*), the instrument focuses on *12 GOE* clusters: Artistic, Scientific, Plants and Animal, Protective, Mechanical, Industrial, Business Detail, Selling, Accommodating, Humanitarian, Leading Influencing, and Physical Performing. The CCQ was designed for group administration with clients from seventh grade through adult and is interpreted through the resulting Career Paths Occupational Profile. Useful as both a stand-alone measure of vocational interest as well as a part of a larger career battery, the CCQ is able to direct clients toward various career interests and educate individuals on the career options available to them (Daniel & Thompson, 1995).

Author:	Chronicle Guidance Publications, Inc.
Availability:	Chronicle Guidance Publications, Inc.
	66 Aurora Street
	Moravia, NY 13118-1190
	(800) 899-0454
	http://www.chronicleguidance.com

Assessments of Career Maturity

Career maturity inventories grew out of developmental approaches to career counseling including Super's life-span theory. Career maturity generally refers to clients' ability to make reasoned career choices based on their skills, readiness, awareness, and experience (Levinson & Ohler, 1998). Zunker and Osborn (2002) cite this category of inventories as one of the greatest growth areas in the field of career assessment. The Career Thoughts Inventory from the theory of cognitive information processing is a career maturity assessment previously discussed in this chapter. Other examples include the following.

Career Maturity Inventory.   The Career Maturity Inventory (CMI) is designed to measure attitudes toward career choice as well as competency to make career decisions. The CMI is considered one of the foremost career maturity instruments (McDivitt, 2002). Intended for students in Grades 6 through 12, the CMI is made up of two separate 25-item tests. An Attitude Scale measures true or false responses to various work-related statements, and a Competence Test measures knowledge considered necessary to make effective career decisions. Suitable for group administration, the inventory can be hand-scored or sent to a machine-scoring service for interpretation. Scores on each test as well as responses to individual items can illuminate clients' needs and serve as the basis for counseling (Zunker & Osborn, 2002).

> *Author:*   John O. Crites and Mark L. Savikas
> *Availability:* Careerware
>   A Division of Bridges
>   808 Commerce Park Drive
>   Ogdensburg, NY 13669
>   (800) 281-1168
>   http://www.careerware.com

Career Factors Inventory.   The Career Factors Inventory (CFI) is designed to assess career indecision in clients age 13 to adult. It focuses on the emotional and informational factors influencing decision-making abilities (Chartrand & Robbins, 1990). Consisting of 21 response items using a Likert scale, the CFI is self-scorable and provides profile scores for scales titled Need for Career Information, Need for Knowledge, Career Choice Anxiety, and Generalized Indecisiveness. This simple and practical measure of career indecision can be swiftly administered and is helpful in counseling settings where readiness to make career decisions is a concern (D'Costa, 2001).

> *Author:*   Judy M. Chartrand, Steven B. Robbins, and Weston H. Morrill
> *Availability:* Consulting Psychologists Press Inc.
>   3803 E. Bayshore Road
>   P.O. Box 10096
>   Palo Alto, CA 94303
>   (800) 624-1765
>   http://cpp-db.com

Assessments of Personality

Measures of personality have long held interest for career counselors because they serve the utilitarian function of illuminating client traits, attitudes, and motivations. Such information is helpful to counselors working with clients about career choices and changes and attempting to predict career fit or satisfaction. Research is limited, however, regarding the relationship between personality factors and career satisfaction (Zunker & Osborn, 2002). Consequently, such instruments should be used with care, and never as a single measure of career need. Rather, personality assessments provide counselors and clients with a point of reference when exploring potential career options.

Sixteen Personality Factor Questionnaire & Personal Career Development Profile.   The Sixteen Personality Factor Questionnaire (16PF) is an objective test of a broad base of personality traits and attributes across 16 dimensions. Intended for use with high school, college, and adult populations, the 16PF is suitable for group or individual administration. The machine scored profile and interpretive report provide an abundance of information for the counselor working with career choice decisions. Supplemental to the 16PF is the Personal Career Development Profile (PCDP), a career-focused computer interpretation of the 16PF. This profile provides information about occupational interest patterns, leadership abilities, and career lifestyle preferences (Zunker & Osborn, 2002).

Author:	Raymond Cattell for 16PF
	Verne Walter for PCDP
Availability:	Institute for Personality and Ability Testing
	PO Box 1188
	Champaign, IL 61824-1188
	(800) 225-4728
	http://www.ipat.com

Myers-Briggs Type Indicator.   One of the most widely used measures of personality preferences available to counselors, the Myers-Briggs Type Indicator (MBTI) provides scores on the dichotomies of Extroversion-Introversion, Sensing-Intuition, Thinking-Feeling, and Judging-Perceiving (Myers & McCaulley, 1985). Available for both computer and hand scoring, the MBTI is best used in situations where the focus is on increasing a client's self-understanding (Mastrangelo, 2001). The manual provides information regarding occupational information and MBTI typology, which may prove valuable to the career-counseling process.

Author:	K. C. Briggs, I. B. Myers, M. H. McCaulley, N. L. Quenk,
	and A. L. Hammer
Availability:	Consulting Psychologists Press Inc.
	3803 E. Bayshore Road
	P.O. Box 10096
	Palo Alto, CA 94303
	(800) 624-1765
	http://cpp-db.com

Student Styles Questionnaire.   The Student Styles Questionnaire (SSQ) is designed to measure personal learning styles and preferences for junior and senior high school students. The instrument is based on Jungian constructs, making it similar in design to the Myers-Briggs Type Indicator. Designed for group or individual administration, with hand- and machine-scoring options, the SSQ provides scores for eight dimensions: Extroverted, Introverted, Practical, Imaginative, Thinking, Feeling, Organized, and Flexible. The SSQ is intended for use in school settings to identify learning styles, gifted students, and students with high-risk behaviors. Counselors may also use information gleaned from the instrument to facilitate vocational and educational choices (Schraw, 2001).

> *Authors:*   Thomas Oakland, Joseph Glutting, & Connie Horton
> *Availability:*   The Psychological Corporation
> 19500 Bulverde Rd.
> San Antonio, TX 78259
> 1-800-872-1726
> http://www.psychcorpcenter.com

Comprehensive Personality Profile.   The Comprehensive Personality Profile (CPP) was designed to measure compatibility between clients and specific occupations. A series of 88 true-false questions, this machine-scored instrument provides clients with an assessment of their personal characteristics and ideal characteristics of given jobs. The CPP is intended for adults, is machine scored, and can be administered to individuals or groups. The general focus of the CPP is on occupations in the service industry, including positions in sales or customer service (Cohn, 2001).

> *Author:*   Larry L. Craft
> *Availability:*   Wonderlic, Inc.
> 1795 N. Butterfield Rd.
> Libertyville, IL 60048-1238
> (800) 323-3742
> http://www.wonderlic.com

Jackson Personality Inventory—Revised: The Jackson Personality Inventory-Revised (JPI-R) measures a range of personality variables in adolescents and adults. An intended primary use of this measure is career counseling related to hiring decisions (Zachar, 1998). The instrument is divided into five clusters: Analytical, Emotional, Extroverted, Opportunistic, and Dependable. The interpretive information found in the computer scored profile provides a base for career counseling.

> *Author:*   Douglas Jackson
> *Availability:*   Sigma Assessment Systems
> PO Box 610984
> Port Huron, MI 48061-0984
> (800) 265-1285
> http://www.sigmaassessmentsystems.com

Computer-Assisted Career Guidance Systems (CAGS)

With the advent of widely available assessment technology, career assessments built on computer foundations have emerged as a specialized area of career counseling. Often used to supplement existing career counseling methods, CAGS may be used in test administration, scoring, profiling, interpreting, or multimedia interpretation (Sampson, 2000). CAGS are beneficial to career counselors through their ability to rapidly and efficiently update large quantities of information not feasible through paper-pencil instruments (Gati, Saka, & Krausz, 2001). In a recent review of a comprehensive compilation of career assessment tools, roughly half of the instruments utilized computer assistance in some form (Sampson, Lumsden, & Carr, 2002).

It must be noted that CAGS best function in addition to the counselor providing services to the client, not as a replacement for the counselor (Sampson, Lumsden, & Carr, 2002). Counselors may best serve clients by explaining the computer application prior to testing, intervening at selected points during testing to ensure the client is gaining maximum benefit from the process, and following up during the interpretive phase to assure the client integrates new information (Zunker & Osborn, 2002). As with any assessment tool, counselors must be thoroughly familiar with CAGS before using them in practice. Some of the more popular computer-based tools for career counseling are presented here.

Discover.   DISCOVER is a broad application to career planning for clients ages high school through adult. Clients enter "halls" within a virtual "World of Work" center, where they complete self-assessments, choose occupations, plan their educations, and plan for work (Zunker & Osborn, 2002). Clients are assessed using the Inventory of Work Related Abilities and the Inventory of Work Preferences (ACT, 2001). The results are interpreted through the World-Of-Work Map, an extension of Holland's hexagon, to provide a comprehensive yet easy-to-understand overview of the work world (ACT, 2001).

> *Availability:*   ACT
> 500 ACT Drive
> P.O. Box 168
> Iowa City, Iowa 52243-0168
> (319) 337-1000
> http://www.act.org

Choices CT.   Choices CT is intended for clients in postsecondary institutions seeking ongoing educational or occupational direction. Using the Choices CT Road Map, the user participates in guided career exploration. The program connects to an Internet component allowing clients access to college links, financial aid sources, and over 650 Occupational Information Network (O*net) occupations (Zunker & Osborn, 2002). Site licensing makes Choices CT an affordable option for school and college counselors.

Availability: Bridges.com
808 Commerce Park Drive
Ogdensburg, NY 13669
(800) 281-1168
http://www.bridges.com

Sigi Plus System of Interactive Guidance Information.   The SIGI PLUS system provides counselors with a more comprehensive assessment tool for career decision making (Zunker & Osborn, 2002). Created with multiple modules, the use of which can be varied to meet the needs of the test taker or client, SIGI PLUS contains a self-assessment, a search for compatible career options, and information needed to prepare for, and plan, tentative career plans (Kivlighan & Johnston, 1994). Updated annually by Educational Testing Service, SIGI PLUS is available in PC, Internet, and institutional intranet versions (Zunker & Osborn, 2002).

Availability: SIGI Plus
Educational Testing Service
Rosedale Road
Princeton, NJ 08541
1-800-257-7444
http://www.ets.org/sigi

Career Key.   The Career Key is available free via the Internet. Clients can take the assessment online or print and complete a paper version. Because the Career Key is offered as a public service by the author, duplication of the instrument for group administration is possible (Jones, 2003). Clients rate 24 statements about their activities, values, interests, and preferences, as well as their interest in 42 occupations. The results are then interpreted in terms of Holland's six personality types as they relate to career decision making (Levinson & Zeman, 2002). The Website offers supplemental information useful to career counselors, including the *Career Key Professional Manual* and career information resources (Jones, 2003).

Author: Lawrence K. Jones
Availability: North Carolina State University
520C Poe Hall
PO Box 7801
Raleigh, NC, 27695
(919) 515-6359
http://www.ncsu.edu/careerkey

Coin.   The COIN Career Guidance System was developed to assist high school through adult populations with a series of career exploration tools. The instruments provided include a self-assessment and the ability to match clients to occupations specific to their interests and geographical location. Additionally, this product has the capability to integrate scores from other career inventories the client may have taken, such as the SDS, CDM, ASVAB, and COPS/CAPS.

> *Availability:* COIN Educational Products
> 3361 Executive Parkway
> Suite 302
> Toledo Ohio 43606
> (800) 274.8515
> http://coin3.com

Magellan. Magellan, an interactive CAGS for school-based application, contains eight assessments related to career choice. Developed to pique student interest in career decision-making, this lively tool contains occupational video clips, career biographies, and a large occupational database. Also linked to the *Guide for Occupational Exploration* and the *Occupational Outlook Handbook,* Magellan is most appropriate for middle and high school career-counseling settings.

> *Availability:* Valpar International Corporation
> 2450 W. Ruthrauff Road, Suite 180
> Tucson, AZ 85705
> (800) 633-3321
> http://valparint.com

Qualitative Assessment

While the majority of this chapter is dedicated to the use of standardized instruments, such approaches may leave clients feeling more like test takers than active participants in their own career futures (Croteau & Slaney, 1994). A more flexible and unique process of career counseling and assessment can occur through the use of qualitative methods. Typically presented in the form of simulations, games, or card-sorting activities, qualitative methods are emerging as feasible options for career counselors (Croteau & Slaney, 1994). Goldman (1992) outlines several general traits of qualitative tools, including their more informal manner, the minimal need for statistical expertise, the enhanced level of client involvement, a tendency to be open-ended and flexible, and applicability to group settings.

Counselors must take care when selecting qualitative methods. These exercises are not intended to replace standardized assessment measures (Goldman, 1992). Qualitative methods require that counselors possess a unique knowledge base related to the use of these tools. Additionally, excellent interpersonal skills are needed due to the increased dependence on the collaborative client-counselor relationship (Okacha, 1998). Finally, the lack of standardized interpretation assistance for qualitative activities places the responsibility for facilitating career exploration and decision making on the counselor (Goldman, 1992).

Numerous methods that are traditionally considered therapeutic may be used by career counselors as qualitative assessments. One example is Life Lines, a system in which clients recall and chart significant life events, resulting in individualized descriptions of client interests and values (Goldman, 1992). Likewise, an occupational Genogram elicits information about career choices in the client's family of origin (Okocha, 1998). A third type of qualitative measure is the card sort.

Career Values Card Sort.   The Career Values Card Sort Planning Kit was designed for adults in order to foster an understanding of values critical to client satisfaction. During the activity, the client sorts 41 occupational values into degrees of interest. These prioritized values are then compared to corresponding career exploration concerns that facilitate the client's awareness of how values impact work decisions. This learning activity is most helpful as an exploratory measure rather than a predictive tool (Kinnier, 1998).

> *Author:*   Richard L. Knowdell
> *Availability:*   Career Research and Testing, Inc.
>   3629 W. MacArthur Blvd. #201
>   Santa Ana, CA 92704
>   (800) 888-4945
>   http://www.careertrainer.com

Assessments of Special Populations

Career counselors need to be aware of their client's special needs, cultural backgrounds, and experiences and how these relate to the formation of his or her vocational identities. What may appear typical of the majority culture in our society might not be generalizable to those who are different in race, language, acculturation, and geography. Career counselors must take into consideration the characteristics of a career instrument's norming group. They must seek out research supporting its relevance with their targeted population as well as engage in a thorough analysis of the implications of intervening with this particular instrument with their particular group.

Earlier in this chapter, the importance of comparing and contrasting the makeup of a test's norming group with a client's demographic profile was emphasized. Oftentimes counselors must make subjective decisions regarding the relevance of a particular career inventory or technique and its applicability to their current client population. Frequently, few guidelines are offered to determine when a client's characteristics are too divergent for use with a particular career assessment tool.

Leung (1996) offered six guidelines for career assessment with ethnic minorities but may be applicable for testing special populations in general. First, counselors must have adequate training in multicultural counseling including awareness of the most recent research on cross-cultural assessment for ethnic minorities. Second, test selection must ensue only after a thorough assessment of client needs and relating these to the purpose, structure, norms, psychometric properties, and limitations of each instrument. Third, assessment of the cultural histories of minority clients must recognize the large within-group differences generic to each ethnic group. Fourth, counselors must be aware of the client's verbal and nonverbal responses when test data is presented to ensure proper test interpretations by each client. Fifth, assessment data, scores, and individual item responses can be used as stimuli to promote further exploration of the client's career development. Finally, career assessment can serve to empower clients to take control of their lives through the role they play and the choices they make in the career counseling process.

Some commonly used instruments already discussed in this chapter that have some research supporting their potential appropriateness with multicultural populations include the Strong Interest Inventory, Self-Directed Search, My Vocational Situation and Career Maturity Inventory (Leung, 1996). Other instruments that may prove useful when working with multicultural populations are acculturation inventories such as the Cross-Cultural Adaptability Inventory (CCAI; Kelley & Myers, 1992) and the Suinn-Lew Asian Self-Identity Acculturation Scale (SL-ASIA; Suinn, Rickard-Figueroa, Lew, & Virgil, 1987).

Author: Colleen Kelley & Judith Meyers (CCAI)
Availability: Pearson Assessments
                 5601 Green Valley Dr.
                 Bloomington, MN 55437
                 (800) 627-7271
                 (Fax) 800-632-9011
                 http://pearsonassessments.com

Finally, one other instrument that may be applicable to not only multicultural clients, but also those populations with varying degrees of physical, emotional, verbal, and cognitive limitations is the Wide Range Interest and Opinion Test.

Wide Range Interest and Opinion Test.   The Wide Range Interest and Opinion Test (WRIOT) is a pictorial instrument intended for educationally or culturally disadvantaged clients or with those whose severe disabilities render other interest inventories unfeasible (Zunker & Osborn, 2002). Similar to other interest inventories, the test-taker selects most and least preferred choices from a series of triads. The stimulus items were redrawn in the late 1970s to enhance inclusion of gender and cultural minorities (Hsu, 1985). The instrument may be administered individually or in groups, is machine-scored, and is intended for ages 5 to adult. Results provide scores for 18 occupational clusters such as art, office work, and biological science (Zunker & Osborn, 2002).

Authors: Joseph Jastak and Sarah Jastak
Availability: Wide Range
                P.O. Box 3410
                15 Ashley Place, Suite 1A
                Wilmington, DE 19804
                (800) 221-9728
                www.widerange.com

SUMMARY

From standardized to qualitative tests and from computer-assisted to pen-and-paper formats, career assessment instruments are available in a variety of forms to meet the unique needs of career counselors and their clients. While no one type is superior, each has its own advantages and limitations. Counselors must be well-informed consumers of career assessment products to make appropriate decisions regarding their applicability to the unique needs of their clients.

CAREER ASSESSMENT WEBSITES

http://www.acinet.org/acinet/library.asp?category=1.7

Comprehensive site providing links to basic employment outlook and trend data, assessment resources, and local job banks.

http://www.apa.org/science/fairtestcode.html

The Code for Fair Test Practice in Education provides guidelines for professionals and consumers of testing services.

http://www.careerbookstore.com/assessment_testing.shtml

Listing of career resource materials, including self-assessments as well as those administered by professionals.

http://www.careercc.com/links/

Includes links to instructional materials, reference books, and numerous assessment tools, including purchasing information.

http://www.ncda.org/

Links to the homepage of the National Career Development Association, a division of the American Counseling Association, which provides support and resources to career professionals and the public.

http://www.schoolcounselor.org/

Includes a variety of support materials for counselors practicing in a school setting.

http://www.apa.org/science/fairtestcode.html

The Code of Fair Testing Practices in Education provides guidelines for professionals and consumers of testing services.

REFERENCES

ACT. (2001). DISCOVER a world of possibilities: Research support for DISCOVER assessment components. Retrieved November 15, 2003, from http://www.act.org/discover/pdf/research_support.pdf

Albanese, M. A. (2001). Review of the Career Occupational Preference System Professional Level Interest Inventory (COPS-P). In B. S. Plake & J. C. Impara (Eds.), *Fourteenth mental measurements yearbook* (Vol. 65, pp. 225–227). Lincoln, NE: Buros Institute of Mental Measurements.

American Counseling Association. (1995). *American counseling association code of ethics and standards of practice*. Alexandria, VA: Author.

American Psychological Association. (2002). *American Psychological Association ethical principles of psychologists and codes of conduct*. Washington, DC: Author.

Benson, P. G. (1988). Minnesota Importance Questionnaire. In J. T. Kapes & M. M. Mastie (Eds.), *A counselor's guide to career assessment instruments* (2nd ed., pp. 144–149). Alexandria, VA: National Career Development Association.

Borgen, F. H., Weiss, D. J., Tinsley, H. E. A., Dawis, R. V., & Lofquist, L. H. (1968). The measurement of occupational reinforcer patterns. *Minnesota Studies in Vocational Rehabilitation*, XXV. Minneapolis: University of Minnesota.

Chartrand, J. M., & Robbins, S. B. (1990). Using multidimensional career decision instruments to assess career decidedness and implementation. *Career Development Quarterly*, *39*, 166–178.

Cohn, S. (2001). Review of the Comprehensive Personality Profile. In B. S. Plake & J. C. Impara (Eds.), *Fourteenth mental measurements yearbook* (Vol. 92, pp. 310–313). Lincoln, NE: Buros Institute of Mental Measurements.

Cronbach, L. J. (1951). Coefficient alpha and the internal structure of tests. *Psychometrika*, *16*, 197–334.

Croteau, J. M., & Slaney, R. B. (1994). Two methods of exploring interests: A comparison of outcomes. *Career Development Quarterly*, *42*, 252–262.

Daniel, L. G., & Thompson, D. (1995). Review of the Chronicle Career Quest™. In J. C. Conoley & J. C. Impara (Eds.), *Twelfth Mental Measurements Yearbook* (Vol. 79, pp. 193–197). Lincoln, NE: Buros Institute of Mental Measurements.

Dawis, R. V. (1980). Personnel assessment from the perspective of the theory of work adjustment. *Public Personnel Management*, *9*, 268–273.

D'Costa, A. (2001). Review of the Career Factors Inventory. In B. S. Plake & J. C. Impara (Eds.), *Fourteenth Mental Measurements Yearbook* (Vol. 63, pp. 219–221). Lincoln, NE: Buros Institute of Mental Measurements.

Donlon, T. F. (1998). Review of the Wonderlic Basic Skills Test. In J. C. Impara & B. S. Plake (Eds.), *Thirteenth Mental Measurements Yearbook* (Vol. 362, pp. 1137–1139). Lincoln, NE: Buros Institute of Mental Measurements.

Drummond, R. J. (2000). *Appraisal procedures for counselors and helping professionals* (4th ed.). Upper Saddle River, NJ: Merrill.

Drummond, R. J., & Ryan, C. W. (1995). *Career counseling: A developmental approach*. Englewood Cliffs, NJ: Prentice Hall.

Erchul, W. P. (1989). Review of the Survey of Personal Values. In B. S. Plake & J. C. Ingram (Eds.), *Tenth Mental Measurements Yearbook* (Vol. 354, pp. 800–801). Lincoln, NE: Buros Institute of Mental Measurements.

Fontaine, J. H. (1999). Review of the Career Thoughts Inventory. In B. S. Plake & J. C. Impara (Eds.), *Fourteenth Mental Measurements Yearbook* (Vol. 63, pp. 228–230). Lincoln, NE: Buros Institue of Mental Measurements.

Gati, I., Saka, N., & Krausz, M. (2001). "Should I use a computer-assisted career guidance system?" It depends on where your career decision-making difficulties lie. *British Journal of Guidance and Counselling*, *29*, 301–321.

Goldman, L. (1992). Qualitative assessment: An approach for counselors. *Journal of Counseling and Development*, *70*, 616–622.

Educational Testing Service. *GRE for Test Takers*. (n.d.). Retreived November 11, 2003, from http://www.gre.org

Hanna, G. S., & Hughey, K. F. (2002). Wonderlic Basic Skills Test. In J. T. Kapes & E. A. Whitfield (Eds.), *A counselor's guide to career assessment instruments* (4th ed., pp. 178–182). Alexandria, VA: National Career Development Association.

Harmon, L. W., Hansen, J. C., Borgen, F. H., & Hammer, A. L. (1994). *Strong Interest Inventory: Applications and technical guide.* Palo Alto, CA: Consulting Psychologists Press.

Harrington, T. F., & Schafer, W. D. (1996). A comparison of self-reported abilities and occupational ability patterns across occupations. *Measurement and Evaluation in Counseling and Development, 28,* 180–191.

Herman, J. (1998). Review of the Vocational Interest Inventory and Exploration. In J. C. Impara & B. S. Plake (Eds.), *Thirteenth Mental Measurements Yearbook* (Vol. 357, pp. 1083–1084). Lincoln, NE: Buros Institute of Mental Measurements.

Holland, J. L. (1985). *Vocational Preferences Inventory Manual.* Palo Alto, CA: Consulting Psychologists Press.

Holland, J. L. (1992). *Making vocational choices* (2nd ed.). Odessa, FL: Psychological Assessment Resources.

Holland, J. L. (1994a). *The occupation finder—Form R* (4th ed.). Lutz, FL: Psychological Assessment Resources.

Holland, J. L. (1994b). *Self-directed search: Assessment booklet—Form R* (4th ed.). Lutz, FL: Psychological Assessment Resources.

Holland, J. L. (1994c). *You and your career—Form R* (4th ed.). Lutz, FL: Psychological Assessment Resources.

Holland, J. L., Fritzsche, B. A., & Powell, A. B. (1997). *Self-directed search: Technical manual.* Lutz, FL: Psychological Assessment Resources.

Holland, J. L., & Gottfredson, G. D. (1994). *Career attitudes and strategies inventory: An inventory for understanding adult careers.* Odessa, FL: Psychological Assessment Resources.

Holland, J. L., Powell, A. B., & Fritzsche, B. A. (1997). *Self-directed search: Professional user's guide.* Lutz, FL: Psychological Assessment Resources.

Hood, A. B., & Johnson, R.W. (1991). *Assessment in counseling: A guide to the use of psychological assessment procedures.* Alexandria, VA: American Counseling Association.

Hsu, L. M. (1985). Review of the Wide Range Interest-Opinion Test. In J. V. Mitchell (Ed.), *Ninth Mental Measurements Yearbook* (Vol. 2, pp. 1737–1739). Lincoln, NE: Buros Institute of Mental Measurements.

Ivens, S. H. (1995). Review of the Miller Analogies Test. In J. C. Conoley & J. C. Impara (Eds.), *Twelfth Mental Measurements Yearbook* (Vol. 235, pp. 617–620). Lincoln, NE: Buros Institute of Mental Measurements.

Joint Committee on Testing Practices. (1988). *Code of fair testing practices in education.* Washington, DC: Author.

Jones, L. K. (2003). The Career Key. Available online at: http://www.careerkey.org. Retrieved March 13, 2005.

Kapes, J. T. & Mastie, M. M. (2002). *A counselor's guide to career assessment instruments* (4th ed.). Alexandria, VA: National Career Development Association.

Keesling, J. W. & Healy, C. C. (1988). The General Aptitude Test Battery. In J. T. Kapes & M. M. Mastie (Eds.), *A counselor's guide to career assessment instruments* (2nd ed., pp. 71–75). Alexandria, VA: National Career Development Association.

Kehoe, J. F. (1992). Review of the Career Assessment Inventory. In B. S. Plake & J. C. Ingram (Eds.), *Eleventh Mental Measurements Yearbook* (Vol. 59, pp. 148–151). Lincoln, NE: Buros Institute of Mental Measurements.

Kelly, K. R. (2002). Kuder Occupational Interest Survey. In J. T. Kapes & E. A. Whitfield (Eds.), *A counselor's guide to career assessment instruments* (4th ed., pp. 265–275). Alexandria, VA: National Career Development Association.

Kelly, C., & Meyers, J. (1992). The cross-cultural Adaptability Inventory (CCAI). Minneapolis, MN: National Computer Systems.

Kinnier, R. T. (1998). Review of the Career Values Card Sort. In B. S. Plake & J. C. Impara (Eds.), *Thirteenth Mental Measurements Yearbook* (Vol. 47, pp. 183–185). Lincoln, NE: Buros Institute of Mental Measurements.

Kivlighan, D. M., Jr., & Johnston, J. A. (1994). Who benefits from computerized counseling? *Journal of Counseling and Development, 72,* 289–293.

Krumboltz, J. D. (1991). *Manual for the career beliefs inventory.* Palo Alto, CA: Consulting Psychologists Press.

Krumboltz, J. D. (1994). The Career Beliefs Inventory. *Journal of Counseling and Development, 72,* 424–429.

Krumboltz, J. D. (1998). Debate: Counsellor actions needed for the new career perspective. *British Journal of Guidance and Counselling, 26,* 559–565.

Kuder, G. F., & Richardson, M. W. (1937). The theory of estimation of test reliability. *Psychometrika, 2,* 151–160.

Law, J. (1998). Review of the Vocational Interest Inventory and Exploration. In J. C. Impara & B. S. Plake (Eds.), *Thirteenth Mental Measurements Yearbook* (Vol. 408, pp. 1083–1084). Lincoln, NE: Buros Institute of Mental Measurements.

Layton, W. L. (1992). Review of the Minnesota Importance Questionnaire. In J. T. Kramer & J. C. Conoley (Eds.), *Eleventh Mental Measurements Yearbook* (Vol. 243 pp. 544–546). Lincoln, NE: Buros Institute of Mental Measurements.

Leung, S. A. (1996). Vocational assessment across cultures. In L. A. Suzuki, P. J. Meller, & J. G. Ponterotto (Eds.), *Handbook of Multicultural Assessment* (pp. 475–508). San Francisco: Josssey-Bass.

Levinson, E. M., & Ohler, D. L. (1998). Six approaches to the assessment of career maturity. *Journal of Counseling and Development, 76,* 475–483.

Levinson, E. M., & Zeman, H. L. (2002). A critical evaluation of the Web-based version of the Career Key. *Career Development Quarterly, 5,* 26–36.

Mastrangelo, P. M. (2001). Review of the Myers-Briggs Type Indicator. In B. S. Plake & J. C. Impara (Eds.), *Fourteenth Mental Measurements Yearbook* (Vol. 251, pp. 818–819). Lincoln, NE: Buros Institute of Mental Measurements.

McDivitt, P. J. (2002). Career Maturity Inventory. In J. T. Kapes & E. A. Whitfield (Eds.), *A counselor's guide to career assessment instruments* (4th ed., 336–342). Alexandria, VA: National Career Development Association.

Miner, C. U., & Sellers, S. M. (2002) Career Assessment Inventory. In J. T. Kapes & E. A. Whitfield (Eds.), *A counselor's guide to career assessment instruments* (4th ed., pp. 202–209). Alexandria, VA: National Career Development Association.

Mitchell, K. E., Levin, A. S., & Krumboltz, J. D. (1999). Planned happenstance: Constructing unexpected career opportunities. *Journal of Counseling and Development, 77,* 115–124.

Myers, I. B., & McCaulley, M. H. (1985). *Manual: A guide to the development and use of the Myers-Briggs Type Indicator.* Palo Alto, CA: Consulting Psychologists Press.

National Board of Certified Counselors. (1997). *National board for certified counselor code of ethics.* Charlotte, NC: Author.

Okocha, A. A. G. (1998). Using qualitative appraisal strategies in career counseling. *Journal of Employment Counseling, 35,* 151–160.

Pennock-Román, M. (1988). Differential Aptitude Test. In J. T. Kapes & M. M. Mastie (Eds.), *A counselor's guide to career assessment instruments* (2nd ed., pp. 65–68). Alexandria, VA: National Career Development Association.

Peterson, G. W., Sampson, J. P., Jr., Reardon, R. C., & Lenz, J. G. (1996). Becoming career problem solvers and decision makers: A cognitive information processing approach. In D. Brown &

L. Brooks (Eds.), *Career choice and development* (3rd. ed., pp. 423–475). San Francisco, CA: Jossey-Bass.

Pope, M. (1995). Review of the Kuder General Interest Survey. In J. C. Conoley & J. C. Impara (Eds.), *Twelfth Mental Measurements Yearbook* (Vol. 209, pp. 543–545). Lincoln, NE: Buros Institute of Mental Measurements.

Pope, M. (2002). Kuder General Interest Survey. In J. T. Kapes & E. A. Whitfield (Eds.), *A counselor's guide to career assessment instruments* (4th ed., pp. 257–264). Alexandria, VA: National Career Development Association.

Roe, A. (1956). *Psychology of occupations.* New York: Wiley.

Roe, A. (1957). Early determinants of vocational choice. *Journal of Counseling Psychology, 4,* 212–217.

Sampson, J. P., Lumsden, J. A., & Carr, D. L. (2002). Computer-assisted career assessment. In J. T. Kapes & E. A. Whitfield (Eds.), *A counselor's guide to career assessment instruments* (4th ed., pp. 202–209). Alexandria, VA: National Career Development Association.

Sampson, J. P., Peterson, G. W., Lenz, J. G., Reardon, R. C., & Saunders, D. E. (1996a). *Career thoughts inventory.* Odessa, FL: Psychological Assessment Resources.

Sampson, J. P., Peterson, G. W., Lenz, J. G., Reardon, R. C., & Saunders, D. E. (1996b). *Improving your career thoughts: A workbook for the career thoughts inventory.* Odessa, FL: Psychological Assessment Resources.

Sampson, J. P., Jr. (2000). Using the Internet to enhance testing in counseling. *Journal of Counseling and Development, 78,* 348–356.

Sanford, E. E. (1995). Review of the Rokeach Values Scale. In J. C. Conoley & J. C. Impara (Eds.), *Twelfth Mental Measurements Yearbook* (Vol. 334, pp. 879–880). Lincoln, NE: Buros Institute of Mental Measurements.

Schoenrade, P. (2002). Review of the Values Scale. In J. T. Kapes & E. A. Whitfield (Eds.), *A counselor's guide to career assessment instruments* (4th ed., pp. 298–302). Alexandria, VA: National Career Development Association.

Schraw, G. (2001). Review of the Student Styled Questionnaire. In B. S. Plake & J. C. Impara (Eds.), *Fourteenth Mental Measurements Yearbook* (Vol. 375, pp. 1197–1199). Lincoln, NE: Buros Institute of Mental Measurements.

Sharf, R. (2002). *Applying career development theory to counseling* (3rd ed.). Pacific Grove, CA: Brooks/Cole.

Suinn, R. M., Rickard-Figueroa, K., Lew, S., & Virgil, P. (1987). The Suinn-Lew Asian Self- Identity Acculturation Scale: An initial report. *Educational and Psychological Measurement, 47,* 401–407.

Super, D. E., & Osborne, W. L. (1992). Developmental career assessment and counseling: The C-DAC model. *Journal of Counseling and Development, 71,* 74–83.

Thompson, J. M., & Blain, M. D. (1992). Presenting feedback on the Minnesota Importance Questionnaire and the Minnesota Satisfaction Questionnaire. *Career Development Quarterly, 41,* 62–66.

U.S. Department of Labor. (1991). *Dictionary of occupational titles* (4th ed., rev. Stock No. 1191-295-302). Washington, DC: U.S. Government Printing Office.

U.S. Military Entrance Processing Command. (2002). *ASVAB Student and Parent Guide.* North Chicago, IL: Author.

Walsh, B. D. (1995). The Career Beliefs Inventory: A review and critique. *Measurement and Evaluation in Counseling and Development, 28,* 61–62.

Wang, L. (2002). Differential Aptitude Test. In J. T. Kapes & E. A. Whitfield (Eds.), *A counselor's guide to career assessment instruments* (4th ed., pp. 123–131). Alexandria, VA: National Career Development Association.

Wickwire, P. N. (2002). COPSystem. In J. T. Kapes & E. A. Whitfield (Eds.), *A counselor's guide to career assessment instruments* (4th ed., pp. 210–217). Alexandria, VA: National Career Development Association.

Worthen, B. R., White, K. R., Fan, X., & Sudweeks, R. R. (1999). *Measurement and assessment in schools* (2nd ed.). New York: Longman.

Zachar, P. (1998). Review of the Jackson Personality Inventory—Revised. In B. S. Plake & J. C. Impara (Eds.), *Thirteenth Mental Measurements Yearbook* (Vol. 162, pp. 555–561). Lincoln, NE: Buros Institute of Mental Measurements.

Zunker, V. G., & Osborn, D. S. (2002). *Using assessment results for career counseling* (6th ed.). Pacific Grove, CA: Brooks/Cole.

Zytowski, D. G. (1988). Salience Inventory. In J. T. Kapes & M. M. Mastie (Eds.), *A counselor's guide to career assessment instruments* (2nd ed., pp. 150–154). Alexandria, VA: National Career Development Association.

CHAPTER 6

USING INFORMATION AND TECHNOLOGY IN CAREER COUNSELING

DEBORAH P. BLOCH

University of San Francisco

The Association of Computer-Based Systems for Career Information (ACSCI) was formed in 1978. At that time, a few states and locales and a few publishers had begun to offer information on occupations and colleges by means of computers. This was before the invention of the personal computer or the advent of the World Wide Web. The systems ran on mainframe computers, which, generally speaking, had less computing power than today's laptops. The computers were connected to teletype-like printers, primarily in high schools, by means of modems. The modem itself was about the size of a shoebox and had two rubber cups on top. A telephone handset placed with the earpiece and speaker in the cups provided the link between the mainframe computer and the terminal, which, incidentally, could only print in capital letters.

This brave movement to provide career information using technology began despite limitations no one would tolerate today. Because the mainframes had limited memory and the career systems were often considered secondary users, every bit of information was valuable. That is a literal statement, with the emphasis on the word *bit*. The number of bits, translated into bytes, and from there to words and numbers, had to be calculated precisely. Similarly, the number of users dialing in at any one time was limited by the number of telephone lines the mainframe could accommodate. Furthermore the equipment was expensive—and exotic. An individual school or the occasional library certainly did not have more than one terminal. Therefore, use by students and others was carefully rationed. Counselors were completely unfamiliar with all aspects of the systems. They had to be trained in "keyboarding," in placing the telephone receiver in the model, and, most important, in changing their roles from information disseminators to facilitators of information analysis. Finally, the systems were fragile. A good thunderstorm usually meant the end of communication for the day.

Twenty-five years later, as this chapter is being written, the challenge has shifted from scarcity to overwhelming riches. Not only have many of the original systems continued to operate and expand in content, in technological savvy, and in types of users served, but the free-flowing World Wide Web has also added dimensions and layers of information previously unthought of. The challenge to understanding the riches of career information is met in two ways in this chapter. First, the need for career information is placed in a theoretical perspective. This perspective presents information as essential in a world in which individuals strive to find order in a dynamic, apparently random universe. The perspective goes beyond the idea of information as good in itself, instead situating information within the relatively new ideas about career development drawn from complexity and chaos theories (Bloch, 2005). Second, three kinds of resources, with specific examples, are described: organized systems, job-search sites, and corporate sites. The organized systems are themselves further grouped according to comprehensive national and state-based systems, occupational information systems, and educational information systems. Third, the chapter includes information about research and evaluation as related to computer-based career information.

THE NEED FOR CAREER INFORMATION— A THEORETICAL PERSPECTIVE

The Theory: Complexity, Connections, and Career

Fixed in school or work, people are thrust into change. The change may come from an expected source, such as graduation from high school, choosing a new job, or beginning retirement, or from an unexpected source, such as a layoff or firing, a change in family circumstance, or an illness. These latter changes may seem unnatural and unasked for. Moreover, whether anticipated or not, changes often provoke uncertainty and discomfort. People feel adrift. They believe there is some sequence of work roles that they are expected to follow. They believe that others make career decisions based on logical links of past experience and expect this logic of them as well, but that is not what most people experience. The reality of most careers consists of a tension between order and disorder. This tension is at the heart of living systems, systems as diverse as single-cell organisms and the evolution of species. Indeed, it is this tension between order and disorder of the individual living entity as well as its place in a completely interconnected universe that is explored and explained through chaos and complexity theories.

Chaos and complexity theories focus on entities and their relationships. These theories, as applied to career development, enable us to see each career as a complex adaptive entity—a living system. This set of theories enables career practitioners to understand and explain what otherwise appears to be the messiness of life by revealing the underlying order in what otherwise appears to be random. In the section that follows, 11 characteristics of complex adaptive entities are identified and applied to career development (Bloch, 2005).

1. Autopoesis.   Complex adaptive entities have the ability to maintain themselves, although their components and even their shapes may change. In this sense, they have life. Life is the ability of the entity to maintain itself, or *autopoesis*. Life is self-organizing, not controlled externally. Life is also the ability to adapt to changing environments.

Autopoesis or self-regeneration in career development.   People continually reinvent their careers, moving freely among, within, and outside the macro-cycles and roles previously identified as the anticipated career paths of "healthy" individuals. Whether or not people receive career counseling or participate in any career education programs, they have careers. This is not to suggest that the efforts of the career-counseling profession are in vain or even unnecessary, but to point out that the original idea that career development is a natural, internal process is borne out by the acceptance of the career as a complex adaptive entity.

2. Open Exchange.   Entities are *open*. They maintain themselves through the continuous flow and interchange of components or energy. There is an ongoing interplay of the internal and external.

Open exchange in career development.   Career requires a living human body, in which it functions in continuing exchange with all the entities of that body. In addition, career cannot take place for the individual alone. By its very nature, career requires participation of give and take in the outside world, that is, in labor markets. These relationships are complex and dynamic but nevertheless hark back to the foundational work of Frank Parsons (1909).

3. Networks.   In these exchanges, entities are part of *networks*. Any entity is part of many networks, which can be depicted, not only as concentric circles, but also as ever-widening links to nodes beyond itself. At the same time, a particular entity may have networks operating within it.

Networks in career development.   The relationships among the physical, psychological, neural, and spiritual aspects of the individual are neither unitary nor linear, but rather exist in interweaving networks. So, too, career is an entity within the system of the individual, as well as part of the surrounding networks of education, occupations, industries, particular employers, cultures, the needs of the community, and the local and global economies—to mention just a few. These are ongoing relationships, which operate, affect, and are effected by the entity of each career.

4. Fractals.   Entities are parts, or *fractals*, of other entities. Each fractal has the entirety of the organism within its shape, and every organism is a fractal of the universe. Fractals reveal themselves as irregular structures that are self-similar at different scales of manifestation (Mandelbrot, 1982). Like a hologram, fractals show the same features at different levels of examination, from the closest look at the smallest elements to the most distant view of what appears to be the entire organism.

Fractals in career development.   The career of any person is a fractal of that person's entire life experience. Because career is a fractal of one's life, in examining a career, one sees the patterns and dynamics of the whole life. In addition, the careers of many people are fractals of the workforce experience. They are fractals in that the parts are similar to the whole.

5. Phase Transitions.   Entities are dynamic. In the constant exchange of forms, components, and energy, they move between order and chaos. These *phase transitions* are comparable to the movement of water among its three phases: liquid, solid or ice, and gas or steam. Phase transitions are the opportunity for creativity and the emergence of new forms.

Phase transitions in career development.   From a state of being fixed in school or work, one is thrown into change, thus moving from order to chaos. These career changes occur because of any combination of the relational networks busily and openly in exchange with the entity of career. In this model, graduation, being fired, ambition, illness, the influence of significant others, and virtually any other event are all potential sources of phase transitions.

6. Fitness Peaks.   During phase transitions, entities seek *fitness peaks*, that is, the state that will yield the greatest chance of survival. Kauffman (1995) wrote in *At Home in the Universe:*

> I suspect that the fate of all complex adapting entities in the biosphere—from single cells to economies—is to evolve to a natural state between order and chaos, a grand compromise between structure and surprise. . . . The edge-of-chaos then also arises as a potential general law. In scaling the top of the fitness peaks, adapting populations that are too methodical and timid in their explorations are likely to get stuck in the foothills, thinking they have reached as high as they can go, but a search that is too wide ranging is also likely to fail. (p. 15)

Fitness peaks in career development.   During phase transitions, career is characterized by the search for the best that each individual can imagine for her- or himself. However, like all entities, the career search for fitness peaks may be limited by excessive timidity or excessive risk taking, as well as the ongoing (and continual) networked relationships and exchanges.

7. Nonlinear Dynamics.   Phase transitions are best explained by *nonlinear dynamics.* In linear dynamics, there is an expectation that changes of equal sizes will produce equal effects. There is also the assumption that causation is, if not unidimensional, then at least easily studied through multiple regression methods. Complex entities, however, behave in nonlinear ways. Because the transitions between order and chaos draw on multiple causes from multiple network relationships, the dynamics are fuzzy.

Nonlinear dynamics in career development.   Each person's career development pattern makes sense in terms of that entire person's work life, the specific dynamics of the environment in which the career occurs, and the internal dynamics of that person. So, too, people experience parts of their careers that seem to form patterns for them, yet these patterns are either not explicable or only partially explained in terms of the patterns of other careers. The career development of each individual is a series of choices that have internal harmonics or resonances for that individual and can only be understood in terms of that particular person.

8. Sensitive Dependence.   Small changes bring about large effects. Within the non-recurring, nonlinear patterns, small changes may be seen to bring about large effects. This phenomenon, known as *sensitive dependence*, is a quality of all complex entities. No matter how similar the starting states of dynamic entities may be one can be sure that they will "drift apart" after a while. The difference in results stems not from the external cause alone but also from the condition of the organism or body itself. Relative degrees of sensitivity change the effects.

Sensitive dependence in career development.   Apparently random, often small, events may lead to major career shifts.

9. Torus Attractors and Bagel Patterns.   As the entity moves through its transition, it may retain its life by repeating similar but not identical patterns, which are said to be held in place by *torus attractors*. The oxymoron *nonrecurring patterns* describes entities in this state. Patterns formed by torus attractors are often described as dough-nuts, or bagels, as the events continually go around the same circle, never exactly repeating themselves yet never leaving the circumscribed area.

Torus attractors in career development.   Some careers appear to be formed by torus attractors, that is, the patterns are clearly repeated with slight differences in each repetition, even for already experienced negative results. Individuals whose careers are formed by torus attractors may feel comfortable at times, yet the awfulness of the repeated pattern lies in the illusion of change followed by the recognition of being stuck.

10. Strange Attractors and Emergence.   However, as the entity moves through its transition, it may retain life through the creation of new forms, a quality known as *emergence*. *Strange attractors* yield entity shapes that are neither linear nor contained. When they are plotted mathematically, the patterns will each form unique figures or fractals.

Strange attractors in career development.   Strange attractors allow careers to take new shapes and emerge in forms quite varied from those seen before. Life has surprises; unexpected opportunities arise. Even in careers in which an individual has stayed in one occupation and industry, emergence is present to the extent that the individual continues to learn, and therefore, to emerge. This apprehension of emergence creates a sense of satisfaction, of flow, even of joy.

11. Spirituality.   Complex adaptive entities exist only as part of nested inseparability or connectedness. In other words, there are no living entities without interdependence. *Spirituality* is the experience of this unity.

Spirituality in Career Development.   As a complex adaptive entity, career can only exist as part of nested inseparability or connectedness. In other words, there are no careers without interdependence. In experiencing this interdependence, one experiences spirituality in work. Career counseling can thus be seen as spiritual counseling. Seeing work as spiritual enables each person to consider his or her contribution to the world and to the ongoing creation of the universe. This view gives value to each career and may save one from self-centeredness. It also encompasses a perspective that: "Our individual microscale activity in all its uniqueness can count in a way classical science never imagined" (Goerner, 1995, p. 36). Finally, seeing one's career as spiritual avoids a moral split between life and work. It adds both an ethical dimension and a dimension of love.

The webs of relationships that are revealed in the examination of complex adaptive entities can lead to an understanding that "the world is totally connected: that is to say that there are no events anywhere in the universe which are not tied to every other event in the universe" (Bronowski, 1978, p. 58). This sense of connection is the essence of spirituality. Jacobsen (1997) and Mitroff and Denton (1999) conducted separate investigations into the definition of spirituality. Mitroff and Denton, in *A Spiritual Audit of Corporate America*, asked executives, managers, and workers at all levels in a variety of industries to define spirituality. Jacobsen queried a panel of educators, corporate executives, community leaders, and clergy. Striking similarities were found in the responses. In essence, the definition of spirituality had two components: first, that spirituality included a sense of connection to something beyond the individual, and second, that spirituality is a search for meaning, purpose, and integration in life.

Wuthnow (1998) has described contemporary spirituality as a "seeking spirituality," one in which people "increasingly negotiate among competing glimpses of the sacred, seeking practical knowledge and practical wisdom" (p. 3). Another way of looking at spirituality was provided by Roof (1999), who studied hundreds of baby boomers since 1988. Spirituality, he discovered, encompassed four themes: "a source of values and meaning beyond oneself, a way of understanding, inner awareness, and personal integration" (p. 35). A survey by Gallup and Jones published in 2000 showed that more than three-fourths of Americans feel the need to experience spiritual growth in their lives. This was up from 20 percent in 1994.

The sense of unity described here can come from religious experience, art, nature, or reflection. However, it is often difficult to keep the sense of unity in focus. Bloch and Richmond (1998) developed seven connectors to help people stay focused on the underlying integration or unity of life, particularly in terms of career. These seven connectors provide an additional dimension in the discussion of the need for career information and its place in individual development. The connectors may be summarized as follows:

- *Change:* Being open to change in yourself and the world around you;
- *Balance:* Achieving balance among the activities of your life, such as work, leisure, learning, and family relationships; being able to leave behind that which is no longer useful and to retain core values and useful skills;

- *Energy:* Feeling that you always have enough energy to do what you want to do;
- *Community:* Working as a member of a team or community of workers and understanding you are part of communities of companionship; communities of culture; and the cosmic community;
- *Calling:* Believing that you are called to the work you do by your particular mix of talents, interests, and values;
- *Harmony:* Working in a setting that harmonizes with your talents, interests, and values; and
- *Unity:* Believing that the work you do has a purpose beyond earning money and in some way serves others.

Applying the Theory: Complexity, Spirituality, and Career Information

This section places career information into the theoretical context developed previously. It is clear that people always use career information. In other words, people make decisions based on their understanding of the networked relationships they are part of and their understanding of how to achieve the best in a given situation. Unfortunately, sometimes that information is incomplete, inaccurate, or simply wrong. In addition, people are not always fully aware of the influences that affect their choice of career information. The job of the counselor is, therefore, twofold: first to make clients aware of their need for objective and accurate career information, and second to help them identify the sources of this information. Four links to career information can be derived from the theory described previously (Bloch, 2004).

Phase Transitions, Change, and Career Information.   The first link is to the concept of *phase transitions.* In the physical sciences, some phase transitions can be predicted. For example, in ordinary circumstances, the substance H_2O will move between a liquid and a solid at 32° Fahrenheit. Similarly, some phase transitions in career are predictable. A graduating senior will leave the school and move into work, further education, or a combination of the two. A retiring person will have more time for leisure pursuits. Other career phase transitions are unpredictable. However, phase transitions—that is, the moments between order and chaos—are the most fruitful times for creative change. That is why the acceptance of change as a condition of life is a spiritual connector. Therefore, the responsibility of the career counselor is not solely to provide accurate career information. The responsibility of the counselor is also to provide the client with knowledge of the sources of career information and tools for interpreting and understanding these resources.

Open Exchange, Networks, Community, and Career Information.   The second link is to the concepts of *open exchange*, and *networked relationships.* Too often, clients see themselves as isolated. They may feel isolated because they are willingly leaving a familiar situation or because they perceive they have been thrust out of one. Sometimes there is a sense of connection to a family or community, to a particular occupation, employer, or industry. However, there is rarely a sense of the impact and potential of the full array of connections to the labor market and the general economic world. The concept of networked interpersonal relationships is encapsulated in the spiritual connector of "community." The role of the counselor in this regard is to open the world and its connections through career information. Opening the connections in the world means enabling clients to look at career information in its broadest sense—from specific job descriptions to an understanding of the role of economics in the relative growth of different occupational opportunities. Opening the connections means helping clients understand the swirling dynamics of the world. Furthermore, making changes can be uplifting or dispiriting. For those who are dispirited, a lack of immediate success may bring about a sense of unconquerable failure. An understanding of the dynamics can help clients see that, while they have the power to move in chosen directions, the results that are sought will not always be immediate or lasting.

Attractors, Calling, and Career Information.   The third conceptual link is to *attractors*. Attractors can be salutary or deleterious, even though the word *calling* suggests a positive force. Those attractors that lead individuals toward growth and emergence help keep careers alive. Torus attractors, which keep individuals spinning around the same circles, create a sense of being stuck. Career interests, career anchors, social and socio-economic constraints, habits of mind, and other internal and external factors are examples of possible attractors. An unwillingness to stay with discomfort of change can itself be an attractor that pulls clients into precipitous, frequently unsatisfying, decisions. It is the responsibility of the counselor to listen to the stories that help individuals find the links and nodes of their networks and to identify the attractors that have operated in their careers. It is also important to introduce the client to the wealth of career information available. Many of the career information resources allow for personal exploration as well as exploration of occupational and educational opportunities. Counselors can use career information to help clients create new career scenarios, narratives that can challenge or support the attractors of the past.

At the same time counselors challenge clients to accept change and seek those attractors that promote growth, it is important to remain open to one's own discomfort with change. To be an ever-improving professional and counselor is to be present with one's own mental wellness. Change is often uncomfortable. Getting used to working with one's own feelings of discomfort and still being willing to experiment or make mistakes is how counselors reach fitness peaks of practice. You may ask yourself whether your sense of discomfort is coming from taking too great a risk and, conversely, if that sense of comfort is coming from stagnation, from playing it safe (M. Stauffer, personal communication, August 14, 2004).

Fitness Peaks, Harmony, and Career Information.   The fourth and final link is to the concept of *fitness peaks*, or the spiritual connector of *harmony*. The most familiar use of career information brings us back to the work of Frank Parsons (1909), in which, through true reasoning, individuals make choices based on a knowledge of self and of occupations. While this synthesis of self and search remains at the heart of career counseling (Bloch, 1989a), the concept of fitness peaks suggests that career information is not neutral in the eyes of clients. Career information is sorted and presented in ways which the authors or publishers believe is most helpful. However, not all information is equal or equally useful to each client. The responsibility of the counselor is to help the client identify the issues—interests, skills, and values—that are of greatest importance to that client and then to identify the career information resources that will provide that information. Through self-analysis that goes beyond career interests combined with skills and action based on the analysis of career information, clients can move toward settings in which they are most likely to flourish and experience harmony.

SOURCES OF CAREER INFORMATION: TIPS ON READING THIS SECTION

As you move into the sections that describe the sources of career information, you may want to work at your computer, opening and exploring the sites that are identified. It is suggested that you read through this section as a whole so that you can grasp the wide array of types of sites. Then go back and examine those sites that are available to you and of potential interest. Finally, you may want to open a word-processing file into which you copy the addresses (URLs) of interesting sites along with comments as to how you would utilize the information. For example, you might include the population or populations for which the site is most appropriate. You might include comments on the career issues the site most readily addresses. Finally, you might include how much assistance clients would need in utilizing the site. The description of some sources of information may prove tantalizing as the site is not open for exploration by nonmembers or nonsubscribers. Most publishers are interested in having their sites explored by members of the counseling profession. An e-mail or telephone call will often yield at least temporary access.

SOURCES OF CAREER INFORMATION: ORGANIZED SYSTEMS

This portion of the chapter identifies major organized systems for providing career information. An organized system for providing career information includes one or more of the following major elements:

- Occupational descriptions and one or more methods for sorting and searching the descriptions
- Information about educational programs and institutions with one or more methods for sorting and searching the information
- One or more instruments for identifying individual interests, skills, or values and relating these to occupational and/or educational information
- Links among those major elements of the system as well as links between the files within the elements

Comprehensive systems include all these elements. Historically, two terms have been used to describe comprehensive systems: career information delivery systems (CIDS) and computer-assisted career guidance systems (CACGS). While the origin of the two different terms may be of interest to historians of the field, suffice it to say they are now used interchangeably. For consistency in this chapter, the term CIDS is used.

CIDS are described first, followed by descriptions of systems that provide only occupational information or only educational information. CIDS themselves fall into two groups: those offered nationally and those available within particular states or other locales. In other words, the potentially confusing mix of systems will be described in the following order:

- National CIDS
- State-based CIDS
- Occupational information systems
- Educational information systems

National CIDS

There is always a danger in writing about resources, particularly electronic resources, that the author will inadvertently omit a valuable resource. To determine the national CIDS to be included in this chapter, I contacted the current president of ACSCI for its current membership list. Each of the CIDS described was a member of ACSCI as of September 2003 (C. Buhl, personal communication, October 13, 2003), maintained an Internet-based CIDS, and provided Internet-based information on its system.

The national CIDS include the following:

- Career Cruising (http://www.careercruising.com)
- CIS (http://cis.uoregon.edu), available from Into Careers at the University of Oregon
- COIN Educational Products (http://www.coin3.com)
- Discover (http://www.act.org/discover), available from ACT
- eChoices (http://www.echoices.com), available from Bridges.com
- Keys2Work (http://www.keys2work.com)
- SIGI Plus (http://www.ets.org/sigi), available from the Educational Testing Service (ETS)

Many of the national CIDS offer a variety of products and modes of delivery, including both Internet-based and CD-ROM systems. It can be expected that as technology changes, so will the systems. However, what is at the heart of the systems is not their technology, but what they include. Occupational information includes the following: a description of the occupation; characteristics of the work being performed; levels of skills and knowledge required; physical demands; entry requirements; wage information; and anticipated demand for the occupation. Educational information includes descriptions of postsecondary educational programs and descriptions of educational institutions that provide the programs. The postsecondary institutions include public and private colleges and universities and, sometimes, technical schools, career schools, and trade schools. Educational institution information usually includes the characteristics that prospective students most often consider important in choosing a place to study, but minimally it includes the location, Website, and contact person (Association of Computer-based Systems for Career Information [ACSCI], 2002). Many CIDS also provide information on financial aid, including not only general information on federal assistance, but also the specifics of scholarship requirements and grants.

CIDS offer much more than databanks of information. All of the CIDS listed provide methods for self-exploration and for linking self-exploration to lists of occupations. Within occupational information, the systems provide links that allow clients to identify related occupations. In addition, the systems provide for seamless movement from occupational information to educational information. The information and self-exploration can prove useful in many types of phase transitions. The needs at the phase transition from school to additional schooling or work are obvious. In addition, CIDS can prove useful for adults in transition from one occupation to another. The CIDS can be used to identify occupations which require skills developed on one job that can be used on another. In addition, the occupational descriptions of CIDS can be used to power a resumé with terms appropriate to a new occupation.

The original CIDS began with the needs of high school students in mind. However, with the growth in technological capacity and the pervasiveness of computers, CIDS have expanded their base. Some CIDS now offer modules that focus on the needs of younger students and decisions they must make about skills improvement. Other CIDS offer modules that can be tailored to the needs of business organizations for the development of career ladders and succession planning.

While all the CIDS offer the same general sorts of information, they differ greatly in how they present the information and in the types of self-exploration and searches they provide. In comparing CIDS, a counselor will notice variety in the number of occupations described. In general, this reflects a conscious decision on the level of detail appropriate to the audience. All CIDS attempt to capture the complete occupational structure of the United States. However, they differ in how they cluster and describe occupations. In addition, CIDS may offer special features such as files on entrepreneurship, Holland Code–related self-exploration, values-based self-exploration, military occupational information, and more. In selecting a CIDS, the counselor first needs to consider the nature and needs of the intended audience, the amount of time needed to move meaningfully through the modules in relation to the time generally available online, and the methods of delivery available in relation to the equipment and culture of the organization. In addition, the accuracy and comprehensiveness of the information needs to be evaluated. Some suggestions for information sources related to CIDS evaluation and research are presented in the last section of this chapter. Among these, the ACSCI Standards (ACSCI, 2002) are particularly important in evaluating the comprehensiveness, accuracy, and development of a CIDS. All of the CIDS listed above allow for an online tour or provide temporary passwords for full exploration of their systems. CIDS are generally licensed to sites, although some may allow subscriptions by individual users, and some national CIDS are also used as the basis for state-based systems.

State-Based CIDS

State-based CIDS have all the general information, self-exploration characteristics, and linkage characteristics described for the national systems. They therefore have the same utility in working with clients. However, the state-based systems generally provide a deeper level of local data than the national systems. State-based systems provide wage and employment outlook information that is accurate for their state and often for regions within the state. Similarly, education information on institutions, programs of study, and financial aid within the state may be more detailed than in the national CIDS. In addition, state-based systems often provide information about employers and local job or training opportunities. Both state-based and national CIDS are responsible for collecting and presenting information with rigor, accuracy, and comprehensiveness.

The underlying software and the information files that drive the self-exploration, searches, and information may be developed by the state, based on one of the national CIDS, or a combination of the two. ACSCI has been in the process of collecting information from the state-based CIDS since 1999. While the survey remains a work in progress (C. Buhl, personal communication, October 20, 2003), draft data shows that 32 states and Puerto Rico reported that they had state-based CIDS. Of these, 12 reported that their systems were based on the Career Information System (http://cis.uoregon.edu); seven reported that their systems were based on Choices (http://www.echoices.com); and one reported that its system was based on COIN (http://www.coin3.com). Of these, five augmented the system with additional software. Six state-based CIDS reported that they had developed their own software. The remainder did not respond to this question.

A look at the sites in which state-based CIDS are offered shows the growth of the systems since their original use in high schools. The types of sites listed by the CIDS responding to the ACSCI survey include the following:

- Elementary, junior high, and middle schools
- Two- and four-year colleges and universities
- Employment services offices
- Correctional institutions
- Rehabilitation agencies
- Counseling agencies
- Military bases
- Public libraries
- Private businesses

In addition, state-based CIDS usually provide training often customized to audiences such as displaced worker programs, vocational rehabilitation programs, job centers, and equity programs. A number of CIDS offer newsletters or career tabloids to their sites.

State-based CIDS, like national CIDS, are in a state of perpetual development. The information with the systems is itself dynamic. Maintaining up-to-date information is the most important aspect of change. On a larger scale, technological advances, demands from existing and new audiences, and funding opportunities (or the lack thereof) lead to changes in delivery modes and design. Nevertheless, one should not expect that the turn-around time for changes in design is like that between new models of a laptop. Given the importance of the information and the need to validate any self-assessment changes, both national and state-based CIDS require adequate time for design and testing before changes can be implemented.

State-based CIDS generally license the systems to sites within the state. The costs vary with the nature of the funding for the CIDS. ACSCI (http://www.acsci.org/acsci_states.asp) is a good source of information as to whether your state has a CIDS.

Occupational Information Systems

Unlike comprehensive CIDS, occupational information systems offer information, as their name suggests, only on occupations. However, that is not a limitation, but an increase in specialization. Three government systems are discussed: O*Net, the *Occupational Outlook Handbook*, and the *Career Guide to Industries*, as well as one proprietary system, ERI.

O*Net.   O*Net, perhaps the most comprehensive source of occupational information, has been developed by the U.S. federal government and is offered online and at no cost to individuals on organizations. In fact, many of the CIDS described previously use the O*Net information either as the basis for their career information or as one element in their research. All one need do is go to the Website. O*Net (http://online.onetcenter.org/) allows the client to access a searchable database of occupations using keywords, or ordinary language, O*Net-SOC code numbers, job families, or the complete list of occupations included in the database. The O*Net-SOC Codes are the basic numbering system used by O*Net and related government and other sources. Each occupation has a unique number so that information found in one source can be utilized with information from another. If you or the client have found occupations using another classification system, such as Military Occupational Classifications (MOC), you can use a "crosswalk" to find matching O*Net occupations.

The O*Net occupational database has information on more than 900 occupations. For each occupation, information is provided on the following:

- Tasks
- Knowledge
- Skills
- Work activities
- Work context
- Interests
- Work values
- Related occupations
- Job zones

Interests are described in terms of Holland Codes. Job Zones refers to a method of grouping occupations by the level of overall experience, job training, and education required. There are five job zones, with zone 5 requiring the highest levels. The work values are directly related to the Work Importance Locator. At the end of the description, there is a "Wages and Employment" link, which takes the client to a pulldown menu of states and, from there, to state information. All of this information is provided by selecting "Summary" under the "Reports" heading next to the list of relevant occupational titles. Summary is generally the most useful tool in working with clients. Selecting "Details" will, as the name suggests, give details, that is, numeric information related to each of the items under Summary. Selecting "Custom" allows the user to preset the levels for information that will be displayed. The Details and Custom reports are more useful to analysts or system developers than to individual counselors.

The same Web page also takes the client to the skills search (http://online. onetcenter.org/gen_skills_page). By answering questions in one or more of six broad skills areas, the client will generate a list of occupations. The six skill areas are: Basic Skills, Social Skills, Complex Problem Solving Skills, Technical Skills, System Skills, and Resource Management Skills. The online directions suggest that the client begin by selecting one or more skill groups. Then, within the skill group or groups, the client is advised to select as many skills as the client has or plans to acquire. In general, the fewer the skills selected the larger the number of occupations that will be generated. The selected skills are compared to skill ratings for each occupation. If a selected skill is rated "Very Important" for a particular occupation, it is considered a match. "Very Important" includes skills rated 69 or above on a standardized scale. Occupations matching all the selected skills are shown first, followed by those matching all but one of the selected skills, and so on. Within these groupings, occupations are subgrouped by "Job Zones."

O*Net offers two other tools for searching the database of occupations. These are also offered without cost, but they must be downloaded and "unzipped" with the proper software to make them usable. At the top of the O*Net site (http://www. onetcenter.org/tools.html), there is a selection menu. From this menu the "Computerized Interest Profiler" and the "Work Importance Locator" can be downloaded. The "Computerized Interest Profiler" utilizes the Holland hexagon classification system of Realistic, Investigative, Artistic, Social, Enterprising, and Conventional. The client is presented with a series of work activities. For each one, he or she must choose "like," "dislike," or "uncertain." Upon completion, a list of occupations for exploration is generated. The "Work Importance Locator" is based on the client's ranking of how important various values are to him or her on the job. The items refer, for example, to the desire to be "busy all the time," to have fair supervision, to be innovative, to get steady employment, to be recognized for one's achievement. The questions relate to six groups of values:

- Achievement
- Independence
- Recognition
- Relationships
- Support
- Working conditions

Upon completion of the "Work Importance Locator," a list of occupations for exploration is provided.

O*Net provides an ever-increasing array of tools and information for the counselor. From the home page of O*Net, the counselor can go to the Job Accommodation Network or the Searchable Online Accommodation Resource for assistance in working with clients who have a health problem or disability. A link to Career OneStop (http://www.careeronestop.org/) provides services to job seekers such as a resume posting service and services to employers such as a job posting service as well as links to America's Job Bank. America's Job Bank (http://www.ajb.org/), a cooperative venture of the U.S. Department of Labor and state-operated public employment services, allows the client to search for job openings by category of work or job title and location, even down to zip code. USAJOBS (http://www.usajobs.opm.gov/) offers searchable information for jobs in the federal government. In addition, the O*Net database is now available in Spanish and can be requested directly from O*Net or through its parent government agency. O*Net was developed and supported by the U.S. Department of Labor, Employment and Training Administration (www.doleta.gov).

It is impossible to capture the myriad services offered by O*Net. Instead, the counselor is urged to go to the site and begin exploring. The first exploration suggested would be of the occupational information database and its search tools. The database will be useful to some clients, but many may find it overwhelming. Excellent facilitation skills are needed by the counselors as well as complete familiarity with the system. While this is true of the use of all information, it is particularly true of O*Net because of its complexity. An ancillary site to O*Net (http://www.workforceaguirre.org) provides downloadable documents to help counselors utilize O*Net. The O*Net Online Desk Aid is recommended for convenience: it is a two-sided card that provides an overview of all the features and links.

The Occupational Outlook Handbook. The *Occupational Outlook Handbook* (*OOH*; http://www.bls.gov/oco/) is provided by the Bureau of Labor Statistics (BLS) of the U.S. Department of Labor. The *OOH* has been used for many years predating the Internet, and many publishers have sold the *OOH*, printing the information provided by the BLS.

The *OOH* contains narrative descriptions of approximately 275 occupational groups including descriptions of what workers do on the job, working conditions, the training and education needed, earnings, expected job prospects, and sources of additional information in a wide range of occupations.

As an example, the *OOH* identifies these sources of additional information for counselors:

- For general information about counseling, as well as information on specialties such as school, college, mental health, rehabilitation, multicultural, career, marriage and family, and gerontological counseling, contact: American Counseling Association, 5999 Stevenson Ave., Alexandria, VA 22304–3300; http://www.counseling.org
- For information on accredited counseling and related training programs, contact: Council for Accreditation of Counseling and Related Educational Programs,

American Counseling Association, 5999 Stevenson Ave., 4th floor, Alexandria, VA 22304; http://www.counseling.org/cacrep

■ For information on national certification requirements for counselors, contact: National Board for Certified Counselors, Inc., 3 Terrace Way, Suite D, Greensboro, NC 27403–3660; http://www.nbcc.org

■ For information on certification requirements for rehabilitation counselors and a list of accredited rehabilitation education programs, contact: Commission on Rehabilitation Counselor Certification, 1835 Rohlwing Rd., Suite E, Rolling Meadows, IL 60008. http://www.crcertification.com

The database of occupations can be searched by entering a job title in the "A–Z" index of occupational titles, through a selection of one or more job clusters, or by examining the entire array of occupations, letter by letter. In addition to the database of occupational information, the BLS provides information on trends in employments. (An overview can be accessed at http://www.bls.gov/oco/oco2003.htm, and from this site, there are also links to more detailed information.)

Career Guide to Industries.   In addition to the descriptions of occupations provided in the *OOH*, the BLS provides narrative descriptions of 42 industry groupings in the *Career Guide to Industries* (at http://www.bls.gov/oco/cg/home.htm). The *Career Guide to Industries* provides information on available careers by industry. The current edition provides information on 70 percent of wage and salary jobs. The information includes the nature of the industry, working conditions, employment, occupations in the industry, training and advancement, earnings and benefits, employment outlook, and lists of organizations that can provide additional information.

Economic Research Institute.   Economic Research Institute (ERI; http://www.erieri.com/index.cfm), another member of ACSCI, offers a specialized occupational information system. The institute describes itself as most useful for "career changers and those who assist them." The ERI contains about 15,000 job descriptions and 15,000 alternate titles. Prior to the development of O*Net, the primary data-gathering schematic for the Bureau of Labor Statistics was the *Dictionary of Occupational Titles (DOT)*. ERI maintains a database of the *DOT*, which it updates using information from surveys it compiles. In addition, ERI provides software and databases that calculate salary and cost-of-living differentials between any of over 7,200 cities in the United States and Canada. A "Salary Assessor" and "Relocation Assessor" provide additional information for job changers and for employers.

As with all other systems, there is more to ERI than can be described briefly here. ERI describes itself as more useful with job changers than with job entrants. As with comprehensive CIDS, it is available, at a cost, by subscription.

Educational Information Systems

Following the principle of including only ACSCI members or government systems as examples in this chapter, there is only one specialized educational information system described: Peterson's. However, there are other systems available that offer similar information and services. Before making a selection or recommendation, the counselor is urged to search Google (www.google.com), using the phrase "college search" (including the quotation marks). In addition, if the client has access to a national or state-based CIDS, that system will include much of the same information.

Peterson's.   Peterson's (http://www.petersons.com/) is the only educational information system that is a member of ACSCI. Peterson's includes detailed information about colleges and universities as well as a search tool. The search allows the client to select colleges based on location, major, tuition, size, student-faculty ration, GPA, sports offered, religion, and type (all men, all women, or co-ed; private or public; two-year or four-year).

In addition to the college information, Peterson's includes information about financial resources, ranging from federally guaranteed loans of "Sallie Mae" loans to over 1.6 million scholarships and grants, presented in a searchable database. The site includes admissions essay help and direct links to selected financial providers. Some of the services provided by Peterson's are free to the user. Others are offered on a fee-paying basis.

The obvious use of educational information systems is to prepare for the transition from secondary to postsecondary education. However, the systems are also useful in working with those clients for whom graduate education is under consideration. Finally, it is useful for clients who are considering a major shift in occupation and so may also want to consider additional formal education.

JOB SEARCH INFORMATION

Using Internet Job Search Sites

In addition to the organized career-information delivery systems and the specialized systems, there are many sites on the Internet that can provide valuable assistance in working with clients, particularly those in the job search stage of a phase transition. These sites offer an array of information and services. These may include occupational descriptions, articles on trends in the marketplace, or tips on job seeking. However, their most important use is in identifying current job openings and letting clients respond to them.

While Internet career sites come and go, there are several that have exhibited longevity. Hotjobs (http://www.hotjobs.com) and Monster.com (http://www.monster.com) are two of these. Both sites provide information on job openings, a resumé posting service, tips on writing resumés, and access to other career advice. The client can search for job openings using ordinary occupational titles, location, salary requirements, and other features. Once a job opening has been identified, the client can apply directly by e-mail or by sending a resumé posted to the site. While there are no fees to individual users, registration is required.

Employers seeking new college and university graduates list jobs on Monstertrak (http://www.monstertrak.com/). This site is available only through participating colleges and universities, but many career centers at colleges and universities subscribe. According to the Website, it is the "the most-visited college-targeted site on the Internet." Founded in 1987 as JobTrak, it provides a link between active job seekers on and off campus and employers offering jobs and internships. Subscribing colleges provide passwords to their students and alumni to use this site.

Another specialized job search site is IMDiversity.com (http://www.imdiversity.com/). As the name suggests, it provides job search information and resumé-posting services, with particular emphasis on serving the needs of historically under-represented populations, specifically, as stated on the Website "African Americans, Asian Americans, Hispanic Americans, Native Americans and Women." The Website was founded by the magazine *The Black Collegian* and has operated since 1970 to provide African American college students with information on career and job opportunities. The goals of IMDiversity are to provide access to a database of employers committed to workplace diversity and to help its users find jobs and the tools and information needed for job success. In addition, the Website offers information specific to the needs of its targeted groups.

Using Technology to Respond to Resumé Requests

Whether responding to job postings on the Internet sites mentioned here or those that come from newspapers and other traditional sources, more and more requests from potential employers are for faxed or e-mailed resumes. There are four ways, other than mailing a printed copy, in which technology can be used to compile and submit a resumé. Each of the methods calls for different techniques of layout, general style, and even the choice of words and is described below with suggestions for use with clients.

- The client can send a printed resumé by fax directly to an employer or to an agency working on behalf of the employer. Whether the resumé is faxed or mailed, it is likely that it will be scanned into a database for further use. This section is about creating the scannable resumé.
- The client can send a resumé as an attachment to an e-mail. This section is about creating an attached file for submission by e-mail.
- The client can list the resumé on a resumé-listing service on the Internet, either in response to a job listing on the Web or to self-advertise. This section is about creating the online resumé.
- The client can create a unique Web page to attract prospective employers. This section is, very briefly, about creating a Web page of one's own as a way of attracting employers.

Creating a Scannable Resumé.   Scanners are often attached to computers to enter data quickly from print to images that the computer can read. After the image is read into the computer, optical character recognition (OCR) software looks at the image and translates what it sees into letters and numbers. Then other software is used to identify important information about such as the client's name and address, work history, experience and skills.

OCR software is imperfect, or perhaps, too perfect. When it is looking for perfect matches between the images being supplied and letters and numbers, it can only translate what it sees against the set of characters it has been given. If it has been given asterisks, for example, and the client uses bullets to highlight different responsibilities, unlike a human, it cannot think, "Oh yes, this person has used bullets." Instead, it will try to match your bullets against some character, perhaps periods, thereby creating strange sentences indeed. It may not recognize or be able to translate italics or underlining. Parentheses may be misinterpreted as part of the letter they adjoin or as some other symbol. Smudges may become characters and broken letters may be omitted altogether.

Once the resumé has been scanned, other software is used to place it in the potential employer's database and then to search it for the key words that the employer has identified for the job under consideration. While there are a number of different programs for scanning and searching, the rules to increase the chances of being selected for the next step in the review process are generally the same.

The rules for creating a scannable resumé, then, are fairly simple. In fact, that is the rule: "Keep it simple!" Here are eight pointers to share with clients.

- Use white, 8 ½ by 11 inch paper, printed on one side only.
- Use a standard font such as Arial, Optima, Universe, Times New Roman, or Courier, in 12-point typeface. Do not condense or expand the type.
- Avoid all "fancy" type—no italics, underlining, boxes, graphics, bullets, or columns. Do use capital letters and line spacing to help organize your resumé.
- Be sure to put each of the following on separate lines: name, address, phone number, fax number, and e-mail address. Put your name only at the top of each additional page.
- Use a structured resumé format, with clear headings.
- Increase your use of key words, particularly nouns and industry jargon, to increase your chances that the key word search will select your resumé.
- Be sure to print your resumé on a laser or ink jet printer. Dot matrix print and less than perfect photocopies do not scan well.
- Do not staple or fold your resumé. Either of these can make marks that will "confuse" the OCR software. Mail it in a large, protective envelope.

Sending Your Resumé by E-Mail.   Employers in every field, not just those in "high tech" industries, are asking for e-mailed resumes. Using e-mail has probably made you aware of the limited ability to format the material you are sending. In addition, depending upon the program the other party has, the e-mail may arrive with even less style than originally included. Although communication by e-mail across the Internet improves almost day by day, it is still difficult to know how well the page that is sent will resemble the page that is received. Very often, the first page of an e-mail is taken up by a header that contains a raft of information about the machine-to-machine transmission of the letter. If your client sends a resumé by e-mail, the only thing the employer may receive on the first screen will be the person's name. In addition, employers who want to print the resumé or store it in a database must find where it begins and separate that from the unneeded header.

Your client can exercise some control over the appearance of the e-mailed resumé by sending it as an attached file to the e-mail rather than as a part of the e-mail itself. Because there is no way of knowing which word-processing program the potential employer has, the best way to ensure compatibility of sending and receiving is to send the resumé as an ASCII file. ASCII (pronounced *askee*) is a simple form of text recognized by virtually all computer platforms (for example, both Windows and Macintosh) and all computer applications of interest. (ASCII stands for American Standard Code for Information Interchange.)

Without getting into technicalities of binary coding, one of the reasons why ASCII works is because it is used to communicate in text that has no frills and virtually no formatting. The client can use all of the resumé ideas developed for a scannable resumé, with five additional pointers.

- Do not use any centering. Keep all text left-justified, straight on the left margin.
- The computer programs that will read your resumé prefer simple, left-justified text. However, if you want to indent, do not use a tab key, but rather type in the number of spaces you want.
- Before you send your resumé, save it in "text only" mode. On most programs, this is called "rich text format" (RTF). Often, you will have to save your resumé file and close it before you can attach it to an e-mail message.
- Of course, you will not be printing your resumé and sending it. You will be transmitting by e-mail, so you need not worry about paper and print quality. However, you should print a copy of your resumé to see what it looks life *before* you send it.
- Finally, when you are sending your e-mail response, direct the attention of the reader to the attached file and be sure to attach the file before hitting the "send" button.

Using a Web-Based Resumé Listing Service.   The Websites identified in this section of the chapter—Monster.com, Hotjobs.com, Monstertrak.com, and IMDiversity.com—provide structures for posting a resumé. In addition, they allow the client to respond to a specific job listing as well as to post a resumé to a database that may be searched by prospective employers. The client can take advantage of both types of services.

The client can find other resumé-listing services that serve his or her field by using one of the search engines (such as www.google.com or www.dogpile.com). In the search box, put the name of the job and the word resumé. For example, enter "sales resumés" or "accountant resumés" and then carry out the search. The disadvantage to this approach is that the client will also find many resumé-writing services available for a fee. Depending on the client's level of career sophistication and tolerance for frustration, you may want to facilitate the search.

The resumé-listing services generally provide forms that are completed by the client and that they then format to fit their database. The client may need assistance in being brief and to the point, stressing skills, and working within a rigid framework.

A word of caution: Some people prefer not to put home addresses and telephone numbers on the Web. Remember, just as your clients can get to the site to list their resumés and look at those of others, so others can get to your clients' resumés. Some people will list their city, state, and e-mail address. Some prefer to list only their e-mail address and to include the location of the work they are seeking in the objective box. In fact, some resumé-listing services will provide a free e-mail address to aid in maintaining security for one's identity.

A Few Words on a Web Page Resume. Your clients can use the most sophisticated tools of the Internet, including multimedia capabilities and links to other parts of the Web, to create their own Web pages as an advertisement for their services. The techniques for creating such Web pages are beyond the scope of this chapter; however, here are four simple tips for your client.

- Remember, the purpose of the resumé is to get you a job interview. Restrict your information to that which serves the purpose.
- Consider that if you send your readers off on links to other parts of the World Wide Web, you may never see them again. Consider how each link contributes to *you* getting a job.
- Be sure to make your information accessible. Consider how a potential employer will know that your Website is out there advertising your services.
- Do not include every graphic or auditory feature you can dream up. Do include those that demonstrate that you are the best person for the job you are seeking.

Using Corporate Web Sites for Career Information

The final sources of career information are the Websites of corporations and other organizations. These provide a level of specificity that is not available in any of the career-information delivery systems or specialized occupational information systems. In addition to looking at job listings on an Internet site created for that purpose, your client can also get information about organizations in general and, sometimes, about job vacancies by going directly to a company's Website. Most companies, not-for-profit agencies, and government organizations have homepages on the World Wide Web. Web addresses are often part of companies' advertisements, and they can also be found through Google or other search engines.

There are three ways in which information about an organization can be used in the job search. First, many companies now list their vacancies directly on their Websites. Second, information about a company's direction and its products and services can be used in tailoring a resume and a planning for an interview. Finally, information about a company's mission and values, as stated on the Website, can be used to assess the likelihood of finding harmony or a good fit between the client and the prospective employer.

You can use Internet sites to help clients reach the person in the organization who can advance their chances of success in the hiring process. Once you or the client has found the Website, help the client look for a link to company or organization news. This may include articles written about the company and published in newspapers, magazines, trade journals, and the like. Now use the "find" command in the "E"dit menu of your Internet browser. Look for words like *said, commented, noted*. You will find the names, and often the titles or positions, of key people in the organization. Your client may want to e-mail, telephone, or write to that person. Given the ever-present possibility of transitions, it is important that you teach your clients these skills rather than execute the searches yourself.

To help clients prepare for an interview, ask them to go to the Website of the organization for which they will interview. Once there, help them look at the listing for the specific job, if posted, and then help them look beyond the listings. Look for publicity releases and news items. These often give clues to directions the company plans to take or to problems it has solved. Look at mission statements or other general information. All of these are clues to what the company hopes to accomplish. They are also clues as to what clients can stress about the match between their backgrounds and an organization's needs.

Use online indexes to newspapers, the *New York Times*, the *San Jose Mercury News*, and others to search for articles about the organization. The company's Website will have only the information the company chose to put there. News articles may present more objective information both favorable and unfavorable, and information about changes in the organization that the company did not care to include in its Website. Look for information about the industry as a whole and the company's competitors as well. The more prepared clients are with information, the better they can respond to the questions that will be asked.

Finally, use online news groups and weblogs (called Blogs), to get the unofficial news, the "virtual" water cooler gossip about organizations. Because there are no organizational filters on the information, the material in news groups may be more or less accurate than information in other sources. For this reason, you and your clients will need to exercise more caution in using the news group information. The purpose behind all of this searching is threefold: first, to ascertain if this is an organization in which your client will want to work; second, to prepare the resumé and prepare for the interview in a way that shows a client's responsiveness to the organizational needs and requirements; and third, to identify organizations that need the client's skills but may not have posted or advertised a job.

RESEARCH AND EVALUATION

Although the need for career information has been axiomatic in the career development field since its inception, there is little empirical research on its effectiveness. Early research focused on counselors' opinions on what career information should include and how it was being used (Bloch, 1989b; Bloch & Kinnison, 1988, 1989; McCormac, 1988; McDaniels, 1988; McKinlay 1988; Thompson, 1988). Members of the Center for the Study of Technology in Career Development and Counseling at Florida State University have been active in documenting the content and costs of CIDS. In 1998, Sampson and colleagues produced the eighth edition of *A Differential Feature-Cost Analysis of Seventeen Computer-Assisted Career Guidance Systems*. In 1999, Sampson, Lumsden, Carr, and Rudd produced *A Differential Feature-Cost Analysis of Internet-Based Career Information Delivery Systems (CIDS)*. Both these major reports provides analysis of selected features, including site content; user-friendly features;

support; access policy; and costs, generally as license fees. Information is derived from use of the systems, support materials, and interviews with the developers. The reports, (which can be accessed at http://www.career.fsu.edu/techcenter/) are models for collecting information but have less utility as time passes because of the changes in systems discussed earlier in this chapter. Additional reports along these lines are under consideration (J. Sampson, personal communication, October 2003).

Recently, there has been some attempt to assess the relationship between client outcomes and aspects of CIDS use (Gati, Saka, & Krausz, 2001; Kim & Kim, 2001; Mau, 1999; Osborn, Peterson, Sampson, & Reardon, 2003). While each of these studies found positive relationships, they were limited in scope. All, with the exception of the Gati et al. study, had small samples; all of the studies used "convenience" samples; and none of the studies compared entire systems with each other. Nevertheless, the belief in the importance and efficacy of career information, particularly of comprehensive CIDS persists—and, I must confess, I too subscribe to this belief.

Although there is limited research, there are definite attempts to set standards for the field. The National Career Development Association has developed *Guidelines for the Preparation and Evaluation of Career and Occupational Information Literature* ([NCDA], 1991). *Guidelines for the Preparation and Evaluation of Video Career Media* (NCDA, 1992), and *Guidelines for the Use of the Internet for Provision of Career Information and Planning Services* (NCDA, 1997). All of these are available on the NCDA Website (http://www.ncda.org/). Other organizations have provided ratings of systems from time to time. For example, the *Career Planning and Adult Development Journal* published a special issue, "Using the Internet for Career Development," under the editorship of Hohenshil and Brott in 2002.

However, the professional association that has made the provision of career information its primary business is ACSCI. In 2002, ACSCI published its *Standards Implementation Handbook*. This handbook is the fourth edition, replacing the standards that were originated in 1981 and revised in 1982 and 1999. These changes reflect both continuity and change—continuity of efforts to explain what is meant by a high-quality career-information delivery system and change that reflects new technology and a growth in the user base for career information.

The standards are organized into four major groups:

- Core standards apply to all career information products and services. They include the requirements for information, delivery, support, evaluation, disclosure, and confidentiality.
- Component standards are used to assess the components of a particular system. They include the requirements for assessment, search and sorting, career planning and management, occupational information, industry information, education and training information, financial aid information, and job search information.
- Integration standards apply to systems with multiple components and include integrity, transparency, and integration of the relationships among components.
- Comprehensive system standards, or standards for CIDS (as defined earlier in this chapter), include requirements for accessibility, privacy and confidentiality, services and support, localization of key information, feedback and evaluation, and accountability.

The standards and checklists for assessing a system are provided in print or online by ACSCI (http://www.acsci.org/acsci_pubs1.htm).

SUMMARY

This chapter has explored the purpose and sources of career information. The sources of career information range from comprehensive career information delivery systems through specialized systems offering only occupational or educational information to uses of the Internet for job search success. Throughout the chapter the emphasis has been on two aspects of the world in which we live, both of which are exemplified by complexity theory. The first aspect is interconnectedness, and the second aspect is change. Just as the lives of clients and counselors are affected by many circumstances and technological advances, so are the systems. Even as the chapter is being written, more is being added to the systems described, other systems are beginning to decline, and still others are at the beginning of their design cycle. Thus, the final step advised in this chapter is to stay abreast. Use the Websites of the identified professional organizations, ACSCI and NCDA, to watch for changes in the field, conferences about career information, and new statements of standards. Use search engines such as Google and Dogpile to identify new sources of information. Use the Educational Resources Information Center (ERIC) to find research as it continues to be reported. This entire chapter has been filled with Websites. Here are the websites for additional information that were just mentioned.

WEBSITES FOR ADDITIONAL INFORMATION

http://www.acsci.org
http://www.ncda.org/
http://www.dogpile.com/info.dogpl/
http://www.google.com
http://www.askeric.org/

REFERENCES

Association of Computer-based Systems for Career Information. (2002). *Standards implementation handbook* (4th ed.) Tulsa, OK: Author.

Bloch, D. P. (1989a). From career information to career knowledge: Self, search and synthesis. *Journal of Career Development, 16*, 119–128.

Bloch, D. P. (1989b). Using career information with dropouts and at-risk youth. *The Career Development Quarterly, 38*, 160–171.

Bloch, D. P. (2004). Spirituality, complexity, and career counseling. *Professional School Counseling, 7*, 343–350.

Bloch, D. P. (2005). Complexity, chaos, and non-linear dynamics: A new perspective on career development theory. *Career Development Quarterly*.

Bloch, D. P., & Kinnison, J. F. (1988). A method for rating computer-based career information delivery systems. *Measurement and Evaluation in Counseling and Development, 21,* 177–187.

Bloch, D. P., & Kinnison, J. (1989). Occupational and career information components: A validation study. *Journal of Studies in Technical Careers, 11,* 101–110.

Bloch, D. P., & Richmond, L. J. (1998). *SoulWork: Finding the work you love, loving the work you have.* Palo Alto, CA: Davies-Black.

Bronowski, J. (1978). *The origins of knowledge and imagination.* New Haven, CT: Yale University Press,

Gallup, G., Jr., & Jones, T. (2000). *The next American spirituality: Finding God in the twenty-first century.* Colorado Springs, CO: Cook.

Gati, I., Saka, N., & Krausz, M. (2001). "Should I use a computer-assisted career guidance system?" It depends on where your career decision-making difficulties lie. *British Journal of Guidance and Counselling, 29,* 301–321.

Goerner, S. J. (1995). Chaos, evolution and deep ecology. In R. Robertson & A. Combs (Eds.), *Chaos theory in psychology and the life sciences* (pp. 17–38). Mahwah, NJ: Erlbaum.

Hohenshil, T. H., & Brott, P. (2002). Using the Internet for career development [Special issue]. *Career Planning and Adult Development Journal, 18.*

Jacobsen, S. (1997). *Heart to God, hands to work: Connecting spirituality and work.* Bethesda, MD: Alban Institute.

Kauffman, S. (1995). *At home in the universe.* New York: Oxford University Press.

Kim, T.-H., & Kim, Y.-H. (2001). The effect of a computer-assisted career guidance program on secondary schools in Korea. *Asia Pacific Education Review, 2,* 111–118.

Mandelbrot, B. B. (1982). *The fractal geometry of nature.* San Francisco: Freeman.

Mau, W.-C. (1999). Effects of computer-assisted career decision making on vocational identify and career exploratory behaviors. *Journal of Career Development, 25,* 261–274.

McCormac, M. E. (1988). The use of career information delivery systems in the states. *Journal of Career Development, 14,* 196–204.

McDaniels, C. (1988). Virginia VIEW: 1979–1987. *Journal of Career Development, 14,* 169–176.

McKinlay, B. (1988). Oregon's contribution to career information delivery: 1972–1987. *Journal of Career Development, 14,* 160–168.

Mitroff, I. I., & Denton, E. A. (1999). *A spiritual audit of corporate America: A hard look at spirituality, religion and values in the workplace.* San Francisco: Jossey-Bass.

National Career Development Association (NCDA). (1991). *Preparation and evaluation of career and occupational information.* Tulsa, OK: Author. Retrieved November 10, 2003, from http://www.ncda.org

NCDA. (1992). *Guidelines for the preparation and evaluation of video career media.* Tulsa, OK: Author. Retrieved November 10, 2003, from http://www.ncda.org

NCDA. (1997) *Guidelines for use of the Internet for provision of career information and planning services.* Tulsa, OK: Author. Retrieved November 10, 2003, from http://www.ncda.org

Osborn, D. S., Peterson, G. W., Sampson, J. P., Jr., & Reardon, R. C. (2003). Client anticipations about computer-assisted career guidance system outcomes. *The Career Development Quarterly, 51,* 356–367.

Parsons F. (1909). *Choosing a vocation.* Garrett Park, MD: Garrett Park Press.

Roof, W. C. (1999). *Spiritual marketplace: Baby boomers and the remaking of American religion.* Princeton, NJ: Princeton University Press.

Sampson, J. P., Jr., Lumsden, J. A., Carr, D. L., & Rudd, E. A. (1999). A differential feature-cost analysis of Internet-based career information delivery systems (CIDS) (Technical Report Number 24). Tallahassee, FL: Center for the Study of Technology in Counseling and Career Development.

Retrieved October 15, 2003, from http://www.career.fsu.edu/documents/technical%20reports/Technical%20Report%2024/Technical%20Report%2024.html

Sampson, J. P., Jr., Reardon, R. C., Reed, C., Rudd, E., Lumsden, J., Epstein, S., Folsom, B., Herbert, S., Johnson, S., Simmons, A., Odell, J., Rush., Wright, L., Lenz, J. G., Peterson, G. W., & Greeno, B. P. (1998). A differential feature-cost analysis of seventeen computer-assisted career guidance systems (Technical Report Number 10; (8th ed.). Tallahassee, FL: Center for the Study of Technology in Counseling and Career Development. Retrieved October 15, 2003, from http://www.career.fsu.edu/documents/technical%20reports/Technical%20Report%2010/Technical%20Report%2010.doc

Thompson, S. D. (1988). Data—people—aspirations: The career information delivery system the Maine way. *Journal of Career Development, 14,* 177–189.

Wuthnow, R. (1998). *After heaven: Spirituality in America since the 1950s.* Berkeley: University of California Press.

CHAPTER 7

DEVELOPING COMPREHENSIVE CAREER DEVELOPMENT PLANS FOR YOUR CLIENTS

RICH W. FELLER

Colorado State University

"[Career planning is] a straightforward process of understanding, exploring, and decision making, reflecting on your life, family, and work in a wider context. What complicates it is that careers and organizations are constantly changing. [Thus,] . . . careers have been defined as a set of improvisations based on loose assumptions about the future."

—*Business: The Ultimate Resource* (Perseus, 2000, p. 418)

Focused on developing comprehensive career development plans, this chapter reflects beliefs and practices about one of life's most challenging processes—the interplay between career decisions and self or identify. Chapter authors in this text focus on important knowledge and skills needed to gain insights about clients, counseling, and development processes. Culled from working with clients, students, and colleagues, this chapter illustrates the author's beliefs about developing comprehensive career plans.

Stimulating clients to integrate insights and feedback, which leads to choices about affirmation and change, is critical. Working alliances that articulate unmet needs, identify strategies, and evaluate remedies is essential. Developing competencies that build on strengths and learning to compensate for strength overuse and neutralize weaknesses are key to planning. As clients explore development and gain feedback, the goal of motivating them to enhance lifestyle satisfaction, career adjustment, and performance takes center stage. Commitments tied to allies and timelines promotes accountability. Since counselors serve individual clients and organizations, this chapter attends to both.

Initially, this chapter addresses the evolution of career development to support thoughts on policy issues and their implications for opportunities. Throughout, insights into the far-reaching perspectives and skills career counselors need to appropriately and adequately work with clients are offered. To assist career counselors and consultants in understanding their pivotal roles, I introduce current thinking and research about individual and organizational motivations and goals set within local, national, and global contexts. Challenges confronted by career development planning across its multiple venues, despite its value to organizational and individual success, are highlighted. Ultimately, the practical and human dimensions of career development are woven into an array of useful strategies and resources applicable to both individual clients and organizations.

THE EVOLUTION OF CAREER DEVELOPMENT

Writing this chapter thirty-five years ago would have meant focusing on how to build a supportive relationship with clients to fit them into jobs or traditional learning options through a rather mechanistic trait-and-factor approach. Many believed career work could be separated from personal counseling, and vocational guidance was best done with youth rather than helping clients manage their career development throughout life. With the advent of portfolio careers, free agency, and downsizing that has changed expectations about "jobs for life," today we know that matching people to jobs is much too narrow a perspective. As Simonsen (1997) states:

> John Krumboltz, a Stanford University professor holding an international reputation for theories on career choice and development, suggested in a 1994 presentation that, " . . . instead of taking people and matching them to a job, we need to help them determine career direction, overcome real and perceived obstacles, learn job search skills, avoid burnout, and prepare for new opportunities." (p. 205)

Twenty-five years ago, this chapter would have referenced the merits of "fit models" that included behavior modification methods and Job Clubs (Azrin & Besalel, 1980). Awareness about planning life roles beyond work for a more affluent society taught workers that no job could meet all needs. In 1972, Richard Bolles' *What Color Is Your Parachute?* popularized and expanded access to career development principles and exposed the "hidden job market." Past achievement skill analysis, adapted from Haldane's (1960) success acknowledgment, helped clients break out of the "three boxes of life" (Bolles, 1978), and *Parachute*-related workshops paralleled creation of the career self-help book industry, which broadened perceptions of careers and career counseling. The quickly changing nature of work and the unraveling of the social employment contract moved counselors to advocate for lifelong learning, and challenge lifetime employment assumptions.

New vocational education legislation, the National Occupational Information Coordinating Committee (NOICC), and the National Career Development Association helped stimulate a career development counselor training renewal by promoting occupational, career and labor market information-delivery systems, and developing products to teach individuals the full range of career self-management skills.

U.S. Department of Labor training programs such as the Comprehensive Employment and Training Act (CETA) and Job Training Partnership Act (JTPA), through partnerships among education, business, and private industry councils, moved career development issues to the top of their agenda.

Today, this chapter is written with greater appreciation for holistic career development. In acknowledging the complexity and diversity of current career interventions, new taxonomies of school career development interventions have emerged (Dykeman et al., 2001). Moreover, local, national and international crises—shootings in schools; the attack of September 11, 2001; the *Challenger* explosion; the war in Iraq; "jobless growth"—have prompted self-reflection at the most basic of human levels. We have come to realize that career development, as with all of life, includes a sense of tentativeness or "positive uncertainty" (Gelatt, 1998), a renewed commitment to self-advocacy and self-management, heightened resiliency, and a call to make meaning out of one's existence.

CAREER DEVELOPMENT PLANNING AND POLICY IMPLICATIONS

Career development is a complex field wherein specialists freely interchange the terms *career interventions, career assistance, career counseling, career planning,* and *career coaching* as they propose change models and techniques. It is increasingly accepted as a lifelong strategy, impacting, not only individuals, but also organizations and national economies. When "expressed in terms of measureable impacts on personal, community, economic and workforce development [it] can capture the attention of legislatures, policy makers and administrators" (Jarvis, Zielke & Cartwright, 2003, p. 269); and it has the potential to foster efficiency in the allocation and use of human resources, as well as promote social equity through expanding educational and occupational access (Watts, Dartois, & Plant, 1986).

The extent to which workers do not share in the success of their companies, live in poverty, and have difficulty accessing education is directly proportionate to their need for external support. Reich (2002) argues that those workers who are most adversely entrenched need strong interventions from their companies and communities to stem a widening income gap. If individuals are neither infinitely nor readily malleable, especially in the adult years, and when work roles change more rapidly than the individual's capacity to adapt, Lowman (1996) suggests: "individuals will suffer transitional casualties: persons will be unable to work at levels compatible with their economic wants and demands. Depression, anxiety, and other mental disorders related to work will accelerate under such circumstances, and mental health professionals will be increasingly called upon to address career and work-related issues" (p. 206).

Watts (1996) proposes that although the field of career counseling has been dominated by psychologists, career counseling is also a sociopolitical activity that "operates at the interface between personal and social needs, between individual aspirations and opportunity structures, between private and public identities . . . [Thus], the rationale for public funding for such services stems from their value to society and the economy, as well as to individuals" (p. 229). While research illustrates its value, national support for more comprehensive career development planning is presently hampered by shifts in political priorities and mounting government deficits. However, as employers place more responsibility on workers for managing their careers, health care, and retirement options, it has never been more important.

Career Planning Makes a Difference

Individuals, organizations, and government policy makers are not easily convinced that comprehensive career development planning is a sound investment, despite contrary evidence. A report titled *The Education, Social, and Economic Value of Informed and Considered Career Decisions* (America's Career Resource Network Association [ACRNA], 2003) synthesized the existing research and found that comprehensive career counseling provides several benefits:

Educational
a. improved educational achievement;
b. improved preparation and participation in postsecondary education;
c. better articulation among education levels; and
d. higher graduation and retention rates.

Social
a. higher levels of worker satisfaction and career retention;
b. shorter paths to primary labor markets for young workers;
c. lower incidence of work-related stress and depression; and
d. reduced likelihood of work-related violence.

Economic
a. lower rates and shorter periods of unemployment;
b. lower costs of worker turnover;
c. lower incarceration and criminal justice costs; and
d. increased worker productivity.

Herr (1995, 1999), citing several studies, avows career counseling's positive effects on eliminating both career information deficits and client needs for support, as well as assisting clients in identifying and selecting available options (Campbell, Connel, Boyle, & Bhaerman, 1983; Spokane, 1990; Spokane & Oliver, 1983). Complementing these findings, Holland, Magoon, and Spokane's (1981) meta-analysis shows that effective career interventions include (a) occupational information organized by a comprehensive method easily accessible to a client (e.g., using the Harrington-O'Shea Career Decision Making System (Harrington & O'Shea, 2000); (b) assessment materials and devices that clarify a client's self-picture and vocational potentials (see Feller, 2004); (c) individual or group activities that provide rehearsals of career plans or problems (see Barry, 2001); (d) support from counselors, groups, or peers (e.g., model reinforcement counseling session; see Krumboltz & Thoresen, 1964); and (e) a cognitive structure for organizing information about self and occupational alternatives (e.g., the CASVE Cycle; see Sampson, Peterson, Lenz, & Reardon, 1992).

CHANGING PERSPECTIVES AND SKILLS FOR CAREER COUNSELORS

As the comprehensiveness of career development increases, so does the need for counselor skills and strategies. Facilitating comprehensive development planning means that counselors need (a) to operate within well-defined roles, (b) to gain knowledge about the needs and idiosyncrasies of various groups of clients, and (c) to understand changes in the workplace and learning options.

Career Counselors: Developing Self

Learning about the value of diversity (Miscisin, 2001, Myers & McCaulley, 1985; Petersen & Gonzalez, 2000a), strength themes (Buckingham & Clifton, 2001), and career success strategies (Derr, 1986), coupled with courage to examine traditional career assumptions (Barry, 2001, Feller, 2003; Gray & Herr, 2000; Hansen, 1997) and the willingness to question counseling conventions (Amundson, 2003), are all integral skills for career counselors to master. Further, providing development plans asks counselors to continually explore *their* own worldviews and expose themselves to experiences, models, and techniques that broaden their understanding and empathy. Accumulating varied experiences and practicing humility enhances counselor wisdom and openness to the ways others choose to live their life (Dominquez & Robin, 1992; Whitmyer, 1994). By cultivating broader perspectives, counselors become effective at instilling hope (Snyder, Feldman, Shorey, & Rand, 2002) and belief in the self, in even the hardest client cases (e.g., "career stallers and career stoppers"; Lombardo & Eichinger, 2002a).

Career Counselors: Providing More Than "Test and Tell"

To suggest that one can plan for a lifelong career by finding the perfect job is as naive as thinking contemporary career counseling is driven by test administration. However, "vocational" or career counseling has often been introduced to counselors-in-training as a mechanistic, linear process of (a) meet and greet, (b) take charge of the process by administering interest and personality tests, (c) interpret results to find congruence tied to labor market availability, and (d) measure success by level of client focus.

Helping clients fashion comprehensive plans requires approaches beyond individual "talk therapy." Creativity, spontaneity, active engagement, and understanding how people effectively make life transitions are necessary counselor assets. Staying current with workplace, learning tool, technological, and organizational changes prepares career counselors for the often daunting, and always unique, task of building client action plans.

The traditional trait-factor-matching model seems most helpful when a person needs a job right away or simply needs a job to meet survival needs. However, it lacks comprehensiveness and does little to develop the client competencies needed to build satisfying lifestyles or improve performance. With workplace turbulence, pervasive learning and lifestyle choices, and a burgeoning appreciation for questions such as, "What kind of person do I want to be?," "What am I doing with my life?," and "Am I living the way that I want to live?," career planning needs to be holistic. Particularly among clients without security and economic concerns, work has become an expression of meaning. Meeting needs tied to career satisfaction comes from evaluating, prioritizing, and developing life roles. Many clients are no longer satisfied with working *for* a living, but instead want to work *at* living (Boyatzis, McKee, & Goleman, 2002).

Career Counseling: Integrating "Humanistic" Elements

Mental health practitioners have learned that a dichotomy between personal and career counseling rarely exists. Career counselors have learned that career counseling is not devoid of psychological processes. As Peterson and Gonzalez (2000b) note, "it is impossible to separate vocational concerns from emotional factors, family interactions and social well-being" (p. 70). Herr (1999) suggests that work and mental health are interwoven, and Niles and Pate (1989) propose that all counselors be trained in both the career and non career domains. Feller and Whichard (2005) argue that counselors need to empathize with the differing traits of "knowledge nomads" and the "nervously employed".

Tools for Acquiring Counseling Skills

Counselors need a practical organizing tool that can help them acquire the skills necessary for their burgeoning roles. One option is offered by Hansen's (1997) Integrative Life Planning (ILP) approach. Combining accepted theories and proven practices about how people (a) choose jobs or educational pursuits, (b) make the transition through life stages and cycles, and (c) negotiate psychological and environmental barriers that can immobilize them during career changes, Hansen (1997) gives a comprehensive, interdisciplinary, and eminently practical template for working with clients. Subsuming fundamental and broad life-choice questions, it concentrates on six key life tasks:

1. Finding work that needs to be done in changing global contexts.
2. Weaving lives into a meaningful whole.
3. Connecting family and work.
4. Valuing pluralism and inclusivity.
5. Exploring spirituality and life purpose.
6. Managing personal transitions and organizational change.

Further, Hansen (1997) poses seven provocative questions to guide career counselors and consultants in strategizing individual or organizational change.

1. How do we help people move from the old to new paradigm, see the big picture, and understand the connection between local and global needs and the changes that the twenty-first century is likely to bring?
2. How can individuals achieve greater wholeness when our educational and occupational institutions are still structured on the old Newtonian paradigm, when

actual work structures do not keep up with human needs, and when the traditional work ethic, especially in upper management of corporations and institutions, still dominates?

3. How can career professionals help their clients understand the importance of both women's and men's lives and the need for self-sufficiency and connected-ness for both? How can both men and women become self-directed agents in their life plans?

4. How can individuals and organizations be helped to understand the link between work and family and to work toward change that will facilitate their connection rather than erect barriers between them?

5. How can career professionals best help clients negotiate in a different world? How can they help them understand their own uniqueness while valuing the differences of "the other" in the workplace and in other areas of their lives?

6. How can clients be helped to become agents for change themselves?

7. How can career professionals help clients learn to negotiate the various parts of their lives, set priorities, and put the pieces of their own quilts together in meaningful ways? (p. 263).

Unique in both its comprehensiveness and incisiveness, the ILP encourages coun-selors to carefully scrutinize all pivotal life choices impacting career development. Career counselors benefit immeasurably in personal and professional growth by challenging themselves to ask and answer these questions.

COMPREHENSIVE CAREER DEVELOPMENT PLANNING: ITS MYRIAD CHALLENGES

Although the need for career planning assistance is well documented, many efforts fall short of the mark. Typically, such efforts are the result of well-intentioned, but mis-guided, plans impacted by scarce resources, inadequately trained and informed profes-sionals, disinterested systems, and competing priorities.

Career Planning with Students: Promoting Its Use

Despite its importance in life role success, career planning is not a major compo-nent in a student's secondary education. Most students have little experience with comprehensive career guidance or computerized career planning systems. Those who do typically come from settings with more recently trained staff, significant technology support, integration of academic and career and technical education, and a high level of administrative commitment to a cohesive career development program. Mandated individual career plans for students with special needs offer models useful to all.

As "educators assume that the changing economy simply requires more education, resulting in a misguided belief that all students should attend college" (Rosenbaum & Person, 2003, p. 252), career and technical education wanes. Exploring where students can learn job skills and how those not intending following a college path can be motivated to learn in preparation for something in which they will not participate is essential (Bailey, Hughes & Moore, 2004).

Community colleges enroll 53 percent of public higher education students and 71 percent of all students with disabilities enrolled in public postsecondary institutions (Pacifici & McKinney, 1977). Unfortunately, only 12 percent of those students with disabilities enrolled in community colleges actually complete their planned program (Edger & Polloway, 1994; Fairweather & Shaver, 1991). Most often, colleges and universities provide student advising and placement services that seldom reach those students with the greatest information needs. Moreover, those students taught by faculty with strong ties to employers find network advantages that exceed those of students in general areas of study.

The report *Decisions without Direction: Career Guidance and Decision-Making among American Youth* (Ferris State University Career Institute for Education and Workforce Development, 2002) found that students perceive a lack of career guidance in their schools, and often cannot name anyone other than their parents who has influenced career choices. Further, most admit that parental guidance is limited to a few hours over a few months. The study also identified a pervasive bias toward a four-year degree, even though only 28 percent of 25- to 29-year-olds obtain a bachelor's degree, ignoring those fields that need employees and require only technical training.

A report titled *High School Guidance Counseling* (Parsad, Alexander, Farris, & Hudson, 2003) found that helping students with their academic achievement in high school was the most emphasized goal of high school guidance programs (48 percent of all public high schools), and another 26 percent of programs reported that the most emphasized goal of their guidance program was helping students plan and prepare for postsecondary schooling. Helping students with personal growth and development was noted by only 17 percent as the most emphasized, while helping students plan and prepare for their work roles after high school was the least emphasized goal of school guidance programs (8 percent).

Student "Presenting" Problems.   Most students entering career counseling begin with questions such as, "I need to pick a college to attend," or "I don't know what to major in." Typically, such questions are socially acceptable ways of saying "I'm confused about who I am," "I'm nervous I won't find a place in the adult world," "I'm afraid of letting my parents down," or "I feel my worth is tied to achievement." Developmentally, this is to be expected as most students experience little meaningful career development planning in schools, and most college courses offer little integration with career exploration experiences. Consequently, students often present problems needing imminent responses. Unfortunately, resolution usually means longer-term relationships, requiring developmental activities beyond "quick fixes." (See Chapter 10 for further information on school counseling).

Career Planning with Nonschool Clients: Understanding Its Diversity

As individuals try to integrate life roles, seek balance, improve performance, and self-advocate for lifelong learning, they find that developing and managing their careers takes on greater value. Regardless of age, carrying out development plans is indispensable since few individuals succeed in new roles by simply repeating past successful behaviors.

> It is essential that employees understand the changing employment contract, hear a clear message about the requirements for success in the future, know clearly the business needs and competencies expected for contribution on the present job, and have the resources necessary for development in order to take ownership of their own careers and development. (Simonsen, 1997, p. 196)

Adults Want Career Planning.   Gallup Organization (1989) surveys have found that nearly two-thirds of American adults would seek more information about career options if they were starting their careers over again. The 1987 Gallup survey reported that 32.2 percent had no help in career development. Of the 41.2 percent of respondents who sought help, they typically did so through self-directed activities. Fewer than 1 in 5 sought assistance from school or college counselors, and fewer than 9 percent had used publicly supported employment counselors.

Unfortunately, 10 years later, little had changed. A 1999 Gallup survey found that 42 percent of adults indicated that friends or relatives were their most frequent source for career help, and 59 percent did not start their job or career through conscious choice. Only 2 percent were influenced by school, college, or career counselors; and 3 percent were influenced by a counselor, job or career specialist, or public service placement office. Just under 10 percent of all adults reported that they needed help annually in career planning and making a career change. Even when using professional services, Herr, Cramer, and Niles (2004) observed that clients typically have interactions with trained career counselors that are "short-lived and limited to points of crisis rather than to career planning and to helping an individual come to terms with the future" (p. 31).

Job Satisfaction Matters.   Palmore's (1969) findings that job satisfaction is the best predictor of longevity (better than a physician's ratings of physical functioning, use of tobacco, or even genetic inheritance) complement Dawis's (1984) comprehensive review of research on job satisfaction. Dawis notes that "from a cognitive standpoint, job satisfaction is a cognition, with affective components, that results from certain perceptions and results in certain future behaviors. As a cognition, it is linked to other cognitions, or cognitive constructs, such as self-esteem, job involvement, work alienation, organizational commitment, morale, and life satisfactions" (p. 286). He also reports that job dissatisfaction is correlated with mental and physical problems, including psychosomatic illnesses, depression, anxiety, worry, tension, impaired interpersonal relationships, coronary heart disease, alcoholism, drug abuse, and suicide.

Adult "Presenting" Problems.   Adults, who are often responsible for multiple life roles, may see few degrees of freedom when they present themselves in counseling. Issues related to burnout and stress, transitions in relationships, sudden loss of employment, conflicts at work, poor communication with significant others, unrealized career goals, or a sense of defeat commonly are interwoven with career-counseling needs. Financial problems and caregiving responsibilities force a sense of urgency and necessitate a focus on immediate coping strategies rather than longer-range objectives like finding satisfaction and meaning in daily experiences, redefining success to match a preferred lifestyle, or living intentionally based on clear priorities.

Weinrach (2003) and McDonald (2002) remind counselors about the often overwhelming needs of welfare-to-work clients as they try to plan and integrate development needs, concrete goals, and action plans. One's social class generally determines economic realities, with higher social classes perceiving work as integrally tied to personal satisfaction and meaning and lower social classes viewing work primarily as a means to economic survival (Bluestein et al., 2002). Often, immediate job opportunities are more important than personal interests to clients with basic survival needs. Crisis intervention methods and highly directive career counseling may be needed for such clients who have few internal resources from which to draw (Janosik, 1994; Sandoval, 2002; W. Stewart, 2001).

Research on work addiction (Fassel, 1990) provides insight into the personal costs of the inability to control compulsive work habits. Schlossberg's (1994) Transition Coping Guidelines, Leider's (1985) Purpose Profile, Krumboltz's (1991) Career Beliefs Inventory, Sampson, Peterson, Lenz, Reardon, and Saunders's (1996) Career Thoughts Inventory, Moris's (1988) Individual Life Planning, Richardson's (1999) What's Draining You? Inventory, and Simonsen's (2000) Career Compass all provide creative ways to help adult clients gain or regain mastery of the self in work situations.

Herr and colleagues (2004) cited numerous studies that suggest that many workers are inadequately coping with typical life problems and need skill-building approaches organized around specific life crises to better manage themselves.

> For a growing number of people the real problem lies not in a lack of job-specific skills, but in a surplus of social pathologies—[there are] too many people with too little self-discipline, self-respect, and basic education to fit easily into any workplace. For another group, the problem lies with age. Most firms prefer 20-year-old recruits to 45-year-old ones because 20-year-olds usually cost less and because they are thought—rightly or wrongly—to be more flexible, more malleable, more likely to turn into "company men." ("Training for jobs," 1994, p. 19)

Although employee assistance programs (EAP) have some measure of success in alleviating employee issues, they tend to focus on symptomatic mental health issues rather than encompassing broader life and career development issues. Attending to job satisfaction as part of the intervention can often result in both career stimulation and enhancement opportunities within the employment setting, and the consequent amelioration of social pathologies. Business's current performance review practices could be appreciably enhanced by providing meaningful and accountable development plans concomitant with EAP support. This would require a strong commitment from senior management to an employee development culture, including mentoring and coaching for managers.

Adult career counselors in workforce centers, private practice, community centers, or within EAPs serve heterogeneous populations at various life stages. Because of competing work-family priorities, career counselors need to help clients develop what the Families and Work Institute (Galinsky, 2003) calls a "dual-centric work-life." Galinsky (2003) found that those who put equal priority on work and their personal/ family life—who are dual-centric—have the highest ratings in feeling successful at both work and home, with appreciably less stress overall.

Adults will deal increasingly with skill obsolescence, age discrimination, and technological illiteracy. Seeking help in coping with feelings of loss, incompetence, job change, or voluntary or involuntary retirement is becoming more and more common-place. Early retirement, especially among white males who prospered during the 1990s or worked for paternal organizations providing lucrative pensions, as well as aging clients with better health and longer life spans, may still want to work. Preparing for what Curnow and Fox (1994) call the "Third Age"—that period of life beyond the career job and parenting, which can last for anywhere up to 30 years—presents addi-tional challenges for career counselors. Acting as interpreters of "lives in progress rather than as actuaries who count interests and abilities" (Savickas, 1992, p. 338), the tasks of career counselors include much more than working to help clients find a job that fits.

Career Planning and Development with Organizations

Organizations seek career development models when faced with the challenge of attracting and keeping talented people (Pink, 2001). They invest in employee develop-ment to induce performance, build employee strength at key positions, capture intel-lectual capital, foster innovation to drive patents, and define or enhance organizational identity (T. A. Stewart, 2001).

Organizational Planning: Initiating the Process.   Simonsen's (1997) *Promoting a Development Culture in Your Organization: Using Career Development as a Change Agent* offers a comprehensive roadmap for creating a development culture in organizations.

1. First, employee development plans must be linked to, and driven by, business needs.
2. The organization needs to create and promote a vision and philosophy of career development.
3. Senior management must actively and publicly support all efforts.
4. Clear communication and comprehensive education for all employees across all organizational levels needs to precede and accompany the plan's imple-mentation.
5. Management involvement in learning and mastering all phases of the plan is essential.
6. Employees must be given incentives and taught how to assume ownership of and responsibility for their own growth.
7. Adequate and appropriate career development resources must be available to all employees.

Organizational Planning: Maximizing Employee Contributions.   In the Gallup Organization–supported publication, *Follow This Path: How the World's Greatest Organizations Drive Growth by Utilizing Human Potential* (Clifton & Gonzalez-Molina, 2002), the path to maximize individual employee contributions with positive business outcomes is highlighted in eight steps.

1. Identify Strengths: Identifying an employee's dominant strength themes and refining them with knowledge and skills. (Strengths are a person's ability to provide consistent, near-perfect performance in given activities.)
2. The Right Fit: Placing the right people in the right roles with the right managers.
3. Great Managers: Developing managers who will (a) opt for talent, not simply experience, intelligence, or determination; (b) define the right outcomes, not the steps to get there; (c) focus on the person's strengths, not the weaknesses; and, (d) use the Gallup Q12 (defined next) as a guide to understand and develop employees.
4. Engaged Employees: Developing employees so they can answer all the questions in the Gallup Q12 with strong affirmative responses.
5. Engaged Customer: Developing employees who engage customers to experience products or services in a superior fashion.
6. Sustainable Growth: Producing efforts that are metrically measurable such as revenue per store, revenue per product, or number of services used per customer.
7. Real Profit Increase: Producing sales growth tied directly to stock value.
8. Stock Increase: Sustaining profit increases that drive ongoing increases in stock value.

Further, this work offers career counselors and consultants 12 questions for organizations and their employees to tangibly measure their mutual effectiveness. Referred to as the Gallup Q12, the questions evoke responses indicating satisfaction levels.

1. Do I know what is expected of me at work?
2. Do I have the materials and equipment I need to do my work right?
3. At work, do I have the opportunity to do what I do best every day?
4. In the last seven days, have I received recognition or praise for doing good work?
5. Does my supervisor, or someone at work, seem to care about me as a person?
6. Is there someone at work who encourages my development?
7. At work, do my opinions seem to count?
8. Does the mission or purpose of my company make me feel my job is important?
9. Are my coworkers committed to doing quality work?
10. Do I have a best friend at work?
11. In the last six months, has someone at work talked to me about my progress?
12. In the last year, have I had opportunities at work to learn and grow?

Career consultant Nicholas Lore states that only "approximately ten percent of people report that they love their work" (Rockport Institute, 2003). However, he notes that "when fit is optimal, workers find numerous indicators of increased job satisfaction, including experiencing work as a natural expression of one's talents and personality." Gallup's research indicates that as more of the Q12 questions are responded to as "strongly agree," work satisfaction grows, spurring on higher levels of organizational performance.

It has been found that career classes, workshops, and structured groups are useful career interventions that produce a variety of documented outcomes (Peterson, Long, & Billups, 1999, 2003; Reed, Lenz, Reardon & Leierer, 2000; Spokane & Oliver, 1983; Whiston, Brecheisen, & Stephens, 2003; Whiston, Sexton, & Lasoff, 1998). These venues could easily be built around the Gallup Q12, as each question is both a developmental goal and a strategic objective for employee growth.

Organizational Planning: Developing Human Capital with Performance Incentives.   When career development interventions such as employee development plans are used by employers, evidence indicates improved performance, a more engaged workforce, and more effective management (Wilms & Zell, 1993). As Michaels, Handfield-Jones, and Axelrod (2001) explain in *The War for Talent*, career planning and management are becoming an important weapon in an employer's retention efforts, as well as a strategy for heightened competitiveness. In a knowledge-based, technology-enhanced, globally competitive workplace, where success hinges on human capital, there is no issue more important than developing people to increase performance. Product innovation, timeliness, and quality earn customer satisfaction, as loyalty promotes brand recognition. These intangible assets are achieved chiefly through developing human capital.

However, what does developing human capital entail? Becker, Huseld, and Ulrich (2001) state that "even when human resource professionals and senior line managers grasp this potential, many of them don't know how to take the first steps to realizing it" (p. 4). The most productive response seems to be dedication to developing people in three distinct ways: (a) presenting challenging tasks; (b) providing feedback before, during, and after; and (c) ongoing learning (Lombardo and Eichinger, 2002b). If organizations and their workers are to prosper, a culture encouraging workers to plan and assume responsibility for their career development must be actualized (Simonsen, 1997).

DEVELOPING COMPREHENSIVE CAREER PLANS

Gysbers, Heppner, and Johnston (2003) note, "client presenting problems . . . are only a beginning point, and . . . as counseling unfolds, other problems emerge. Career issues frequently become personal-emotional issues, and family issues, and then career issues again" (p. 3). Amundson (2003) adds that "most people come to counseling with life problems that do not fall neatly into the categories of career or personal: life just does not define itself that neatly" (p. 16). However daunting the individual's needs appear, career counselors assume responsibility for helping clients address issues of career satisfaction and adjustment resolved by initially identifying their desires, needs, competencies, and challenges. Ultimately, their alliance will construct concrete career development goals on which to build action plans.

Identifying Career Competencies

Bringing attention to competency-based education helped sustain the school-to-work movement, as well as adding a persuasive argument for implementing contextual and work-based learning in public schools. Subsequent taxonomies of career-development intervention identified school practices (Dykeman et al., 2001; Feller & Whichard, 2005) as part of a system to determine competencies necessary for goal attainment, and ways to evaluate student progress toward those goals.

Emerging career development assumptions are challenging traditional beliefs (Feller, 2003) about the competencies needed for navigating a career, and fostering progressive policies and practices to improve transitions from high school to college and then to jobs (Rosenbaum & Person, 2003). The National Occupational Information Coordinating Committee's (1996) Career Development Competencies, the National Life/Work Centre's (2001) Blueprint for Life/Work Designs, and 40 developmental assets promoted by the Search Institute (1997) are powerful tools to help determine and focus on needed client competencies. Spawned by business leaders, attention to competencies helps clients prepare for greater career satisfaction and improved performance. Research consistently notes that "to sustain superior performance, emotional competence matters—twice as much as IQ and technical skills combined" (Kivland & Nass, 2002–3, p. 136). Dubois and Rothwell (2000) suggest that competencies are more enduring than jobs and are inherent to individuals rather than resident in the work employers do.

Identifying Individual Strengths

"Strengths models" represent some of the more recent developments and thinking in career planning. Arguing that discovering and capitalizing on one's strength increases the potential of performance excellence, as well as work success and satisfaction in life, strength models have become available commercially. The StrengthsFinder, an online adult assessment within the framework of *Now Discover Your Strengths* (Buckingham & Clifton, 2001), as well as its youth counterpart in *StrengthsQuest: Discover and Develop Your Strengths in Academics, Career, and Beyond* (Clifton & Anderson, 2001), help clients identify their top 5 of 34 strength themes. This feedback helps to uncover dormant or neglected talents and serves as a foundation for goal setting and planning. Savickas (2003) offers a career adaptability framework to assess development delays and distortions in building human strengths and then offers interventions to build strengths needed to cope with newly encountered situations.

Lombardo and Eichinger (2002b) have identified 67 competencies, falling into 6 factors: Strategic Skills, Operating Skills, Courage, Energy and Drive, Organizational Positioning Skills, and Personal and Interpersonal Skills. Their work (2002a) provides a common language for assessing and developing individuals. It identifies 10 performance dimensions and 19 career inhibitors and stoppers, while proposing client competencies in positive and straightforward language. Called the Career Architect (Lombardo & Eichinger, 2002a), in its simplest application counselors ask clients to sort 67 cards into three roughly equal piles in response to the question, "What are my 22 highest, middle, and lowest skills?" They find that the forced sorting, although sometimes resisted by clients, is critical for more accurate outcomes as people tend to be overly positive or negative without a forced-choice method. Because self-assessments may be only partially accurate (people tend to be fairly accurate about their strengths and less so about their "unskilled" areas), counselors recommend that clients validate the card sort with others who know them well. Counselors next review the competency sorts, arranging the cards into larger clusters and identifying themes in the highest and lowest skills. Once the skills have been rated, the system offers the counselor and client a map to which each of the skills is tied, thus helping the client tangibly "see" the relative importance of each skill in successfully mastering career competencies.

In my experiences with these instruments, I have found that clients are able to gain tremendous insights into previously undiscovered proficiencies, aptitudes, and talents. Additionally, clients are helped to understand why some tasks come more readily than others, and how they can't compensate for more difficult to master or overused competencies. The concrete suggestions for competency enhancement, carefully couched in encouraging terms, allow clients to appreciate their inherent value while negotiating their intrinsic challenges.

Developing Individual Competencies

Clients experience tension anytime a gap between a vision of what they want and their current reality exists. Feedback about a mistake, failing at something important, or seeing a need to learn are examples of instances where gaps and consequent tension surface. Handled prudently, this tension can be used to motivate clients to master competencies at higher levels of effectiveness. However, where and when it occurs is pivotal. Lombardo and Eichinger (2002a) state, "The odds are that [tension leading to subsequent] development will be about 70% from on-the-job experience, working on tasks and problems; about 20% from feedback or working around good and bad examples . . . ; and 10% from courses and reading" (p. v.). Moreover, they argue that feedback, even when informed, is not adequate by itself for client development. Because tensions most often occur in situations where counselors are not present, providing as many coping techniques and tools for skill mastery as possible that clients can use outside of sessions allows clients to maximize develoment opportunities. Lombardo and Eichinger (2002a) give 10 "remedies" for overcoming skill weaknesses for each of the 67 competencies, 10 performance dimensions, and 19 career stallers and stoppers that counselors can process with clients. While it is understood that no client would be expected (or need) to be good at all 67 competencies at any one point, the need for all competencies tend to come into play over a career as positions, functions, and levels of responsibility change.

I believe that such systems offer tremendous resources for counselors trying to help clients enhance strengths, develop "middle skills" into strengths, remedy weaknesses, work on untested areas, or compensate for overused strengths. Following Lombardo and Eichinger's (2002b) argument: The secret of success is continuously learning to do what you do not know how to do. This should be the basic tenet of any development plan.

Articulating Concrete Goals

Regardless of the client population, good counseling traits and strong working alliances (Bordin, 1979) are fundamental for successful counseling outcomes. Bordin suggests three essential parts needed to facilitate goal creation: (a) agreement between the client and the counselor on the outcomes expected in counseling, (b) agreement on the tasks involved to achieve the outcomes, and (c) a commitment between the client and counselor on the importance of the outcomes and tasks to both of them.

In the *Career Counselor's Handbook*, Figler and Bolles (1999) list 12 key skills of the career counselor. They align with requirements needed to effectively move clients from presenting problems through identifying competency needs, to development plans, to articulating goals and taking action.

1. Clarifying content: restating the essence of the client's needs.
2. Reflecting feeling: identifying and restating the emotional quality of the client's needs.
3. Open-ended questioning: asking questions that encourage a wide range of possible responses.
4. Identifying skills: naming specific areas of talent or strength revealed through past experiences.
5. Clarifying values: identifying sources of enjoyment and satisfaction via a client's description of past activities and experiences.
6. Value imaging: encouraging clients to envision possibilities through open-ended brainstorming, imaging, visualization, and fantasizing.
7. Information giving: giving key job or career information, enabling clients to better understand the need for all parts of the counseling process.
8. Role-playing: providing practice in roles clients may face.
9. Spot-checking: asking for feedback to keep the process on track.
10. Summarizing: collecting all the information clients have and reviewing it for purposes of moving forward.
11. Task setting: asking clients to gather information or engage in experiences relevant to development objectives.
12. Establishing the "yes, buts": identifying main concerns, obstacles, or roadblocks standing in the way of development plans, remedies, or goals.

Goal Setting: An Iterative Process.   Developing comprehensive career plans is seldom a sequential, linear process. Clients start and stop, reframe, try out new thoughts, feelings, and behaviors as they explore feedback and options. Further, most client needs are not easily anticipated as explained in Harrington's (2003) "dual track model." The dual-track model communicates the career counseling process to users, with Track 1 including the provision of career information with a cognitive orientation. Track 2 involves the integration of the information into self-awareness and the affective domain. The dual-track model allows professionals to personalize the process and "create a contract for specific services that may require an established time commitment with the client" (p. 80). This helps the counselor and client mutually envision preferred outcomes at any specific point. Within Track 1, the counselor responds to client inquiries about career information, self-information, job-finding information, and job preparation information. Often, this omits "bringing unconscious material to the conscious level such as integrating self-knowledge with career information [in order] to reflect a manifestation of the self-concept, developing the readiness to make decisions, and using self-knowledge of personality type with corresponding knowledge about work environments [Track 2]" (p. 83). For a holistic understanding of a person, cognitive informational-seeking behavior must be integrated with affective development. Understanding that clients move between the two tracks, counselors can keep focused on the overall goals, while allowing clients room for exploration and experimentation.

Another approach to help clients articulate concrete goals is Figler's "1-2-3 career counseling" system. This model (Figler & Bolles, 1999) submits that the themes of career counseling are captured in three questions and woven together throughout the entire process (p. 111). The three questions are: (a) What do you want to do? (b) What is stopping you from doing it? and (c) What are you doing about it?

Understanding human development, particularly age and stage, gender, and diversity issues, helps counselors negotiate the context within which goals are articulated. A useful acronym to guide goal selection, while keeping context in mind, is SMART. SMART proposes that goals should be kept **s**pecific, **m**easurable, **a**chievable, **r**ealistic, and **t**imebound. Creating goals within the SMART framework assists the counselor in integrating the client's unique contextual issues into a manageable development plan.

Creating Action Plans

Helping clients look inward, outward, and forward helps move them toward developing action plans (Simonsen, 1993). Developing action plans is a dynamic, energy-driven process, and counselors must work hard to maintain client motivation. One strategy often employed is encouraging clients to find "allies of support" to help keep them focused on completing tasks within the action plan. At times, the action phase will need to be modified and perhaps expanded. Counselors should be ready for such eventualities, preparing clients for the necessary flexibility while recognizing their need for closure. Providing homework assignments, Websites, and additional resources are ways to keep clients continuously engaged between sessions. Renewing client commitments, following timelines, focusing on the ultimate outcomes, and measuring progress concretely are all effective tools for ensuring success throughout the action plan phase.

RECENT AND EMERGING TRENDS IN CAREER COUNSELING

Herman, Olivo, and Gioia (2003) state that "interest in career planning is at an all-time high and will become even stronger as we move into the future" (p. 108). Concurrently, they note that individuals, particularly younger ones, do not trust employers to control their careers and are seeking ways to manage independently their professional and personal development. This demand has given rise to a proliferation of career development opportunities and choices—computerized, video-enhanced, Internet-based, and curriculum-based instruction; eCareer Development programs in corporate Websites; and career coaching to cite just a few.

Career Coaching Plays a Greater Role

Formerly provided only to executives, career coaching is now used at least as often as EAPs or career counseling "by managers and employees in a variety of work settings" (Chung and Gfroerer, 2003, p. 141). Defined as strategists in "promoting continuous resilience and performance in persons and organizations . . . [career] coaches are often asked about personal evolving, succession planning, career shifting, work performance, high performance work teams, outplacement, burn-out, scenario building, leadership training, work-home balance, and individual and organizational renewal" (Hudson, 1999, p. 4). (See Chapter 9 for further information on supervision, coaching, and consultation).

Life coaching appears to use a solution-focused, results-oriented, systematic process driven by "the assumption that clients are capable and not dysfunctional" (Grant, 2003, p. 254), and what Hudson calls "experiential learning that results in future-oriented abilities" (1999, p. 6). Presently, professionally licensed counselors point out that there is little empirical research attesting to the effectiveness of the unregulated industry of coaching. As it grows in popularity, there is a burgeoning interest in defining its psychology (Grant, 2002). With traces of consulting and counseling in the coaching background, as well as the application of contemporary management theory (Whitworth, Kimsey-House, & Sandahl, 1998, p. xi), Coach University (1999) suggests that career coaches are as much a part of life as personal fitness trainers.

Career Development Facilitators: Expanding Career Counseling Accessibility

Responding to the need for career development training by staff other than professional career counselors, the National Career Development Association has implemented an advanced training program to develop career development facilitators (CDFs). Designed for those working in diverse career development settings, this training prepares CDFs to serve as career group facilitators, job search trainers, career resource-center coordinators, career coaches, career development case managers, intake interviewers, occupational and labor market information resource people, human resource career-development coordinators, employment or placement specialists, or workforce development staff. CDFs are trained in career-planning techniques and development strategies commonly included in most professional career counselor programs. Although career counselors, coaches, and CDFs may differ in their emphasis on practices as well as professional and ethical issues, many of the same career-planning techniques and development strategies are used by all three, regardless of the helper's title.

Emotional Intelligence: Its Emerging Role in Comprehensive Career Development

Emotional intelligence (EI) is increasingly linked to success in school, family, and work. Goldman (1995) states that "EI is the ability to motivate oneself and persist in the face of frustrations, to control and delay gratification, to regulate one's moods, to empathize and to hope" (p. 34). His Emotional Competence Framework, which includes Self-Awareness, Self-Regulation and Motivation as Personal Competence, and Empathy and Social Skills as Social Competence (1998, p. 26), has provided focus for counselors and human resource experts identifying and cultivating competencies for maintaining high-performance workers and workplaces (Dubois, 2002–3). Ground-breaking EI-based competency models, skills, strengths, and competency lists are currently available and are being used to enhance connections among lifelong learning, development plans, and performance improvement goals.

Helping Clients Readily Access Career Planning

Many individuals are ready to change their lifestyles or set development goals, or want help coping with searching for jobs in workplaces that change faster than they adapt. Some landed in jobs and lifestyles with little planning; many lack awareness of their skills, abilities, and interests or have little experience making decisions. Some are self-directed learners, seeking permission and encouragement to plan for a new life direction.

One of the largest groups of clients increasingly stating their needs for career development is the group commonly referred to as the "boomer population" in *Age Power: How the 21st Century Will Be Ruled by the New Old* (Dychtwald, 2000). Many of this group have benefited from economic growth, medical advances, and significant educational opportunities, which results in a different view on career development issues. Valuing their personal time, finding expression and meaning in multiple outlets, questioning their life purpose, and seeking connections through spirituality, they want relevant career information succinctly, but incisively. This might well mean that career counselors implement career planning interventions in more creative ways, such as weekend workshops or retreats; ongoing, onsite employee development trainings; or interactive multimedia projects such as Ellis's (2000) *Falling Awake*. Presenting engaging activities that help these clients capture insights into personal happiness, yet highlight the realities needed to attain their goals, surely demands heightened levels of counselor creativity.

SUMMARY

Fraught with a history of "testing and telling" clients what to do and "fitting round pegs into square holes," planning careers is evolving into a holistic approach around which individuals create and live their lives. No longer seen as merely job placement, career development has a growing presence in organizations promoting development cultures (Simonsen, 1997), giving and enhancing both corporate and individual purpose and meaning. It has moved from something done at key decision points with youth in search of a destination, to a lifelong process using techniques from numerous disciplines. It has become a sociopolitical instrument, infusing economic vitality into communities, etching humanistic values into turbulent workplaces, and enhancing personal engagement and organization alignment.

The work of building comprehensive career development plans is more exciting and important than ever before. It attends to the very personal emotional domain of individuals on their journeys, searching for satisfaction, quality, and meaning in every choice. Helping create and achieve these work life designs, practitioners in a wider range of settings with greater variety in titles and levels of training are driven to keep pace with change. The only constant is that the number of individuals needing comprehensive career development plans will grow. This growth will spawn new and dynamic career counseling tools, career-planning strategies, and development opportunities needed to help clients achieve desired levels of excellence.

Comprehensive career development planning's value lies in the degree to which it helps clients make career decisions congruent with a healthy view of self, and a sense of hope about future transitions.

> When development is on schedule or career counseling succeeds, individuals approach occupational choices and work roles with a concern for the future, a sense of control over it, conceptions of which roles to play and conviction about what goals to pursue, confidence to design the occupational future and execute plans to make it real, commitment to their choices, and connections to their coworkers and organization. (Savickas, 2003, p. 242)

Hopefully, this chapter provides useful insights, strategies, and resources to align client needs with comprehensive plans, as well as help career counselors progress in their own development. The following Websites provide additional information relating to the chapter topics.

WEBSITES RELATED TO CHAPTER TOPICS

www.ncda.org
National Career Development Association
http://www.shrm.org
Society for Human Resource Management

http://www.jobhuntersbible.com
Job Hunter's Bible, Richard Bolles
http://www.newwork.com
New Work News, free daily news service on work, education and career development
http://www.coe.ohio-state.edu/jwheaton/bookmarks/counseling.htm
Counseling theory sites
http://www.blueprint4life.ca
Blueprint for Life Work Designs
http://www.newdream.org
Center for the New American Dream
http://www.readyminds.com
Customized Career Counseling Programs
http://www.cdm.uwaterloo
Career Development eManual
http://www.familiesandwork.org
Families and Work Institute
http://www.search-institute.org
Search Institute
http://www.career.fsu.edu/techcenter
Center for the Study of Technology in Counseling and Career Development
http://www.nccte.org
National Centers for Career and Technology Education
http://www.eric.ed.gov
The New ERIC System (in process of transition)
http://www.cete.org/acve
ERIC Archives
http://www.lominger.com
Career Architect Site
https://www.strengthsfinder.com
StrengthsFinder
http://www.strengthsquest.com
StrengthsQuest
http://www.realgame.com
The Real Game Series
http://www.jff.org/jff
Jobs for the Future
www.fallingawake.com
Falling Awake
http://online.onetcenter.org
O*Net

REFERENCES

America's Career Resource Network Association. (2003). *The educational, social, and economic value of informed and considered career decisions.* Bismarck, ND: Author.

Amundson, N. E. (2003). *Active engagement: Enhancing the career counseling process.* Richmond, B.C., Canada: Ergon Communications.

Azrin, N. H., & Besalel, V. A. (1980). *Job club counselor's manual.* Baltimore, MD: University Park Press.

Bailey, T. R., Hughes, K. L., & Moore, D. T. (2004). *Working knowledge: Work-based learning and educational reform.* New York: RoutledgeFalmer.

Barry, B. (2001). *The Real Game series* (Rev. ed.). St. John's, Newfoundland, Canada: The Real Game.

Becker, B. E., Huseld, M. A., & Ulrich, D. (2001). *The HR scoreboard: Linking people, strategy, and performance.* Cambridge, MA: Harvard Business School Press.

Bluestein, D. L., Chaves, A. P., Diemer, M. A., Gallagher, L. A., Marshall, K. G., & Sirin, S. (2002). Voices of the forgotten half: The role of social class in the school-to-work transition. *Journal of Counseling Psychology, 49,* 311–323.

Bolles, R. (1972). *What color is your parachute?* Berkeley, CA: Ten Speed Press.

Bolles, R. (1978). *Three boxes of life and how to get out of them: An introduction to life/work planning.* Berkeley, CA: Ten Speed Press.

Bordin, E. S. (1979). The generalizability of the working alliance. *Psychotherapy: Theory, Research and Practice, 16,* 252–260.

Boyatzis, R., McKee, A., & Goleman, D. (2002, April). Reawakening your passion for work. *Harvard Business Review, 80*(4), 86–94.

Buckingham, M., & Clifton, D.O. (2001). *Now discover your strengths.* New York: Free Press.

Campbell, R. E., Connel, J. B., Boyle, K. K., & Bhaerman, R. (1983). *Enhancing career development: Recommendations for action.* Columbus: Ohio State University, National Center for Research in Vocational Education.

Chung, Y. B., & Gfroerer, M. C. (2003). Career coaching: Practice, training, professional, and legal issues. *The Career Development Quarterly, 52,* 141–152.

Clifton, C., & Gonzalez-Molina, G. (2002). *Follow this path: How the world's greatest organizations drive growth by utilizing human potential.* New York: Warner Books.

Clifton, D. O., & Anderson, E. (2001). *StrengthsQuest: Discover and develop your strengths in academics, career, and beyond.* Washington, DC: Gallup Organization.

Coach University. (1999). Coach University electronic media kit. Retrieved September 7, 1999, from http://www.mediakit@coachu.com (No longer accessible. Document available from Y. Barry Chung, from bchung@gsu.edu)

Curnow, B., & Fox, J. M. (1994). *Third age careers.* Brookfield, VT: Gower.

Dawis, R. V. (1984). Job satisfaction: Worker's aspiration, attitudes and behavior. In N. C. Gysbers (Ed.), *Designing career counseling to enhance education, work and leisure.* San Francisco, CA: Jossey-Bass.

Derr, C. B. (1986). *Managing the new careerists.* San Francisco, CA: Jossey-Bass.

Dominguez, J., & Robin, V. (1992). *Your money or your life.* New York: Penguin Books.

Dubois, D. D. (2002–2003, Winter). Special issue: Competencies from the individual's viewpoint. *Career Planning and Adult Development Journal, 18*(4).

Dubois, D. D., & Rothwell, W. J. (2000). *The competency toolkit.* Amherst, MA: Human Resource Development Press.

Dychtwald, K. (2000). *Age power: How the 21st century will be ruled by the new old.* New York: Putnam.

Dykeman, C., Herr, E. L., Ingram, M., Wood, C., Charles, S., & Pehrsson, D. (2001). *The taxonomy of career development interventions that occur in America's secondary schools.* University of Minnesota, National Research Center for Career and Technical Education.

Edger, E., & Polloway, E. A. (1994). Education for adolescents with disabilities: Curriculum and placement issues. *The Journal of Special Education, 27,* 438–452.

Ellis, D. (2000). *Falling awake.* Rapid City, SD: Breakthrough Enterprises.

Fairweather, J. S., & Shaver, D. M. (1991). Making the transition to postsecondary education and training. *Exceptional Children, 57,* 264–267.

Fassel, D. (1990). *Working ourselves to death: The high cost of workaholism and the rewards of recovery.* New York: HarperCollins.

Feller, R. (2003). Aligning school counseling, the changing workplace, and career development assumptions. *Professional School Counseling, 64,* 262–271.

Feller, R. (2004). Using career assessments with adults (Special issue). *Career Planning and Adult Development Journal, 19.*

Feller, R., & Whichard, J. (2005). Knowledge nomads and the nervously employed: Workplace change and courageous career choices. Austin, TX: ProEd.

Ferris State University Career Institute for Education and Workforce Development. (2002). *Decisions without direction: Career guidance and decision-making among American youth.*

Figler, H., & Bolles, R. N. (1999). *The career counselor's handbook.* Berkeley, CA: Ten Speed Press.

Galinsky, E. (2003). *Dual-Centric: A new concept of work-life.* Retrieved November, 22, 2003, from http://www.familiesandwork.org/summary/dual-centric.pdf

Gallup Organization. (1987). *A Gallup survey regarding career development.* Princeton, NJ: Author.

Gallup Organization. (1989). *Work in America.* Princeton, NJ: Author.

Gallup Organization. (1999). *National survey of working America.* Princeton, NJ: Author.

Gelatt, H. B. (1998). Positive uncertainty: A new decision making framework for counseling. *Journal of Counseling Psychology, 36,* 2.

Goldman, D. (1995). *Emotional intelligence.* New York: Bantam Books.

Goldman, D. (1998). *Emotional intelligence at work.* New York: Bantam Books.

Grant, A. M. (2002, June). Towards a psychology of coaching: The impact of coaching on metacognition, mental health and goal attainment. *Dissertation Abstracts International, 63*(12), 6094.

Grant, A. M. (2003). The impact of life coaching on goal attainment, metacognition and mental health. *Social Behavior and Personality, 31,* 253–264.

Gray, K. C., & Herr, E. L. (2000). *Other ways to win: Creating alternatives for high school graduates* (2nd ed.). Thousand Oaks, CA: Corwin Press.

Gysbers, N. C., Heppner, M. J., & Johnston, J.A. (2003). *Career counseling: Process, issues, and techniques.* Boston, MA: Allyn & Bacon.

Haldane, B. (1960). *How to make a habit of success.* Englewood Cliffs, NJ: Prentice-Hall.

Hansen, L. S. (1997). *Integrative life planning: Critical tasks for career development and changing life patterns.* San Francisco, CA: Jossey-Bass.

Harrington, T. F. (2003). Career counseling strategies. In T. Harrington (Ed.), *Handbook of career planning for students with special needs* (pp. 77–108). Austin, TX: Pro-Ed.

Harrington, T. F., & O'Shea, A. J. (2000). *The Harrington-O'Shea Career Decision-Making System manual* (Rev. ed.). Circle Pines, MN: American Guidance Service.

Heppner, M. J., Multon, K. D., & Johnson, J. A. (1994). Assessing the psychological resources during career change: The development of the career transitions inventory. *Journal of Vocational Behavior, 44*, 55–74.

Herman, R., Olivo, T., & Gioia, J. (2003). *Impending crisis: Too many jobs, too few people.* Winchester, VA: Oakhill Press.

Herr, E. L. (1995). *Counseling employment bound youth.* Greensboro, NC: ERIC/CAPS Publication.

Herr, E. L. (1999). *Counseling in a dynamic society: Opportunities and challenges.* Alexandria, VA: American Counseling Association.

Herr, E. L., Cramer, S. H., & Niles, S.G. (2004). *Career guidance and counseling through the life span: Systematic approaches* (5th ed.). Boston, MA: Allyn & Bacon.

Holland, J. L., Magoon, T. M., & Spokane, A. R. (1981). Counseling psychology: Career interventions, research, and theory. *Review of Psychology, 32*, 279–300.

Hudson, F. M. (1999). *The handbook of coaching: A comprehensive resource guide for managers, executives, consultants and human resource professionals.* San Francisco, CA: Jossey-Bass.

Janosik, E. H. (1994). *Crisis counseling: A contemporary approach* (2nd ed.). Boston: Jones & Bartlett.

Jarvis, P., Zielke, J., & Cartwright, C. (2003). From career decision making to career management: It's all about lifelong learning. In G. Walz & R. Knowdell (Eds.), *Global realities: Celebrating our differences, honoring our connections* (pp. 269–280). Greensboro, NC: CAPS Press.

Kivland, C. M., & Nass, L. M. (2002–2003, Winter). Applying the use of emotional intelligence competencies: A business case report. *Career Planning and Adult Development Journal.*

Krumboltz, J. D. (1991). *Career Beliefs Inventory.* Palo Alto, CA: Consulting Psychologists Press.

Krumboltz, J. D., & Thoresen, C. E. (1964). The effect of behavioral counseling in groups and individual settings on information-seeking behavior. *Journal of Counseling Psychology, 17*, 324–333.

Leider, R. J. (1985). *The power of purpose.* New York: Ballantine.

Lombardo, M., & Eichinger, R. W. (2002a). *The career architect development planner.* Minneapolis, MN: Lominger.

Lombardo, M. W., & Eichinger, R. W. (2002b). *The leadership machine: Architecture to developing leaders for any future.* Minneapolis, MN: Lominger.

Lowman, R. (1996). Who will help us work more functionally? In R. Feller & G. Walz (Eds.), *Career transitions in turbulent times: Exploring work, learning and careers* (pp. 205–210). Greensboro, NC: ERIC/CASS.

McDonald, D. L. (2002). Career counseling strategies to facilitate the welfare-to-work transition: The case of Jeanetta. *The Career Development Quarterly, 50*, 326–330.

Michaels, E., Handfield-Jones, H., & Axelrod, B. (2001). *The war for talent.* Cambridge, MA: Harvard Business School Press.

Miscisin, M. (2001). *Showing our true colors.* Riverside, CA: True Colors Publishing.

Moris, A. (1988). *Individual life planning.* Seattle, WA: Sabah House/Individual Development Center.

Myers, I. B., & McCaulley, M. H. (1985). *Manual: A guide to the development and use of the Myers-Briggs Type Indicator.* Palo Alto, CA: Consulting Psychologists Press.

National Occupational Information Coordinating Committee (NOICC). (1996). *National career development guidelines: K–adult handbook.* Stillwater, OK: NOICC Training Support Center.

National Life/Work Centre, Canada Career Information Partnership & Human Resources Development Center, Canada. (n.d.). *Blueprint for life/work designs.* Retrieved January 7, 2004, from http://www.Blueprint4life.ca

Niles, S. G., & Pate, P. H. (1989). Competency and training issues related to the integration of career counseling and mental health counseling. *Journal of Career Development, 16*, 63–71.

Pacifici, T., & McKinnery, K. (1977). *Disability support services for community college students* (ERIC Document Reproduction Service NO. ED 409972).

Palmore, E. (1969). Predicting longevity: A follow-up controlling for age. *Gerontologist, 9,* 247–250.

Parsad, B., Alexander, D., Farris, E., & Hudson, L. (2003). *High school guidance counseling.* (NCES 2003-015). Washington, DC: U.S. Department of Education, National Center for Educational Studies.

Perseus. (2000). *Business: The ultimate resource.* Cambridge, MA: Bloomsbury.

Petersen, N. & Gonzalez, R. C. (2000a). *Career counseling models for diverse populations: Hands-on applications for practitioners.* Belmont, CA: Wadsworth.

Petersen, N. & Gonzalez, R. C. (2000b). *The role of work in people's lives: Applied career counseling and vocational psychology.* Belmont, CA: Wadsworth.

Peterson, G., Long, K., & Billups, A. (1999). The effect of three career interventions on educational choices of eighth grade students. *Professional School Counseling, 3,* 34.

Peterson, G., Long, K., & Billups, A. (2003). *How do career interventions impact the educational choices of eighth grade students?* National Center for School Counseling Outcome Research. Retrieved August 25, 2003, from http://www.umass.edu/schoolcounseling/ResearchBrief1.2.pdf

Pink, D. (2001). *Free agent nation: The future of working for yourself.* New York: Warner Books.

Reed, C., Lenz, J., Reardon, R., & Leierer, S. (2000). *Reducing negative career thoughts with a career course.* The Center for the Study of Technology in Counseling and Career Development. Retrieved August 25, 2003, from http://icdl.uncg.edu/ft/091001-02.html

Reich, R. B. (2002). *I'll be short: Essentials for a decent working society.* Boston, MA: Beacon Press.

Richardson, C. (1999). *Take time for your life.* New York: Broadway.

Rockport Institute. (2003). An interview with Rockport founder Nicholas Lore about career fit and satisfaction. Retrieved January 7, 2004, from http://rockportinstitute.com

Rosenbaum, J. E., & Person, A. E. (2003). Beyond college for all: Policies and practices to improve transitions into college and jobs. *Professional School Counseling, 64,* 252–260.

Sampson, J. P., Peterson, G. W., Lenz, J. G., & Reardon, R. C. (1992). A cognitive approach to career services: Translating concepts into practice. *The Career Development Quarterly, 41,* 67–74.

Sampson, J. P., Peterson, G. W., Lenz, J. G., Reardon, R. C., & Saunders, D. E. (1996). *Career thoughts inventory: Professional manual.* Odessa, FL: Psychological Assessment Resources.

Sandoval, J. (Ed.). (2002). *Handbook of crisis counseling, intervention, and prevention in the schools* (2nd ed.). Mahwah, NJ: Erlbaum.

Savickas, M. L. (1992). New directions in career assessment. In D. H. Montross & C. J. Shinkman (Eds.), *Career development* (pp. 336–355). Springfield, IL: Charles C. Thomas.

Savickas, M. L. (2003). Toward a taxonomy of human strengths: Career counseling's contribution to positive psychology. In W. B. Walsh (Ed.), *Counseling psychology and optimal human functioning* (pp. 229–249). Mahwah, NJ: Erlbaum.

Schlossberg, N. K. (1994). *Transition coping guidelines.* Minneapolis, MN: Personal Decisions International.

Search Institute. (1997). *The asset approach: Giving kids what they need to succeed.* Minneapolis, MN: Author.

Simonsen, P. (1993). *Managing your career within your organization.* Rolling Hills, IL: Career Directions, Inc.

Simonsen, P. (1997). *Promoting a development culture in your organization: Using career development as a change agent.* Palo Alto, CA: Davies-Black.

Simonsen, P. (2000). *Career Compass: Navigating your career strategically in the new century.* Palo Alto, CA: Davies-Black.

Snyder, C. R., Feldman, D. B., Shorey, H. S., & Rand, K. L. (2002). Hopeful choices: A school counselor's guide to the hope theory. *Professional School Counseling, 5,* 298–307.

Spokane, A. (1990). Supplementing differential research in vocational psychology using nontraditional methods. In R. A. Young & W. A. Borgen (Eds.), *Methodological approaches to the study of careers* (pp. 25–36). New York: Praeger.

Spokane, A. R., & Oliver, L. W. (1983). The outcomes of vocational intervention. In S. H. Osipow & W. B. Walsh (Eds.), *Handbook of vocational psychology* (Vol. 2, pp. 99–136). Hillsdale, NJ: Erlbaum.

Stewart, T. A. (2001). *The wealth of knowledge: Intellectual capital and the twenty-first century organization.* New York: Doubleday.

Stewart, W. (2001). *An A–Z of counseling theory and practice* (3rd ed.). Hampshire, U.K.: T. J. International, Ltd.

Training for jobs. (1994, March 12). *The Economist, 330*(7584), 19–20, 26.

Watts, A. G. (1996). The changing concept of career: Implications for career counseling. In R. Feller & G. Walz (Eds.), *Career transitions in turbulent times: Exploring work, learning and careers* (pp. 229–235). Greensboro, NC: ERIC/CASS.

Watts, A. G., Dartois, C., & Plant, P. (1986). *Educational and vocational guidance services for the 14–25 age group in the European Community.* Brussels, Belgium: Commission of the European Communities, Directorate-General for Employment, Social Affairs and Education.

Weinrach, S. (2003). A person-centered perspective to Welfare-to-Work services: In pursuit of the elusive and the unattainable. *The Career Development Quarterly, 52,* 153–161.

Whiston, S. C., Brecheisen, B. K., & Stephens, J. (2003). Does treatment modality affect career counseling effectiveness? *Journal of Vocational Behavior, 62,* 390–410.

Whiston, S. C., Sexton, T. L., & Lasoff, D. L. (1998). Career intervention outcome: A replication and extension of Oliver and Spokane. *Journal of Counseling Psychology, 45,* 150–165.

Whitmyer, C. (1994). *Mindfulness and meaningful work.* Berkeley, CA: Parallex Press.

Whitworth, L., Kimsey-House, H., & Sandahl, P. (1998). *Co-active coaching: New skills for coaching people toward success in work and life.* Palo Alto, CA: Davies-Black.

Wilms, W. W., & Zell, D. M. (1993). *Reinventing organizational culture across international boundaries* (Working Paper 94-3). Pittsburgh, PA: Carnegie Bosch Institute for Applied Studies in International Management.

CHAPTER 8

PROGRAM PROMOTION, MANAGEMENT, AND IMPLEMENTATION

DONALD A. SCHUTT, JR.

University of Wisconsin–Madison

The effective management of people, processes, and resources—in career development programs or any setting—requires specific competence in the areas of human resource management, strategic planning and continuous improvement, budgeting, and marketing. The particular combination of these competencies is often influenced by the context where the career development program resides. Understanding whom the career development program serves and how the services are delivered to meet their needs should guide program implementation. A one-person career center in a public library might demand a different blend of competencies and roles than a school counselor who is responsible for systemwide career development delivery targeted at kindergarten through high school students. The focus of this chapter are the competencies necessary to develop, plan, implement, and manage comprehensive career development programs in a variety of settings.

The chapter begins with a discussion of management responsibilities and leadership characteristics that can apply to a variety of contexts. Following that discussion are areas critical to effective program management: strategic planning and continuous improvement, budgeting, and marketing and promotions. The first area, planning, is vital for establishing a foundation from which the other areas can build. The planning process articulated in this chapter is very intentional and emphasizes the importance of systematic planning, which drives programmatic initiatives. Examples from different career development programs are interspersed and a case study utilizing the Letters and Science/Human Ecology Career Services office at the University of Wisconsin–Madison has been integrated with the discussion to illustrate effective program management.

MANAGING PEOPLE

Regardless of the size and scope of the career development program, there are fundamental human resource roles and functions that must be performed. Those roles include management, counseling, information technology, outreach, and operations. An appropriate staffing plan is congruent with priorities and initiatives identified through the planning process, which will be described later in the chapter.

The management role is typically filled by an individual manager, coordinator, or director. That individual must:

> have a strong understanding of the field of career development, as well as the components that are critical to developing and supporting comprehensive career development programs, and insights into successful management processes. Experience writing grants or soliciting funding would be additional desirable skills. Lastly, the manager should be competent in using technology and systems to manage the use and future needs of technology.
>
> The tasks of a manager/coordinator/director include: supervising staff, managing the day-to-day operations, searching for financial resources (when needed), developing collaborative partnerships with other organizations including schools and business/industry, and directing the continuous planning and improvement process guided by the mission and vision. (Schutt, 1999, p. 71)

The manager is also involved in the creation of positions, selection of staff, orientation, training, and performance management decisions. Finally, the management staff is accountable to the other staff for creating a positive and effective workplace environment that provides opportunities to work at one's highest level.

What Managers Do Matters

Management practices are the foundation on which career development programs succeed or fail, regardless of program size or complexity. Effective management creates a workplace culture that is inclusive and welcoming, recognizes the contributions of others in the workplace as critical to the programmatic outcomes, is invested in the growth and development of the contributors, and fosters articulate and frequent communication among those working in the program and with those for whom the work is done. Ineffective management leads to negative feelings about the program, has a negative impact on quality and productivity, and instills negative feelings that employees have about their ability to do the work (Ryan & Oestreich, 1998). The manager, often supported by practices, policies and procedures, establishes the climate and ultimately creates the culture in programs. This was reinforced by the Gallup Organization in an investigation of strong workplaces that attract and retain the most productive workers. They discovered that "the manager—not pay, benefits, perks, or a charismatic corporate leader—was the critical player in building a strong workplace. The manager was the key" (Buckingham & Coffman, 1999, p. 32). It is clear that how managers behave in the workplace matters.

This connection between culture and manager behavior is not just about what managers do, but also about who they are. Buckingham and Coffman (1999) described the key role of a manager:

> Great managers look inward. They look inside the company, into each individual, into the differences in style, goals, needs, and motivation of each person. These differences are small, subtle, but great managers need to pay attention to them. These subtle differences guide them toward the right way to release each person's unique talents. (p. 63)

The focus on the individual differences as a strength invites employees to be "able to bring more of their whole selves to the workplace and identify more fully with the work they do" (Thomas & Ely, 1996, p. 80). In doing so, the workplace culture becomes a welcome and inviting environment for people from a variety of backgrounds and life experiences. It is clear that manager behavior impacts the ability to succeed of those with whom they work, as well as the career development program overall.

Effective Management Behaviors

Being a manager requires skills in a number of different areas, typically outside the education and training received within a discipline such as counseling or psychology. It is often the case that technically competent employees are promoted into management positions because of their expert knowledge or technical skills rather than their ability to manage or lead. One challenge in facing circumstances that are unfamiliar (such as being in a management role for the first time) is the tendency to fall back on experience. Managers begin to manage as they have been managed—for better or for worse—based on personal experiences with previous managers. In some cases this can be very effective; however, in other cases it unintentionally sustains a cycle of poor management. The good news is that management and leadership skills can be taught and—through practice, self-reflection, and more practice—can be learned and integrated into the manager's personal repertoire. The goal for managers is to develop effective skills that they employ in an intentional and purposeful manner with the people, processes, and program in mind.

Zenger and Folkman (2002) captured the most critical elements of leadership. Those elements, summarized here, represent areas in which managers need to be effective:

1. character, including treating people with respect, working collaboratively, and having emotional resilience or the ability to rapidly adjust to change;
2. personal capability, which includes technical competence, professional skills, and using information technology effectively;
3. a focus on results, which is composed of identifying and communicating important organizational goals that translate to the level of the individual worker;
4. interpersonal skills, such as communicating effectively, building positive relationships, and being an effective team member; and

5. the ability to lead organizational change, including both tactical changes, such as process or facility improvements, and strategic changes, like creating a new vision for the program or changing the workplace culture.

Skills in these areas are necessary to effectively manage people, processes, and resources.

Staff Responsibilities

The responsibilities of the manager are determined by the size and breadth of services. Typically, the smaller the staff, the more the manager fills the role of generalist and is involved in all aspects of the program. As the size and breadth of the program grow, the manager may find that significant time is spent on personnel issues, budget discussions, and developing external partnerships and collaborations. If the program is actively engaged in grants or external funding or has a large internal budget produced through revenue streams, the management staff may be expanded to include a person with financial expertise such as an accountant or bookkeeper, or these roles may be outsourced. The disadvantage to having permanent management staff is cost; typically, individuals in management roles are the most highly paid employees, with the possible exception of information technology specialists.

The management staff is charged with ensuring that professional roles in the program are filled by staff that are qualified within their profession, appropriately prepared to work in career development, and committed to program success. Professional counselors and psychologists are those who have been licensed at the state level and/or certified at the national level; Professional Counselors were certified by the National Board for Certified Counselors, and Professional Psychologists are those who have graduated from a graduate program accredited by the American Psychological Association (APA) and are current members of the APA. Career Development Facilitators and Global Career Development Facilitators receive 120 hours of classroom instruction prior to certification and are prepared to provide career development guidance and assistance. Career Development Facilitators are endorsed by the National Career Development Association (NCDA), the National Employment Counseling Association (NECA), and the National Association of Workforce Development Professionals (NAWDP) and certified through the Center for Credentialing and Education, Inc. (CCE), a subsidiary of the National Board for Certified Counselors (NBCC).

Information technology professionals are typically certified on the software with which they are proficient. Companies like Microsoft, Cisco Systems, Oracle through Oracle University, and Novell offer a number of different certifications for the hardware and software they produce.

Administrative professional staff and office professionals can be certified as either a Certified Professional Secretary or a Certified Administrative Professional from the International Association of Administrative Professionals. Each of these certifications requires passing an examination that covers finance and business law, office systems and administration, and management. The Certified Administrative Professional exam also covers organizational planning, which includes team skills, strategic planning, and advanced administration. Other roles in the program may be filled by paraprofessionals, volunteers, or students. When effective management behaviors are accompanied by strategic planning, and continuous improvement skills, managers and the organization are positioned for success.

MANAGING PROCESSES: STRATEGIC PLANNING AND CONTINUOUS IMPROVEMENT

Often the planning process is viewed as having distinct beginning and end points. Effectiveness increases with intentionality; the greater the emphasis placed on the initial planning and ongoing improvement processes, the more likely it is that resources will be concentrated on the areas most important to the program audience and other stakeholders. The approach described in this chapter offers a different and more dynamic framework. Planning and improvement are linked in a continuous process focused on enhancing service and operational excellence. Service excellence is seen as the "complex set of communication processes through which we create and maintain relationships with those with whom we interact" (Ruben, 2004, p. 24). Operational excellence is connected to the effectiveness and efficiency of how our programs function (Ruben, 2004). Excellence is demonstrated in the policies, processes, and functions of the career development program.

At the foundation of the strategic planning and improvement process for the career development program are initiating a needs assessment; creating a mission statement; identifying the core values; setting a vision; and ultimately, articulating organizational strategies, including objectives and measures. Kaplan and Norton (2001) defined these terms:

> The overall *mission* of the organization provides the starting point; it defines why the organization exists or how a business unit fits within a broader corporate architecture. The mission and *core values* that accompany it remain fairly stable over time. The organization's *vision* paints a picture of the future that clarifies the direction of the organization and helps individuals to understand why and how they should support the organization. In addition, it launches the movement from the stability of the mission and core values to the dynamism of strategy, the next step in the continuum. *Strategy* is developed and evolves over time to meet the changing conditions posed by the real world. (pp. 72–73)

These definitions are synthesized in Table 8.1.

The Program-Planning Process (Figure 8.1) depicts the strategic-planning process, moving from needs assessment to the performance measures. These elements set the stage for providing effective career development services as well as guiding the evaluation of human resource management, budget, and marketing and promotional decisions. It is critical to understand how these concepts are developed in order to effectively assess progress and set the direction for ongoing improvement. The

TABLE 8.1   Definitions

TERM	DEFINITION
Mission	"A concise, internally focused statement of the reason for the organization's existence, the basic purpose toward which its activities are directed, and the values that guide employees' activities." (Kaplan & Norton, 2004, p. 34)
Core Values	Articulated or unexpressed principles or ethical guidelines that steer individual and organizational behavior; when unexpressed, individuals make decisions based on what they "think" are the principles; articulating core values is more effective if the goal is to have individuals and the organization moving in the same direction and ensuring that decisions and behaviors are consistent with organizational principles.
Vision	"A concise statement that defines the mid- to long-term (three- to ten-year) goals of the organization. The vision should be external and market-oriented and should express—often in colorful or 'visionary' terms—how the organization wants to be perceived by the world." (Kaplan & Norton, 2004, pp. 34–35)
Strategy	"Specific and detailed actions you will take to achieve your desired future." (Kaplan & Norton, 2001, p. 90)

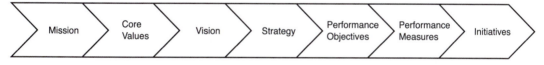

FIGURE 8.1   The Program-Planning Process

measure of success for strategic planning and continuous improvement processes is finding that the needs of the program's target audience have been met or exceeded, as demonstrated in the following case study (see box).

■ ■ ■ ■ ■

INTRODUCTION TO THE CASE STUDY: LETTERS AND SCIENCES/HUMAN ECOLOGY CAREER SERVICES

This case study describes an existing career services organization that operated for many years without incident or reason for change. Students were being served to the extent of the issues and needs they presented; the staff worked hard and were committed to the work they did; and the delivery model and organizational structure fit the services provided. In many ways, it appeared to be a typical organization that could be found on any college campus or any state agency or school. The distinguishing characteristic of this case study is that the organization, while stable, was not maximizing opportunities to reach the organization's

(continued)

■ ■ ■ ■ ■ ▬▬▬▬▬▬▬▬▬▬▬▬▬▬▬▬▬▬▬▬▬▬▬▬▬▬▬▬▬▬

CONTINUED

full potential. The following example—integrated through the chapter—demonstrates how effective leadership and sound program management can escalate to a higher level of performance to meet the greater, previously unidentified, needs of those they serve.

Background.   The Career Advising and Planning Services (CAPS) at the University of Wisconsin–Madison primarily provided resumé-review services and career advising. The CAPS office also focused on assisting in the transition from college to the workforce by hosting employers for on-campus interviewing. Additional programming included hosting a career fair each year and offering a small number of strategy workshops on campus.

One factor in the operation of the CAPS office and the delivery of its services was a lengthy leadership transition period. When the longtime director retired, it was over three years until a permanent director was hired. This extended leadership transition process had a significant impact on the ability of the office to maximize its potential.

Challenges.   There were six primary challenges facing CAPS when the new director came on-board:

1. neither the office nor the services were connected to a college or academic unit, resulting in CAPS serving a broad audience rather than leveraging its resources to focus on a smaller target audience;
2. the lack of connection to an established campus academic unit also impacted CAPS funding, which was primarily driven by state funding;
3. the articulation of the mission was unclear to staff members as well as external audiences;
4. the organization suffered from a lack of consistent leadership during the three-year period of transition between permanent directors;
5. the organizational infrastructure did not position CAPS to keep pace with changing environmental demands; and
6. the cumulative impact of these challenges resulted in low staff morale; more specifically, while individuals were personally satisfied by their work, they lacked an organization-wide sense of connection to a greater purpose.

INITIAL COMPELLING QUESTIONS

The new director faced a daunting task: to decide which of the challenges was most important and determine the point of greatest leverage or greatest opportunity within the system. To effectively respond, a better understanding of the needs was necessary.

Needs Assessment

Developing an effective needs assessment process is essential. Needs assessments consider both organizational and individual needs, depending on the context of the particular career development program. The identification of needs gives direction to the strategic planning and continuous improvement process. "A need has been defined as the discrepancy between *what is* and *what ought to be*. Once identified, needs are placed in order of priority. They are the basis for setting program goals" (Isaac & Michael, 1981/1984, p. 5). This gap analysis approach also considers what is or should be within the scope of the career development program.

Herr and Cramer (1996) described a multiphase process for needs assessment. The first phase is planning and designing the needs assessment, the second phase is conducting it, the third phase is using the results, and the fourth phase is determining the impact of the needs assessment process. Two steps are identified in the first phase: executing preliminary activities and planning and designing the needs assessment.

The first step, executing preliminary activities, includes setting up a needs assessment committee, identifying external priorities or limiting factors, determining the scope of assessment, establishing the needs assessment schedule, and reviewing committee resources and obtaining commitment. The planning and designing step includes specifying process and product goals, defining process goals as the intervention process itself, and defining product goals as student or employee outcomes as a result of the intervention process. The second step also includes developing statements of needs assessment program objectives with clarity, precision, measurability, feasibility, appropriateness, relevance, and logic; identifying the kind of data to be gathered (performance, description, opinion, attitude, perception); identifying the sources of data, sampling methods (groups, sizes, strategies/methods), and quantitative and qualitative methods and instruments; and determining the strategy for analyzing variables.

Before moving to the second phase—conducting the needs assessment—the National Occupational Information Coordinating Committee (NOICC) identified a "Career Guidance and Counseling Program Model" (Perry, 1995) that has relevance for process and product goals. Career development and counseling programs may want to consider the content, processes, and structures outlined in this model as areas in which to gather needs assessment data. Aspects of content included self-knowledge, educational and occupational exploration, and career planning. The processes identified were outreach, instruction, counseling, assessment, career information, work experience, placement, consultation, referral, and follow-up. Structural components were leadership, management, personnel, and facilities and resources. These three areas may be useful starting points when trying to decide where to begin the needs assessment.

The second phase described by Herr and Cramer (1996) involved implementing the assessment, a process comprised of obtaining, organizing, summarizing, analyzing, and interpreting the data collected, followed by an analysis of relationships to determine how the factors connect with needs and their timing. The third phase, using the needs assessment results, involved selecting priorities, as well as program planning and implementation. Program planning and implementation will be discussed in greater detail in this chapter as will the fourth phase, which is determining the impact of the change process.

Whether beginning a new career development program or evaluating a program that has been in place for years, the needs assessment process is vital to overall program planning and management as it connects directly to the individuals and organizations served by the career development program. It gives definition to the direction of the organization. The case study provides insights into one process.

CASE STUDY: RESPONDING TO THE NEEDS

A campuswide group assembled to review CAPS during the transition between the retired director and the permanent director provided a solution to the first challenge. CAPS became connected to two colleges within the university—the College of Letters and Science and the School of Human Ecology. This was a critical shift. The College of Letters and Science was, and remains, the largest academic unit on campus, with 39 departments, five professional schools, and nearly 60 interdisciplinary research and teaching programs. In 2002–2003, the college enrolled 17,495 students, just over 60 percent of the students at University. The School of Human Ecology, home of five academic departments with 1,005 students (approximately 3.5 percent of the undergraduate student population), is considerably smaller but is still a partner under the new organization. Narrowing services to declared majors in these two colleges allowed CAPS to begin to identify appropriate marketing and image strategies. In addition, the new move, to the school-college connection, meant a new home for CAPS with the Advising Group in Student Academic Affairs in the College of Letters and Science, as well as peer status with other academic support programs. CAPS could participate as a partner in a seamless advising system for students with divisional support. Furthermore, the academic connection clarified reporting lines and, ultimately, clarified the target audience for services; it also meant that the new director reported to an associate dean in an academic college.

The most compelling question that remained for CAPS was that of mission. What should the organization do? What infrastructure and delivery model strategies would best serve 18,500 students in a timely, efficient, and pertinent manner?

Mission Statements

A program's mission statement answers the question, "Why does the program exist?" and is driven from the results of the needs assessment. It helps to differentiate the program from others as well as to provide clarity related to the target audiences, both internally and externally. Effective mission statements inspire change, are long term in nature, and are easily understood and communicated (Niven, 2002). One example of an effective mission statement is from the U.S. Department of Labor, Employment and Training Administration (ETA):

> The mission of the Employment and Training Administration is to contribute to the more efficient functioning of the U.S. labor market by providing high quality job training, employment, labor market information, and income maintenance services primarily through state and local workforce development systems. (2005)

Another example is from Career Services at the University of Louisiana at Lafayette (2005):

> The mission of Career Services is to assist students and alumni in developing and implementing their career goals by providing skill enhancement, career and employer

information, and maintaining quality university-employer relationships which provide a link between students and potential employers.

Last, the Missouri Division of Vocational Rehabilitation created a phrase that captured the essence of their mission statement: "Making a positive difference through education and service." They then followed it up with an expanded mission statement:

> The Department of Elementary and Secondary Education is a team of dedicated individuals working for the continuous improvement of education and services for all citizens. We believe that we can make a positive difference in the quality of life for all Missourians by providing exceptional service to students, educators, schools, and citizens. (Missouri Division of Vocational Rehabilitation, 2005.)

The purpose of a mission statement is to orient the career development program staff, program participants, and other stakeholders to the central focus of your work. As Niven (2002) stated: "It acts as a beacon for your work, constantly pursued but never quite reached. Consider your mission to be the compass by which you guide your organization" (p. 73).

CASE STUDY: CREATING A MISSION STATEMENT

To create a mission statement for the new CAPS office, the director turned to professional organizations for the answers. One source that guided her was the National Association of Colleges and Employers (NACE) Principles for Professional Conduct, which are:

> Maintain an open and free selection of employment opportunities in an atmosphere conducive to objective thought, where job candidates can choose optimum long-term uses of their talents that are consistent with personal objectives and all relevant facts; maintain a recruitment process that is fair and equitable to candidates and employing organizations; support informed and responsible decision making by candidates. (National Association of Colleges and Employers, 2005)

Next, she identified and investigated two different career services operations in college settings. One was similar in terms of position within the institution and one was similar in terms of target audience served (in this case, college majors). The information collected from these sources was used to create clarity of purpose, as well as mission, strategic, and annual goals.

A new mission statement was developed: "To educate and support L&S and Human Ecology students with their career development process, enabling them to integrate their academic and life experiences with their career goals, and transition to the world of work"

(*continued*)

CONTINUED

(Letters and Science Career Services/Human Ecology Career Services, 2003a). The mission statement articulated specific strategies:

- Advise and assist Letters and Science and Human Ecology students and recent alumni with self-assessment, career exploration, decision making, planning and implementing a job search, and making decisions about how graduate school fits in with their career path.
- Provide support by storing and sending letters of recommendation for students considering graduate and professional schools.
- Encourage active student participation in planning our programs, and value students' voices and suggestions regarding our services.
- Offer a richer experience for our students by actively partnering and collaborating with campus constituencies, community, alumni, and employers.
- Present students with a variety of connections with employers to position them for success after graduation. (Letters and Science Career Services/Human Ecology Career Services, 2003a)

The first two points captured the CAPS mission; the last three points propelled the new organization in a different direction.

Core Values

Core values answer the question, "For what does your program stand?" Niven (2002) defined values as "the timely principles that guide an organization. They represent deeply held beliefs within the organization and are demonstrated through the day-to-day behaviors of all employees. An organization's values make an open proclamation about how it expects everyone to behave" (p. 77). Collins and Porras (1997), in their study of visionary companies, described core values as "the organization's essential and enduring tenets—a small set of general guiding principles; not to be confused with specific cultural or operational practices; not to be compromised for financial gain or short-term expediency" (p. 73). They added:

> Visionary companies tend to have only a few core values, usually between three and six. In fact, we found none of the visionary companies to have more than six core values, and most have less. And, indeed, we should expect this, for only a few values can be truly *core*—values so fundamental and deeply held that they will change or be compromised seldom, if ever. (p. 74)

The Virtual Career Center, which is a part of Career Management Services at Old Dominion University (2003), listed their core values as customer service, integrity, dependability, teamwork, accountability, and productivity. Core values are the unwavering principles supporting the mission and guiding the program through decision making.

LETTERS AND SCIENCE CAREER SERVICES/HUMAN ECOLOGY CAREER SERVICES CORE VALUES

A core values statement was developed that connected to the mission statement. The core values are:

- We are committed to treating all students with respect at all times.
- We value diversity, openness of communication, and a safe work environment for individuals and groups.
- We value a strong work ethic, and a sense of passion and fun in whatever we do, and a sense of balance between work and life.
- We are committed to continually assessing our operations to ensure the best possible service to our customers.
- We are committed to growing our staff through professional development and continuing education opportunities. (Letters and Science/Human Ecology Career Services, 2001, February, p. 3)

In 2001–2002, four strategic planning goals were projected:

> To become a proven cutting edge leader in providing career services, to use a developmental model of career services in expanding our programs and services, to focus on coalition and partnership building and establishing collaborations across campus and with alumni and employers, and to promote and instill the value of a liberal arts education. (Letters & Science/Human Ecology Career Services, 2001, February, p. 4)

Further, goal initiatives were articulated for each strategic planning goal. Examples of goal initiatives driven by the first strategic planning goal—to "become a proven cutting edge leader"—were (a) determining how the office was currently "cutting edge" by assessing its strengths, (b) benchmarking with the NACE Professional Standards for College and University Career Offices, and (c) investigating other career services operations. The other goal initiatives under this strategic planning goal included a gap analysis and an initiative for record-keeping process improvement. This progression from mission to the expanded mission statement and then to the core values statement and the strategic planning goals and initiatives refocused the organization.

The mission statement, combined with the formal connection to the colleges, created a new image for CAPS, which included a new name. The Career Advising and Placement Center (CAPS) changed its name to the College of Letters and Science/School of Human Ecology Career Services Office (L&S/Human Ecology Career Services Office). The new name stirred the internal and external perception of the office to move beyond one-on-one advising and placement with a broad audience to more complete career counseling and career development services directed toward three specific audiences: L&S/Human Ecology students, L&S/Human Ecology recent alumni (defined as within one year of graduation), and employers.

Next on the agenda was to develop programmatic strategies, an infrastructure to support those strategies, and a plan for marketing.

Vision

The value of a shared vision in the future direction of the career development program is enormous. The opportunity for people to consider creatively the future services and resources that a career development program might offer is exciting. Kotter (as cited in Niven, 2002) described the purpose of shared vision, particularly during times of change:

1. By clarifying the general direction for change, the vision simplifies hundreds or thousands of more detailed decisions.
2. The vision motivates people to take action in the right direction, even if the initial steps are personally painful.
3. Actions of different people throughout the organization are coordinated in a fast and efficient way based on the vision statement. (p. 84)

One challenge is that there are many different definitions that try to capture the vision component of the strategic-planning process, which creates an unclear picture of the importance of vision statements, as well as the process of creating one. Collins and Porras (1994/1997) eliminate the confusion with their vision framework. The vision framework is created through a balance between preserving the core of what your program is about while also stimulating new growth and progress.

> [Vision] builds on the interplay between these two complementary yin-and-yang forces: it defines "what we stand for and why we exist" that does not change (the core ideology) and sets forth "what we aspire to become, to achieve, to create" that will require significant change and progress to attain (the envisioned future).
>
> To pursue the vision means to create organizational and strategic alignment to preserve the core ideology and stimulate progress toward the envisioned future. Alignment brings the vision to life, translating it from good intentions to concrete reality. (Collins & Porras, 1994/1997, p. 221)

Effective vision statements are: concise, appeal to all the stakeholders, are consistent with the mission and values, are verifiable and feasible, and are inspirational (Niven, 2002). One example comes from the U.S. Department of Labor, Employment and Training Administration (2003) Web site: "Our vision is to promote pathways to economic liberty for individuals and families working to achieve the American Dream. On behalf of American taxpayers, the Employment and Training Administration will administer effective programs that have at their core the goals of enhanced employment opportunities and business prosperity." Building a shared vision strengthens the relationship between the program and the stakeholders.

Strategy

Strategy is the game plan through which a career development program implements the vision and, ultimately, the mission. Kaplan and Norton (2001) described the relationship between the vision and the strategy: "The vision creates the picture of the destination. The strategy defines the logic of how this vision will be achieved. Vision and strategy are essential complements" (p. 74). More specifically, strategy could be defined as "the specific and detailed actions you will take to achieve your desired future" (Niven, 2002, p. 90). Niven (2002) reported on some key principles of strategy as: generates understanding, consists of programmatic activities that distinguish the program from others, focuses the program to make decisions about what it is to do and what the program will not do, fits with the other strategies to create an integrated whole, provides continuity, and combines conceptual as well as analytical components. The purpose of defining strategy is to align programmatic activities with the identified needs of a program's target audience or users.

While strategy is the action-planning phase, it is also the vehicle through which program staff comes to understand the vision and their contributions to the overall program. Kaplan and Norton (2001) make the following point:

> Strategy does not (or should not) stand alone as management process. A continuum exists that begins in the broadest sense, with the mission of the organization. The mission must be translated so that the actions of the individuals are aligned and supportive of the mission. A management system should ensure that this translation is effectively made. Strategy is one step in a logical continuum that moves an organization from a high-level mission statement to the work performed by frontline and back-office employees. (p. 72)

Identifying the strategy or strategic themes is an important preparation for fully engaging the strategic-planning and continuous improvement process.

The National Career Development Guidelines, originally developed in 1986, were revised with the new version released in 2005 (America's Career Research Network, http://www.acrnetwork.org/ncdg.htm). Like the original guidelines, the new guidelines provide three strategic career development themes around which career development interventions can be framed: personal social development, educational achievement and life-long learning, and career management. Within each of the three areas, called "domains" in the revision, are sets of goals similar to the competencies identified in the previous guidelines. Table 8.2, National Career Development Guidelines Domains and Goals, provides an overview of the new structure. This goal-competency structure provided the stimulus necessary to begin integrating career development concepts into curriculum, services, and organizational structures. Career centers began to organize materials around the thematic areas. Career development activity books connected the activities to the NCDG thematic areas. The strategic themes increased awareness of career development concepts and assisted the delivery systems in moving down a common path. "Organizations don't execute unless the right people, individually and collectively, focus on the right details at the right time" (Bossidy & Charan, 2002, p. 33). The National Career Development Guidelines generated the necessary focus, as was also demonstrated in the case study.

TABLE 8.2   National Career Development Guidelines Domains and Goals

STRATEGIC THEME AREA (DOMAIN) GOALS

Personal Social Development Domain
- Develop understanding of self to build and maintain a positive self-concept.
- Develop positive interpersonal skills including respect for diversity.
- Integrate growth and change into your career development.
- Balance personal, leisure, community, learner, family and work roles.

Educational Achievement and Lifelong Learning Domain
- Attain educational achievement and performance levels needed to reach your personal and career goals.
- Participate in ongoing, lifelong learning experiences to enhance your ability to function effectively in a diverse and changing economy.

Career Management Domain
- Create and manage a career plan that meets your career goals.
- Use a process of decision-making as one component of career development.
- Use accurate, current and unbiased career information during career planning and management.
- Master academic, occupational and general employability skills in order to obtain, create, maintain and/or advance your employment.
- Integrate changing employment trends, societal needs and economic conditions into your career plans.

Note: Modified from America's Career Resource Network (ACRN) (n.d.). *The National Career Development Guidelines.* Retrieved March 19, 2005, from http://www.acrnetwork.org/ncdg.htm

CASE STUDY: IMPLEMENTATION, INFRASTRUCTURE, AND BEYOND

One significant change that the Career Services Office (formerly CAPS) needed was to modify the programmatic strategy of primarily serving students through individual meetings to a model that served a greater number of students, who could utilize existing resources in a different manner. The Career Services Office decided to preserve a core of individual advising appointments and improve the quality of appointments process by developing client intake protocol at the front desk. They then increased the number of students with whom they had contact by hosting workshops, panels, and career fairs.

This new model was very successful. For example, there was an increase from one career fair a year to seven different career fairs in 2002–2003. During 2002–2003, the L&S/Human Ecology Career Services Office connected with 4,600 students, an increase from 2,825 the previous year. These students had contact with 291 employers, up from 250 employers the previous year. Table 8.3 shows the number of students and employers at each fair during 2002–2003.

One effect of this programmatic shift was that an expansion of services to students through fair-type events resulted in a significant increase in event revenue, which, in turn, increased the overall budget for the office. This shift also affected the type of services requested. The number of students seeking advising appointments declined, which

TABLE 8.3   Participation in Career Events

CAREER FAIR	STUDENTS	EMPLOYERS
Career Expo	900	61
Graduate School Fair	700	70
Majors Fair	700	45[a]
Fall Internship Fair	400	18
Sciences & Life Sciences Fair	500	40
Spring Internship Fair	400	12
Multicultural Career Fair	350	40
Government & Non-Profit Fair	650	50
Total	4600	291[b]

[a]These were all L&S departments.
[b]Excluding L&S departments.

resulted in fewer walk-in appointments. In one year, the number dropped from approximately 1,500 appointments a year to 1,000 appointments. To support this change in services, an increased Web presence was created, and now some of the needs of students that were previously met through individual appointments are met through the Web page (http://www.lssaa.wisc.edu/careers/).

Students still submit resumés for review and critique. Due to a process change that guarantees a 48-hour turnaround, the actual number of resumés critiqued has continued to increase. The office also began to bundle services into packages, which contributed to this increase. For example, students who register for on-campus recruiting are required to have the resumé reviewed by staff prior to loading it into the electronic database of resumés.

The mission statement demanded that the organizational structure shift to fit the new model. Under CAPS, the 1999–2000 flat organizational structure (Figure 8.2) had little differentiation within the unit in terms of work flow and provided little support beyond the director level. This old organizational structure fit with the CAPS model of focusing on individual appointments with one-half of the positions dedicated to advising. As the new delivery model under L&S/Human Ecology Career Services Office emerged, greater specialization and delineation of roles and expectations was necessary. The organizational structure was divided into three operational units: an administrative unit, an employer relations unit, and an advising unit. In response, position descriptions were updated or modified to fit within the unit structure. Figure 8.3 also shows the addition of an

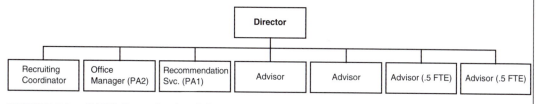

FIGURE 8.2   CAPS Organizational Structure

(*continued*)

■ ■ ■ ■ ■

CONTINUED

associate director dedicated to managing the internal operational activities. The role defini-tion was useful in clarifying the responsibilities and operational areas in the organization.

Two additional structural changes occurred: the creation of the Alumni Advisory Board and a shift from staff marketing to student-driven marketing. The Alumni Advi-sory Board provides insight into the changing marketplace needs of employers, insight into the demands on students entering the marketplace, and a flow of new ideas into the operation. Student-driven marketing under the employer relations and event coordinator has reaped multiple benefits, including more appealing advertising based on student experiences, a clearer understanding of the career development needs of students at the university, and an opportunity for Career Services to practice what it preaches by offering an internship opportunity to students. The identification of, and connection to, the three target audiences led to significant changes in the service-delivery strategy, organizational structure, and marketing.

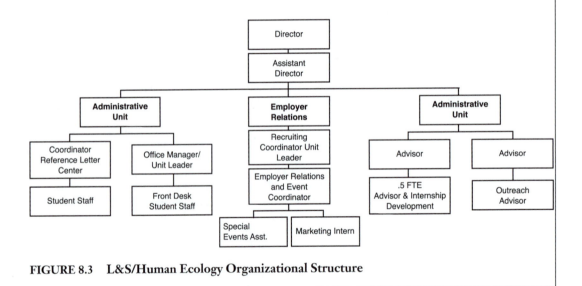

FIGURE 8.3 **L&S/Human Ecology Organizational Structure**

Fully Engaging Strategic Planning and Continuous Improvement

Once the mission, values, and vision foundations have been set and the strategy areas identified, the strategic-planning process is well under way. This process moves from strategy to performance objectives, measures, initiatives, and then personal objectives that define the work of individuals. Kaplan and Norton (2001) noted an important caveat: "The strategic planning process should use initiatives to help the organization to achieve its strategic objectives, not as ends in themselves. Public sector and nonprofit organizations are especially guilty of often confusing initiative completion as the target rather than improvements in mission objectives and agency effectiveness" (p. 294). Once the initiatives are identified, it is critical to identify the performance targets that will best demonstrate success relative to the objectives. The measure, in effect, becomes how well the initiative improves the program's ability to meet the strategic objectives, which is different than processes that assume success has occurred once the initiative is completed.

Identifying Performance Objectives.   Performance objectives "describe what you must do well in order to execute your strategy. Objective statements are just that—concise statements that describe the specific things you must perform well if you are to successfully implement your strategy" (Niven, 2002, p. 107). Objectives tell the story of your strategy in action. The Career Connection to Teaching with Technology (2002) Web site offered four objective statements:

> Objective 1: Identify reading, writing, mathematics and science achievement standards, benchmarks and accountability measures for students.

> Objective 2: Create a career connection to integrated core academic studies that increases the relevancy and authenticity of learning.

> Objective 3: Train teachers and students to access and utilize existing technologies, to create original instructional materials, and to collaborate with business partners in co-development of resources.

> Objective 4: Contribute to national educational networks using telecommunications to disseminate products and best practices. (Career Connection to Teaching with Technology, 2002)

Objectives link the strategy to the performance measures. Niven (2002) suggested conducting "objectives and measures generation sessions" with the goal of creating a number of objectives and measures.

With the National Career Development Guidelines competencies as an example of career-focused performance objectives, the strategic domain "personal social development" had four performance indicators, called *goals*. Each of the goals within the guidelines served as objectives working toward shared vision, and each of the objectives had *indicators* that served as performance measures. With the addition of the indicators, the measure was then linked to the strategy through the objective.

Performance Measures.   Performance measures are the tools that gauge progress against the objectives. These tools come in varying forms, from informal measures such as short pen-and-paper evaluations at the end of events or traffic headcounts on a daily basis, to formal evaluations such as satisfaction surveys, transaction surveys, or user complaint management processes. The goal of any measure is to gather information and increase knowledge about the ability of the career development program to meet the needs of clients and also about the program's efficiency and effectiveness in managing processes, people, and resources.

Niven (2002) offered criteria to use when selecting performance measures. He recommended that performance measures be linked to strategy, quantitative, accessible, easily understood, counterbalanced against other measures, relevant to the area being measured, and clearly defined. For example, If the target audience was veterans, the career development program could create a needs assessment based on the National Career Development Guidelines domains and goals to gauge where each program participant was currently functioning, develop initiatives based on the pattern of needs, and then measure the growth or development of the individuals over time. A pattern that might emerge is that low self-concept appears when the veterans are interviewing for jobs. Accordingly, one initiative under this competency area—which would follow the pattern of needs identified—might be a workshop on effective interviewing techniques and mock interviews. If the veterans who took the workshop ultimately improved their skills in maintaining a positive self-concept (relative to the initial assessment), it could be inferred that the initiative (interviewing workshop) met the objectives (enhanced self-concept), as measured by the performance measures (mock interview). Furthermore, the success of meeting the objectives in the strategic theme area (personal social development) thereby fulfilled the mission: strengthening career development programs at all levels and enhancing student/client achievement. This scenario emphasizes the links from the mission statement to the performance measures while also highlighting the importance of creating initiatives that are driven from the planning process rather than another source.

CASE STUDY: MEASURING EFFECTIVENESS

Effectiveness in achieving the goals is enhanced through an assessment plan, which is developed annually to respond to critical issues that have emerged over the previous year or is based on new initiatives that are introduced. The assessment plan for 2003–2004 (Letters and Science Career Services/Human Ecology Career Services, 2003b) included process components and traditional measures. The process components were forming an internal assessment team and a Web page redesign. The traditional measures were tracking student traffic at events, tracking advising use, event and workshop evaluations, office traffic reports, and student satisfaction surveys. One tool used by the unit to measure major events was a Web-based product called Zoomerang (www.zoomerang.com) that offered free basic memberships. The results of the assessment plan were delivered through an annual report composed of an update on the strategic-planning goals, a staff activity report, and numerical data representing the three units within the Career Services Office.

Morale. The final challenge the Letters and Science Career Services/Human Ecology Career Services dealt with was assessing employee morale. The director reported that following the reorganization, the office culture became energized and more responsive to the needs of the newly identified target audiences—the student, recent alumni, and employers. In addition, staff members sought continuous feedback from customers, viewed planning as a necessary organizational tool, and appeared comfortable taking risks while respecting and honoring the history of the office (A. Groves Lloyd, personal communication, October 2, 2003). This case study also demonstrates the positive impact that collaboration and partnerships can have on outreach efforts, marketing, and the ability to connect with the target audiences.

Initiatives.   Initiatives are the program components with which program staff and users are most familiar. Examples of initiatives include career fairs that connect job seekers with employers or a rescue helicopter landing on the elementary school playground to kick off "Careers in Health Care Day." Other examples of initiatives are day-one professional development plans (detailed plans for individuals charting necessary learning and skill development areas over the course of employment), portfolio workshops, succession preparation courses, and workshops that enhance an employee's ability to be successful at work. Initiatives might also include working with managers or supervisors to help them understand the importance of ongoing professional development for both the career development needs of the individuals and the success of the organization. Initiatives should be driven by the objectives. The landing of the rescue helicopter at the elementary school should have intentional connections back to the broader career development plan at that school, not just because the students love it and it has been done for the last five years. Initiatives that are most visible need to contribute to the results defined by the shared vision and mission for the career development program. The measure of success is not only at the programmatic level, but also in response to the question, "How does this initiative positively contribute to the strategy?"

Where to Begin?

Creating an effective strategic plan begins with selecting a planning committee. The initial steps are to identify the "individual who will oversee the process—the strategic planner—and to consider who should be the members of the committee" suggested Dolence, Rowley, and Lujan (1997, p. 6) in their discussion of strategic planning on a university campus. The strategic planner oversees the process and is responsible for organizing and making operational decisions about how the process unfolds.

> [The committee] should include people who are dedicated to the well-being of the institution and who also reflect the broad constituency base of the campus. This broadness is needed to assure that the major elements of the institution or unit are adequately represented while at the same time the size of the group is kept manageable. (Dolence et al., 1997, p. 6)

Following the selection and charge to the planning committee, the planner should begin the process of educating committee members on the process and expectations.

The process should flow in this manner: select initial committee; introduce the process; initiate the needs assessment process (with members from the planning committee participating on the needs assessment committee); identify the needs; review the mission, identify the values and create the shared vision; establish broad-based support and understanding relative to the mission, values, and vision; determine the strategy; name the objectives and performance measures; identify and execute the initiatives; continue to measure, reviewing the needs assessment findings and keeping track of changes in the economy, state, organization, community and workplace; and evaluate and continue to make adjustments as necessary.

Strategic Planning and Continuous Improvement as the Foundation

The process of creating the components for the strategic plan and then utilizing those components to continuously measure effectiveness and success, while time intensive, are critical as a map to guide the management decisions in human resources, budgeting, and marketing and promotion. Earlier in the chapter, these areas were described as building from the foundation established in the planning and improvement process; the larger goal of strategic planning is to create alignment among the organization's staff and resources and move toward increased effectiveness and success.

BUDGETING

There are a number of different budget and fiscal management systems from which to choose. The allocation of resources receives direction, in part, from the strategy identified earlier. From the strategy, initiatives are identified, each of which requires resources to execute. Budgets can be used to prioritize which initiatives have the greatest impact on the objectives relative to the strategy. Kaplan and Norton (2001) described resource allocation as evolving from two different processes: the operational budget and the strategic budget. The operational budget recognizes that:

> only a small percent of the spending and expenses in an annual (or quarterly) budget is discretionary. Most expenses are determined by the volume and mix of goods produced, services delivered, and customers served. The budget for such expenses reflects an expected level of spending based on forecasted revenue and the mix of products, services, and customers to generate the revenue. (p. 288)

Examples of the operational budget items are the costs related to the operations and infrastructure, such as telephones, Web pages, salaries, employee benefits, heat, electricity, and other ongoing costs related to getting the work done. Kaplan and Norton (2001) estimate those costs at 65 percent of the total budget and resource allocations. Also in the operational budget are the costs of maintaining existing customers, with some adjustments for improvements or enhancements to existing services. They estimate that this portion of the operating budget is an additional 25 percent, so the operational budget comprises 90 percent of the total budget, with the remaining 10 percent available for the strategic budget process.

The strategic budget draws returns to the idea that initiatives are not intended to be the endpoint of the funding, but rather a means to explore a new level of service or expand the program.

> The strategic budget authorizes the initiatives required to close the planning gap between desired breakthrough performance and that achievable by continuous improvement and business as usual. The strategic budget identifies what new operations are required; what new capabilities must be created; what new products and services must be launched; what new customers, markets, applications, and regions must be served; and what new alliances and joint ventures must be established. (Kaplan & Norton, 2001, p. 288)

As a program manager, decisions regarding the budget process are challenging. The importance of working with the shared vision created through teamwork and open communication is felt during difficult budget times. It is never easy to reallocate funding or to reduce programs or positions, but the choices are less complicated when the pattern of decision making over time has been consistent with the mission, values, and objectives.

MARKETING AND PROMOTIONS

Connecting career development programs and services to participants and users begins with the needs assessment. The needs assessment, if properly planned, creates awareness on the part of potential or current users of what services and programs exist and what could exist. The question of target audience, and understanding their needs, drives the system that was created.

Developing a comprehensive marketing and promotion plan takes time. Effective marketing and promotion extend well beyond merely pulling together a couple flyers and handing them out to existing program participants. Marketing plans involve alignment between your internal and external communications and the mission, values, goals, and objectives. Middleton (n.d.) proposed a marketing strategy based on positioning, packaging, promotion, persuasion, and performance.

Positioning communicates to potential users the unique aspects provided by the career development program. This area can "tell the program's story" to potential service users and program participants.

Packaging is the plan for presenting the program's services to prospective users, generating interest and responses from potential users through marketing brochures, creating an image with a business identity package (like letterhead and a logo), and identifying a way to connect with potential users. The purpose of packaging is to demonstrate to existing and potential users what the program is all about—the mission, the vision, the objectives, and how the program sees itself. Packaging also tells prospective users how they will be treated if they choose to utilize the career development program.

Promoting career development services includes: networking, well-crafted communications sent to existing mailing lists, a Web strategy (or at least a Web page), and getting out and speaking at community events, or writing for community newspapers. One example is a workforce development center that partnered with a local newspaper to have it profile interesting and unusual jobs once a week. The newspaper ran the profile, and the workforce development center provided the occupational background information to the reporter.

The persuasion process includes having a clear and concise description of the program prepared when asked "What is it that you do?" Persuasion emphasizes the value of sending consistent messages in incoming and outgoing communications, and sharing success stories (when appropriate, always protecting the identity of individuals).

Performance includes scheduling regular marketing meetings and making marketing a priority, keeping track of short-term and long-term marketing projects, and ensuring that programmatic actions match promises made to existing and new users.

A marketing and promotion plan is only as effective as the time and thought expended in its development. Promotion is the process of having the program noticed, considered, and selected; marketing is delivering the services to the users and program participants in a timely and effective manner. Effective marketing and promotion serve to showcase the results of effective management behaviors and planning processes.

CONCLUSION

The process of planning, supported by strong management behaviors, can build effective and successful organizations that are aligned around mission, core values, and shared vision. The Appendix provides additional Web resources related to the areas discussed in this chapter.

■ ■ ■ ■ ■ ▬▬▬▬▬▬▬▬▬▬▬▬▬▬▬▬▬▬▬▬▬▬▬▬▬▬▬▬▬▬▬▬▬▬

CASE STUDY: SUMMARY

The management practices employed by the new director, including the creation of structures and services that met the needs of the target audiences, positioned the organization to maximize opportunities. At the beginning of the case study, six challenges were identified. Through the execution of sound management practices, the organization effectively connected with established academic units that articulated the audience, created and implemented an organizational mission and planning process, identified new funding sources to supplement existing state funding, stabilized executive leadership and called on leadership from within the organization during the organization restructuring, revised the organizational structure to fit the mission, and gathered feedback from current students, alumni, and employers to guide the future direction of the services.

The case study demonstrated the transition from a management approach that was less focused on planning and improvement to an organization that is driven by planning and continuous improvement. The organization created programming initiatives that are aligned with its mission, values, vision, and objectives and that significantly expanded the base of program participants. Through creative strategy, the program promotion shifted to have students market to students. Further, these changes created a positive impact on the office climate and made employees feel a balance of challenge and support, causing them to demonstrate risk-taking behaviors that will continue to develop the organization.

Successful career development programs are based on many factors. This chapter has demonstrated the importance of strategic planning and continuous improvement in all aspects of program planning. The skills of managing people, processes, and resources are applicable to many settings; the ability of a career development program manager to customize these concepts for the context in which they work and transfer this knowledge to program staff is essential.

APPENDIX: WEB RESOURCES

SOURCE	URL
American Psychological Association	http://www.apa.org
American School Counselor Association National Model	http://www.schoolcounselor.org/content.asp?contentid=134
California Department of Education Career Counseling	http://www.cde.ca.gov/spbranch/ssp/careercounsel.html
Career Development Facilitators	http://www.ncda.org
Cisco Systems	http://www.cisco.com/en/US/learning
Global Career Development Facilitators	http://www.cdf-global.org/index2.htm
International Association of Administrative Professionals	http://www.iaap-hq.org/
International Career Development Library	http://icdl.uncg.edu/index.html
Microsoft	http://www.microsoft.com/traincert/mcp/default.asp
National Association of Colleges and Employers	http://www.naceweb.org/
National Board for Certified Counselors	http://www.nbcc.org
National Career Development Association Career Counseling Competencies	http://ncda.org/about/polccc.html
National Center for Research in Vocational Education 1988–1999	http://ncrve.berkeley.edu/
NOICC Guide to Planning	http://icdl.uncg.edu/pdf/030900-01.pdf
NOICC/SOICC Network	http://icdl.uncg.edu/noicc.html
Novell	http://www.novell.com/training/certinfo/

Oracle	http://education.oracle.com/
University of Minnesota Career and Lifework Center	http://www.lifework.umn.edu/indicator/index.html
University of Waterloo Career Development eManual	http://www.cdm.uwaterloo.ca/

Note: Retrieved November 13, 2003.

REFERENCES

America's Career Resource Network (ACRN). (n.d.). *The National Career Development Guidelines.* Retrieved March 19, 2005, from http://www.acrnetwork.org.ncdg.htm

Bossidy, L., & Charan, R. (2002). *Execution: The discipline of getting things done.* New York: Crown Business.

Buckingham, M., & Coffman, C. (1999). *First, break all the rules: What the world's greatest managers do differently.* New York: Simon & Schuster.

Career Connection to Teaching with Technology. (2002). *Objectives.* Retrieved November 13, 2003, from http://www.cctt.org/summaries/year5.asp

Collins, J. C., & Porras, J. I. (1997). *Built to last: Successful habits of visionary companies.* New York: HarperBuisness. (Original work published 1994)

Dolence, M. G., Rowley, D. J., & Lujan, H. D. (1997). *Working toward strategic change: A step-by-step guide to the planning process.* San Francisco: Jossey-Bass.

Herr, E. L., & Cramer, S. H. (1996). *Career guidance and counseling through the lifespan: Systematic approaches* (5th ed.) New York: HarperCollins.

Isaac, S., & Michael, W. B. (1984). *Handbook in research and evaluation: A collection of principles, methods, and strategies useful in the planning, design, and evaluation of studies in education and the behavioral studies* (2nd ed.). San Diego, CA: EdITS Publishers. (Original work published 1981)

Kaplan, R. S., & Norton, D. P. (2001). *The strategy-focused organization: How balanced scorecard companies thrive in the new business environment.* Boston: Harvard Business School.

Kaplan, R. S., & Norton, D. P. (2004). *Strategy maps: Converting intangible assets into tangible outcomes.* Boston: Harvard Business School.

Letters and Science/Human Ecology Career Services. (2001, February). *Letters and Science/Human Ecology Career Service 2000–2001 Annual Report.* Madison, WI: Author.

Letters and Science Career Services/Human Ecology Career Services. (2003a). *From college to work: Educating students on the tools for life* [Brochure]. Madison: University of Wisconsin–Madison.

Letters and Science Career Services/Human Ecology Career Services. (2003b). *2003–04 assessment plan draft.* Unpublished manuscript, University of Wisconsin–Madison.

Middleton, R. (n.d.). *5Ps of professional service business marketing: Plan and clarify your marketing direction.* Retrieved November 13, 2003, from http://www.actionplan.com/6psmarkt.html

Missouri Division of Vocational Rehabilitation. (n.d.). *Mission statement.* Retrieved March 19, 2005, from Missouri Division of Vocational Rehabilitation, at http://vr.dese.mo.gov/vr/co/VRWebsite.nsf/web/MissStmnt?opendocument

National Association of Colleges and Employers. (2005). *Principles for professional conduct for career services and employment professionals.* Retrieved March 19, 2005, from http://www.naceweb.org/principles/principl.html

Niven, P. R. (2002). *Balanced scorecard step-by-step: Maximizing performance and maintaining results.* New York: John Wiley & Sons.

Old Dominion University, Career Management Center, Virtual Career Center. (2003). *Core values.* Retrieved November 13, 2003, from http://www.odu.edu/ao/cmc/mission.html

Perry, N. (1995). *Program guide—Planning to meet career development needs: School-to-work transition programs.* Washington, DC: National Occupational Information Coordinating Committee.

Ruben, B. D. (2004). *Pursuing excellence in higher education: Eight fundamental challenges.* New York: John Wiley & Sons.

Ryan, K. D., & Oestreich, D. K. (1998). *Driving fear out of the workplace: Creating the high-trust, high-performance organization.* San Francisco: Jossey-Bass.

Schutt, D. A. (1999). *How to plan and develop a career center.* Chicago: Ferguson.

Thomas, D. A., & Ely, R. J. (1996, September–October). Making differences matter: A new paradigm for managing diversity. *Harvard Business Review*, 79–90.

U.S. Department of Labor, Employment and Training Administration. (2005). *ETA mission.* Retrieved March 19, 2005, from http://www.doleta.gov/etainfo/mission.cfm

University of Louisana at Lafayette Career Services. (2005). *Mission statement.* Retrieved March 19, 2005, from http://careerservices.louisiana.edu/about_us/index.html

Zenger, J. H., & Folkman, J. (2002). *The extraordinary leader: Turning good managers into great leaders.* New York: McGraw Hill.

CHAPTER 9

CONSULTATION, COACHING, AND SUPERVISION

LAURA R. SIMPSON

Counseling, in general, is a multidimensional occupation, and career counseling is no exception. Meeting the various needs and interests of each client can be a counselor's greatest challenge. Thus, considering how to best meet the identified needs requires special attention. Career counselors may be asked to assume many diverse roles when working with individuals. As a student, comprehending the similarities and differences among these assorted roles is the first step in determining how to best meet the needs of clients. This chapter is designed to explore some of the specific roles that career counselors may engage in while working with clients.

Too often, individuals try to fit themselves into a job and end up patterning their lives around it. According to Hayes (2001), a survey of 400 college-educated workers between the ages of 30 and 55 revealed that almost half would choose a different major if they could do it over. Career counselors can assist people in matching their values, interests, skills, and capabilities with occupations or professions that meet their personal needs. Career counselors are most appropriate for people who need encouragement to enter into, change, or reevaluate their career or life goals or who need to evaluate retirement career options. When tailoring an approach to assist a client, a career counselor may engage in many roles, including consultant, coach, and supervisor. While these roles are somewhat similar, each is also distinctly separate. This chapter examines the roles of consultation, coaching, and supervision in relation to career counseling, as well as providing practical examples of how these roles might be applied to the counseling process.

THE MANY ROLES OF CAREER COUNSELING

Consultant

Consultation frequently occurs within the hierarchical relationship between a supervisor and supervisee, as well as in relationships between peers of equal status. There is little doubt that consultation activities are distinctly different from those that involve administrative or evaluative functions (Hays & Brown, 2004a). "It is essentially a problem solving process in which the two participants in the process identify the relevant diffi-culties, collaborate on some intervention, and then assess the results, making adjust-ments as needed" (Bradley & Kottler, 2001, p. 14). Consultation provides an indirect service to a client or group for whom the helping intervention is intended (Backer, 2003; Drapela, 1983).

Consultation as an activity and consultant as a career label became increasingly prevalent in the last generations of the twentieth century. Although generally recog-nized as originating in the medical profession, today, endless varieties of professions use the label *consultant*. The characteristics and models of consultation are easily applied to career counseling.

Characteristics of Consultants

Regardless of the vocational arena, there are a variety of components that charac-terize consultation. Some include the following: (Brown, Pryzwansky, & Schulte, 1991; Dougherty, 1995; Gibson & Mitchell, 1999; Gladding, 1996; O'Roark, 2002; Scholten, 2003):

1. The consultant is considered an expert, whether a master counselor or, in the case of career consultation, an individual with extensive training and experience in the area of need.
2. The consultee is considered capable. Whether the individual is a counselor looking for assistance in dealing with a client or an employee seeking career intervention, they are accepted as potentially capable. If the consultant does not view the consul-tee as such, the effectiveness of the consultation may be threatened.
3. The relationship between the consultant and consultee must be well matched and complementary. The role of the consultant is to help with personal and profes-sional development, competency development, and the institution and continua-tion of accountability. The primary role of the consultee is to seek, and benefit from, the consultant's expertise in the attainment of responsible self-development.
4. A need exists that cannot be met by the individual or organization requesting the consultation.

Career consultants provide career counseling and placement services. The focus is generally on job search strategies and support. Consultants are typically degreed profes-sionals with experience in business, industry, or the public sector. Executive placement consultants, or "headhunters," work for employers, not the job seeker. Headhunters seek qualified people to fit existing positions, and they are paid by the employer. While not useful for career changers, headhunters perform a valuable service for employers and for job seekers with recent and relevant transferable skills and experience.

Models of Consultation

Consultation and its application to counseling have been widely recognized and defined, although not nearly as well publicized as their business counterparts (Gibson &

Mitchell, 1999). However, consultation as an activity for counselors has led to an examination of various models appropriate to the consultation process and their adaptation to counselor use. This section will examine a number of commonly used consultation models.

A traditional model that highlights the basic consultation process is the triadic model (Gibson & Mitchell, 1999; Newman, 1993). The triad is made up of a consultant, a consultee, and the consultee's client. In this model, consultation services are offered indirectly, through an intermediary, to target clients. The consultant has direct contact with the consultee, yet the issues discussed and assistance offered are focused on a third party. All consultation efforts proceed to the third party through the consultee, and none proceed directly from consultant to clients. The consultee derives some professional and personal benefits from the consultation process as well.

Kurpius (1988) and Kurpius and Fuqua (1993) suggest that consultants can function effectively in several ways. They may provide a direct service to a client through prescribing a solution to a specific problem identified by a consultee, assist a consultee in developing a plan for problem solving, or take a more directive approach by actually defining a problem and proposing a solution. These functions are organized into four consultation modalities.

Provision Mode.   The provision mode of consultation is used when a client is confronted with a problem and lacks the resources of time, interest, or competence to define the problem objectively, generate possible solutions, or implement a problem-solving strategy. In this case, a consultant is requested to provide a direct service to the client, with minimal or no intervention by the consultee after the referral is in place. For a career counselor functioning in this mode, the consultee could be an agency with a specific employee issue. For example, a board of directors of a nonprofit organization might engage a career counselor to assist a new agency director in expanding fund-raising skills to better meet the needs of the position requirements.

Prescriptive Mode.   This mode is utilized when a consultee is looking for a specific solution, or "prescription," for a specific problem. The consultant and consultee work together to ensure that all information needed to define and solve the problem is available and accurate, and that the consultee accepts the plan prescribed and will implement the program as designed by the consultant, and to specify who will evaluate the process and outcomes. In this case, a career counselor might provide consultation to the board directly and prescribe specific training opportunities to aid the new director's development.

Collaboration Mode.   If this mode is utilized, the consultant functions more as a facilitator than a technical expert. The consultant's efforts are aimed at assisting the consultee in maximizing resources, realizing abilities, and developing a plan for problem solving. This process may include providing feedback, making suggestions, and examining circumstances that may either impede or, alternately, assist the resolution of the problem at hand. As a career counselor functioning in the collaboration mode, the consultation will involve meeting with the board (consultee) to explore potential resources among current staff to best meet the agency's fund-raising needs.

Mediation Mode. Mediation is uniquely different from the previous three modes of consultation, in which the consultee initiates contact and requests help for solving a problem. In mediation, it is the consultant who recognizes a problem, gathers and interprets information, and determines an appropriate intervention, ultimately resulting in contacting the persons who have the greatest potential for implementing change and sharing a proposed solution. Thus, a career counselor who has been working with an agency may recognize that the board and the director are not communicating and note a high employee turnover rate. The consultant then approaches the board, makes suggestions on how to reduce turnover, and brings the two sides together to address the identified problem.

Some models break down the consultation process into even more specific roles. Blocher (1987) identifies seven models of consultation, which help identify many of the specific roles of consultants. They include the following.

Triadic Consultation. Characterized by three distinct roles, this model utilizes a consultant who provides specific expertise; the mediator, who applies the feedback of the consultant; and the client, who is the focus of the service.

Technical Consultation. A narrow and specific intervention, this model is focused on specific expertise in relation to a specific problem. A career counselor with experience in a specific vocational arena might be utilized for technical consultation. For example, a career counselor with experience as a teacher might provide consultation for a school with teachers in need of classroom management techniques.

Collaborative Consultation. A cooperative relationship between consultant and consultee, this model combines the collective resources of the two, and the pair work as equal partners. For example, a career counselor might provide collaborative consultation for a police department through the provision of assessment techniques to determine strengths and weaknesses of new officers.

Facilitative Consultation. The consultant facilitates the consultee's access and use of resources in this model. Moreover, the consultant expresses legitimate interest in the functioning of the consultee.

Mental Health Consultation. In this model, the consultant assists a counselor in gaining better understanding of the interaction with a client through such means as analyzing the treatment approach, consideration of the consultee's responses to the client, and providing general education and support. This approach is the same as the consultation mode of Bernard's discrimination model of supervision (1979), which is discussed later in this chapter.

Behavioral Consultation. This model is focused on the consultant teaching the consultee behavior management techniques, which, when understood and implemented, influence the behavior of the consultee's clients. For example, a career counselor may provide consultation for a business to develop specific responses to customer issues on customer service lines.

Process Consultation.   In this model, the consultant provides services to an organization as a means to increasing the effectiveness of a work group in reaching its goals. This approach examines the interactions among groups of individuals who work with each other and the existing relationships. A career counselor may provide process consultation when two banks merge employees retaining all employees. The consultation can assist employees who were formally competitors in working together successfully.

Regardless of model choice, counselor consultants must recognize that they are involved in a process that provides structure and direction for their consultation efforts. It is naive to think that knowledge or experience in itself qualifies one to consult. An understanding of the process of consultation and the acquisition of skills for consultation are prerequisites to success as a consultant. While experience is important, these skills and knowledge are typically acquired through special courses in consultation.

Consultative Relationship

The consultative relationship is distinct from other relationships between counselor and client. A consultant is usually an expert in a field who consults with or offers expertise to others, both within and outside the career area. Consultation occurs when the expertise is requested by another party or organization. The consultant's role is an advising or enhancing one, not a supervisory one. Likewise, unlike counseling, it is not a therapeutic relationship.

While not traditional counseling, consultation does share certain special skills, which are needed if the counselor is to function effectively as a consultant. Some skills include the following (Backer, 2003; Brown et al., 1991; Dougherty, 1995; Gladding, 1996):

- the expertise needed to address the identified need and provide effective intervention;
- knowledge of, and experience in, the consultation process; and
- the recognition and understanding of differing environments and their impacts on populations and organizations.

The counselor who is functioning in the consultation role should possess and employ those skills that are essential in the counseling process. Critical communication and specialized interpersonal skills such as attending, listening, questioning, and giving feedback are essential. Respect and understanding should be emphasized. Consultants should possess expertise in systematic problem-solving techniques and evaluation procedures as well. Moreover, skills in facilitating groups can be very helpful. These characteristics combine to equip the career counselor to make the transition from facilitator, mediator, planner, educator, and motivator as needed.

Career counselors acting as consultants must be mindful that requests for consultation may be based on a foundation of unresolved personal problems of the consultee. For instance, a manager of a local business who wishes to consult about an employee may end up discussing her own personal problems. A counselor who realizes that the initial consultation is shifting toward counseling will likely respond to the personal needs of the manager but avoid losing sight of the primary professional responsibility to the employees of the business. After providing short-term assistance to the manager, the counselor may suggest additional counseling elsewhere and provide information regarding available counseling opportunities in the community. Such an approach will help the counselor uphold professional priorities and maintain an ongoing consulting relationship with the manager that will focus on the needs of the employees for whose benefit the helping intervention was initiated.

There is an inherent overlap between counseling and consultation in the area of occupational issues. If occupational issues are closely linked to personal problems, they are dealt with through counseling. For example, an employee who experiences a reactive depression because of job-related pressures needs counseling assistance. If occupational issues are related to problems of a third party, they may fall within the perimeter of consultation. This could be the case if an employer asks for consultation because of excessive insubordination of employees. In the process of consultation, it becomes evident that the problem lies with the employer, who lacks management skills and needs personalized instruction in this area.

The qualified career counselor will have multiple opportunities to consult. The effective consultant will always be mindful that for consultation to be effective, it must be wanted. Even when requested, the consultant should proceed with tact and understanding in providing ideas, opinions, and solutions to others.

Ethical and Legal Concerns

Traditional counseling differs from consulting relationships in several primary ways. These differences require special deliberation in evaluating ethical considerations. The code of ethics for the helping professionals provide only limited guidance for consultation practice, leaving clinicians to bear vast personal responsibility for their professional actions and decisions.

Relationship Issues.   At the most fundamental level, the triadic nature of consulting relationships must be considered. Ethical issues are complicated by the involvement of three parties within the relationship: the consultant, the consultee, and the consultee's client. Snow and Gersick (1986) define the problem as the fact that it is "conceptually awkward to consider clients of the consultee agency to be part of the consultation agreement since they are not present, do not have the opportunity to articulate their own priorities, and most often do not even know that a consultation is taking place" (p. 401). Thus, the consultee's client is affected by the consultation process, without the opportunity of participation (Newman, 1993). As a result, it is generally agreed that the consultant's responsibility extends to these individuals (Backer, 2003; Brown et al., 1991; Newman, 1993; Newman & Robinson, 1991).

Confidentiality.   Confidentiality represents an individual's right to privacy and establishes the foundation of trust that is essential to successful outcomes. Although confidentiality has been widely addressed, the special circumstances of consultation require particular consideration.

"Given the practical limits of a consultant's ability to protect the confidentiality of information obtained during the consultation, individual's rights to privacy may be difficult or even impossible to guarantee" (Newman, 1993, p. 150). Clearly, the consultant has an ethical responsibility to ensure that participants understand what information will be used, as well as whom it will be used with and for what purpose. The limits of confidentiality must be plainly and unanimously understood by all participants. Consider this: a career counselor is called to provide consultation for a school interested in determining why a teacher is having difficulty disciplining her students. The teacher reveals to the consultant that she has a history of childhood abuse. Clearly, it would be important for the teacher to know from the start that her employer will be informed of any information provided to the consultant.

Power.   Within the consultation process, power—or the ability to influence—is typically irregularly distributed among participants. Thus, the potential misuse or abuse of power is a concern within the consultation process (Hays & Brown, 2004b). This irregular distribution of power may exist between the consultant and the consultee organization or within the organization itself. Power differentials may be real or perceived, but either type may exert substantial influence on the process and outcomes on consultation.

As the consultant role is one of expert, there becomes potential for an "imbalanced power relationship" (Tokunga, 1984). Consultants must make every effort to ensure their power is used to facilitate the goals and welfare of the consultee. "Collaborative definition of organizational interests and goals with the consultee will reduce the likelihood that the consultant will exploit this influence to facilitate unilaterally defined objectives" (Newman, 1993, p. 152). Power differentials within the organization itself may receive a positive influence from the consultant's own responsible use of power. Consultants are in a unique position to educate consultees in constructive methods for using power to extract cooperation from employees and for strengthening cooperative commitments to organizational goals (Merrell, 1991). The issue of power could be pertinent to a career counselor if consultation is requested for a situation in which the consultant has a personal interest. For example, the consultant may be called into an elementary school setting to assess student preparation for high school. Perhaps this consultant has a strong interest in foreign language. He or she must be careful not to misuse power in the role of expert by pushing a personal agenda onto the consultee.

Competence.   It has been written that the most basic requirement for consultants wishing to ensure competent practice is a thorough understanding of their own limitations (Newman, 1991; Snow & Gersick, 1986). Consultants must develop means for evaluating their own skills, knowledge, and expertise relative to the specific demands of the practice of consultation. They must recognize the margins of their competence and confine their practice accordingly. Equally important, consultants must be aware of personal and interpersonal characteristics that might influence their perceptions, judgments, decisions, and actions (Schein, 2003). Consultants must maintain awareness in order to avoid defining organizational problems through conforming to their specific areas of expertise and resist pressure to provide services outside the boundaries of their competence (Gallesich, 1982; Scholten, 2003; Snow & Gersick, 1986). To assist in avoiding this risk, cautiously defining parameters of proficiency with the consultee before engaging in the consulting relationship is recommended. Finally, consultants have an ethical responsibility to be conscientious of new developments in theory, research, and technology that might affect the quality of their services to consultees (Newman, 1993; O'Roark, 2002).

The complex nature of consulting relationships creates unique issues and challenges for career counselors. The need to balance the interests of multiple parties while maintaining awareness of personal strengths and limitations is imperative. Consultants must recognize and accept responsibility for the impact of their professional decisions and actions while adhering to professional and ethical standards (O'Roark, 2002).

Coach

Career coaching is a relatively new practice that combines the concepts of career counseling, organizational consulting, and employee development (Chung & Gfreorer, 2003). It is much less defined than consultation and involves considerable controversy among counseling professionals.

Think of a career coach as a job counselor. Your coach can help you identify your sharpest skills, define your career goals, be more productive, set strategies to earn more money, and make you more valuable to your current or next boss (Chung & Gfroerer, 2003; Hube, 1996). A career coach can guide your professional development, identifying and opening doors (Myers, 1996; Wasylyshyn, 2003). "You might even enlist a coach to help you become more creative, live with chemotherapy or attention-deficit disorder, resolve conflicts, market a book, or play in a rock 'n' roll band" (Campbell, 1999).

Career coaches have been around for some time under other names such as *mentor, management consultant,* and *human resource specialist* (Hagevik, 1998). Career coaching has emerged as an individualized service to professionals who wish to enhance their personal effectiveness by improving their communication and negotiating skills, professional presence, and other interpersonal abilities while remaining in their present job. Many career coaches provide their services via telephone or online (Harrington, 1998).

There is considerable comparison between career coaching and career counseling as an occupation. Both address career planning, accomplishment of career alternatives, and the interaction of personal and vocational issues. However, the two specialties differ in some significant ways. Career counselors are trained professional counselors with a specialization in career interventions and with national and state credentialing available, whereas the field of career coaching is fundamentally unregulated, with only a few coaching institutions offering a certificate or ethical code (Chung & Gfroerer, 2003).

Initially, career coaching was an expansion of managers acting as coaches to their employees (Rich, 1998). However, the managers themselves found need for improvement in management styles and assistance with strategic planning or organizational development (Hudson, 1999b). Thus, career counselor found themselves with an extended role, and professional career coaches were an expansion of this need. Virtually nonexistent as recently as 1990, an estimated 1,500 coaches advised about 20,000 workers a year by 1996 (Hube, 1996). By 1999, with an estimated 10,000 coaches worldwide, coaches were helping start businesses, straighten out finances, and improve personal and business relationships (Campbell, 1999).

The tasks of a career coach include facilitating continuity and change, clarifying core values and beliefs, identifying key social roles, tapping emerging developmental challenges, and developing a continuous learning agenda (Hudson, 1999a). Often, however, what coaches offer is common sense. Many people in stable work situations are so immersed in their day-to-day job duties that they lack the perspective and objectivity to make major changes on their own. Hiring a coach can also be the route to moving up or even out. Career coaches make long-term commitments to work with clients as they move through job and life transitions, acting as an advisor during the transitions and helping clients reach their full career potential (Myers, 1996). Coaches attend to specific problems through the implementation of strategies designed to bring about change (Grant, 2003). It has even been suggested that coaches are needed for clients "so someone will hold them accountable for taking action when they say they will" (Campbell, 1999, p. 4). An example of how a career counselor might function as a coach is an insurance agent requesting assistance to improve sales. The coach would assist the agent in maximizing skills to increase productivity.

Coaches should have interpersonal, communication, team or group, and change-mastery skills in order to assist clients in developing a new skill set, learn the workplace culture, and build a new support network (Clarke, 1999). However, there are no universal requirements for career coaching. Depending on the state, some counselors must undergo rigorous state-licensing requirements and have advanced degrees in counseling or social work (Hayes, 2001). On the other hand, some coaches draw solely on years of work experience and simply hang out a shingle. Regardless of training, ethical coaches realize that when clients' problems exceed their scope of practice, they should be referred to the appropriate specialists. If an athlete tears a ligament, the coach does not fix it himself, he sends the athlete to the doctor. Similarly, if stress on the job is caused by difficulties at home, a qualified counselor is in order.

There are many dynamics within the career counselor's relationship with a client that may call for the role of coach instead of counselor. Although both career coaches and career counselors work with clients in a confidential work relationship, career coaching is largely task and problem-solving oriented, as opposed to career counseling, in which psychological interventions are often employed. Counselors work with clients to achieve self-understanding and awareness in career planning and may use professional instruments to assess personality traits to aid in the awareness process. Conversely, career coaches who have not been trained as counselors generally do not have the skills or credentials to use professional assessment instruments or to work with mental health issues such as abuse, clinical depression, or addiction. Coaches suspecting damage or a need for healing within a client should be prepared to make a referral to a counseling professional.

Counseling and coaching can complement one another, and it is not uncommon for someone to work with both a coach and a counselor simultaneously. While working with a counselor, past experiences and patterns that cause blocks or challenges may be examined. A coach focuses on the future to assist individuals in defining what they want to be and do and designs a step-by-step plan for accomplishment. Generally, career counselors assist clients in finding direction and focus, whereas in coaching, clients arrive with certain goals and the coach helps them reach those goals. For example, a career counselor might work with a salesperson to condense a current level of sales calls from six days into five.

Thus, career counselors are typically utilized by individuals who want to find a field to enter or by experienced workers trying to reevaluate their career. Career coaches help you achieve specific goals to improve your current career. Goals may include such issues as finding more time to spend with your family, how to cultivate new business, and how to delegate duties to others. It is an individualized service to professionals who wish to enhance their personal effectiveness by improving their communication and negotiating skills, professional presence, and other interpersonal abilities while remaining in their present job.

Coaching Models

While many career coaches do not have professional training, career counselors who are utilizing the role of coach should be familiar with coaching models. According to Price and Llevento (1999), there are three major arenas of coaching, including:

- coaching for leadership, with focus on leadership support;
- coaching for development and success, with emphasis on current or future assignments and opportunities; and
- coaching for performance, with focus on enhancement for current and future challenges.

Within each of the major approaches to coaching, there are specific models and techniques. One such coaching model is coactive coaching (Whitmore, Whitmore, Kimsey-House, & Sandahl, 1998). Developed by professional career coaches, this model is similar to person-centered counseling theory, as it upholds the premise that the client has the answers and that the job of the coach is to listen and empower rather than inform and advise. This approach asserts that all people are naturally creative, resourceful, whole, and completely capable of finding their own answers to whatever challenges they face. Based on this assertion, strategies and techniques specifically forward actions in the specific direction identified by the client. The intent is to deepen the client's understanding of personal motivation and enjoyment. The key outcome for this approach is to assist the client in creating genuine fulfillment and balance while engaging more fully in the process of life as it unfolds. It is a holistic approach built on the principle that all parts of people's lives are interrelated. In contrast to a consulting model, in which one person is an expert and the other is in need of expertise, participants using a coaching model recognize their complementary strengths and weaknesses. Thus, a career counselor functioning within this role might observe an employee at work to illuminate strengths that promote success and assist in identifying barriers that detract from it. Consider a fitness trainer. As a consultant, the trainer would write a workout plan. As a coach, the trainer would push the individual to run farther.

Another counseling model that is applicable to career coaching is Hershenson's (1996) model of work adjustment, which addresses relationships among three interacting intrapersonal domains and the individual's work environment. This model is parallel to career coaching, as it takes an approach focusing on personality, work competencies, work habits, and work goals while considering the work setting.

According to Hershenson (1996), each individual has "three sequentially developing, interactive subsystems of work personality (WP), work competence (WC), and work goals (WG)" (p. 444). Work adjustment is accomplished through the interaction of these three subsystems in relation to the work environment. There are three components of work adjustment: work role behavior (RB), task performance (TP), and worker satisfaction (WS). These three components are connected to intrapersonal subsystems and work settings.

Three environments largely shape the development of the three intrapersonal subsystems. Initially, the family affects the development of work personality, which includes the individual's self-concept as a worker, system of work motivation, and system of work-related needs and values. Second, school experience primarily affects the development of work competencies, which consists of work habits, interpersonal skills, and physical and mental skills. Promptness, neatness, and reliability are examples of work habits. Finally, work goals are influenced by an individual's peer or reference group. Comprehensible, reasonable work goals should be consistent with the individual's work personality and competencies.

"In counseling for work adjustment, the counselor focuses on the relationship between the person and the work setting. The counselor must determine if the work problem is one of work role behavior, task performance, worker satisfaction, or some combination of the three" (Hershenson, 1996, p. 444). Upon determining the specific nature of the problem, the role of coach may be useful in determining and implementing a solution-focused approach to improving the problem.

Coaching Relationship

Because career coaches typically engage in a longer-term relationship than some career interventions, the dynamic between the coach and the client is critical. Work styles and backgrounds among career coaches differ. Thus, when choosing a coach, the client should verify that he or she has the knowledge and expertise to help develop the tools and strategies to achieve goals (Wasylyshyn, 2003).

The chemistry between the career coach and the client is important, as trust and commitment are key elements to predicting success. Additionally, because career coaches are less restricted by traditional boundaries and may assume a more active role in providing assistance, the relationship is critical. Career coaches "may interact with their clients in the clients' homes, places of employment, or over the telephone or Internet and may participate in the clients' work activities in order to observe, provide instant feedback, and implement career plans with clients" (Chung & Gfroerer, 2003, p. 142). Counselors typically configure their interactions with their clients in scheduled, face-to-face meetings in their counseling offices and tend to facilitate change rather than actively participate in the process of change.

Like the counseling relationship, career coaches depend on accurate interpersonal skills to facilitate a successful interaction. Listening and attending skills are emphasized, as well as strengths in behavioral observations, as coaches often observe the clients functioning within their work environment. As coaches tend to be more proactive in their interactions with clients, creativity and enthusiasm are necessary tools when assisting individuals in making a personal change.

Ethical and Legal Concerns

Training. Of primary interest when considering the ethical issues inherent in the current practice of career coaching is the fact that there is no recognized professional organization that stipulates required guidelines for training and practice (Chung & Gfroerer, 2003). While career counselors have nationally recognized bodies that accredit counselor-training programs (e.g., Council for Accreditation of Counseling and Related Educational Programs), national certificates or state licenses for counselors or counseling psychologists (e.g., National Board for Certified Counselors), and relevant professional codes of ethics (e.g., American Counseling Association, American Psychological Association, and the National Career Development Association), the field of career coaching is limited to specific coaching institutes that offer specific training certificates. Thus, there is no national accrediting body to regulate training or continuing education. This is potentially hazardous for clients in need of specialized assistance because there are no guarantees of training or expertise. Approximately 90 percent of all career coaches hold at least a bachelor's degree, whereas only 50 percent hold a graduate degree (Chung & Gfroerer, 2003). Any individual that chooses to identify him- or herself as a "career coach" may do so. Many counseling professionals do not even recognize career coaching as a legitimate profession. While the United States has many training programs for career coaches, none is accredited by a nationally recognized body. In addition, some training programs do not screen applicants for relevant educational background (Crockett, as cited in Chung & Gfroerer, 2003). As a result of the lack of training and governing of credentials, it has been posited that standards of competence are called for when the goal is behavioral change (Brotman, Liberi, & Wasylyshyn, 1998). Wasylyshyn (2001) wrote, "Coaches who have not had training in psychology or in related behavior science are less likely to be successful in handling . . . a deeply entrenched and dysfunctional behavior pattern" (p. 17). This supports the concept that career coaching as one of many roles of a career counselor makes for better preparation for dealing with situations that arise during the coaching process. Without training in the multiple roles of career counseling, career coaches may lack the skill to deal with difficult and potentially dangerous situations, which may leave both coaches and their clients at a critical disadvantage.

Cultural Competency. As one common goal of career coaching is to facilitate personal success and life satisfaction, sensitivity to individual values, beliefs, and cultural practices is imperative. Specialized training in cultural sensitivity, including the meaning and importance of work, the roles of family and significant others in an individual's career decision making, and the value of individual career development, is imperative to the success of career coaching and may be impeded by lack of exposure or training related to these issues.

There is clear evidence of the importance of the role coaches can play in the career-counseling process. While some counseling professionals believe career coaches' training and ethical guidelines should be more regulated, the benefits of coaching are evident. Focusing on the individualized needs of employed individuals, coaches offer dynamic exploration into action-oriented solutions to specific problems in an effort to maximize potential, control careers, and manage personal and professional development. For example, a career counselor needs to be culturally sensitive in efforts to make a salesperson more productive. If you coach the client on employing a hearty handshake and eye contact without taking into account that in his or her culture, eye contact could be considered rude, you may create feelings of inadequacy in the client.

Supervisor

Counseling supervision has emerged as an increasingly important component for career counselors. Clinical supervision has been defined as "regular, ongoing supervision of counseling provided by another trained and experienced professional" (Remley, Benshoff, & Mowbray, 1987, p. 53). During the past decade, supervision has matured into a distinct specialty (Riordan & Kern, 1994). The importance of extensive, high-quality supervision has become recognized as critical to learning, maintaining, and improving professional counseling skills (Benshoff, 1994). Supervision is important to the ongoing professional development of counselors, as well as the counseling profession as a whole (Cobia & Boes, 2000). Supervision within the educational process coordinates a "major avenue of entry into the ranks of new professionals" (Pitts & Miller, 1990, p. 300). Additionally, empirical research suggests that "supervision is an essential feature" of successful therapists (Emanuel, Miller, & Rustin, 2002, p. 581). Thus, supervision plays an essential role in the comprehensive development of practicing career counselors. Magnuson, Norem, and Wilcoxen (2000) report that during the 1980s, authors asserted that the existing knowledge related to the counseling supervision process was insufficient. Today, however, contemporary supervisors have an abundance of texts and journals to guide their work. Refinement of supervision theory and practice has been addressed by credentialing bodies such as the National Board for Certified Counselors, with the implementation of the Approved Clinical Supervisor credential (Magnuson et al., 2000). Relevant literature has identified specific roles and goals of supervisors, including supervision of career counselors (Bronson, 2001; Dye & Borders, 1990). Competent supervisors are able to convey their counseling knowledge and skills in a way that promotes a supervisee's effectiveness and professional identity.

Primary functions of the supervisor include monitoring and evaluating, instructing and advising, modeling, consulting, and supporting and sharing (Bernard & Goodyear, 1998; Bronson, 2001). Within these functions are many tasks, including teaching counseling and intervention skills, case conceptualization, professional roles, emotional awareness, and self-evaluation (Bernard & Goodyear, 1998). Because it is concerned with the professional and personal growth of the counselors, counseling supervision offers a direct service to professional staff members (Drapela, 1983).

The blending of supervision theory with the goals of career counseling affords the practitioner the flexibility to function with other career counselors as well as clients in an effective and meaningful fashion.

Models of Supervision

According to Bernard and Goodyear (as cited in Baker, Exum, & Tyler, 2002), "there has been considerable interest in developing models to explain the development of counselors and considerably less interest in models that attempt to explain the development of clinical supervisors" (p. 15). Research suggests several reasons why experience is not sufficient preparation of clinical supervisors. Specifically, not only are accreditation bodies insisting on training in supervision, but clinicians are recognizing the importance of training in supervision (Baker et al., 2002). Leddick (1994) suggests, "Clinical supervision is the construction of individualized learning plans for supervisees working with clients. The specific manner in which supervision is applied is called a 'model'" (p. 1).

According to the literature, three specific types of models have emerged: developmental models, integrated models, and orientation-specific models (Leddick, 1994).

Developmental Model. Developmental models approach supervision from the perspective that people grow continuously. In combining our experience and hereditary dispositions, we develop strengths and growth areas. Stoltenberg and Delworth (1987) described a developmental model with three levels of supervisees: beginning, intermediate, and advanced. Particular attention is paid to self- and other-awareness, motivation, and autonomy (Leddick, 1994).

Integrated Model. Integrated models combine several theories into a consistent practice. Bernard's discrimination model (1979) combines attention to three supervisory roles with three areas of focus. Supervisors may take on the role of teacher, counselor, or consultant, dependant on the supervisory need within the session (Leddick, 1994).

Orientation-Specific Model. Counselors who practice a particular type of therapy may engage in a supervision style that employs theory-specific premises. In this situation, it can be related to "the sports enthusiast who believes the best future coach would be a person who excelled in the same sport at the high school, college and professional levels" (Leddick, 1994, p. 2). Thus, psychoanalytic supervision approaches the process in stages. Behavioral supervision views client problems as learning problems. Supervision adheres to the theoretical principles specific to the approach.

The discrimination model is one popular approach to supervision. Bernard's (1979) combination of the roles of teacher, counselor, and consultant effectively encompasses the shifts that occur within any given session. "It is an eclectic model that attempts both parsimony and versatility" (Bernard & Goodyear, 1998, p. 28). This fits hand-in-hand with any career-counseling theoretical perspective that embraces the idiosyncrasies of individuals and adapts approach to the individual needs of the client. Working within the discrimination model allows for shifting roles to best meet the needs of supervisees. According to Bernard and Goodyear (1998), it is called the discrimination model because "it implies that supervisors will tailor their responses to the particular supervisee's needs" (p. 30).

As described in Nelson, Johnson, and Thorngren (2000), this combination of roles results in "three foci for supervision: (1) intervention skills, (2) conceptualization skills, and (3) personalization skills of the trainee" (p. 48). Supervisors may take on the role of teacher, counselor, or consultant dependant on the supervisory need within the session (Leddick, 1994). This approach allows for consideration of the skills of the supervisee in general and specific types of issues. It allows for use with novice supervisees, as well as more skilled and confident supervisees. This model is synonymous with attention to the specific needs of supervisees. Any of the three roles may be used with each of the three foci, depending on the situational needs of the trainee.

The three specified foci of the discrimination model also represent three of the primary areas of emphasis in counseling supervision. Intervention skills involve technique and strategy (Nelson et al., 2000). Dependent on the developmental level of the supervisee, the focus may be on the actual implementation of the skills rather than treatment planning toward their use. Supervisors routinely place emphasis on how supervisees draw conclusions and make choices in the development of treatment plans. For example, a career counselor providing supervision within the discrimination model might deal with assessment instruments as teacher; counsel a supervisee, if countertransference issues are impacting the supervisee; or serve as consultant in development of vocational planning.

Conceptualization allows the supervisor to recognize cognitive skill that reflects deliberate thinking and case analysis (Nelson et al., 2000). To what extent a supervisee understands what is occurring in the session, identifies patterns, and chooses interventions is imperative to understanding both areas of strength and issues of concern.

Personalization skills are critical, as they involve a supervisee's comfort with the self as he or she responds to the counseling experience (Nelson et al., 2000). One responsibility as a supervisor is to understand how well supervisees blend personal style within the counseling relationship, while keeping their counselor-client relationships free from personal issues.

As the discrimination model of supervision is very flexible, one element of this approach includes establishing expectations at the outset of the supervision relationship. As noted by Ladany and Friedlander (1995), "Presumably, when supervisors and trainees discuss expectations, set goals, and agree on the tasks of supervision within the context of a positive relationship, trainees are less likely to experience confusion or conflict in supervision" (pp. 220–221). At the onset, it may be necessary to assume a teaching and counseling role, as attempting to be a consultant sometimes results in confusion. Initiating any supervisory relationship with a great deal of information can reduce misunderstanding. The tone and rapport established during this stage are critical, and the supervisor's role of counselor can be helpful in establishing a positive working relationship.

Regardless of which approach is employed, it is vital to recognize that supervisees may possess latent resources that can be developed. "If, in addition to training, a supervisor accepts the challenge of facilitating a supervisee's development, the supervisor is more like a sculptor who is attempting to bring to the surface the supervisee's potential" (Presbury, Echterling, & McKee, 1999, p. 148).

Supervisory Relationship. A discussion of the supervision process leads naturally to comparisons with the counseling process. Many comparisons can be drawn between the two, allowing counseling skills and techniques to translate well into supervision (Pearson, 2000).

Despite the similarities between counseling and supervision, many differences are also evident. In the counseling relationship, the growth and welfare of the client are the primary concern. Similarly, in the supervisory relationship, the professional growth and welfare of the counselor are a major concern. However, while focusing on the counselor's growth, this must be balanced with protection of the client.

Evaluation. Evaluation of the counselor by the supervisor is another factor that differentiates supervision from counseling (Pearson, 2000). As the supervisor's purpose is to improve a supervisee's skills and ensure accuracy, evaluation of the supervisee's skill is imperative. This element of the relationship can be intimidating and create issues, including anxiety, power, and games, between the supervisor and supervisee (Borders et al., 1991). A structured approach to supervisee assessment and evaluation produces several beneficial outcomes (Harris, 1994). Supervisors can reduce their own, as well as their supervisee's, anxiety about the process and, when evaluation is viewed as a process of formative and summative assessment of the skills, techniques, and developmental stage of the supervisee, both supervisees and their clients benefit. A variety of strategies and methods are available to supervisors for use with counselors (Hart, 1994). Establishing a plan for supervision at the beginning of the supervisory relationship allows for insight building concerning the supervisee's self-described strengths and weaknesses, as well as the individual goals for supervision. Additionally, it allows an opportunity to initiate goals for the supervisee that can be evaluated, adjusted, and expanded throughout the supervision process.

Supervisor evaluation can also be of great importance to the growth and development of the supervisor in training. Having feedback from the supervisee can illuminate strengths and areas for improvement. Supervisee feedback may also assist in understanding that person's needs and perceptions. For a career counselor this translates into reinforcement for staying competent and up-to-date and for creating a safe environment for honest exchange between the supervisee and supervisor.

Diversity Issues. In addition to the challenges of power differential, the supervisory relationship is subject to influence by personal characteristics of the participants and by a great many cultural variables. Such factors include gender and role attitudes, as well as supervisor's style, age, race and ethnicity, and personality characteristics (Dye, 1994). Paisley (1994) suggests cultural variables can affect issues the client brings to counseling, the perspective of the counselor, and the choice of interventions. Review of current literature advocates discussing diversity issues early and often in supervision, with the result of increasing supervisee satisfaction and developing trust and openness between the supervisee and the supervisor (Britton, Goodman, & Rak, 2002).

As the supervisory relationship itself takes place within the same societal context as other cultural issues, supervisors must be diligent in identifying any ways in which bias in expectations or actions might be occurring in supervision, such as identifying cultural influences on client behavior, on counselor-client interactions, and on the supervisory relationship (Fong, 1994). Supervisors must provide culturally sensitive support and challenge to the supervisee. As all supervision is some form of multicultural supervision, supervisors will need to be proficient in multicultural competencies. It is the supervisor's responsibility to address cultural biases and to encourage diverse thinking (Britton et al., 2002).

Cultural influences within the supervisory relationship can be managed to some extent by mutual respect. The complex goals of client and counselor development within a supervisory relationship require the counselors to trust their supervisors and supervisors to trust the counselors being supervised. "Such a trusting relationship helps to increase the protection of the client, the professional growth of the counselor, and the assurance to the supervisor that ethical concern are being addressed" (Pearson, 2000, p. 285).

There are numerous characteristics that promote a positive supervisory experience. Some characteristics that prepare a student for growth within the supervisory relationship include demonstrating a capacity for openness to learning, curiosity, thoughtfulness, initiative, self-reflection, emotional and interpersonal self-monitoring, recognition of interpersonal patterns, flexibility, and motivation to change (Binder & Strupp, 1997; Kaufman, Morgan, & Ladany, 2000).

Characteristics of the effective supervisor include self-reflection and self-monitoring of the interpersonal process associated with the supervisor-supervisee interactions, along with the ability to move between identifying with, and observing, the experiences of both the supervisee and the clients (Binder & Strupp, 1997).

Ethical and Legal Concerns.   The importance of supervision to the ongoing professional development of counseling is being increasingly recognized and regulated. Supervision is a complex professional endeavor that places participants at increased risk for involvement in ethical conflicts related to competence, conflicting roles, dual relationships, evaluation, and confidentiality (Cobia & Boes, 2000). As gatekeepers of the profession, supervisors must be diligent about their own, and their supervisees', ethics. "In this case, perhaps more than in any other, supervisors' primary responsibility is to model what they hope to teach" (Bernard & Goodyear, 1998, p. 198).

Supervisory arrangements increase legal exposure and pose unique ethical challenges for the supervisor (Sutter, McPherson, & Geeseman, 2002). Because supervision is a triadic relationship, the supervisor must always attend to the need for balance between the counseling needs of clients and the training needs of the counselor (Bernard, 1994). While there is no way to prevent ethical dilemmas, there are several ways to minimize the potential for their occurrence. One such method is the implementation of a professional disclosure statement. Risk to supervisees and potential ethical dilemmas related to misunderstanding about the expectations, goals, and evaluative aspects of supervision can be minimized by developing and adhering to a specific supervision plan (Cobia & Boes, 2000).

Supervision is an invaluable tool in helping career counselors provide holistic, effective counseling. It is just one of many roles the counselor may choose to engage in as an aid in promoting the client's understanding of his or her interests, strengths, and weaknesses.

Roles of the Career Counselor

Table 9.1 contrasts the three roles of career counseling we have examined in a number of dimensions.

TABLE 9.1 Comparisons among Three Roles of Career Counseling

	CONSULTATION	COACHING	SUPERVISION
Focus	Focuses on developing a plan that will improve professional functioning with a specific client, program, or policy.	Focuses on action-oriented, solution-focused intervention for an existing employee within a specific job.	Focuses on reviewing service provision, including the skills and competencies of the counselor and the client's proposed treatment plan.
Goal	Advise and educate the consultee and assist in developing a program or policy to improve a problem.	Actively engage in interaction with the client to identify skills, goals, and talents that will maximize potential.	Provide feedback for career counselors to be better equipped to serve clients and grow as professionals.
Example	Police chief asks for help in developing ongoing program to deal with interpersonal problems between veteran officers and new officers.	A sales manager wants to own his own business and needs to chart a career course that will give him the experience he needs, including retail and marketing roles.	A counselor needs assistance in working with Kathy, a 20-year-old college sophomore with depression who is having difficulty choosing a major.
Role and Responsibilities	Responsible for assessing problem, recognizing the source of difficulty, and preparing a course of action.	Observe the client's career situation, determine a plan of action, and assist the client in implementing the plan.	To assist counselors in providing holistic career counseling and address the overlap and interplay of personal and career concerns.

Many Roles in "Role Model"

As counselors explore the many possible roles that may become part of the process of career counseling, it is important not to lose sight of the impact an individual may have by modeling professional, ethical, competent practice. Being available and approachable for the questions and answers needed to assist young professionals in growth often facilitates mentoring among professionals.

Mentoring is considered to be an important element of career development in relation to career advancement. Mentor relationships develop slowly, through mutual trust and commitment, patient leadership, and emotional maturity (Myers, 1996). It is estimated that over 90 percent of executives have had mentors sometime in their careers, and that of those, 80 percent considered their mentors to be important to their career advancement (Hagevik, 1998).

The ripple effect of mentoring spreads its benefits to mentees, mentors, and their organizations. Mentees benefit because someone cares enough to support them, advise them, and help interpret inside information. That level of interest enhances mentees' sense of self-worth. The mentoring relationship also allows mentees to try out new ideas, skills, and roles in a real-world context.

Mentors experience the fulfillment of passing along hard-earned wisdom, influencing the next generation, and receiving appreciation from a younger worker, all of which enhances their sense of accomplishment. The relationship between a senior member of the profession and a more junior member of that profession also provides mentors a place to learn about generational and cross-cultural differences and about the benefit of giving.

The organization benefits when the optimism and energy of younger and more culturally, technologically, and ethically diverse employees is combined with the efficiency and confident decision-making skills of more experienced personnel. Ideally, mentoring of younger workers reduces turnover, helps mentees deal with organizational issues, and accelerates mentees' assimilation into the culture. Figure 9.1 represents the strengths and benefits of mentoring.

In the ever-turbulent world of work, the need for career development services is growing. New career specialties have emerged to meet the needs of adults in transition and young people preparing for work, some of which blend the roles of coach, consultant, supervisor, and mentor. For example, career development facilitators (CDFs) work in an organization that provides career services to its employees under the supervision of a qualified career counselor. CDFs are utilized to help individuals make informed career and job decisions, develop a career plan of action, and conduct a successful job search (Brawley, 2002). According to the National Career Development Association, as cited in Kerka (2000), a CDF may "serve as a career group facilitator, job search trainer, career resource center coordinator, career coach, career development case manager, intake interviewer, occupational and labor market information resource person, human resource career development coordinator, employment/placement specialist, or workforce development staff person" (p. 6). CDFs serve as an example of the myriad of functions a career counselor can serve in the world of work.

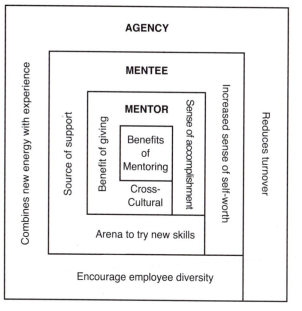

FIGURE 9.1   The Benefits of Mentoring

SUMMARY

Career counseling can be defined as an activity that helps individuals achieve greater flexibility, renew their self-definition, and live in a transformational relationship with themselves and the environment (Miller, 1995). Career counselors encourage people to transform limiting, dysfunctional conceptions of themselves into possibilities that reflect greater opportunities for self-expression, expand restricted roles, and become more responsive to fundamental needs and talents. Through a variety of roles, career counselors assist individuals in accumulating new information about themselves and their environment, help identify unarticulated fundamental values and needs, explore the competing beliefs that leave those values unexpressed, and translate the implications of this exploration into viable actions that are also authentic responses.

Throughout this chapter, conceptual awareness and clarity among the diverse roles in which career counselors may need to engage to operate as a professional are provided. An integrated perspective of counseling, consultation, coaching, and supervision within counselor functioning is necessary for the enhancement of professionalism and the increase of the overall effectiveness of career counselors. We spend roughly 11,000 days of our lives between ages 21 and 65 at work (Koonce, 1995). With such an astounding amount of time spent on any one activity, planning carefully to make the most of a career is imperative. Counselors who understand the relationship of their own helping functions are in a better position to select helping strategies for the various situations that they encounter. The following Web sites provide additional information relating to the chapter topics.

USEFUL WEBSITES

http://www.ncda.org/

This Web site is sponsored by the National Career Development Association. It explains the functions of a career development facilitator, describes the CDF training curriculum, and provides links to the NCDA registry of CDF instructors and programs.

http://www.coachfederation.org

The International Coach Federation is the largest association of professional coaches, and the site provides an opportunity to search for coaches by race, business specialty, or region.

http://www.boomercareer.com/members/department19.cfm

This online publication offers access to dozens of articles written about career-counseling issues.

REFERENCES

Backer, T. E. (2003). Consulting psychology as creative problem solving: Lessons from my first 3 decades. *Consulting Psychology Journal: Practice and Research, 55,* 107–112.

Baker, S. B., Exum, H. A., & Tyler, R. E. (2002). The developmental process of clinical supervisors in training: An investigation of the supervisory complexity model. *Counselor Education and Supervision, 42,* 15–30.

Benshoff, J. M. (1994). *Peer consultation as a form of supervision.* Greensboro, NC: Clearinghouse on Counseling and Student Services. (ERIC Document Reproduction Service No. EDO-CG-94-20)

Bernard, J. M. (1979). Supervisor training: A discrimination model. *Counselor Education and Supervision, 19,* 60–68.

Bernard, J. M. (1994). *Ethical and legal dimensions of supervision.* Greensboro, NC: Clearinghouse on Counseling and Student Services. (ERIC Document Reproduction Service No. EDO-CG-94-17)

Bernard, J. M., & Goodyear, R. K. (1998). *Fundamentals of clinical supervision.* Needham Heights, MA: Allyn & Bacon.

Binder, J., & Strupp, H. (1997). Supervision of psychodynamic psychotherapies. In C. E. Watkins (Ed.), *Handbook of psychotherapy supervision* (pp. 44–62). New York: Wiley.

Blocher, D. H. (1987). *The professional counselor.* New York: Macmillan.

Borders, L. D., Bernard, J. M., Dye, H. A., Fong, M. L., Henderson, P., & Nance, D. (1991). Curriculum guide for training counselor supervisors: Rationale, development, and implementation. *Counselor Education & Supervision, 31,* 58–77.

Bradley, L. J., & Kottler, J. A. (2001). Overview of counselor supervision. In L. J Bradley & N. Ladany (Eds.), *Counselor supervision* (3rd ed., pp. 3–21). Philadelphia, PA: Brunner-Rutledge.

Brawley, K. (2002). *Working ahead: The national one-stop workforce system and career development facilitator curriculum training for instructors.* (ERIC Document Reproduction Service No. ED-465-911)

Britton, P. J., Goodman, J. M., & Rak, C. F. (2002). Presenting workshops on supervision: A didactic-experiential format. *Counselor Education and Supervision, 42,* 31–39.

Bronson, M. K. (2001). Supervision of career counseling. In L. J. Bradley & N. Ladany (Eds.), *Counselor supervision* (3rd ed., pp. 222–242). Philadelphia, PA: Brunner-Rutledge.

Brotman, L. E., Liberi, W. P., & Wasylyshyn, K. M. (1998). Executive coaching: The need for standards of competence. *Consulting Psychology Journal: Practice and Research, 50,* 40–46.

Brown, D., Pryzwansky, W. B., & Schulte, A. C. (1991). *Psychological consultation.* Needham Heights, MA: Allyn & Bacon.

Campbell, D. S. (1999, October 20). Coaches also help put skills to work on job, in life! *Orlando Sentinel.* Retrieved August 15, 2003, from http://www.triumph-of-change.com/article1099.htm

Chung Y. B., & Gfroerer, M. C. A. (2003). Career coaching: Practice, training, professional, and ethical issues. *The Career Development Quarterly, 52,* 141–152.

Clarke, R. D. (1999). Making the right moves. *Black Enterprise, 30,* 56.

Cobia, D. C., & Boes, S. R. (2000). Professional disclosure statements and formal plans supervision: Two strategies for minimizing the risk of ethical conflicts in post-masters supervision. *Journal of Counseling and Development, 78,* 293–296.

Dougherty, A. M. (1995). *Consultation: Practice and perspectives in school and community settings* (2nd ed.). Pacific Grove, CA: Brooks/Cole.

Drapela, V. J. (1983). Counseling, consultation, and supervision: A visual clarification of their relationship. *The Personnel and Guidance Journal, 62*(3), 158–162.

Dye, A. (1994). *The supervisory relationship.* Greensboro, NC: Clearinghouse on Counseling and Student Services. (ERIC Document Reproduction Service No. EDO-CG-94-11)

Dye, H. A., & Borders, D. (1990). Counseling supervisors: Standards for preparation and practice. *Journal of Counseling and Development, 69,* 27–29.

Emmanuel, R., Miller, L., & Rustin, M. (2002). Supervision of therapy of sexually abused girls [Electronic version]. *Clinical Child Psychology and Psychiatry, 7,* 581–594.

Fong, M. L. (1994). *Multicultural issues in supervision.* Greensboro, NC: Clearinghouse on Counseling and Student Services. (ERIC Document Reproduction Service No. EDO-CG-94-14)

Gallesich, J. (1982). *The profession and practice of consultation.* San Francisco, CA: Jossey-Bass.

Gibson, R. L., & Mitchell, M. H. (1999). *Introduction to guidance and counseling.* Upper Saddle River, NJ: Prentice-Hall.

Gladding, A. T. (1996). *Counseling: A comprehensive profession* (3rd ed.). Englewood Cliffs, NJ: Prentice-Hall.

Grant, A. M. (2003). The impact of life coaching on goal attainment, metacognition, and mental health. *Social Behavior and Personality, 31,* 253–264.

Hagevik, S. (1998). Choosing a career counseling service. *Journal of Environmental Health, 61*(4), 31–33.

Harrington, A. (1998). A sounding board in cyberspace. *Fortune, 138,* 301–302.

Harris, M. B. C. (1994). *Supervisory evaluation and feedback.* Greensboro, NC: Clearinghouse on Counseling and Student Services. (ERIC Document Reproduction Service No. EDO-G-94-16)

Hart, G. M. (1994). *Strategies and methods of effective supervision.* Greensboro, NC: Clearinghouse on Counseling and Student Services. (ERIC Document Reproduction Service No. EDO-CG-94-09)

Hayes, C. (2001). Choosing the right path. *Black Enterprise, 31*(9), 109–112.

Hays, K. F., & Brown, C. H. (2004a). Consultant efforts that hinder performance. In K. F. Hays & C. H. Brown (Eds.), *You're on!: Consulting for peak performance* (pp. 233–246). Washington, DC: American Psychological Association.

Hays, K. F., & Brown, C. H. (2004b). A good fit: Training, competence, and ethical practice. In K. F. Hays & C. H. Brown (Eds.), *You're on!: Consulting for peak performance* (pp. 249–280). Washington, DC: American Psychological Association.

Hershenson, D. B. (1996). Work adjustment: A neglected area of career counseling [Electronic version]. *Journal of Counseling and Development, 74,* 442–449.

Hube, K. (1996). A coach may be the guardian angel you need to rev up your career. *Money, 25*(12), 43–45.

Hudson, F. M. (1999a). Career coaching. *Career Planning and Adult Development Journal, 15*(2), 69–80.

Hudson, F. M. (1999b). *The handbook of coaching: A comprehensive resource guide for managers, executives, consultants, and human resource professionals.* San Fransisco, CA: Jossey-Bass.

Kaufman, M., Morgan, K. J., & Ladany, N. (2001). Family counseling supervision. In L. J. Bradley & N. Ladany, (Eds.), *Counselor supervision* (3rd Ed., pp. 245–262). Philadelphia, PA: Brunner-Routledge.

Kerka, S. (2000). *Career development specialties for the 21st century.* (ERIC Document Reproduction Service No. ED-99-CO-0013)

Koonce, R. (1995). Becoming your own career coach. *Training and Development, 49,* 18–26.

Kurpius, J. J. (1988). *Handbook of consultation: An intervention for advocacy and outreach.* Alexandria, VA: American Counseling Association.

Kurpius, D. J., & Fuqua, D. R. (1993). Fundamental issues in defining consultation. *Journal of Counseling and Development, 71,* 598–600.

Ladany, N., & Friedlander, M. (1995). The relationship between the supervisory working alliance and trainees' experience of role conflict and role ambiguity. *Counselor Education and Supervision, 34,* 220–231.

Leddick, G. R. (1994). *Models of clinical supervision.* Greensboro, NC: Clearinghouse on Counseling and Student Services. (ERIC Document Reproduction Service No. EDO-CG-94-08)

Magnuson, S., Norem, K, & Wilcoxon, A. (2000). Clinical supervision of prelicensed counselors: Recommendations for consideration and practice [Electronic version]. *Journal of Mental Health Counseling, 22,* 176–190.

Merrell, D. W. (1991). Back to basics: Things you have always known about consulting but tend to forget in the heat of battle. *Consulting Psychology Bulletin, 43,* 64–68.

Miller, M. J. (1995). A case for uncertainty in career counseling. *Counseling and Values, 39*(3), 62–168.

Myers, W. S. (1996). Finding a career coach. *Women in Business, 48*(6), 24–28.

Nelson, M., Johnson, P., & Thorngren, J. (2000). An integrated approach for supervising mental health counseling interns [Electronic version]. *Journal of Mental Health Counseling, 22,* 45–59.

Newman, J. L. (1993). Ethical issues in consultation [Electronic version]. *Journal of Counseling and Development, 72,* 148–157.

Newman, J. L., & Robinson, S. E. (1991). The best interests of the consultee: Ethical issues in consultation. *Consulting Psychology Bulletin, 43,* 23–29.

O'Roark, A. M. (2002). The quest for executive effectiveness: Consultants bridge the gap between psychological research and organizational application. *Consulting Psychology Journal: Practice and Research, 54,* 44–54.

Paisley, P. O. (1994). *Gender issues in supervision.* Greensboro, NC: Clearinghouse on Counseling and Student Services. (ERIC Document Reproduction Service No. EDO-CG-94-13)

Pearson, Q. M. (2000). Opportunities and challenges in the supervisory relationship [Electronic version]. *Journal of Mental Health Counseling, 22,* 283–295.

Pitts, J. H., & Miller, M. (1990). Coordination of supervision in practicum and internship programs [Electronic version]. *Counselor Education and Supervision, 29,* 291–300.

Presbury, J., Echterling, L. G., & McKee, J. E. (1999). Supervision for inner vision: Solution-focused strategies [Electronic version]. *Counselor Education and Supervision, 39,* 146–156.

Price, D. & Llvento, J. (1999). *License to sell: Professional field guide to selling skills & market trends.* New York: Applied Business Communications.

Remley, T. P., Benshoff, J. M., & Mowbray, C. A. (1987). A proposed model for peer supervision. *Counselor Education and Supervision, 27*(2), 53–60.

Rich, G. A. (1998). The constructs of sales coaching: Supervisory feedback, role modeling and trust. *Journal of Personal Selling and Sales Management, 18*, 53–63.

Riordan, R. J., & Kern, R. (1994). Shazam!!! You're a clinical supervisor [Electronic version]. *Family Journal, 2*, 259–261.

Schein, E. H. (2003). Five traps for consulting psychologists: Or, how I learned to take culture seriously. *Consulting Psychology Journal: Practice and Research, 55*(2), 75–83.

Scholten, T. (2003). What does it mean to consult? In E. Cole & J. A. Seigel (Eds.), *Effective consultation in school psychology* (2nd ed., pp. 87–106). Ashland, OH: Hogrefe & Huber.

Snow, D. L., & Gersick, K. E. (1986). Ethical and professional issues in mental health consultation. In F. V. Manning, E. J. Trickett, M. F. Shore, M. G. Kidder, & G. Levin (Eds.), *Handbook of mental health consultation* (pp. 393–431). Rockville, MD: Missouri Institute of Mental Health (MIMH).

Stoltenberg, C. D., & Delworth, U. (1987). *Supervising counselors and therapists.* San Francisco, CA: Jossey-Bass.

Sutter, E., McPherson, R. H., & Geeseman, R. (2002). Contracting for supervision [Electronic version]. *Professional Psychology: Research and Practice, 33*, 495–498.

Tokunaga, H. T. (1984). Ethical issues in consultation: An evaluative review. *Professional Psychology: Research and Practice, 15*, 811–821.

Wasylyshyn, K. M. (2001). On the full actualization of psychology in business. *Consulting Psychology Journal: Practice and Research, 53*, 10–21.

Wasylyshyn, K. M. (2003). Executive coaching: An outcome study. *Counseling Psychology Journal: Practice and Research, 55*, 94–106.

Whitmore, J., Whitmore, L., Kimsey-House, H., & Sandahl, P. (1998). *Co-active coaching: New skills for coaching people toward success in work and life.* Palo Alto, CA: Davies-Black.

PART III

CONTEXTUAL PERSPECTIVES ON CAREER AND LIFESTYLE PLANNING

This section of the text provides an overview of the basic environments in which today's career counselors are most likely to be hired and work. This section begins with Chapter 10, "Career Counseling in Schools." After a brief history of key events, trends, legislation, and people influencing the development of career and lifestyle planning in U.S. schools, the chapter discusses career and lifestyle planning as a developmental, systemic, and systematic process that involves all students and is the responsibility of all educators. The chapter presents a comprehensive description of system delivery and system support and the associated interventions and tools needed to help students at all grade levels develop and implement career, and associated lifestyle, identities.

Chapter 11, "Career Counseling in Mental Health and Private Practice Settings," presents information useful to those counselors who wish to work in these settings. It discusses the mental health issues typically found in these environments and offers suggestions on how people with mental health concerns can be productively engaged in the workplace through career counseling interventions.

Many clients with disabilities face challenges and barriers that are not the same as those of clients who do not have disabilities. Topics such as the impact of the Americans with Disabilities Act, issues and attitudes of employers and other employees that affect workplace satisfaction and productivity, and reasonable accommodation are explored and discussed in Chapter 12, "Career Counseling in Vocational Rehabilitation Settings."

Chapter 13, "Career Counseling with Couples and Families," addresses questions such as, "How does work affect couples and families?" and "How do families make decisions about what is important?" Consideration of family life cycles, family composition, and family problems are examined in the context of their relationship to adjustment at work and career satisfaction. Practical considerations and techniques for working with challenges faced by couples and families are also presented.

CHAPTER 10

CAREER COUNSELING IN SCHOOLS

REBECCA M. DEDMOND AND PAT SCHWALLIE-GIDDIS
The George Washington University

HISTORY OF CAREER PLANNING

Vocational guidance was started by Frank Parsons and Jessie Davis early in the twentieth century. It became organized in some schools as early as 1911 and continued to spread during the decades of the 1920s and 1930s. By 1939 the federal Department of Labor became interested and assisted by publishing the *Dictionary of Occupational Titles* (U.S. Department of Labor, 1991). Following World War II, business and industry saw vocational guidance as a means to improve the emerging workforce. By 1959, the federal government became involved by funding the National Defense Education Act, to improve the teaching of mathematics and science and the training of counselors to encourage pursuit of these subjects. When Sidney Marland became the U.S. Commissioner of Education in 1970, he promoted the concept of career education (Zunker, 2002, pp. 9–20).

As more and more schools developed programs of career education, the concepts of career development and career guidance emerged. The last 30 years of the twentieth century saw many refinements in the processes and techniques utilized in career guidance. The emergence of Tech Prep and School-to-Work movements, with funding support from the federal government, helped to promote career planning for all students. The U.S. Department of Labor supported many efforts through the National Occupational Information Coordinating Committee (NOICC), with the cooperation of each State Occupational Information Coordinating Committee (SOICC). These efforts at school reform have been a unique effort of cooperation between the federal and state governments to provide the opportunity for career planning to each student in the U.S. public school systems.

Now, as we enter the twenty-first century, schools are once again being evaluated. The standards movement appears to emphasize the academic programs. Counselors, therefore, need to work for balance in education, so that students will be able to develop strong lifetime career plans. Gray and Herr (2000) proposed a new goal for secondary education in their book *Other Ways to Win*. They wrote:

> every student should graduate with a plan for success. This goal will be achieved if counselors will take the lead in their schools to see that each student begins to develop a career plan upon entering secondary education. This plan should be implemented and reviewed annually, so that upon graduation they will have a plan for future success in life. (p. 16)

CAREER PLANNING OVERVIEW

Career planning has progressed through the years and is widely accepted as a developmental, sequential process that involves *all* students—all genders, all ethnicities, all ages. Delivered as an integral component of a comprehensive school counseling program (American School Counselor Association [ASCA], 1995, 2003), career planning is dependent on the integration of a host of competencies, behaviors, and attitudes into all academic instruction that supports state and division standards of learning, kindergarten through Grade 12.

As society has become more complex, expectations for public schools to play a role in life and career preparation have increased to the point that career planning has become a prominent component of school counseling programs throughout the United States (ASCA, 2003). Career planning reflects the changing needs of today's students. School counselors, educators, parents, and community members actively seek ways to engage youth in curriculum and activities designed to assist them to become productive, contributing citizens.

Career counseling acknowledges the unique and individual needs of each student and the need to continuously plan and revise education and career plans as a result of changing interests and of economic and world situations. It focuses on attitudes, behaviors, values, and skills needed in the changing, global world. It is the responsibility of, and requires the cooperation of, all educators, the home, and the community. Recent research has documented the effects of systemic change, which includes career planning. Counselors and educators have long suspected that educational achievement is profoundly affected when resources of the school, home, and community are integrated into the total school program.

The desired outcome of career planning is that students acquire and demonstrate competencies to recognize and analyze their own self-knowledge, behaviors, and attitudes, as reflected in self-esteem and self-worth. Systematic career planning facilitates the ability to learn to recognize, analyze, and exhibit abilities, interests, values, and personality traits compatible with job and career choices. As students progress through a carefully planned and implemented comprehensive program, they learn to set goals and identify the process skills needed to achieve them. Learning to identify the relationship between academic content learned in school and how it applies to life and career choices is the cornerstone of the career planning system. This concept will be more fully explored in the classroom and schoolwide programs section later in the chapter.

The evolving concept of career counseling in schools is based on the continuous development of new theories, processes, and practices in career development and counseling. This chapter expands on the background and foundation of career counseling described previously. It highlights selected components of a career planning system. Select examples of what has worked are offered throughout the chapter. A description of the importance of support groups and the roles they play in building a career planning system is offered. A school counselor, with the myriad of required tasks, cannot do the job alone. The resources section in the Appendix is recommended to the practitioner. It is extensive and meant to be used as an exploration tool to find the products and resources that best fit school populations and needs. Closing comments support how the expectations of the twenty-first century will continue to call for a balance between education and the delivery of student career planning.

THE CAREER PLANNING SYSTEM

The Foundation

Career development is an evolutionary process that begins in infancy and extends through adulthood. Career development competencies and indicators are the basis for integrating career planning into the total school program. Exemplary education programs consistently place and reinforce career education and career planning within a framework of career and life skills competencies and indicators, from kindergarten through Grade 12. Career planning provides youth with timely and accurate labor market and educational information, coupled with educational planning activities, to help them select focused strategies necessary to become productive and contributing members of society.

A Framework of Competencies

For over a decade the competencies and indicators of the National Occupational Information Coordinating Committee (NOICC)'s *The National Career Development Guidelines Project* (1992) have served as a foundation for career counseling and career planning. The *Guidelines* (1992) provide a comprehensive set of competencies and indicators in three areas: self-knowledge, educational development, and career planning and exploration. These areas encompass the functional competencies individuals need to acquire academic skills and to prepare for, obtain, and progress in satisfying and productive life and career choices.

The competencies serve as broad general goals. The indicators describe specific knowledge, skills, and attitudes critical to lifelong career development tasks. As currently outlined, the competencies and indicators are consistent with the general developmental capabilities of individuals at the primary school, middle and junior high school, senior high school, and adult levels. Utilizing them as a guiding framework, counselors and curriculum teams have designed curriculum and programs to ensure that the skills are covered in required courses at the various grade levels. In some cases, where it is not appropriate or desirable to design new curriculum, activities and focus events are created that ensure that the competencies are covered. Many educators believe that emphasizing the relevance of curriculum to the world of work provides depth of meaning to courses so that students are more likely to remember what they have learned.

The *Guidelines* (1992) correspond to developmental levels and tasks that are fully described in the accompanying materials. To review, awareness of careers is the focus at the elementary level. Activities and programs are designed to heighten student knowledge of the broad range of life development skills. It is a time when youth become aware of workers, work responsibilities, and jobs and occupations, mainly in their own neighborhoods. Career awareness activities range from limited exposure to the world of work and occasional field trips and classroom speakers to comprehensive exposure.

Students at the middle and junior high school level engage in learning and activities that help them learn more about themselves in relation to the world of work. It is a time of exploration and discovery of how they might one day fit into that world. Students are introduced to a wide span of career options. Successful integration of career planning at this level has included curriculum redesign that focuses on relevancy of subject matter to the world of work, studying career pathways, identifying potential job opportunities within the pathways, designing and writing individual learning plans, and starting to develop a career portfolio. It is important to provide many resources, including print media and computerized information, to learn about job and labor market information. Most states have their own computerized information system, which probably includes accompanying print materials, some curriculum suggestions, and, often, information for parents, either through the department of labor or education. Care is taken to include information on jobs and opportunities that youth might not have previously considered traditional for their age, gender, and ethnicity.

Building on career awareness and career exploration skills and competencies, students at the high school level learn to access and analyze job and labor market information in relation to their interests, skills, and abilities. They explore further educational and training opportunities that might be viable in their community, in a surrounding area, and globally. Successful strategies during high school include, but are not limited to, career information that is infused into the existing curriculum, apprenticeship programs, game simulations, academies, and job shadowing and mentoring opportunities. Information throughout all the stages is incorporated into a learning and career plan that can be reviewed at least yearly and revised as necessary. Some states stress parental involvement as a necessary component to formulate and review career plans.

The *Guidelines* (1992) are currently being reviewed, revised, and updated under the leadership of the National Career Development Association (NCDA) to more accurately reflect the changing needs of today's workplace and of society. An ultimate goal is to affect the way the United States prepares youth to enter, and be productive contributors in, the competitive global workplace. Counselors will want to follow these revisions and use them as the basis and foundation for career counseling and career planning programs.

Assessing Needs

While the national guidelines movement provides a comprehensive framework for career counseling, career education, and career planning, it is not expected that a school can cover every competency and indicator at one time. Counselors, as advocates for youth, must ask themselves each schoolyear where the focus of the career planning program should lie. What are the most pressing career planning needs of all stakeholders? What methods will be used to determine these needs? How will these identified needs be used to design the most effective career planning program?

In today's world, stakeholder needs change rapidly. When polled, stakeholders readily express and articulate their needs. Career planning designs are then based on the findings of formal needs assessments. The design considers and ensures that the needs of students, the concerns of parents, the requirements of the community and the workplace, and the economic and social trends affecting the community are all considered.

Career planning system design is accomplished when there is total agreement, understanding, and endorsement by community leaders, school administration, counselors, teachers, and parents that career planning, an integral part of the comprehensive school counseling program, is integrated into the total school curriculum. The plan must be clear and concise, state desired outcomes for students, delineate roles of stakeholders, be consistent with school policy and priorities that support learning competencies, be achievable, and be easily communicated to others. Educators and schools listen to the needs, reach out to determine how the needs can best be met, collaborate to respond, and are enabled to document the successes and impacts of their programs.

The Process.   Counselors take a lead role to plan with administrators and faculty to administer the needs assessment instruments that are used to ascertain concerns. Needs assessment instruments can be found in the National Career Development Association's *Career Counseling Competencies* (1997), obtained from state departments of education, or locally designed. Completed assessment instruments are analyzed and data reported to administration, leadership, advisory groups, and curriculum specialists for the purpose of career planning system building and/or improvement.

The needs assessment instrument items correspond to competency framework items in the *Career Counseling Competencies* (1997). Using this companion instrument facilitates and validates program planning. A committee or an advisory group with representative students, parents, teachers, community leaders, and employers reviews the data gleaned from the assessments. After discussion and consideration of the collective stakeholder needs, the group selects a reasonable number of expressed items, which become the focus goals of instruction, learning, and school projects for the schoolyear, at each of the elementary, middle, and high school levels. Curriculum and activities are designed to incorporate the selected career goals that correlate to, and enhance, state and local school division initiatives. To ensure total buy-in, the school vision statement is rewritten to incorporate the new focus. The curriculum objectives and plan are highlighted in school communications, posted on the Website, and shared with the local media.

The career planning goals that have been selected for the schoolyear become the focus of curriculum and instruction for every student at every grade level. Special consideration is given to the diversity of students in the schools. In the initial stages of planning, special consideration is also given to students who learn differently and to those who are from different cultures. Counselors serve as advocates who ensure that resources are provided for every student to access appropriate levels of career planning information. For example, counselors determine if interpreters are needed for those with hearing impairments, if special software is needed on computers used by those with visual impairments, if recorded books are needed, or if more time is needed for some students to participate in targeted learning activities. Counselors ensure that information and resources can be analyzed by different cultures. Careful assessment of materials and resources, speakers, and fieldtrips must be made. A variety of speakers, placements, and fieldtrips should be considered.

Workplace Needs.   In the early 1990s the Secretary's Commission on Achieving Necessary Skills (SCANS) was appointed by the U.S. Secretary of Labor to examine the skills that workers need in order to succeed in the workplace. Specifically, the commission was directed to advise the secretary on the level of skills required to enter employment. The commission was asked to define the skills needed for employment, propose acceptable levels of proficiency, suggest effective ways to assess proficiency, and develop a dissemination strategy for the nation's schools, businesses, and homes.

Leaders from business, unions, and the workplace identified five workplace competencies, a foundation of skills and personal qualities, and eight core skills they deemed essential to successful preparation of all workers for the workplace. The commission articulated its view of how schools prepare young people for work: "[s]chools do more than simply prepare people to make a living. They prepare people to live full lives—to participate in their communities, to raise families, and to enjoy the leisure that is the fruit of their labor. A solid education is its own reward" (SCANS, 1991, p. v).

Expectations articulated in the SCANS report were that schools would teach youth to combine reading, writing, computing, and creative problem solving with personal work behaviors, attitudes, and skills (i.e., required workplace competencies). Career counseling and career planning were expected to become an integral part of education to prepare youth for the world of work awaiting them; therefore it was expected that career planning programs needed to be integrated with existing school-wide policies. Ongoing and more current assessment of business and industry needs remains unchanged. Today employers consistently contend that the work of schools should focus on preparing youth for the world that awaits them.

Advisory Councils

Career planning is clearly dependent on the interrelationship of the school with the community. A positive work ethic, competency in basic skills, employability skills, and education for life are of concern to all persons assisting youth with career planning. Community councils are widely accepted as beneficial in helping the transition of students from school to work.

Establishing an advisory council is one of the most tangible pieces of evidence of community collaboration and support. The council assists in gathering community needs data, which is used to ensure that a valid career planning program is built and sustained. It serves as the communications link between the community and the counselor. The counselor serves as the link between the advisory council, the school curriculum committee, and school administration at all levels.

Articulating the Vision.   Involving the greater community in the educational process provides broad-based support for career planning. Relating curriculum to life and career needs makes academic content more concrete. Career planning that builds on basic academic competencies can be easily understood by students, parents, and community members. Career planning is a motivator for academic achievement as well as a means of building positive attitudes toward self, work, and lifelong learning. It provides an opportunity to extend classroom instruction into the business, industry, and cultural work sites of the community.

Clear and constant communication with all stakeholders must be ongoing. Each group must see the benefits that can be derived. Articulation of benefits is used in program planning, promotion materials, gathering the support of the community, and keeping parents informed of each child's educational program.

Roles and Responsibilities of the School Team

The goal of career planning within the comprehensive counseling program is to provide youth with timely and accurate labor market and education information, coupled with educational planning activities, to help them plan the focused strategies necessary to become productive and contributing citizens. Career planning is the responsibility of the total school and involves counselors, teachers, administrators, parents, community members, and employers working as a team.

Role of counselors.   Increased attention is focused on the preparation of students for their futures in the context of today's technological and information society. Students are faced with vast amounts of information for consideration in the career planning process. Clients (students) seeking career assistance want easily accessible information about themselves and the world of work. Therefore, counselors attend to individual needs and develop and manage career information services that encourage independent self-exploration (Sampson, Reardon, Peterson, & Lenz, 2004, p. 195). While the extent of the counselor's involvement may vary from activity to activity, basic helping responsibilities usually include articulating the focus of the total career planning program with all educators so that expectations are mutual and achievable, incorporating individual planning into a counseling program using national standards and guidelines, planning group guidance programs for students, conducting student evaluation inventories of activities they have completed (internships, mentoring, apprenticeships, service learning), and conducting research on the career planning program and process.

The supportive services encompassed in comprehensive counseling programs have long been recognized as being critical to career planning implementation. The counselor is the primary communications link between school personnel and shares responsibility for the planning and delivery of educational services. Within the educational services of career guidance, career information, staff development, curriculum infusion, instructional materials, community involvement, and services coordination that Gysbers and Moore (1987) describe, counselors participate in implementation planning as it directly relates to school counseling within the school division and as it meets the local and state guidelines for career counseling.

Throughout the career planning process, the counselor acts as a resource to help teachers secure materials appropriate to the delivery of career guidance in the classroom setting, to utilize and promote resources that enhance guidance practices and program activities, and to facilitate an information exchange between guidance personnel and teachers regarding career guidance strategies and techniques. Counselors acquaint administrators and staff with the most current evaluation techniques and materials appropriate to the delivery of career guidance practices.

For students, counselors identify and use appropriate instruments to help them explore interests, attitudes, and aptitudes relative to life roles and career choices. In individual and small-group settings, counselors assist students to develop, clarify, and assimilate work values that are personally meaningful. Counselors provide career planning services to all students, including handicapped, disadvantaged, potential dropout, and high-risk students.

Career planning and guidance sessions are specifically designed to help students acquire job-seeking, -keeping and -changing skills within the structure of a comprehensive school guidance and counseling program. Further, counselors gather and disseminate information to students concerning work permits, labor laws, and other regulations governing employment and counsel students on such topics as life goals, personal problems, education requirements for graduation, postsecondary education, or immediate employment. They also assist middle and high school students with the development of individual career plans and career portfolios.

Counselor Competencies in Career Counseling.   Professional organizations have identified competencies required of school counselors and career counselors. The National Career Development Association (NCDA) Website lists competencies for career counselors. In addition, NCDA has created ethical standards that govern the delivery of career services, including the counseling relationship, measurement and evaluation, research and publication, consulting, private practice, and procedures for processing ethical complaints. (These are accessible on the NCDA Website, http://ncda.org/).

Role of Educators.   With the ever-increasing demand to address the needs of students in a complex society and to attempt to meet those needs through existing courses of study and competency-based education, infusing career education and planning into the curriculum is both a cost-effective and time-efficient delivery system. The schoolday does not need to be extended. New staff or redistribution of existing staff responsibilities do not need to occur. Focusing on only one delivery system, identifying specific audiences that need more assistance than others, and providing separate programming serves to fragment the concept rather than permeate it into a total school philosophy and delivery system. A commitment to planning, designing, implementing, and assessing the progress of career-planning integration into all academic content, at all levels, for all students is the philosophy that guides and engages educators.

Often educators must rethink the way in which they instruct students. A more holistic approach to subjects and curriculum is required to help students see the relevance of what they are learning in school to the world of work that awaits them. Materials and resources, current information, and time for planning and coordination are necessary. Most important, staff must be provided with courses and encouraged to participate in professional development opportunities to understand how to integrate career education and career planning concepts into the curriculum.

Student Benefits

There are many reasons why students benefit from career planning and career counseling. As the career planning program progresses in design and implementation, these become readily apparent. Including students in the design and planning phases of career program development often highlights, focuses, and facilitates the career-planning process at every step and, every level. Students confirm that benefits they derive include, but are not limited to:

- broadened academic program and application to life skills and career choices
- heightened decision-making learning and processes
- increased understanding of economics and work
- increased knowledge of job or career opportunities within local environs and globally
- added advantage of recording job or career insights and knowledge for future referral
- opportunity to document experiences and activities and incorporate them into a self-marketing tool, often a portfolio
- observed reality of women and men working successfully in traditional and nontraditional career fields

Curriculum Design

A primary purpose of education is to develop informed, responsible individuals capable of making decisions and interacting in a meaningful way within the context of their home, family, workplace, and society. Career education is the totality of experiences that contribute to the development of such individuals. These experiences begin early, continue throughout life, and result in competencies, attitudes, and behaviors necessary to function effectively in society and to envision work as a meaningful part of a valuable life. Career education program models are recognized as a critical component of the total education program and provide school divisions with a systematic process that integrates the best of high-quality educational practices and basic skills with the best of career and life planning. The goals of career education focus on the student's self-concept, attitudes and appreciations, interpersonal skills, decision making skills, acquisition of occupational information, planning for education and training, economic awareness, and achievement of employability skills (Dedmond & Duffy, 1989, p. 11; Hoyt, 1981).

A comprehensive, developmental school counseling program enhances the student's opportunity to gain, analyze, and use information throughout the schoolyears to identify interests, strengths, areas in which to improve, and areas for career exploration. "Students use career assessment, information, and instructional resources within the context of a learning relationship with an instructor in an educational setting. The instructor is typically responsible for selecting, locating, sequencing, and using career resources for groups of students, as well as evaluating student outcomes" (Sampson et al., 2004, p. 9).

Classroom Instructional Strategies

Teachers and counselors collaborate to create interactive and interdisciplinary hands-on experiences and simulations and to infuse career planning into the existing curriculum or into teacher advisory periods. A variety of methods and intensities of design are employed. An example of individual curriculum infusion with a schoolwide focus is briefly described. Educators and counselors will want to design similar programs that take careful planning and execution, require great commitment, that document measurable results, and that result in satisfaction for the school and community.

One inner-city elementary school was successful in obtaining an antilitter and beautification grant. The counselor, who had been grappling with her concerns over the lack of care that students exhibited for their environment, expressed these concerns in the grant application. She proposed a study intended to change student attitudes and ultimately result in a cleaner, more attractive school campus. Her contention was that integrating environmental concerns and habits into existing curriculum would serve the purpose of motivating students to exhibit improved attitudes and habits in caring for their school, home, and community environments. After securing administrative backing, she designed and conducted staff development for all teachers, staff, and curriculum coordinators. In preparation for the yearlong theme, and in order to facilitate improved curriculum design for a year of focused studies, a series of field trips, speakers, related worksite visits, and days spent in workplaces that deal with environmental issues was conducted. Each session culminated with time for teachers to reflect on their experiences and use the information to update curriculum information and plans designed to motivate students to greater responsibility. For example, mathematics curriculum activities included gathering trash in certain areas of the school grounds and weighing it to determine where litter was most prevalent. Early elementary students gathered debris, then analyzed the contents to determine the kind of snacks their class most preferred. As a result they successfully learned skills of research, analysis, and reporting. They were rewarded for their efforts when a neighborhood restaurant donated pizza for lunch.

A science class studied the effects of biodegradable trash found on school grounds. Older youth in a social studies class collected litter, analyzed the kinds of snack food wrappers they found, and displayed the results in graphs and charts. Articles were written on the findings and debates were conducted on general eating habits of students at the school. Based on the same findings, a nutritionist, a pediatrician, and a school lunchroom manager participated in a panel discussion for the parents that focused on good eating habits. Students and parents collaborated in the computer lab to write letters to the editor of the local newspaper and articles on good nutrition, which were published. At all grade levels, research projects were conducted and reports were written on the effects of littering. Findings were highlighted in local media.

This total school project elicited activities and results too numerous to describe in this chapter, but a few are worthy of note. Student projects, speakers, field trips, and even electronic mentoring became an integral part of curriculum throughout the year, resulting in greater parent, employer, and community involvement in the school. Visible environmental results were clearly evident in the condition of the school and school grounds. In the academic area, teachers reported that youth exhibited greater interest in coursework and that students going to middle school planned to take higher-level English, science, and mathematics courses. Parents reported that their children were more aware of careers and jobs that relate to the environment and could realistically discuss those they might consider. Finally, students presented their findings in the form of verbal and written reports and PowerPoint presentations to administrators and the school board. As a result, the board provided funding for new playground equipment.

Simulations.   Simulations are especially useful in rural areas, where student insurance and liability are issues, and in communities with few businesses. Business leaders can be recruited to conduct small businesses within classrooms. The focus is on teaching students business practices as they develop, market, and sell a product. It can be expanded to teach students to form a community, complete with partnerships, governing structures, and the challenges of real community and life issues.

The Real Game series (America's Career Resource Network Association, 2002) addresses the competencies of the National Career Development Guidelines, the SCANS employability skills and competencies, and the American School Counselor Association's (ASCA, 2003) National Model. In the Real Game series, students assume work and life roles and learn about planning and setting goals; discovering and enhancing personal skills and talents; connecting school, work, and life roles; participating in teamwork situations; improving and exploring communication skills; and understanding local and global communities. The series is divided by grade levels into five different topics: the Play Real Game for Grades 3 and 4; the Make It Real Game for Grades 5 and 6; the Real Game for Grades 7 and 8; the Be Real Game for Grades 9 and 10; and the Get Real Game for Grades 11 and 12.

In addition to simulations, other strategies can be integrated into classroom instruction. Some of the most widely used include career journals, classroom resource speakers, "classroom of the future" activities, "passport to the world of work," gender equity instruction, minority achievement awareness, dropout prevention, cultural awareness, and economic exploration activities. Field trips, college fairs, career newsletters, internship programs, bulletin boards and showcase displays, and pupil recognition events should closely relate to the curriculum. Schoolwide programs may include linkages with community and four-year college programs.

Alternative Curriculum Designs.   Career majors integrate academic and occupational learning, blend school-based and work-based learning, and establish linkages between secondary schools and postsecondary institutions that foster smooth transitions for students (Kobylarz & Associates, 2001). Many high schools are being restructured around the career majors and career pathways model to create career academies. The academy, often called a "school within a school," focuses on a career cluster and organizes careers into a broad group with a common set of foundational knowledge and skills and similar interests. Students usually enter an academy of their choice by no later than 10th grade and follow a career pathway throughout the remainder of high school.

Another trend that closely parallels the career major theme is the magnet school, in which the entire student body follows the same career path. Some magnet school programs have highly competitive entrance requirements. However, the basic concepts should be considered for students with all levels of academic achievement.

Careers within a related cluster range from entry-level opportunities to professional jobs. They enable students to focus their tentative career goals and interests by incorporating a sequence of career-related courses and related academic material. Career clusters serve as the foundation for "career majors," which are sequences of courses or fields of study that help students expand, rather than limit, their career options and develop a sense of purpose when planning their courses of study. Students learn about the skills needed to be successful in a career path and often become involved in extracurricular activities and experiences related to their cluster of interest. Examples of career clusters are agriculture and natural resources, science and medicine, human services, arts and communications, and business and marketing (Ettinger, 1999, p. 24).

Service learning projects allow students to make a contribution to society and their community as they apply academic information and content concerning a specific subject they are studying. Counselors may also coordinate programs that incorporate volunteering and/or service learning opportunities to introduce students to the world of work (Cobia & Henderson, 2003). For example, at one university, psychology majors provide services in the local hospital, social worker candidates design an activity program for residents in the home for the aging, community counseling students work in a community outreach center, and computer and technology students teach assistive and adaptive technology and equipment usage in a learning center for people with disabilities. Service learning provides opportunities for participants to strengthen skills, make appropriate judgments about the needs of the population being served, and maintain academic performance standards that relate to the activity. The process for securing a placement involves the student outlining and presenting a service plan to the chosen agency or site for consideration and then completing an interview. A culminating self-assessment inventory that details learning or gaps in learning is discussed with the major instructor. It is the responsibility of career planners and instructors of service learning projects to ensure that staff, students, and the cooperating agency understand the purpose, nature, and benefits of the experience of all involved; provide instruction or help in identifying skills needed for effective experiences; articulate responsibilities and methods for recording experiences; and provide the necessary counseling to reduce any anxiety so that all parties realize benefits of the experience.

Other Learning Strategies and Interventions

Given the diversity of workplace, student, and educator needs, there are basic strategies and interventions that can be successfully implemented for students of all ages and at all stages of career awareness, exploration, and implementation, most of which will have measurable positive results. Interventions assist students to gather, analyze, synthesize, and organize information related to their futures. Schwallie-Giddis and Kobylarz (2000, pp. 214–215) define the following broad areas of interventions: outreach, classroom instruction, counseling, assessment, career information, career information delivery systems, work experience, placement, consultation, referral, and follow-up.

Building on the history and background of career development and acknowledging the more recent national counseling models and guidelines, school counselors and educators have agreed on a myriad of practices in the process of building a system of career planning that needs to be learned and achieved by all youth. Some of the more commonly accepted practices are briefly discussed.

Individual Planning.   Career counseling within the comprehensive counseling program provides, through individual or small group sessions, a forum to help students explore personal issues that are related to their plans for the future. Students examine ways to apply information and skills they have learned to their personal plans and to the development of their individualized education and career plans.

Individual planning is the means that counselors use to help students make informed decisions by exploring many options, utilizing many resources, and identifying probable outcomes. Students document the support, skills, and knowledge they need to use to set goals and to systematically monitor their progress toward the goals (Gysbers & Henderson, 2000; VanZandt & Hayslip, 2001). Individual learning plans are developed through group counseling, consultation with parents and teachers, coordination of community resources, classroom guidance focused on career education, and use of information in career resource and information centers. Career life plans that are consistent with students' personal/social, academic, and career goals are accomplished through student appraisal, advisement, placement, and follow-up (Gysbers & Henderson, 2000).

In order to have a written plan and to track management of career services as they relate to student career decision making and problem solving, counselors and students work together to formulate the individual learning plan, which provides the student with a strategy for relating specific career resources to goals, monitors progress of the student toward achieving goals, provides self-directed career decision making opportunities, strengthens client-counselor understanding, and improves client understanding of his or her expectations and of the service delivery.

Commonly accepted activities include assessing one's skills and interests and learning to access and use education, career, and labor market information. These experiences have the benefit of experiential learning through classroom and volunteer and community service projects to assess information related to self. The ultimate goal is that students learn to use information to design a flexible, long-range individualized education and career plan. Individual learning plans facilitate student work to prioritize selected activities the student has identified, delineate the purpose and expected outcome, and estimate the time needed to complete the activity (Sampson et al., 2004).

Career Information.   According to Sampson et al. (2004), career information is used to enhance knowledge of occupational, educational, training, and employment options. Information is categorized into occupational information, educational information, training information, and employment information. The purpose is to clarify and change self-knowledge. Students gain more information about career options, evaluate and narrow career options, and prepare for career implementation.

Career information is delivered through two types of formats: noninteractive (print, microform, audio, video, public presentations, assessment) and interactive (Internet Websites, computer-assisted career guidance systems, computer-assisted instruction, CD-ROM or DVD, card sorts, programmed instruction, structured interview, role playing or games, instruction, simulated work environments, direct observation, direct exploration, social interaction). Interactive formats allow the student to control selection and sequencing. Advantages are that the interactive information has the ability to provide broader and more detailed topic coverage at a low cost and that today's students are motivated to use technology in their learning.

Career information is typically disseminated through career days and career fairs. While no single strategy is applicable to all communities, certain guidelines and procedures should be followed to ensure successful career days and career fairs. Degree of involvement by teaching staff, students, and community members is critical.

Many elementary schools make a commitment to career days and career fairs. It is important to keep in mind that career information at the elementary level should be organized, focused, and introduced in small bits and segments.

At any level, organizing career days to feature a different career cluster each month is effective. Themes such as "Wellness Works," "Math Counts," "Heritage Day," "Fitness and Wellness Awareness," "Communication Counts," and "Motivating for Success" help students define who they are and build confidence in determining their strengths and abilities as they relate to career opportunities.

Career Portfolios.   A widely adopted strategy used for career planning is the development of a career portfolio. Career portfolios are valuable tools that promote informed career decision making and motivate students to become interested in, and enthusiastic about, career planning. Through structured creation and use of portfolios, students learn the techniques of assessing, recognizing, and developing their own abilities, interests, physical attributes, personal and social behaviors, values, and preferences. Relating these factors to potential career opportunities realigns student accountability.

A well-designed career development portfolio guides the student through the career planning process and serves as a sequential career-planning journal. It is both a process and a product that parallels the NOICC *Program Guide* (1994) domains: Self-Knowledge, Educational and Occupational Exploration, and Career Planning. Beginning at the elementary level and continuing through secondary school, students participate in counseling sessions, as well as classroom and small-group guidance activities, that enhance portfolio development. The portfolio serves as a depository for samples of best work, achievements and skills, certificates, letters of recommendation, and a place to record short- and long-range plans. The process of designing and keeping career portfolios current ensures that students are well on the way to becoming self-directed achievers who create their own vision for their future, set priorities and goals, and take responsibility for pursuing them (Dedmond, Sherrod, & Bryant, 1994).

Used as a career-planning journal, the portfolio guides the student through the career planning and development phases of self-knowledge, informed career decision making, and understanding the connections between education and employability skills. It allows students to document interests, abilities, skills, and discoveries. It houses important accomplishments and progress in career development. There are two broad types of career portfolios, those that have career development as a primary focus and those that have employability skill demonstration as a major focus.

Related to computer and technology access, electronic portfolios have gained popularity. Current job and labor market information, data and fact sheets, and instructions are easily accessed, updated, and stored for individual and group use in counseling and career centers. Ease of access and ability to continuously make entries and store electronic files are appealing to teachers, counselors, and students.

Computerized Career Information.   Students accessing computerized career information delivery systems gain a wealth of information to assist them in exploring career and educational options. Through interactive processes, they learn to set priorities, expand awareness of alternatives, and make short- and long-range plans. The most useful systems organize information around the NCDA (1997) and ASCA model (2003) domains and competencies. Most states have designed or adopted a system with specific state information. These are available through state career development supervisors, who are usually housed in either state education or labor departments.

Work Experience.   Matching predicted workforce needs to worker skills availability has become one of public education's greatest challenges. National labor reports estimate that only one in four new employees will have the skill levels needed to function productively in the workplace. Increased emphasis is being placed on matching academic excellence to workforce literacy skills and employment needs. In addition to acquiring skills, youth need to be aware of how to plan for advancement, how to transfer skills from level to level in a chosen career sequence, and, when changing jobs or career paths, how to transfer skills from one job to the next.

Work-based learning experiences allow students to see the relation of their studies to the world of work. Some of the more popular experiences include interviews with workers on their jobs, organized job shadowing, field trips, summer work experiences, internships, service learning, and apprenticeships. The recent emphasis on job shadowing has heightened nationwide participation. Some school districts begin shadowing at the elementary level. Others encourage shadowing in middle and junior high school. Students can explore areas of interest, learn about careers they have never thought about, and combine the information with better course selection at the secondary level. Some high schools expand shadowing experiences to include actual job placement, work experience, internships, and mentoring, thereby extending the students' involvement, exposure and knowledge of work, lifestyle, and societal responsibilities. Each activity has merit if it is prefaced by classroom instruction, carefully coordinated with community workers, role models, mentors, and human resource agencies, and continually evaluated to determine effectiveness.

In addition to work-based activities, summer camps are gaining recognition as exploration experiences for youth. Popular themes include technology, the 4-H program, Scouting, faith and spirituality, and historical, heritage, and cultural exploration.

Entrepreneurial Opportunities.   Designed to introduce youth to the entrepreneurial career option, a popular two-week residential camp, housed at a local university, immerses youth aged 14 to 18 in exploratory and hands-on activities. Electronic commerce sessions, community outings, job shadowing, attending professional and community meetings with successful local entrepreneurs, being guests at civic organization meetings, participating in a job development fair, and conducting online information searches are among the activities participants use to design their own business plan. A culminating presentation of each student's business plan is made to a panel of judges. The student judged to have the most promising business plan is awarded a trip to a national entrepreneurship conference. Though only one student is selected to attend the national conference, all participants gain the advantage of developing relationships with successful local entrepreneur role models in their community. Camp participants are invited to return to the camp the following year to serve to serve as camp counselors and role models to new campers.

Student Appraisal Inventories.   Student appraisal inventories identify career interests, levels of career development, and career maturity to be used in career planning. Standardized testing assists with individual appraisal and enables students to gather information for informed decision making. Increasing numbers of schools are using online career assessments to assimilate information on student interests, skills, personalities, and aptitudes. This information is further used to research possible occupations, access Websites based on personal priorities (e.g., interests, salary, education level, outlook, favorite school subjects, and work conditions), and access additional online career assessments (e.g., interests, work values, aptitudes and employability skills; Kobylarz & Associates, 2001).

Cobia (2003) organizes standardized career assessment instruments into intelligence tests (group or individual measure of academic promise or as part of a battery to detect learning disabilities); aptitude tests (predict and consider student career potential and ability to achieve); achievement tests (assess academic progress, predict future learning, identify strengths and weaknesses in certain areas of learning, estimate amounts and rates of learning, and compare achievement); and personality tests (describe traits and characteristics of an individual's personality).

The National Career Development Association (1997) delineates competencies for school counselors who conduct assessments. In brief, counselors must have knowledge of measurement principles such as scales, scoring systems, reliability, and validity; standardized tests such as intelligence, aptitude, achievement, interests, and personality instruments; nonstandardized assessment strategies such as card sorts, work samples, and observations; management of a school testing program; assessment issues such as invasion of privacy, test bias, and test anxiety; selection and administration of assessment instruments; and accurate communication of assessment information (Baker, 2000).

Student Reflection and Analysis.   Student reflection and analysis of career planning experiences is becoming a more widely accepted tool that is critical to making the connection between learning and careers. This activity often includes assigning a post-experience activity (diary, journal, video, report, display, news article) that is reviewed with students. It is used to evaluate the activity and determine if a second experience should be planned for comparison, contrast and reinforcement of learning about different work roles and environments. While sometimes considered time consuming, the advantages of a tool to monitor and revise individual career plans are critical to usefulness of the process.

Placement.   Placement strategies and activities vary widely from school to school. Large school divisions often hire student placement coordinators for career resource centers. Small school divisions might recruit the services of volunteers, including retired business partners, to establish community contacts and work in placement centers. Some schools collaborate with their local human resource managers associations to host career fairs where employers showcase their businesses and job opportunities and students even participate in on-site interviews for current job openings.

While no single strategy is applicable to all communities, placement is an integral part of career planning. Placement provides students with a database of jobs and opportunities that serve to increase student understanding of the economics of work, increase student understanding of the skills appropriate to work, and reduce student anxiety about work as they participate in preemployment activities such as job shadowing, mentoring, speaking, field trips, interviews, and attendance at professional and business workshops and meetings. Often placement services involve educators and students in corporate training and education seminars that foster workplace requirements. Employers benefit as they gain a venue to showcase their business. They gain access to a pool of potential job applicants and have the opportunity to review portfolios and conduct mock interview sessions. The employer might even realize the added advantage of reduced employee-training costs as a result of assisting schools with preemployment skills programs and services.

Referral.   One of the strengths of a school and community partnership lies in referring and assisting students who have encountered barriers to career development. Partnerships that facilitate referral of students with needs requiring special assistance share common working terminology, definitions, mission and goals. The partnership facilitates developing a relationship with mentors and role models in community and work settings. Future businesses, products, and services are better understood. In return, business partners are in a position to observe social, academic, and citizenship needs of youth. A partnership that addresses the needs of youth with special issues and concerns fosters positive public relations and, ultimately, demonstrates a common commitment to improving the quality of life for many who might otherwise remain unserved.

Evaluation

The purpose of measuring progress is to gather information on current programs and activities that are supportive of career planning and to provide informal evaluation of ongoing career planning programs and activities. It is critical that counselors are involved in continuous measurement of the effectiveness of the career planning program. Findings and results are used to market the career planning program to administration and persons in charge of budget decisions. Well-designed reports are valuable for forging connections with additional business and community leaders who understand the needs of the workplace. Data and information is used to make revisions to guidance strategies and curriculum for increased student achievement.

Data collection and assessment is used to increase community involvement and support and includes recording observations of all community mentors, evaluation data, and areas of student interest. Findings facilitate discussion on ways programs expose students to real-life and work environments and support consideration of additional ways to provide life skills and employability information for students.

Whatever the means of collecting and analyzing data, the counselor's responsibility is to identify ways to optimally utilize the information. Career and educational information is shared with appropriate educators for curriculum planning and enhancement and with students and parents for incorporation into their individual short- and long-term career plans (Cobia & Henderson, 2003). Using an annual assessment or evaluation will assist in maintaining a high level of commitment to, and involvement in, strategies for career planning implementation.

Career Planning Program Evaluation.   Evaluation of career planning programs is the basis for improvement and maintenance of the implemented initiatives. Measures are conducted to provide informal and formal evaluation of career planning programs and activities. Evidence must be shown that the career planning program is designed to serve all students: gifted, handicapped, disadvantaged, potential dropouts, special needs students, and those interested in postsecondary education or training. Documentation should show that programs are monitored through the review and update of student education and career plans, include sequential plans and curriculum for all grades, and are assigned appropriate leadership and resources. A visible means of communicating and interpreting data to staff, students, parents, and community members enhances the program viability.

Documentation of these results, similar to a year-end business report, makes an important statement about career planning. Employer members of the advisory committee may be willing to advise how to report data and statistics that elicits the desired attention from all stakeholders. Members may volunteer to have their own staff design and print reports to distribute. Finally, the career advisory committee realizes that presentation of the report to board members will be most impressive when it involves, and perhaps is delivered by, key stakeholders who are beneficiaries of the program—an advisory committee member, parent, and student.

Student Follow-up.   Follow-up studies of graduates to determine student needs and progress as they transition to become community workers and citizens are effectively led by an advisory panel that meets regularly to recommend and establish new directions for the program. The task of following graduates has improved in the last decade as computerized databanks of contact information are created. Important information that includes profiles of graduating classes can be compiled using both short- and long-term information. The ability to graphically portray post–high school education and training information, chosen career paths, goal attainments, and perceptions of effective elements of career planning are important measures of program enhancement and improvement.

Most important, counselors collect follow-up and assessment information to look holistically at all facets of the career planning program. Data is analyzed and used to determine program strategies that have received "most positive" or "least positive" reactions. Armed with this information, counselors are empowered to meet with appropriate personnel to determine future commitment to career planning programs and to plan for and implement new and improved ways to provide career planning information for students, parents, educators, and the community. Information is analyzed, shared, and utilized for continuous improvement of services and programs.

SCHOOL PARTNERSHIPS

In school partnerships, educators, parents, and business and community leaders work together to ensure that schools provide a variety of experiences that contribute to the development of informed, productive individuals.

Parent Involvement

Research confirms that parents are the number one source that children look to in planning their future. Parents have a critical role to play in helping children think about career goals and options. The growing number of career choices open to youth makes the selection process more complex. There are excellent commercial materials, and many states have created their own parent resource information.

Most states have developed parent guides in response to requests from parents, teachers, and counselors who use the state-developed Websites with their children and students. These are usually organized into resources and activities and can be downloaded from state system Websites. Career information specific to each state, such as financial aid, workforce projections, calendars and timelines, and worksheets, is included. Contact your state department of education.

One popular instrument that has extensive accompanying resources and materials for both parents and youth is the Armed Services Vocational Aptitude Battery (ASVAB; U.S. Department of Defense, 1993). The ASVAB is unique in that it is a multiaptitude test battery that yields three career exploration scores. Interpretations to students and parents help students learn more about themselves and the world of work, identify and explore potentially satisfying occupations, develop an effective strategy to realize goals, and learn a career-planning process. An additional accompanying resource, the *Occupational Outlook Handbook* (U.S. Department of Labor, 2000), is available in print and online (U.S. Department of Labor, 2001).

Business and Community Partners Working with Students

It is important to continue to stress the importance of promoting involvement from the community that surrounds the school and the critical and direct role such involvement plays in the education of students who will become the future citizens and leaders. Community leaders are in a position to provide accurate, up-to-date information about labor needs in a given locality. As with the teacher programs they help students see a direct relationship between academic instruction and life skills and career choices. Such programs provide increased opportunities for students to develop understandings of business operations and their applications.

Employers identify worksites where students can expand classroom instruction, experience involvement in tentative career interests, and learn about diversified career, job, and life roles. Direct involvement of business and community leaders provides opportunities for students to have personal contact with occupational resource persons and facilitates the opportunity to address equity issues and alleviate bias, discrimination, and prejudice in career choice and job tasks. Benefits of community education collaboration should be subject to a continuous review that comes from different perspectives. How will career planning be strengthened by sustained dialogue, relationships, and involvement with representatives from business, industry, labor, government, and human service agencies? How can career planning be enhanced through the cooperative goal setting of education and the community?

Business and Community Partners Working with Educators

Business and community partners work collaboratively with educators to provide leadership, vision, and experiences that support education and ensure a better-educated workforce. They assist teachers in providing educational experiences and motivation that enhance the career planning process.

Educators learn what is going on in their community, and the community, in turn, learns of the goals and aspirations of its future workforce. Partners provide educators with information about specific clusters of occupations; advise on the types of knowledge, skills, and attitudes needed for entry-level employment in specific occupations; recommend competency standards for employment and promotion within specific occupational fields; and offer assistance in recruiting students, providing internship programs and apprenticeships, and locating appropriate jobs for qualified graduates. Partners assist with the design of, and advocate for, community service and volunteer projects as part of student graduation requirements.

Workplace learning is a popular program that takes the educator out of the classroom and into the world of work in an experiential-learning activity. It has long been recognized that if they are to deliver the diverse educational programs needed by today's students, educators need the opportunity to develop their own knowledge of the world beyond the classroom so they can prepare their students to enter that world. Educators must model a commitment to lifelong learning in order to instill that value in students. The reward will be an enriched learning climate in which all students are prepared to envision and plan for work in their chosen careers as a meaningful part of quality living. Business and community partners are instrumental in the design of activities and strategies that connect the necessary workplace skills to the classroom curriculum. Infusing this workplace information into the curriculum is a skill that can be quickly refined when the educator takes part in workplace activities.

Benefits of working with business and community partners are well documented. Students report that they understand the relevance of what they are learning and its relation to the world of work that awaits them. The benefits to educators are that students show more interest, are more motivated, and realize greater academic achievement when students make the connections between curriculum and work. Business and community partners benefit by gaining a platform and voice that serve to guide student preparation toward the competencies needed to become the next leaders.

SUMMARY

Today's students and tomorrow's workers will be better able to make decisions about their futures if they are given the opportunity to explore tentative interests and career choices while completing their formal education. Social skills, academic skills, and job and career information can be acquired through a variety of experiences. Students' interest in academic subject matter and career planning can be stimulated through their awareness of personal development, life roles, and career path choices. When educators take students into the community and bring community resources into the school, students make the connections between work, learning, and career planning.

It is critical for all youth to participate in comprehensive career development programs and activities. Career development is the responsibility of all educators, counselors, parents, and community and business partners. Effective career education and career-planning implementation depend on focused educational programs, services, and activities at all education levels and designed and delivered by administrators, teachers, counselors, parents, and community members. The combined involvement and commitment of key participants is critical, from system design to evaluation and continuous improvement. The desired results are skills, knowledge, attitudes, and competencies that facilitate transitions from school level to school level, from school to work, from job to job, and among chosen life roles.

APPENDIX: RESOURCES FOR DESIGNING AND IMPLEMENTING CAREER PLANNING IN THE SCHOOL SETTING

American Counseling Association. (1999). Ethical standards for Internet on-line counseling. Online at http://www.counseling.org

American School Counselor Association (ASCA). *National Standards for School Counseling Programs; ASCA Standards for Academic and Career Development; ASCA Ethical Standards for School Counselors; ASCA Competencies in Assessment and Evaluation for School Counselors; The Role of the Professional School Counselor; The Get a Life Portfolio.* 800-306-4722; online at www.schoolcounselor.org

America's Career InfoNet. Online at http://www.acinet.org/acinet

Association for Assessment in Counseling. (1998). Competencies in assessment and evaluation for school counselors. Online at http://aac.ncat.edu/documents/atsc_cmptncy.htm

Bloom, D. J. (1998). *The school counselor's book of lists.* West Nyack, NY: Center for Applied Research in Education.

Campbell, C. A., & Dahir, C. A. (1997). *Sharing the vision: The national standards for school counseling programs.* Alexandria, VA: American School Counselor Association.

Career Communications Inc. *Career Magazine.* Online at http://www.careermag.com/

Career Options Institute. Information on topics including diversity and career options for women. Online at http://careeroptions.neric.org

Dahir, C. A., Sheldon, C. B., & Valiga, M. J. (1998). *Vision into action: Implementing the national standards for school counseling programs.* Alexandria, VA: American School Counselor Association.

Educational Resources Information Center. Online at www.ed.gov/edres/edfed/eric.html

Gladding, S. T. (1996). *Counseling: A comprehensive profession* (3rd ed.). Upper Saddle River, NJ: Merrill.

Harris-Bowlsbey, J., Dikel, M. R., & Sampson, J. P. (1998). *The Internet: A tool for career planning.* Columbus, OH: National Career Development Association.

Individuals with Disabilities Act. Online at http://www.ed.gov/offices/OSERS/OSEP/ Job Shadowing. Online at www.jobshadow.org

Kapes, Jerome T., & Whitfield, Edwin A. (Eds.). (2001). *A counselor's guide to career assessment instruments* (4th ed.). Columbus, OH: National Career Development Association.

Kobylarz & Associates. (2001). *Guidelines: National career development, K–Adult Handbook* 2001. DesMoines, WA: National Training Support Center (NSC). Online at www.learningconnections.org/ntsc.htm

Myrick, R. D. (1997). *Developmental guidance and counseling: A practical approach* (3rd ed.). Minneapolis, MN: Educational Media.

National Board for Certified Counselors. (1997). *Standards for the ethical practice of web counseling.* Greensboro, NC: Author.

National Consortium for State Guidance Leadership, Center on Education and Training for Employment (2000). *A state guidance leadership implementation and resource guide: A companion to the national framework for state programs of guidance and counseling.* Columbus: Ohio State University.

National Job Shadowing. Online at www.jobshadow.org

National Occupational Information Coordinating Committee, U.S. Department of Labor. (1992). The *national career development guidelines project.* Washington, DC: U.S. Department of Labor.

National Training Support Center. Online at www.learningconnections.org

Occupational Outlook Quarterly. Online at http://stats.bls.gov/opub/ooq/ooqhome.htm

Perry, N. S. (1994). Skills for success in the 21st century: A developmental school counseling program. In D. G. Burgess & R. M. Dedmond (Eds.), *Quality leadership and the professional school counselor* (pp. 57–70). Alexandria, VA: American Counseling Association.

Reardon, R. C., Lenz, J. G., Sampson, J. P., Jr., & Peterson, G. W. (2000). *Student handbook for career development and planning: A comprehensive approach.* Pacific Grove, CA: Brooks/Cole.

Remley, T. P., Jr., & Herlihy, B. (2001). *Ethical, legal and professional issues in counseling.* Upper Saddle River, NJ: Merrill.

Sabella, R. A. (2000). School counseling and technology. In J. Wittmer (Ed.), *Managing your school counseling program: K–12 developmental strategies.* Minneapolis, MN: Educational Media Corporation.

Sherrod, S. S., & Dedmond, R. M. (1998). *Parent's planner.* Chapel Hill, NC.

Sherrod, S. S., & Dedmond, R. M. (1999). *Helping today's students prepare for tomorrow's careers: Train the trainers manual.* Chapel Hill, NC.

Take Our Daughters to Work Homepage. Online at www.ms.foundation.org

U.S. Bureau of Labor Statistics. *Occupational Outlook Handbook, Occupational Outlook Quarterly, Career Guide to Industries,* and *Career Information for Kids.* Online at www.bls.gov/home.htm

U. S. Department of Education. Online at http://www.ed.gov/

U.S. Department of Labor. *Teacher's Guide to the Bureau of Labor Statistics Career Information.* Online at http://stats.bls.gov/k12/html/edu_tch.htm

U.S. Department of Labor Employment and Training. Online at www.doleta.gov. Links to O*net Resource Center, www.onetcenter.org; America's Job Bank, www.ajb.org; America's Learning Exchange, www.alx.org; and America's Service Locator, www.servicelocator.org

U.S. State and Local Gateway. Online at www.statelocal.gov/links.html

Zunker, V. E, (2002). *Career counseling: Applied concepts of life planning* (6th ed.). Pacific Grove, CA: Brooks-Cole, pp. 9–20

COMPUTERIZED CAREER INFORMATION SYSTEMS

Career Ways and Career Visions, Career Development Systems, 888-237-9297. Online at www.cdsways.com

CHOICES CT, ISM-Careerware, P.O. Box 129, 38465 NYS Route 12, Clayton, NY, 13624; 800-26-1544. Online at http://www.can.ibm.com/ism/careeerware/

DISCOVER for Windows, American College Testing, 800-498-6068. Online at http://www.act. org/discover/

SIGI Plus (SIGI+), Educational Testing Service, Center for Occupational and Professional Assessment, 800-257-7444. Online at http://www.ets.org/sigi/index.html

REFERENCES

America's Career Resource Network Association. (2002). *The Real Game series.* www.Realgame.org

American School Counselor Association. (1995). *Get a life personal career planner.* Alexandria, VA: Author.

American School Counselor Association. (2003). *The ASCA national mode: A framework for school counseling programs.* Alexandria, VA: Author.

Baker, S. B. (2000). *School counseling for the twenty-first century* (3rd ed.). Upper Saddle River, NJ: Merrill.

Cobia, D. C., & Henderson, D. A. (2003). *Handbook of school counseling.* Upper Saddle River, NJ: Merrill/Prentice Hall.

Dedmond, R. M., & Duffy, P. (1989). *Choices and challenges, career education in Virginia: Program management guide.* Richmond, Virginia Department of Education.

Dedmond, R. M., Sherrod, S. S., & Bryant, S. L. (1994). A quality approach to career development. In D. G. Burgess & R. M. Dedmond (Eds.), *Quality leadership and the professional school counselor* (pp. 73–99). Alexandria, VA: American Counseling Association.

Ettinger, J. (1999). *Career development programs for high schools.* Madison, WI: Center on Education and Work.

Gray, K. C., & Herr, E. L. (2000). *Other ways to win: Creating alternatives for high school graduates* (2nd ed.). Thousand Oaks, CA: Corwin Press.

Gysbers, N. C., & Henderson, P. (2000). *Developing and managing your school guidance program* (3rd ed.). Alexandria, VA: American Counseling Association.

Gysbers, N. C., & Moore, E. J. (1987). *Career counseling: Skills and techniques for practitioners.* Englewood Cliffs, NJ: Prentice Hall.

Hoyt, K. B. (1981). *Career education: Where it is and where it is going.* Salt Lake City, UT: Olympus Publishing Company.

Kobylarz & Associates. (2001). *Guidelines: National career development, K–Adult handbook.* DesMoines, WA: National Training Support Center (NSC).

National Career Development Association. (1997). *Career counseling competences: Revised version 1997.* Tulsa, OK: Author.

National Occupational Information Coordinating Committee, U.S. Department of Labor. (1992). *The national career development guidelines project.* Washington, DC: U.S. Department of Labor.

Sampson, J. P., Jr., Reardon, R. C., Petersen, G. W., & Lenz, J. G. (2004). *Career counseling and services.* Belmont, CA: Thompson Brooks/Cole.

Secretary's Commission on Achieving Necessary Skills. (1991). *What work requires of schools: A SCANS report for America 2000.* Washington, DC: U.S. Department of Labor.

Schwallie-Giddis, P., & Kobylarz, L. (2000). Career development: The counselor's role in preparing K–12 students for the 21st century. In J. Wittmer (Ed.), *Managing your school counseling program: K–12 developmental strategies* (2nd ed., pp. 211–218). Minneapolis, MN: Educational Media Corporation.

U.S. Department of Defense. (1993). *Armed Services Vocational Aptitude Battery.* Washington, DC: U.S. Government Printing Office.

U.S. Department of Labor. (1991). *Dictionary of occupational titles.* Washington, DC: U.S. Government Printing Office.

U.S. Department of Labor. (2000). *Occupational outlook handbook.* Washington, DC: U.S. Government Printing Office.

U.S. Department of Labor. (2001). *Occupational information network (O*net).* Available online from http://www.doleta.gove/program/onet

VanZandt, C. E., & Hayslip, J. B. (2001). *Developing your school counseling program: A handbook for systemic planning.* Pacific Grove, CA: Brooks/Cole.

CHAPTER 11

CAREER COUNSELING IN MENTAL HEALTH AND PRIVATE PRACTICE SETTINGS

MARY H. GUINDON

Johns Hopkins University

Historically, career counseling has taken place in public schools, higher educational settings, within the military, in vocational rehabilitation centers, and, more recently, in business and industry. The assumption has been that career-related issues are somehow separate, and qualitatively different, from personal issues. More recently, however, there has been recognition that human beings must be viewed in a more holistic way. Research indicates that clients' career and personal concerns, including their emotional issues, often appear together (Lewis, 2001). There is a close relationship between the processes of psychotherapy and career counseling (Niles, Anderson, & Cover, 2000) and "career is central to general life satisfaction and mental health" (McAuliffe, 1993, p. 13). Work for many Americans is the central organizing feature of life, and they spend more time at work than in any other single activity. It plays a significant role in mental well-being. Individuals exist in a dynamic relationship with their work environments, and they seek to develop satisfactory relationships by making continual adjustments. For some, the results are psychologically unhealthy. Mental health problems can result from the interaction of interests, personality characteristics, and such workplace issues as stress (Osipow, 1983), and problems of career choice may be viewed as personality problems (Crites, 1981). However, it is difficult to know whether some individuals bring mental illness into the workplace or if the workplace induces mental illness (Herr & Cramer, 1992). The likelihood is that both influence each other. The challenges of job insecurity, balancing work and family roles, harassment, discrimination, underemployment, workplace stress, and unemployment can motivate individuals to seek counseling for mental health concerns.

It should be no surprise, then, that some clients in mental health and private practice settings need assistance with career development issues, whether or not the work domain is part of the presenting concern. In fact, clients may have career-related concerns in almost every setting in which counseling takes place (Niles & Harris-Bowlsbey, 2002). These clients, however, receive such services only insofar as the counselor's level of knowledge, comfort, and expertise in career counseling allow. In private settings, career-related issues and career life planning rarely receive the same kind of urgency as mental health–related issues. As a rule, mental health counselors are not well versed in career issues or lack enthusiasm for career counseling. Conversely, career counselors may not have the expertise needed to assist clients for whom mental health issues are primary. Nevertheless, those private practice and mental health counselors who are well versed in both mental health and career counseling can offer a full range of counseling interventions to their clients. Herr (1992) suggested that unless one "is willing to look at the interaction of career counseling and behavior health or mental health problems, there is little likelihood that [one] can be effective in assisting persons with job adjustment problems, dislocated workers, spouses of those experiencing job dislocations, or recovering alcoholics" (p. 26).

Many clients who seek help for career-related matters often must come to terms with issues related to their mental health and, conversely, many clients who seek help with mental health concerns inevitably want to seek out and implement career-related goals once their mental health issues have been successfully resolved. This chapter, therefore, presents information useful to those counselors who wish to work in mental health and private practice settings. It discusses some of the mental health issues typically found in these settings and offers suggestions on how people with mental health concerns can be productively engaged in the workplace through career-counseling interventions. A glossary of mental health terms is provided in Table 11.1.

THE NATURE OF MENTAL HEALTH CLIENTS

A clinical or mental health counselor may work independently in a sole proprietorship or group practice, a private mental health center, a community-based mental health agency, an affiliated psychiatric hospital, an employee assistance program, or a vocational rehabilitation center, or as a consultant in any of these settings. Each of these settings provides unique and different opportunities to offer direct career- and lifestyle-planning services to clients with mental health issues.

A number of considerations determine the necessity of, and opportunity for, career counseling with clients in any setting. In most cases, the presenting concern may not be directly work related. On the other hand, workers sometimes suffer from stress reactions, depression, anxiety, or other disorders for which they need treatment. Generally, clients who present with mental health concerns and who may also have job-related issues fall into several broad categories: (a) individuals with severe mental disorders (SMD), usually chronic and of long-standing duration, such as schizophrenia, dissociative disorders, and the like; (b) those with personality disorders; (c) those who suffer from various forms of depression; (d) those who exhibit symptoms of anxiety-related disorders, including social phobia and posttraumatic stress disorder; and (e) those with substance-related disorders. Other clients may present directly with work-related issues that affect their mental health. Most common are (f) those

TABLE 11.1 Glossary of Mental Health Terms

Anxiety Disorder	A general term used to describe a number of related disorders distinguished by uneasiness, discomfort, worry, and fear that has no known basis or imminent threat. Physical symptoms may include sweating, trembling, heart palpitations and other symptoms associated with stress.
Cognitive-Behavioral	A counseling approach in which counselors use a variety of techniques to bring client's ineffective thinking and behavioral patterns into awareness. Direct, goal-oriented methods are used to assist the client in changing thoughts and actions.
Depression (Depressive Disorder)	A general term used to describe a number of related disorders distinguished by extreme sadness, hopelessness, despair, and low energy. Symptoms can range from mild to severe, short-term or chronic.
Diagnostic and Statistical Manual of Mental Disorders (DSM-IV-TR)	The publication of the *American Psychiatric Association* that codifies and delineates mental disorders used in diagnosis and treatment planning. The most recent is the fourth edition, text revised (*IV-TR*)
Dissociative Disorder	A disorder in which the individual experiences an altered state of consciousness that includes a change in personality and/or memory loss, usually of a traumatic or stressful nature and that is not organic or psychotic in character
Dual Diagnosis	The identification in an individual of two or more mental disorders, one of which is usually a substance abuse disorder (e.g., alcoholism and depression)
Generalized Anxiety Disorder	Excessive emotional fear, worry, and apprehensive expectation of a general nature about events or activities, usually involving the inability to control or "turn off" worrisome thoughts
Guided Imagery	A technique in which the counselor assists the client in imagining various specific scenarios and the related feelings, thoughts, and behaviors evoked
Journaling	A cognitive-behavioral technique used to bring thoughts, feelings, and behaviors into awareness and to recognize significant themes and patterns
Mood Disorder	Mental disorders that have a predominantly excessive or inappropriate emotional basis, including depressive disorders
Personality Disorder	An inflexible, enduring pattern of maladaptive thoughts, behaviors, or emotional responses that interfere with functioning across a broad range of social and work situations and cause impairment in interpersonal relationships and living

(continued)

TABLE 11.1 Continued

Posttraumatic Stress Disorder (PTSD)	A type of anxiety disorder that may follow exposure to a traumatic event where the individual experienced an actual threat or danger to self or others and responded with intense fear or horror
Rational Emotive Behavioral Therapy (REBT)	A type of cognitive-behavioral technique developed by Albert Ellis in the 1950s, in which the counselor confronts the client about dysfunctional thoughts. Thoughts about events rather than the events themselves are seen as the cause of emotional difficulties and inappropriate behaviors.
Schizophrenia	A severe mental disorder in which the individual is out of touch with reality and experiences delusions, hallucinations, speech incoherence, disorganized behavior, and/or other thought abnormalities for a significant period of time
Self-esteem	The evaluative component of the self; the affective judgments placed on the self-concept, consisting of feelings of worth and acceptance, awareness of competence, and sense of achievement
Severe Mental Disorder (SMD)	A general term used to describe any number of psychiatric disorders or mental illness, usually chronic and of long-standing duration, in which the ability to function normally is impaired or disrupted
Social Phobia (Social Anxiety Disorder)	An extreme, unreasonable, and persistent fear of a social or performance situation in which the individual will be embarrassed, scrutinized, or humiliated by unfamiliar persons. Exposure to the feared situation results in intense anxiety or distress.
Stress	A state of physiological tension caused by an imbalance between external demands in the environment and the individual's capacity to adequately respond to these demands
Systematic Desensitization	A step-by-step and gradual behavioral technique in which the client's anxiety is reduced by pairing thoughts/fears with incompatible behaviors: Anxiety-provoking thoughts are paired with relaxation techniques and calming guided imagery.
Thought Stopping	A cognitive-behavioral technique in which clients are taught to use an external cue (such as snapping a rubber band on the wrist) that will interrupt an inappropriate or unproductive thought

suffering mental health disorders due to job loss; and (g) those who seek help with occupationally related stress reactions. Each of these types of clients and their possible career-related issues are discussed, with the understanding that these categories are not mutually exclusive. It is common that these concerns present together, that those experiencing anxiety, for example, may have stress-related disorders, exhibit symptoms of depressive disorders, have substance-related problems, or have lost a job. Individuals with severe mental disorders often experience many other mental health problems as well. Since the purpose of this chapter is to discuss the career-counseling process for people with mental health issues, only limited explications of these disorders are presented. The reader is referred to the *Diagnostic and Statistical Manual of Mental Disorders (DSM-IV-TR;* American Psychiatric Association, 2000) for information about the diagnostic criteria for each mental health disorder.

TYPICAL ISSUES IN MENTAL HEALTH AND PRIVATE PRACTICE

People with Severe Mental Disorders (SMD)

Many individuals with severe, chronic psychiatric disorders may have interrupted training and educational opportunities, fragmented work histories, or lack work experience altogether, and thus they have limited understanding of the world of work and employment opportunities (Ford, 1995). Reports indicate that 80 to 90 percent of those with severe mental illness do not participate in the labor market (National Institute on Disability and Rehabilitation Research, 1992). New drugs for treating severe mental illness have brought hope and possibility to these clients. As new techniques for managing severe mental illness and early interventions have been developed, greater numbers of individuals are better able to manage their disorders and lead more productive lives. For some, career and life planning interventions are now possible, whereas they were routinely out of the question previously.

Career development for those with any type of disability, including those with mental illness, can be described through five constructs (individual, contextual, mediating, environmental, and outcome; see Szymanski, Hershenson, Enright, & Ettinger, 1996) and six processes (development, decision making, congruence, socialization, allocation, and chance; see Syzmanski & Hershenson, 1998). These constructs and processes are discussed in Chapter 12.

Early life experiences or expectations of others may determine how people with SMD view themselves as workers, especially when the mental disability is central to their self-concept. Apathy is common in those with severe mental illness, who all too often have been the recipients of stigmatizing attitudes. Apathy results from poor self-efficacy beliefs along with negative expectations about career choice in the world of work (Chartrand & Rose, 1996). Human development theory suggests that expectations of parents, teachers, and counselors shape self-perceptions. Therefore, the positive expectation of counselors in the career- and life-planning process is essential in assisting those with SMD in developing and maintaining their concepts as successful workers. According to Fabian (1999), three key counselor strategies affect the entry of those with SMD into the labor force: endorsing the value of work, focusing on careers rather than just obtaining jobs, and stressing client strengths rather than deficits.

Americans with Disabilities Act.   The elimination of barriers to employment has led to fuller and more productive lives for people with disabilities. Covered in the definition of a "disability" is any individual who has a mental impairment that substantially limits major life activities, which includes those with SMD who have recovered from a mental illness. Instrumental in breaking down barriers, the Americans with Disabilities Act (ADA) has allowed our society to benefit from the skills and talents of those with disabilities. Under ADA, employment discrimination is prohibited against qualified individuals with disabilities. Individuals are considered to have a qualified disability if they meet legitimate skill, experience, education, or other requirements of an employment position that they hold or seek and can perform the "essential functions" of the position, either with or without reasonable accommodation. The ADA prohibits discrimination in all employment practices, including job application procedures, hiring, firing, advancement, compensation, and training. This applies to all employment-related activities. Hence, career and employment counseling for individuals with mental illness is not only possible, but also mandated by law.

Career development is a complex, lifelong process of developing and implementing an occupational self-concept (Super, 1980). For those with severe and chronic mental disorders, this process is compromised in oftentimes irreparable ways. The preponderance of career- and employment-counseling interventions for people with SMD takes place in vocational rehabilitation centers (see Chapter 12) or community-based mental health facilities in collaboration with vocational rehabilitation centers. Counselors in community mental-health counseling centers are committed to providing preventive and developmental mental-health programming to the general public. Counselors in these centers hold the belief that assessment, treatment, and consultation services should respond to the unique needs of individuals, families, and communities, with the goal of promoting harmony among the psychological, emotional, physical, spiritual, interpersonal, and vocational elements of each person's life. Combining services can be effective. For example, for those with schizophrenia, providing vocational rehabilitation services in conjunction with ongoing psychiatric treatment and counseling increases the efficacy of both approaches (Lamb & Mackota, 1997).

Numerous persons with severe psychiatric disabilities are generally impaired significantly enough to prevent them from holding jobs without some kind of adaptation, as required by the ADA. Persons with disabilities in general are a diverse group, and disability itself does not necessarily hinder career development (Syzmanski & Hershenson, 1998). "Some individuals with marked pathology can manage work tasks quite well, often at high levels" (Spokane, 1991, p. 249). However, disability is a risk factor that may influence the course of career development. Many persons suffering with severe psychiatric disorders can work initially only in supported employment, highly supervised settings most commonly known as sheltered workshops. These settings offer opportunities for counselors to focus on vocational strategies and life-skills training to address individual performance and best practices within the limitations posed by the client's disorder (Fabian, 1999). Common practices include either individual job placement and support or transitional placement during rehabilitation in anticipation of higher-level employment. Some critics argue, however, that such an artificial separation between actual work and the nonwork domains found in sheltered community programs hinders opportunities for those with SMD to explore possible appropriate careers, to develop self-efficacy, or to anticipate participation in the real world of work (Fabian, 1999). Consequently, counselors take care not to impose their own assumptions regarding the nature of meaningful work or the value of specific careers on those with SMD. In fact, counselors understand that they are asking people with severe mental disabilities to manage two careers: employment and their mental illness (Fabian, 1999).

Combining vocational and mental health services to address on-the-job issues assists SMD individuals in making successful transitions to the workplace. Services that counselors typically offer include (a) assessing the client's level of vocational maturity, self-concept, and developmental life stage; (b) referring clients for formal vocational assessment through rehabilitation services; (c) facilitating the setting of realistic career plans and implementing them; and (d) addressing the impact of unrealistic/inappropriate career plans on the client's self-concept and level of success. Special care is taken to assist the client in understanding communications and overcoming communications barriers common to those with SMD. Counselors target interventions in which clients can form and maintain suitable relationships. Clients can learn to respond to social cues correctly and to give and receive appropriate feedback. Expectation and conveyance of possible success on the counselor's part are essential. As an example, Kyle and Persinger (2000) described a community-based, integrated, vocational life-planning model for people with chronic mental illness that focuses on the individual rather than the disorder to allow the client to exercise control over career choice. This model assesses "the client's intellectual abilities, his personality, and his educational achievement to identify areas of difficulties that need to be addressed in order to be successful" (p. 198). The intervention includes a thorough vocational assessment and an individualized plan to address needs and develop interests, skills, and abilities.

When work experience programs allow clients to experience success within a supportive environment, the client's self-efficacy beliefs and confidence in his or her capacity for meaningful work increase (Fabian, 1999). Persons with long-term mental illness can overcome barriers when programs offer speedy placement into real, rather than sheltered, worksites. Loughead and Black (1990) found that people with mental illness who participated in career development programs appropriate to them showed a significant change in vocational identity. Their findings supported the selection of Holland's (1994) Self-Directed Search (SDS) and its concomitant activities as a feasible career development service. Other career interventions include helping clients with personal future planning, seeking out flexible educational programs, workplace mentorship, and interagency collaboration (Hagner, Cheney, & Malloy, 1999), and offering individual or group instruction and coaching in job-search skills. Ultimately, for this population, job placement at the highest functional level possible is the goal.

Personality Disorders

Personality can be a significant factor in workplace functioning and success. Personality is a pattern of cognitive, affective, and behavioral traits that endure over extended periods of time and manifest in a learned and predictable structure of overt and covert behaviors. A normal or healthy personality allows people to cope with and adapt to their environments effectively through individual, specific personality styles (see Sperry, 1995). In fact, Holland (1973) saw career and personality as interrelated and used this perspective to develop the Holland Codes, which are widely used as part of career counseling. People with personality disorders, however, attempt to cope with everyday activities and relationships with inflexibility and maladaptive behavior. Their perceptions of self and the environment are self-defeating and ineffective. In an informal study of clients in a career-counseling practice, 18 percent exhibited sufficient criteria to indicate one or more personality disorders (Musgrove, 1992). Because of the prominence of work in the lives of most individuals, those with personality disorders experience many work-related difficulties and problematic career choices.

Personality disorders vary in level of dysfunctional behaviors. Millon and Everly (1985) differentiated personality behaviors along a continuum, from normal personality style to mildly severe and then moderately and markedly severe, or dysfunctional. The more severe disorders are less amenable to treatment in general and can be categorized according to treatability as high amenability (dependent, histrionic, obsessive-compulsive, and avoidant personality disorders); intermediate amenability (narcissistic, borderline, and schizotypal personality disorders); or low amenability (paranoid, schizoid, and antisocial personality disorders; Stone, 1993). Those with low amenability and many with intermediate amenability will also be less amenable to career- and life-planning interventions than those with high amenability. Career counseling can be difficult with people with moderately severe personality disorders and is less effective with individuals with markedly severe personality disorders. Consequently, people with mildly severe personality disorders are more likely to benefit from career-related interventions.

Several behaviors are delineated in the *DSM-IV-TR* (American Psychiatric Association, 2000) as diagnostic criteria for personality disorders, including factors such as indecisiveness, dependence on others' advice, self-defeating behaviors, anxiety, perfectionism, instability, and difficulties in interpersonal relationships (Kjos, 1995). In the presence of personality disorder, career decision making and work performance are compromised. It is important to note that career and mental health counselors do a disservice to their clients when the career implications of personality disorders are not taken into consideration in the counseling process (Kjos, 1995). Counseling interventions for those with personality disorders combine psychodynamic counseling with emotional, interpersonal, and cognitive-behavioral restructuring techniques. The goal is to facilitate movement from the personality disorder to a more functional personality style (Sperry, 1995). Career counseling is a cognitive-behavioral, psychoeducational modality and can be valuable in facilitating this move. Kjos (1995) pointed out that effective career counseling for people with personality disorders includes the ability to (a) recognize the traits that make up specific personality disorders that may inhibit (or enhance) career development; (b) develop treatment plans that capitalize on the positive aspect of each client's personality style, and (c) work with such clients to maximize their strengths. She described interventions that are targeted toward those with dependent, borderline, and obsessive-compulsive personality disorders and discussed positive and negative characteristics of each of these disorders that should be considered in clients' career choices.

Depression

Depression is a widespread and costly disorder and is present to some degree in most clients. Almost 11 million people suffered from major depression in 1990 (Greenberg, Stiglin, Finkelstein, & Berndt, 1993). Depression is not one entity; it is several different, but related, mood disorders and can be susceptible to misdiagnosis. Depression can range in symptomology from mild to actively suicidal. According to the *DSM-IV-TR* (American Psychiatric Association, 2000), the major symptoms of depressive disorders include depressed mood for most of the day and for a number of days; a diminished interest in activities; significant weight loss or weight gain; poor appetite or overeating; insomnia or sleeping too much; low energy level, fatigue or psychomotor agitation; low self-esteem; feelings of worthlessness and inappropriate guilt; inability to concentrate; difficulty making decisions; feelings of hopelessness; and recurrent suicidal thoughts. When two or more of these symptoms are present during the same two-week period, the existence of a minor depressive episode is likely. When five or more are present during the same two-week period, a major depressive episode is probable. Mild, chronic depression of long-standing duration is known as dysthymia. The symptoms are similar, but less severe, than other depressive disorders. Major Depressive Disorder, Single Episode (*DSM-IV-TR*), is a common type of depression encountered among people who lose their jobs. It is situational in nature and often, but not always, lifts when the situation changes. Stress is a significant contributor to depression, and threats to career can precipitate both stress and depression. Occupational stress and job loss are discussed later in this chapter.

Research indicates significant positive relationships between depression and career indecision and between depression and dysfunctional career thought, and a significant negative relationship between depression and vocational identity (Saunders, Peterson, Sampson, & Reardon, 2000). Role ambiguity is significantly related to depression (Smith, 1989). Engagement in work is problematic for some depressed clients, and stress in this population can lead to either temporary or long-term inability to work. Typically, depressed clients who are not able to work began their work lives expecting failure and rejection and "react to the inevitable setbacks of work life with some combination of confusion, frustration, anger, and demoralization" (Axelrod, 1999, p. 71).

Since inability to make decisions is a common symptom in depressed clients, career-counseling strategies associated with decision making can be effective. A significant component of career indecision is dysfunctional career thought. Crites (1969) differentiated indecision from indecisiveness. Indecision is the inability of a person to commit to a course of action that will result in preparation for, and entering into, a specific career or occupation. Career indecison is addressed by using techniques common to career development and life-planning interventions, such as facilitating the discovery of skills, interests, abilities, and values and teaching the client goal setting, world-of-work information, and, again, decision-making skills. Indecision is ameliorated through gaining information about careers, job search, and the like and learning how to make decisions in order to sort through alternatives. Indecisiveness, on the other hand, is a personality dysfunction and generally involves pain and anxiety of making any decision. An indecisive person is incapable of making a decision even after career counseling and interventions of a more psychotherapeutic nature are indicated.

The counselor working with a depressed client on career issues must first attend to the depression, through personal counseling, by referral for therapy or medications, or both. Counseling is required before career development techniques are indicated. Most important is conveying to the depressed client that satisfaction and pleasure in work activities are real possibilities. The implementation of skills, talents, and interests in and of itself can have a therapeutic effect (Axelrod, 1999).

Self-esteem and depression are highly correlated. Therefore, interventions targeted toward enhancing self-esteem may also improve depressive symptoms and prepare the client for career and life planning when appropriate. Low self-esteem affects individuals' perception about their abilities and their willingness to take action and to make healthy choices in their lives. Self-esteem is significantly related to physical and mental well-being and appears to be correlated with functional behavioral and life satisfaction (Bednar & Peterson, 1995). Self-esteem involves that part of the individual that makes a judgment about all the constituent pieces of the self; it is the evaluative component of the self-concept. Self-esteem can be described in terms of attitudes of approval or disapproval people hold about themselves and all their many characteristics. It appears to vary across different areas of one's experience and fluctuates depending upon the different roles one plays (see Guindon, 2002b). What this means is that in different situations, individuals' feelings about their self-worth will change (they might have high self-esteem in one situation and low self-esteem in another). Therefore, the counselor first ascertains in which situations low self-esteem predominates and on which elements of the self the depressed client places the most importance. He or she assists the client to *realistically* evaluate the various constituent elements of the self through assessment of authentic interests, values, and the like and through challenging irrational thought processes and helping the client bring these thought processes into awareness. Thought stopping, journaling, and other cognitive-behavioral techniques are commonly prescribed. Group work is especially helpful, and career- and life-planning workshops are structured around life-skills training as well as job-search skills.

Anxiety Disorders

The diagnostic category of anxiety disorders includes panic attack, agoraphobia, specific phobia (to an object or situation), social phobia, obsessive-compulsive disorder, posttraumatic stress disorder, acute stress disorder, and generalized anxiety disorder. Counselors in mental health and private practice may find that persons with any of these disorders may have career-related concerns because of the nature of anxiety itself. Anxiety produces feelings of apprehension and fearfulness and may be severe enough to limit everyday workplace behaviors. The work environment itself can be predictive of generalized anxiety disorder (Smith, 1989). Bordin (1986) suggested that clients could best confront career-related problems only when anxiety is minimized. Social phobia and posttraumatic stress disorder (PTSD) are discussed here because of their prevalence within mental health settings and their impact on workplace functioning, with the understanding that there may be a need to facilitate career- and life-planning skills with those experiencing other kinds of anxiety as well.

Social Phobia (Social Anxiety Disorder).   Social phobia affects approximately 13 percent of the population at some time in their lives and thus poses a significant mental health threat (Kessler et al., 1994). Those with social phobia fear meeting new people, situations in which they must be assertive, and performance appraisal. Consequently, work situations can be difficult for them. Research indicates that social phobics are underemployed and are more anxious than healthy persons about beginning a job but show no less job satisfaction than their healthier counterparts (Bruch, Fallon, & Heimberg, 2003). Nonetheless, social phobics' anxiety significantly interferes with occupational functioning (Turner, Beidel, Dancur, & Keys, 1986)

Posttraumatic Stress Disorder.   Unique among anxiety disorders, posttraumatic stress disorder (PTSD) is a condition that can manifest at any age in those with no predisposing conditions. It is distinguishable from other anxiety disorders because symptoms develop only after exposure to a traumatic event or extreme stressor. However, personality characteristics, social support, and the nature of the trauma itself can impact the duration and severity of the disorder. Although estimates of its prevalence vary widely, one study found that 60.75 percent of males and 51.2 percent of females reported experiencing a traumatic event (Kessler, 1995). However, only 25 percent of such people develop symptoms severe enough to be classified as PTSD. About half of these go untreated, despite the impact on overall levels of functioning (Strauser & Lustig, 2001). The *DSM-IV-TR* (American Psychiatric Association, 2000) states that community-based studies indicate a lifetime prevalence of PTSD at approximately 8 percent of the adult population. The highest rates of PTSD are found among victims of rape, military combat, internment, and genocide. However, workplace violence is a risk factor as well.

Symptoms of PTSD can affect understanding and memory, concentration, persistence, social interaction, and adaptation and can significantly reduce stress tolerance. Each of these factors can have a significant influence on workplace functioning and can result in difficulty in completing long-term tasks or weaken a person's ability to complete standard workweek activities, meet deadlines, and handle stressors. These clients may have trouble working closely or interacting socially with coworkers. Even mild impairments may affect the person's capacity to respond effectively to changes, to match skills and abilities to suitable worksettings, and to set appropriate goals independently.

Individual counseling begins by addressing the clients' evaluation of his or her self-image and how realistic it is. Early counseling also addresses congruence of the clients' person/ environment fit. Introducing standard self-exploration career assessment to ascertain interests, skills, and values and using more objective aptitude testing are interventions of choice. Counseling addresses the clients' understanding of the disorder and knowledge of available mental health and rehabilitation services. Because support is critical for PTSD clients, group counseling can be especially effective. Full-service career counseling groups that include job-search skills for those who are out of work can be effective. With those who are appropriately employed but experiencing difficulties at work, cognitive-behavioral techniques (e.g., systematic desensitization, thought stopping, rational emotive behavior therapy, guided imagery, and music) commonly used in addressing a range of other anxiety disorders, along with communications skills and assertiveness training, can be effective as can some alternative counseling techniques.

Substance-Related Disorders

Alcohol and other drugs (AOD) pose a serious health risk, including a risk to mental health. The impact of substance abuse and addictions on education, career development, and employment is well documented, as is the relationship between AOD and workplace stressors. A substance abuse problem is present if "a client's use of alcohol or another mood-altering drug has undesired effects on his or her life or on the lives of others," whereas addiction is a problem "only when physical symptoms of withdrawal or tolerance to the substance are present" (Lewis, Dana, & Blevins, 2002, p. 4). Those with AOD problems manifest in nearly every counseling setting, and counselors must be prepared to facilitate their treatment through their own interventions or by referral to qualified substance abuse counselors. The Center for Substance Abuse Treatment (2000) recommends that "an individual needing treatment will be identified and assessed and will receive treatment, either directly or through appropriate treatment no matter where he or she enters the realm of services" (p. 14).

Alcohol continues to be the most common problem in the general population and in counseling settings. According to the ADA, alcoholics are considered to be persons with a disability and thus, as is the case with people with SMD, are protected under the law if they are qualified to perform the essential functions of the job. In fact, an employer may be required to provide an accommodation to an alcoholic but can require that employees not be under the influence of alcohol. A person who is actively using alcohol is not automatically denied protection, but an employer can discipline, discharge, or deny employment to an alcoholic whose use of alcohol adversely affects job performance or conduct. Users of illegal drugs are not protected under the provisions of the ADA.

Those with AOD problems may present in counseling settings at any point along a continuum of abuse, and thus may need a variety of services along a prevention-intervention continuum as well. General categories of AOD usage are "nonuse; moderate, nonproblematic use; heavy, nonproblematic use; heavy use associated with moderate life problems; heavy use associated with serious life problems; and substance dependence/addiction associated with life and health problems" (Lewis et al., 2002, p. 7). Depending upon the category of use, counseling programs are targeted toward prevention or intervention of AOD, and many of these programs combine at least some elements of career or employment counseling. The point is that counseling services for this population are multidimensional, individualized, and targeted toward ameliorating life problems across many domains. Because substance abuse can permeate all aspects of life, addressing all relevant life domains is part of appropriate and necessary intervention.

Career and life planning for these clients includes setting and implementing career goals, usually after the client is committed to recovery or, in the case of early intervention, in conjunction with other activities. Job-search skills and other employment-related services are common in AOD treatment settings. Such interventions can assist the client in meeting immediate financial and survival needs and may be instituted early in counseling. At the same time, a more comprehensive career development and life-planning process may be undertaken for long-term goals. A common perspective says that people who are addicted to alcohol or other substances stopped growing developmentally at about the time when AOD became a problem. Thus, these clients must work through the developmental tasks that have not yet been accomplished. This perspective applies to the area of career knowledge and awareness as well. Many of these clients, regardless of age, lack vocational identity and are stuck somewhere between two of Super's (1980) developmental stages: the growth stage, with its need to develop a realistic self-concept, and the exploratory stage, wherein the individual learns about world-of-work opportunities. These clients may need assistance with the vocational developmental tasks associated with the crystallization stage (ages 14–18; Super, Starishevsky, Matlin, & Jordan, 1963). At this stage, clients set a general vocational goal through learning possible interests and values, learning about available resources, and beginning to plan for preferred occupations. Thus, it is not unusual, for example, to see a midlife recovering alcoholic with the same career identity issues and lack of world-of-work knowledge as a typical adolescent. Thus, the same career counseling strategies used with secondary school students can be effective with this population. Chapter 18 discusses AOD issues in greater detail.

People with co-occurring substance abuse and mental disorders make up a portion of client populations, especially in the public-supported system of mental health care. In any given year, at least 10 million people in the United States have a combination of mental and substance abuse disorders, and this number may, in fact, be significantly higher (Substance Abuse and Mental Health Services Administration, 2003). Although some of these dually diagnosed clients may have substance abuse disorders along with the less severe personality disorders, most are people with SMD, who need a plethora of services. Unfortunately, many settings are inadequately prepared to help people with both substance abuse and mental health disorders. This means that many of these clients do not get the full care they need, but rather receive treatment for only one of their disorders (Substance Abuse and Mental Health Services Administration, 2003). Moreover, they make up a disproportionate number of the homeless and those in the criminal justice system. Unfortunately, no single social service or care system is equipped to provide these individuals with the range of services they need. Career and life planning, when appropriate, is most often absent in any systematic meaningful way.

Job Loss and Mental Health

Job loss and unemployment are significant factors in the American labor force. Throughout the twentieth century, mental health consequences of unemployment were constant and unchanged (Liem & Liem, 1996). In 2001, job cuts topped 1 million (CNN America, 2001), and the fallout from the events of September 11, 2001, has resulted in significant disruptions to local and national economies and continues to have long-term employment consequences (U.S. Bureau of Labor Statistics, 2001). Many workers are unemployed or have been downsized into jobs well below their skill levels. They continue to search for employment at pre-job-loss levels.

Unemployment takes an emotional toll. Research shows that loss of employment is connected to a number of mental health concerns. Those who involuntarily lose their jobs can be psychologically harmed in various ways. Evidence suggests that "absence of work . . . [is] reflected in behaviors which suggest various problems in living, or, indeed, mental illness" (Herr, 1989, p. 5). In a study of the employment status of mental health clients of private practitioners, 64.7 percent of those treated by psychiatrists and 80.5 percent of those treated by psychologists were unemployed during treatment (Taube, Burns, & Kessler, 1984). Of course, many of these mental health clients are people with severe and chronic mental disorders. However, a significant number suffer from emotional trauma because of recent job loss. In fact, admissions to psychiatric hospitals can be associated with unemployment and economic decline (Brenner, 1973; Hanisch, 1999), and high levels of unemployment have also been associated with increased rates of chemical dependency (Herr & Cramer, 1992).

Feelings of isolation, rejection, and shame are common in clients experiencing job loss. Among the most frequent presenting concerns are stress reactions, depression, and anxiety (Guindon & Smith, 2002). Each of these disorders is discussed elsewhere. Crites (1981) noted that when counseling the unemployed, traditional assumptions that career counseling takes place only after mental health counseling is established must be discarded. He viewed the relationship between career and mental health counseling as dynamic and interactive. He went further to suggest that career counseling often goes beyond personal counseling and is more effective and more difficult than psychotherapy; moreover, the need for career counseling is greater than the need for psychotherapy.

Borgen and Amundson (1987) compared the loss of employment to an emotional roller coaster. They applied the stages of grieving delineated in the Kubler-Ross (1969) model of grief and loss to this population and described feelings of denial, anger, bargaining, depression, and frustration following job loss. In the job-loss process, the client may experience all or some of the stages of grieving. Mental health and private practice counselors help their clients work through these emotional stages so that they successfully reach the acceptance stage, at which point the client is ready to undertake an effective job search and career-life planning can begin.

Unlike employed individuals, who tend to engage in group activities as part of their workday, those who are unemployed experience minimal engagement. Employment offers opportunities for external social and internal work group activities. The unemployed tend to have less contact with coworkers and engage in social activities less often or not at all, contributing to the experience of latent deprivation (Waters & Moore, 2002). Because self-esteem may plummet during job loss, self-esteem interventions should be instituted.

Gender is an important consideration; males and females react to job loss in different ways. For example, Malen and Stroh (1998) found that male and female managers who are unemployed had different styles for managing their loss of employment. Men were found to use networking more and to rely more extensively on support systems than did women. Hence, women may need additional assistance in identifying support systems to help them with tasks associated with an employment search.

Occupational Stress

In 1987, a Gallup survey partially sponsored by the National Career Development Association (NCDA) found that over 30 percent of those surveyed ($N = 1006$) reported that job stress interfered with their ability to do their jobs and with their personal relationships as well as affected their physical health (Smith, 1989). Stress can be a threat to mental health in the workplace. Feelings of hopelessness and powerlessness, racial anger, disparity in earnings, and rapid change also can be stressors (Parmer & Rush, 2003). The turbulence of the work world and possibility of violence in and out of the workplace contribute further to stress.

Although stress itself is neither good nor bad, there are optimal levels of stress. The nature, intensity, and duration of stress can vary, as can the resources with which the individual responds (Selye, 1956). Stress occurs when there is an imbalance between perceived external demands and the individual's perceived capability to adequately respond to these demands. The individual may be unable to muster the internal and personal resources necessary to counteract stress effectively.

Stressors such as role overload, role ambiguity, interpersonal conflict, underemployment, and job loss are major causes of psychological and physiological strain. Caplan, Cobb, French, Harrison, and Pinneau (1975) defined strain as resulting "from discrepancies between either environmental demands and an individual's abilities to meet them or between an individual's needs and environmental supplies to meet those needs" (p. 47). Strain manifests itself in an array of symptoms. Included are such common conditions as headaches, sleep disorders, anxiety and depression, lowering of self-esteem, substance abuse, and family disruption and abuse (Guindon & Smith, 2002). Physiological problems, such as many cardiovascular and digestive disorders, are commonly attributed to stress reactions. Accidents, interpersonal conflicts, marital and family discord, apathy, and dissatisfaction are often attributable to strain. Many of these symptoms may also be indicative of depression and anxiety. Thus, many of the disorders discussed in this chapter are interrelated and appear together, either during the intake and treatment-planning stages or during later stages of treatment.

Mental health practitioners and career counselors alike can play a major role in helping their clients manage stress in the workplace. Initially, they can assist their clients in recognizing symptoms of stress. Perhaps this is one of the most important roles counselors can assume. Stress is so closely related to other mental health disorders that managing stress may serve as preventive intervention. Stress management techniques can be incorporated into career- and life-planning programs for the disorders discussed in this chapter. Table 11.2 delineates common reactions to stress (see also Guindon & Smith, 2002).

INTAKE, ASSESSMENT, TREATMENT PLANNING, AND INTERVENTION

Intake and Assessment

Whether they work in career or mental health settings, counselors use assessment methods in making sound decisions so that their interventions fit the needs of their clients (Ridley, Li, & Hill, 1998). By using both objective and subjective methods of appraisal, counselors in either setting are better able to develop plans that aid their clients in identifying problems and discovering effective problem-solving strategies.

TABLE 11.2   Some Common Reactions to Stress

DOMAIN	SYMPTOM
Behavioral	Increased use of alcohol, prescriptions, or illegal drugs
	Difficulty sitting still
	Frequent frowning
	Tight or hunched shoulders
	Nail biting
	Teeth grinding
	Increased speech and/or rate of speech
	Short temper and/or mood swings
	Impulsive or pressured actions
	Lashing out verbally or physically
	Withdrawal from normal activities
	Family disruption
	Prone to accidents
Physical	Upset stomach
	Diarrhea
	Frequent need to urinate
	Hives
	Headache or neck pain
	Chest pain
	Cardiovascular concerns
Cognitive	Forgetfulness
	Mental block
	Nightmares
	Inward preoccupation/ruminating
	Difficulty organizing thoughts
	Apathy
Emotional	Feelings of hopelessness
	Feelings of helplessness
	Decreased interest in sex
	Feelings of being "overwhelmed"
	Impatience
	Urge to lash out at others
	Resentment toward others or "fate"
	Anxiety about the future
	Anxiety about being disapproved of by others

Regardless of whether the presenting concern is mental health or career related, "assessment can stimulate discussion about the direction and goals of counseling. It can also stimulate independent thinking and reflection on the part of the client about what he or she wishes to achieve during the counseling experience" (Guindon, 2002a, p. 335). Hohenshil (1995) pointed out that counselors cannot establish the best treatment interventions unless they diagnose effectively. This is especially true when career- and life-planning concerns are not evident at the outset of counseling. Use of assessment instruments allows the counselor to gain information, not only on the client's presenting concern, but also on the contributing factors associated with the problem (Cormier & Cormier, 1998). It can diagnose those factors that may hinder developmental growth and evaluate individual strengths and weaknesses. Assessing interpersonal and academic skill deficiencies can aid in identifying the need for treatment, remedial training, or skills development (Zunker & Norris, 1998).

An intake interview is a routine procedure in mental health and private practice settings. Standard procedures such as administering a mental status exam are undertaken to ascertain the presenting concern, the major issues, and appropriate treatment planning. Medical, personal, and family history information is gathered. The counselor takes note of appearance, speech, behavior, emotions, concentration and attention, orientation to reality, thought processes and content, memory and intelligence, perception, and insight and judgment. Whether or not the presenting concern is work related, the intake procedure should include some assessment of the client's capacity to work (Lowman, 1993). Life-span issues are included to help the counselor better understand the client's personal and vocational identity. When a career issue is indicated, the counselor should assess vocational and career maturity and consider the inclusion of appropriate career assessments instruments as needed.

Lowman (1993) stated that the initial task of the counselor is to "(a) assess the type of work problems, if any, presented by the client and (b) determine the relation of such problems to other aspects of personality and psychopathology for purposes of (c) formulating a diagnosis and (d) developing an initial intervention strategy" (p. 40). For further information on intake and diagnosis, several guides are available. Spokane (1991) offers a thorough diagnostic taxonomy of adult career concerns that can be incorporated into the intake assessment stage in either career or mental health settings. Campbell and Cellini (1981) offer another useful taxonomy of problem categories and subcategories of work dysfunctions.

Treatment Planning and Interventions

Treatment for mental health disorders can be classified as primary, secondary, or tertiary. *Primary treatment* means that through promoting healthy behaviors, many disorders may be prevented altogether, before problems reach a critical point and before they exact a psychological toll. Prevention as a psychological goal gained acceptance when the negative effects of mental disorders became clearer (Spokane, 1991). *Secondary treatment* means that existing disorders can be minimized by early identification and treatment. *Tertiary treatment* means providing interventions for fully developed disorders so that their effects and symptoms can be managed.

Albee (1982) suggested a competency model of mental disturbance instead of a mental illness model. The field of career counseling and life planning offers such a competency model. Table 11.3 delineates the threats to mental health described in this chapter and relates them to possible appropriateness or suitability of career interventions in mental health and private practice settings.

TABLE 11.3   Typical Presenting Concerns of Clients in Mental Health and /or Private Practice Settings and Suitability of Career and Life Planning

PRESENTING CONCERN	LEVEL OF CAREER TREATMENT/INTERVENTION		
	Primary	*Secondary*	*Tertiary*
Mental Illness Concerns of People with Severe Mental Disorders		X	X
Personality Disorders		X	X
Depressive Disorders	X	X	X
Anxiety Disorders	X	X	X
Substance-Related Disorders		X	X
Job-Loss Issues	X	X	
Occupational Stress Reactions	X	X	

Primary: Career and lifestyle planning may prevent threats to mental health.
Secondary: Career and lifestyle planning may moderate effects of existing mental health disorders and/or minimize severity of disorder through early identification and treatment of work-life issues.
Tertiary: Career and lifestyle planning may be possible and/or suitable in concert with mental health counseling for people with a fully developed disorder.

Assisting individuals to gain career competence through implementing authentic career-related goals is a mental health modality—a primary treatment intervention. For example, people who have lost their job may experience feelings of sadness and despair. Many feel at least temporarily without hope. It is not unusual, and may even be expected, that many will experience symptoms of loss and grieving. Providing the many interventions and techniques associated with career and life planning and assisting clients in performing activities necessary to conduct a thorough job search may prevent some forms of depression and anxiety from reaching psychopathological levels. Thus, to provide interventions that lead to employment and career satisfaction is to address significant and important mental health areas. When depression, anxiety, or other mental health issues exist, career counseling can ameliorate the severity of these threats through early identification and treatment of work-life issues.

For people with personality disorders, career counseling may be an appropriate secondary treatment objective. Since personality disorders are longstanding and enduring patterns of thoughts, behaviors, and emotional responses, they are less likely to be amenable to primary intervention. However, career- and life-planning techniques can assist these individuals so that the severity of their disorder may be minimized. For example, these clients can learn more effective ways of interacting in the world of work or minimize the effects of their disorders through life-skills training. Tertiary treatment may also be appropriate for individuals diagnosed with severe personality disorders.

Those with schizophrenia, those with long-standing substance abuse disorders, and others who have severe mental disorders that keep them from functioning normally in society may benefit from career counseling at either a secondary or tertiary level. Vocational counseling can be a secondary treatment intervention when it assists clients to maximize their potential through suitable work and may moderate the effects of some disorders through early identification. Mentioned earlier was the importance of sheltered workshops for those who cannot work in more traditional settings. For these individuals, experiential programs that provide opportunities for practicing appropriate workplace behaviors offer a tertiary treatment intervention.

Importance of diversity issues.   Counselors should understand clients and their needs in context. Career- and life-planning interventions in private practice or community mental health settings attend to issues of diversity. The National Career Development Association's (NCDA) (1988) minimum career competencies address the need for knowledge and skills about diverse populations that impact on career counseling and include the demonstrated ability to identify the developmental needs unique to populations with regard to gender, sexual orientation, ethnic group and race, and physical and mental capacity. Thus, counselors must take these differences into account in each of these areas of mental health concern. For example, gender differences in symptoms of stress have been widely reported. Women report higher levels of depression, psychological distress, and anxiety than do men (Nelson & Hitt, 1992), as do gay, lesbian, and bisexual individuals. Certainly, the deleterious effects of racism on mental health are well documented (Spokane, 1991). Consequently, multicultural and contextual factors, although beyond the scope of this chapter, must be incorporated into any treatment plan. Refer to Chapters 15, 16, and 17 for additional information.

Career and Life Planning for Those with Mental Health Concerns

Career- and life-planning programs in mental health and private practice settings have much in common with standard programs offered by career counselors in more traditional settings. With clients who do not possess cognitive clarity, counselors should postpone addressing career concerns until cognitive clarity is attained (Brown & Brooks, 1991). The exceptions are those whose best career-related option is work in sheltered workshops. Individuals with SMD or those recovering from AOD addictions are provided opportunities to work despite this lack of cognitive clarity. For others whose disorders do not require a supported work environment and for whom career and workplace concerns are a legitimate area of treatment, career counseling is very much as it is for clients without mental health problems. Mental health, of course, is always the treatment goal, and career counseling is the vehicle toward that goal. Individual career and mental health assessments are administered, interpreted, and integrated into overall diagnosis and treatment planning.

Hands-on experiential programs provide many mental health clients opportunities to assess and reevaluate their current belief systems and self-concepts, to challenge outdated and dysfunctional values, and to reduce those beliefs and values that prevent progress toward a more fulfilling career and personal life. Some programs focus on challenges to mental health and provide clients with opportunities for emotional healing and growth. Clients can thus reevaluate their self-defeating behaviors and perceptions to gain an understanding of themselves as successful workers. They learn that, although their mental health problems are real, some barriers to success are self-imposed. They begin to clearly define and work toward achieving realistic long- and short-term goals and learn the decision-making process. Personal step-by-step action plans prepare clients to move toward their own pragmatic, self-defined goals.

Group work is useful for those who are ready to undertake career and life planning as part of their mental health treatment goals. After being screened for suitability, members of these preestablished, closed groups serve as a support for each other as they make lifestyle changes and reinforce continued growth under the direction of a properly trained counselor. In the process, external and internal barriers to employment are identified. Where external goals are present, participants can be assisted with workplace modifications as mandated by the ADA. Most important, internal barriers are challenged. Examples of topics facilitated by the counselor include managing mental illness, developing and refining effective communication skills, understanding and using community resources, risk taking, goal setting, problem solving and decision making, learning about world-of-work information and resources, developing life skills, and, ultimately, practicing job-search skills. Life-skills training contributes to empowerment and self-sufficiency and may include stress management, time management, assertiveness training, AOD education, work-life balance strategies, budgeting and financial management, self-esteem enhancement, and coping with transitions. Job-skills training consists of employment-counseling activities and may include assistance with preparing resumés and job applications, interview preparation sessions, dress-for-success workshops, practical world-of-work speakers, and, when appropriate, field trips, informational interviewing, job shadowing, and referrals.

Job retention groups are effective for those who are currently employed or who begin employment during the course of their mental health treatment. Additional topics covered in these psychoeducational groups include employer expectations, work-related communications skills, sexual harassment and discrimination, customer service skills, conflict resolution skills, and many more.

Because the nature of mental illness may preclude some individuals from reaching the level of career achievement that others may achieve, it is important to bear in mind that the definition of career includes, not only work, but all other life roles as well. Niles and Harris-Bowlsbey (2002) stated, "When work is lacking in personal satisfaction, other life roles may be useful in offsetting this lack of meaning and satisfaction" (p. 6). Attending to the place and significance of other life roles can assist these clients in living fuller, more meaningful lives even when the worker role is limited.

COLLABORATION AND REFERRAL

Few counselors are skilled in offering services to all clients with all disorders. Consequently, counselors skilled in mental health issues as well as counselors skilled in career development issues must be willing to make appropriate referrals when their clients' concerns are beyond the scope of their own expertise and training. Our ethical codes demand it. Chapter 4 discusses ethical issues in detail.

Although it is true that career counselors need to broaden their conception of career counseling to consider their clients' mental health concerns and that they should become more aware of the relationship between mental health and employment conditions (Brown, 1990), it is essential that they receive adequate training and credentialing to provide some mental health services. The same applies to mental health counselors with regard to career issues. Unless the professional counselor is skilled in both areas, he or she must cultivate relationships with colleagues in all the related helping professions and work collaboratively to offer a full range of necessary services to the betterment of clients. Our clients deserve nothing less.

SUMMARY

Decisions about work affect the totality of one's life. The need is great for assisting individuals trying to manage effectively the influence of work in their lives (Niles & Harris-Bowlsbey, 2002). Career-counseling interventions in mental health and private practice settings are similar to those services provided by career counselors in more conventional settings and include activities such as clarifying values, determining interests, imparting world-of-work information and resources, and setting career goals and providing coaching about how to achieve them. Counselors in mental health practice who offer these services do so in concert with the mental health services they provide, and only when career-related needs arise as a focus of treatment.

In formulating career interventions, the counselor should keep in mind that vocational development is a normal developmental process. Those with mental health issues "have had significant physical, mental, or emotional barriers to normal development ... [and may] experience difficulty in choosing and implementing work that is satisfying and interesting to them" (Musgrove, 1992, p. 47). Consequently, counselors must strive to discover the factors that interfere with the normal process of career development. As mental health counseling progresses, clients can try new behaviors in the workplace, if they are employed, and risk fresh behaviors in the job search process, if they are not. Both types of clients can benefit from implementation of a new self-concept, redefinition of workplace roles, and personal change management.

Mental illness and career development are not mutually exclusive, and counselors in all settings must be aware that clients may need assistance in both parts of their lives, either through referral or through the interventions of a counselor trained and experienced in both domains. Professional counseling is one profession with many subspecialties. Mental health counseling and career counseling are complementary specialties that, when practiced together, offer many clients fuller opportunities for positive change and life satisfaction. The following Websites provide additional information relating to the chapter topics.

USEFUL WEBSITES

www. nmha.org

The National Mental Health Association (NMHA) is the country's oldest and largest nonprofit organization, addressing all aspects of mental health and mental illness through advocacy, education, research and service.

www. nami.org

The purpose of the National Alliance of the Mentally Ill (NAMI) is the eradication of mental illnesses and the improvement of the quality of life of all whose lives are affected by these diseases. It offers articles and links to related sites.

www.nimh.nih.gov

This is the Website of the National Institute of Mental Health (NIMH), the lead federal agency for research on mental and behavioral disorders.

www.mentalhealth.samhsa.gov

This is the Website of Substance Abuse and Mental Health Services Administration (SAMHSA). Part of the National Mental Health Information Center, it provides information about mental health.

www.adda.org

The Anxiety Disorders Association (ADDA) promotes the early diagnosis, treatment, and cure of anxiety disorders.

www.depression.org

The National Foundation for Depressive Illnesses (NAFDI) offers information and promotes diagnosis, treatment, and management of depressive disorders.

www.workhealth. org

The Job Stress Network Website offers public dissemination of information about, and related to, job strain and work stress.

www.workplaceblues.com

Work Place Blues provides information about physical and mental health in the workplace and offers articles, resources, and Web links to related sites.

www.mental health matters.com

This Website supplies information and resources to mental health consumers, professionals, and students and provides links to related sites.

REFERENCES

Albee, G. W. (1982). Preventive psychopathology and promoting human potential. *American Psychologist, 37,* 1043–1050.

American Psychiatric Association. (2000). *Diagnostic and statistical manual of mental disorders* (4th ed., text revision). Washington, DC: Author.

Axelrod, S. D. (1999). *Work and the evolving self: Theoretical and clinical considerations.* Hillsdale, NJ: Analytic Press.

Bednar, R. L., & Peterson, S. R. (1995). *Self-esteem: Paradoxes and innovations in clinical theory and practice* (2nd ed.). Washington, DC: American Psychological Association.

Bordin, E. S. (1986). The effectiveness of psychotherapy: An introduction. *American Journal of Orthopsychiatry, 56,* 500.

Borgen, W. E., & Amundson, N. E. (1987). The dynamics of unemployment. *The Journal of Counseling & Development, 66,* 180–184.

Brenner, M. H. (1973). *Mental illness and the economy.* Cambridge, MA: Harvard University Press.

Brown, D. (1990). Issues and trends in career development: Theory and practice. In D. Brown, L. Brooks, & Associates. *Career choice and development* (2nd ed., pp. 506–517). San Francisco: Jossey-Bass.

Brown, D., & Brooks, L. (1991). *Career counseling techniques.* Boston: Allyn & Bacon.

Bruch, M. A., Fallon, M., Heimberg, R. G. (2003). Social phobia and difficulties in occupational adjustment. *Journal of Counseling Psychology, 48,* 109–117.

Campbell, R. E., & Cellini, J. V. (1981). A diagnostic taxonomy of adult career problems. *Journal of Vocational Behavior, 19,* 178–180.

Caplan, R. D., Cobb, S., French, J. R. P., Jr. Harrison, R. V., & Pinneau, S. R., Jr. (1975). *Job demands and worker health: Main effects and occupational differences.* Washington, DC: U.S. Government Printing Office.

CNN America (2001). Announced job cuts fell in August but top 1M for year. Retrieved Sept. 5, 2001, from http://cnnfn.cnn.com/2001/09/05/economy/job_cuts

Center for Substance Abuse Treatment. (2000). *Changing the conversation: Improving substance abuse treatment: The national treatment plan initiative* (Vol. 1). Rockville, MD: U.S. Department of Health and Human Services.

Chartrand, J. M., & Rose, M. S. (1996). Career interventions for at-risk populations: Incorporating social cognitive influences. *The Career Development Quarterly, 44,* 341–362.

Cormier, S., & Cormier, B. (1998). *Interviewing strategies for helpers* (4th ed). Pacific Grove, CA: Brooks/Cole.

Crites, J. O. (1969). *Vocational psychology.* New York: McGraw-Hill.

Crites, J. O. (1981). *Career counseling: Models, methods, and materials.* New York: McGraw-Hill.

Fabian, E. (1999). Rethinking work: The example of consumers with serious mental health disorders. *Rehabilitation Counseling Bulletin, 42,* 302–317.

Ford, L. H. (1995). *Providing employment support for people with long-term mental illness: Choices, resources, and practical suggestions.* Baltimore, MD: Brookes.

Greenberg, P. E., Stiglin, L. E., Finkelstein, S. N. & Berndt, E. R. (1993). Depression: A neglected major illness. *Journal of Clinical Psychiatry, 54,* 419–424.

Guindon, M. H. (2002a). Assessment. In B. E. Erford (Ed.), *Transforming the school counseling profession* (pp. 331–356). Upper Saddle River, NJ: Prentice Hall.

Guindon, M. H. (2002b). Toward accountability in the use of the self-esteem construct. *Journal of Counseling and Development, 80,* 204–214.

Guindon, M. H., & Smith, B. (2002). Emotional barriers to successful reemployment: Implications for counselors. *Journal of Employment Counseling, 39,* 73–82.

Hagner, D., Cheney, D., & Malloy, J. (1999). Career-related outcomes of a model transition demonstration for young adults with emotional disturbance. *Rehabilitation Counseling Bulletin, 42,* 228–242.

Hanisch, K. A. (1999). Job loss and unemployment research from 1994–1998: A review and recommendations for research and intervention. *Journal of Vocational Behavior, 55,* 188–220.

Herr, E. L. (1989). Career development and mental health. *Journal of Career Development, 16,* 5–18.

Herr, E. L. (1992). Types of career counseling practices. In A. A. Hafer (Ed.), *The nuts and bolts of career counseling: How to set up and succeed in private practice* (pp. 23–32). Garrett Park, MD: Garrett Park Press.

Herr, E. L., & Cramer, S. H. (1992). *Career guidance and counseling through the lifespan: Systematic approaches.* New York: HarperCollins.

Hohenshil, T. (1995). Editorial: Role of assessment and diagnosis in counseling. *Journal of Counseling and Development, 75,* 64–67.

Holland, J. L. (1973). *Making vocational choices: A theory of careers.* Englewood Cliffs, NJ: Prentice-Hall.

Holland, J. L. (1994). *Self-Directed Search.*™ Odessa, FL: Psychological Assessment Resources.

Kessler, R. C. (1995). Posttraumatic stress disorder in the national comorbidity survey. *Archives of General Psychiatry, 52,* 1048–1060.

Kessler, R. D., McGonagle, K. A., Zhao, S., Nelson, C. B., Hughes, M., & Eshleman, S. (1994). Lifetime and 12-month prevalence of DSM-III-R psychiatric diagnosis in the United States. *Archives of General Psychiatry, 51,* 8–19.

Kjos, D. (1995). Linking career counseling to personality disorders. *Journal of Counseling and Development, 73,* 592–597.

Kubler-Ross, E. (1969). *On death and dying.* New York: Macmillan.

Kyle, M. T., & Persinger, S. (2000). Chronic mental illness and work: An integrated vocational life-planning model. In N. Peterson & R. C. Gonzalez (Eds.), *Career counseling models for diverse populations: Hands-on applications by practitioners* (pp. 197–204). Belmont, CA: Wadsworth/Brooks Cole.

Lamb, H. R., & Mackota, C. (1997). Vocational rehabilitation for patients with schizophrenia. In J. Lonsdale (Ed.), *The Hatherleigh guide to vocational and career counseling* (pp. 161–175). New York: Hatherleigh Press.

Lewis, J. (2001). Career and personal counseling: Comparing process and outcome. *Journal of Employment Counseling, 38,* 82–90.

Lewis, J. A., Dana, R. Q., & Blevins, G. A. (2002). *Substance abuse counseling* (3rd ed). Pacific Grove, CA: Brooks/Cole.

Liem, R., & Liem, J. H. (1996). Mental health and unemployment: The making and unmaking of psychological casualties. In M. B. Lykes, A. Banuazizi, R. Liem, & M. Morris (Eds.), *Myths about the powerless: Contesting social inequalities* (pp. 105–127). Philadelphia: Temple University Press.

Loughead, T. A., & Black, D. R. (1990). Selection criteria for a career development program for the mentally ill: Evaluation of the Self-Directed Search (SDS). *Journal of Counseling and Development, 68,* 324–326.

Lowman, R. L. (1993). *Counseling and psychotherapy of work dysfunctions.* Washington, DC: American Psychological Association.

Malen, E. A., & Stroh, L. K. (1998). The influence of gender on job loss coping behavior among unemployed managers. *Journal of Employment Counseling, 35,* 26–39.

McAuliffe, G. J. (1993). Career as imaginative quest. *American Counselor, 1,* 23–28, 36.

Millon, T., & Everly, G. S. (1985). *Personality and its disorders: A biosocial learning approach.* New York: John Wiley & Sons.

Musgrove, M. (1992). Psychological aspects of career counseling. In A. A. Hafer (Ed.), *The nuts and bolts of career counseling: How to set up and succeed in private practice* (pp. 45–52). Garrett Park, MD: Garrett Park Press.

National Career Development Association. (1988). *The professional practice of career counseling and consultation: A resource document.* Alexandria, VA: Author.

National Institute on Disability and Rehabilitation Research. (1992). *Strategies to secure and maintain employment for people with long-term mental illness.* Washington, DC: Author.

Nelson, D. L., & Hitt, M. A. (1992). Employed women and stress: Implications for enhancing women's mental health in the workplace. In J. C. Quick, L. R. Murphy, & J. J. Hurrell, Jr. (Eds.), *Stress and well-being at work* (pp. 164–177). Washington, DC: American Psychological Association.

Niles, S. G., Anderson, W. P., Jr., & Cover, S. (2000). Comparing intake concerns and goals with career counseling concerns. *Career Development Quarterly, 49,* 135–145.

Niles, S. G., & Harris-Bowlsbey, J. (2002). *Career development interventions in the 21st century.* Upper Saddle River, NJ: Merrill/Prentice Hall.

Osipow, S. H. (1983). *Theories of career development* (3rd ed.). Englewood Cliffs: NJ: Prentice-Hall.

Parmer, T., & Rush, L. C. (2003). The next decade in career counseling: Cocoon maintenance or metamorphosis? *Career Development Quarterly, 52,* 26–34.

Ridley, C., Li, L., & Hill, C. (1998). Multicultural assessment: Reexamination, reconceptualization, and practical applications. *Counseling Psychologist, 26,* 827–910.

Saunders, D. E., Peterson, G. W., Sampson, J. P., & Reardon, R. C. (2000). Relation of depression and dysfunctional career thinking to career indecision. *Journal of Vocational Behavior, 56,* 288–298.

Selye, H. (1956). *The stress of life.* New York: McGraw Hill.

Smith, R. L. (1989). Work and mental health: Stress as a major factor. In D. Brown & C. W. Minor (Eds.), *Working in America: A status report on planning and problems* (pp. 82–96). Alexandria, VA: National Career Development Association.

Sperry, L. (1995). *Handbook of diagnosis and treatment of the DSM-IV personality disorders.* New York: Brunner/Mazel.

Spokane, A. R. (1991). *Career intervention.* Englewood Cliffs, NJ: Prentice-Hall.

Stone, M. (1993). *Abnormalities of personality: Within and beyond the realm of treatment.* New York: Norton.

Strauser, D. R., & Lustig, D. C. (2001). The implications of posttraumatic stress disorder on vocational behavior and rehabilitation planning. *Journal of Rehabilitation, 67*(4), 26–30.

Substance Abuse and Mental Health Services Administration. (2003). *Strategies for developing treatment programs for people with co-occurring substance abuse and mental disorders* (SAMHSA Publication No. 3782). Rockville, MD: Author.

Super, D. E. (1980). A life-span, life-space approach to career development. *Journal of Vocational Behavior, 16,* 282–298.

Super, D. E, Starishevsky, R., Matlin, N., & Jordan, J. P. (1963). *Career development: Self-concept theory.* New York: College Entrance Examination Board.

Szymanski, E. M., & Hershenson, D. B. (1998). Career development of people with disabilities: An ecological model. In R. M. Parker & E. M. Szymanski (Eds.), *Rehabilitation counseling: Basics and beyond* (3rd ed., pp. 327–278). Austin, TX: Pro-Ed.

Szymanski, E. M., Hershenson, D. B., Enright, M. S., & Ettinger, J. (1996). In E. M. Szymanski & R. M. Parker (Eds.), *Work and disability: Issues and strategies in career development and job placement* (pp. 79–126). Austin, TX: Pro-Ed.

Taube, C. A., Burns, B. J., & Kessler, L. (1984). Patients of psychiatrists and psychologists in office-bound practices: 1980. *American Psychologist, 39,* 1435–1447.

Turner, S. M., Beidel, D. C., Dancu, C. V., & Keys, D. J. (1986). Psychopathology of social phobia and comparison to avoidant personality disorder. *Journal of Abnormal Psychology, 95,* 389–394.

U.S. Bureau of Labor Statistics. (2001). Employment situation summary. Retrieved October 3, 2001, from http://www.bls.gov/news.release/empsit.nr0.htm

Waters, L. E., & Moore, K. A. (2002). Reducing latent deprivation during unemployment: The role of meaningful leisure activity. *Journal of Occupational and Organizational Psychology, 75,* 15–32.

Zunker, V. G., & Norris, D. (1998). *Using assessment results for career development* (5th ed.). Pacific Grove, CA: Brooks/Cole.

CHAPTER 12

CAREER COUNSELING IN VOCATIONAL REHABILITATION SETTINGS

JERRY A. OLSHESKI
Ohio University

One of the core values of American society is that everyone has a right to work. For individuals with disabilities, however, this value has been more of a dream than a reality. Individuals with disabilities have substantially higher unemployment rates than people without disabilities. According to the President's Committee on the Employment of People with Disabilities (1992), 31 percent of people with disabilities were employed or actively seeking employment, while over 78 percent of Americans without disabilities work or actively seek work. The lack of participation of people with disabilities in the world of work is of major concern to society as the human and financial costs associated with disability continue to escalate. This concern was expressed in the congressional findings contained in the Workforce Investment Act of 1998. Congress concluded that people with disabilities, as a group, experience very high rates of unemployment, and that reasons for this chronic unemployment include discrimination, lack of accessible and available transportation, fear of losing health care benefits under Medicaid or Medicare, and a lack of education, training, and supports to secure, retain, or advance in employment (Andrew, 2000).

Vocational adjustment is a complex process that involves the interaction of the individual's physical, educational, academic, psychosocial, and cultural traits with the physical, social, and cultural dimensions of the work environment. The presence of a disability complicates the interactive relationship of these important work adjustment components (Szymanski & Parker, 2003). The disabling condition may result in functional limitations that hinder the person's ability to perform job tasks or restrict his or her exposure to specific types of work settings. There may also be a number of environmental barriers, including discrimination, that restrict or undermine the individual's career development and vocational functioning. The negative stereotype of the person with a disability in the employment community has been well documented (Bordieri, Drehmer, & Comninel,

1988; Hallock, Hendricks, & Brodbent, 1998; Nordstrom, Huffaker, & Williams, 1998). Some of the stereotypical beliefs regarding employers' attitudes towards hiring people with disabilities include anticipation of high accommodation costs, difficulty in supervising and communicating with the employee, problem behavior, poor attendance, low productivity, and problems with coworker acceptance (Blessing & Jamieson, 1999; Lee & Newman, 1995).

People with disabilities have unique career needs and face challenges in securing and maintaining employment. Interventions must not only address personal issues but also be sensitive to the contextual and environmental factors that impact the person's career development and opportunities for employment.

This chapter presents information that may be useful in providing career- and life-planning services to people with physical disabilities. The following information is included in this chapter: career development issues for people with disabilities; the use of functional capacity and job analysis information in vocational planning and job accommodation; the impact of the Americans with Disabilities Act on the employment of people with disabilities; and vocational rehabilitation services that may be useful in facilitating career development and employment of people with disabilities.

CAREER DEVELOPMENT AND DISABILITY

The Relevance of Career Theory to People with Disabilities

Because disability is often defined as the inability to work in American society, it is of little surprise that the career and vocational needs of people with disabilities have largely been ignored by career development researchers. Consequently, the relevancy of mainstream career development theory and research to the career development issues that are typically experienced by people with disabilities and other minority groups has been questioned (Gysbers, Heppner, & Johnston, 2003; Lent, Brown, & Hackett, 2000; Syzmanski, Enright, Hershenson, & Ettinger, 2003). Osipow (1976) noted that people with disabilities have largely been omitted from career research because most of the participants in this research involved middle-class, white males. The systematic, linear model of career development that emerged from this type of "class-biased" research was based on the assumptions of freedom of choice in career decisions, and little attention was given to the role that contextual and environmental factors play in hindering or restricting career development. Consequently, these theories were not relevant to people with disabilities, whose career and vocational experiences were more often characterized by discontinuous development, constricted choices, limited employment opportunities, chronic unemployment, and a variety of contextual and environmental barriers to career development (Szymanski et al., 2003). Conte (1983) and Curnow (1989) concluded that many theories are insensitive to the unique career-development issues faced by people with disabilities. They noted that people with disabilities often have experiences related to their career development that are not encountered by other people. Disability may limit the individual's early vocational development, restrict vocational exploration, and hinder the development of career decision-making skills and a positive self-concept. Szymanksi and Trueba (1994) cautioned that most theories incorporate the basic trait and factor philosophy of "matching people to jobs." This mechanical matching may result in a type of "castification" of minority groups, in which people are relegated to stereotyped occupations because of their membership in a particular group, for example, matching the functional limitations of people with disabilities to certain stereotypical occupations.

More Appropriate Models for Individuals with Disabilities

More recently, alternative models of career theory and research have emerged that recognize the unique career development experiences of women and other minority groups. These models are more ecologically sensitive and consider the effects of cultural or environmental factors on career development, as well as the impact of bias and discrimination (Arbona, 1996; Beveridge, Heller Craddock, Liesener, Stapleton, & Hershenson, 2002; Gysbers et al., 1998; Hershenson, 1996; Lent et al., 2000; Szymanski et al., 2003).

Hershenson's Theory.   Hershenson (1996) developed a model of work adjustment that is useful in understanding career-development issues of people with disabilities. He emphasized the developmental nature of work adjustment and identified the personal and environmental components of work adjustment that dynamically interact in the developmental process. The personal domains of work adjustment include the *work personality, work competencies,* and *appropriate work goals.* These domains develop sequentially within the person, and each domain is influenced by a specific formative environment. The first domain to develop is the work personality, which includes two components: the person's self-concept as a worker and his or her system of work motivation. The work personality develops during the preschool years, when the family is the primary environmental influence. The second domain involves the development of work competencies. Work competencies include work habits, physical and mental skills used in jobs, and interpersonal skills required in the work setting. Work competencies develop during the school years and are mainly influenced by both positive and negative experiences in meeting the demands of the school environment (Szymanski et al., 2003). The last domain to develop is appropriate work goals. This domain, which is developed as the person prepares to make the transition from school to work, is mostly influenced by the individual's peer or reference group.

In the sequential development of the work-adjustment domains, each domain is influenced by the others. The domains that emerge earlier in the developmental process influence the level of development achieved in the domains that emerge later. Thus, a negative self-concept (work-personality domain) may hinder success in school (work-competency domain). There is also a reciprocal relationship among the domains and subsequent domains may influence those that developed earlier. For example, success in school (work-competency domain) may result in the modification of a negative self-concept (work-personality domain) that developed in a dysfunctional family environment (Szymanski et al., 2003).

Work personality, work competencies, and appropriate work goals continue to develop over the individual's life span, as they establish a dynamic balance so that changes in one domain affect changes in the others (Hershenson, 1996). Individuals achieve a positive work adjustment by fulfilling the task performance requirements of the job (work competency); maintaining appropriate behavior at the workplace (work personality); and feeling a sense of satisfaction or gratification from one's work (appropriate work goals). Disability may limit the development of the work-adjustment domains and disrupt the balance among them. The effect of disability in the early years of development may restrict the development of the work personality as the result of exposure to a nonsupportive family environment. Likewise, the onset of disability in mid-career may impact the person's work competencies and necessitate a re-evaluation of work goals. Hershenson (1981) observed that disability typically affects the work-competency domain of work adjustment by imposing functional limitations that restrict the person's physical or mental abilities. The changes in work competencies may "spread" to the work personality (i.e., self-concept, motivation to work), and vocational goals may no longer be appropriate. The degree of spread to the other domains depends on the level of development of the domains and the degree to which the disability disrupts the compatibility between the person and his or her current or planned occupation.

Counselors may find Hershenson's model useful in guiding assessments and designing interventions to serve the career needs of the person with a disability. Problems with the development of the work personality may require an assessment of the individual's career maturity (Crites, 1978) or interventions that promote the development of appropriate work behaviors and skills. Specific vocational rehabilitation services, such as work-adjustment programs, vocational evaluation, and supported employment, may be useful interventions in addressing problems related to the development of the work personality. There may also be a need to provide interventions to enhance work competencies. Vocational- and academic-training programs, physical conditioning, and other services that strengthen the physical, cognitive, and psychological abilities of the individual to perform work may be appropriate. In addition to providing a framework to conceptualize the personal components of work adjustment, Hershenson's model allows for the analysis of potential environmental factors that may pose barriers to work adjustment and career development. Interventions may be designed to modify the various environments of the work-adjustment domains. Examples of these types of interventions include family counseling (family environment), special-education interventions (school environment), and modifications to the work setting (peer group/coworker environment). Hershenson's model of work adjustment is outlined in Table 12.1.

Ecological Model of Vocational Behavior.   Szymanski and Hershenson (1998; Szymanski et al., 2003) incorporated Hershenson's developmental model of work adjustment as well as the theories developed by Lent and Hackett (1994) and Fitzgerald and Betz (1994) in their *Ecological Model of Vocational Behavior*. This model is composed

TABLE 12.1 Hershenson's Model of Work Adjustment

PERSONAL DOMAIN	DOMAIN ELEMENTS	WORK ADJUSTMENT BEHAVIORS	PRIMARY ENVIRONMENT
Work Personality	Self-Concept Motivation Needs / Values	Work-Role Behaviors	Preschool Family
Work Competencies	Work Habits Physical / Mental Skills Interpersonal Skills	Task Performance	School Education
Appropriate Work Goals		Work Satisfaction	Peer Groups

of five *constructs* and six *processes*. Career development is organized around common theoretical constructs, which are organized into five interrelated groups: *individual, context, mediating, environment,* and *outcome*. The model also contains seven processes, which affect the interaction among the constructs: *development, decision making, socialization, allocation, congruence, chance,* and *labor market forces*. Particular attention is given to the influence of disability and other minority-group factors that influence the interactions of concepts and processes.

Individual constructs include the physical and psychological traits of the person. Factors like race, gender, values, interests, needs, and limitations are classified as individual constructs. The personal, not social, aspects of disability are also viewed as individual constructs. *Context* constructs include factors that are external to the person, such as socioeconomic status, family, educational opportunities, and also non-normative influences such as natural disasters, war, and relevant legislation. *Mediating* constructs describe individual, cultural, and social beliefs that impact the interaction of people with their environments. Individual mediating constructs include personal beliefs about abilities, self-efficacy, self-concept, adjustment to disability, and work personality. Cultural mediating constructs consist of beliefs that are influenced by the individual's larger cultural group. These cultural beliefs influence how the person perceives and acts on his or her environment. Examples of these beliefs include a person's worldview, racial and ethnic identity, religious orientation, and possible minority group status (e.g., deaf culture, disability rights advocacy). Social-mediating constructs describe the societal belief structures that influence the interaction of the person and environment. These beliefs include stereotypes, discrimination, marginalization of certain groups, and attitudes toward persons with disabilities.

Environmental constructs describe characteristics of the work environment. These characteristics include task requirements, organizational factors, interpersonal requirements, and issues concerning disability-related access and accommodation. *Outcome* constructs refer to the product of the interaction among the other construct groups and processes. These outcomes may include a positive work adjustment, as characterized by job satisfaction, tenure, productivity, and competitiveness, or negative outcomes, including chronic unemployment, underemployment, job dissatisfaction, and termination.

The processes of the ecological model of vocational behavior are used to describe factors that influence the interaction among the construct groups. These processes include *congruence* (the degree of fit between the person and environment); *development* (systematic changes in the person over time); *decision making* (the person's ability to process information and make career decisions); *socialization* (how people learn about work and life roles); *allocation* (how societal gatekeepers such as parents, teachers, and employers direct individuals toward or away from specific career directions); *chance* (unforeseen events or encounters); and *labor market forces* (health of the economy, technological changes, changing corporate structures).

According to the *ecological* model, career development is viewed as the interaction of the individual, mediating, contextual, environment, and outcome concepts with the processes of congruence, decision making, development, socialization, allocation, chance, and labor market forces (Szymanski et al., 2003). The ecological model is useful in conceptualizing the career-development process for people with disabilities. Assessment questions and interventions may be organized around the constructs or the processes of the model, which serves as a framework for analyzing individual, contextual, and environmental factors that influence career development. For example, it may be necessary to evaluate the work skills and functional capacities of the client with a disability and to provide additional vocational training or physical conditioning in order to enhance these individual traits. Evaluating an individual's skills and providing vocational training are illustrations of possible client assessments and interventions that are related to the *individual* construct.

Individuals with disabilities may also face a number of *contextual* and *environmental* issues that limit their career development, and the ecological model is useful in guiding both assessments and interventions that are designed to remove or minimize these types of barriers. From a contextual standpoint, it may be important to assess the influence of the family and socialization processes on the person's perceptions of career opportunities and use such interventions as exposure to role models or mentors and participation in supported employment experiences to overcome contextual barriers. Evaluating the need for job accommodations and implementing job modifications are examples of assessment and intervention methods related to the *environmental* construct. It may also be appropriate to evaluate the impact of such *mediating* factors as the discrimination and stereotyping that the person with a disability may experience in the career-development process and world of work.

The applicability of career-development theories to people with disabilities remains a concern. However, more recently developed approaches, such as the ones just discussed, provide models that are sensitive to the unique developmental, contextual, individual, and environmental experiences of individuals with disabilities. These ecologically oriented approaches provide a conceptual framework that is useful for evaluating the impact of disability on career development and for designing interventions aimed at removing individual and environmental barriers to the developmental process. Components of the ecological model of vocational behavior are outlined in Table 12.2.

TABLE 12.2 The Ecological Model of Vocational Behavior

CONSTRUCT	CONSTRUCT COMPONENT	PROCESS
Context	Socioeconomic Status Family Education Nonnormative Events	Development
Individual	Gender Race Physical/Mental Abilities Impairments	Decision Making Congruence
Mediating	*Individual* Work Personality Self-Efficacy Outcome Expectations Adjustment to Disability Career Maturity *Cultural* Beliefs/Values Acculturation Racial Identity *Societal* Discrimination Prejudice Stereotypes Castification	Socialization Allocation
Environment	Organizational Culture Task Requirements Reinforcement Systems Physical Structure	Labor Market Forces Chance
Outcome	Job Satisfaction Satisfactoriness Job Stress Occupational Attainment Productivity Competitiveness	

IMPLICATIONS OF THE AMERICANS WITH DISABILITIES ACT

Like other minority groups, people with disabilities face discrimination and limited participation in many aspects of social life, particularly the world of work. In the 1960s, civil rights legislation was passed to protect women, as well as racial and other ethnic minority groups. Although previous legislation, such as the Rehabilitation Act of 1973, afforded civil rights protection for people with disabilities, this protection was limited in the private sector to employers who had contracts with the federal government and public agencies that were recipients of federal funds. It was not until 1990 that civil rights protection was extended to essentially all of the private sector and state and local governments, regardless of their status as either federal contractors or fund recipients, when the Americans with Disabilities Act (ADA) was passed. Just as women and members of racial and ethnic minority groups advocated for laws to protect their civil rights, people with disabilities began to perceive themselves as members of a marginalized minority group in American society. As noted in the congressional data gathered to document the need for disability-related civil rights legislation, people with disabilities, as a group, occupy an inferior status in U.S. society and are severely disadvantaged socially, vocationally, economically, and educationally (Rubin & Roessler, 1995). The passage of the ADA was viewed as a major victory for the long-fought efforts of the disability rights movement and the advocacy organizations representing people with disabilities. Because of the discrimination that people with disabilities face in the workplace, it is important for career counselors to have a basic understanding of the ADA.

The Five Titles of the ADA

The ADA contains five separate titles that guarantee equal access to employment, public accommodations, transportation, state and local government resources, and communication services. The enforcement provisions of the ADA are the same as those used to enforce Title VII of the Civil Rights Act of 1964 (Montgomery, 1996). The Equal Employment Opportunity Commission (EEOC) is the agency that receives and investigates allegations of discrimination. Based on the findings of the investigation, EEOC may grant the individual who files a complaint a "right to sue" letter. If unlawful discrimination occurs, possible relief may include reinstatement to a job, accommodations, compensatory damages, payment of legal fees, and punitive damages.

The basic provisions contained in the five titles of the ADA are as follows:

1. *Title I* prohibits discrimination in *access to employment.* This section of the law applies to private sector employers, unions, employment agencies, and all government bodies with the exception of the federal government that employ 15 or more employees in 20 or more calendar weeks during a calendar year. Because *Title I* pertains to employment rights, it will be discussed in further detail in the next section.

2. *Title II* prohibits discrimination by any public entity in providing *public services,* including transportation, to individuals with disabilities. Public entities include agencies, special purpose districts, departments, and other instrumentalities of state and local government.

3. *Title III* prohibits discrimination on the basis of disability in places of *public accommodation.* This includes such places as restaurants, lodging facilities, places of exhibition or entertainment, places of public gathering, retail establishments, educational institutions, and places of commerce.

4. *Title IV* contains the *telecommunication provisions*, which require common carriers of wire or radio communications to provide accommodations for individuals with hearing and speech impairments, such as telephone-operator relay services.

5. *Title V* contains *miscellaneous provisions* of the act, such as prohibiting retaliation against an individual who takes action to exercise his or her rights under the ADA and the relationship of the ADA to other federal and state laws.

The five titles of the ADA provide a comprehensive safeguard for protecting the civil rights of individuals with the most severe disabilities. According to the ADA, an individual with a disability is defined as someone who has a physical or mental impairment that substantially limits one or more major life activities. Major life activities include walking, seeing, speaking, breathing, hearing, thinking, performing manual tasks, learning, caring for oneself, and working. Individuals may also be protected by the ADA if they have a record of some disability (e.g., recovered alcoholic), or if they are regarded as having a disability even though it is not functionally limiting in nature (e.g., facial disfigurement). Title I of the ADA, which prohibits discrimination in the workplace, is of particular importance in career-service programs that serve people with disabilities.

Title I: Prohibiting Discrimination in the Workplace

Title I of the ADA prohibits discrimination in all phases of the employment process, including job-application procedures, hiring, advancement, compensation, training, and other terms, conditions, and privileges of employment. The provisions contained in Title I also provide certain safeguards during the job application process. For example, it is now unlawful for an employer to ask questions about a person's disability or medical status on application forms or during the pre–job offer interview. These include questions about previous hospitalizations, workers' compensation claims, medications, and so on. These types of questions may only be asked after a conditional job offer has been made. Once the job has been offered to the individual, disability-related questions are permitted. An employer may condition a job offer on the satisfactory result of a post–job offer medical examination or medical inquiry if this information is required of all entering employees in the same job category. If it appears that the person may have difficulty performing the essential functions of the job, the employer may ask about the types of reasonable accommodations needed or the person may request accommodations. If an individual is denied a job because of a postoffer medical exam or medical inquiry, the reasons for not hiring must be job related and consistent with business necessity. The employer must also demonstrate that no reasonable accommodation that would enable the person to perform the essential job functions was available or that implementing such an accommodation would pose an undue hardship.

It is important for counselors who serve the career needs of people with disabilities to be familiar with the provisions of Title I of the ADA. Specifically, Title I prohibits discrimination against a qualified individual with a disability who can perform the essential functions of a job, with or without reasonable accommodations. A qualified individual with a disability is one who not only meets the ADA definition of disability, but also satisfies the requisite skill, experience, education, and other job-related requirements of the employment position that the individual holds or desires and can perform the essential functions of the position, with or without reasonable accommodations (Olsheski & Breslin, 1996).

Determining whether an individual with a disability is "qualified" under Title I of the ADA involves a series of steps. First, the presence of a disability that substantially limits one or more major life activities must be documented by collecting the appropriate medical or psychological information. Second, the traits of the individual must be evaluated to determine if he or she possesses the necessary skills, education, certifications, and other traits to perform the essential functions of the job. Next, an assessment is needed to determine if the person can perform the essential functions of the job, with or without a reasonable job accommodation. Included in this step is a comparison of the individual's functional capacities with the physical and environmental demands of the job. Information specifying the demands of the job is obtained through the use of job analysis data or the performance of an on-site job analysis (Weed, Taylor, & Blackwell, 1991). By synthesizing this information, the degree of compatibility between the person's capacities and job requirements may be determined. If discrepancies between the person's capacities and job demands are identified, an evaluation of potential reasonable accommodations that may be implemented to remove or reduce the discrepancies is conducted.

General guidelines included in the ADA regarding the job accommodation process include: analyze the job to determine its purpose and essential functions; evaluate the physical and mental capacities of the individual; consult with the individual who needs the accommodation in order to ascertain the precise job-related limitations and how those limitations could be overcome with certain accommodations; identify the potential accommodations and assess the effectiveness that each would have in giving the individual the opportunity to perform the essential functions of the job; consider the preference of the individual to be accommodated and select the accommodation that would be most appropriate for both the employee and employer (U.S. Equal Employment Opportunity Commission [EEOC], 1991). Blanck, Anderson, Wallach, and Tenney (1994) summarized the following guidelines for assessing reasonable accommodations: get the facts regarding essential job functions and the capacities of the employee with a disability; identify what specific disability-related limitations need to be accommodated; assess the need for expertise and objective review; assess costs and undue hardship; engage in a problem-solving dialogue; develop an accommodation plan; and evaluate the effectiveness of the accommodation.

Reasonable Accommodations

Reasonable accommodations are modifications or adjustments to the job or work environment that allow the person with a disability the opportunity to perform the job. The ADA mandates reasonable accommodations in all phases of the employment process, including job-application procedures. Reasonable accommodations in the application process may involve assistance to an individual who is unable to complete the application form because of manipulative or visual impairments. Examples of reasonable accommodations cited in the ADA include restructuring a job by reallocating or redistributing marginal job functions; altering when or how an essential function is performed; part-time work or modified work schedules; modifying equipment; using assistive technological devices; and reassignment to another job (EEOC, 1991).

Examples of Reasonable Job Accommodations

The following examples of actual job accommodations have been provided by the U.S. Department of Labor (USDOL, 2002):

> *Example 1.* An assembler for a furniture manufacturer has spinal degeneration, which results in an uncoordinated gait and problems with balance. This limits her abilities to walk, carry materials, and balance herself. This worker was accommodated by installing a plywood platform to raise part of the work station; tools were suspended from the ceiling to balance their weight; and a cart was provided to move materials and prevent the need for carrying materials. The cost of this accommodation was $200.

> *Example 2.* A well-drilling rig operator with a lower back condition is having difficulty performing his job because of the constant vibration of the standard seat in the rig. This worker was accommodated by removing the seat in the rig and installing an ergonomically designed mechanical seat that allowed him to adjust his position and avoid most of the vibration. The cost of this accommodation was $1,100.

> *Example 3.* An administrative assistant with amyotrophic lateral sclerosis (ALS) was having difficulty with using the phone, typing, computer input, completing forms and reports, and doing filing. Accommodations for this worker included providing a cordless headset for the telephone, using armrest extensions from the edge of the desk to reduce the strain on arms and wrists, and having a new, effortless lock and handle installed on the restroom door. The cost of the accommodation was $450.

> *Example 4.* An airline programmer with post-polio fatigue brought on by stress could not be on call 24 hours a day and work overtime as needed. This worker was accommodated by waiving the requirements of the 24-hour on-call duty and overtime work. This change in policy cost the company nothing to implement.

As illustrated in the previous examples, accommodations often do not involve considerable cost. Information from the Job Accommodation Network (JAN) indicated that in more than 100,000 cases of job accommodations, 20 percent of the accommodations cost nothing, 51 percent cost between $1 and $501, and only 25 percent cost more than $501 (Rubin & Roessler, 2001). Similarly, Sears, Roebuck and Company reported that for the period of 1978 to 1992, a total of 436 employees were provided with job accommodations, and that out of this number, 69 percent involved no costs, 28 percent cost less than $1,000, and only 3 percent cost more than $1,000 (Cameron & Sharp, 1998).

Undue Hardship/Direct Threat

Although Title I of the ADA mandates reasonable accommodations in the workplace for people with disabilities, the issue of what is "reasonable" may be unclear or subject to debate between the employee and the employer. Therefore, there are some criteria contained in the ADA that address situations in which the proposed accommodations are not reasonable. These provisions are expressed by the concepts of *undue hardship* and *direct threat.* In general, employers may defend their decision to not accommodate a particular worker by alleging that the accommodation would impose an undue hardship. The nature of the undue hardship could involve the cost of the proposed accommodation or the argument that the accommodation would be disruptive or fundamentally alter the nature or operation of the business.

The determination of whether a particular accommodation constitutes an undue hardship is done on a case-by-case basis. Cameron and Sharp (1998) outlined the following factors that should be considered in determining if an accommodation poses an undue hardship: the nature and cost of the accommodation; the overall financial resources of the employer, including the number of employees, type of business, number of locations, and other company resources; and the type of operation or operations of the employer, including the composition, structure, and functions of the workforce.

Another defense that employers may use to refuse an accommodation for a person with a disability is the concept of *direct threat.* A direct threat exists if it can be established that the presence of the individual in the work setting would cause a significant risk to his or her own safety and health or the safety and health of others and that this threat cannot be eliminated by reasonable accommodation. The factors that must be considered in determining whether an individual would pose a "direct threat" include the duration of the risk; the nature and severity of the potential harm; the likelihood that the potential harm will occur; and the imminence of the potential harm (EEOC, 1991).

USING FUNCTIONAL CAPACITY AND JOB ANALYSIS DATA IN CAREER PLANNING

Career planning for individuals with disabilities requires an assessment of how their particular illness or disease impacts the ability to function in an actual or desired work environment. This analysis involves a comparison of the person's functional capacities with job analysis data and is similar to the trait and factor approach that is central to many theories of career development. Therefore, an accurate assessment of the person's functional capacities and accurate job analysis information are essential in selecting appropriate vocational goals and identifying reasonable job accommodations. Without this type of information, the chances of achieving a positive work adjustment or implementing effective accommodations are greatly reduced. This section of the chapter discusses the use of functional-capacity and job-analysis information in the career-planning process for people with disabilities.

Functional Limitations

Functional limitations refer to the hinderance or negative effect in the performance of tasks or activities and other adverse or overt manifestations of a mental, emotional, or physical disability (Wright, 1980). A clear understanding of how the individual's disability impacts his or her functional capacities is essential to the career and vocational planning process. It is important to differentiate between the concepts of *disability* and *functional limitation*. Disability describes a physiological, anatomical, mental, or emotional impairment resulting from disease or illness. Functional limitation describes the impact that the disability has on the person's abilities to *perform* certain tasks in a life-adjustment context (Wright, 1980). For example, an individual with a below-the-knee amputation of the left leg (disability) may be limited to standing for no more than one hour at a time and be unable to ambulate on uneven surfaces or maintain balance on ladders (functional limitations). These limitations may preclude working in certain occupations unless the limitations can be removed or minimized via reasonable accommodations. Vocational and career planning, therefore, require an understanding of how the person's disability impacts his or her ability to perform specific job tasks and tolerate certain work conditions.

Although the functional limitations that arise from disabilities are many and varied, there have been some attempts to group the most common into general categories (Mueller, 1990; Wright, 1980). Brodwin, Parker, and DeLaGarza (2003) developed a list of functional limitation categories that expanded previous classification models and include the following 18 categories: difficulty in interpreting information; limitations of sight and total blindness; limitations of hearing and total deafness; susceptibility to fainting, dizziness, and seizures; incoordination; limitation of stamina; limitation of head movement; difficulty in reaching, lifting and carrying; difficulty in handling and fingering; inability to use the upper extremities; difficulty in sitting; difficulty in using the lower extremities; poor balance; cognitive limitation; emotional limitation; limitation due to disfigurement; substance abuse; and pain limitation. A brief overview of the more common categories is provided below.

Difficulty in interpreting information.   Individuals with this limitation have an impaired ability to read or understand written or verbal communication. This limitation may result from a variety of disabilities including stroke, learning disabilities, traumatic brain injury, mental retardation, and other neurological impairments. The individual may experience limitations in expressive and/or receptive communication abilities. Impairment in interpreting information impacts a large number of occupations, ranging from jobs that have information processing as essential job functions (secretary, computer programmer) to less skilled jobs that require the employee to follow written or verbal instructions (assembler, order filler). Counselors must evaluate the specific job functions that are affected and implement accommodations or the use of assistive technology to facilitate job performance. For example, if the employee's limitation is primarily related to expressive communication skills, an attempt could be made to rely more on written than verbal communication. Alternately, complicated communications may be reduced to more understandable units for an individual who is cognitively impaired.

Limitations of Sight and Blindness.   This limitation includes a variety of visual impairments, including total blindness. Visual impairments are related to such disabilities as glaucoma, periocular disease, macular degeneration, diabetic retinopathy, corneal diseases, optic nerve damage, central nervous system damage, and other conditions. As noted by Brodwin, Parker, and DeLaGarza (2003), the functional limitations of an individual with a visual impairment are related to the amount and type of the impairment, environmental conditions such as lighting and contrast, the individual's degree of motivation to function in a particular environment, and the individual's ability to use any remaining vision. From a vocational standpoint, it is important to evaluate the specific nature of the vision loss in conjunction with specific work tasks. Panek (2002) noted that the functional limitations caused by a visual disability are best described in a visual task–related manner. This approach focuses on the individual's ability to perform different types of visual tasks. Colenbrander (1977) developed a model for classifying the degree of functional limitations for visual disability. The model is based on the degree of ability to perform various visual tasks such as reading. A person with slight disability performs visual tasks without special aids (often with glasses alone). Moderate visual disability indicates that the person cannot perform fine tasks without special aids. Severe disability describes the person who needs visual aids to function even with difficulty. Profound visual disability indicates that the person cannot perform most detailed tasks like reading and has difficulty with gross visual tasks such as mobility. Total visual disability means the individual must rely on other senses and vision contributes nothing to functional ability.

Accommodations for employees with residual vision may include changes in illumination, color and contrast, size (enlarged print), and distance and space arrangements. Assistive technology in the form of low-vision devices such as magnifiers and telescopes is also commonly used. Computers may also be modified to include print magnification, speech output, and optical-scanning features. For individuals with total blindness, accommodations rely on tactile and auditory senses. These types of accommodation include the use of Braille printers and labels, speech output on computers, talking calculators, and the use of speech synthesizers, combined with both a Braille and a regular printer. Orientation and mobility specialists may be used to teach a person with blindness or low vision how to safely move about in the work environment. Services for the visually impaired are also available in the public rehabilitation program that exists in each state. These agencies provide a variety of vocational-rehabilitation and independent-living services for individuals who are legally blind.

Limitations of Hearing and Deafness.   People with hearing impairments have difficulty in comprehending usable speech, either with or without amplification. Deafness is defined as a hearing impairment that limits the ability to understand normal conversation. The level of functional limitation depends on the degree of impairment in auditory discrimination of speech frequencies and the age of onset (Harvey, 2002). Functional limitations associated with hearing problems are rated in severity by the degree of decibel (dB) loss associated with the impairment. These problems exist on a continuum of severity and range from conditions involving a slight hearing loss to a profound hearing loss or deafness (Moores, 2001). For example, a "moderate" hearing impairment involves a loss of between 26 and 40 dB. With a moderate loss, the person can hear conversation at a distance of 3 to 5 feet but understanding speech is difficult and the full-time use of a hearing aid is necessary. A "severe" hearing impairment involves a loss of 71 to 90 dB, and the person can hear only very loud speech, about 1 foot from the ear. Hearing aids may of limited use for a person with a severe loss, and lipreading and sign language may also be necessary. Workplace accommodations include the use of interpreters, amplified telephones, flashing lights and alarms, communication aids, and telecommunication devices for the deaf (TDD). Environmental restrictions related to hearing impairments may include avoiding loud noise work settings or exposure to hazards such as moving machinery.

Limitations in Lifting, Reaching, and Carrying.   These types of limitations may be related to a variety of disabling conditions that result in decreased range of motion and strength in the upper extremities and back, including spinal cord injuries, musculoskeletal injuries, multiple sclerosis, arthritis, neurological diseases, and other permanent injuries. Limitations may involve the magnitude, frequency, and duration of a person's ability to lift, carry, push and pull, and reach. In severe cases, paralysis of one or both of the upper extremities requires substantial modification to work tasks that require handling, reaching, lifting, and carrying. Ergonomic evaluation of the work station may be needed to identify job accommodations for limitations involving the upper extremities (Olsheski & Breslin, 1996). The use of work-site physical and occupational therapy may also be useful in transitioning individual's who have these types of functional limitations back to work (Breslin & Olsheski, 1996).

Difficulty in Using the Lower Extremities.   Functional limitations associated with impairments of the lower extremities include slowness of gait, and impairment of the ability to walk, stand, kneel, and climb stairs or ladders. These limitations may be related to spinal cord injuries, degenerative joint diseases, arthritis, congenital deformities, amputation, cardiovascular or pulmonary diseases, and stroke, peripheral neuropathy, and other neurological impairments. Functional limitations include impaired ability to ambulate, stoop, bend, lift, balance, kneel, climb, carry, and stand (Andrew, 2000). Workplace accommodations may involve the use of wheelchairs or other motorized vehicles for mobility, minimization of job tasks that require prolonged periods of standing, and use of foot controls (Brodwin et al., 2003).

Limitations Related to Fainting, Dizziness, and Seizures.   These limitations involve conditions in which the person experiences periods of unconsciousness from fainting or seizures and a loss of balance because of dizziness. People with these types of limitations may have such diseases as epilepsy, cerebral palsy, brain injury, vertigo, migraine headaches, hypertension, or other various neurological or cardiac impairments (Brodwin et al., 2003). These types of impairments may restrict the individual from being exposed to certain environmental risk factors (e.g., unprotected heights, hazardous machinery, extreme temperatures). For individuals with epileptic seizures, the severity and frequency of the seizure, the effectiveness of antiseizure medication, and the time needed to recover after having a seizure will influence the degree of environmental restriction and need for accommodation. Individuals having problems with dizziness may need such accommodations as using supportive grab bars, and avoiding exposure to unprotected heights, slippery surfaces, and hazardous machinery (Mueller, 1990).

Functional Capacity Evaluation

In order to make appropriate educational and vocational decisions, people with disabilities must have an accurate understanding of their functional assets and limitations. This information is essential in all phases of the career-planning process, including the development of vocational goals, selecting appropriate training or educational programs, and identifying the need for potential accommodations. Functional capacity evaluations may be conducted by physical and occupational therapists who also have expertise in job analysis methods. This information quantifies the person's functional capacities by measuring standing tolerance, sitting tolerance, lifting capacity, ability to assume various postures, pushing and pulling capacity, fine and gross manipulation abilities, reaching, range of motion, strength, endurance, and abilities to tolerate exposure to various work environment conditions (Lynch & Lynch, 1998). By comparing information about the person's functional capacities with job analysis data, the degree of compatibility between the worker's capacities and the requirements of the job can be determined. Reasonable accommodations may be used to remove or reduce specific areas of incompatibility between the worker's capacities and the job requirements.

Job Analysis Information

Job analysis is the gathering, evaluating, and recording of accurate, objective, and complete job data (University of Wisconsin–Stout, 1992). Job analysis describes in a systematic manner: *what* the worker does; *how* the work is done; *results* of the work; *worker characteristics*; and the *context* of the work in terms of environmental and organizational factors (USDOL, 1982). Job-analysis data includes the essential job tasks performed by the worker and the tools, equipment, or work aids that are used on the job. In addition, job analysis data describes the general educational development, training, aptitudes, interests, and skills that are required to perform a job. Job-analysis data is used to classify the physical demands of the occupation and assign it to a strength category; specify the frequency and duration of various physical traits such as handling, reaching, bending, climbing, and so forth; and describe various factors in the work environment, such as exposure to hazardous machinery, dust, fumes, or temperature extremes.

Occupations may be classified in various strength categories based on the amount of standing, sitting, walking, lifting and carrying, and pushing and pulling. These factors are used to define the five "physical demand" categories, as defined in the *Dictionary of Occupational Titles* (USDOL, 1991). These categories include: *sedentary work; light work; medium work; heavy work;* and *very heavy work.* Sedentary work requires the worker to lift up to 10 pounds occasionally and to work primarily in a seated position. Light work requires the worker to lift up to 20 pounds occasionally and items weighing 10 pounds or less on a frequent basis. Medium work requires the worker to lift up to 50 pounds occasionally and up to 25 pounds frequently. Heavy work requires the worker to lift up to 100 pounds occasionally and up to 50 pounds frequently. Very heavy work requires the worker to occasionally lift 100 pounds or more and to lift up to 50 pounds or more on a frequent basis. Most of the occupations that exceed the sedentary classification typically require standing or walking for approximately 6 out of 8 hours.

Having a physical disability not only impacts the individual's physical capacities for meeting the physical demands or strength factors required to perform a specific occupation, but also impacts the type of *work environment* in which the individual is able to function. Job-analysis data is useful for evaluating environmental factors that workers may be exposed to in the course of performing job duties. These factors may hinder successful job performance and pose a threat to safety. For example, a person who experiences epileptic seizures may not be able to tolerate extremely hot temperatures in the workplace if the seizures are precipitated by exposure to high amounts of heat. Similarly, individuals with pulmonary impairments may be restricted to work environments that are free of dust and fumes. Environmental conditions are defined as specific *physical working conditions* to which the worker is exposed while performing assigned work tasks (Materials Development Center, 1992). Environmental conditions include: exposure to weather; extreme cold; extreme heat; wet and/or humid conditions; noise (noise intensity is rated on the Occupational Safety and Health Administration decibel continuum ranging from quieter exposures [10 dB] to very loud exposures [115 dB and above]); vibration; atomspheric conditions; moving mechanical parts; electric shock; high, exposed places; radiant energy; explosives; toxic or caustic chemicals; and dust, fumes, gases, and odors.

Although the most accurate job-analysis data is obtained from performing an on-site analysis of the job, there are a number of generic sources of job analysis information that are also useful in career planning. There are a number of U.S. Department of Labor publications that contain valuable job analysis information including *The Dictionary of Occupational Titles* (USDOL, 1991), *A Guide to Job Analysis* (USDOL, 1982), and the recently developed Internet tool known as the *Occupational Information Network or O*Net* (Peterson et al., 1997). The O*Net is designed to replace the *Dictionary of Occupational Titles* (DOT), which was last updated in 1991. The DOT contained descriptions of over 12,000 discrete occupational titles. However, O*Net groups a number of similar occupations into 1,172 occupational units. The O*Net database is relational in nature and is more useful in evaluating transferable work skills. The O*Net model merges information from the DOT and other Department of Labor publications such as the *Guide for Occupational Exploration* (USDOL, 1979) and the *Occupational Outlook Handbook* (USDOL, 2003). Information contained in the O*Net model includes: experience requirements (training, experience, licensing); worker requirements (basic skills, cross-functional skills, general knowledge, education); worker characteristics (abilities, interests, work styles); occupational characteristics (labor market information, occupational outlook, wages); occupational requirements (generalized work activities, organizational context, work conditions); and occupation-specific requirements (occupational knowledge, occupational skills, tasks, duties, machines, tools and equipment). The O*Net offers easy access to job-analysis data and vocational information that is useful in career planning, assessing transferable skills, and identifying reasonable accommodations (Olsheski & Schelat, 2003).

Vocational and career planning for individuals with physical disabilities requires an accurate assessment of their functional capacities and an integration of this information with job analysis information (i.e., the physical demands, job requirements, and work conditions). By synthesizing these two important sets of data, appropriate vocational choices and career paths may be selected that enhance the likelihood of a successful work adjustment. In addition, this information is critical in identifying reasonable accommodations that may be implemented to minimize or eliminate any discrepancies between the worker's abilities and the requirement of the job.

VOCATIONAL REHABILITATION SERVICES

Vocational rehabilitation services are defined as continuous and coordinated services that are designed to enable a person with a disability secure and retain suitable employment (Wright, 1980). In the United States, vocational rehabilitation services have developed over time as new models of service delivery have emerged and federal legislation has broadened the scope of services as well as the types of disabling conditions served (Jenkins, Patterson, & Szymanski, 1998). Originally, vocational rehabilitation services were limited to veterans. The passage of the Soldier Rehabilitation Act of 1918 authorized vocational training and placement for World War I veterans with disabilities. Rehabilitation services for civilians began in 1920 with the passage of the Smith-Fess Act. Permanent funding for vocational rehabilitation services was not established until the passage of the Social Security Act in 1935. Other key legislative acts included the Barden-LaFollette Act of 1943, which made services available to people with mental illness, mental retardation, and blindness.

In 1956, the Social Security Administration (SSA) initiated cash disability payments for workers over age 50 who were considered permanently and totally disabled. Today, the SSA provides medical and financial disability benefits for totally disabled workers, regardless of their age, through two major disability benefits programs: Social Security Disability Insurance Title II (SSDI) and Supplemental Security Income Title XVI (SSI). The SSDI program provides medical and cash benefits to disabled workers who are insured as a result of their contributions, made through Federal Insurance Contribution Act (FICA) payroll deductions, to the Social Security trust fund. The SSI program provides medical and cash benefits to disabled individuals who have not earned insured status but are unable to engage in substantial gainful activity. Unlike the SSDI program, the person with a disability must also meet financial need criteria to be eligible for SSI benefits. There may also be individuals who are simultaneously eligible for both SSDI and SSI benefits. Vocational rehabilitation services for SSDI and SSI recipients are available through both public and private rehabilitation programs. The passage of the Ticket to Work and Work Incentives Improvement Act in 1999 expanded vocational rehabilitation services for beneficiaries and provided safeguards for continued health-care coverage and income during employment attempts (Radtke, 2000).

The passage of a number of rehabilitation and disability-related legislative acts has shaped the structure and function of today's comprehensive public (state/federal partnership) vocational rehabilitation program. This system is implemented through state rehabilitation agencies and is referred to as the "state-federal" program. Federal funding is provided to state vocational rehabilitation agencies in the form of grants under the authority of the Rehabilitation Act of 1973 (Brabham, Mandeville, & Koch, 1998). A federal-state matching formula is used in the funding process, with the federal contribution amounting to nearly 80 percent. The program is administered by the U.S. Department of Education's Rehabilitation Services Administration, a federal agency that monitors state program operations, oversees requirements for program implementation, and interprets legislation.

Counselors who provide career services to people with disabilities should become familiar with their local public vocational rehabilitation agency and the many services that are available. In order to be eligible for public vocational rehabilitation services, it must be demonstrated that the individual has a physical or mental impairment that constitutes or results in substantial impediments to employment. Furthermore, it must be determined that the individual is able to benefit in terms of employment outcomes as a result of vocational rehabilitation services, and that vocational rehabilitation services are necessary to prepare for, secure, or retain employment (Andrew, 2000). Vocational rehabilitation services may include funding for academic or vocational training programs, physical restoration services, vocational counseling, vocational assessment, rehabilitation engineering, job-search and placement assistance, and other interventions that help the individual achieve his or her vocational objectives.

Besides public-sector vocational rehabilitation programs, a number of privately based programs have also emerged. Vocational rehabilitation services are often provided by private insurance carriers who underwrite compensable occupational disability policies such as workers' compensation and short- and long-term disability (Rasch, 1985). Additionally, a number of employers have developed their own disability-management programs and use vocational-rehabilitation services to prevent or minimize lost work time and control disability-related costs (Olsheski, 1996). Some larger companies employ rehabilitation specialists as part of their internal human resource staff, while others contract services with external providers (Rosenthal & Olsheski, 1999).

The primary objective of private-based vocational-rehabilitation services is to return the individual to suitable employment in an expeditious manner. Therefore, private-based vocational-rehabilitation services tend to be more time-limited than public-sector interventions and place more emphasis on physical conditioning, disability case management, job placement, job accommodation, and the development of early return-to-work programs (Lynch & Lynch, 1998).

A number of specialized vocational rehabilitation services have emerged in both the public and private sectors. These services are designed to meet the unique career and vocational development needs of people with disabilities. Some of the major types of vocational rehabilitation services are discussed in the next section.

Vocational Rehabilitation Services

Work-Adjustment Training. Work-adjustment training consists of a series of activities designed to teach people appropriate work behaviors (Rubin & Roessler, 1995). Work-adjustment training is a type of behavior modification program that emphasizes eliminating undesirable work behaviors and reinforcing appropriate behaviors in areas related to job responsibilities, task production, and social-vocational competence (McCuller, Moore, & Salzberg, 1990). Marr and Roessler (1994) noted that work-adjustment interventions are useful in ameliorating problems related to fluctuating production output, social skills deficits, and poor responses to coworkers and supervision. Work-adjustment training is used for people with various disabilities, including cognitive impairments resulting from mental retardation, brain injury, mental illness, or other neurological impairments.

Inappropriate work behaviors may also be the result of developmental problems. Individuals with severe disabilities may experience problems in developing a healthy work personality, vocational self-efficacy, and career maturity (Hershenson, 1996). These developmental problems may have impeded the development of appropriate work behaviors and impair the person's ability achieve a positive work adjustment. Work-adjustment training is useful as a remedial intervention that may help restore the person's work personality, enhance the motivation to work, develop feelings of self-efficacy, and teach appropriate work behaviors.

Marr (1982) recommended the development of an individualized work-adjustment treatment plan that would take into consideration the person's behavioral assets and limitations. The treatment plan should specify the problems and objectives in terms of observable behaviors and the products of these behaviors. Other components of the work-adjustment treatment plan include measuring behaviors prior to interventions; selecting intervention procedures based on research evidence; continually measuring the target behavior to evaluate success; and attributing any failure of the intervention to the technique used, not to the person.

Work-adjustment training occurs in different settings ranging from rehabilitation facility–based programs to professionally supervised programs in competitive work settings (Rubin & Roessler, 1995). Facility-based programs use either real work tasks, which are developed by contracting work form local businesses and industries, or simulated work activities in their training process. The most effective programs are those that occur in actual competitive work settings and use supported employment interventions (Wehman & Kregel, 1992). Supported employment approaches to work-adjustment training involve the use of job coaches who supervise and train workers with disabilities in integrated work settings.

Work Evaluation. Work evaluation represents an approach to vocational assessment that combines the principles of psychometric testing with performance-based techniques (Rubin & Roessler, 1995). Work evaluation allows for observation of the individual's performance on actual or simulated work tasks in real or simulated work settings. Caston and Watson (1990) noted that the purpose of work evaluation is to provide reliable and valid data concerning the person's ability to work, preferences for different jobs and work activities, need for training in specific and general skills, and capacity to perform in various vocational roles.

The three basic work-evaluation methodologies include work samples, the situational approach, and on-the-job evaluation (Rubin & Roessler, 1995). Work samples involve the use of real or simulated work tasks that are used in various occupations. Simulated work samples are designed by professionals and include work activities of specific occupations. Work samples include a sample of the procedures, tools, and materials used in actual jobs. By using real tools, materials, and tasks, the individual's vocational exploration is facilitated and the evaluator is provided with the opportunity to observe important work behaviors. Work-sample testing allows for a comparison of the individual's performance with performance standards that have been developed from competitive or industrial norms. Test results indicate whether the individual is performing tasks at the competitive employment or noncompetitive employment levels in terms of quantity and quality.

Several commercial work-evaluation systems have been developed, including the JEVS System, developed by the Philadelphia Jewish Employment and Vocational Services; the Singer/Graflex Work Sample System; and the Valpar Component Work Sample Series (Power, 1991). Many of these systems are available in rehabilitation facilities that provide work-evaluation services.

The situational approach to work evaluation involves an assessment of the individual who is performing either contract or simulated work in a rehabilitation facility. The individual's performance is evaluated regarding the quality and quantity of work tasks performed as well as the behaviors demonstrated during task performance. In situational assessment, the individual responds to the realistic expectations of a work supervisor and productivity demands, which enables the evaluator to assess a wider range of work behaviors and employability characteristics (Power, 1991). The individual's work potential may be evaluated in regard to such work behaviors as getting along with coworkers and supervisors, staying on task, maintaining production, and tolerating frustration (Neff, 1985).

On-the-job evaluation consists of evaluating the person under the real conditions of the worksite (Rubin & Roessler, 1995). This approach allows the evaluator to observe how the person responds to the environment and how the environment impacts the person. The on-the-job approach gives the individual an opportunity for self-evaluation of task performance and work behaviors in a work setting that is presumed to be compatible with his or her interests and skills. The evaluator rates the performance of tasks and work behaviors. In addition, work supervisors may provide supplemental information on the individual's suitability for the job.

Work-evaluation services are provided to individuals with a wide range of disabilities, including mental retardation, psychiatric impairments, orthopedic impairments, brain damage, educational deficiencies, and multiple types of disability (Rubin & Roessler, 1995). Work evaluation is appropriate for individuals with disabilities who have little occupational information and who learn best by direct exposure to work activities. Nadolsky (1983) observed that the experiential nature of work evaluation enabled many individuals to develop more concrete images of a job or jobs and to seek more occupational information.

The work evaluation report contains important information regarding the nature of the person's disability and background information; a discussion of why the person was referred for evaluation; vocational history and transferable skills analysis, if applicable; vocationally significant behavioral observations; results of psychometric tests and work samples; information related to activities of daily living and social skills; recommendations for vocational rehabilitation services; and appropriate job options for the person to consider (Cutler & Ramm, 1992).

Supported Employment. Supported employment is a vocational rehabilitation service for individuals with severe disabilities who otherwise would not be able to obtain or maintain competitive employment (Hanley-Maxwell, Szymanski, & Owens-Johnson, 1998). The supported-employment model is based on the principals that job preparation for many people with severe disabilities should take place in a competitive setting, and that intensive follow-along interventions at the worksite should be provided to the client (Wehman & Kregel, 1985). This approach departs from the traditional "train and place" model of vocational rehabilitation for individuals with severe disabilities, which operates on the belief that job readiness and other types of skills training should occur prior to placement in a competitive job. The supported employment approach allows individuals to be placed in competitive jobs who do not possess all of the required skills and behaviors required for immediate occupational success. Through the use of professional support services at the worksite, the individual becomes job ready by performing tasks in a competitive, integrated work setting. This "place-train-follow-up" approach to supported employment includes four major components: job placement, job-site training and advocacy, ongoing assessment, and job retention (Wehman, 1986, p. 23).

The most common form of support is job coaching (Rubin & Roessler, 1995), which may be provided in either individual or group models. Job coaches function as trainers and supervisors by helping the person acquire the vocational skills required of the job as well as critical work behaviors, including appropriate relationships with coworkers and supervisors. The duration of supported-employment services varies according to the needs of the individual. Some individuals may need support for a specified amount of time and professional interventions may be systematically decreased as natural supports in the workplace emerge through enhanced social and physical integration. With improved integration, coworkers and supervisors may assume the supportive functions that the job coach provided. However, other individuals with significant disabilities may need long-term or permanent support to maintain competitive employment (Hanley-Maxwell et al., 1998). Although supported employment was initially used for individuals with developmental disabilities, it has also proved valuable for other types of disabilities, including chronic mental illness, traumatic brain injury, deafness, and visual impairments (Wehman, & Kregel, 1992).

Job-Seeking Skills Training (JSST). JSST programs are used to address skill deficiencies that people with disabilities have in the job-search process. These problems may include poor interviewing skills and difficulties in finding job leads, preparing resumés, explaining skills to employers, completing applications properly, and understanding employment rights. Some common problems experienced by job seekers with disabilities include difficulties in explaining their skills to employers, dealing with issues related to a marginal work history with gaps in periods of employment, and discussing or disclosing the nature of their disability or need for accommodations during the interview (Roessler, Hinman, & Lewis, 1987).

JSST is usually offered in a group format, and most programs follow an established curriculum of instruction. Specific training methods include the use of videotapes, instruction manuals, computer resources, occupational and labor market information, counseling, and supervision of job search activities (Roessler & Rumrill, 1994). Training involves the use of video equipment for developing appropriate interviewing skills and the development of resumés, cover letters, and other documents related to the job search. Participants also receive instruction in using labor market information and learning how to identify job leads. An important aspect of the training involves helping the person respond appropriately to disability-related issues, including an understanding of employment rights and strategies for requesting job accommodations (Rubin & Roessler, 1995).

Assistive Technology/Rehabilitation Engineering.   The Technology-Related Assistance for Individuals with Disabilities Act of 1988 (Tech Act) authorized financial assistance to the states to plan and implement a consumer-responsive assistive technology service delivery system for individuals with disabilities (Rehabilitation Services Administration, 1998). Assistive technology devices are defined in the Tech Act as "any item, piece of equipment, or product system, whether acquired commercially off the shelf, modified, or customized, that is used to increase, maintain, or improve functional capabilities of individuals with disabilities" (DeWitt, 1991, p. 315). By extending or replacing the capacities of the person, assistive technology removes barriers to participation in various social, personal, and vocational environments (Rubin & Roessler, 1995).

Categories of assistive technology applications have been defined by the Rehabilitation Services Administration's Institute on Rehabilitation Issues (1998). These categories include: aids for daily living; augmentative communications; computer applications; environmental control systems; home or worksite modifications; prosthetics and orthotics; seating and positioning; aids for vision or hearing impairments; wheelchairs and mobility aids; and vehicle modifications.

Assistive technology devices used to enhance capacities for activities of daily living typically include low-tech, self-help tools that provide assistance with such activities as preparing food, cleaning, bathing, and dressing. Augmentative and alternative communication devices include picture or letter communication boards or electronic speech synthesizers to assist people who have difficulty speaking or are unable to speak. Environmental control units help a person with mobility limitations operate and control home appliances and other equipment. Vision aids include devices such as magnifiers, Braille labels, voice synthesis computers, and audio clocks and alarms.

Rehabilitation engineers are qualified technologists that assist people with disabilities and counselors in assessing the need for assistive-technology services and in selecting or designing the devices to be used. The Rehabilitation Engineering and

Assistive Technology Society of North America (RESNA) conducts exams for licensing and certification of qualified professionals (Rehabilitation Services Administration, 1998). Rehabilitation engineering has been defined by Reswick (1980) as a combination of engineering technology and medicine designed to improve the life of people with disabilities. In addition to expertise in the application of assistive technologies, the skills of the rehabilitation engineer are also useful in evaluating environmental modifications that can remove or minimize barriers to participation in the home, community, or workplace. Workplace applications may include an ergonomic evaluation of the workstation for the purpose of fitting the job to the person and modifying tools and equipment used by the worker (Olsheski & Breslin, 1996).

Physical Restoration Services.   A number of vocational rehabilitation services involve those that are designed to enhance the physical capabilities of people with disabilities. Many of these services are provided by medical and allied health-care professionals. Physical medicine and rehabilitation physicians, also known as *physiatrists*, specialize in the treatment and rehabilitation of people with disabilities. Physiatrists establish treatment goals and collaborate with various health-care specialists, including physical therapists, occupational therapists, nurses, other physician specialists, speech pathologists, audiologists, prosthetic and orthotic specialists, and others related to the physical restoration of the individual (Rubin & Roessler, 1995).

Physical therapy is used to increase and maintain range of motion, strength, stamina, and balance and to teach proper body mechanics such as lifting techniques (Falvo, 1991). Occupational-therapy services are designed to rehabilitate the functional deficits of the individual with a disability. Occupational-therapy services include training and therapy to help improve the person's ability to function in activities of daily living, the community, and the workplace. Occupational therapists are also useful in designing orthotic devices such as splints and braces and for consultation concerning the adaptation of the physical environment. Occupational and physical therapists are also used to perform functional capacity evaluations, to make recommendations for job accommodations, and to provide clinical supervision of workers who are transitioning back to employment (Olsheski & Breslin, 1996).

Specialists in prosthetics and orthotics provide services related to the design, modification, and maintenance of artificial devices that increase a person's functional capacities (Rubin & Roessler, 1995). Orthotists specialize in fitting people with braces to provide support and stability for weakened parts of the body. These may include braces for the lower extremities, upper extremities, or spine. Prosthetists provide care for people by fitting them with prosthetic devices to replace missing limbs or parts of missing limbs (Clawson, 2002).

Speech therapy services are provided for individuals with various speech-language pathologies. These services may include evaluating, diagnosing, and treating various disorders of speech including problems of articulation, fluency, and voice. These conditions may include disorders of the oral-pharyngeal functions, cognitive communication disorders, and developing augmentative and alternative communication systems (Rubin & Roessler, 1995). Speech-therapy services have been used for such disabilities as stroke, brain injury, degenerative diseases, learning disabilities, cerebral palsy, and autism (Rehabilitation Services Administration, 1992). Audiologists evaluate hearing impairments and make recommendations for utilizing residual hearing ability. They also provide assistance in the selection and fitting of hearing aids or other listening devices as well as training the person in the proper use of the device (Harvey, 2002).

SUMMARY

Like other minority groups, people with disabilities continue to be underrepresented in many aspects of social and economic life. The negative stereotyping and discrimination experienced by people with disabilities is perhaps the most poignant in the world of work. Restricted opportunities for participation in meaningful work not only result in the high poverty rates among people with disabilities, but also contribute to their exclusion from other life activities in the context of where they live.

In order to better meet the career-development needs of people with disabilities, counselors need to be aware of each person's unique developmental experiences and the influence of contextual or environmental factors that make it difficult to obtain and maintain employment, and to advance in the world of work. The information presented in this chapter may be useful in helping people with physical disabilities overcome both personal limitations and environmental barriers to career development and work adjustment. The following Websites provide additional information relating to the topics discussed in this chapter.

USEFUL WEBSITES

1. *Rehabilitation Agencies*

Rehabilitation Services Administration: www.ed.gov/offices/osers/rsa

Information on the Office of Special Education and Rehabilitation Services; RSA organization, programs, grants, state plans, monitoring, and policy.

State Vocational Rehabilitation Agencies: http://trfn.clpgh.org/srac/state-vr.html

Links to all state vocational rehabilitation agencies.

2. *Disability Policy and Legislation*

Americans with Disabilities Act Document Center: http://janweb.icdi.wvu.edu/kinder

Information on statutory law, regulations, accessibility guidelines, federally reviewed technology checklists, and other assistance documents.

Center for the Study and Advancement of Disability Policy: http://www.disabilitypolicycenter.ogr

Information on advocacy training, ADA, Individuals with Disabilities Education Act, court decisions, Rehabilitation Act, Temporary Assistance for Needy Families, Ticket to Work and Work Incentives Improvement Act, vocational rehabilitation, and Workforce Investment Act.

National Council on Disability: www.ncd.gov

An independent federal agency that makes disability-related policy recommendations to the U.S. President and U.S. Congress.

3. Job Accommodations, Assistive Technology, and Employment

Abledata: http://www.abledata.com

Abledata Bulletin provides information on vendors and organizations that design and manufacture custom-made products; AbleData Fact Sheets cover various types of assistive technology, including components, accessories, applications, and manufacturers; Abledata Informed Consumer Guides presents information on assistive technology from a consumer's standpoint.

Job Accommodation Network (JAN): http://www.jan.wvu.edu/

Practical information on accommodating a specific person with a disability in a specific work situation as well as information on ADA and employment tips for individuals with disabilities.

RESNA Technical Assistance Project: http://www.resna.org/reshome.htm

Information on the Technical Assistance Project funded by the U.S. Department of Education, National Institute on Disability Rehabilitation Research, a grant providing technical assistance and information to 56 assistive-technology projects located throughout the United States.

*President's Committee on Employment of People with Disabilities:*http://www.pcepd.gov/

Information on the costs and benefits of accommodations; a business guide for hiring people with disabilities; and the use of job analysis as an employment tool.

REFERENCES

Andrew, J. (Ed.). (2000). *Disability handbook.* Fayetteville: University of Arkansas Department of Rehabilitation Education and Research.

Arbona, C. (1996). Career theory and practice in a multicultural context. In M. L. Savikas & W. B. Walsh (Eds.), *Handbook of career counseling theory and practice* (pp. 45–54). Palo Alto, CA: Davies-Black.

Beveridge, S., Heller Craddock, S., Liesener, J., Stapleton, M., & Hershenson, D. (2002). INCOME: A framework for conceptualizing the career development of persons with disabilities. *Rehabilitation Counseling Bulletin, 45,* 195–206.

Blanck, P., Anderson, J., Wallach, E., & Tenney, J. (1994). Implementing reasonable accommodations using ADR under the ADA: The case of a white-collar employee with bipolar mental illness. *Mental and Physical Disability Law Review, 18,* 458–464.

Blessing, L., & Jamieson, J. (1999). Employing persons with a developmental disability: Effects of previous experience. *Canadian Journal of Rehabilitation, 12,* 211–221.

Bordieri, J., Drehmer, D., & Comninel, M. (1988). Attribution of responsibility and hiring recommendations for job applicants with low back pain. *Rehabilitation Counseling Bulletin, 32,* 140–149.

Brabham, R., Mandeville, K., & Koch, L. (1998). The state-federal vocational rehabilitation program. In R. M. Parker & E. M. Szymanski (Eds.), *Rehabilitation counseling: Basics and beyond* (3rd ed., pp. 41–70). Austin, TX: Pro-Ed.

Breslin, R., & Olsheski, J. (1996). The impact of a transitional work return program on lost time. *NARPPS Journal, 11*(2), 35–40.

Brodwin, M., Parker, M., & DeLaGarza, D. (2003). Disability and accommodation. In E. M. Szymanski & R. M. Parker (Eds.), *Work and disability: Issues and strategies for career development and job placement* (2nd ed., pp. 201–246). Austin, TX: Pro-Ed.

Cameron, D., & Sharp, T. (1998). *ADA resource manual.* Columbus, OH: Ohio Rehabilitation Services Commission.

Caston, H., & Watson, A. (1990). Vocational assessment and rehabilitation outcomes. *Rehabilitation Counseling Bulletin, 34,* 61–66.

Clawson, L. (2002). Orthotics, amputation, and prosthetics. In M. Brodwin, F. Tellez, & S. Brodwin (Eds.), *Medical, psychosocial, and vocational aspects of disability* (2nd ed., pp. 305–316). Athens, GA: Elliott & Fitzpatrick.

Colenbrander, A. (1977). Dimensions of visual performance. *Transactions—American Academy of Ophthalmology and Otolaryngology, 83*, 332–337.

Conte, L. (1983). Vocational development theories and the disabled person: Oversight or deliberate omission. *Rehabilitation Counseling Bulletin, 26*, 316–328.

Crites, J. (1978). *Theory and research handbook for the career maturity inventory.* Monterey, CA: CTB, McGraw Hill.

Curnow, T. (1989).Vocational development of persons with disability. *Vocational Guidance Quarterly, 37*, 269–278.

Cutler, F., & Ramm, A. (1992). Introduction to the basics of vocational evaluation. In J. Siefker (Ed.), *Vocational evaluation in private sector rehabilitation* (pp. 31–66). Menomonie: University of Wisconsin–Stout, Materials Development Center, Stout Vocational Rehabilitation Institute.

DeWitt, J. (1991). Removing barriers through technology. In J. West (Ed.), *The Americans with Disabilities Act: From policy to practice* (pp. 313–332). New York: Milbank Memorial Fund.

Falvo, D. (1991). *Medical and psychosocial aspects of chronic illness and disability.* Gaithersburg, MD: Aspen.

Fitzgerald, L., & Betz, N. (1994). Career development in cultural context: The role of gender, race, class, and sexual orientation. In M. L. Savickas & R. W. Lent (Eds.), *Convergence in career development theories: Implications for science and practice* (pp. 103–117). Palo Alto, CA: Consulting Psychologists Press.

Gysbers, N., Heppner, M., & Johnston, J. (2003). *Career counseling: Process, issues, and techniques* (2nd ed.). Boston: Allyn & Bacon.

Hallock, K., Hendricks, W., & Broadbent, E. (1998). Discrimination by gender and disability status: Do worker perceptions match statistical measures? *Southern Economic Journal, 65*, 345–263.

Hanley-Maxwell, C., Szymanski, E., & Owens-Johnson, L. (1998). School-to-adult life transition and supported employment. In R. Parker & E. Szymanski (Eds.), *Rehabilitation counseling: Basics and beyond* (3rd ed., pp. 143–180). Austin, TX: Pro-Ed.

Harvey, E. (2002). Hearing disabilities. In M. Brodwin, F. Tellez, & S. Brodwin (Eds.), *Medical, psychosocial, and vocational aspects of disability* (2nd ed., pp. 143–156). Athens, GA: Elliott & Fitzpatrick.

Hershenson, D. (1981). Work adjustment, disability, and the three r's of vocational rehabilitation: A conceptual model. *Rehabilitation Counseling Bulletin, 25*, 91–97.

Hershenson, D. (1996). Work adjustment: A neglected area in career counseling. *Journal of Counseling and Development, 74*, 442–448.

Jenkins, W., Patterson, J., & Szymanski, E. (1998). Philosophical, historical, and legislative aspects of the rehabilitation counseling profession. In R. Parker & E. Szymanski (Eds.), *Rehabilitation counseling: Basics and beyond* (3rd ed., pp. 1–40). Austin, TX: Pro-Ed.

Lee, B., & Newman, K. (1995). Employer responses to disability: Preliminary evidence and a research agenda. *Employee Responsibilities and Rights Journal, 8*, 209–229.

Lent, R., Brown, S., & Hackett, G. (2000). Contextual supports and barriers to career choice: A social cognitive analysis. *Journal of Counseling Psychology, 47*, 36–49.

Lent, R., & Hackett, G. (1994). Sociocognitive mechanisms of personal agency in career development: Pan theoretical prospects. In M. Savickas & R. Lent (Eds.), *Convergence in career development: Implications for science and practice* (pp. 77–101). Palo Alto, CA: Consulting Psychologists Press.

Lynch, R. K., & Lynch, R. T. (1998). Rehabilitation counseling in the private sector. In R. Parker & E. Szymanski (Eds.). *Rehabilitation counseling: Basics and beyond* (3rd ed., pp. 71–106). Austin, TX: Pro-Ed.

Marr, J. (1982). Behavioral analysis of work problems. In B. Bolton (Ed.), *Vocational adjustment of disabled persons* (pp. 127–148). Baltimore, MD: University Park Press.

Marr, J., & Roessler, R. (1994). *Supervision and management: A guide to modifying work behavior.* Fayetteville: University of Arkansas Press.

McCuller, G., Moore, S., & Salzberg, C. (1990). Programming for vocational competence in sheltered workshops. *Journal of Rehabilitation, 56,* 41–44.

Montgomery, J. (1996). Legal aspects of ergonomics. In A. Bhattacharya & J. McGlothlin (Eds.), *Occupational ergonomics: Theory and applications* (pp. 685–698). New York: Marcel Dekker.

Moores, D. (2001). *Educating the deaf: Psychology, principles, and practices* (5th ed.). Boston: Houghton Mifflin.

Mueller, J. (1990). *The workplace workbook: An illustrated guide to job accommodation and assistive technology.* Washington, DC: Dole Foundation.

Nadolsky, J. (1983). The development of vocational evaluation services. In R. Lassiter, M. Lassiter, R. Hardy, & J. Cull (Eds.), *Vocational evaluation, work adjustment, and independent living for severely disabled persons* (pp. 5–17). Springfield, IL: Charles C. Thomas.

Neff, W. (1985). *Work and human behavior.* New York: Aldine.

Nordstrom, C., Huffaker, B., & Williams, K. (1998). When physical disabilities are not liabilities: The role of applicant and interviewer characteristics on employment interview outcomes. *Journal of Applied Social Psychology, 28,* 283–306.

Olsheski, J. (1996). Contemporary issues in disability management. *NARPPS Journal, 11*(2), 5–7.

Olsheski, J., & Breslin, R. (1996). The Americans with Disabilities Act: Implications for the use of ergonomics in rehabilitation. In A. Bhattacharya & J. McGlothlin (Eds.), *Occupational ergonomics: Theory and applications* (pp. 669–684). New York: Marcel Dekker.

Olsheski, J., & Schelat, R. (2003). Reasonable job accommodations for people with psychiatric disabilities. In D. Moxley & J. Finch (Eds.), *Sourcebook of rehabilitation and mental health practice* (pp. 61–76). New York: Plenum.

Osipow, S. (1976). Vocational development problems of the handicapped. In H. Rusalem & D. Malikin (Eds.), *Contemporary vocational rehabilitation* (pp. 51–60). New York: New York University Press.

Panek, W. (2002). Visual disabilities. In M. Brodwin, F. Tellez, & S. Brodwin (Eds.), *Medical, psychosocial, and vocational aspects of disability* (2nd ed., pp. 157–170). Athens, GA: Elliott & Fitzpatrick.

Peterson, N., Mumford, M., Borman, W., Jeanneret, P., Fleishman, E., & Levin, K. (1997). *ONET final technical report, Vol. II.* (Vol. 2). Salt Lake City: Utah Department of Workforce Services.

Power, P. (1991). *A guide to vocational assessment* (2nd ed.). Austin, TX: Pro-Ed.

President's Committee on the Employment of People with Disabilities. (1992). *Report.* Washington, DC: Author.

Radtke, M. (2000). *Effective strategies to improve the employment of SSI/SSDI participants.* Washington, DC: Stout Vocational Rehabilitation Institute.

Rasch, J. (1985). *Rehabilitation of workers' compensation and other insurance claimants.* Springfield, IL: Charles C. Thomas.

Reswick, J. (1980). Rehabilitation engineering. In E. Pan, T. Backer, & C. Vash (Eds.), *Annual Review of Rehabilitation* (Vol. 1, pp. 55–79). New York: Springer.

Rehabilitation Services Administration. (1992). *Rehabilitation-related professions.* Washington, DC: Office of Special Education and Rehabilitation Research.

Rehabilitation Services Administration, Institute on Rehabilitation Issues. (1998). *Achieving successful employment outcomes with the use of assistive technology: Twenty-fourth institute on rehabilitation issues.* Menomonie, WI: University of Wisconsin–Stout.

Roessler, R., Hinman, S., & Lewis, F. (1987). Job interview deficiencies of "job ready" rehabilitation clients. *Journal of Rehabilitation, 53*, 33–36.

Roessler, R., & Rumrill, P. (1994). *Enhancing productivity on your job: The "win-win" approach to job accommodations.* New York: Multiple Sclerosis Society.

Rosenthal, D., & Olsheski, J. (1999). Rehabilitation counseling and disability management: Present status and future opportunities. *Journal of Rehabilitation, 65*, 31–38.

Rubin, S., & Roessler, R. (1995). *Foundations of the vocational rehabilitation process* (4th ed.). Austin, TX: Pro-Ed.

Rubin, S., & Roessler, R. (2001). *Foundations of the vocational rehabilitation process* (5th ed.). Austin, TX: PRO-ED.

Szymanski, E., Enright, M., Hershenson, D., & Ettinger, J. (2003). Career development theories, constructs, and research: Implications for people with disabilities. In E. Szymanski & R. Parker (Eds.), *Work and disability: Issues and strategies for career development and job placement* (2nd ed., pp. 91–153). Austin, TX: Pro-Ed.

Szymanski, E., & Hershenson, D. (1998). Career development of people with disabilities: An ecological model. In R. Parker & E. Szymanski (Eds.), *Rehabilitation counseling: Basics and beyond* (3rd ed., pp. 327–378). Austin, TX: Pro-Ed.

Szymanski, E., & Parker, R. (Eds.). (2003). *Work and disability: Issues and strategies in career development and job placement* (2nd ed.). Austin, TX: Pro-Ed.

Szymanski, E., & Trueba, H. (1994). Castification of people with disabilities: Potential disempowering aspects of classification in disability services. *Journal of Rehabilitation, 60*(3), 12–20.

U.S. Department of Labor. (1979). Guide for occupational exploration. Washington, DC: U.S. Government Printing Office.

U.S. Department of Labor. (1982). *Handbook for analyzing jobs.* Washington, DC: U.S. Government Printing Office.

U.S. Department of Labor. (1991). *Dictionary of occupational titles* (4th ed.). Indianapolis, IN: JIST Works.

U.S. Department of Labor. (2002). *Accommodations get the job done.* Washington, DC: Author.

U.S. Department of Labor. (2003). *Occupational outlook handbook.* Washington, DC: U.S. Employment Services.

U.S. Equal Employment Opportunity Commission. (1991). *The Americans with Disabilities Act: Your responsibilities as an employer.* Washington, DC: U.S. Government Printing Office.

University of Wisconsin–Stout, Materials Development Center. (1992). *A guide to job analysis.* Stout, WI: Author.

Weed, R., Taylor, C., & Blackwell, T. (1991). Job analysis for the private sector. *NARPPS Journal, 6*, 153–158.

Wehman, P. (1986). Competitive employment in Virginia. In F. Rusch (Ed.), *Competitive employment issues and strategies* (pp. 23–33). Baltimore, MD: Paul H. Brooks.

Wehman, P., & Kregel, J. (1985). A supported work approach to competitive employment of individuals with moderate and severe handicaps. In P. Wehman & J. Hill (Eds.), *Competitive employment for persons with mental retardation* (pp. 20–45). Richmond: Virginia Commonwealth University, Rehabilitation and Training Center.

Wehman, P., & Kregel, J. (1992). Supported employment: Growth and impact. In P. Wehman, P. Sale, & W. Parent (Eds.), *Supported employment: Strategies for integration of workers with disabilities* (pp. 3–28). Stoneham, MA: Butterworth-Heinemann.

Wright, G. (1980). *Total rehabilitation.* Boston: Little, Brown.

CHAPTER 13

CAREER COUNSELING WITH COUPLES AND FAMILIES

KATHY M. EVANS

University of South Carolina

Until very recently, career planning was directed toward a single individual and his or her specific personality characteristics, values, interests, skills, and desires. Family issues may have been considered, but they seldom were treated as central to the individual's career-planning needs. The counseling profession has evolved over the years and has moved from conceptualizing clients as isolated individuals to viewing clients in the context of their environment (e.g., their families, partners, and other significant people in their lives). This move has been heavily influenced by (a) multicultural counseling, which introduced the notion that the Anglo-American value of the rugged individualist is contrary to the values of many ethnic and cultural minority groups; (b) feminists, who pointed out that women tend to be more relationship oriented and that use of individualism as the norm pathologizes women's experiences; (c) postmodern philosophy, which asserts that individuals make their own meaning of their experiences and that counselors should honor their clients' perception of the world; and (d) family therapy, which states that an individual is part of a family system and that there is a reciprocal influence between an individual and his or her family.

SYSTEMS THEORY

Although family influence on the careers of its members is an ancient process, as more research is conducted, we become more aware of the reciprocal influences between family and individuals concerning career planning. Children have been going into the "family business" for centuries. It is not uncommon for a family to produce generations of doctors, lawyers, farmers, teachers, or business owners (Evans & Rotter, 2000). Research shows that most people seek family support and approval of their career decisions and that, in fact, rather than lose that family support, individuals are willing to compromise their career aspirations (Gottfredson, 1981). When a family member does choose an occupation without receiving family support, there is often upheaval in the family and stress on the defector.

The reciprocal influences of individuals and their families is a concept from general systems theory, adapted to family therapy to understand family dynamics. General systems theory was originally a mathematical theory developed by Norbert Wiener (1948) and extended to biology and medicine by Von Bertalanffy (1968). Simply put, the first part of general systems theory asserts that systems are made up of many parts that interact and relate to one another. The interrelationships between parts affect the functioning of the entire system. A change in any one of these parts results in a change in all the other parts as well as the entire system. Any change in the system affects all of its parts. This is called *circular causality*. Second, the system works to maintain homeostasis, meaning stability and equilibrium. That is, the system works to keep the status quo. Goldenberg and Goldenberg (1994) use the thermostat as an example of homeostasis, stating that the thermostat will maintain a constant temperature, keeping the house from getting too hot or cold.

To relate general systems to family therapy, each member of the family is part of the larger family system, and when one family member displays problematic behavior, it is understood that this behavior is a manifestation of a change in the interactional process of the family system as a whole (circular causality) and that the problematic behavior is an attempt to get back the stability and equilibrium (homeostasis) in the family. If Tyreeq suddenly starts to pick fights with fellow classmates, he may be reacting to decreased attention he is receiving from his parents, who spend most of their time arguing over a new addition to their home. His behavior is an attempt to regain his parent's attention and return family interaction to the status quo. The family is also affected by other, even larger systems (e.g., ethnic group, neighborhoods, schools, communities, workplaces, economic and political institutions, etc.), and changes in those systems affect the family and, in turn, its individual members (Goldenberg & Goldenberg, 1994; Ivey, D'Andrea, Ivey, & Simek-Morgan, 2002).

Systems theory has gained general acceptance in counseling and psychology as a way to better understand individuals. However, it is not without its critics. Feminists have criticized systems theory because it assumes that everyone in the family has equal power and can affect the system equally when change occurs. Less powerful individuals (women and children), they say, cannot be equally as responsible for what happens as those who are more powerful. Multicultural counselors state that systems theory is based on a white, middle-class model of the family and does not take into account different family configurations and the effects of race, gender, ethnicity, and culture (Evans & Rotter, 2000; Sciarra, 1999). Given these caveats, systems theory helps counselors to understand the workings of families and may help them develop interventions that will be useful for their clients. Before counselors can really understand families, however, they need to have an understanding of the meaning of "family" in the twenty-first century.

THE TWENTY-FIRST-CENTURY FAMILY

The notion of family has changed so much over the past few decades that it is not surprising that Paniagua (1996) recommends that counselors ask their clients to identify who is family to them. Carter and McGoldrick (1999b) described the contemporary American family with various configurations: (a) two-parent families, which may be heterosexual, gay, or lesbian, married or unmarried, with children who may or may not be their biological offspring; (b) single parents, who may be heterosexual, gay, or lesbian and may or may not be the biological parents to their children; (c) extended families that may or may not be biologically related to one another; (d) couples (heterosexual, gay, or lesbian) without children; and (e) single adults (heterosexual, gay, or lesbian) without children. Family configurations are often determined by cultural influences. However, even within cultural groups, there is diversity. For example, Billingsley (1992) was able to identify 32 different configurations of African American households. Carter and McGoldrick said it best when they wrote "It is high time we gave up on our traditional concept of family and expanded our very definition of the term" (1999b, p. 10).

CONNECTION BETWEEN FAMILY AND WORK

Sigmund Freud described a healthy individual as one who has the ability to love and work. The wisdom of that observation is not lost on today's researchers and practitioners. Zedeck and Mosier (1990) stated that family and work are the two "central institutions in life," and Burke (1996) states that the major life roles for most employed adults are as worker and family member. Individuals in the United States spend, on average more than one-third of their days and approximately two-thirds of their lives at work (Dawis & Lofquist, 1984). It is not surprising that many people spend the better part of their lives juggling the responsibilities of work and family.

A great deal of the research that has been conducted on family and career connections support the belief that there is a predictable relationship between how well a person functions at work and how well he or she functions in familial relations. Most of the research is driven by one or more theories that have evolved regarding the work and family connection. They include compensation theory, segmentation theory (Gysbers, Heppner, & Johnston, 1998), instrumental theory, spill-over theory, and conflict theory.

Compensation theory purports that individuals compensate for what is missing in their families by increasing their commitment to work, or vice versa. For example, with a bachelor's degree in marketing, Marie is underemployed as an administrative assistant at an advertising firm and compensates by spending more time on activities involving her children. She has taken on the tasks of Little League baseball coach, Sunday school teacher, and president of the parent-teacher organization.

According to the segmentation theory, individuals are able to compartmentalize their lives, keeping family life and work life completely separated. For example, at work, Johnny does not display pictures of his family on his desk, nor does he discuss family problems or issues with his coworkers. Johnny also refuses to take work home and does not discuss his work with his family. He concentrates on only one facet of his life at a time because he believes he would be less effective in his role as a worker if he were to let his family interfere and less effective as a parent and spouse if he were to let his work interfere.

Instrumental theory purports that individuals work to provide their families, not only with what they need, but also with luxuries. For example, by putting in overtime and weekends during the winter months, Annie is able to buy a wide-screen television, send her children to camp for two weeks in the summer, take a family vacation, and have a membership in the local athletic club.

Most of the research on family and work is devoted to spill-over theory and conflict theory. In spill-over theory, boundaries between work and family are very fuzzy. Spill-over theory is the complete opposite of compartmentalization theory. For example, Bill shares his frustrations about his family with his coworkers and shares his disappointments in his work with his family. He conducts family business during work hours and frequently takes work home.

Conflict theory describes how conflict can arise from the roles that individuals play at work and at home. They are often forced to choose one role over the other due to the conflict. For example, as a supervisor, Thea must work evenings to oversee a special project that has a critical deadline. Thea's daughter, Shani, has the lead in the school play that takes place on the very evenings Thea must work.

These theories illustrate very clearly that work and family are intertwined and to work out these problems, counselors may have to work with more than one member of the family. Therefore, family-counseling skill competencies are indeed essential for career counselors. In fact, Blustein (2001) stated that

> the artificial barriers between work and relationships are finally beginning to be understood and perhaps diminished in scope. Once we can fully internalize the fact that work and relational functioning are integrated aspects of human life, we may be able to generate theory, research, and practice models that truly embrace the full scope of human life in the 21st century. (p. 189)

Family Life Cycle

One of the ways that we can internalize the relationship between work and relational functioning is to take a close look at the family life cycle. The family life cycle approach illustrates the development of the traditional nuclear family by describing six stages of development and the emotional processes that the family experiences during these stages (Carter & McGoldrick, 1999). The authors present developmental examples of each stage as well as the changes that the family needs to make to continue to develop. The stages are leaving home, joining families through marriage, families with young children, families with adolescents, launching children, and families in later life. Each stage primarily reflects major transitions that mostly coincide with the age of the children in the family. As the child grows, the interactions and relationships that the parents have to that child and to each other change, resulting in changes in other family members as well. Families that do not effectively make the adjustment from one stage to another tend to have difficulties that may result in a need for therapy. The adjustments that the family makes are referred to as second order change, during which the generations must shift their status in their relationship and reconnect in a new and different way.

What is clearly apparent from the family life cycle is that it was developed on the model of a nuclear family: two married, heterosexual parents and their biological children, with a wife who stays at home and works full time as a homemaker while the father works outside the home. In 1999, Carter and McGoldrick stated that in the current U.S. society, the idea of the "traditional family" needs to be abandoned because it does not describe the majority of households. "It is becoming increasingly difficult to determine what family life cycle patterns are 'normal,' causing great stress from family members, who have few consensually validated models to guide them through the passages they must negotiate" (1999a, p. 1).

Because the stages are based on the traditional White (Anglo), middle-class family of old, Hines, Preto, McGoldrick, Almeida, and Welman (1999) warn that to understand how families move through their life cycle, we have to determine the importance of their cultural and ethnic backgrounds. Different ethnic and cultural groups may place more importance on some stages and transitions than they do on others. For example, Irish and African American families place a great deal of importance on the wake after the death of a family member. Italian and Polish Americans emphasize weddings, and Jewish families stress the bar mitzvah or bat mitzvah. There are often different generational patterns among ethnic groups that may call into question the timing of the life-cycle stages. In some cultures, launching does not take place until marriage; in others, interdependence lasts a lifetime. When second and third generations of a cultural group are in close contact, there is often conflict because the younger generation wants to adopt the dominant culture's traditions while members of the older generation want to pass on their legacy. The traditional family life cycle would not explain the struggles for families of every cultural group, so it is important for counselors to have an understanding of their clients' cultural traditions and view their family as a unique example in the life cycle of a particular cultural group. Hines et al. warn that "any life cycle transition can trigger ethnic identity conflicts, since it puts families more in touch with the roots of their family traditions" (p. 70).

There are other very important transitions that modern-day families encounter that are not included in the Carter and McGoldrick model. Some examples include open adoption, artificial means of conceiving, reunions of families separated by state social services department, separation of nonmarried couples, gay and lesbian marriage or commitment, and biracial and bicultural marriages. One of the largest issues in most of these transitions is that they involve alternative lifestyles that the larger society rejects, and that as a result, the families involved are seldom likely to get the kind of support that is available in more traditional transitions (Imber-Black, 1999). Carter and McGoldrick's (1999) family life-cycle approach is not predictable for all families and may have to be reconfigured to reflect culturally different families and families with different life style patterns. Consider the Connor family (see box on next page).

CONNOR FAMILY

Judy Connor is a 23-year-old African American woman who has an 8-year-old daughter, Taylor. Judy and Taylor live with Judy's parents and two siblings, Troy, 15, and Ricky, 17. Judy has limited contact with Taylor's biological father, Joe, 30, who is employed at a local discount store and who sends child support payments to Judy sporadically. Judy became pregnant while she was in high school, but was able to finish and go on to study computer-aided graphic design at the community college. Her parents have been very supportive and have helped her with her tuition as long as she took care of her child and worked full time while she was in college.

While Judy was able to take on the responsibilities of an adult by becoming a parent, she remained financially and emotionally dependent on her parents. However, the extended family support will enable her to become truly independent in the near future. Judy has not married, though she shares parenthood with Joe. The two families are related and, on occasion, they interact. Judy's parents are also involved in several other family life stages at this time. They have teen-aged boys (families with adolescents) and a grandchild (launching). Grandparenthood, too, came earlier for the elder Connors than the original family life cycle suggests.

The career issues reflected in the family life cycle model are implied and may need further explanation. By juxtaposing Super's career development stages with the family life cycle, one can begin to see the impact of career issues (see Table 13.1).

Young adults leaving home do not only test out their independence from their family of origin but also examine their initial career choices. As they marry and join with their spouse's family, they are solidifying their career choices and beginning to make advances in their careers. Once they start to have children, their careers may begin to soar and the role conflicts will become critical. Their children, however, are just beginning to understand what careers are about as well as just discovering what they are capable of doing. When the children become adolescents, the parents' careers are beginning to level out, and they do not rise as quickly after that. Some have reached as high as they will go by this time. The children, however, are beginning to explore careers, trying them out through part-time work and extracurricular activities in school. As the children leave home, their parents begin to lose their own parents, they are settled in their careers and attempt to maintain what they have gained. The children have started exploring their own careers at this point and are trying out their first jobs. Finally, when the parents reach later life, they enjoy being grandparents and scale down their work or retire altogether while their children are climbing their own career ladders.

Some of the current career issues individuals may encounter throughout the family life cycle are listed next.

1. Leaving home: Many young people today find it difficult to find their first job, especially if they leave formal education before or right after completing high school. If they do find a job, it may be difficult for them to earn enough to live on

TABLE 13.1   Comparison between Carter and McGoldrick's Stages of the Family Life Cycle and Super's Career Development Stages

CARTER & MCGOLDRICK'S FAMILY LIFE CYCLE STAGES		SUPER'S STAGES OF CAREER DEVELOPMENT
Leaving home:	Young adult begins life on his or her own	Exploration: Young adult tries out career opportunities.
Marriage:	Commits to a new family system	Exploration/Establishment: Young adult completes exploration of careers and begins to establish him- or herself.
Families with young children:	Takes on responsibility of parenthood	Establishment: Parents grow and develop in their careers. Growth: Children begin to learn and fantasize about careers and try out new abilities.
Families with adolescents:	Grants children more independence	Maintenance: Parents settle into their careers. Growth/Exploration: Children begin to learn interests and abilities through participation in academic work, extra-curricular activities, and part-time work.
Launching children:	Accepts family members leaving; both new beginning and endings	Maintenance: Parents continue to work in careers and begin to think about retiring. Exploration: Children try out career opportunities.
Families in later life:	Accepts new generational roles	Disengagement: Retirement or reduced hours for parents.

their own. Therefore, leaving home is occurring later and later for many adult children (Fulmer, 1999).

2. Joining: This lifestyle stage is also being delayed because people are leaving home later in their lives. Also, once they get married, most couples find it is necessary for both spouses to work. The couple will need to decide on the lifestyle they want to live based on their income and the commitment they want to make to their careers.

3. Young children: Since both parents are likely to work, decisions have to be made about child care and how parental roles are to be shared. One or both spouses will start to experience role conflicts between work and family obligations. Decisions will need to be made regarding chores for school-aged children.

4. Adolescents: Work and family role conflicts lessen as adolescents become more independent. The teenager may begin work to earn his or her own money or may be frustrated by a lack of available jobs.

5. Launching children: Parents may see that retirement may not occur as soon as they thought because of financial need. Children remain dependent longer as they enroll in higher education or stay at home until they can afford to move or get married. Children may be starting their own careers and may be experiencing the reality of that career choice. Some children will decide they have made a poor decision after all.

6. Later life: More and more retired people are returning to work to supplement their income and to remain physically and mentally active.

The family life cycle and the related career development issues will become even clearer when we explore the specific career issues of families and couples.

TWO-INCOME FAMILIES

The literature on issues for heterosexual dual-career and dual-earner couples is vast. It is the most researched area for family- and career-related issues. For the purposes of this discussion, two-income families will be defined as two heterosexual, married or unmarried, parents and their children. The discussion will also include blended families, where parents have remarried and the children may be stepchildren to an otherwise childless stepparent, children of both stepparents, or biological children of both parents. Today 20 percent of American children live in homes that are blended in some way (U.S. Census Bureau, 2001–2002). In today's society, it is necessary for both parents to earn an income. Two-parent, married families make up only 25 percent of the total population of families in the United States (U.S. Census Bureau, 2001–2002). Overall, both parents work in at least 63 percent of the two-parent families (U.S. Census Bureau, 2001–2002).

It is necessary to make a distinction between two groups of two-income families. The first is dual-career families, in which both members of the couple are engaged in a managerial or professional position that (a) requires high levels of effort and energy for success, (b) commands high commitment to excel, and (c) offers advancement in responsibility and pay status (Cooper, Arkkelin, & Tielbert, 1994; Duxbury & Higgins, 1994). Dual-earner couples, on the other hand, are involved in jobs rather than careers. They tend to have gainful employment with no expectation of a high degree of commitment or advancement and with lower levels of energy and effort involved. A couple could be considered a dual-earner couple even if one spouse were in a pursuit of a career. Many of the problems encountered by dual-earner couples are also felt by dual-career couples, but there are different issues as well.

Gysbers et al. (1998) suggest it is helpful to develop a vocabulary of family and work problems to clarify any potentially fuzzy issues. They suggest categorizing problems into life roles (worker role, family role), life events (work-related events, family-related events), and life setting (home or work). These categories have been used to discuss the issues for two-income families.

Problems with Life Roles

When two parents work, there are many concerns: child care, household duties, and managing the spillover from work to home and from home to work. However, the overarching theme for dual-career and dual-earner families involves gender-role expectations and socialization. Women have been socialized to be the caretakers of the young, and men have been socialized as the providers. Although these roles have been evolving (especially since the majority of women now work outside the home), little has changed in society as to the expectations for mothers and fathers (Duxbury & Higgins, 1994). When young men and women prepare for a career, women are more likely to consider their future family in their career decision making. They have the expectation and, for many, the desire to subordinate their career interests for the sake of raising their children. McGoldrick (1999) stated that there are three marital types of dual-career families: traditional/conventional, modern/participant, and egalitarian/role-sharing. In traditional/conventional families, parenting and household work are the wife's duties. In the modern/participant marriages, parenting is shared but the woman does the housework. In the egalitarian/role-sharing marriage, both spouses do the parenting and the housework (only a third of all dual-career couples have this kind of a division of labor). McGoldrick (1999) states that the difference in how the family is divided is the result of a variety of factors, including gender-role socialization and cultural factors. When couples have difficulty agreeing on a fair division of work and power, there will be disharmony in the relationship. If they agree, there will be satisfaction (Goldenberg & Goldenberg, 1994).

On average, women work 12 more hours per week on home-related activities than men (Stohs, 1995). Today's men, however, have placed more importance on family and relationships than ever before and spend more time caring for children. However, the work that is done in the home is typically divided by gender. Women do more work in meal preparation, while men do yard work and home repairs (Silberstein, 1992). Silberstein found that there was a more equal division of role sharing when children were added to the dual-career couple's family.

In dual-earner families, many women work to supplement the man's income, and they are more likely to downgrade career or work concerns to take care of the family (Brines, 1994). In their research on dual-earner couples, Becker and Moen (1999) found that couples try to buffer their families from the demands of work by scaling back their career pursuits. Some of the strategies they use include deciding on a one-career marriage, limiting work hours and travel, or alternating who has the job and who has the career. Part-time work seemed to be another scaling-back strategy practiced by women with children under six years of age whose husbands earned a high income. Most of these wives worked fewer hours than career women with higher pay (Risman, Atkinson, & Blackwelder, 1999). In fact professional women's commitment is expected to mirror that of professional men, whether or not they have a family. If they have a family, there is an expectation that the children will be given priority, but husbands who perceive that their wives are highly committed to their careers are more likely to participate in domestic work (Gilbert, 1985). However, couples pay the price for sharing the work both at home and outside the home (Mackey, 1995). Men with children and a working spouse earn about the same as single men and married men with no children but less than men with children and a stay-at-home spouse. Women with children and a working spouse did make more than single women but about the same as married women with no children (Schneer & Reitman, 1993).

Problems with Life Events

Job stress is likely to have a negative impact on marital relationships and the worker's mood at home. This may be especially true for women. Barnett (1994) found that women in dual-career couples experienced stress when their marital or family experiences were negative. Women, also, are more likely to suffer from spillover and role conflict when things are not going well at home. This reaction occurs because women's salaries are often thought of as supplemental and their primary duty is to their family (Duxbury & Higgins, 1994). When things are going well at home, stressful situations at work for both men and women are lessened.

Other life events that can be problematic for dual-career couples can occur in their relationship. At times there is competition between the individuals in a couple because they are both chasing a career (Goldenberg & Goldenberg, 1994). Resentment may arise if one partner is advancing more quickly than the other or if one's salary is higher than the other's. Also, equity in the relationship may become an issue, since it is closely related to money. If the male partner makes more money, then he is likely to assume more power. Since women typically earn less than men even if they are employed in the same career, men will maintain the power. However, competition issues may arise if the woman makes more than her partner because such a situation defies gender socialization.

Problem in Life Settings

One of the most difficult issues for dual-career couples is geographical mobility. Typically, the goal is for each partner to find an ideal position in the same city. However, in many dual-career couples, one partner's career is at a higher level than the other's, and there are fewer opportunities at the highest levels than at the lower levels (Rhodes, 2002). More often than not, the man's career is the one at the higher level so that the geographic moves are based on his career.

When both spouses are intensely career minded and committed to their respective careers and their relationship, a commuter marriage may result. One spouse chooses to stay in City A while the other spouse goes to City B, and they meet on weekends or monthly (depending on time and distance). Commuter marriages require a great deal of sacrifice. The couple is separated most of the time and there is the cost of running two households. It is particularly stressful if there are children involved. The parent that stays with the children is virtually a single parent while the other parent is out of town. More often than not, commuting is temporary. Most couples prefer not to be separated or uproot their families for advancement. Even when companies are willing to assist couples in finding work for the two of them, it is difficult to get them to leave their positions and move their families.

Employers are slowly responding to the family needs of their employees. These adjustments include flex time, telecommuting, on-site day-care centers, parental leave for fathers and mothers, financial assistance for day care, job sharing, and part-time options for workers (Goldenberg & Goldenberg, 1994). However, men are less likely to take advantage of these benefits. Even when they are self-employed, an avenue many tend to take to gain work-time flexibility and autonomy, men do not tend to utilize this flexibility and autonomy to better balance their work and family life the way women do (Loscocco, 1997).

Counseling Two-Income Families

Before counselors begin to work with two-income families, they should recognize that each family is unique in terms of its ethnicity and culture. In order to connect with their clients, counselors need to understand the clients' perspectives of their culture and the expectations that the family is attempting to meet. Goldenberg and Goldenberg (1994) suggest a number of strategies for counseling two-income families. They recommend that counselors involve both partners in what Hazard and Koslow (1992) call *conjoint career counseling*, in which the counselor treats each partner evenhandedly. It defeats the purpose of counseling if one person perceives that the counselor is on the other person's side and feels ganged up on. Couples should be encouraged to reevaluate their career expectations and, if necessary, redefine success in their careers if they are having problems with role conflict and spillover. Often, conflicts that parents experience may be improved by stress- and time-management strategies. Sometimes it will be necessary to have the members of the couple resolve any unfinished business that they have with their family of origin that seems to be repeating itself in their current family relationships. Gender-role socialization is one area where counselors will need to examine both partners to help them find the source of their conflicts (Forrest, 1994). Remarried couples may need to mourn the loss of their previous lifestyle and adjust to their present situation. Stepparenting can be a challenge to a previously childless parent, and the couple has to negotiate stepparent involvement, not only in disciplining, but also in taking on parental responsibilities that will influence their work.

In addition, it is essential to draw on the couple's positive assets (commitment to one another, extended family, cultural values, etc.) to help them work through their relationship problems that occur due to stressful work and family experiences. Couples should be encouraged to approach their respective employers about making family-friendly changes in their policies. Sometimes, just working out a flexible schedule will go a long way toward smoothing out the families' rough edges.

SINGLE-PARENT HOUSEHOLDS

The term *single-parent households* is preferred to *single-parent families* because it avoids the exclusion of the noncustodial parent, which the latter term tends to imply (Amato, 2000). For the sake of discussion, single-parent households include parents who are widowed, divorced, and never married. The number of single-parent households is increasing, not only due to divorce, but also due to the increased numbers of affluent, never-married career women, either having their own children or adopting (Gottfried & Gottfried, 1996; Okun, 1996). Twenty-five percent of the children in the United States live in single-parent households, and of those, 37 percent have divorced parents and 36 percent have parents who were never married (Saluter, 1996). Nearly 12 percent of all families are headed by a single woman, and 4 percent are headed by a single man (U.S. Census Bureau, 2001–2002). The racial breakdown for single-parent households is telling. Twenty-two percent of white families have a one-parent head of household, 29 percent of Hispanic homes are headed by one parent, and 56 percent of African American households have a single parent heading them (U.S. Census Bureau, 2001–2002).

Traditionally, single-parent households were considered "broken homes" and the children were believed to be damaged by having only one parent in the home. Research has shown that this is a myth. The truth is that the difficulties encountered by single parents have more to do with socioeconomic status than with the number of parents the child has at home. When poverty is factored out, researchers have found that children from single-parent households have no more problems adjusting than those from two-parent households (Anderson, 1999).

Challenges for Single-Parent Households

Single-parent households are not without significant concerns. The most common concerns include child care, role overload, financial strain, and negative perceptions of society. Child care for single, working parents needs to be reliable and flexible. Finding such child care can be elusive, which means that single parents must develop a primary support system that can assist with child care as well as provide social support and adult connections (Jackson, 1993). Female-headed single families are prone to be more vulnerable to financial strain than their male counterparts. Women typically earn less than men and use more of their time for child care and other nonpaid labor, making it difficult for them to increase their income by working longer hours, getting a second job, or training for a better, higher-paying job.

It may seem reasonable to expect that in the twenty-first century, societal taboos against single parenting would be a distant memory, but this is not the case. Single parents are still the victims of stereotypes and bias (Anderson, 1999; Goldenberg & Goldenberg, 1994). The commonly held stereotype of a single parent is of a young, unwed, African American woman living on welfare with several children under the age of five. The assumption is that she is lazy and, rather than find employment, she will just have more babies. Also, the children of such families are assumed to be juvenile offenders and dangerous to society. Bias regarding single-parent households is often based on these negative stereotypes, and society is reluctant to provide financial assistance or other types of support for them.

Divorce

Divorce accounts for most of the increase in single-parent households over the past 20 years. On the scale of stressful life events, divorce is ranked at the top of the list (Ahrons, 1999). The trauma of divorce may go on for months and years, even though the divorce decree has a day and date. Divorce lowers the income for both parents; however, mothers typically take longer than fathers to recover from the financial effects of divorce, and households led by women likely experience greater hardships and are more likely to be poor. Often when divorce occurs after the children have grown, women find themselves with limited income and no retirement (Ahrons, 1999). Single-father households have different problems. They may have more money than female-headed households, but the drop in income may be more pronounced because they typically must buy housekeeping and child-care services.

Women who held part-time work or who were stay-at-home mothers while they were married are likely to struggle with finding work and shouldering the burden for keeping a job to support the family. The older the woman is, the more difficulty she may have and the more desperate she may feel. Women who have been employed full time and have children may find it necessary to seek better jobs to compensate for lost income.

The divorce process is a highly emotional one, and the anger, despair, anxiety, loneliness, and helplessness that each person experiences is likely to affect his or her job performance (Carter & McGoldrick, 1999a). Employers are also challenged to have patience to adjust to the change in the availability of their employees who are attempting to survive this process.

Counseling for the Single-Parent Household

The fact that society tends to frown on single-parent households is not one that is exclusive to the general public. Because of the high percentage of single-parent households among African Americans, the bias is often twofold, involving both race and family configuration. Counselors must be willing to explore their own biases toward these families and work with supervisors and other counselors to overcome any biases that they may have. Acceptance of the client is the first priority.

Counseling the newly divorced client is a very challenging task, and the client will need to seek counseling just to work on divorce issues. Career counselors may focus on work-related stressors of the newly divorced and the single-parent head of household. The most important task is to help parents develop a sense of confidence in their abilities as parents and workers. They will need to develop problem-solving skills and learn to draw on existing supports and develop new ones. Since money is an overriding problem in many single-parent households, counselors may want to focus on debt management skills and work with the client on the depression and hopelessness that often accompanies money worries. Equally important is helping the newly single parent assess his or her ability to prepare for crises such as his or her illness or death.

FAMILIES HEADED BY GAYS AND LESBIANS

Although gays and lesbians are more visible than ever in our society, acceptance of the lifestyle of gays and lesbians has been slow in coming. Only after gay rights advocates have challenged discriminatory practices and laws have gays and lesbians been able to improve their lives and reduce some of the risks of "coming out of the closet" (Goldenberg & Goldenberg, 1994). However, hostility and discrimination against gays and lesbians is still socially acceptable (Gysbers et al., 1998). Lack of acceptance from the larger society colors all experiences of gay and lesbian couples and families. To begin with, joining together as a couple is complicated by each partner's level of disclosure of his or her sexuality. One partner may be completely open about his or her sexual orientation at work and with family members, yet the other may not have revealed his or her sexual orientation to anyone. Typically, if couples cohabitate, they will reveal their sexual orientation to some extent. However, because gays and lesbians are still discriminated against at the workplace, many will stay closeted to coworkers and employers. Those who are "out" at work risk harassment or dismissal from their jobs. Furthermore, on becoming a couple, gays and lesbians are prohibited from getting married in most states. Without marriage, they are deprived of spousal privileges ranging from family insurance coverage to spousal considerations in job relocation. In the case of those who are not out at work, employers may perceive them to be unmarried and expect a greater commitment to the job than the heterosexual married employees (Johnson & Colucci, 1999).

Parenting Issues

Parenting for lesbian and gay couples occurs in a number of ways: (a) children from a previous heterosexual marriage or relationship, (b) artificial insemination, (c) surrogate mothers, or (d) adoption. Regardless of how they become parents, nonbiological parents must safeguard their parental rights legally. It is not always a given that lesbians and gays can depend on their family of origin to support their relationship with their partners or their children. Original families of gays and lesbians have varying levels of support, which is reflective of homophobia in the general society. The parents of gays and lesbians often do not know how to handle grandchildren and partners of these unions. Though societal bias against lesbian motherhood has led the general public to believe that children of lesbian parents are damaged from the experience, research has shown that children of lesbians develop as normally as children of heterosexual parents (Patterson, 1996). As a result of the unpredictable nature of familial assistance, it is not uncommon for gays and lesbians to garner support from a network of close friends. Weston (1991) refers to this network as the chosen family.

Most gay and lesbian couples are dual-earner or dual-career couples and tend to be committed to their work and their relationships (Eldridge & Gilbert, 1990). They share problems of child care, role conflict, and spillover with heterosexual dual-career couples, but their gender-role restrictions differ. While heterosexual couples haggle over gender-appropriate tasks at home, lesbian and gay couples are more likely to share household duties equally. The gender differences that have been found are the differences between lesbians and gay males. Lesbians tend to strive for equality in their relationships more than gay male couples (Blumstein & Schwartz, 1983). Other work-related issues that gay and lesbian couples must contend with are work discrimination and fear of being outed or fired.

Counseling Gay and Lesbian Couples and Families

The most challenging problem for counselors of gay and lesbian clients is the counselor's own homophobia. Research has shown that a large percentage of counselors are homophobic, and before they can be successful with their gay and lesbian clients, they need to be free of this prejudice. The most challenging problem for gays and lesbians as individuals and couples is "coming out." Counselors can assist the couple in this process and help them to accept each other's current stage. Counselors can also assist gays and lesbians in finding support networks and groups that will help them along the way. Networks can also be helpful in locating employers who are safe and friendly to gays and lesbians. If that fails, clients will also need to learn strategies for coping with discrimination and hostility in the workplace.

OTHER CHALLENGES AFFECTING FAMILIES AND WORK

Unemployment

Unemployment, underemployment, and low-paying unskilled and semiskilled jobs all contribute to a family's financial distress. Though the unemployment figures have declined in recent years, they only reflect those individuals who are eligible for benefits and are actively seeking employment. The growth of homeless families may tell more about the true unemployment level in the United States. Economic uncertainty has plagued the country in recent years and has had devastating effects on many families. Unemployment affects all the family types discussed so far. A 1996 *New York Times* poll reported that 75 percent of families in the United States had encountered layoffs between 1980 and 1996 (Uchitelle & Kleinfield, 1996). Traditionally, unemployment was experienced by low-level employees, those involved in seasonal work, and part-time workers, most of whom were ethnic minorities. However, in the last 15 years, companies have been downsizing to compensate for the fluctuating economy, and for the first time, the white middle class has experienced layoffs in large numbers. Even so, the racial breakdown of the unemployed is not evenly distributed. The 2001 unemployment figures for all races was 4.8 percent. When race is factored in, this amounted to 4.2 percent of whites, 6.6 percent of Hispanics, and 8.7 percent of African Americans (U.S. Census Bureau, 2001–2002).

Counselors can help clients with feelings of anger at the employer and themselves, their feelings of loss and shame, and doubt in their abilities, all of which accompany job termination. They need to help clients focus on solutions rather than on their loss. Counselors can help the client to develop job-search strategies that might improve the chances for finding a new position. Families cope with unemployment in a variety of ways, but they should start by cutting back on buying luxuries and by soliciting assistance from family and friends.

Once the crisis issues have been addressed, the counselor might want to discuss finance issues with clients for future planning. Various personal finance books have recently highlighted that one of the greatest gifts a family can offer the next generation is to educate its youngsters about money matters. Families should have age-appropriate discussions about such issues as wills, living wills, inheritance, investment, loans, taxes, and family finances. It can be as simple as having children spend 80 percent of money they earn, give 10 percent to the community (nonprofits or the church, etc.), and save 10 percent.

Poverty

One of the most far-reaching and disturbing trends in the United States is the poverty of its people (Rank, 2000). In 2000, 15 percent of the total population lived below the poverty line (which is adjusted every year based on a number of factors). Again, African Americans had the highest percentage of poor, at 22 percent, while 21.2 percent of Hispanic families were below the poverty level, as were 10.7 percent of whites. The number of families with children who lived in poverty was even higher: 12.3 percent of white families, 27 percent of Hispanic families, and 30 percent of African American families had incomes below the poverty level.

The gap between those who are affluent and those who are struggling to survive is steadily increasing and difficult to ignore. While the middle and upper classes tend to dismiss and rebuke those who are on welfare, arguments of laziness and fraud cannot be applied to the plight of the working poor. These are individuals who are employed in low-wage, low-security jobs that do not supply sufficient income to raise the family's income over the poverty level. They struggle to meet even the most basic family needs of food, clothing, and shelter, and health care is nonexistent for them. Often they must sacrifice meeting one need in favor of another. Today, the working poor are getting publicity because they defy the American work ethic that if you work hard, you will get ahead. These families work hard yet have little to show for it. Many would not think of welfare as an alternative, but welfare is the one way that many single-parent households can keep food on the table. The early reports on welfare reform are encouraging. It seems that poor families were able to raise their family income a fraction higher, and many were able to leave welfare. However, some of these families have not moved out of poverty, they have simply moved off the welfare lists. One of the saddest results of the increasing large population of working poor is that they often are not covered by health insurance at the jobs they are able to secure. Recent studies have shown that those who do not have health insurance often pay two to four times the price insured clients pay for hospital services.

Homelessness

Lindsey (1994) states that extreme poverty resulting from reduced requirements for unskilled workers is responsible for homelessness in the United States. Due to the reduction in welfare payments, the scarcity of low-income housing, and increases in housing costs, unemployment and even welfare can deteriorate into homelessness. Families with children are the fastest growing group of homeless people in the country today (Mihaly, 1991). Most of those families (80 percent) are headed by single women, who typically have inconsistent work histories (Reyes & Waxman, 1989). In fact, Burt and Cohen (1989) found that 50 percent of the homeless mothers they studied had been jobless for more than 2 years, with an average jobless time span of 46 months. Substance abuse and psychiatric histories among homeless mothers are similar to those of homeless persons generally, but many homeless mothers have been abused sexually and physically. Besides joblessness, other reasons for homelessness include leaving abusive relationships, moving from condemned and fire-damaged buildings or buildings used for drug sales, or being asked to leave by friends or relatives who had housed them.

Counseling poor and homeless clients may often require crisis intervention strategies, depending on how dire the client's circumstances. The homeless client will need to find shelter and a job that pays enough to pay for housing. Poor clients may need to explore more ways to increase their income. It is imperative that counselors focus on the strengths and resourcefulness of their clients and explore each client's extended network of support (family, church, etc.). As with the unemployed, the counselor's knowledge of the labor market and employment opportunities is essential for these clients. Equally as important is the counselor's involvement in advocacy for the poor and homeless. The most effective way to assist the poor is to change the system that is designed to support them.

Violence

Family violence is a disturbing problem that endangers the lives of the elderly, children, and, usually, their mothers. Because of the physical harm that is inflicted on family members, it is reasonable to assume that the violence involves aggression to some extent but involves power even more (McGoldrick, Broken Nose, & Potenza

1999). The stronger family members assert their power over the weakest. Therefore, greatest violence is usually against children and includes physical abuse and neglect as well as sexual abuse (Gelles, 1994; McGoldrick et al., 1999). Abuse and neglect of the elderly is a disturbing trend because the elderly population is growing and their lack of resources necessitates that they live with relatives, putting them at greater risk for abuse. Researchers estimate that 20 to 40 percent of all homicides are the result of intrafamily violence (Gelles, 1994). Other consequences that result from family violence are that abused children are more likely to commit violent crimes and abuse drugs and that abused spouses have higher rates of anxiety, depression, and suicide (Gelles, 1994).

The family violence that receives the greatest media attention is spousal or partner abuse, which is as prevalent in gay and lesbian relationships as it is in heterosexual relationships (McGoldrick et al.; Potenza, 1999). The victims of the abuse lose days from work to recover, report to court, and interact with social service agencies. Partners who are abusive tend to exert their power and control in other ways as well. They will attempt to keep their partner from gaining independence by getting a job, have complete control of the family income, and make all the major decisions about the family.

Counseling families that have suffered from violence often takes the form of crisis intervention. Since the victims of abuse hold family secrets and because society has been known to blame the victim, it is important for counselors to be accepting and supportive of their clients. Knowing that violence is an abuse of power will help counselors to work with their clients from abusive homes. McGoldrick et al. (1999) recommend that rather than focusing only on the victims of the abuse, counselors should become active in communities to help stop violence and challenge the values in our society that allow violence to continue.

OVERALL COUNSELING STRATEGIES

Gysbers et al. (1998) suggest that counselors separate work and family problems into life roles, life settings, and life events and then identify underlying dynamics in family or work that affect the problem. They suggest 11 tasks for career counselors to complete for clients with issues involving the relationship between work and family. They range from helping clients to see the connection between family and work to helping them to turn frustrations into positive solutions. Hazard and Koslow (1992) suggested that counselors use family systems theory as well as a career-stage theory in their work with couples. What occurs in counseling will depend on each partner's career stage (apprenticeship, independence-specialization, interdependence-managerial, and director of organization) and the couple's family stage (early, middle, and late).

Strategies for career and lifestyle planning for couples and families overlap family-counseling and career-counseling specialty areas. Theories of family counseling and career counseling really do not adequately address the family-career connection. Clearly the counseling field needs more complex and comprehensive theories to accommodate today's families (Forrest, 1994). There are two models that have been proposed that have some promise in integrating these theories, those of Hansen (2001) and Gold, Rotter, and Evans (2002).

Hansen's integrative life-planning model takes a "holistic approach by encouraging people to connect various aspects of life" (Niles & Bowlsbey, 2002, p. 85). The assumptions of the model are (a) new ways of knowing about career development are needed because there have been so many changes in the nature of knowledge, and (b) an expanded view of career requires broader self-knowledge in addition to interests, abilities, and values, such as multiple roles, identities, and critical life tasks in diverse cultures. The integrative life-planning model is based on six career development tasks, which reflect social justice, social change, connectedness, diversity, and spirituality. They are:

1. Finding work that needs doing in a changing global context
2. Weaving our lives into a meaningful whole
3. Connecting family and work
4. Valuing pluralism
5. Managing personal transitions and organizational change
6. Exploring spirituality and life purposes

The model is designed to help, not only individuals, but also partners and families, in their exploration of the way the various priorities in their lives fit together and in developing an awareness of how life choices and decisions are affected by the changing contexts of our lives.

Gold and colleagues (2002) introduced the out of the box (OTB) model for synthesizing family, culture, and career counseling. Rather than a theoretical model, it is a practice model that is designed to get counseling practitioners to see the importance of family, culture, and career issues in their clients' lives, giving each of these areas equal attention in assessing the client's problem and then focusing on the issue of the greatest importance to the client when counseling is started.

The OTB model has the following assumptions: (a) the notion that there is one truth for all people is not feasible, (b) the stories of families and cultural groups explain the common social reality imprinted on individuals, (c) the building blocks of an individual's worldview are his or her family and cultural stories, (d) the individual's personal worldview is confirmed or amended through interaction with family and significant others, (e) individuals develop their own stories through their own experiences while incorporating family and cultural group stories into their own reality, (f) the individual's story reveals the person's knowledge of self, symbols, and meanings that the individual values about the world and makes meaning of the individual's life, and (g) it is imperative, therefore, from a conceptual and interventional perspective, that counseling reflect narrative approaches to helping. The OTB model was designed to help counselors help their clients tell the whole of their stories and encouraged clients to reauthor their stories to overcome the pressures of society. As a process of finding a "truer" career and life direction, one begins to connect with one's true career dreams, values, beliefs, and commitments. Table 13.2 describes the process for using the OTB model with clients.

TABLE 13.2   The Counseling Process for the Out of the Box Model

Step 1 Counselors determine how well they understand the client's worldview.	a. Counselors assess client problem from multiple perspectives. b. Counselors listen for client priorities with an open mind. c. Counselors become aware of client's lifestyle focal point.
Step 2 Counselors determine how their own cultural values and biases affect their approach to their client	a. Counselors are aware of their theoretical biases. b. Counselors are aware of their cultural biases. c. Counselors work on letting go of biases.
Step 3 Counselors evaluate the usefulness of their interventions.	a. Counselors base intervention on client's lifestyle focal point. b. Counselors move easily into the sphere of counseling that best fits the client's needs.

Source: Adapted from Gold, Rotter, & Evans (2002)

SUMMARY

The changing family dynamics in the United States along with changing work environments have made it evident that there is a significant relationship between family and work that needs to be addressed by counselors. There are countless configurations of families in this country, yet each is defined as a "family." The systems perspective of the family emphasizes circular causality. That is, individual members have an effect on the family, and as they change, the family changes. In addition, changes from larger systems have an effect on the family and thus change individuals in the family. Work influences the different configurations of families in different ways, and counselors need to keep those influences in mind when they work on family issues. In addition, poverty, violence, and unemployment can affect any family, and each of these issues cuts across all family configurations. Life planning for couples and families is a developing area for counselors, and although there are no comprehensive theories available at this time, work is being done to fill the void. The following Websites provide additional information relating to this chapter's topics.

USEFUL WEBSITES

http://ncda.org
National Career Development Association
www.iamfc.com
International Association of Marriage and Family Counselors

www.aglbic.org

Association for Gay, Lesbian, and Bisexual Issues in Counseling

http://npin

National Parent Information Network

www.amcd-aca.org

Association for Multicultural Counseling and Development

www.familyresource.com

Family Resource.com

www.ncfr.org

National Council on Family Relations

REFERENCES

Ahrons, C. R. (1999). Divorce: An unscheduled family transition. In B. Carter & M. McGoldrick (Eds.), *The expanded family life cycle: Individual, family, and social perspectives* (pp. 381–398). Boston: Allyn & Bacon.

Amato, P. R. (2000). Diversity within single-parent families. In D. H. Demo, K. R. Allen, & M. A. Fine (Eds.), *Handbook of family diversity* (pp. 149–172). New York: Oxford University Press.

Anderson, C. J. (1999). Single-parent families: Strengths, vulnerabilities, and interventions. In B. Carter & M. McGoldrick (Eds.), *The expanded family life cycle: Individual, family, and social perspectives* (pp. 399–416). Boston: Allyn & Bacon.

Barber, B. L., & Eccles, J. S. (1992). Long-term influence of divorce and single parenting on adolescent family- and work-related values, behaviors, and aspirations. *Psychological Bulletin, 111*, 108–126.

Barnett, R. C. (1994). Home-to-work spillover revisited: A study of full-time employed women in dual-earner couples. *Journal of Marriage and the Family, 56*, 647–656.

Becker, P. E., & Moen, P. (1999). Scaling back: Dual-earner couples' family strategies. *Journal of Marriage and the Family, 61*, 995–1007.

Billingsley, A. (1992). *Climbing Jacob's ladder: The enduring legacy of African-American families*. New York: Simon & Schuster.

Blumstein, P., & Schwartz, P. (1983). *American couples: Money, work, and sex*. New York: Morrow.

Blustein, D. L. (2001). The interface of work and relationships: Critical knowledge for 21st century psychology. *The Counseling Psychologist, 29*, 179–192.

Brines, J. (1994). Economic dependency, gender, and the division of labor at home. *American Journal of Sociology, 100*, 652–688.

Burke, R. J. (1996). Work experiences, stress and health among managerial and professional women. In M. J. Schabracq, J. A. M. Winnubst, & C. L. Cooper (Eds.), *Handbook of work and health psychology* (pp. 259–278). New York: Wiley.

Burt, M. R., & Cohen, B. E. (1989). Differences among homeless single women, women with children, and single men. *Social Problems, 36*, 508–524.

Carter, B. & McGoldrick, M. (1999a). The divorce cycle: A major variation in the American family life cycle. In B. Carter & M. McGoldrick (Eds.), *The expanded family life cycle: Individual, family, and social perspectives* (3rd ed., pp. 373–380). Boston: Allyn & Bacon.

Carter, B., & McGoldrick, M. (1999b). *The expanded family life cycle: Individual, family, and social perspectives* (3rd ed.). Boston: Allyn & Bacon.

Cooper, S. E., Arkkelin, D. L., & Tielbert, M. J. (1994). Work-relationship values and gender role differences in relation to career-marriage aspirations. *Journal of Counseling and Development, 73,* 63–68.

Dawis, R. V., & Lofquist, L. H. (1984). *A psychological theory of work adjustment.* Minneapolis: University of Minnesota Press.

Duxbury, L., & Higgins, C. (1994). Interference between work and family: A status report on dual-career and dual-earner mothers and fathers. *Employee Assistance Quarterly, 9,* 55–80.

Eldridge, N. S., & Gilbert, L. A. (1990). Correlates of relationship satisfaction in lesbian couples. *Psychology of Women Quarterly, 14,* 43–62.

Evans, K. M., & Rotter, J. C. (2000). Multicultural family approaches to career counseling. *The Family Journal: Counseling and Therapy for Couples and Families, 8,* 67–71.

Forrest, L. (1994). Career assessment for couples. *Journal of Employment Counseling, 31,* 168–187.

Fulmer, R. (1999). Becoming an adult: Leaving home and staying connected. In B. Carter & M. McGoldrick (Eds.), *The expanded family life cycle: Individual, family, and social perspectives* (pp. 215–230). Boston: Allyn & Bacon.

Gelles, R. J. (1994). Family violence, abuse and neglect. In P. C. McKenry & S. J. Price (Eds), *Families and change: Coping with stressful events* (pp. 262–280). Thousand Oaks, CA: Sage.

Gilbert, L A. (1985). *Men in dual-career families: Current realities and future prospects.* Hillsdale, NJ: Erlbaum.

Gold, J. M., Rotter, J. C., & Evans, K. M. (2002). Out of the box: A model for the twenty-first century. In K. M. Evans, J. C. Rotter, & J. M. Gold (Eds.), *Synthesizing family culture and career: A model for counseling in the twenty-first century* (pp. 3–15). Alexandria, VA: ACA.

Goldenberg, H., & Goldenberg, I. (1994). Counseling today's families (2nd ed.). Pacific Grove, CA: Brooks/Cole.

Gottfredson, L. S. (1981). Circumscription and compromise: A developmental theory of occupational aspirations. *Journal of Counseling Psychology, 28,* 545–579.

Gottfried, A., & Gottfried, A. (1996). A longitudinal study of academic intrinsic motivation in intellectually gifted children: Childhood through early adolescence. *Gifted Child Quarterly, 40,* 179–183.

Gysbers, N. C., Heppner, M. J., & Johnston, J. A. (1998). *Career counseling: Process, issues, and techniques.* Boston: Allyn & Bacon.

Hansen, L. S. (2001). Integrating work, family and community through holistic life planning, *Career Development Quarterly, 49,* 261–274.

Hazard, L., & Koslow, D. (1992). Conjoint career counseling: Counseling dual-career couples. In H. D. Lea & Z. B. Leibowitz (Eds.), *Adult career development: Concepts, issues, and practices* (pp. 218–233). Alexandria, VA: National Career Development Association.

Hines, P. M. (1999). The family life cycle of African American families living in poverty. In B. Carter & M. McGoldrick (Eds.), *The expanded family life cycle: Individual, family, and social perspectives* (pp. 327–345). Boston: Allyn & Bacon.

Hines, P. M., Preto, N. G., McGoldrick, M., Almeida, R., & Welman, S. (1999). Culture and the family life cycle. In B. Carter & M. McGoldrick (Eds.), *The expanded family life cycle: Individual, family, and social perspectives* (pp. 69–87). Boston: Allyn & Bacon.

Imber-Black, E. (1999). Creating meaningful rituals for new life cycle transitions. In B. Carter & M. McGoldrick (Eds.), *The expanded family life cycle: Individual, family, and social perspectives* (pp. 202–214). Boston: Allyn & Bacon.

Ivey, A. E., D'Andrea, M., Ivey, M. B., & Simek-Morgan, L. (2002). *Theories of Counseling and Psychotherapy: A Multicultural Perspective.* Boston: Allyn and Bacon.

Jackson, A. P. (1993). Black, single, working mothers in poverty: Preferences for employment, well-being, and perceptions of preschool-age children. *Social Work, 38,* 26–34.

Johnson, T. W., & Colucci, P. (1999). Lesbians, gay men and the family life cycle. In B. Carter & M. McGoldrick (Eds.), *The expanded family life cycle: Individual, family, and social perspectives* (pp. 346–361). Boston: Allyn & Bacon.

Lindsey, E. W. (1994). Homelessness. In P. C. McKenry & S. J. Price (Eds.)., *Families and change: Coping with stressful events* (pp. 281–302). Thousand Oaks, CA: Sage.

Loscocco, K. A. (1997). Work-family linkages among self-employed women and men. *Journal of Vocational Behavior, 50,* 204–226.

Mackey, W. C. (1995). U.S. fathering behaviors within cross-cultural context: An evaluation by an alternate benchmark. *Journal of Comparative Family Studies, 26,* 443–458.

McGoldrick, M. (1999). Women and the family life cycle. In B. Carter & M. McGoldrick (Eds.), *The expanded family life cycle: Individual, family, and social perspectives* (pp. 106–123). Boston: Allyn & Bacon.

McGoldrick, M., Broken Nose, M. A., & Potenza, M. (1999). Violence and the family life cycle. In B. Carter & M. McGoldrick (Eds.), *The expanded family life cycle: Individual, family, and social perspectives* (pp. 470–491). Boston: Allyn & Bacon.

McLanahan, S. S., & Booth, K. (1989). Mother-only families: Problems, prospects, and policies. *Journal of Marriage and the Family, 51,* 557–580.

Mihaly, L. (1991). Beyond the numbers: Homeless families with children. In J. H. Kryder-Coe, L. M. Salamon, & J. M. Molnar (Eds.), *Homeless children and youth: A new American dilemma* (pp. 11–32). New Brunswick, NJ: Transaction.

Niles, S. G. & Bowlsbey, J. (2002). *Career Development Interventions in the 21ˢᵗ Century.* Columbus, OH: Merrill Prentice Hall.

Okun, B. F. (1996). *Understanding diverse families: What practitioners need to know.* New York: Guilford Press.

Paniagua, F. A (1996). Cross-cultural guidelines in family therapy practice. *The Family Journal: Counseling and Therapy for Couples and Families, 4,* 127–138.

Patterson, C. (1996). Lesbian mothers and their children. In J. Laird & R. Green (Eds.), *Lesbians and gays in couples and families: A handbook for therapists* (pp. 420–437). San Francisco: Jossey-Bass.

Peterson, N., & Gonzalez, R. C. (2000). *The role of work in people's lives: Applied career counseling and vocational psychology.* Belmont, CA: Brooks/Cole-Wadsworth/Thompson Learning.

Rank, M. R (2000). Poverty and economic hardship in families. In D. H. Demo, K. R. Allen, & M. A. Fine (Eds.), *Handbook of family diversity* (pp. 293–315). New York: Oxford University Press.

Reyes, L. M., & Waxman, L. D. (1989). *A status report on hunger and homelessness in America's cities: 1989: A 27-city survey.* Washington, DC: U.S. Conference of Mayors.

Rhodes, A. R. (2002). Long-distance relationships in dual-career couples: A review of counseling issues. *The Family Journal: Counseling and Therapy for Couples and Families, 10,* 398–404.

Risman, B. J., Atkinson, M. P., & Blackwelder, S. P. (1999). Understanding the juggling act: Gendered preferences and social structural constraints. *Sociological Forum, 14,* 319–344.

Saluter, A. (1996). *Marital status and living arrangements, March 1995* (Current Population Reports P20-49). Washington, DC: U.S. Department of the Census.

Schneer, J. A., & Reitan, F. (1993). Effects of alternate family structures on managerial career paths. *Academy of Management Journal, 36,* 830–843.

Sciarra, D. T. (1999). *Multiculturalism in counseling.* Itasca, IL: F. E. Peacock.

Silberstein, L. R. (1992). *Dual-career marriage: A system in transition.* Hillsdale, NJ: Erlbaum.

Stohs, J. H. (1995). Predictors of conflict over the household division of labor among women employed full-time. *Sex Roles, 33,* 257–275.

Super, D. E. (1992). Toward a comprehensive theory of career development. In D. H. Montross & C. J. Shinkman (Eds.), *Career Development: Theory and Practice* (pp. 35–64). Springfield, IL: Charles C. Thomas.

U.S. Census Bureau. (2001–2002). *Statistical abstract of the United States.* Retrieved November 13, 2003, from http://www.census.gov/prod/www/statistical-abstract-02.html

Uchitelle, L., & Kleinfield, N. R. (1996, March 3). On the battlefields of business, millions of casualties. *New York Times.*

Von Bertalanffy, L. (1968). *General systems theory: Foundation, development, application.* New York: George Braziller.

Weston, K. (1991). *Families we choose: Lesbians, gays, kinship.* New York: Gardner.

Wiener, N. (1948). *Cybernetics, or control and communication in the animal and the machine.* Cambridge, MA: Technology Press.

Weiss, R. S. (1984). The impact of marital dissolution on income and consumption in single-parent households. *Journal of Marriage and the Family, 46,* 115–127.

Zedeck, S., & Mosier, K. L. (1990). Work in the family and employing organizations. *American Psychologist, 45,* 240–251.

CAREER AND LIFESTYLE PLANNING WITH SPECIFIC POPULATIONS

In previous sections of this text, foundational background, skills and techniques, and contextual perspectives for career and lifestyle planning with clients were all presented to the reader. In Part IV, "Career and Lifestyle Planning with Specific Populations," the preceding information is applied to a number of specific populations with whom a career counselor may work. Each of these specific populations demands a unique combination of skill, knowledge, and experience from counselors engaged in career counseling.

The concept of "careers," as related to gender and valuing what is "male" and what is "female," provides an interesting and pertinent backdrop for Chapter 14, "Gender Issues in Career Counseling." This chapter examines the underlying causes of gender inequities in the world of work and describes problems that contemporary women and men encounter in their careers and occupations. Suggestions for gender-aware career counseling are offered. Case studies are presented to give readers an opportunity to apply the concepts and strategies that are discussed.

Chapter 15, "Career Counseling with Gay, Lesbian, Bisexual, and Transgender Clients," explores the career development of gay, lesbian, bisexual, and transgender (GLBT) persons across the life span. Institutional and demographic factors that facilitate or hinder career and lifestyle planning with these clients are discussed, as well as environmental influences such as state laws, workplace nondiscrimination policies, and the strength of GLBT communities, since these are phenomena that may be outside the typical scope of a career counselor's preparation. In addition to the discussion of other issues such as isolation, lack of role models, and mentorship, several case examples are used to assist career counselors to provide services to a diverse cross-section of individuals who have a minority sexual orientation or gender identity.

Chapter 16, "Career and Lifestyle Planning with Visibly Recognizable Racial and Ethnic minority Groups," touches upon the spectrum of attitudes and values regarding career and lifestyle planning in different cultures. Some discussion of the complexity of racial identity as it relates to career is provided, along with an analysis of how acculturation and assimilation affect individual and group career options, choices, and values. The career counselor's role as an advocate is also considered.

Counselors in every setting need to be prepared to help clients struggling with both their career development and addictive behaviors. Chapter 17, "Career Counseling for Clients with Addictive Behaviors," provides excellent guidelines and case examples for counseling clients simultaneously dealing with career and addictive concerns and presents a stages of change model that can be used in the counseling process.

CHAPTER 14

GENDER ISSUES IN CAREER COUNSELING

BARBARA RICHTER HERLIHY AND ZARUS E. WATSON

University of New Orleans

There has been "women's work" and "men's work" throughout most of human history, although the relative worth accorded them by society has not remained constant. A clear division of labor existed in societies of the Old Stone Age: men were the hunters and women were the gatherers of vegetables and grains. In these primitive clan societies, women had equal economic and social status with men because they contributed equally to the group's subsistence, as food gatherers and as bearers of the children who would ensure the clan's continued existence (Leavitt, 1971).

Gender equity began to erode with the dawn of the New Stone Age, along with agricultural advances and the domestication of animals. As a result of agricultural improvements and the rise of herding societies, women's contributions to the food supply grew less important and their economic value to society gradually diminished (Atkinson & Hackett, 2004). At that time, occupational gender equity was lost, and it has never been fully regained.

In the United States of the twenty-first century, occupational segregation still exists, with men and women being concentrated in different clusters of occupations. Women today are overrepresented in low-paying, low-status, "pink collar" jobs, while men dominate the ranks of the high-paying, high-status, upper echelons of corporate management. Wage discrimination based on gender has been against the law in the United States for more than 40 years, yet women earn an average of 76 cents for every dollar earned by men (U.S. Department of Labor, 2002).

This chapter examines the underlying causes of gender inequities in the world of work and describes problems that contemporary women and men encounter in their careers and occupations. Suggestions for gender-aware career counseling are offered, and two case studies are presented to give readers an opportunity to apply the concepts and strategies that have been discussed.

GENDER ROLE SOCIALIZATION

To understand the profound effect of gender on the occupational and career decision making of women and men, it is essential to recognize that gender is socially constructed. Gender is not synonymous with sex, which refers to biological differences. A considerable body of research has shown that biological differences between the sexes are few. Learned differences, however, are great. These learned differences are a result of *gender role socialization*, which is based on assumptions about women and men that have been conditioned into our thinking over multiple generations.

Gendered behaviors are learned from birth. From the beginning of life, boys and girls are socially supported and encouraged to develop very different characteristics and behaviors. This pervasive gender-role socialization is carried out, often unconsciously, by virtually every significant force in a child's life, including parents, teachers, peers, schools, and religious organizations. Stereotypical beliefs about what is "masculine" and "feminine" are reinforced in myriad ways, through language, clothing, toys, games, movies, books, gendered play experiences, and television and other mass media. Children's experiences with these influences form the foundation for complex cognitive schemas that they then use to organize the world into gendered categories. Over time, an individual's gender schemas become a powerful, unconscious mechanism for processing information (Bem, 1993).

Gender-role socialization has a cumulative effect on boys and girls, to which parents and teachers alike contribute by expecting boys to be more active and aggressive and girls to be more passive and dependent (Atkinson & Hackett, 2004; Basow, 1992; Doyle, 1983). Throughout their school years, boys are reinforced for competition, skill mastery, achievement, and ambition, while girls are reinforced for connectedness, nurturing, emotiveness, and cooperation (Gilligan, 1982; Niles & Harris-Bowlsby, 2002).

Even very young children have already acquired stereotypical views of masculinity and femininity and of the occupational choices open to each gender (Enns, 2000, 2004; Gilbert & Sher, 1999). Occupational stereotyping begins so early that two- and three-year-old children are able to identify gender-stereotyped occupations for women and men (Gettys & Cann, 1981). By the time children are six to eight years old, they have developed what Gottfredson (1996) has called their "tolerable sex type boundary," a set, narrow range of perceived occupational choices. Children's perceptions of acceptable career options for their gender become increasingly rigid from kindergarten to fourth grade (Matlin, 1996). As girls and boys mature, these socially conditioned occupational gender stereotypes become deeply engrained. They also interact in complex ways with other cultural variables that must be considered along with gender in order to understand the context in which people engage in the career and occupational planning processes.

Gender, Culture, and Individual Differences

Although gender has a powerful influence on occupational and career aspirations, it is not the only force that operates to shape people's occupational development. Race, ethnicity, social class, and culture are also extremely influential. All people have multiple cultural identities, and the relevance and importance of these identities vary according to the situation. In some contexts, gender is likely to be a highly salient cultural variable, while in other situations, it may have a secondary role. As an example, for a 50-year-old man who is contemplating a return to college to gain further education to make a career change, age may be a primary consideration. However, if he is thinking about a traditionally female-dominated occupation such as elementary school teaching, gender may have a more prominent role in his deliberations.

At the same time, it is important to keep in mind that individual differences play an equally crucial role. If gender and other cultural variables were the sole determinants of career choice, it would be difficult to explain how the two coauthors of this chapter made the same career choice to become counselor educators. One of us is male and African American and was reared in a middle-class home in an urban area in the southern United States. His family structure included two working parents. He was expected to attend college and earn a degree. College, though intimidating, was seen as almost the sole path to economic and social success both for him and for his family.

The other of us is female and was raised as white and upper middle class in the northeastern and midwestern regions of the United States. Her family structure was a traditional one in which the mother did not work outside the home and the father, a corporate executive, was the sole income provider. Although she was expected to attend college, she was not expected to persist and earn a degree. College was primarily a venue for ensuring that she would find a well-educated husband who would be a good provider.

That two such disparate sets of influences could converge at the same career choice is a testament to the complexity of the interactions among myriad factors in career decision making. Gender-role socialization is a powerful force, but it cannot be isolated from other aspects of identity, nor can individual differences be ignored.

Outcomes of Gender-Role Stereotyping

With an understanding of the pervasive influence of gender-role socialization, we can now look more closely at the effects of gender-role stereotyping on the occupational and career development of females and males. The consequences of gender-role stereotyping are profound. Girls and boys internalize societal messages regarding gender expectations, and as a result, their career decision-making processes are shaped while they are still very young. For girls, two of the most well-documented outcomes are math avoidance and lowered expectations for success. For boys, consequences that have lifelong effects include an intense need to compete and succeed and the development of a restricted emotionality.

Consequences for Girls.   One of the most devastating outcomes of gender-role stereotyping for female career attainment is *math avoidance* (Gysbers, Heppner, & Johnston, 1998). In elementary school, girls outperform boys on math tasks, report liking math more than boys, and believe they are better at math than boys (Boswell, 1985). By late high school, however, boys have gained a clear advantage in math skills.

There is evidence to suggest that, even though girls may enter high school with confidence in their math ability, teachers and other adult figures communicate a stereotyped belief that girls are not as competent as boys in this realm of learning (Welfel & Patterson, 2005). This strongly affects girls' willingness to pursue math-related careers (Greenberg-Lake, 1991).

Mathematics appears to be a "critical filter" (Betz, 1994, p. 22) that operates to narrow the career choices of females. Even when boys and girls enter college with enough high school math courses to pursue a science major, only one in five females does so, as compared to half of males (Betz). As Gysbers et al. (1998) pointed out, math will become an increasingly important prerequisite for high-paying, high-status jobs as our society continues to become more technologically advanced.

A second consequence for girls of growing up in a gendered context is that they learn to consistently underestimate their abilities and develop *lowered expectations of success*. Even when girls earn good grades in school, they get less attention and fewer comments about the intellectual quality of their work (Barnett & Rivers, 1996). By the time they enter college, they have lower expectations of success on exams (Matlin, 1996) and lower estimates of their present abilities and future success than males, even if their objective performance is actually higher (Meece, Parsons, Kaczala, Goff, & Futterman, 1982). These underestimates seem to be particularly true when women assess their ability to succeed in nontraditional careers. Because many fields that are nontraditional for women require math and science backgrounds, it becomes evident that the forces of gender stereotyping interact with each other to compound their impact.

Consequences for Boys.   Because theories of career development and normative work patterns were all developed from a male perspective, little attention has been paid to the effects on males of a gendered career decision-making context (Gysbers et al., 1998). Only recently has it been recognized that gender-role stereotyping takes a significant toll on boys as well as girls. From early childhood, boys are socialized to be *more aggressive and competitive* than girls. A clear example is the influence of sports as a major socializing experience for boys (Gysbers et al.; Skovholt, 1990). In football, basketball, baseball, wrestling, and other sports, there are winners and losers, and boys are taught to compete and win. Winning is perceived as necessary to maintain the masculine role (Smith & Inder, 1993). Therefore, when boys grow up, they translate the values of the sports field into the workplace and judge their success by their ability to compete, win, and acquire status. Of course, not every boy can win, and the outcome of failure often can be a diminished sense of self-worth.

Along with the expectation to compete and succeed comes a parallel societal message to boys that they must be tough and avoid showing weakness. Thus, adolescence becomes a time of *restricted emotionality* for boys, which results in a narrowing of their range of coping behaviors when faced with stressful situations (Gysbers et al., 1998) and can lead to stress-related health problems in adulthood. The fear of femininity, of being seen as weak or as a sissy, influences boys to avoid anything that might be considered feminine (Slattery, 2004). They internalize and come to avoid expressing feelings of grief, sadness, pain, or uncertainty because such expressions are perceived as unmanly

(Lindsey, 1990). Not only do they learn to avoid self-disclosing and admitting their vulnerabilities, they become reluctant to consider careers that are traditionally female dominated or to seek help, including career guidance (Rochlen & O'Brien, 2002). This culturally maintained "walling off" of emotions can result in difficulties with intimate relationships and with being full partners in raising children (Welfel & Patterson, 2005).

Gender Differences in Career Decision Making

By young adulthood, when choosing an occupation or career is a major life task, the influence of the deeply embedded gender-role socialization of males and females is so profound that there are marked differences in their career decision-making processes (Gilligan, 1982). The pattern that is more characteristic of women's decision making is contextual and embedded in relationships with others. Women often make decisions based on relationship and connectedness, considering the effects of their decisions on others. With respect to occupational and career development, women's decisions have been described as *dichotomous* (Jackson & Scharman, 2002). Women are socialized to perform the primary family role of nurturer and caregiver. This role is expressed through interactions within the family. Thus, women's perspective is that family and career do not run parallel with each other; rather, they conflict. When women frame their career issues in this dichotomous way, they are forced to choose between family and career, or they may lower their career aspirations to maintain a balance between the two responsibilities. Women tend to assign lower importance to the centrality of work in their lives than do men (Harpaz & Fu, 1997).

While women tend to emphasize relatedness, the pattern more characteristic of men is based on separation, logic, and individuality. The isolated decision presented to men is quite different from the dichotomous choice presented to women. Male gender-role socialization has taught men that their identity is defined primarily through work (Skovholt, 1990). Historically, men were socialized to be the family's financial provider, or breadwinner, a role expressed through career endeavors. Thus, men's family and career obligations ran parallel and were *synchronous* with each other, rather than in competing positions. Career decision making simultaneously fulfilled both family and career imperatives for men. Today, however, there is increasing recognition that men pay a price for working long hours and expending so much of their energy in fulfilling the breadwinner role. They may become isolated from the family and come to resent their peripheral status. Thus, men's decisions have become more dichotomous, too, in that success in the work role may compete with meaningful involvement in family life.

These decision-making patterns have deleterious effects on both women and men: the perceived dichotomy forces women to make career compromises in order to fulfill their nurturing roles, while the isolated decision making experienced by many men places them under tremendous pressure to succeed in their careers, often at the expense of family inclusion. In addition, external reality operates to reinforce stereotypical perceptions of occupational choice. The world of work does not present the same opportunities to men and to women.

THE GENDERED WORKPLACE

This section of the chapter explores gender-based issues inherent in the world of work, including occupational segregation, the earnings gap between the sexes, and barriers to women's advancement. Each of these issues affects both women and men, although women generally bear the brunt of the associated costs.

Occupational Segregation

Women and men tend to be concentrated in different clusters of occupations (Moen, 1992). Men are overrepresented in craft, laborer, and senior executive jobs in corporations, while women are overrepresented in clerical, sales, and services jobs (Herz & Wootton, 1996; Maume, 1999; Moen). Some traditionally masculine jobs are physician (especially surgeon), math/science careers, electrician, plumber, and teamster. Traditionally female jobs are almost always lower paying and lower status, *"pink collar"* (Howe, 1977) jobs such as beautician, secretary, social worker, nurse, elementary school teacher, child-care worker, and waitress. The gender disparities in many of these stereotyped job categories are distinct: only 10 percent of engineers and 2 percent of electricians are women. In 1998, 84 percent of elementary school teachers were women, but the majority of school administrators were male (U.S. Department of Labor, 2002). Although women have made inroads into some traditionally male-dominated occupations such as accountant or police officer, jobs that have been traditionally female-dominated have tended to remain segregated. For instance, the Bureau of Labor Statistics reported that in 1983, about 99 percent of secretaries were female; in 1995 the percentage was still 99 percent (U.S. Department of Labor, 1995).

Occupational segregation has become further entrenched as the United States has moved toward a service economy (the vast majority of workers—between 80 and 92 percent—are now in the service sector) and as more women with young children have entered the workforce. Along with the growth of the service economy, the number of part-time and temporary jobs (more than two-thirds of which are held by women) has increased significantly. Employers recruit this "contingent workforce" because it is less costly. This situation creates a double bind for women: part-time jobs offer the flexibility to better manage home and work responsibilities, but they also tend to be low-wage positions with little or no opportunity for advancement and few fringe benefits. The proliferation of mothers of young children in the workforce also has led to an increased need for child-care workers, restaurant workers, and sales clerks to staff expanded retail business hours, all of which are low-paying, "female" occupations (Moen, 1992). This situation, in which low-paying jobs generate more low-paying jobs, has produced what has been called the "occupational ghetto" (Reskin & Hartmann, 1986).

These occupational disparities are not due to a "natural" inclination of women and men toward certain types of occupations, although occupational segregation is often justified on the basis of women's and men's different strengths or as a result of "choices" they have made. Occupations that are stereotypically viewed in our society as male or female can in fact be gender equitable. For example, in the United States, only 3 percent of all full-time university faculty in physics are women, while in Hungary almost half (47 percent) are women (Hyde, 1997).

The Earnings Gap

In the United States, the overwhelming majority (nearly 99 percent) of women will work for pay at some time in their lives (Betz, 1994; Costello & Stone, 2001; U.S. Department of Labor, 1995). Most work out of economic need. Levels of workforce participation often have been higher for women of color than for white women. For many women of color, the need to balance personal and work lives is a "given" (Atkinson & Hackett, 2004). Their income is especially important to the family because African American and Latino men earn less than white men (U.S. Department of Labor, 1995).

Wage discrimination based on gender has been against the law for more than 40 years. The Equal Pay Act of 1963 prohibits employers from paying women less than men for substantially equal work. Title VII of the Civil Rights Act of 1964 prohibits paying women less than men even when their jobs are different if the reason for the pay difference is gender. Title VII also prohibits discrimination against women in hiring, promotion, training, and discipline and makes sexual harassment against women workers illegal (www.aflcio.org/yourjobeconomy/women). Despite the existence of these laws, women still do not receive equal pay for equal or similar work. In 2002, women earned, on average, 76 cents for every dollar earned by men. When race or ethnicity is factored in, the disparity is even greater: African American women in 2001 were earning 67 cents and Latina women were earning 56 cents for every dollar earned by white men (U.S. Census Bureau, 2002). In the two decades between 1978 and 1998, the earnings gap between men and women narrowed by 15 percent, but it has been pointed out that the narrowing of the gap had more to do with men's real wages declining than with improvements in women's circumstances (Costello & Stone, 2001).

The median salary for men in 2000 was approximately $37,000, while for women it was just over $28,000 (U.S. Department of Labor, 2002). This difference can be explained in large measure by occupational segregation by gender. The earnings gap is wider in traditionally female occupational categories; managerial and professional women earn 76 percent of what men in those occupations earn, but they earn only 60 percent of what men earn in sales occupations. Men earn more than women even in female-dominated occupations (Whittock, Edwards, McLaren, & Robinson, 2002).

Barriers to Advancement for Women

Gender discrimination in the workplace often occurs when a woman is hired for a job. "The inequality of level and compensation experiences between women and men is early written in stone, because comparable male and female candidates enter the field at different levels" (Canning & Kaltreider, 1997, p. 246). When married women interview for jobs, they may be perceived as having less economic need for a position and as unlikely to be geographically mobile. They may be offered a lower starting salary than men hired into comparable positions, a practice that persists in part because many women are reluctant or unprepared to negotiate wages (Canning & Kaltreider). Rather, they focus on getting hired and then expect to be promoted when they prove themselves (Hymowitz, 2004).

Once hired, women are penalized in their career trajectories for taking time off due to pregnancy and child-care responsibilities, for moving because of their spouse's career, and for lack of geographic mobility. Women who take time off to attend to family responsibilities are seen as lacking commitment to the organization. Additionally, they are subjected to many subtle workplace "micro-inequities" (Rowe, 1990), such as holding meetings at the end of the day, when women employees may have to pick up children at day care, not mentioning women as likely candidates for promotion, and not giving women high-profile assignments. Women who aspire to leadership positions often are penalized by a lack of mentors. Not only do men prefer to mentor men (Garland, 1991; Hymowitz, 2004), but there are few women in leadership positions to provide the needed mentorship.

More women are in the professions and in management positions today, but they are still disproportionately absent from the top echelon. Less than one-tenth of one percent of chief executive officers (CEOs) of *Fortune* 500 companies are women (Costello & Stone, 2001). Institutional power structures, values, and promotion policies create a *"glass ceiling"* composed of artificial barriers that prevent women from advancing into midlevel and senior management positions (Vega, 1993 Welfel & Patterson, 2005;).

Women who aspire to advancement have to contend with a double bind situation. On the one hand, they need to counter the gender-role expectation that women do not "know how to play hardball" (Spielvogel, 1997). On the other hand, they are often penalized for exhibiting the very characteristics and behaviors that would be valued in a male leader. A woman might be called arrogant, abrasive, and overbearing, while a man who displayed the same behaviors would be called self-confident, outspoken, and assertive.

Finally, more women than men have to contend with *sexual harassment* in the workplace. Sexual harassment has been called the single most widespread occupational hazard for women (Lott, 1994). According to various estimates, 35 to 70 percent of women have experienced sexual harassment on the job (Barnett & Rivers, 1996; Welfel & Patterson, 2005). In nontraditional occupations, the percentage is much higher (Gutek & Done, 2001).

CONTEMPORARY ISSUES

This section of the chapter explores issues that today's men and women commonly confront as they establish and negotiate their career paths. For many people, balancing work and family responsibilities, including child and elder care, is an ongoing struggle. Women attempting reentry into the workforce face difficulties as they attempt to restart their careers. Male socialization, with its emphasis on achievement and

CHAPTER 14   GENDER ISSUES IN CAREER COUNSELING

competition, can exact a heavy toll on men's health. Dual-career couples often have to make tough sacrifices in order to maintain both careers. Men and women alike have adopted new roles, and employers are beginning to adopt new policies to accommodate changes in the world of work.

Work-Family Conflicts

It is a challenge for contemporary Americans, particularly for women, to build a life that includes both family and career. Young women who aspire to have successful life-long careers and to have children often end up being doubly penalized. Taking time out of the labor force or working part time while the children are young can wreak havoc on a long-term career trajectory. "The difficulty is that the child-nurturing years are also the career nurturing years. What is lost in either case cannot be 'made up' at a later time" (Moen, 1992, p. 133).

Some young women with children get shunted onto a *mommy track*, which is an alternative career path for women who are committed to both raising children and having a career. These women often are held in less esteem in the workplace and are sidetracked for advancement. Other young women choose to *delay child bearing*, a decision that has particular consequences for professional women in "front-loaded careers" (Denmark, 1992) such as medicine, law, academia, and business management. Because the education and training for these professions is lengthy and because the early years in the profession require a great investment of time and commitment to establish oneself, women who decide to postpone child bearing can find themselves in a race with their biological clock.

Despite evidence that suggests that men participate increasingly in household work and that women have decreased the amount of time they devote to household tasks, the division of household labor has not even begun to approach equity (Fitzgerald, Fassinger, & Betz, 1995). Women still do 80 percent of time-consuming, routine household tasks and continue to provide most of the child care (Barnett & Rivers, 1996; Moen & Yu, 1997). Balancing the demands of work and family can cause *role overload*, which occurs when the demands of a role exceed a person's resources.

This *superwoman* ideal of having and managing both career and family has been fostered by women's perception that they need to "do it like a man." Self-help books and seminars on how to dress for success, handle confrontation, and learn to be assertive are a growth industry with a largely female audience, despite the fact that the ideal of a woman who can do it all has been attacked as impossible and even life-threatening to women who attempt it (Ponton, 1997). Many women who start out with the expectation that they can manage children and career are forced to modify these expectations and reevaluate their priorities. As they cut back on their personal time for exercise, pleasure reading, hobbies, friends, and time alone, they may begin to wonder whether career success is worth the price.

A growing body of evidence suggests that career-family conflict is no longer primarily a women's problem. Studies have indicated that contemporary men experience their family life as more psychologically significant than their jobs. They want to spend more time with their families and are willing to adapt their working lives considerably to do so. Many contemporary men struggle equally with women with difficulties related to child care (Luzzo & McWhirter, 2001), dual careers, and balancing work and family life (Barnett & Rivers, 1996). Increasingly, younger men (of Generations X and Y) are placing greater importance on family than on career (Ebenkamp, 2001).

Child and Elder Care

A lack of adequate *child care* may be the biggest unresolved issue for working couples (Reardon, Lenz, Sampson, & Peterson, 2000). The percentage of working women with children under the age of six was only 12 percent in 1950; by 1992 it had grown to 57 percent (National Commission on Children, 1993) Despite growing evidence that employer-provided child care is actually cost-effective in that it reduces absenteeism and tardiness and increases productivity (Burud, Aschbacher, & McCroskey, 1984; Lambert, Hopkins, Easton, & Walker, 1992; Stewart & Burge, 1989), growing numbers of women and men must coordinate their work demands with their spouses' jobs and child care (Moen, 1992).

In response to this need, more employers are now offering *parental leave*, which can be an important asset in managing work and family commitments. However, taking paternity leave is a "tricky area for men" (Barnett & Rivers, 1996, p. 67). Gender stereotypes still exist, and the cultural message remains in force that it is somehow "unmasculine" for men to take time off work to care for children. Because paternity leave requires formal approval and is often unpaid, men who take paternal leave often do so under the guise of sick leave or vacation time (Barnett & Rivers).

For members of the *sandwich generation*, child care concerns may be compounded by the need to care for elderly parents. It has been estimated that more than half of baby boomers will find themselves caring for children and elders at the same time (Michaels & McCarty, 1993). *Elder care* can take a toll on worker productivity: one study showed that the elder care responsibilities of employees at a large insurance corporation cost an estimated $2,500 annually per worker (Scharlach, Lowe, & Schneider, 1991). Nonetheless, today's employers do not seem to address this need.

Some *divorced* women and men have children who depend on them emotionally, physically, and financially. Both women and men who have dependent children are challenged to balance the responsibilities of parenthood and household management with work demands (Zunker, 1998).

Reentry women, who are returning to the labor force after a lengthy absence, face some unique difficulties. Reentry women, broadly defined, are women ranging in age from 35 to 55 who are married with children still in the home, single parents, empty nesters, or displaced homemakers. Among those who are the most disadvantaged are *displaced homemakers*, women over 35 who have been out of the labor force for an extended period of time (Zunker, 1998). Their occupational problems are acute because they often lack job-search skills and current training that would be useful in the modern work world. For example, a woman who worked 15 years ago as a secretary and was skilled at taking dictation by shorthand would now need computer skills instead.

Stress and Health Concerns

Through traditional male socialization, boys learn that they are expected to work outside the home throughout their lifetimes and provide for their families. It has been suggested that the most powerful gender stereotype or schema for males is the concept of *breadwinner* (Reardon et al., 2000). Work becomes the primary means for them to achieve an identity. Internalized messages to achieve and succeed put pressure on men to strive to get ahead and be "on top," even though there is very little room at the top (Gysbers et al., 1998). Because men have few other avenues for their identity, failure to succeed in the work role can lead to discouragement, stress-related physical illnesses, psychological distress, and even a shortened life span (Pedersen, Draguns, Lonner, & Trimble, 2002; Sharpe & Heppner, 1991). Gysbers et al. suggested that differences in longevity (on average, women live seven years longer than men) are largely attributable to gender-role behaviors of men.

An intense drive to compete and succeed is often associated with Type A behavior and workaholism. Workaholism has been described as an addiction to work or a need to work that is so excessive that it negatively affects a person's physical health and marital and family relationships (Seybold & Salomone, 1994). Similarly, people with Type A personalities have been described as being overcommitted to their work and highly achievement oriented. Although Type A behavior is more common among men than among women, many professional women display Type A behavior patterns as well (Greenglass, 1991).

There appear to be strong links among workaholism and competitiveness, Type A behavior, and heart disease (Booth-Kewley & Friedman, 1987; Machlowitz, 1980). Although the consequences of a workaholic lifestyle include marital failure and family estrangement (Bartolome, 1983; Klaft & Kleiner, 1988; Spruell, 1987), workaholism is still the addiction that is most rewarded in our society (Spruell).

Dual-Career Couples

Dual-career couples or *dual wage-earning couples* are more the norm than the exception today. These couples have developed strategies for managing work-family conflicts such as buying services (e.g., hiring a housekeeper); learning to negotiate both at home and at work; and developing support systems with partners, friends, relatives, and colleagues. Still, they face many stressors as they attempt to negotiate the complexities of their lives. Relocation is very stressful for dual-career couples, who face difficult decisions when the career of the husband or wife requires them to relocate. There is still an expectation that the man will be mobile and the woman will follow her husband. Typically, the woman sets aside her career or consciously alters her career aspirations. A man's decision to refuse to relocate is still nontraditional, and he is likely to be seen as lacking professional commitment (Kaltreider, 1997).

Commuter marriages are becoming more common as increasing numbers of wives and husbands choose to maintain their own employment even though this requires them to live in geographically separate locations. Dual-career relationships, in all their permutations, often require sacrifices. However, many couples have reported that the rewards are substantial, including personal fulfillment and increased income (Kaltreider, Gracie, & Sirulnick, 1997).

New Roles for Women and Men

Jobs traditionally allocated to men are now more available to women (Zunker, 1998). In 2001, women comprised nearly half (47 percent) of workers in executive, administrative, and managerial occupations and slightly more than half (52 percent) of those in professional specialty occupations (U.S. Department of Labor, 2001). Men have been more reluctant to move into occupations that are nontraditional for them (Reardon et al., 2000), possibly because they face the double disincentive of low wages and a socialized fear of being perceived as feminine. Nonetheless, it is no longer startling to encounter a male nurse or a man who is an elementary school teacher.

As more women have entered the workforce and as women increasingly have pursued full-time careers, the relatively new role of *househusband* has emerged. Although it is unknown how many men are now staying at home while their wives work outside the home, it has been estimated that the range is between 325,000 and 2 million (Rauch, 1996). This reversal of the stereotypical marital roles may start out as a temporary arrangement that stretches into years, as a logical division of labor when the wife is making more money than the husband, or when adequate child care is not available at the workplace or in the community. Alternately, it may occur because the father wants the opportunity of watching his children grow. Whatever the reasons for a man to take on the househusband role, he can expect that friends and family may find it odd and wonder what he does all day.

More women are taking responsibility for the breadwinner role in the family. Statistics gathered in 1996 indicated that 55 percent of working women were providing at least half of the family income and that 29 percent were earning more than their husbands (Barnett & Rivers, 1996; Clark, 1996). Men married to successful businesswomen may find themselves in the uncharted role of *first husband*. Although traditional male socialization may make it difficult to men to share the limelight with their wives, relinquish the provider role, be a subordinate earner, and be a more involved parent (Reardon et al., 2000), these new configurations afford both men and women opportunities to move away from traditional gender roles. Recent career development literature provides some support for the existence of a trend toward changing gender-role ideology (Abowitz & Knox, 2003).

Entrepreneurship among women and couples is increasing. Women own approximately half of small businesses. The number is growing, despite barriers not usually faced by men, such as discrimination by lenders, exclusion from informal "old boy" networks, and lack of information on how to obtain capital (Gould & Parzen, 1990). Advantages for women to owning their own businesses may include flexible work schedules and the opportunity to take control of their economic lives (Reardon et al., 2000). Shared entrepreneurship—husbands and wives running their own businesses—is one of the fastest-growing areas within the business world (Granfield, 1993). Although there are obvious challenges to making such an arrangement work, successful couples generally share a common vision, have distinct roles, and make a strong effort to protect their private lives (Granfield, 1993).

The Changing World of Work

Over the past 25 to 30 years, employers have become more responsive to the needs of the changing workforce. The federal government, the nation's largest employer, provides "flexitime" in many of its agencies and is more likely than private-sector employers to provide employer-sponsored day care. Flex time is used regularly by mothers and fathers alike to deliver and collect children and to spend time with the family (Lewis & Lewis, 1996). Private-sector initiatives, led by several large corporations (such as IBM, Xerox, Kodak, and Corning), have adopted new policies including assistance for child care, part-time employment, work-at-home options such as telecommuting, job sharing, flex time, flexible time off, parental leave, and relocation support for "trailing spouses" (Moen, 1992). Still, these workplace accommodations are by no means routinely available.

In conclusion, there is ample evidence that the world of work is changing, although it still has far to go to be gender equitable. Women and men are finding new, creative ways to accommodate their desire to have both a family and a meaningful career. Career counselors will need to be creative, as well, if they are to serve their clients effectively and in a gender-fair manner.

STRATEGIES FOR GENDER-AWARE CAREER COUNSELING

This concluding section of the chapter focuses on strategies to help counselors ensure that their career-counseling practices are gender-aware. As a first step, it is essential for counselors to realize that they are not immune to society's gender-conditioning messages. Counselors are products of their gender-role socialization processes and have developed their own deeply embedded gender schemas. Because the forces of gender-role socialization operate at an unconscious level, they can lead counselors to see gender differences when none exist and to pay attention to behavior that conforms to gender expectations while ignoring behavior that is inconsistent with their beliefs about gender.

Recommendations for Gender-Fair Career Counseling

Career counselors need to constantly check their assumptions. Research has confirmed the existence of gender-biased attitudes and practices in career counseling (Crawford & Unger, 1992; Fitzgerald & Cherpas, 1985; Haring & Beyard-Tyler, 1984; Robertson & Fitzgerald, 1990). Thus, counselors need to be aware of how their own internalized gender schemas, as well as the gender stereotyping that exists in the larger social system, may limit the perspectives and choices of women and men (Atkinson & Hackett, 2004). This points to the need for career counselors to constantly self-monitor and check the assumptions they are making. The goal is to develop a culturally competent, nonassumptive stance.

It is equally important not to lose sight of individual differences, both within and between genders (Betz, 1994). All women are not alike, nor do they all share the same value of willingness to compromise their careers for family reasons. This principle also applies to men; for some men, family considerations are as important as the stereotypical motivators of power and prestige in their career choice process (Pedersen et al., 2002).

Although it is true that women generally are more relational in their orientation and that men are generally more achievement oriented, not all women are relationally oriented, nor are all men driven to compete and achieve. Counselors should inquire into the *meaning of work* for their female and male clients alike and should ascertain what needs these clients hope to meet through their career or occupational choices. Even when clients conform to gender-role expectations, there are some women who are relationally oriented but choose to fulfill their relational needs outside the work arena, just as there are some men who choose to channel their needs to compete and win into sports and other nonwork activities.

Another assumption to be avoided is that women who have young children must choose between pursuit of a full-time career (which would entail leaving child care to others) and being part-time employees with little opportunity for advancement or career development. Women studied by Jackson and Scharman (2002) were able to creatively construct their careers to allow them to work less than the standard 40-hour week, thus striking a balance between work and child care. Joint decision making with their spouses and children was a key component in making arrangements work. For career counselors, such studies highlight the importance of *including spouses, and even entire families*, in the career counseling process when appropriate.

Gender-aware career counseling should begin early, in the elementary school years. Because occupational gender stereotyping starts very early in life, *school counselors* have unique opportunities to help boys and girls to move out of their traditional "gender boxes." Children at the elementary-school level can be exposed to a wide range of career options and encouraged to explore jobs that are nontraditional for both sexes. They can be connected with mentors and role models who have been successful in careers and occupations that are nonstereotypical. School counselors are well positioned to address the barriers of insufficient career exploration, gender-role expectations, and restrictive internalized beliefs that work to limit the career development of boys and girls (Perusse & Goodnough, 2004).

Counselors should work from career development theories that apply equally to women and men. Traditional models of career development need to be examined with a critical eye. Historically, career development theories were patterned on life-stage models created from studying the experiences of men. They were based on assumptions such as (a) career choices are made autonomously, (b) equal opportunity is open to all, (c) work is the most important aspect of people's lives, (d) career decisions are made through a rational matching of a person's traits to the characteristics of occupations, and (e) career development progresses in linear stages, moving upward toward greater responsibility, rank, and financial reward (Betz, 1994; Gysbers et al., 1998). Well into the 1960s, descriptions of women's career paths were based on the premise that women's normative life role was that of homemaker. Women who gave equal or greater emphasis to their careers were described as "innovative" (Ginzberg, 1966) or "unusual" (Zytowski, 1969).

In more recent decades, there has been a growing awareness that neither women's nor men's occupational life cycles follow a rigid progression, but rather that both are influenced by factors and events such as marriage, child rearing, financial resources, and cultural values (Sanguiliano, 1978). It has become evident that counselors need to consider barriers to career development as well as interests and aptitudes (Farmer, 1976; Harmon, 1977). Some of these barriers are internal (psychological). They include (primarily for women) fear of success, home-career conflict, math avoidance, and low expectations of academic success and (primarily for men) fear of failure, avoidance of occupations that are traditionally feminine, and restricted emotional expressiveness. Other constraints are external (societal), such as sex discrimination, sexual harassment on the job, lack of child care, and gender-biased counseling (Herlihy & Watson, 2003).

Cook, Heppner, and O'Brien (2002) have suggested that an ecological model can help counselors broaden their perspectives by focusing on both individual and environmental interventions. Individual interventions can be targeted toward helping clients analyze and develop skills for dealing with environmental barriers (Luzzo & McWhirter, 2001). Environmental interventions can focus on creating supportive networks that include mentors and role models, working to create change in child-care policies, and designing educational strategies to reduce sexual harassment and increase gender equity in the workplace. Counselors can function as change agents as well as providers of individual counseling services.

Betz (2002) cautioned that, although ecological models may improve career counseling, attention must be given to individual differences within, as well as between, genders. Whatever the counselor's approach to career development, that approach may need to be adapted so that it is free of gender-role stereotyping (Betz & Fitzgerald, 1987), considers internal and external barriers, and accounts for individual differences as well as differences between women and men.

Counselors should take a holistic approach to career counseling.   It is important to remember that cultural issues, including gender, are inextricably interwoven with career-planning issues. This is particularly evident when clients need assistance in achieving a balance between work and family. Work-family conflicts are common among working couples. Rather than concentrating exclusively on career and workplace issues, interventions can address broader goals. For example, Tennent and Sperry (2003) focused on optimizing clients' physical health by combining physical activities with family time. They found such interventions to be effective. There was a positive spillover in both the family and work spheres when clients' physical health was increased. Family members were positively affected and clients' productivity at work increased.

Counselors should use caution in interpreting career interest inventories.   Most career assessment inventories have been revised to be more gender sensitive, but counselors still need to be alert to inherent biases. For example, most women tend to score high on the artistic, social, and conventional scales of Holland's hexagon, while men are more likely to score high on the realistic, investigative, and enterprising themes (Zunker, 1998).

When these typical scoring patterns are accepted without questioning, the ghettoization of women in clerical and service occupations is perpetuated and men lose the opportunity to explore careers that are nontraditional for them. Prior to test interpretation, counselors can incorporate a self-reflection phase, during which clients are encouraged to explore the impact of their gender-role socialization on their career interests and goals.

Counselors need to be prepared to assist women and men with gender-based concerns that they may bring to career counseling. Male clients (and some female clients) might benefit from learning (a) how the gender-role socialization process influences their career behavior, (b) how to increase their emotional expressiveness, (c) strategies for managing and reducing stress, and (d) ways to participate more fully in family life and other nonwork roles (Niles & Harris-Bowlsby, 2002). Female clients (and some male clients) might find it helpful to (a) explore and learn how to transcend restrictive gender-role messages about careers, (b) increase their self-efficacy and expectations for success, (c) develop skills for challenging workplace and home inequities, (d) find ways to achieve a satisfying balance between work and family roles (Atkinson & Hackett, 2004), (e) find mentors, and (f) deal with sexual harassment. Both men and women might benefit from assistance in finding adequate and affordable child care, and garnering support for their aspirations to enter nontraditional occupations.

In closing, we offer two case examples and invite you, the reader, to think about how you might apply the concepts in this chapter in conducting career counseling with these clients.

CASE EXAMPLE 1: MARIA

Maria Rodriguez is a 24-year-old unmarried woman who lives at home with her parents and her two younger siblings. She seeks counseling because she wants to learn to be less self-critical and figure out "some goals in my life." She works in a technical support staff position at a cellular communications company. She says she enjoys her work, but that she just took the first job she was offered after she graduated from a community college and has stayed there ever since. She would like to pursue a four-year degree but questions whether she would be able to succeed academically. When asked how she fared with her grades at the community college, she replies that she graduated with a 3.7 grade-point average but that a "real university would be much harder." Besides, even if she could do well in her studies, she has no idea what major she would pursue or what career goal might suit her.

Maria adds that it would be difficult for her to juggle the demands of her job, college studies, and her household responsibilities. Her youngest brother, age 16, has cystic fibrosis and her mother depends on her to help with his physical care as well as with the cooking, cleaning, and other household chores. Her other brother, age 19, works at a full-time job and is rarely home when he is off work. She describes her father as the dominant force in the family, even though he is sometimes absent for extended periods of time as a result of "getting into trouble when he starts drinking." She states that she realizes she would have more control over her time if she were to move out on her own, but that would not be possible, because "my mother could never manage without me during the times when my father is gone."

In our view, a holistic approach is indicated in Maria's case, one that considers cultural issues along with career exploration. Maria seems to have internalized several gender-role expectations, such as the belief that females are responsible for caregiving and household chores. She also appears to have lowered self-efficacy expectations with respect to her academic abilities. She questions her ability to succeed in a four-year university despite having achieved a 3.7 grade point average at the community college. She may lack assertiveness skills as well, as she has remained in the same position at work since she was hired.

Maria's career counselor needs to remain sensitive, not only to gender issues in working with Maria, but also to expectations associated with Latino culture that may be influencing her decision making. If her counselor is culturally different from Maria (e.g., Caucasian, male), the counselor might assume she could benefit from learning to be more independent, moving out on her own, and pursuing her baccalaureate degree. If her counselor is culturally similar to Maria (e.g., Latina, female), the counselor will need to remain alert to the possibility that cultural differences are present even though counselor and client are trait-factor matched. In any event, the counselor must understand and respect Maria's cultural values.

The counselor should explore Maria's self-efficacy beliefs with her. Cognitive-behavioral techniques might be used to help her identify her cognitive distortions with respect to her ability to succeed academically. Feminist therapy strategies such as gender-role analysis and power analysis might be useful to increase Maria's awareness of her competencies and personal power. Then, Maria will be able to choose which of her internalized gender role expectations she wants to continue to live by and which ones she may wish to modify.

Maria's counselor needs to ascertain the role of work in Maria's life. Does Maria envision that she will get married and have children? If so, how will her work role relate to her roles as wife and mother? Depending on her answers to these questions, she may or may not want to focus her career exploration on jobs that have flexibility to allow her to balance work and family responsibilities.

Career counseling with Maria needs to include helping her explore her interests. Because she enjoys her work providing technical support services, a career in the technology field, although nontraditional for women, might be an option she would want to investigate. At the age of 24, with her academic talents, Maria has a vast world of possibilities open to her. The counselor's task is to help her become aware of her choices and make decisions that are in accordance with her values.

CASE EXAMPLE 2: RICHARD

Richard Johnson, age 52, has sought counseling at the suggestion of an emergency room physician. Richard had made four trips to the hospital emergency room within the past three months, each time because he was certain he was having a heart attack. Each time, his electrocardiograms (EKGs) and other medical tests were normal and he was discharged.

(continued)

CONTINUED

In his first session with the counselor, Richard described the symptoms that had led the physician to refer him. They were textbook symptoms of panic attacks. Richard's wife accompanied him to the counselor's office, and she was included in the first 15 minutes of the session while initial information was gathered. She appeared to be very supportive of Richard's decision to seek counseling and provided this occupational information about herself: she works part-time in a small gift shop, taking care of sales, inventory, and general store management duties.

The counselor noted that Richard is highly verbal and articulate. He is well read and can quote entire passages from Kafka and Tolstoy. He did not finish high school. At age 20, he enrolled in several courses to complete his GED but quit because they were boring. He has been employed for 18 years as a forklift machine operator in a warehouse. He and his wife have been married for 24 years, and they have no children.

Richard describes his work as dull and unchallenging, but adds that it compensates him well financially. He says he is lucky to have such a good job despite his lack of education. When he is asked about what he does for enjoyment, he talks at length about his love of woodworking. His wife chimes in, stating that he does beautiful work refinishing old furniture and has designed and created many small wooden objects as gifts for friends. Richard's goals for counseling, other than to "stay out of emergency rooms," are ill defined. He feels as though his life has no meaning and that he is just "drifting through."

If we were counseling Richard, we would want to deal with his immediate presenting problem first. Cognitive-behavioral techniques could be applied to reduce the frequency and severity of his panic attacks. Then, Richard and his counselor would be able to focus on longer-term goals. The counselor, working from a holistic framework, would want to understand what brought on Richard's series of panic attacks at the age of 52. They may be related to his sense of meaninglessness, and his belief that he has no alternative work options to his "dull and unchallenging" job. He may be feeling trapped, not only by his lack of formal education, but also by gender-stereotyped thinking that he must be a good "breadwinner" even though he does not enjoy his job. His physical problems could also be a result of long-suppressed emotions.

A positive asset search would reveal that Richard has some important strengths: he is intelligent, is a steady and reliable employee, and has a stable and supportive marital relationship. Despite his intelligence, returning to school may not be a viable option for Richard, given this experience with GED courses. He and the counselor might, instead, work from his demonstrated interests and talents and explore ways he could convert his love of woodworking into a paying occupation. He might be interested in entrepreneurship. Possibly, he could take a course or two in small business ownership at a community college without having to enroll for course credit. Opening a business that would offer a service (restoration of antique and old furniture) and a product (his own creations) might give him a sense of control over his life and provide him with work that he loves to do. It is possible, too, that he and his wife would want to consider making the business a shared entrepreneurship, as she already has skills in sales and small business management.

USEFUL WEBSITES

www.aflcio.org/yourjobeconomy/women/equalpay/

Information on what workers can do if they believe their rights have been violated, up-to-date statistics on wages

www.library.wisc.edu/libraries/WomensStudies/womened/

Subject listings of women and gender resources

www.e.ac.uk/careers/genderissues.htm/

Gender issues in employment

www.eoc.org.uk/cseng/research/pay_and_income.asp/

Equal Opportunities Commission

www.jobseekersadvice.com

Information and advice for job seekers

http.//www.womenissues.about.cum/gemderdisc/

Gender discrimination resources, links, and information

www.workfamily.com/model.htm>

List of companies that have developed model family-friendly programs

http://www.women.com/work/best/

Rating of the best companies for working couples

http://www.dol.gov/dol/wb/

Information from the Women's Bureau in the Department of Labor

REFERENCES

Abowitz, D., & Knox, D. (2003). Goals of college students: Some gender differences. *College Student Journal, 37,* 550–557.

Atkinson, D. R., & Hackett, G. (2004). *Counseling diverse populations* (3rd ed.). Boston: McGraw-Hill.

Barnett, R. C., & Rivers, C. (1996). *He works, she works.* San Francisco: HarperCollins.

Bartolome, F. (1983). The work alibi: When it's harder to go home. *Harvard Business Review, 61,* 66–74.

Basow, S. A. (1992). *Gender: Stereotypes and roles* (3rd ed.). Pacific Grove, CA: Brooks/Cole.

Bem, S. L. (1993). *The lenses of gender: Transforming the debate on sexual equality.* New Haven, CT: Yale University Press.

Betz, N. E. (1994). Basic issues and concepts in career counseling for women. In W. B. Walsh & S. H. Osipow (Eds.), *Career counseling for women* (pp. 1–42). Hillsdale, NJ: Erlbaum.

Betz, N. E. (2002). Explicating an ecological approach to the career development of women. *Career Development Quarterly, 50,* 335–338.

Betz, N. E., & Fitzgerald, L. F. (1987). *The career psychology of women.* Orlando, FL: Academic Press.

Booth-Kewley, S., & Friedman, H. S. (1987). Psychological predictors of heart disease: A quantitative review. *Psychological Bulletin, 101,* 343–362.

Boswell, S. L. (1985). The influence of sex-role stereotyping on women's attitudes and achievement in mathematics. In S. F. Chipman, L. R. Brush, & D. M. Wilson (Eds.), *Women and mathematics: Balancing the equation* (pp. 175–198). Hillsdale, NJ: Erlbaum.

Burud, S. L., Aschbacher, R., & McCroskey, J. (1984). *Employer-supported child care: Investing in human resources.* Dover, MA: Auburn House.

Canning, M., & Kaltreider, N. B. (1997). Heads up: Strategies to deal with gender discrimination and harassment. In N. B. Kaltreider (Ed.), *Dilemmas of a double life: Women balancing careers and relationships* (pp. 237–252). Northvale, NJ: Jason Aronson.

Clark, K. (1996, August 5). Women, men, and money. *Fortune,* pp. 60–61.

Cook, E. P., Heppner, M. J., & O'Brien, K. M. (2002). Career development of women of color and white women: Assumptions, conceptualization, and interventions from an ecological perspective. *Career Development Quarterly, 50,* 291–305.

Costello, C. B., & Stone, A. J. (Eds.) (2001). *The American woman, 2001–2002: Getting to the top.* New York: W. W. Norton.

Crawford, M., & Unger, R. (2000). *Women and gender: A feminist psychology* (3rd ed.). Boston: McGraw-Hill.

Denmark, F. L. (1992). The thirty-something woman: To career or not to career. In B. R. Wainrib (Ed.), *Gender issues across the life cycle* (pp. 71–76). New York: Springer.

Doyle, J. A. (1983). *The male experience.* Dubuque, IA: William D. Brown.

Ebenkamp, B. (2001, February). Chicks and balances. *Brandweek, 42*(7), 16.

Enns, C. Z. (2000). Gender issues in counseling. In S. D. Brown & R. W. Lent (Eds.), *Handbook of counseling psychology* (3rd ed., pp. 601–638). New York: Wiley.

Enns, C. Z. (2004). Counseling girls and women: Attitudes, knowledge, and skills. In D. R. Atkinson & G. Hackett, *Counseling diverse populations* (3rd ed., pp. 285–306). Boston: McGraw Hill.

Farmer, H. S. (1976). What inhibits achievement and career motivation in women? *Counseling Psychologist, 6,* 12–14.

Fitzgerald, L. F., & Cherpas, C. C. (1985). On the reciprocal relationship between gender and occupation: Rethinking the assumptions concerning masculinity and career development. *Journal of Vocational Behavior, 27,* 109–122.

Fitzgerald, L. F., Fassinger, R. E., & Betz, N. E. (1995). Theoretical advances in the study of women's career development. In W. B. Walsh & S. H. Osipow (Eds.), *Handbook of vocational psychology* (2nd ed., pp. 67–110). Mahwah, NJ: Erlbaum.

Garland, S. D. (1991, August 19). Throwing stones at the glass ceiling. *Business Week,* p. 29.

Gettys, L. D., & Cann, A. (1981). Children's perceptions of occupational sex stereotypes. *Sex Roles, 9,* 597–607.

Gilbert, L. A., & Sher, M. (1999). *Gender and sex in counseling and psychotherapy.* Boston: Allyn & Bacon.

Gilligan, C. (1982). *In a different voice.* Cambridge, MA: Harvard University Press.

Ginzberg, E. (1966). *Lifestyles of educated American women.* New York: Columbia University Press.

Gottfredson, L. S. (1996). A theory of circumscription and compromise. In D. Brown, L. Brooks, & Associates, *Career choice and development* (3rd ed., pp. 179–281). San Francisco: Jossey-Bass.

Gould, S., & Parzen, J. (Eds.). (1990). *Enterprising women*. Columbus, OH: Clearinghouse on Adult, Career, and Vocational Education. (ERIC Report No. ED 335 463).

Granfield, M. (1993, June). Till debt do us part. *Working Woman*, pp. 33–35.

Greenberg-Lake, E. (1991). *Shortchanging girls, shortchanging America*. Washington, DC: The Analysis Group.

Greenglass, E. R. (1991). Type A behavior, career aspirations, and role conflict in professional women. In M. J. Strube (Ed.), *Type A behavior* (pp. 277–292). Newbury Park, CA: Sage.

Gutek, B. A., & Done, R. S. (2001). Sexual harassment. In R. Unger (Ed.), *Handbook of the psychology of women and gender* (pp. 367–387). New York: Wiley.

Gysbers, N. C., Heppner, M. J., & Johnston, J. A. (1998). *Career counseling: Process, issues, and techniques*. Boston: Allyn & Bacon.

Haring, M. J., & Beyard-Tyler, K. C. (1984). Counseling with women: The challenge of nontraditional careers. *School Counselor, 31*, 301–309.

Harmon, L. W. (1977). Career counseling for women. In E. Rawlings & D. Carter (Eds.), *Psychotherapy for women* (pp. 197–206). Springfield, IL: Thomas.

Harpaz, P. J., & Fu, L. (1997). Work centrality in Germany, Israel, Japan, and the United States. *Cross-Cultural Research, 31*, 171–200.

Herlihy, B. R., & Watson, Z. E. (2003). Ethical issues and multicultural competence in counseling. In F. D. Harper & J. McFadden (Eds.), *Culture and counseling: New approaches* (pp. 363–378). New York: Allyn & Bacon.

Herz, D. E., & Wootton, B. H. (1996). Women in the workforce: An overview. In C. Costello & B. K. Krimgold (Eds.), *The American woman, 1996–97* (pp. 44–78). New York: W. W. Norton.

Howe, L. K. (1977). *Pink collar workers*. New York: Avon.

Hyde, J. S. (1997). Gender differences in math performance. In M. R. Walsh (Ed.), *Women, men, and gender: Ongoing debates* (pp. 283–287). New Haven, CT: Yale University Press.

Hymowitz, C. (2004, February). Women put noses to the grindstone, and miss opportunities. *Wall Street Journal, Eastern Edition, 243*, B1.

Jackson, A. P., & Scharman, J. S. (2002). Constructing family-friendly careers: Mothers' experiences. *Journal of Counseling and Development, 80*, 188–196.

Kaltreider, N. B. (Ed.). (1997). *Dilemmas of a double life: Women balancing careers and relationships*. Northvale, NJ: Jason Aronson.

Kaltreider, N. B., Gracie, C., & Sirulnick, C. (1997). Love in the trenches: Dual-career relationships. In N. B. Kaltreider (Ed.), *Dilemmas of a double life: Women balancing careers and relationships* (pp. 121–140). Northvale, NJ: Jason Aronson.

Klaft, R. P., & Kleiner, B. H. (1988). Understanding workaholics. *Business, 38*, 37–40.

Lambert, S., Hopkins, K., Easton, G., & Walker, J. (1992). *Added benefits: The link between family responsive policies and work performance at Fel-Pro, Inc.* Chicago: University of Chicago Press.

Leavitt, R. R. (1971). Women in other cultures. In V. Gornick & B. K. Morgan (Eds.), *Woman in sexist society* (pp. 393–427). New York: New American Library.

Lewis, S., & Lewis, J. (1996). *The work-family challenge*. Thousand Oaks, CA: Sage.

Lindsey, L. L. (1990). *Gender roles: A sociological perspective*. Englewood Cliffs, NJ: Prentice-Hall.

Luzzo, D. A., & McWhirter, E. H. (2001). Sex and ethnic differences in the perception of educational and career-related barriers and levels of coping efficacy. *Journal of Counseling and Development, 79*, 61–67.

Machlowitz, M. (1980). *Workaholics: Living with them, working with them*. Reading, MA: Addison-Wesley.

Matlin, M. (1996). *The psychology of women*. New York: Holt, Rinehart, & Winston.

Maume, D. J. (1999). Glass ceilings and glass escalators. *Work and Occupation, 26,* 483–510.

Meece, J. L., Parsons, J. E., Kaczala, C. M., Goff, S. B., & Futterman, R. (1982). Sex differences in math achievement: Toward a model of academic choice. *Psychological Bulletin, 91,* 324–348.

Michaels, B., & McCarty, E. (1993). Family ties and bottom lines. *Training and Development, 47*(3), 70–72.

Moen, P. (1992). *Women's two roles: A contemporary dilemma*. New York: Auburn House.

Moen, P., & Yu, Y. (1997). *Does success at work compete with success at home?* (Bronfenbrenner Life Course Center Working Paper 97-06). Ithaca, NY: Cornell University Press.

National Commission on Children. (1993). *Just the facts: A summary of recent information on America's children and their families*. Washington, DC: Author.

Niles, S. G., & Harris-Bowlsby, J. (2002). *Career development interventions in the 21st century*. Upper Saddle River, NJ: Merrill/Prentice Hall.

Pedersen, P. B., Draguns, J. G., Lonner, W. J., & Trimble, J. E. (Eds.). (2002). *Counseling across cultures* (5th ed.). Thousand Oaks, CA: Sage.

Perusse, R., & Goodnough, R. (2004). *Leadership, advocacy, and direct service strategies for professional school counselors*. Belmont, CA: Brooks/Cole-Thompson Learning.

Ponton, L. E. (1997) Career and parenting: Women make it work. In N. B. Kaltreider (Ed.), *Dilemmas of a double life: Women balancing careers and relationships* (pp. 141–164). Northvale, NJ: Jason Aronson.

Rauch, S. (1996, January 9). Dads at home. *Tallahassee Democrat*, pp. 3D, 6D.

Reardon, R. C., Lenz, J. G., Sampson, J. P., & Peterson, G. W. (2000). *Career development and planning: A comprehensive approach*. Pacific Grove, CA: Brooks/Cole.

Reskin, B. F., & Hartmann, H. D. (Eds.). (1986). *Women's work, men's work: Sex segregation on the job*. Washington, DC: National Academy Press.

Robertson, J., & Fitzgerald, L. F. (1990). The (mis)treatment of men: Effects of client gender roles and life-style on diagnosis and attribution of pathology. *Journal of Counseling Psychology, 37,* 3–9.

Rochlen, A. B., & O'Brien, K. M. (2002). Men's reasons for and against seeking help for career-related concerns. *Journal of Men's Studies, 11,* 55–64.

Rowe, M. (1990). Barriers to equality: the power of subtle discrimination to maintain unequal opportunity. *Employees' Responsibilities and Rights Journal, 3,* 153–163.

Sanguiliano, I. (1978). *In her time*. New York: Morrow.

Scharlach, A. E., Lowe, B. F., & Schneider, E. L. (1991). *Eldercare and the work force*. Lexington, MA: Lexington Books.

Seybold, K. C., & Salomone, P. R. (1994). Understanding workaholism: A review of causes and counseling approaches. *Journal of Counseling & Development, 73,* 4–9.

Sharpe, M. J., & Heppner, P. P. (1991). Gender role, gender-role conflict, and psychological well-being in men. *Journal of Counseling Psychology, 38,* 323–330.

Skovholt, T. M. (1990). Career themes in counseling and psychotherapy with men. In D. Moore & F. Leafgren (Eds.), *Problem-solving strategies and interventions for men in conflict* (pp. 39–52). Alexandria, VA: American Association for Counseling and Development.

Slattery, J. M. (2004). *Counseling diverse clients: Bringing context into therapy*. Pacific Grove, CA: Brooks/Cole.

Smith, A. B., & Inder, P. M. (1993). Social interaction in same and cross gender pre-school peer groups: A participant observation study. *Educational Psychology, 13,* 29–42.

Spielvogel, A. M. (1997). Women in leadership. In N. B. Kaltreider (Ed.), *Dilemmas of a double life: Women balancing careers and relationships* (pp. 189–208). Northvale, NJ: Jason Aronson.

Spruell, G. (1987). Work fever. *Training and Development Journal, 41,* 41–45.

Stewart, D. L., & Burge, P. I. (1989). *Assessment of employee satisfaction, stress, and childcare at Dominion Bankshares Corporation.* Blacksburg, VA: Virginia Polytechnic Institute and State University Press.

Tennent, G. P., & Sperry, L. (2003). Work-family balance: Counseling strategies to optimize health. *Family Journal, 11,* 404–408.

U.S. Census Bureau. (2002). *Census 2002.* Washington, DC.

U.S. Department of Labor, Bureau of Labor Statistics. (2002). *Employment and earnings.* Washington, DC.

U.S. Department of Labor, Bureau of Labor Statistics. (2001). *Highlights of Women's Earnings in 2001.* Washington, DC.

U.S. Department of Labor, Bureau of Labor Statistics. (1995). *Employment and Earnings.* Washington, DC.

Vega, J. (1993, spring). Crack in the glass ceiling? *Career Woman,* pp. 43–45.

Welfel, E. R., & Patterson, L. E. (2005). *The counseling process: A multitheoretical integrative approach* (6th ed.). Pacific Grove, CA: Brooks/Cole.

Whittock, M., Edwards, C., McLaren, S., & Robinson, O. (2002). The tender trap: Gender, part-time nursing and the effects of "family-friendly" policies on career advancement. *Sociology of Health and Fitness, 24,* 305–327.

Zunker, V. G. (1998). *Career counseling: Applied concepts of life planning* (5th ed.). Pacific Grove, CA: Brooks/Cole.

Zytowski, D. (1969). Toward a theory of career development of women. *Personnel and Guidance Journal, 47,* 660–664.

CHAPTER 15

CAREER COUNSELING WITH GAY, LESBIAN, BISEXUAL, AND TRANSGENDER CLIENTS

DAVID H. WHITCOMB

KARA BRITA WETTERSTEN

CHERYL L. STOLZ
University of North Dakota

WORKPLACE ISSUES FOR GAY, LESBIAN, BISEXUAL, AND TRANSGENDER PERSONS: SOME OPENING THOUGHTS

Although your perspective will vary depending on whether you are heterosexual, gay, lesbian, bisexual, or transgender, we think it would be helpful for you to imagine what it is like for a gay, lesbian, bisexual, or transgender (GLBT) person to look for a job, hold a job, and advance in a career. One of the key decisions a GLBT person makes is whether to come out to others as gay (or lesbian, bisexual, or transgender), given the perceived and real experiences of harassment and discrimination for being "gay." In some cases there is an identifiable moment in which a person decides to come out to others, an event that transforms one's entire life. Still, to some extent it is a daily decision if and when to come out to others, who will often assume that the individual is heterosexual or of the biological sex that corresponds with his or her outward appearance.

Now imagine yourself working in a large corporation and hiding your sexual identity for fear of being teased, harassed, looked over for promotions, or even fired. Do you ever tell anybody at work? How do you decide whom and when to tell? If you do not tell people, how do you deal with the feelings of hiding or not being yourself? Do you deny your partner or hide his or her gender when questions come up at work? These and many other concerns affect the day-to-day working lives of gay, lesbian, bisexual, and transgender individuals.

It is often the case that a person will be out as GLBT to friends and some family members but not out with other family members or coworkers. This is important because research has begun to show that career paths and job satisfaction vary according to the degree of "outness" of an individual on the job (Fassinger et al., 2003; Waldo, 1999). For example, a recent study showed that the degree of being open at work about one's sexual orientation as GLB (one's "outness") was positively related to experiences of direct heterosexism (that is, being in an environment in which workers and work policies consider heterosexuality to be the norm or preferred sexual orientation for employees), such as antigay jokes, but negatively related to indirect experiences of heterosexism, such as assumptions of heterosexuality (Waldo, 1999).

One's outness may vary according to how receptive or hostile the workplace is perceived to be toward employees' sexual orientation or gender identity. Workplace heterosexism had a strong effect on job satisfaction in a large, national sample (Fassinger et al., 2003). Specifically, the more heterosexism there was on the job, the less job satisfaction lesbian and gay employees had. The authors concluded that the person-workplace fit may be even more important for the job satisfaction of lesbian and gay people than for the general population. In another recent study, Waldo (1999) found that GLB employees who believed that their organization tolerated heterosexism were likely to experience considerably more heterosexism than those who believed their organization was intolerant. Not surprisingly, experiencing heterosexism at work was associated with adverse psychological, health, and job-related outcomes, a finding in support of the minority stress theory (Meyer, 1995; Waldo, 1999), which suggests GLB individuals are invariably in the minority during their day-to-day lives and that reminders of their minority status result in psychological distress.

The findings of recent studies help us understand how important decisions about coming out at work are and that being out on the job can have both positive and negative consequences. It should be noted at this point that, whereas coming out at work is usually a personal decision, sometimes the decision is made by others at work who "out" the employee (publicly identify the person as GLBT) or assume a GLB sexual orientation or transgender identity for an employee who has not self-identified as such. These situations frequently occur to persons who have decided not to come out as GLBT at work (or perhaps they have decided to wait or have told only one or two trusted coworkers) and are "passing" as heterosexual or traditionally gendered. Working with GLBT persons whose self-determination and privacy have been violated in terms of public disclosure is a challenging issue in career counseling.

This chapter explores career development of GLBT persons across the life span. Institutional and demographic factors that facilitate or hinder career and lifestyle planning for GLBT persons are discussed. Environmental influences such as state laws, workplace nondiscrimination policies, and the strength of local GLBT communities are phenomena outside the typical scope of career interests and skills that play an important role in the career adjustment of GLBT persons. Several case examples are used to assist current and prospective career counselors to provide services to a diverse cross-section of individuals who have a minority sexual orientation or gender identity.

Later in this chapter we consider many other workplace issues that affect career decisions and career development of GLBT persons. Among these, the interrelated issues of isolation, role models, and mentorship are discussed in terms of integrating an often marginalized segment of the workforce into the "mainstream." Issues facing couples in intimate same-sex relationships are also highlighted. After reading the chapter, the reader will be familiar with theories and research in the field of GLBT career development and career counseling as well as strategies to apply these theories and research findings to the practice of culturally competent career counseling with GBLT clients. At this point, however, we will step back from career-specific topics to review some basic GLBT terminology.

THE LEXICON OF SEXUAL ORIENTATION AND GENDER IDENTITY

It is important to note the advantages and limitations in presenting career-counseling and lifestyle-planning issues for four groups that share many similarities but also represent important and complex differences. The terms *gay, lesbian,* and *bisexual* all refer to a person's sexual orientation, whereas *transgender* refers to one's gender identity. Whereas sexual orientation most often refers to the biological sex of the persons to whom one is primarily sexually attracted, gender identity refers to one's identity as male, female, or a combination thereof. To elaborate, the word *gay* is sometimes used to include gay men, lesbian women, and bisexual women and men, but other times refers specifically to gay men and gay adolescent boys.[1] *Lesbian* is the preferred term by most women who are primarily sexually attracted to other women, though some self-identify as gay and many consider themselves to be included under umbrella terms such as *gay rights.* Men and women who identify as bisexual affirm their capacity to be sexually attracted to members of each traditionally recognized gender (i.e., women and men; Fox, 2000). As with persons of every sexual orientation, while in an intimate relationship, monogamy is the most common practice for bisexual men and women and attractions to other persons are not acted upon.

Gender identity is conceptualized as separate from sexual orientation. For example, a person who is biologically male may prefer traditionally masculine clothes, activities, and mannerisms and also be attracted to women. This combination of biology, sexual orientation, and gender identity has been regarded as the norm for heterosexual men. A person who is biologically female, prefers to wear clothes and engage in activities that are traditionally masculine, and is also attracted to women most likely identifies herself as a lesbian and fits with common stereotypes about lesbian gender roles. In contrast, a biological male who prefers to dress as a woman and is most comfortable with activities and mannerisms traditionally regarded as feminine may self-identity as a woman. Such a person is transgender and may be sexually attracted to men or women. As the gender

---

[1]Although we will use the terms "boys" and "girls" to refer specifically to persons below the age of 18, when discussing gender groups generally, we will use "men" and "women" even when the topic applies to adolescents or younger children.

crossing is from a biologically male origin, this is referred to as MTF (male to female), whereas the reverse pattern is called FTM (female to male). If attracted to women, this biological man may self-identify as lesbian, whereas if attracted to men, the sexual orientation identity may be that of a heterosexual woman. If this person undergoes biological procedures, which range from hormonal treatment to breast implantation or sex reassignment surgery, this person would be referred to as *transsexual*. These gender identity issues are complex and are experienced as such by clients, counselors, and the general public.

Over the years, several classification systems have been developed to help locate a person's sexual orientation along a continuum of homosexual to heterosexual. Sell (1997) summarized the most commonly used systems, noting their strengths and weaknesses. His own scale (Sell, 1996) is arguably the best, as it accounts for an individual's sexual interests and sexual contact to vary, independently of each other, on a continuum of opposite sex to same sex, while one's sexual orientation identity varies on a continuum of homosexual to heterosexual. As such, it adds dimension to the classic 0–6 Kinsey Scale (Kinsey, Pomeroy, Wardell, & Martin, 1948), which is presented in Table 15.1, and conceptualizes sexual orientation similarly to Bem's (1974) mapping of gender roles. That is, just as an androgynous person has considerable masculine as well as considerable feminine qualities, a bisexual person can have high heterosexual interests in conjunction with high homosexual interests. Similar scales that include gender identity, conceptualized independently from sexual orientation, will be an important addition to the literature.

To work effectively with GLBT clients, career counselors must be familiar with how terminology concerning sexual orientation and gender identity are used in the academic literature, the popular media, and the clientele in one's own geographic region. To complicate matters further, preferred terminology can vary according to the client's age, race or ethnicity, sexual orientation, gender identity, and level of identity development. Persons questioning their sexual orientation or gender identity may not be comfortable with any label. In response to these challenging issues, some academicians, as well as members of the general public, are using the term *queer* to encompass all GLBT

TABLE 15.1   The Kinsey Scale of the Continuum of Human Sexual Experience

KINSEY RATING	DESCRIPTION
0	Exclusively heterosexual in psychological response and behavior
1	Predominantly heterosexual; incidental homosexual behavior
2	Predominantly heterosexual; more than incidental homosexual behavior
3	Equally heterosexual and homosexual in psychological response behavior
4	Predominantly homosexual; more than incidental heterosexual and behavior
5	Predominantly homosexual; incidental heterosexual behavior
6	Exclusively homosexual in psychological response and behavior

concerns. Whereas *queer theory* and *queer identity* are considered affirmative and appropriate terms for some GLBT persons, many other GLBT persons and their allies still take offense to this historically oppressive term. For the purposes of this chapter, standard terminology current in the counseling field will be used (cf. Barret & Logan, 2002). For best practice with your own clients, we suggest using the terminology they are most comfortable with, provided that those terms are respectful of their current identity and potential for further identity development (Barret & Logan, 2002; Fukuyama & Ferguson, 2000).

Within the current chapter, we try to be as inclusive of all four populations (the G, L, B, and T) as possible, but with certain caveats. First, in the areas of vocational psychology and career counseling, there has been much more research on gay men and lesbians than on bisexual or transgender persons. Even between gay men and lesbian women there are differences in the extent of research on certain topics, as well as the findings. For example, there are more studies about the lesbian than the gay male experience of discrimination in the workplace, yet findings for the two groups are more similar than different. In studies that sample both groups, however, findings may be quite different. One pioneering study comparing the four groups of heterosexual men, heterosexual women, gay men, and lesbian women found that on career choice uncertainty, the scores of gay men were highest and those of lesbian women were lowest (Etringer, Hillerbrand, & Hetherington, 1990). Therefore it is often unwise to generalize findings from one group (e.g., lesbians) to another group (e.g., gay men).

The literature on bisexual career issues is smaller than for gay men or lesbians (Croteau, Anderson, Distefano, & Kampa-Kokesch, 2000), whereas the literature on transgender career issues is most extensive in legal cases of discrimination and has only started to appear in counseling journals and textbooks. The cautions that apply to generalizing findings between gay men and lesbians are even more salient when dealing with the more understudied groups of bisexual and transgender persons. Therefore, many of our suggestions for career counseling with bisexual and transgender persons will be based on theory and practice with gay and lesbian clients more than on empirical findings, and therefore will be stated more tentatively than our recommendations for gay and lesbian clients.

A DEVELOPMENTAL LOOK AT GLBT CAREERS

With these cautions about different groups of GLBT individuals in mind, we return to career issues, using a developmental framework to understand the careers of GLBT persons across the life span. In a predominantly heterosexual society, virtually everyone is socialized to become a heterosexual person (Hetrick & Martin, 1987; Matthews & Lease, 2000). Most children are reared by heterosexual parents, with the vast majority of boys socialized according to traditional norms of masculinity and most girls socialized to assume traditionally feminine gender roles (Katz, 1979, 1996). Gender roles are usually well established by the time a child starts school, whereas awareness of one's sexual orientation may occur in early childhood, crystallize during adolescence, or change over the course of one's life (Cass, 1996; Rust, 1992; Sophie, 1985–1986; Troiden, 1989). In the case of a child who does not develop the stereotypical interests of his or her assigned gender, early career exploration may gravitate toward occupations traditionally held by the opposite gender. Whereas some lesbians may benefit from feeling liberated to pursue occupations dominated by men (Fassinger, 1995, 1996), other LBT women and perhaps most GBT men may perceive gender-atypical occupations as being unavailable, despite their interest in them.

Although most transgender and many GLB individuals have gender-atypical interests in childhood, many other GLB individuals are more gender conforming (Gagné & Tewksbury, 1998; Gainor, 2000; Ossana, 2000). Although empirical evidence is lacking, anecdotal evidence suggests that more traditionally gendered GLB persons explore careers along a developmental path similar to their heterosexual peers, at least until the time when they start to come out to themselves and others. Therefore it is important to examine briefly the coming-out process and its potential effects on career development.

Several studies have indicated that the most common developmental period for individuals to come out as gay, lesbian, or bisexual is middle to late adolescence, with a possible historical trend toward coming out at younger ages (Savin-Williams, 1995). For youth, coming out is fraught with consequences of oppression, discrimination, and concomitant setbacks to mental and physical well-being, such as substance abuse, anxiety, depression, suicidality, and high-risk sexual behaviors (Hershberger & D'Augelli, 2000). These negative consequences are often a result of rejection by one's family, though family communication can gradually improve once the family adjusts to having a GLB member (Savin-Williams, 1998). Whether one comes out during adolescence or adulthood, the process has been described as scary, exciting, and disruptive to career development (Boatwright, Gilbert, Forrest, & Ketzenberger, 1996; Morrow, Gore, & Campbell, 1996; Schmidt, Nilsson, & Rooney, 2003). While coming out, attention to career concerns is often overshadowed by a focus on sexual identity development. Although career concerns often take a back seat to redefining oneself as GLBT and establishing a support system for a newfound identity, coming out is also marked by increasing awareness of harassment and discrimination of GLBT people in all realms of society, including the workplace (Croteau, 1996; Savin-Williams, 1994).

Several studies of career development have demonstrated the importance of role models and mentorship for women and racial minorities (e.g., Richie et al., 1997). Fassinger (1995) noted the paucity of role models as a barrier in lesbian career development, largely due to the lack of lesbians who are out at their jobs. Lacking real-life role models, many GLBT youth feel isolated in their sexual orientation and gender identity. Nauta, Saucier, and Woodard (2001) presented data conflicting with this notion, in that the GLB college students in her study reported having more career role models than their heterosexual peers. The sample, however, was not representative, but instead demonstrated that attendees of a GLB student organization were able to identify career role models and preferred them to be of their own sexual orientation. Knowing that most GLBT youth are not so well integrated in the community, we hypothesize that they may therefore try to identify with career role models in the popular media, such as pop music stars and characters in television shows and film, a topic considered further in the section on stereotypes.

CASE EXAMPLES

Let us consider the issue of coming out at work by examining the cases of two young people applying to their first full-time job. To illustrate issues such as the choice of passing as heterosexual, lack of perceived career opportunity, and dual-career dilemmas, we will look at the hypothetical cases of an 18-year-old male high school graduate, Bill, and a 23-year-old female college graduate, Sarah.

Case 1

Bill self-identifies as bisexual but has not had a long-term boyfriend or girlfriend. His family lives in a town of 7,000 people, over an hour away from the nearest metropolitan area, where his family is one of several African American families in the neighborhood. Only his older sister and two young men his age with whom he has been romantically involved know of his bisexuality. Vocationally, he is aware of test results showing that he has a high mechanical aptitude and is thinking of becoming an airplane mechanic. He knows that such a career would require continued formal education, but for the time being, he would like to work at a neighbor's automotive repair shop. Bill's neighbor has known his family for years and is almost like an uncle to Bill. He notices that Bill has not had a recent girlfriend and sometimes hints that their mutual neighbors have attractive daughters his age that he should ask out on dates. Even more frequently he hints that Bill would make a fine worker in his shop.

What issues does Bill face in terms of sexual identity development and career development if he applies for a full-time job at his neighbor's shop? How might his employment at this work setting influence his decision to come out to people as bisexual both at work and elsewhere in the community?

Case 2

Sarah came out to her parents as a lesbian two years ago, and they are starting to accept her sexual orientation but still occasionally ask about her high school boyfriends. She has been in an intimate relationship with another woman, Lynn, for the past year. The couple decided to put their relationship on hold for the time being, as both graduated from the same college four months ago and moved back to their respective home cities, 600 miles apart, to live with their families while looking for work. Sarah majored in marketing while Lynn graduated with a degree in finance. Within a month, Lynn was employed with a top business firm in her city, whereas Sarah was just starting to freelance in small-scale, fee-for-services marketing assignments. Three weeks ago, Lynn called Sarah with news that her firm was hiring a marketer for an 18-hour-per-week position. Although Sarah wanted a full-time position, the job in Lynn's city provided steady employment, enough for her to afford to move in with Lynn. She interviewed for the position and was offered the spot the following week. Just as she was packing her belongings to start her career in her partner's home city, she was offered a full-time position at her latest freelance assignment. Unlike the part-time job at Lynn's firm, this one offers full benefits. They are a growing firm with positions in Lynn's field, but none that are currently open.

What are some of the key decisions Sarah faces in terms of her career, financial security, and intimate relationships? Would there be any advantages or disadvantages for Sarah to tell either potential employer about her relationship status? What additional information would Sarah need to make the best career decision possible? How might her situation be different if her partner were a man?

These two cases illustrate the need for culturally competent career counseling for persons early in their careers. Below are two cases, one from a middle-aged lesbian and the other from an older transsexual woman, whose career issues and personal issues are even harder to separate than the first two cases.

Case 3

Marisol is a 41-year-old Latina woman who divorced her husband, Carlos, three years ago. Their 14-year-old daughter and 11-year-old son live with her during the week and live with their father, who lives across the city, on the weekends and some holidays. Marisol works full time as a paralegal and started dating Leah, an attorney in another local law firm, last year. Although this is her first same-sex relationship, Marisol now self-identifies as a lesbian and, upon her invitation, Leah moved in with her a few months ago. With Leah's encouragement, Marisol is now applying to two local law schools, though she worries how she will be able to balance work, family, and going back to school. Leah, a Caucasian woman who has been fairly active in the city's lesbian community, is now running for city council. She knows that being a lesbian will be raised as an issue by her opponents in the race, so she has decided to come out in her campaign and has asked Marisol to appear by her side as her partner at fundraisers and speeches.

Marisol has disclosed her sexual orientation to her children and ex-husband, but not her employer, nor was she planning to come out as a lesbian during her law school interviews over the next two weeks. Carlos, who is a family physician affiliated with St. Mary's Hospital, does not like the idea of Marisol's public disclosure of her sexual orientation and has told Marisol that the children are too young for her to "put their lives on display like that." Feeling distraught, she makes an appointment with you for "personal counseling."

How do the paths of career development and sexual identity development intersect in Marisol's life? How can you, as a counselor, utilize theories and practices of career counseling and personal counseling to help Marisol with life-planning decisions? How might issues of race or ethnicity, gender, job discrimination, and parenting affect how Marisol perceives her situation and which counseling interventions might be most appropriate to use?

Case 4

Hallie is a 58-year-old widow, whose partner of 15 years died suddenly last year. She is a Caucasian male to female (MTF) transsexual who is very private about the details of her gender transition. In her first counseling session, she relates to you a career history in which, as a young man (by the name of Hal), she held a sequence of short-term jobs as an office clerk and home appliance sales representative. She dropped out of school at age 17, but completed a GED 12 years ago "just because I wanted to show everyone I could still do it at my age." Hal was fired from his last full-time job at age 25 when word got out that he was performing at a drag show in town. After that, Hal decided to make what had been a hobby as a drag queen into a career. By age 30, Hal mostly appeared in public as a woman and legally changed his name to Hallie. Hallie supplemented her income as a drag show performer by filling in for bartenders at the club and taking female roles in local theater company productions. As Hallie, she never had employee benefits or earned enough to save for retirement. When she moved in with her partner, Jack, her immediate financial needs were met and she gradually reduced her hours at work, stopping completely six years ago. When he died, there was only enough money to last for two years. Hallie wonders if times have changed enough for her to start working in an office again, but knows her skills are rusty and worries about holding down a mainstream job. She is also curious about a career in cosmetology. Finally, she has no intention of leaving the town where she has lived all of her life.

How can you help Hallie acquire an accurate appraisal of her job skills and vocational interests? Which occupations and employers would provide a good job match for Hallie? How might you use knowledge of gender stereotypes and gender-typed occupations in your work with her? What transgender issues do you need more knowledge about before you can effectively help Hallie? How might you assist her with appropriate retirement planning while also helping her transition back into the workforce?

As these cases illustrate, GLBT persons face a multitude of challenges across the life span, many of which are quite different from those typically encountered within the dominant culture. Awareness of these developmental issues is key to developing appropriate career counseling interventions, but specific recommendations will not be offered until other essential issues, such as the effects of stereotypes and discrimination and the importance of vocational theory, are reviewed.

STEREOTYPES AND DISCRIMINATION: ISSUES IN GLBT CAREER COUNSELING

This section will discuss prominent issues and challenges GLBT individuals face across stages of career development, with particular attention to key points of career choice.

Stereotypes—Society's Portrayal of GLBT in the Workforce

A stereotype is a belief about the personal attributes of a group of people, which can be overgeneralized, inaccurate, and resistant to new information (Myers, 1999). For example, a common stereotype of a gay man is that his occupation is most likely a photographer, nurse, or interior designer, while lesbians are believed to prefer occupations such as mechanic, plumber, or truck driver (Botkin & Daily, 1987; Whitam & Mathy, 1986). Related to these narrow stereotypes is the belief that GLBT individuals are unsuitable for certain careers. These stereotypical beliefs assert that gay men and lesbians are unfit to serve in the military due to their alleged propensity to sexually harass heterosexual counterparts. In occupations where individuals interact with children, such as pediatrician and child-care worker, GLBT individuals are seen as unfit due to the stereotype that they are child molesters (Chung, 1995). This misperception also applies to the teaching profession; gay and lesbian teachers are reluctant to disclose their sexual orientation, fearing such stereotypes will be applied and result in job termination (Griffin, 1992; Woods & Harbeck, 1992).

Despite research refuting such allegations (e.g., Herek, 1993), these stereotypes persist in many cultures. In fact, it has been hypothesized that GLBT individuals may internalize these presumably widely held stereotypical beliefs, thus affecting their career choice (Mobley & Slaney, 1996). As a result, career barriers become instituted and ingrained, leaving GLBT individuals with the perception that fewer vocational choices exist.

Stereotypes in the Media

Stereotypes are often perpetuated through popular media, particularly in the case of gay men. For adolescents, who are at the point in their lives where choosing a vocation is considered a key developmental task, the depiction of media role models can be very influential (Nauta et al., 2001). Social learning theory asserts that children often learn through observation and subsequent imitation (Bandura, 1997). Considerable empirical evidence supports this theory (e.g., Thelan, Frautsh, Roberts, Kirkland, & Dollinger, 1981), as well as extensive research supporting the use of role models in career counseling interventions (Almquist, 1974; Fisher, Reardon, & Burck, 1976; Pallone, Rickard, & Hurley, 1970; Thoresen, Hosford, & Krumboltz, 1970). The "others" observed in an individual's life may be his or her parents, extended family members, people in the child's community, even older brothers and sisters. With the extensive role that media plays in the lives of today's youth, characters from television, movies, newspapers, and advertising have become important influences in our lives, from early childhood onward. These high-profile media role models may become a key element for children and adolescents in the gradual process of choosing a career.

Prior to the 1970s, the media primarily portrayed gays and lesbians as either wicked in character or as the suffering victim (Gross, 1994), and this population was virtually always characterized in a stereotypical way, with gay men shown as effeminate and lesbians as masculine (Shugart, 2003). Although the gay rights movement witnessed popular media progress toward more positive portrayals of gays and lesbians (Capsuto, 2000; Dow, 2001; Gross, 2001; Walters, 2001), stereotypes continue to persist. These individuals are depicted as primarily minor characters inside a heterosexual setting, often devoid of any GLBT social or political reference, with their primary purpose to be supportive to, and understanding of, the heterosexual characters (Brookey, 1996; Brookey & Westerfelhaus, 2001; Dow, 2001; Walters, 2001). Although we were unable to locate data concerning the assigned careers of such characters, their secondary status suggests they did not generally fill positions in society to which most young people aspire.

Although the number of openly GLBT celebrities is rapidly increasing, it is still the case that most came out, or in some cases were forced out of the closet, after having attained celebrity status. Popular athletes, musical performers, and stars of television and film in the 1990s and early 2000s, including Ellen DeGeneres, Elton John, Rosie O'Donnell, Martina Navratilova, Melissa Etheridge, Boy George, and Greg Louganis have all discussed their coming out in the popular press, with many noting how their careers suffered as a result, at least in the short term. In the political arena, U.S. Representatives Barney Frank (D-Massachusetts) and Tammy Baldwin (D-Wisconsin), as well as Winnipeg, Canada, mayor Glen Murray, also came out after being elected to office. Although many of the individuals listed could provide good career role models for GLBT youth wondering about their potential for success, young people may internalize the implicit message that a minority sexual orientation or gender identity is something to conceal until one has established a successful career.

A number of potentially detrimental effects that media role models can have on young GLBT individuals when choosing a career have been postulated (Fejes & Petrich, 1993). For example, while some GLBT persons do, in fact, choose stereotypical careers, such portrayals can limit what a young person might perceive as viable career choices. Specifically, the authors of this chapter have heard statements from young men such as, "I thought I couldn't be gay because I didn't want to be an interior designer."

Gender Stereotypes (Nonconformity)

According to Gottfredson's (1981, 1996) theory of circumscription and compromise, children between the ages of 6 and 8 begin to develop a sense of appropriate careers based on perceived gender role. After the age of 14, children begin to develop more self-awareness and explore careers partially based on this awareness.

Society's determination of what is and is not a gender-appropriate career is learned in early childhood, but may conflict with a child or adolescent's gender identity and stand apart from that individual's sexual identity. It has been suggested that careers seen as gender inappropriate may result in reduced social support by parents (Morrow et al., 1996). Denial of parental support, whether financial, emotional, or both, may result in GLBT individuals choosing careers that may not be congruent with their interests or abilities. It is imperative for counselors to be aware how children or adolescents may be struggling through this very trying time of life and to provide guidance in career decision making.

Economic Stereotypes

Gay men and lesbians have long been perceived to have a surplus of money, creating a growing advertising market targeting "gay disposable income." This myth has been supported by the common stereotype that gay individuals are primarily white, wealthy males (Goldberg, as cited in Badgett, 1998) who are typically free from the economic "burdens" of supporting a spouse and children. Badgett (1998) explored whether these economic beliefs were in fact true for GLB individuals. Badgett's report indicates that GLB individuals in fact do not earn more than their heterosexual counterparts and, in the case of gay males, often earn less than heterosexual males in similar positions. In fact, GLB earnings range on a normal distribution from low to high, with the majority of incomes somewhere in the middle.

While stereotypes in which GLBT individuals are depicted as affluent may not necessarily appear negative, they may serve to perpetuate the mythical gay life. As well, this misperception may lead people to believe that GLBT individuals "have it all" financially; therefore, same-sex rights, such as employee benefits, become a nonissue. This misrepresentation of the gay lifestyle as affluent ignores the fact that GLBT individuals are an oppressed minority that does indeed have to continue to fight for equal employment rights.

Geographic Stereotypes

A disproportionate number of GLBT individuals live in urban areas. In reporting the number of same-sex couples, data from the U.S. Census (Gaydemographics.org, n.d.; U.S. Census Bureau, 2003) depict a distinct difference between urban and rural states. For example, data from the District of Columbia (urban) indicate that same-sex couples make up 5.14 percent of all couples, while figures from the state of North Dakota (rural) indicate that same-sex couples comprise only 0.47 percent of all couples. This geographical variance may be a product of GLBT individuals in urban areas experiencing higher degrees of tolerance and more opportunities for career and social support, such as living with one's partner. In fact, geographic location has been found to be one of the most significant predictors of career selection for gay men and lesbians (Elliott, 1993).

GLBT individuals growing up in rural areas may choose to move to an urban setting in order to access this more tolerant and supportive environment. The result of such an exodus may be detrimental to society and the workforce in a number of ways. First, there is a depletion of positive GLBT role models for rural GLBT adolescents. Second, without a visible GLBT presence in rural communities, tolerance, much less acceptance, is not likely to develop there, which in turn can perpetuate hate crimes. The stereotype of a GLBT person as a resident of a large city reduces the attention to the needs of rural GLBT persons.

One question that arises when considering rural GLBT individuals is where are these individuals employed? How are job opportunities for GLBT individuals different between urban and rural settings? Although there are obviously GLBT individuals in every state and county in the United States, we know little about their employment patterns. We suggest that this is an important area for future research, and may provide a potential resource for GLBT role models within a particular community or area.

DISCRIMINATION IN THE CAREERS OF GLBT PERSONS

Discrimination within a career context can be defined as negative behavior toward individuals, which may be targeted at an individual who is deemed to not "belong" within the organization. "Negative behaviors" may consist of nonhiring policies, firing policies, and lack of advancement opportunities within an organization. A distinction may also be made between overt and covert discrimination. *Overt discrimination* constitutes outward and unconcealed negative behaviors against GLBT individuals. *Covert discrimination* is more subtle negative behavior and can occur even in light of nondiscrimination policies. For example, a workplace may have an antifiring policy based on sexual orientation, but a gay or lesbian individual may be fired under other pretenses.

Although legal protections for gay men and lesbians do exist in some domains, particularly in the public sector, there is no national standard with regard to employment discrimination based on sexual orientation (Lee & Brown, 1993), and even less with regard to gender identity. Since the early 1980s, many states and counties throughout the United States have incorporated nondiscrimination legislation for GLBT individuals (Graham, 1986; Seal, 1991; Susser, 1986). Similar policies have been adopted by private enterprise (Neely Martinez, 1993); however, there remains a fear among GLBT individuals of discrimination on the job (Levine & Leonard, 1984). In fact, the most recent literature available states that GLBT individuals still see workplace discrimination as a serious obstacle (Croteau, 1996; Croteau & Lark, 1995; Croteau & von Destinon, 1994).

Anticipating discrimination, the GLBT individual may be less concerned with his or her ability to perform in a career than what will happen if he or she *does* choose a certain career (Morrow et al., 1996). The fear of discrimination may result in GLBT individuals choosing careers that are "safe" rather than those that are appropriate for their vocational interests and abilities. Whether this fear of discrimination is based on reality or assumptions, the result is marginalization of GLBT individuals into careers that provide a sense of safety. Skilled career counselors should therefore learn to assess the level of affirmation or discrimination in work environments (Gelberg & Chojnacki, 1996).

Although some GLBT persons compromise their interests and abilities for the safety of more affirming workplaces, others knowingly enter systems known to be hostile to their own minority group. Herek (1993), for example, cited the historical function that military service has provided for minority groups seeking social equality. Herek also cited extensive evidence from U.S. and international military services that gay men and lesbians have served their countries effectively and often openly in terms of their sexual orientation. A third argument he presented against current U.S. policy is that rather than being a same-gender issue in the military, male to female sexual harassment is a prevalent problem. A decade after that article's publication, the "don't ask, don't tell" policy remains the most commonly enforced form of legal discrimination used to terminate GLBT employees in the United States, while around the world, more and more countries are realizing success in their inclusion of GLBT recruits in their armed services.

In between the presumably friendly and hostile work environments for GLBT persons are occupational fields that seem to emit mixed signals. For example, Woods and Harbeck (1992) studied the identity management of lesbian physical educators, an occupation commonly stereotyped for lesbians, yet within the historically GLBT-chilly climate of the K–12 education system (Harbeck, 1992). Within higher education, GLB student affairs professionals seem more likely than employees in most departments to be out at work, yet 44 percent still feared future job discrimination related to their sexual orientation (Croteau & Lark, 1995). The pros and cons of coming out to one's students in the college classroom have also been empirically studied and critiqued (Waldo, 1998). In contrast to what we have learned about GLB educators, we know relatively little about the work environment in many other fields where GLBT people are employed, such as skilled and unskilled trades.

Discrimination in Relation to Employee Benefits

As of 1999, approximately 10 percent of employers, both private and public, had instituted what is referred to as domestic partnership benefits (Kohn, 1999). Among this 10 percent are approximately 570 companies, including more than half of the *Fortune* 500 (Gore, 2000), as well as foundations, nonprofit organizations such as the United Way, 87 counties and states, and 141 universities across the United States.

While many companies have incorporated nondiscrimination policies into their workplace, many of these same companies have not provided same-sex employee benefits (Kohn, 1999). As well, many GLBT individuals fear that, even with the option of such benefits, revealing oneself as GLBT in order to take advantage of these benefits may result in other forms of workplace discrimination (Kohn, 1999). Paradoxically, there exists an underlying fear of discrimination despite organizations implementing nondiscrimination policies. One manifestation of such fears pertains to the historical stigma of HIV/AIDS for GBT men. Awareness that a person can lose one's job and not be eligible for health insurance at the next job due to AIDS-related discrimination factors into some gay men's decision not to be tested for HIV (Siegel, Levine, Brooks, & Kern, 1989).

Racial and Ethnic Discrimination Issues

Discrimination against minorities has been evident throughout history. Therefore, for some individuals, for example an African American lesbian, discrimination within the workforce increases as a direct result of the triple minority status in gender, race, and sexual orientation (Garnets & Kimmel, 1991). Therefore, race and ethnicity may augment the effects of discrimination in the workplace (Morrow et al., 1996). Although little has been written within the fields of vocational psychology and career counseling on specific issues for people of color, career counselors can gain insight into career challenges faced by this population by reading books in the popular press. For example, Keith Boykin has provided thought-provoking reflections in his social critique *One More River to Cross: Black and Gay in America* (1996), in which he discusses the tensions between the African American heterosexual and Caucasian gay communities from his perspective as a White House attorney.

GLBT COUPLES AND THEIR CAREERS

There is another set of challenging workplace issues for GLBT persons who are in a committed intimate relationship with a same-sex partner (note that *same-sex partner* is a term that applies better to GLB persons than to transgender persons, for whom having a partner of any gender may raise questions for those not familiar with transgender issues). In this section, we consider issues faced by dual-career gay and lesbian couples. Questions such as "whose career is most important?" are addressed. Similarities to and differences from heterosexual couples are noted, as well as the lack of information available about the relationship between career and intimate relationships for bisexual and transgender persons.

Certain unique issues arise for same-sex couples that may affect career counseling with the individual GLBT client. Some of the key issues include one individual being out and the other being closeted, lack of dual-career role models, discrepant incomes between the two individuals, and implications of one person within the relationship relocating (Pope, 1995). Some of these issues, such as disclosing one's relationship, may seldom occur with heterosexual couples, whereas other issues, such as job relocation, are common. Still, family support networks and employment policies that assist heterosexual couples with career changes are often absent for same-sex couples.

The degree to which one partner is out is often different from that of the other (Fassinger et al., 2003). Day and Schoenrade (1997) measured the discord within a couple related to differences in how much each partner communicated about his or her sexual orientation at work. The authors found a significant relationship between discord level in the work environment and the conflict they experience at home. These same authors also noted that individuals who more openly communicated about their sexual orientation at work (i.e., were out at work) were more likely to perceive their work atmosphere as supportive. However, the authors were quick to indicate that people are more likely to be out when the work atmosphere is supportive, and that there are no clear answers for handling role strain (deciding whether or not to hide one's roles as a GLBT person) within a work environment.

Here is an example of how a couple who is discordant in degree of outness may face challenges in the workplace. It is very common for companies and agencies to have social gatherings for their employees. At these events, special recognition of outstanding employees may occur, food and entertainment are often provided, and employees' spouses or significant others are often invited and, in some cases, implicitly expected to attend. A lesbian employee who is out on the job may want to bring her partner to such an event and may have good reason to believe that the partner would be generally welcomed by others. The partner, however, may feel very uncomfortable at such an event and may worry that news about her sexual orientation would spread through the community and even to her job, where she is passing as heterosexual. The discordance in their degree of outness may therefore cause a strain in their relationship, as deciding upon attendance will be stressful and it is likely that neither will be satisfied with the outcome of attending or not attending the employer's social event.

Many authors have recommended that, to help a client with these relationship issues, individual career counseling for GLBT clients should be combined with dual-career *couples* counseling when appropriate (Belz, 1993; Elliott, 1993; Morgan & Brown, 1991; Orzek, 1992). For example, with regard to one person within the relationship being out and the other being closeted, it may prove important to work with the couple in terms of how each wishes to present the other to colleagues. As well, if one person within the relationship relocates, how might this affect the partner? What career opportunities, if any, exist in this new location for the other person within the relationship? The couple may have to decide whose career is more important to advance at this point in their lives, a difficult decision that may be facilitated by career counseling.

Income differentials within lesbian couples may also be an issue, as any substantial variances in earnings may create discord within the egalitarian lesbian relationship (Fassinger, 1995). Income differentials within gay male couples may pose a challenge to the socialized male gender role of breadwinner, though this possibility has not yet been empirically studied. For a bisexual person, the issues discussed previously may be more relevant if he or she is currently in a same-sex relationship, but less important if one's life partner or current relationship is with a person of the opposite sex. As with gay male couples, dual-career issues for bisexual persons have not been systematically studied. This situation also holds true for transgendering persons, though we may speculate about these issues. If, for example, an MTF transsexual employee discusses her intimate partner at work, whether or not the partner is male or female, homophobic responses among coworkers, supervisors, and, if applicable, customers and clients, may be greater than if the employee were to conceal her relationship status at work.

Issues such as inclusion of a partner at employee social functions, placing a picture of one's partner in one's office, employee benefits, and job relocation may not only affect career decisions within a dual-career relationship, but may ultimately affect the quality of a couple's relationship as well. Current events may propel researchers and clinicians to investigate at greater depth the issues affecting same-sex couples in careers. In the United States, for example, the debates around same-sex marriage have reached the level of major lawsuits and a proposed amendment to the U.S. Constitution. Counselors working with same-sex couples who are married or who have formed a civil union may more often encounter couples' life planning and divorce issues than the familiar issue of degree of "outness" of each partner. In the meantime, career counselors are advised to attend to relationship issues that their clients may not disclose, and to stay abreast of advocacy efforts, such as the American Psychological Association's proposal for legal benefits for same-sex couples (Levant, 1999) and resolution supporting the legalization of same-sex civil marriages (American Psychological Association, 2004).

THEORIES OF CAREER COUNSELING

Whether or not counselors have a specific career-counseling focus, the variety of settings in which GLBT individuals seek help for work-related issues calls for a theoretical understanding of the issues and concerns faced by this population. The purpose of this section is to review three broad categories of the career theories and discuss them in the context of concerns pertinent to a GLBT population. The three broad theories discussed here are trait-factor theories, developmental theories, and learning theories. Given space limitations, our goal is to highlight theories that address issues raised in this chapter, as well as theories that have already engendered discussion in the GLBT literature.

Trait-Factor Theories

Trait-factor theories vary in their complexity and sophistication, but they are unified by the assumption that knowledge of specific individual characteristics (particularly interests and abilities) and specific occupational characteristics (such as entry require-ments, tasks performed, and the nature of working environment) aid in the career choice and attainment process (Parsons, 1909; Sharf, 2002). Two trait-factor theories, Holland's theory of career decision making and the theory of work adjustment, are considered next, with close attention given to their implications for GLBT individuals.

Holland's (1997) hexagon theory posits that six basic constellations of characteris-tics ("Holland Codes") are believed to describe individuals and that the same six codes also apply to work environments. Much attention has been paid to whether Holland's model holds up across cultures (Ryan, Tracey, & Rounds, 1996), with many investigators indicating that, with minor modifications, the model is appropriate for people from a variety of backgrounds (Rounds & Tracey, 1996). However, Mobley and Slaney (1996) argued that while matching an individual's characteristics (Holland Codes) to the appro-priate work environment is relevant to gay men and lesbians, it is less relevant than finding a work environment that is gay or lesbian affirming. According to the authors, gay men and lesbians will have more job satisfaction, and consequently more life satisfac-tion, if the work environment is tolerant or supportive of homosexuality, regardless of how well "matched" the person is in terms of vocational interests or abilities.

Several authors have suggested that the Holland Codes themselves have implica-tions for GLBT individuals. For example, Chung and Harmon (1994) indicated that gay men, as compared to heterosexual men, were more likely to score higher in artistic and socially oriented Holland Codes. Likewise, Fassinger (1996) argued that lesbians are more likely than heterosexual women to express interest in jobs that are more tra-ditionally associated with men, including jobs that have more traditionally masculine Holland Codes, such as Realistic and Investigative. Many writers (Chung & Harmon, 1994; Hetherington & Orzek, 1989; Mobley & Slaney, 1996) have proposed that the process by which these differences are brought about is related to gender identity development, with gay men and lesbians having developed a self-concept of their own gender role that is less traditional. Although this hypothesis was not supported in a study that compared highly educated gay and heterosexual men in terms of differ-ences in the development of nontraditional gender identity (Chung & Harmon, 1994), similar investigations of the hypothesis with a broader population (women and less educated men) are worth conducting before dismissing this notion.

Like Holland's theory, the theory of work adjustment (TWA; Dawis & Loftquist, 1984) holds that career attainment is a result of a match between individuals and their environments. In the case of TWA, however, this match is broken down into the key constructs of satisfaction and satisfactoriness. Specifically, satisfaction happens when a working environment provides adequate reinforcement for an individual's value system, and satisfactoriness occurs when an individual adequately completes the tasks and demands of employment in a manner deemed appropriate (or valuable) by the employer (Dawis, 1994). In this sense, then, TWA is a theory of mutual reinforce-ment; when mutual reinforcement is achieved, job tenure is obtained. When mutual reinforcement is not achieved (by one or both parties), either changes are made or employment is terminated.

For GLBT individuals, TWA may provide a better explanatory system of career attainment than Holland's theory, primarily due to a broader interpretation of what makes for a matched environment. For example, a transgender individual may place a high value on acceptance of his or her gender presentation, and consequently may seek a working environment based largely on that value alone. Likewise, work environments that value traditional male and female roles may discriminate against individuals who present with a nontraditional gender identity. In the latter example, GLBT individuals must often make difficult decisions, including whether to continue employment without making changes (and possibly deal with significant discrimination, harassment, or termination for not conforming to societal norms), whether to make personal changes at work (such as trying to pass as heterosexual or traditionally gendered), whether to attempt to change the work environment (through education or possibly litigation), or whether to seek employment elsewhere (cf., Dawis, 1994). In an empirical test of the TWA model among a GLB population ($N = 397$), Lyons, Brenner, and Fassinger (2004) did indeed find that workplace heterosexism accounted for 10.4 percent of the variance in job satisfaction.

In regard to the application of TWA, Degges-White (2002) provides a thorough review of the literature in its implications for working with lesbian clients. Specifically, Degges-White indicated that, from a TWA perspective, work decisions are made based on the reinforcement value (or intensity) of the particular issue under consideration. For example, Degges-White presented the notion that a lesbian who values congruence between her personal life and her work life may decide to be out at work, despite the possible consequences of harassment or discrimination. In light of the relevant literature, Degges-White suggested that the effective counselor working with a lesbian client would do well to explore the reinforcement value for (a) the salary differences for lesbians who are out (Ellis & Riggle, 1996), (b) the absence of discrimination and/or harassment (Croteau et al., 2000), (c) the degree of openness about sexual orientation (Mohr & Fassinger, 2000), (d) the desire to work in nontraditional (gender) occupations (Morgan & Brown, 1991), (e) the impact of passing or not passing on developing meaningful relationships at work (Driscoll, Kelley, & Fassinger, 1996), and (f) the impact of being a token and the possible isolation and concomitant stress that may result (Degges-White, 2002).

Developmental Theories

Like trait-factor theories, developmental theories look at the match between individuals and their working environment. However, unlike trait-factor theories, developmental theories focus on how an individual's characteristics develop and change throughout the life span (Savickas, 2002). Consequently, developmental theories focus on how the self-concept is formed, on what role environmental and genetic factors play in its formation, and, more generally, on the subjective view of the individual. With reference to the lives of GLBT persons, two developmental theories are considered next: Super's life span, life-space theory (Super, 1990) and Gottfredson's theory of circumscription and compromise (Gottfredson, 2002).

As the title suggests, Super's (1990) theory of career development is based on two intersecting life dimensions. The first, life span, refers to the developmental periods (or tasks) that come to shape our self-concept. Super identified five primary developmental periods, including growth (ages 4–13), exploration (14–24), establishment (25–44), maintenance (45–65), and disengagement (65 and over). While Super suggested specific ages for each of these developmental periods, he also recognized the importance of both recycling (moving back through the stages in the course of a career change) and adaptability (the ability to deal with the changes inherent in today's world of work). The second dimension, life space, refers to the different roles played by an individual, including that of worker, student, citizen, parent, child, and spouse (in Super's terminology), Super argued that different roles can take on greater or lesser importance depending on the developmental period in question.

Super's theory directly addresses vocationally oriented developmental tasks but only indirectly addresses other more general developmental issues. Nonetheless, several authors (Boatwright et al., 1996; Dunkle, 1996; Hetherington, 1991; Schmidt et al., 2003) have integrated the two core issues of sexual identity development and gender identity development into the framework of Super's model, resulting in clinically and theoretically constructive conceptualizations. For example, Dunkle (1996) reviewed Cass's (1979) model of gay and lesbian identity development and overlaid it on Super's developmental stages. Belz (1993), Boatwright et al. (1996), and Hetherington (1991) all discussed the notion that attention to sexual orientation (identity confusion, discrimination, coming out issues) often come at the expense of vocational development issues. Specifically referring to adolescence, Hetherington hypothesized that attention to sexual orientation creates a "bottleneck" effect. The bottleneck effect holds that the majority of a GBLT youth's psychological energy will be devoted to coming out concerns rather than career concerns—a hypothesis that was recently supported in a comparison study of gay, lesbian, and heterosexual high school students (Schmidt et al., 2003).

In looking beyond the adolescent years, Boatwright and colleagues (1996) identified several vocationally oriented themes among lesbians they interviewed. One such theme supported the presence of a recycling process that happens as part of coming out, with some women describing this period as a "second adolescence," and others describing it as the adolescence they never had. Most of the women (9 of 10) also indicated that coming out either slowed down, stalled, or changed their career process, adding merit to the idea that coming out takes psychological energy. This, combined with homophobia and job discrimination, can thwart the career paths of both adolescents and adults. Importantly, Fassinger (1995, 1996) pointed out positive aspects of being a lesbian on women's career development, including the freedom to explore a range of occupational options.

The life-roles component of Super's theory may also be useful in understanding the issues within the GBLT population. Though never discussed by Super, the lack of recognition given to same-sex intimate relationships brings to the forefront the role that a "partner" plays in one's career. Super does discuss at some length how roles can conflict with each other, and for members of the GLBT community, this can be particularly true if the two persons involved in a relationship are at different degrees of outness (Day & Schoenrade, 1997; Fassinger et al., 2003).

The second developmental theory under consideration, Gottfredson's (2002) theory of circumscription and compromise, is predicated on the notion that as individuals develop, they increasingly restrict (circumscribe) their job choices based on perceptions of acceptable occupational sex type and prestige (known as the zone of acceptable alternatives). Individual interests and perceptions of ability facilitate the determination of choices only within the already developed (or circumscribed) zone of acceptable alternatives. Gottfredson's (2002) theory also delineates a series of developmental stages (only two are reviewed here). The first stage is the orientation to power and size (ages 3–5), and the second is orientation to sex roles (ages 6–8).

In regard to this latter stage, Gottfredson (2002) has written at length about how individuals come to understand that different jobs are stereotyped on a scale of masculinity-femininity. However, little is discussed regarding an individual's own gender identity or how a nontraditional gender identity might intersect with an individual's perceptions of acceptable job choices (however, see Henderson, Hesketh, & Tuffin, 1988; Kim, 2002; Leung & Harmon, 1990; for vocational studies with gender identity as a primary component). For example, if a nine-year-old boy exhibits traditionally feminine interests, how (or when) does he integrate that into his own self-concept? How do his gender atypical interests affect the development of his zone of acceptable occupational alternatives (particularly on the masculinity-femininity scale)? How does the conflict between self-perceptions of nontraditional gender identity, coexisting with conscious awareness of societal stereotypes regarding femininity and masculinity, impact his occupational decision making? Gottfredson's theory opens the door to discussing the role of gender identity within career decision making, but only part way. Much more theoretically (and empirically) driven work needs to be done to address this complex issue within the GLBT community (Chung, 1995), including outcome evaluations of interventions aimed at impacting occupational sex-role stereotypes (Gottfredson & Lapan, 1997).

In addition to significance of including sex-role stereotyping in our understanding of career choice and attainment, Gottfredson (2002) discussed two additional constructs that are particularly relevant to the career issues of GLBT persons. The first construct is the notion of accessibility (as a component of compromise). Accessibility refers to the perceptions individuals have about the feasibility of obtaining a particular job, and can include such elements as job availability, family obligations, and the presence or absence of discrimination. For GLBT individuals, the accessibility of a particular career may be constrained by perceptions of homophobia within a given occupation, company, or region of the country.

The second construct worth noting is the notion of a life niche and its interaction with culture. According to Gottfredson (2002):

> The ability to express or implement one's abilities, interests, and other traits on a sustained basis—to create a life niche comporting with them—depends on the availability of cultural channels for their expression. Stated another way, cultural roles and activities are the raw materials that genetically distinct individuals have for building their preferred social niches. We must be public selves to be ourselves in human society, but we must work within the menu of possible public selves (jobs, family roles, and so on) that our particular culture provides or allows. (p. 124)

Akin to self-actualization, Gottfredson's "life niche" becomes a powerful tool for counselors, clients, and researchers to understand the impact of culture on an individual's pursuit of happiness. As career counselors, it is essential to appreciate how some work settings affirm the public expression of an employee's GLBT identity, whereas others serve as a cultural tool to inhibit or punish the attempt to develop a social niche as a GLBT person. Utilizing the notion of life niche may facilitate useful, though at times difficult, dialogues on how culture impacts occupational choice for the GLBT client. Such a dialogue might encompass choices about creating a life niche that is open versus closeted, or one that compromises vocational interests for the sake of a supportive (non-homophobic) work environment.

Learning Theories

Based primarily on the work of Bandura (1986, 1997), theories falling within this framework emphasize the role of learning in addition to the influences of genetic and environmental factors in career development. Two learning theories are prominent in the field of career counseling, Krumboltz's social learning theory for career decision making (Krumboltz, 1996) and social cognitive career theory (SCCT; Lent, Brown, & Hackett, 1994). Because of the demonstrated potential in addressing the career development concerns of GLBT persons (Morrow et al., 1996), only SCCT is considered here.

In writing about SCCT, Lent et al. (1994, 2002) emphasized three key cognitive constructs that, in addition to considerations of genetic and environmental factors, serve to facilitate career development. According to Lent et al., these constructs are self-efficacy (self-perceived ability), outcome expectations (perceived results of an action or behavior), and goals. In line with Bandura (1997), beliefs about self-efficacy, outcome expectations, and goals are gained through direct learning, indirect (vicarious) learning, emotional arousal, and persuasion.

Morrow et al. (1996) reviewed each of the three main SCCT cognitive constructs in the context of GLBT career-related concerns. The authors noted that, developmentally speaking, children's perceptions of self-efficacy begin before sexual orientation is identified, but often at the same time as gender identity development. Consequently, those whose gender identity is nontraditional (a common GLBT theme; Ossana, 2000) may experience a unique set of issues that impact their self-efficacy development, particularly in a culture that values gender-role conformity. For example, the almost exclusive societal role models of male auto mechanics may cause girls to vicariously learn that they do not have the capabilities to pursue this occupation, despite an expressed interest in the area. Likewise, negative outcome expectations may develop around the harassment they foresee if they pursued this goal. According to Morrow et al., "Unpleasant associations with being perceived as different will lead to negative outcome expectations related to behaviors that further draw attention to the child's differentness" (1996, p. 141).

In addition to the possible impact of nontraditional gender identity on early career development, GLBT individuals may also deal with discrimination and harassment of identifying (or being identified) as gay, lesbian, bisexual, or transgender. As noted earlier in the chapter, this discrimination can come in the form of hiring practices, on-the-job harassment, salary differences, isolation, and stereotyping (Croteau et al., 2000; Fassinger, 1991). It also may take the form of family-of-origin discord and/or hostility directed at the GLBT son or daughter—discord that has a significant mental health impact on GLBT youth (Hershberger & D'Augelli, 2000; Morrow et al., 1996).

According to Morrow et al. (1996), these and other barriers to career development and satisfaction may also be framed within a social cognitive model. For example, whether the barrier of on-the-job harassment is only perceived, or perceived and real, such perceptions are likely to change the work behaviors and goals of an individual experiencing them. Likewise, if a particular career is perceived to be "gay friendly," such a perception may encourage an otherwise uninterested person to pursue it due to an outcome expectation of support around GLBT issues. However, these arguments are largely theoretical, though some indirect empirical support does exist. For example, Waldo (1999) found that GLBT persons who experience on-the-job heterosexism were more likely to experience adverse psychological, health, and job-related outcomes.

ASSESSMENT ISSUES IN CAREER COUNSELING

Counselors working with GLBT clients are ethically obligated to develop awareness, knowledge, and skills required for appropriate assessment of their clients' concerns (American Psychological Association, 1999; Chung, 2003). For our purposes, the term *assessment* may include clinical interviews for diagnostic purposes (i.e., understanding the presenting concern) or the administration of formal psychological tests and surveys. In either situation, counselors must be aware of their own biases and potential heterosexism or risk becoming ineffective (or even harmful) in the therapeutic approach (Division 44/Committee on Lesbian, Gay, and Bisexual Concerns Joint Task Force, 2000).

While self-awareness of attitudes regarding GLBT issues is imperative, equally valuable is obtaining the basic knowledge (and skills) of the concerns frequently experienced by GLBT persons. These concerns include, but are not limited to, knowledge of the coming out process; knowledge of the risks of coming out; knowledge of the impact of discrimination and harassment and stereotyping; knowledge of community issues, role models, and resources; knowledge of the impact of internalized stereotyping for the GLBT person; and knowledge of dual-career issues (Chung, 2003). Additional knowledge specific to assessment includes how formal psychological tests and measurements may contain a heterosexist bias.

The issue of heterosexist bias in testing has recently received attention in the GLBT literature. In particular, Morin and Charles (1983) and Chernin, Holden, and Chandler (1997) identified three primary sources of heterosexist bias that counselors should consider in test administration. These sources of bias include omission bias (e.g., omitting language that is inclusive of GLBT persons), connotation bias (e.g., including references to homosexuality in lists of characteristics that have negative connotations), and contiguity bias (e.g., including scales meant to "diagnose" homosexuality with scales that diagnose psychopathology). Prince (1997) also argued that heterosexism is also present in content bias (e.g., omitting content that is GLBT specific) and in the lack of norms specific to a GLBT population.

For example, whereas the Strong Interest Inventory (Harmon, Hansen, Borgen, & Hammer, 1994) does not contain omission, connotation, or contiguity biases (Chernin et al., 1997), the Infrequency Response Scale (a validity scale) is based on gender norms. That is, those who express nontraditional gender interests are more likely to have more infrequent responses, which in turn may make it more likely that the test would be considered invalid (Pope, 1992). Pope (1992) argued that, for GLBT clients, such a finding may be inappropriate, and the counselors may wish to use the inventory for purposes of interpretation, but with the appropriate cautions.

In addition to the importance of scrutinizing assessment for the presence of heterosexual bias, counselors are also encouraged to consider the impact of vocational testing on their clients. Pope (1992) provided several case examples of individuals expressing concerns around psychological assessment, as they believed the tests would reveal their gay, lesbian, bisexual, or transgender status. Consequently, as with counseling in general, counselors must work to understand the impact of testing on their clients, giving due consideration and respect to an individual's stage of sexual identity development and degree of communication about his or her identity.

RECOMMENDATIONS FOR THE PRACTICE OF CAREER COUNSELING

In this section, a list of recommendations will be offered to enhance the practice of career counselors working with GLBT clients. This list is not meant to be exhaustive; instead it should be considered a sample of theoretically and empirically based suggestions for a variety of career-counseling domains.

We can begin to dispel stereotypes and counter the effects of discrimination by following the recommendations listed below to provide quality career counseling to GLBT individuals:

MANAGING STEREOTYPES AND DISCRIMINATION
1. Be aware of the influence and detrimental effects that discrimination, stigma, and stereotypical portrayals can have on GLBT people, and help our clients to place discrimination and these stereotypes in perspective; for example, provide resources to help clients accurately distinguish between real and perceived discrimination, as well as between formal and informal discrimination in the workplace (Chung, 2001).
2. Become aware of our *own* stereotypical beliefs and prejudices toward GLBT individuals; if we ourselves are GLBT, realize that these beliefs and prejudices may be internalized.
3. Provide career resources specifically geared toward GLBT persons. Some career Websites that cater to gay men and lesbians are listed at the end of this chapter. It should also be noted that fewer resources are available for bisexual and transgender persons.
4. Become aware of local, national, and international role models for GLBT clients, especially for youth. In light of the paucity of openly bisexual and transgender individuals, consider the appropriateness of a gay or lesbian role model for bisexual or transgender clients. However, caution should be taken about outing a potential role model. Studies of GLB individuals suggest that whereas they *want* career role models, many potential GLB role models may be hesitant to provide such a service for fear of being outed (Griffin, 1992; Olson, 1987; Woods &

Harbeck, 1992), particularly in rural areas or in careers in which GLBT status is seen as less acceptable, such as K–12 teacher or pediatrician.

5. Look for opportunities to advocate for GLBT persons facing discrimination on the job or when seeking employment. Often, discrimination is institutionalized within a heterosexist organization. A recent study by Brenner, Lyons, and Fassinger (2004), for example, suggested that employees in heterosexist organizations must spend some of their energy managing their sexual orientation identity (e.g., remaining in the closet), which leads to organizational sexual orientation isolation rather than engaging in prosocial organizational citizenship behaviors. Practitioners are in a position to help promote employee wellness through interventions at the organizational level that could change policies and practices in heterosexist work environments (Brenner et al., 2004; Smith & Ingram, 2004). "Safe space" stickers on one's office door is a way that counselors and human resource personnel can indicate knowledge of, and openness to, GLBT issues.

LANGUAGE, LABELING, AND IDENTITY

6. Rather than prematurely labeling your client's experience or identity, use inclusive, nonheterosexist language with GLBT clients (Barret & Logan, 2002; Bieschke & Matthews, 1996).

7. Understand the distinction between sexual orientation and gender identity. For example, do not assume a transgender client is gay, lesbian, or bisexual. Instead, assess the degree to which a transgender client feels affiliated with the GLB community. Similarly, appreciate that some lesbian and bisexual women may appear to enact an exaggeratedly masculine (butch) role, others may act in such a manner even when trying not to, whereas a third set of lesbian and bisexual women will appear to be very traditionally feminine (a femme role), and still others will be characterized by androgyny. Gay and bisexual men's gender roles are similarly diverse. Your client's own comfort with his or her gender identity will likely interact with your own comfort level with that role as well as the fit among the client's gender role, sexual orientation, and work environment.

ETHICS

8. We adhere to the Ethical Codes of the counseling profession (American Counseling Association, 1995) when we act in accordance with basic ethical principles (Kitchener, 1984). With GLBT clients, for example, we can abide by the principle of nonmaleficence (avoiding harmful actions) by understanding our client's worldview as a GLBT person and not treating him or her according to heterosexist assumptions. Similarly, we act with justice when we affirm and advocate for our client's rights by providing opportunities to seek employment that affirms his or her GLBT status or to work toward a fair resolution when facing discrimination with an oppressive employer.

9. No matter what our sexual orientation or gender identity is, we were all raised in a heterosexist environment that also reinforces traditional gender roles. Therefore, even when functioning well, we are prone to activate heterosexist assumptions without being aware of it. In some cases, however, our personal issues or stage of sexual orientation or gender identity development may impede

our ability to provide optimal counseling services to clients dealing with similar issues. Morrow (2000) reviews common distortions in the therapeutic relationship and provides suggestions for handling several challenges. For example, counselors should be able to make decisions about self-disclosing their own sexual orientation without great ambivalence and should refrain from working with clients whose struggles are too similar to their own.

CULTURAL CONTEXT

10. Realize that whereas your GLBT client may be part of the dominant culture in most respects, in other respects he or she is a member of a minority group with special needs. Become familiar with recently published guidelines pertaining to GLB clients (Division 44/Committee on Lesbian, Gay, and Bisexual Concerns Joint Task Force, 2000) and multiculturally competent counseling practice (American Psychological Association, 2003).

11. Be aware of the cultural context of your client outside of the workplace. What issues is he or she facing that may influence readiness for career decision making? An extreme example would be a college student whose parents are threatening to stop paying his tuition, room, and board now that he has come out as gay, whereas a more ordinary example would be the dilemma faced by a lesbian client who is not out at work and must find excuses to leave work on occasion to care for her partner's preschool children. Different still, you may be called upon to help your client come to a decision to move to a geographic location with a richer GLBT culture (Bieschke & Matthews, 1996).

IDENTITY DEVELOPMENT

12. Be sensitive to a client's stage of sexual or gender identity development. Prince (1995) provides an example of the temptation to mislabel as psychopathology the behavior of a man from a repressive home environment who suddenly immerses himself into the gay culture, thereby setting aside career priorities (cf. Boatwright et al., 1996; Schmidt et al., 2003). Understanding such a life-course detour as part of normative development rather than a sign of psychological maladjustment will serve career counselors and their clients well.

GENERAL CAREER COUNSELING SKILLS

13. Despite the many differences across sexual orientation and gender identity to be mindful of when working with GLBT clients, rest assured that your general counseling skills, such as listening, empathy, respect, and well-timed confrontation, will serve you well with GLBT clients. On the other hand, most GLBT people have learned to detect subtle messages of disapproval, dismissal, or insincere expressions of concern and are very likely to terminate services with a counselor soon after any disrespect is perceived.

14. In addition to interpersonal counseling skills, the career counselor's expertise in the world of work and the local job market will be well utilized and even enhanced by working with job-ready GLBT clients.

RECOMMENDATIONS FOR RESEARCH

As an emerging area of inquiry, research in GLBT career development and career counseling is still in its early stages of development. While some prominent vocational psychologists are conducting studies to test a spherical versus hexagonal model of career interests for the general population and beginning to compare data to link over-arching theories of personality, abilities, and vocational interests (Swanson & Gore, 2000), those who study GLBT career issues are working with more basic research problems, such as trying to obtain more representative samples and move beyond studies that report only descriptive statistics.

To the credit of researchers studying GLBT career issues, they continue to investigate societal barriers such as discrimination and harassment, despite preliminary evidence within the broader field of career counseling research that such barriers account for little variance in career intervention outcomes (Brown & Ryan Krane, 2000). It has been suggested, however, that the general lack of support for the importance of career barriers may be an artifact of including relatively few research participants (only a small number of whom are members of minority groups) who have experienced significant societal barriers (Brown & Ryan Krane, 2000). Clearly the barriers faced by GLBT persons in the workforce are worth investigating further; dissemination of the resultant data will inform career counselors and their clients about the extent of such remaining barriers, areas of opportunity revealed as policies and societal attitudes shift, and strategies to manage workplace identity in cases where clients must continue to face anti-GLBT policies and attitudes on the job.

In addition to the continued need for such studies, the link between research and practice would be strengthened if the GLBT career research agenda were broadened. In 1995, Y. B. Chung reviewed the career decision-making literature for GLB individuals, noted the lack of research in several important areas, and made specific recommendations for future studies. In writing this chapter, we suspected that few such studies have since been conducted, a hunch that was supported by the original author (Y. B. Chung, personal communication, October 31, 2003). Specifically, no published studies exist for GLBT workers with lower educational attainment, no research has been conducted to test hypotheses of Gottfredson's (1981, 1996) circumscription and compromise theory of career aspiration as they pertain to atypical gender roles among GLBT persons, and no outcome studies have been conducted on recent interventions that educate individuals in the workplace about GLBT issues. Modest progress over the past decade, however, was reported for a broadened methodological focus from between-group methodology to a few newer studies using within-group comparisons for gay men and lesbian women (Y. B. Chung, personal communication, October 31, 2003). Overall, we continue to learn more about the vocational interests, career barriers, and changing workplace environments for GLBT persons, but the pace seems to have decreased since the late 1980s through mid-1990s, with no new empirically supported interventions for career counselors working with this population. Finally, we encourage researchers to conduct studies including significant numbers of bisexual and transgender persons. Qualitative studies are particularly recommended to begin the exploratory and descriptive work that may help launch this important area of inquiry.

SUMMARY

All counselors will work with GLBT clients during their career. They must therefore acquire the knowledge and skills and develop the attitudes that will increase their cultural competency to work with this minority population. Whether working as a career counselor or in other counseling specialties, counselors are in a distinctive position to facilitate the career exploration and understand the workforce barriers of their GLBT clients and to help them maximize their vocational contribution to society. In this chapter we have provided a variety of information and tools to enable counselors to work more effectively with their GLBT clients' careers. By reviewing and using inclusive and affirmative language; discussing the challenges and opportunities within the workplace; exploring issues of stereotypes, discrimination, role models, and mentorship; and grounding our presentation in theory, research, assessment practice, ethical principles, and multicultural counseling skills, we hope to have provided a foundation for counselors to meet the career needs of GLBT clients. The four detailed and complex case examples may have spawned more questions than the chapter provided answers for. As many concrete answers cannot be provided, we encourage readers to continue to learn about the lives of GLBT individuals and the challenges imposed by a society that often does not grant GLBT persons full human rights and to commit themselves to helping GLBT clients lead productive, rewarding careers.

The following lists of Websites, films, and books provide additional information relating to the chapter topics.

USEFUL WEBSITES

Employment Resources

Gaywork.com (in partnership with Monster.com—job searches, resumé postings, etc.)

www.gaywork.com

GLBT Central (GLBT careers and gay-friendly employers)

www.glbtcentral.com/employment.html

Lavender Xpress (job opportunities with gay and gay-friendly employers)

www.infotycoon.com/lavenderx/careers.htm

Jobsearch.com—gay resource division of Website (job search, writing resumés, etc.)

www.jobsearch.about.com/cs/gayresources

Planetout.com—information on money and careers

www.planetout.com/pno/splash.html

Organizations for Specific Occupational Fields

Aerospace—National Gay Pilots Association

www.ngpa.org

Military—British military Website:

www.rank-outsiders.org.uk

U.S. military website:

www.sldn.org/templates/index.html

Scientific & Technical—National Organization of Gay and Lesbian Scientists and Technical Professionals Inc.

www.noglstp.org

Legal, Educational, and Advocacy Resources

Gay and Lesbian Alliance against Defamation (GLAAD)

www.glaad.org

Gay, Lesbian, and Straight Education Network (GLSEN)

www.glsen.org

Human Rights Campaign

www.hrc.org

Institute for Gay and Lesbian Strategic Studies

www.iglss.org

Lambda Legal

www.lambdalegal.org

National Gay and Lesbian Taskforce

www.ngltf.org

Miscellaneous Resources

The Advocate Magazine

www.advocate.com

Queer Resources Directory

www.qrd.org/qrd

USEFUL FILM DOCUMENTARIES (MANY AVAILABLE AT WWW.WOLFEVIDEO.COM)

Gay Men and Lesbians in Careers

The Times of Harvey Milk, 1984. Rob Epstein, Director. A documentary about the career and assassination of San Francisco's first gay councilor.

Coming Out under Fire, 1994. Arthur Dong, Director. The stories of nine gay and lesbian military veterans who volunteered to fight for the United States yet faced persecution because of their sexual orientation.

Homophobia in the Workplace, 1993. Narrated by Brian McNaught. Explains why companies need to address issues of concern to gay, lesbian, and bisexual employees and how to do so effectively. Los Angeles: Motivated Media Available at: www.trbproductions.com/video.html

Historic GLBT Events

Before Stonewall, 1984. Robert Rosenberg and John Scagliotti, Directors. A history of gay men and lesbians prior to the Stonewall riots, which precipitated the major gay rights movement.

After Stonewall, 1999. John Scagliotti, Director. A companion documentary to *Before Stonewall*, covering the gay rights movement of the last 30 years of the twentieth century.

The Question of Equality, 1995. Robert Byrd, III, and Robyn Hutt, Directors. A four-part historical video series, commencing in the 1960s with the gay rights movement and proceeding to the battle against HIV/AIDS, restrictions of federal policies and laws against GLBT individuals, and the courage and outlook of contemporary gay and lesbian youth.

GLBT Persons in Diverse Populations

Trembling Before G-d, 2001. Sandi Simcha Dubowski, Director. Stories from gay and lesbian Hasidic and Orthodox Jews.

Transgender Story

The Brandon Teena Story, 1998. Greta Olafsdottir and Susan Muska, Directors. An FTM transgender biopic.

USEFUL BOOKS FOR COUNSELING GLBT INDIVIDUALS

Chernin, J. N., & Johnson, M. R. (2002). *Affirmative psychotherapy and counseling for lesbians and gay men.* Thousand Oaks, CA: Sage.

Lev, A. I. (2004). *Transgender emergence: Therapeutic guidelines for working with gender-variant people and their families.* Binghamton, NY: Haworth Press.

Perez, R. M., Debord, K. A., & Bieschke, K. J. (2000). *Handbook of counseling and psychotherapy with lesbian, gay, and bisexual clients.* Washington, DC: American Psychological Association.

REFERENCES

Almquist, E. M. (1974). Sex stereotypes in occupational choice: The case for college women. *Journal of Vocational Behavior, 5*, 13–21.

American Counseling Association. (1995). *Code of ethics and standards of practice.* Retrieved August 16, 2004, from http://www.counseling.org/Content/NavigationMenu/Resources/Ethics/ACA_Code_of_Ethics.pdf

American Psychological Association. (2003). Guidelines on multicultural education, training, research, practice, and organizational change for psychologists. *American Psychologist, 58*, 377–402.

American Psychological Association. (2004). *Resolution on sexual orientation and marriage.* Retrived August 16, 2004, from http://www.apa.org/releases/gaymarriage_reso.pdf

Badgett, M. V. L. (1998). *Income inflation: The myth of affluence among gay, lesbian, and bisexual Americans.* New York: Author, the Policy Institute of the National Gay and Lesbian Task Force (NGLTF), and the Institute for Gay and Lesbian Strategic Studies.

Bandura, A. (1986). *Social foundations of thought and action: A social cognitive theory.* Englewood Cliffs, NJ: Prentice Hall.

Bandura, A. (1997). *Self-efficacy: The exercise of control.* San Francisco: W. H. Freeman.

Barret, B., & Logan, C. (2002). *Counseling gay men and lesbians: A practice primer.* Pacific Grove, CA: Brooks/Cole.

Belz, J. R. (1993). Sexual orientation as a factor in career development. *Career Development Quarterly, 41,* 197–200.

Bem, S. L. (1974). The measurement of psychological androgyny. *Journal of Consulting and Clinical Psychology, 42,* 155–162.

Bieschke, K. J., & Matthews, C. (1996). Career counselor attitudes and behaviors toward gay, lesbian, and bisexual clients. *Journal of Vocational Behavior, 48,* 243–255.

Boatwright, K. J., Gilbert, M. S., Forrest, L., & Ketzenberger, K. (1996). Impact of identity development upon career trajectory: Listening to the voices of lesbian women. *Journal of Vocational Behavior, 48,* 210–228.

Botkin, M., & Daily, J. (1987). *Occupational development of lesbians and gays.* Paper presented at the American College Student Personnel Association Annual Meeting, Chicago, IL.

Boykin, K. (1996). *One more river to cross: Black and gay in America.* New York: Anchor Books.

Brenner, B. R., Lyons, H. Z., & Fassinger, R. E. (2004). *Workplace heterosexism and organizational citizenship behaviors.* Unpublished manuscript, University of Maryland.

Brookey, R. A. (1996). A community like Philadelphia. *Western Journal of Communication, 60,* 40–56.

Brookey, R. A., & Westerfelhaus, R. W. (2001). Pistols and petticoats, piety and purity: *To Wong Foo,* the queering of the American monomyth, and the marginalizing discourse of deification. *Critical Studies in Media Communication, 18,* 141–156.

Brown, S. D., & Ryan Krane, N. E. (2000). Four (or five) sessions and a cloud of dust: Old assumptions and new observations about career counseling. In S. D. Brown & R. W. Lent (Eds.), *Handbook of counseling psychology* (3rd ed., pp. 740–766). New York: Wiley.

Capsuto, S. (2000). *Alternate channels: The uncensored story of gay and lesbian images on radio and television.* New York: Ballantine.

Cass, V. (1996). Sexual orientation identity formation: A Western phenomenon. In R. P. Cabaj & T. S. Stein (Eds.), *Textbook of homosexuality and mental health* (pp. 227–251). Washington, DC: American Psychiatric Press.

Cass, V. C. (1979). Homosexual identity formation: A theoretical model. *Journal of Homosexuality, 4,* 219–235.

Chernin, J., Holden, J. M., & Chandler, C. (1997). Bias in psychological assessment: Heterosexism. *Measurement and Evaluation in Counseling and Development, 30,* 68–76.

Chung, Y. B. (1995). Career decision making of lesbian, gay, and bisexual individuals. *Career Development Quarterly, 44,* 179–189.

Chung, Y. B. (2001). Work discrimination and coping strategies: Conceptual frameworks for counseling lesbian, gay, and bisexual clients. *Career Development Quarterly, 50,* 33–44.

Chung, Y. B. (2003). Ethical and professional issues in career assessment with lesbian, gay, and bisexual persons. *Journal of Career Assessment, 11,* 96–112.

Chung, Y. B., & Harmon. L. W. (1994). The career interests and aspirations of gay men: How sex-role orientation is related. *Journal of Vocational Behavior, 45,* 223–239.

Croteau, J. M. (1996). Research on the work experiences of lesbian, gay, and bisexual people: An integrative review of methodology and findings. *Journal of Vocational Behavior, 48,* 195–209.

Croteau, J. M., Anderson, M. Z., DiStefano, T., & Kampa-Kokesch, S. (2000). Lesbian, gay, and bisexual vocational psychology: Reviewing foundations and planning construction. In R. M. Perez, K. A. DeBord, & K. J. Bieschke (Eds.), *Handbook of counseling and therapy with lesbian, gay and bisexual clients* (pp. 383–408). Washington, DC: American Psychological Association.

Croteau, J. M., & Lark, J. S. (1995). On being lesbian, gay, and bisexual in student affairs: A national survey of experiences on the job. *NASPA Journal, 32*, 189–197.

Croteau, J. M., & von Destinon, M. (1994). A national survey of job search experiences of lesbian, gay, and bisexual student affairs professionals. *Journal of College Student Development, 35*, 40–45.

Dawis, R. V. (1994). The theory of work adjustment as convergent theory. In M. L. Savickas & R. W. Lent (Eds.), *Convergence in career development theories* (pp. 33–44). Palo Alto, CA: Consulting Psychologists Press.

Dawis, R. V., & Lofquist, L. H. (1984). *A psychological theory of work adjustment.* Minneapolis: University of Minnesota Press.

Day, N. E., & Schoenrade, P. (1997). Staying in the closet versus coming out: Relationships between communication about sexual orientation and work attitudes. *Personnel Psychology, 50*, 147–163.

Degges-White, S. (2002). Career counseling with lesbian clients: Using the theory of work adjustment as a framework. *Career Development Quarterly, 51*, 87–96.

Division 44/Committee on Lesbian, Gay, and Bisexual Concerns Joint Task Force on Guidelines for Psychotherapy with Lesbian, Gay, and Bisexual Clients. (2000). *American Psychologist, 55*, 1440–1451.

Dow, B. J. (2001). *Ellen,* television, and the politics of gay and lesbian visibility. *Critical Studies in Media Communication, 18*, 123–140.

Driscoll, J. M., Kelley, F. A., & Fassinger, R. E. (1996). Lesbian identity and disclosure in the workplace: Relation to occupational stress and satisfaction. *Journal of Vocational Behavior, 48*, 229–242.

Dunkle, J. H. (1996). Toward an integration of gay and lesbian identity development and Super's lifespan approach. *Journal of Vocational Behavior, 48*, 149–159.

Elliott, J. E. (1993). Career development with lesbian and gay clients. *Career Development Quarterly, 41*, 210–226.

Ellis, A. L., & Riggle, D. B. (1996). The relation of job satisfaction and degree of openness about one's sexual orientation for lesbians and gay men. *Journal of Homosexuality, 30*, 75–85.

Etringer, B. D., Hillerbrand, E., & Hetherington, C. (1990). The influence of sexual orientation on career decision-making: A research note. *Journal of Homosexuality, 19*(4), 103–111.

Fassinger, R. E. (1991). The hidden minority: Issues and challenges in working with lesbian women and gay men. *Counseling Psychologist, 19*, 157–176.

Fassinger, R. E. (1995). From invisibility to integration: Lesbian identity in the workplace. *Career Development Quarterly, 44*, 148–167.

Fassinger, R. E. (1996). Notes from the margins: Integrating lesbian experience into the vocational psychology of women. *Journal of Vocational Behavior, 48*, 160–175.

Fassinger, R. E., Gallor, S. M., Kolchakian, M. R., Brenner, B., Kellams, I., Perez, R., Morrow, S., & Lyons, H. Z. (2003, January). *Results of the National Gay and Lesbian Experiences Study.* Panel presentation at the National Multicultural Conference and Summit III, Hollywood, CA.

Fejes, F., & Petrich, K. (1993). Invisibility, homophobia, and heterosexism: Lesbians, gay men and the media. *Critical Studies in Mass Communication, 10*, 396–422.

Fisher, T. J., Reardon, R. C., & Burck, H. D. (1976). Increasing information-seeking behavior with a model-reinforced videotape. *Journal of Counseling Psychology, 23*, 234–238.

Fox, R. C. (2000). Bisexuality in perspective: A review of theory and research. In B. Green & G. L. Croom (Eds.), *Education, research, and practice in lesbian, gay, bisexual, and transgendered psychology* (pp. 161–206). Thousand Oaks, CA: Sage.

Fukuyama, M. A., & Ferguson, A. D. (2000). Lesbian, gay, and bisexual people of color: Understanding cultural complexity and managing multiple oppressions. In R. M. Perez, K. A. DeBord, & K. J. Bieschke (Eds.), *Handbook of counseling and therapy with lesbians, gays, and bisexuals* (pp. 81–105). Washington, DC: American Psychological Association.

Gagné, P., & Tewksbury, R. (1998). Conformity pressures and gender resistance among transgendered individuals. *Social Problems, 45*, 81–101.

Gainor, K. A. (2000). Including transgender issues in lesbian, gay and bisexual psychology: Implications for clinical practice and training. In B. Green & G. L. Croom (Eds.), *Education, research, and practice in lesbian, gay, bisexual, and transgendered psychology* (pp. 131–160). Thousand Oaks, CA: Sage.

Garnets, L., & Kimmel, D. (1991). Lesbian and gay male dimensions in the psychological study of human diversity. In J. D. Goodchilds (Ed.), *Psychological perspectives on human diversity in America* (pp. 137–192). Washington, DC: American Psychological Association.

Gaydemographics.org. (n.d.). *2000 census information on gay and lesbian couples.* Retrieved November 24, 2003, from http://www.gaydemographics.org/USA/USA.htm#tables

Gelberg, S., & Chojnacki, J. T. (1996). *Career and life planning with gay, lesbian, and bisexual persons.* Alexandria, VA: American Counseling Association.

Gore, S. (2000). The lesbian and gay workplace: An employee's guide to advancing equity. In B. Green & G. L. Croom (Eds.), *Education, research, and practice in lesbian, gay, bisexual, and transgendered psychology* (pp. 282–302). Thousand Oaks, CA: Sage.

Gottfredson, L. S. (1981). Circumscription and compromise: A developmental theory of occupational aspirations. *Journal of Counseling Psychology, 28*, 545–579.

Gottfredson, L. S. (1996). A theory of circumscription and compromise. In D. Brown & L. Brooks (Eds.), *Career choice and development: Applying contemporary theories to practice* (3rd ed., pp. 179–232). San Francisco: Jossey-Bass.

Gottfredson, L. S. (2002). Gottfredson's theory of circumscription, compromise, and self-creation. In D. Brown & Associates (Eds.), *Career choice and development* (3rd ed., pp. 85–148). San Francisco: Jossey-Bass.

Gottfredson, L. S., & Lapan, R. T. (1997). Assessing gender-based circumscription of occupational aspirations. *Journal of Career Assessment, 5*, 419–441.

Graham, M. A. (1986). Out of the closet and into the courtroom. *Employment Relations Today, 13*, 167–173.

Griffin, P. (1992). From hiding out to coming out: Empowering lesbian and gay educators. In K. M. Harbeck (Ed.), *Coming out of the classroom closet* (pp. 167–196). Binghamton, NY: Harrington Park Press.

Gross, L. (1994). What is wrong with this picture? Lesbian women and gay men on television. In R. Ringer (Ed.), *Queer words, queer images: Communication and the construction of homosexuality* (pp. 143–156). New York: New York University.

Gross, L. (2001). *Up from invisibility: Lesbians, gay men, and the media in America.* New York: Columbia University Press.

Harbeck, K. M. (1992). Gay and lesbian educators: Past history/future prospects. *Journal of Homosexuality, 22*, 121–140.

Harmon, L. W., Hansen, J. C., Borgen, F. H., & Hammer, A. L. (1994). *Strong Interest Inventory: Applications and technical guide.* Stanford, CA: Consulting Psychologists Press.

Henderson, S., Hesketh, B., & Tuffin, K. (1988). A test of Gottfredson's theory of circumscription. *Journal of Vocational Behavior, 32*, 37–48.

Herek, G. M. (1993). Sexual orientation and military service: A social science perspective. *American Psychologist, 48*, 538–549.

Hershberger, S., L., & D'Augelli, A. R. (2000). Issues in counseling lesbian, gay, and bisexual adolescents. In R. M. Perez, K. A. DeBord, & K. J. Bieschke (Eds.), *Handbook of counseling and therapy with lesbian, gay, and bisexual clients* (pp. 225–247). Washington, DC: American Psychological Association.

Hetherington, C. (1991). Life planning and career counseling with gay and lesbian students. In N. J. Evans & V. A. Wall (Eds.), *Beyond tolerance: Gays, lesbians, and bisexuals on campus.* Alexandria, VA: American College Personnel Association.

Hetherington, C., & Orzek, A. (1989). Career counseling and life planning with lesbian women. *Journal of Counseling and Development, 68*, 52–57.

Hetrick, E. S., & Martin, A. D. (1987). Developmental issues and their resolution for gay and lesbian adolescents. *Journal of Homosexuality, 14*, 25–43.

Holland, J. (1997). *Making vocational choices: A theory of vocational personalities and work environments* (3rd ed.). Odessa, FL: Psychological Assessment Resources.

Katz, P. A. (1979). The development of female identity. *Sex Roles, 5*, 155–178.

Katz, P. A. (1996). Raising feminists. *Psychology of Women Quarterly, 20*, 323–340.

Kim, J. H. (2002). The relationships among gender, gender identity factors and career-decisions-situation-specified personality traits. *Dissertations Abstracts International Section A: Humanities and Social Sciences, 62*(12–1), 4073.

Kinsey, A., Pomeroy, W., Wardell, B., & Martin, C. (1948). *Sexual behavior in the human male.* Philadelphia: Saunders.

Kitchener, K. S. (1984). Intuition, critical evaluation and ethical principles: The foundation for ethical decisions in counseling psychology. *Counseling Psychologist, 12*(3), 43–55.

Kohn, S. (1999). *The domestic partnership organization manual for employee benefits.* New York: National Gay and Lesbian Task Force.

Krumboltz, J. D. (1996). A learning theory of career counseling. In M. L. Savickas & W. B. Walsh (Eds.), *Handbook of career counseling theory and practice* (pp. 55–80). Palo Alto, CA: Davies-Black.

Lee, J. A., & Brown, R. G. (1993). Hiring, firing, and promoting. In L. Diamant (Ed.), *Homosexual issues in the workplace* (pp. 45–62). New York: Wiley.

Lent, R. W., Brown, S. D., & Hackett, G. (1994). Toward a unifying social cognitive theory of career and academic interest, choice, and performance. *Journal of Vocational Behavior, 45*, 79–122.

Lent, R. W., Brown, S. D., & Hackett, G. (2002). Social cognitive career theory. In D. Brown & L. Brooks (Eds.), *Career choice and development* (4th ed., pp. 255–311). San Francisco: Jossey-Bass.

Leung, S. A., & Harmon, L. W. (1990). Individual and sex differences in the zone of acceptable alternatives. *Journal of Counseling Psychology, 37*, 153–159.

Levant, R. F. (1999). Proceedings of the American Psychological Association, Incorporated, for the legislative year 1998: Minutes of the Annual Meeting of the Council of Representatives February 20-22, 1998, Washington, DC, and August 13 and 16, 1998, San Francisco, CA, and Minutes of the February, June, August, and December 1998 Meetings of the Board of Directors [Proposed APA policy statement on legal benefits for same-sex couples]. *American Psychologist, 54*, 605–671.

Levine, M. P., & Leonard, R. (1984). Discrimination against lesbians in the work force. *Signs: Journal of Women in Culture and Society, 9*, 700–710.

Lyons, H. Z., Brenner, B. R., & Fassinger, R. E. (2004). *A multicultural test of the theory of work adjustment: Investigating the role of heterosexism and person-environment fit in the job satisfaction of lesbian, gay, and bisexual employees.* Manuscript submitted for publication.

Matthews, C. R., & Lease, S. H. (2000). Focus on lesbian, gay, and bisexual families. In R. M. Perez, K. A. DeBord, & K. J. Bieschke (Eds.), *Handbook of counseling and therapy with lesbian, gay, and bisexual clients* (pp. 249–273). Washington, DC: American Psychological Association.

Mobley, M., & Slaney, R. B. (1996). Holland's theory: Its relevance for lesbian women and gay men. *Journal of Vocational Behavior, 48*, 125–135.

Mohr, J., & Fassinger, R. (2000). Measuring dimensions of lesbian and gay male experience. *Measurement and Evaluation in Counseling and Development, 33*, 66–90.

Morgan, K. S., & Brown, L. S. (1991). Lesbian career development, work behavior, and vocational counseling. *Counseling Psychologist, 19*, 273–291.

Morin, S. F., & Charles, K. A. (1983). Bias in psychotherapy—Heterosexism. In J. Murray & P. R. Abramson (Eds.), *Bias in psychotherapy* (pp. 309–338). New York: Praeger.

Morrow, S. L., Gore, P. A., Jr., & Campbell, B. W. (1996). The application of a sociocognitive framework to the career development of lesbian women and gay men. *Journal of Vocational Behavior, 48,* 136–148.

Morrow. S. L. (2000). First do no harm: Therapist issues in psychotherapy with lesbian, gay, and bisexual clients. In R. M. Perez, K. A. DeBord, & K. J. Bieschke (Eds.), *Handbook of counseling and therapy with lesbian, gay, and bisexual clients.* Washington, DC: American Psychological Association.

Myers, D. G. (1999). *Social psychology* (6th ed.). Boston: McGraw-Hill.

Nauta, M. M., Saucier, A. M., & Woodward, L. E. (2001). Interpersonal influences on students' academic and career decisions: The impact of sexual orientation. *Career Development Quarterly, 49,* 352–362.

Neely Martinez, M. (1993). Recognizing sexual orientation is fair and not costly. *HR Magazine, 38,* 66–72.

Olson, M. R. (1987). A study of gay and lesbian teachers. *Journal of Homosexuality, 13,* 73–81.

Orzek, A. M. (1992). Career counseling for the gay and lesbian community. In S. Dworkin & F. Gutierrez (Eds.), *Counseling gay men and lesbians: Journey to the end of the rainbow* (pp. 23–34). Alexandria, VA: American Counseling Association.

Ossana, S. M. (2000). Relationship and couples counseling. In R. M. Perez, K. A. DeBord, & K. J. Bieschke (Eds.), *Handbook of counseling and therapy with lesbian, gay, and bisexual clients* (pp. 275–302). Washington, DC: American Psychological Association.

Pallone, N. J., Rickard, F. S., & Hurley, R. B. (1970). Key influences of occupational preference among black youth. *Journal of Counseling Psychology, 17,* 498–501.

Parsons, F. (1909). *Choosing your vocation.* Boston: Houghton-Mifflin.

Pope, M. (1992). Bias in the interpretation of psychological tests. In S. Dworkin & F. Gutierrez (Eds.), *Counseling gay men and lesbians: Journey to the end of the rainbow.* Alexandria, VA: American Counseling Association.

Pope, M. (1995). Career interventions for gay and lesbian clients: A synopsis of practice knowledge and research needs. *Career Development Quarterly, 44,* 191–203.

Prince, J. P. (1995). Influences on the career development of gay men. *Career Development Quarterly, 44,* 168–177.

Prince, J. P. (1997). Assessment bias affecting lesbian, gay male and bisexual individuals. *Measurement and Evaluation in Counseling and Development, 30,* 82–88.

Richie, B. S., Fassinger, R. E., Linn, S. G., Johnson, J., Prosser, J., & Robinson, S. (1997). Persistence, connection, and passion: A qualitative study of the career development of highly achieving African American–black and white women. *Journal of Counseling Psychology, 44,* 133–148.

Rounds, J. & Tracey, T. J. (1996). Cross-cultural structural equivalence of RIASEC models and measures. *Journal of Counseling Psychology, 43,* 310–329.

Rust, P. C. (1992). The politics of sexual identity: Sexual attraction and behavior among lesbian and bisexual women. *Social Problems, 39,* 366–386.

Ryan, J. M., Tracey, T. J., & Rounds, J. (1996). Generalizability of Holland's structure of vocational interests across ethnicity, gender, and socioeconomic status. *Journal of Counseling Psychology, 43,* 330–337.

Savickas, M. (2002). Career construction: A developmental theory of vocational behavior. In D. Brown & Associates (Eds.), *Career choice and development* (4th ed., pp. 149–205). San Francisco: Jossey-Bass.

Savin-Williams, R. C. (1994). Verbal and physical abuse as stressors in the lives of lesbian, gay male, and bisexual youths: Associations with school problems, running away, substance abuse, prostitution, and suicide. *Journal of Consulting and Clinical Psychology, 62,* 261–269.

Savin-Williams, R. C. (1995). Lesbian, gay male, and bisexual adolescents. In A. R. D'Augelli & C. J. Patterson (Eds.), *Lesbian, gay, and bisexual identities over the lifespan: Psychological perspectives* (pp. 165–189). New York: Oxford University Press.

Savin-Williams, R. C. (1998). The disclosure of same-sex attractions by lesbian, gay, and bisexual youths to their families. *Journal of Research on Adolescence, 8,* 49–68.

Schmidt, C., Nilsson, J., & Rooney, S.C. (2003). *Career development outcomes of lesbian, gay, and bisexual youth.* Paper presented to the 110th convention of the American Psychological Association, Toronto, Ontario.

Seal, K. (1991). Sexual orientation becomes workplace issue for the 1900s. *Hotel and Motel Management, 206,* 2–29.

Sell, R. J. (1996). The Sell Assessment of Sexual Orientation: Background and scoring. *Journal of Gay, Lesbian, and Bisexual Identity, 1,* 295–310.

Sell, R. L. (1997). Defining and measuring sexual orientation: A review. *Archives of Sexual Behavior, 26,* 643–658.

Sharf, R. S. (Ed.). (2002). *Applying career development theory to counseling* (3rd ed.). Pacific Grove, CA: Brooks/Cole.

Shugart, H. A. (2003). Reinventing privilege: The new (gay) man in contemporary popular media. *Critical Studies in Media Communication, 20,* 67–91.

Siegel, K., Levine, M. P., Brooks, C., & Kern, R. (1989). The motives of gay men for taking or not taking the HIV antibody test. *Social Problems, 36,* 368–383.

Smith, N. G., & Ingram, K. M. (2004). Workplace heterosexism and adjustment among lesbian, gay, and bisexual individuals: The role of unsupportive social interactions. *Journal of Counseling Psychology, 51,* 57–67.

Sophie, J. (1985–1986). A critical examination of stage theories of lesbian identity development. *Journal of Homosexuality, 12*(2), 39–51.

Super, D. E. (1990). A life span, life-space approach to career development. In D. Brown, L. Brooks, and Associates (Eds.), *Career choice and development* (pp. 197–261). San Francisco: Jossey-Bass.

Susser, P. A. (1986). Sexual preference discrimination: Limited protection for gay workers. *Employment Relations Today, 13,* 57–65.

Swanson, J. L., & Gore, P. A. (2000). Advances in vocational psychology theory and research. In S. D. Brown & R. W. Lent (Eds.), *Handbook of counseling psychology* (3rd ed., pp. 233–269). New York: Wiley.

Thelan, M., Frautsh, N., Roberts, M., Kirkland, K., & Dollinger, S. (1981). Being imitated, conformity, and social influence: An integrative review. *Journal of Research in Personality, 15,* 403–426.

Thoresen, C. E., Hosford, R. E., & Krumboltz, J. D. (1970). Determining effective models for counseling clients of varying competencies. *Journal of Counseling Psychology, 17,* 369–375.

Troiden, R. R. (1989). The formation of homosexual identities. *Journal of Homosexuality, 17,* 43–73.

U.S. Census Bureau. (2003, February). Married-couple and unmarried-partner households: 2000: Census 2000 special reports. Retrieved November 24, 2003, from http://www.census.gov/prod/2003pubs/censr-5.pdf

Waldo, C. R. (1998). Out on campus: Sexual orientation and academic climate in a university context. *American Journal of Community Psychology, 26,* 745–774.

Waldo, C. R. (1999). Working in a majority context: A structural model of heterosexism as minority stress in the workplace. *Journal of Counseling Psychology, 46,* 218–219.

Walters, S. D. (2001). *All the rage: The story of gay visibility in America.* Chicago: University of Chicago Press.

Whitam, F. L., & Mathy, R. M. (1986). *Male homosexuality in four societies: Brazil, Guatemala, the Philippines, and the United States.* New York: Praeger.

Woods, S. E., & Harbeck, K. M. (1992). Living in two worlds: The identity management strategies used by lesbian physical educators. In K. M. Harbeck (Ed.), *Coming out of the classroom closet* (pp. 141–166). Binghamton, NY: Harrington Park Press.

CHAPTER 16

CAREER COUNSELING WITH VISIBLY RECOGNIZABLE RACIAL AND ETHNIC MINORITY GROUPS

SHARON L. BOWMAN,

GINA L. EVANS
Ball State University

The American workforce is changing rapidly. Each day the workforce becomes a little more diverse, as racial- and ethnic-minority group members increase their numbers in a variety of occupations. The American workforce is also going global—look at the changes brought about by the North American Free Trade Agreement (NAFTA), connecting U.S., Mexican, and Canadian interests, or consider the changes brought about by the internationalizing of formerly U.S.-owned businesses, for example the connections between American and foreign car companies (Daimler Chrysler, for one).

All of these changes impact the diversity of the American workplace and lead to a demand that counselors become more sensitive to multicultural needs. Evans and Larrabee (2002) noted that counselors must focus on career-counseling competencies, but they must also incorporate multicultural-counseling competencies into their work with clients. This chapter discusses approaches to career counseling that will be beneficial when working with racial and ethnic minority clients.

MULTICULTURAL COMPETENCIES IN COUNSELING

A significant amount of theoretical and empirical literature has been created since the identification of multiculturalism as a fourth force in counseling (Pedersen, 1991). Multicultural issues can be identified in nearly every area of counselor training, from research approaches to marital counseling to rehabilitation counseling. Counselors must become aware that clients are not a homogenous group: they are not all young, attractive, verbal, intelligent, and successful (YAVIS). Some are quiet, ugly, old, indigent and dissimilar culturally (QUOIDs; Sundberg, 1981). The term YAVIS was created to describe the dominant client type preferred by most therapists, and the term QUOIDs was created to describe the least preferred client type. Clients come in all shapes, sizes, and colors, so to speak. Racial- and ethnic-minority clients may bring issues to the counseling that are not easily categorized through mainstream counseling theories. If counselors are not prepared for clients who are unlike themselves, they may cause more harm than good. They will also be doing a disservice to their communities, as they will be unable to provide adequate service to people who need them.

Cultural Encapsulation

The counseling field has historically trained its practitioners to operate from a culturally encapsulated perspective. As introduced by Wrenn (1962, as cited in Pedersen, 2003), this concept includes, first, a belief that there is one set of cultural assumptions. Second, counselors believe that this set of assumptions is the only correct view. Third, counselors believe that their narrow perspective is true despite evidence to the contrary, or even reasonable proof, in some cases. Fourth, counselors will seek simple remedies and may focus on techniques to resolve client issues. Finally, clients' cultural perspectives may be disregarded, and the only important reference point is that of the counselor.

Do counselors continue to hold culturally encapsulated beliefs today? Think about some of the assumptions counselors and counselor trainees make about clients and counseling. Mainstream U.S. culture defines "normal" in a particular way, which may not fit for nonmainstream individuals. U.S. culture also assumes that healthy clients seek to individuate from their families; collectivist beliefs are discouraged as problematic. Even more disturbing, counselors are often taught that the purpose of counseling is to help the client adjust to his or her environment. How often are counselors encouraged to help change the system instead of the individual client? Indeed, encapsulation remains inherent in our training systems.

How can counselors countermand the effects of encapsulation? Doing so requires conscious effort to "step out of the box." Here are some suggestions to get started on escaping cultural encapsulation:

- Keep a journal for a week, noting how often you interact with someone of a different racial or ethnic group (including international contacts). Record whether these interactions are superficial or meaningful, and examine your role in making them that way. Then consider what you can do to change things.
- Read several books (modern novels, nonfiction, biographies) by authors who are racially or ethnically different than you. Pay attention to the portrayal of life in the book, without labeling it inferior or superior. How is it different from your life?

- Attend events presented by or showcasing persons of different racial or ethnic groups. On campuses this can include speakers series, discussion sessions, or other events sponsored by campus organizations. Off-campus this may include festivals, religious services, or philanthropic organization or other community group events. Be a participant observer, not a shadow in the background.
- Become involved in a social-justice or social-change group. Just because injustice is not happening to you personally or to someone of your cultural group does not mean you cannot help to change the situation.
- Listen to what others are saying. Do not assume that you fully understand what is being said or clearly perceive that person's (colleague, friend, acquaintance, client) experience of a situation. Allow yourself to accept that person's version of events and that what is being described could have happened, without negating it through the overlay of your own cultural experience.
- Speak up when you notice injustice, regardless of whether it is happening to you personally. Speak, not to make yourself look good, but to challenge the injustice. You carry more power than you know.

Multicultural Competencies

Arredondo and her associates (Arredondo et al., 1996) developed a set of multicultural competencies that all counselors should strive to achieve. These competencies are sanctioned by the American Counseling Association and the Association for Multicultural Counseling and Development (American Counseling Association, n.d.). There are 31 competencies organized into three broader categories. Space limitations do not permit an in-depth discussion of each competency; the reader is encouraged to review them in their entirety at another point. This chapter will focus on those competencies most significant to career counseling.

The first broad category directs counselors to be become aware of their own cultural values and biases (American Counseling Association, n.d.; Arredondo et al., 1996). As noted earlier, cultural encapsulation restricts our views of the world. Counselors must first acknowledge that they hold biases and that they are products of their own unique cultures. Once these cultural biases are identified, counselors must recognize how those cultural biases affect their work with clients. What does it mean to be raised with those biases? How does it affect assumptions about personal and career choices, internal and external locus of control, luck or fate versus personal control of one's destiny? How does it affect the ability to understand racism and other types of discrimination that clients may experience? In other words, the first category demands that counselors focus on themselves, not on their clients or the other person, as the first step toward multicultural competence.

The second broad category directs the counselor to focus on the client's worldview (American Counseling Association, n.d.; Arredondo et al., 1996). How might the counselor's biases affect the client's perception of the counseling work? Clients, especially those who perceive counselors as part of a mainstream that is biased against persons of their culture, may have a healthy mistrust of counseling services. They may interpret hesitation or uncertainty from a counselor as bias and not some other emotion.

A counselor who is focused on the client's worldview will have a working knowledge of racial-identity models, immigrant-identity models, and the effects of racism and discrimination on client decision making, along with the typical mainstream approaches to working with a client. Developing expertise in this area compels the counselor to move out of the comfort of the office and interact on a more personal level with persons of different cultural groups. For example, a counselor who anticipates working with a predominantly Mexican immigrant population should become familiar with important family and social roles and with common rites of passage, family and religious festivals, and other typical aspects of that cultural group. While it may not be possible to learn everything about a particular group without significant immersion into the group's culture, it is possible to develop enough understanding to know the questions to ask and the patterns to identify. It is also important to know that every aspect gleaned about a cultural group does not attach to every individual member of that cultural group: individual differences do exist within groups.

The third broad category focuses on culturally appropriate intervention strategies (American Counseling Association, n.d.; Arredondo et al., 1996). Counselors working on competencies at this level of development should be aware of the importance of clients' traditional support structures and ways of seeking help; counseling may well be a last resort. Perceived barriers, such as English not being the client's primary language, may have solutions, if the counselor is willing to look for them. Counselors will pay attention to barriers created by educational and occupational sources that may impede the client's progress. Counselors should also be aware of cultural biases inherent in common counseling instruments and tests and treat any results with caution. They are also expected to be cognizant of the impact of both verbal and nonverbal interactions on the counseling process. In addition, counselors who are culturally competent recognize that sometimes they must be advocates for their clients, because it may be that a systemic change is needed, not an individual one.

Counselors who are operating in a culturally competent and ethical manner toward all their clients will have a powerful effect on their clients' well-being and, by extension, the well-being of the greater community. Whether the focus of counseling is personal (e.g., marital, relationship, parenting, or other issues) or vocational (e.g., educational or career choice, vocational development), cultural competence is a significant part of the process.

CAREER-COUNSELING COMPETENCIES

Aside from demonstrating multicultural competence, career counselors must also be competent in career counseling. In 1997 the National Career Development Association (NCDA) delineated 11 areas of competence in career counseling. As Evans and Larrabee (2002) note, some of these areas overlap with the aforementioned multicultural-counseling competencies. One of those competencies, in fact, is an awareness of the needs of diverse populations when providing career-counseling services. The following is a list of the career-counseling competencies (a more in-depth discussion of the competencies is on the NCDA Webpage; see National Career Development Association, n.d.).

CAREER COUNSELING COMPETENCIES AS DEFINED BY THE NATIONAL CAREER DEVELOPMENT ASSOCIATION

- Knowledge of career development theory, individual and cultural differences, life-span development, and planning and placement
- Knowledge and skill in individual and group counseling, including decision-making processes and the impact of contextual conditions on development
- Knowledge in individual and group assessment techniques to assess aptitude, achievement, interests, values, personality, leisure interests, and the possible impact of gender, race or ethnicity, and nationality on the validity of assessment instruments
- Knowledge about career information and the ability to identify local, regional, and national resources that may benefit clients in career and life planning
- Ability to develop, implement, and appropriately evaluate comprehensive career programs across settings and use that information to strengthen such programs
- Utilize skills in coaching, consultation, and performance improvement to work with clients, their employers, and the general public to benefit the process
- Knowledge about, and ability to counsel and advocate for, members of diverse populations, who may bring unique needs to the session
- Ability to provide appropriate supervision to student career counselors and to seek supervision for oneself when necessary
- Appropriate knowledge of the issues involved in the ethical and legal practice of career counseling
- Ability to understand research and evaluation, from developing a research study to conducting a program evaluation
- Appropriate knowledge and ability to use technology in career planning, from computer-based guidance and information systems to Internet services. National Career Development Association (n.d.)

Competent career counselors have the same basic skills expected of any counselor. They understand counseling and career theory and development and are current with the latest theoretical information. They must also understand the context in which their favorite career theories were created. Many of the traditional career theories were created after studying samples of privileged white men. Do such theories continue to be relevant and equally useful for today's diverse working populations? Probably they do not, at least not without some significant caveats and caution about wholesale acceptance of the interpretations made under these theories. Modern theories may be more likely to include information regarding the wide variety of barriers that a client may experience or decision making tied to family happiness.

Competent counselors must also grasp the importance of individual- and group-counseling skills and the potential reactions of minority clients to the relatively foreign experience called counseling. The literature on client trust and mistrust indicates that minority clients prefer counselors who are similar to them in some significant way, that is, counselors who are of the same race (Duncan, 2003). It is also true that some minority clients may be leery of counseling, perceiving it as something only for white people or only for people who are "crazy." Career counseling is often viewed as less intimidating, or more socially acceptable, than personal counseling, so it may be somewhat easier for career counselors to persuade racial- and ethnic-minority clients to come for services. Also, it is possible that minority clients may prefer group experiences over individual counseling, as this can take away the stigma and provide some peer support for the struggles they are experiencing. Ethnic-minority clients may respond to the career counselor through the lens of their racial or ethnic identity, which could affect the counselor's ability to do effective work with the client. Racial identity is discussed later in this chapter.

An additional area of expertise important for career counselors is a knowledge of assessment instruments: how they work, how they are normed, and how to interpret results for clients who do not fit the prototypical model. Counselors must know how to choose assessment instruments wisely, taking into account the client's background, gender, and language abilities. Counselors must read the test manuals and be familiar with how the instrument was created, not just how quickly the clients can finish it. They must also evaluate the client's ability to comprehend the questions on the instrument, either due to reading level or English comprehension. A client who is not comfortable or familiar with mainstream English and is not academically inclined toward higher education would probably not do well on an instrument normed on highly intelligent, English-speaking college-bound students.

Another important area of career competence relates to program evaluation and development. Career counselors are expected to develop career programs, carry them out, and evaluate the outcomes, which would then be used to improve or significantly change the programs. Methodologies for program evaluation and assessment should include a representative number of racial- and ethnic-minority clients or consumers; otherwise, the results may be unnecessarily skewed. Often researchers and program evaluators are simply happy to get any responses back to their surveys; in this case, however, to perform the evaluations it is critical to identify members of subgroups if one is serious about having their input.

Supervision, both as supervisor and as supervisee, is another necessary area of competence for career counselors; this area can also have implications for working with culturally diverse clients. As a supervisor, career counselors have the opportunity to train their supervisees to be aware of racial- and ethnic-minority issues in career development, to focus on the relationship between counselor and client, and to model appropriate counseling technique. A supervisor who is comfortable raising questions about diversity can create a safe space for the supervisee to raise his or her own issues. The supervisor is also a significant source of support for a racial- or ethnic-minority supervisee who is struggling with his or her role in the counseling session. In other words, clients and counselors come in different colors; a minority counselor may have significant struggles with clients of a different race.

A career counselor may also seek peer supervision regarding minority-client career issues if the client is a member of a racial or ethnic group with which the career counselor is unfamiliar. As with any other area of counseling, it is the counselor's responsibility to recognize when he or she is working in an area outside of his or her expertise and to do something to remedy the situation. If the client has to do all the work of helping the counselor develop cultural sensitivity instead of getting the help he or she is seeking, it is likely that he or she will drop out of the sessions and not get the information he or she was seeking.

The oldest article we could locate on barriers to counseling was written by Vontress (1969), who examined counseling barriers for African Americans. The barriers listed at that time included the counselor's and client's racial attitude; the counselor's lack of knowledge about the client's culture; language difficulties; the client's unfamiliarity with the counseling process; the client's fears about self-disclosure; and sexual and racial taboos. Yancy (1984) suggests that these same fears or barriers also affect members of other racial or ethnic groups. While these authors were discussing counseling in general, certainly we can make the short leap to career counseling.

Evans and Larrabee (2002) noted that career counselors must be familiar with both the multicultural competencies and the career counseling competencies. Without both areas of expertise, the counselor will not be as effective as he or she could or should be. In fact, they state, "The competent counselor of the twenty-first century must be educated to meet the challenges of both multicultural and career counseling with diverse clientele in many different settings" (p. 32).

BARRIERS TO CAREER DEVELOPMENT

Traditional career-development theories place a strong emphasis on the manner in which personality, interest, and ability factors influence vocational development. While traditional vocational-development theories measuring these variables may be appropriate for determining the vocational development of Caucasian Americans, these theories do not encompass additional cultural factors or barriers that influence vocational development for visible racial and ethnic minorities (Parham & Austin, 1994). Traditional career-development theories also fail to account for the variability in the influence of these cultural factors on individuals within the same minority group. While members of the same racial or ethnic group may experience similar cultural factors or barriers in their career development, they may differ in the level of influence those factors have. This variability is generally caused by differing levels of racial identity, acculturation, and assimilation across members of the same minority group. The influence of these factors makes it essential to employ cultural-counseling techniques in career counseling with visible ethnic minorities.

What are some factors that could be barriers to career development? Bowman (1989) developed a list of potential barriers to career attainment that still seem relevant 15 years later. The list includes racial discrimination, sexual discrimination, limited financial resources, parental influence, low grades, and difficulty entering the first job, among other potential barriers. Albert and Luzzo (1999) state that students who believe that career-related barriers are caused by external, uncontrollable, stable factors that are out of their control or caused by fate or misfortune are unlikely to try to change those factors. Instead, students holding such a pessimistic view will continue to be blocked by those perceptions. On the other hand, persons who perceive career-related barriers through an internal locus of control will be more likely to try to overcome those barriers rather than be blocked by them (cf. Richie et al., 1997). Career counselors might consider working from a social cognitive perspective to change the pessimistic views.

While there are many barriers to career development that could be discussed, space limits our discussion to cultural values, discrimination, racism, and prejudice. These barriers are among the most frequently mentioned variables in the cross-cultural career-counseling literature.

Cultural Values

Members of racial- and ethnic-minority groups often experience career-related barriers that may not be commonly experienced by Caucasian Americans (Durodoye & Bodley, 1997). These unique experiences are commonly attributed to differences in cultural values and beliefs between visible ethnic minorities and Caucasian Americans. In accordance with Brown (2002), values and beliefs are characterized by individual standards that guide functioning and play a major role in the establishment of personal goals. Thus, values and beliefs can be important to both the personal and career development of racial and ethnic minorities.

It is not uncommon for members of racial and ethnic minority groups to endorse values that are different than those endorsed by the dominant society. Some minority groups, particularly members of African American and Hispanic cultures, tend to value collectivism, cooperation, family, respect, communalism, humanism, honor, and religion (Helms & Piper, 1994). Several of these values are in opposition of the Caucasian culture's values of self-progression, competition, autonomy, and independence. These cultural differences may cause difficulties for members of racial and ethnic minority groups who are forced to function in a vocational system incongruent with their cultural values and beliefs.

Individuals who hold collective social beliefs will be heavily influenced by family and respected others during the career decision-making process (Durodoye & Bodley, 1997). Value-based occupational information may have much less influence in this case than it would with individuals who hold an individualistic value system (Brown, 2002). This collective-based decision-making process is a direct contrast to the mainstream decision-making process. Because individualism and autonomy are valued by the dominant society, a more independent and less family-involved vocational career decision-making process is commonly endorsed, as encouraged by many career-development theories. If the career counselor does not recognize this difference in decision making as cultural, he or she might inappropriately label the client as career immature. Career counselors must pay attention to the context in which clients develop and express their values and the ways in which cultural encapsulation can hinder the counseling process. Other cultural factors or barriers and experiences are also influential in the career development and decision making of visible ethnic minorities. Additional cultural factors or barriers include the influence of prejudice, discrimination, and racism.

Prejudice, Discrimination, and Racism

Prejudice, discrimination, and racism have historically been problematic concerns for members of racial- and ethnic-minority groups. African American college students, for example, have reported daily incidents of what is labeled everyday racism (routine encounters with prejudice and discriminatory behavior based on racial group membership; Swim, Hyers, Cohen, Fitzgerald, & Bylsma, 2003). The inequality created through these factors has negatively influenced self-image (Brooks, 1994, in Durodoye & Bodley, 1997). A low self-image, in turn, may discourage some members of racial- and ethnic-minority groups from pursuing their vocational dreams. That may be especially true if the dream is for a field that has very few minority participants. Those fields may be avoided in favor of fields that do have minority role models and or are sanctioned by friends and family as acceptable for members of a minority group.

Members of racial- and ethnic-minority groups are more likely than Caucasian Americans to perceive career-related barriers directly associated with their ethnicity (Luzzo & McWhirter, 2001). Urban racial- and ethnic-minority youth may perceive that they have few career choices and opportunities and more difficulty obtaining successful jobs (Want, Haertel, & Walberg, 1994, in Constantine, Erickson, Banks, & Timberlake, 1998). This perception of additional career barriers can decrease motivation to pursue a variety of career options (Constantine et al., 1998). This diminished perception may also be due to a limited exposure to careers with job security and career advancement.

Numerous cultural factors or barriers persist in the career development of visible ethnic minorities. Some career theorists have previously attempted to examine the influence of cultural factors by exploring race-related vocational behaviors of ethnic minorities. These studies provided some insight into the variability of vocational behaviors among different racial groups. Unfortunately many of these theorists failed to explore the variability in vocational behavior among individuals of the same racial groups.

INFLUENCE OF RACE
ON VOCATIONAL DEVELOPMENT

Many barriers hinder the career development of visible ethnic minorities. Race salience and racial-identity levels can affect the rate at which these barriers influence the career development of visible ethnic minorities. Empirical studies measuring the influence of race in the career development of visible ethnic minorities has primarily been nominal in nature. These studies have offered information concerning vocational behaviors between groups, but have: (a) neglected to explore individual difference among group members, (b) been atheoretical in nature, and (c) potentially perpetuated vocational-behavior stereotypes onto ethnic minority groups. The utilization of racial identity theory in career counseling provides a solution to these problems.

Race as a contributor to vocational behavior has primarily been examined nominally in the career-counseling literature (Helms & Piper, 1994). In particular, measuring vocational behavior nominally, whereby an individual is assigned to a mutually exclusive racial category and race-related psychological characteristics are inferred from the person's racial classification, has been the primary method used in vocational psychology studies. Many of these studies have focused on investigating racial-group comparisons (Sheffey, Bingham, & Walsh, 1986, in Helms & Piper, 1994) and career maturity (Westbrook, Sanford, & Donnelly, 1990, in Helms & Piper, 1994). These studies have provided valuable information attributing vocational behaviors to various ethnic-minority groups. However, many of the studies were atheoretical and did not examine the effect of individual differences among racial-group members.

Using nominal methods in studies to explore variability of career development among different ethnic groups has also been problematic. Many nominal studies are devoid of theoretical models. Negating to utilize a model in career studies can decrease the usefulness of the results and limit the ability to predict or explain the career-development process. This absence of theoretical framework could account for why the existing nominal studies of race and vocational behavior have yielded inconsistent findings (Smith, 1975, in Helms & Piper, 1994).

The absence of exploration into individual differences has also proven to be problematic in career-counseling studies. Some cultural characteristics may be commonly influential to members of the same racial group. Each person is unique in their conceptualizations, beliefs, and worldviews. Thus, variability in the career-development process occurs among individuals of the same ethnic-minority group (Parham & Austin, 1994). As stated by Smith (1975, in Helms & Piper, 1994), failing to explore individual differences in career development can contribute to the negative stereotypes of minority clients. Exploring the clients' level of racial identity can help career counselors explore individual differences in career development with ethnic-minority clients.

RACIAL IDENTITY AND CAREER DEVELOPMENT

Few career-counseling theories attempt to connect racial identity to vocational assessment and behavior (Walsh & Srsic, 1996). Some theorists (Helms & Piper, 1994; Parham & Austin, 1994) argue that racial identity theory is useful in explaining some aspects of career assessment and development. These theorists have further suggested that racial identity models can be especially useful in understanding the career decision-making process of ethnic minorities. Helms and Piper (1994) indicated that racial identity is influential to vocational behavior, depending on the degree of an individual's race salience. *Race salience* refers to the importance placed on race in the perception of vocational options and vocational decision making (Helms & Piper, 1994).

> Examples of race salience for Black career decision-makers, might include beliefs that certain careers are accessible only to Whites, or that various occupations have more or less status in the Black community, or that the well-being of the Black community as a whole requires certain modes of career-related behavior. In such instances racial identity might serve as a mediator between the objective racial circumstances or stressors and the person's vocational behavior in response to the circumstances. (Helms & Piper, 1994, p. 129)

Thus, the level of race salience and racial-identity development can directly influence the career-development process of visible ethnic minorities.

INFLUENCE OF RACIAL IDENTITY
ON THE CAREER DEVELOPMENT
OF AFRICAN AMERICANS

Although there are multiple models that detail the development of African American racial identity, the Nigrescence model by William Cross (1971) is the most commonly used in the vocational and cross-cultural counseling literature. The study of Nigrescence (a French word that means the process of becoming black) evolved in the late 1960s and explains the development of African American racial identity by the evaluation of the individual and the reference group rather than one's skin color (Helms, 1990). The theory models the direction of healthy African American racial identity development and indicates that "overidentification" with Caucasians and Caucasian culture is a psychologically unhealthy resolution to the identity issues resulting from one's need to survive in a racist culture (Helms, 1990). This model denotes the development of racial identity in African Americans along four stages (Pre-encounter, Encounter, Immersion-Emersion, and Internalization). These stages were thought to depict the linear advancement from negative to positive Afrocentric (developing into "blackness" and embracing black culture) identity development, but the stages can be repeated and reexperienced due to the fact that racial identity is an ongoing, continuous process.

Using the Nigrescence model, Woods (1987, in Helms & Piper, 1994) found small but significant correlations between African American racial-identity Encounter attitudes and the Holland Vocational Preference Inventory scales of Investigative (I), Artistic (A), and Social (S). Woods also found significant correlations between African American Pre-encounter attitudes and Holland's Investigative scale. These findings indicate that racial-identity attitudes influence vocational preferences and perceptions of vocational options. The influence could occur in one of two ways. Persons who pursue vocational interests related to the I, A, or S scales may be exposed to more situations that could stimulate an Encounter reaction. In other words, they may meet more people who would challenge Pre-encounter beliefs. On the other hand, persons who are high on Encounter attitudes may be drawn to I, A, or S vocational interests as a means of resolving some questions. There may be other reasons, as yet unexplored, to explain the correlation between Encounter attitudes and Holland Scale scores.

African American racial identity has also been linked to the perception of work environments and quality of interactions with others. The manner in which individuals express their racial identity or racial-identity conflicts influences their perception of the work environment and quality of interactions with Caucasian Americans in vocational settings (Helms & Piper, 1994). Watts and Carter (1991, in Helms & Piper, 1994) found African American managers in the Pre-encounter stage, who perceived race to be less of a problem, denounced affirmative action policies, and conformed to the environmental climate, reported having favorable views of their vocational environment and experienced more career advancement and promotions. Conversely, African American managers in the Immersion or Emersion stage, who perceived race to be a problem, vocalized their views concerning inequality in the vocational environment, and endorsed affirmative action policies, had a negative view of their work environment and interaction with Caucasian coworkers. Thus, African American racial identity is influential to the perception of vocational environment. Other empirical studies (Thompson, 1985, in Helms & Piper, 1994) indicated that Pre-encounter and Internalization racial identity attitudes may be more stable styles of processing racial information (Helms & Piper, 1994). These results could indicate that stability in one's racial inner world may be indicative of the search or need for stability in one's vocational world (Helms & Piper, 1994).

Researchers and theorists have found a correlation between levels of racial identity and the career-development process of visible ethnic minorities. Many of these studies have focused on the career development of African Americans. Because racial identity development has been proven to be influential to the vocational development of visible ethnic minorities, recognizing the African American client's level of racial identity will substantially contribute to the counselor's understanding of the client, ability to establish rapport with the client, and ability to meet the client's career-development needs (Walsh & Srsic, 1996). Although African Americans were the only group discussed in detail, racial-identity development also influences the career development of Asian Americans (Asher, 2002), Latinos (Gross, 2004), and Asian/Pacific Islanders (Wear, 2000). For more information, the reader is also directed to Gomez et al. (2001), Juntunen et al. (2001), and Leong (1995).

CAREER-COUNSELING NEEDS OF RECENT IMMIGRANTS

Many cultural factors or barriers that affect the career development of American racial- and ethnic-minority group members can also be applied to career development of first- and second-generation immigrants to the United States. However, immigrants' career development may also be influenced by other factors, such as language, adjustment issues and experiences, and loss of occupational and self-identity.

Language

Language difficulties are experienced by individuals in a variety of immigrant groups and are a significant barrier in the career-development process of immigrants and immigrant groups (Westwood & Ishiyama, 1991). Dissimilarities in pronunciation and intonation can cause immigrants to experience difficulties learning, speaking, and communicating in English. Language difficulties are one of the main sources of discrimination against immigrants in the workforce.

Poor language proficiency can lead to miscommunications that affect both the counselor-client relationship and career-development process of immigrants. Career development is influenced by the ability to obtain, comprehend, and process career information (Westwood & Ishiyama, 1991). Possessing strong language proficiency is essential to performing these tasks. Sometimes children, who can quickly learn a new language, serve as translators for their parents or grandparents. This can be both helpful and damaging to the counseling process, helpful because the non–English speaker may feel reassured by the presence of a trusted family member, but damaging to the power structure in the familial relationship. Mistranslations and miscommunications due to difficulties in language proficiency can increase the chances of miscommunication between the client and counselor and hinder the career-development process. As a result, immigrant clients who possess a low level of language proficiency may experience difficulty fully exploring career-development options and opportunities (Penderson & Penderson, 1985, in Westwood & Ishiyama, 1991). Counselors are ill-advised to use children as translators, which can create new problems for the clients and their family members.

Accents have long been a source of discrimination and prejudice for immigrants. Immigrants who speak with a more pronounced accent generally experience more discrimination and prejudice than immigrants who speaks with a less pronounced accent (Westwood & Ishiyama, 1991). This source of racial discrimination or prejudice can impact an immigrant's career-development process. For example, "an employer may not exercise tolerance and understanding of ethnically distinct employees or job applicants who speak with a heavy accent and have culturally distinct manners of communication" (Westwood & Ishiyama, 1991, p. 135). This lack of understanding and tolerance may cause the employer to treat the immigrant applicant negatively or decline to hire him or her based solely on accent.

Adjustment Issues and Experiences

Immigrants new to a society often experience cultural disorientation and adjustment difficulties that interfere with normal daily activities (Lundstedt, 1963, in Westwood & Ishiyama, 1991). Immigrants who move to a culture that is less homogenous than their original culture generally experience more adjustment issues than those moving to a more homogenous culture (Westwood & Ishiyama, 1991). Also, immigrants moving to a less homogenous culture may experience a cultural shock that influences their ability to effectively solve conflict, make decisions, gather information, and find much needed resources (Westwood & Ishiyama, 1991). Additional factors, such as interpersonal problems, have also been associated with the level of cultural shock and adjustment difficulties experienced by immigrants.

Immigrants commonly experience a wide range of emotions associated with moving to a different culture. These feelings are often influenced by their experiences in the new culture. If an immigrant perceives his or her migration experiences to be traumatic and negative, he or she may experience an increase in interpersonal problems such as depression, anxiety, homesickness, and loneliness (Westwood & Ishiyama, 1991). Some recent immigrants come to the United States willingly, with the support of family, and have a relatively easy moving experience. Others, however, come unwillingly, leaving homelands that are suffering economically, in the midst of war, or otherwise inhospitable. The more traumatic and negative the perception of the immigration experience is, the more severe the interpersonal problems may be. These interpersonal problems can "significantly scatter energy, reduce work motivation, and reduce openness to explore new opportunities and advance vocational development" (Westwood & Ishiyama, 1991, p. 139). Because these interpersonal problems frequently influence the clients' vocational development, career counselors must also work with immigrant clients to resolve interpersonal problems as well as advance career development. These interpersonal problems can also occur when an immigrant experiences a loss of identity.

Many immigrants already possess a sense of self-identity before moving to a new culture. This self-identity can be created from various dimensions of life (e.g., social, occupational, ethnic, and spiritual; Westwood & Ishiyama, 1991). Although several dimensions of life may influence self-identity, some aspects may be more influential than others. For example, the move to a different culture and the disconnection from the home community may be threatening to immigrants' self-identity (Ishiyama, 1990, in Westwood & Ishiyama, 1991). For instance, an immigrant's self-identification can be formed through the relationship with family and friends or occupational status. If an immigrant moves to a new culture devoid of family and friends or has to take an occupational position lower than the previous position in the original culture, he or she may experience identity conflict pertaining to the loss of life dimensions that previously formed his or her self-identity.

Language, heightened interpersonal stress, and loss of identity are unique barriers to the career development of immigrants and immigrant groups. While each of these variables may influence the career development of immigrants, variability exists pertaining to the degree of influence. Much of this variability is attributed to differences in individual levels of acculturation and group assimilation.

INFLUENCE OF ACCULTURATION AND ASSIMILATION ON VOCATIONAL DEVELOPMENT

Acculturation and assimilation are influential to the career development of immigrants at the individual and group levels (Oledo & Padilla, 1978, in Miranda & Umhoefer, 1998). Several definitions have been used to describe the concepts of acculturation and assimilation. For the purpose of this chapter, acculturation is defined as a process of learning culture and adapting behavior that takes place when individuals are exposed to a new culture, while assimilation is defined as accepting the values and beliefs of the new culture, while rejecting the original culture (Berry, 1980, in Miranda & Umhoefer, 1998). Although both definitions describe the same concept of cultural change, they represent two distinct processes and are erroneously used interchangeably.

Differences in the two concepts are often implied, but a differentiation of the terms is rarely provided. Acculturation primarily describes the individual process by which an immigrant integrates the worldviews, values, and beliefs of the dominant culture and their original ethnic culture. This concept primarily describes cultural *integration* at the *individual* level. Conversely, assimilation describes the *shedding* of original cultural values and adoption of dominant worldviews, values, and beliefs at the *group* level. Further, "assimilation is commonly viewed as a linear and unidirectional process, while acculturation is viewed as a more complex process with multiple outcomes" (Leong & Chou, 1994, p. 158).

Earlier career and psychotherapy studies examined the effect of assimilation on immigrant personal and career development. The effects of acculturation on immigrant personal and career development were not explored until much later in the career-counseling and psychotherapy literature (Leong & Chou, 1994). Immigrant groups (either voluntarily or involuntarily) become influenced by the host culture. As a result, several immigrant groups have experienced varying degrees of assimilation into the dominant culture. Immigrant vocational development has been influenced by this assimilation process. Immigrant groups, as well as nonimmigrant groups, commonly choose vocational choices that correspond to their values and beliefs. If the values and beliefs of the immigrant group change as a result of the assimilation process, changes in vocational choices and interests will occur to mimic this change. For instance, many immigrant groups are collectivist in nature (e.g., Chinese, Japanese, Mexican, African, etc.). These collectivistic characteristics can influence immigrants to pursue vocational opportunities that endorse group rather than individual success. However, as the immigrant assimilates into the dominant culture and sheds collectivistic values, individuals belonging to this immigrant group may begin choosing vocational opportunities that are more self-rewarding than group rewarding.

Although the assimilation process may account for vocational development among immigrant groups, it does not explain the considerable individual variability in vocational development between members of the same immigrant group. As a way to gain this additional information, career counselors have begun studying this variability through exploring individual levels of acculturation. The information gained from these studies has helped explain the variability in vocational development as well as a broad spectrum of possible outcomes to understand the career development of immigrant clients. As a result, acculturation theory has been found to be one of the most useful theoretical dimensions used to explain observed variability among individual members of a minority groups (Lucero-Miller & Newman, 1999).

The influence of acculturation on immigrant vocational development is commonly assessed according to levels of acculturation. Varying levels of acculturation can influence vocational choices pursued by immigrant clients. More highly acculturated immigrants will pursue career options and experience career development more closely to that of the dominant culture, whereas less acculturated immigrants may pursue career options and experience career development more closely related to their traditional culture. This theory has proven to be accurate with studies measuring vocational development in Chinese American children. For instance, Leong and Chou (1994, p. 164) indicated that "more acculturated Asian Americans will choose occupations based on what they enjoy and less acculturated Asian Americans will view careers more as a means to an end."

Varying levels of acculturation are also influential to individual career development of immigrant clients. Berry (1980, in Chun, Organista, & Marin, 2002) describes four levels of acculturation: marginalization, assimilation, separation, and integration (see Table 16.1).

Individual vocational development may be dependent on the level of acculturation endorsed by the immigrant client. For example, the separation level of acculturation is primarily characterized by an immigrant becoming totally embedded in the traditional culture and refusing to participate in the host culture. An immigrant client who endorses

TABLE 16.1   Stages of Acculturation

Marginalization	Characterizes individuals with little possibility of, or interest in, cultural maintenance and little interest in having relationship with others.
Assimilation	Characterizes individuals who do not wish to maintain their cultural identity and seek daily interactions with other cultures.
Separation	Characterizes individuals who place a value on holding onto their original culture and, at the same time, wish to avoid interacting with others.
Integration	Characterizes individuals who have an interest in maintaining their original culture during daily interactions with other groups.

Berry, J. W. (2003). Acculturation as varieties of adaptations. In K. M. Chun, P. B. Organista, & G. Marin (Eds.), *Acculturation: Theory, models and some new findings* (pp. 1–25). Boulder, CO: Westview.

this level of acculturation will be likely to have career interests more congruent with the needs of traditional immigrants than more acculturated immigrants. Thus, the career counselors should be aware of these levels of acculturation and their influence of career development of immigrant clients.

Counseling Implications with Immigrant Clients

Immigrant clients experience additional barriers (interpersonal problems, difficulty adjusting to a new culture, and loss of identity) to their career-development process. Thus, the career counselor must attend to both interpersonal and career issues when providing services to immigrant clients. Also, vocational development is influenced by both group assimilation and individual acculturation. Thus, it will be important for the career counselor to develop a strategy to meet immigrant clients' needs that takes into consideration both group assimilation and individual acculturation.

To fulfill these needs, career counselors must first obtain a working knowledge of the client's cultural history and group beliefs. This information will help provide a foundation of influential cultural factors to be used as a baseline to measure the client's individual level of acculturation into the dominant society. This information should help guide counselors' use of culturally appropriate theories and techniques. For instance, immigrants who are highly acculturated may benefit from the use of original career theories, whereas less acculturated immigrants may need a more culturally sensitive approach (Helms & Piper, 1994).

IMPLICATIONS FOR CAREER COUNSELING WITH RACIAL- AND ETHNIC-MINORITY CLIENTS

Several excellent articles, chapters, and books on culturally sensitive career counseling already exist (cf. Leong, 1995; Leong & Hartung, 2003; Spokane, Fouad, & Swanson, 2003; Swanson & Fouad, 1999). They all make the same point: career counselors must develop multicultural counseling competencies before working with racial- and ethnic-minority clients. The counselor should understand cultural characteristics important to the client at the group and individual levels. This information should be used to help the counselor develop a culturally sensitive mode of treatment to be incorporated into the career-counseling process.

Spokane et al. (2003) noted that some career clients make decisions from a collectivistic perspective (career in relation to family, to create a work-family balance, or possibly to benefit the ethnic community). For example, a client may want to enter medicine and ultimately work in an underserved minority community. Other minority clients will work toward individual goals or an individualistic perspective, which reflects the more traditional approach to career counseling. For example, such clients may choose a medical career for personal gain, never making a significant link between that choice and ethnic group needs. Career counselors must accept both types of client needs, and guide these clients without judgment; that is, the collectivistic approach is no less valid than the individualistic approach. Cultural and individual differences in needs will also affect what we choose to do in career counseling, that is, traditional approaches work well with individualistic, traditional clients, while more fluid approaches may work better with collectivistic clients.

Barriers to career choices are a fact of life for clients; what they choose to do about them and whether they can identify and employ ways to overcome them is an area in which the career counselor can assist. Racial- and ethnic-minority clients who possess relatively high levels of confidence in their ability to cope with and manage perceived barriers are more likely to overcome these barriers to pursue their particular goals or objectives (Bandura, 1997, in Luzzo & McWhirter, 2001). Thus, it will be important for career counselors to include activities to build self-confidence in the counseling process.

Overly attributing group cultural characteristics to clients can be just as harmful as negating client culture (Sue & Sue, 2003) and can result in attributing stereotypes to the clients. The career counselor should explore the variability of cultural influence on the client's presenting problems and level of racial identity to avoid stereotyping and negatively affecting minority clients.

Bowman (1993) and Spokane et al. (2003) among others advocate the use of group-counseling approaches with racial- and ethnic-minority clients. Racial- and ethnic-minority clients, especially children and adolescents, may feel more comfortable discussing cultural values and career options in a group format, where they can learn as much from each other as from the group leader. They can also provide encouragement to each other and serve as a reminder that the individual is not the only one experiencing this career confusion. Using group techniques will allow the counselor to reach more clients in a shorter time and will have success rates at least equivalent to individual counseling.

Bowman (1993) also noted that role models are an important part of the career-development process. Clients, especially persons from lower-class or working-class backgrounds, often have little exposure to a broad realm of occupations. It is very possible that their few contacts with college-educated persons come through physician and dentist visits. A lack of exposure can equate with assumptions that certain occupations are closed. Identifying racial- and ethnic-minority role models in a variety of occupations can have immeasurable benefits to the career-counseling process. Another aspect of career counseling is helping the client identify a mentor, someone who works in the field of interest and would be willing to spend time with the client, providing guidance. This guidance would include ways to avoid some of the pitfalls of the occupation, methods to overcome perceived barriers to success, and insight into the network connected to that field. While some of us learn these lessons by trial and error, having a mentor available who can help us gain perspective and be a guide into the field is an excellent way to encourage racial- and ethnic-minority workers to remain in the field. Leong and Hartung (2003) and Swanson and Fouad (1999) describe culturally appropriate career-counseling models. Below is a brief interpretation of the steps of Swanson and Fouad's (1999) model on culturally appropriate career counseling.

- Establish a culturally appropriate relationship—Create a comfortable working relationship between counselor and client that incorporates both individuals' cultural backgrounds and typical working styles.
- Identify career issues—Determine what career development areas are salient for the client at this point in his or her development.
- Assess the impact of cultural variables on career issues—Based on the client's cultural background, identify the variables that have shaped the creation and continuation of these issues.
- Set culturally appropriate processes and goals—Determine the goals of career counseling, as defined by the career and cultural issues previously identified.
- Implement culturally appropriate interventions—Utilize career assessments and other intervention approaches that are consistent with the client's cultural background.
- Decision making—Based on the results of the assessment and other interventions, the client makes a decision regarding his or her career choice.
- Implementation—Assist the client in formulating steps to implement the career decision.

CASE EXAMPLE: KIANA

Kiana is a 31-year-old Mexican American woman; she has been married to Tomas for eight years. She has two sons, Tomas (age 5) and Antonio (age 3). She and her husband live in a small apartment in Dayton, Ohio. Kiana currently is a stay-at-home mother and runs an in-home day care center for her boys and two other Latino children. Tomas is an aircraft mechanic for the nearby Air Force base.

Kiana is the youngest of five children and the only girl. Her parents were born in Mexico, but they came to Texas shortly after they were married. Kiana and her youngest brother were born in Texas. Her parents were migrant workers during Kiana's childhood; they traveled from California to the Midwest, picking crops or helping with planting as the seasons changed. For her first seven years of life Kiana spoke mostly Spanish interspersed with only a few words of English; her family and the majority of people in the migrant camp spoke only Spanish to each other. She did not begin attending an English-speaking school on a regular basis until she was 7, when her parents found steady work on a chicken farm. She was held back in second grade because her teacher thought she was a slow learner. Kiana was shy and did not assert herself during school. She was also torn between expectations from school (homework, reading, etc.) and expectations at home. Kiana was considered too small to handle the farmwork, so her parents left her to handle the majority of the cleaning and cooking at home. She continued that role until she finally left home for college at age 18.

Kiana was more successful in school once she learned English. She particularly enjoyed her classes in social studies and history, and she enjoyed math until she hit the nineth grade. She also did well in home economics and Spanish-language courses, but they were not fun for her—she only took them to fulfill requirements. She had not considered going to college until her high school guidance counselor advised her best friend, a Caucasian girl, that she should plan to go. Kiana was then determined to go, too—she did not want to be left behind. Ultimately, Kiana was able to win a partial scholarship to Ohio State University in Columbus. She lived on campus, worked two jobs, and graduated with a 3.2 GPA. Her major was general studies, with minors in home economics and social studies. She wanted to major in something more exciting, like prelaw, but her parents would not hear of it. They were unhappy that she chose to leave home and go to college; her father was especially negative about having a daughter getting a higher education because education is wasted on girls. Kiana is the only member of her immediate family to complete a four-year degree. She met Tomas while in college, and married him during her senior year. Her father was disappointed that she did not quit college after she married, but Kiana wanted to finish her degree. She then worked for a day care center until the birth of her first son.

Kiana has come to you for career counseling because she is frustrated with her current life and wants to return to work. She loves her sons and her husband, but she does not feel that she is living up to her potential. She does not want her sons to think that her college degree was not useful. Tomas, her husband, is not happy about her decision, but he will support her choice if she can wait until Antonio is in kindergarten, in two more years, before she takes a full-time position. Kiana is not sure what she can do with her general studies degree, She still dreams about law school, but does not believe she can handle the workload now and keep up with all of her home responsibilities. She has been thinking about teaching, possibly at the elementary level, which would allow her to be home when the children are home. There is a predominantly Latino school nearby, and she could probably volunteer there until she earned her teaching license. Kiana also knows that her parents are not happy with the idea of her going back to work: they think that she should be happy with the good living that her husband makes, which is better than what she had growing up.

QUESTIONS FOR THE READER:
1. What theory would you use to describe Kiana's vocational path?
2. What barriers might have affected Kiana's career development?
3. How do you interpret the familial issues with Kiana's father and husband?
4. What stage of racial identity might Kiana be in?
5. What, if any, assessment instruments would you want to administer?
6. What would be your next step as Kiana's therapist?

CASE EXAMPLE: REGGIE

Reggie is a 17-year-old biracial male. He lives in St. Louis, Missouri, with his father, who is African American, and his mother, who is Asian American. He is a junior in a predominantly black high school. He is the middle child of three boys. Many of his father's relatives live within five miles of his home (he attends school with several cousins), while most of his mother's relatives live on the West Coast.

Reggie is of average intelligence, as measured by a Wechsler Intelligence Scale for Children, Fourth Edition during middle school. He is in regular classes at school, earning a 3.2 GPA. He is confident that his grades could be higher, but admits that he does not put enough effort into his work. He has not studied seriously for a test since eighth grade; often he does not bring his textbooks home. If he does not finish his homework in study hall, he simply does not do it. His grades have not suffered because he does well on his exams and his class participation (he loves to talk in class, even if he has not read the material). Reggie's best classes are industrial arts and computer technology. His worst class, by far, is English. He almost never finishes a book for that class.

Reggie recently took the Preliminary Scholastic Aptitude Test for a lark; his best friend and his cousin were taking it, so he did, too. He did not study for it, and actually teased his friends who were studying about working too hard, saying his "natural intelligence" would get him by. Halfway through the test, Reggie knew he was in trouble. He had no idea how to answer some of the questions, although he vaguely recognized some of the material. Now he is worried about his parents' impending reaction to his PSAT scores and what this means for his Scholastic Aptitude Test scores if he decides to take the exam next year. He is not sure whether he wants to go to college, anyway, but he thinks he should get prepared now just in case he changes his mind later. Reggie's parents have not pushed him to go to college, but his older brother went and his parents paid his tuition. His parents say only that Reggie should do whatever makes him happy.

Reggie has come to you for counseling so he can make some decisions about what to do with his life. One of his friends took "some kind of career test that told him what to do for a job," and Reggie wants to take the same test. He also wants to know if his PSAT scores mean he will not be successful in any post–high school training.

QUESTIONS FOR THE READER:

1. What theory would you use to describe Reggie's current development?
2. What possible barriers could hamper Reggie's future career development?
3. Would you give Reggie the "test" he is asking for? Why or why not?
4. How would you proceed with this case?

SUMMARY

Career counseling with racial- and ethnic-minority clients requires counselors to develop a solid working knowledge of career theory, career assessment, and basic counseling skills. The National Career Development Association presents a complete set of career-counseling competencies that should be heeded. Career counselors who will be working with racial- and ethnic-minority clients (in other words, nearly every career counselor) should also heed the *Journal of Multicultural Counseling and Development* list of multicultural counseling competencies. The combination of the two will help the counselor be more effective with clients, or at least recognize the problem.

Career counselors should also be aware of barriers to career development that may impede minority clients. Barriers may include cultural values, prejudice, racism, discrimination, parental influence, financial difficulties, or school grades. Clients can accept these barriers as external and stable, and therefore insurmountable, or they can accept the barriers as hurdles to overcome on their way to their career choice. It is the counselor's role to assist in this endeavor.

Career counselors must also be aware of the significance of race, racial identity, and immigrant status to career counseling and the decision-making process. These factors cannot be ignored, as they are overriding factors that determine how the client perceives the workforce and how the workforce may perceive the client. These barriers may also come into the counseling session and create unnecessary tension, or a wall between the members of the dyad. If the career counselor is able to smoothly pay attention to this information, future career-counseling suggestions should be more effective.

Finally, utilizing all of the background information while intervening with a client is a heady task. Career counselors should take care to use culturally appropriate career-counseling intervention models and to be cognizant of the client's needs and reactions to the process. The more adept the counselor is at understanding the client's needs, the more successful he or she will be when working with clients from culturally diverse populations.

The following Websites provide additional information relating to the chapter topics.

USEFUL WEBSITES

www.counseling.org

The American Counseling Organization, with links to the Association of Multicultural Counseling and Development

www.ncda.org

The National Career Development Association, with a section devoted to job seekers and consumers

www.imdiversity.com

This page includes information on "global villages" for African Americans, Asian Americans, Hispanic Americans, Native Americans, and women. It includes graduate and professional school information, news articles, job postings, and links to legal and health-care pages.

http://www.cete.org/acve/docgen.asp?tbl=digests&ID=135

Site to assist students in understanding the influence of racial identity on the career development of ethnic minorities

www.diversityworking.com

A job-hunting/job-posting site

http://www.ericfacility.net/databases/ERIC_Digests/ed421641.html

Site to assist students in understanding the influence of racial identity on the career development of ethnic minorities

www.hirediversity.com

Another job-hunting/job-posting site, with subsections for various ethnic and racial groups, women, and people with disabilities

www.nemnet.com

The official site of the National Employment Minority Network, designed to assist schools and organizations seeking minority students and job candidates

http://www.parentsassociation.com/education/career_develop.html

Site to assist students in understanding the influence of racial identity on the career development of ethnic minorities

www.saludos.com

A job-posting site focused specifically on bilingual Hispanic job candidates

www.quintcareers.com

A job-seeking site that also includes pages for career resources for ethnic minorities, women, and persons with disabilities

www.minoritycareernet.com

A job-posting/job-hunting site with additional resource information

REFERENCES

Albert, K. A., & Luzzo, D. A. (1999). The role of perceived barriers in career development: A social cognitive perspective. *Journal of Counseling and Development, 77,* 431–436.

American Counseling Assocation. (n.d.). *Cross-cultural competencies and objectives.* Retrieved January 7, 2004, from http://www.counseling.org/site/PageServer?pagename-resources_competencies

Arredondo, P., Toporek, R., Brown, S. P., Jones, J., Locke, D. C., Sanchez, J., et al. (1996). Operationalization of the multicultural counseling competencies. *Journal of Multicultural Counseling and Development, 24,* 42–78.

Asher, N. (2002). Class acts: Indian American high school students negotiate professional and ethnic identities. *Urban Education, 37,* 267–296.

Berry, J. W. (2003). Acculturation as varieties of adaptations. In K. M. Chun, P. B. Organista, & G. Marin (Eds), *Acculturation: Theory, models and some new findings* (pp. 1–25). Boulder, CO: Westview.

Bowman, S. L. (1993). Career intervention strategies for ethnic minorities. *Career Development Quarterly, 41,* 14–25.

Bowman, S. L. (1989). An examination of the career development of black college students. *Dissertation Abstracts International, 50*(6-A): 1598.

Brown, D. (2002). The role of work and cultural values in occupational choice, satisfaction, and success: A theoretical statement. *Journal of Counseling and Development, 80,* 48–56.

Chun, K., Organista, P., & Marin, G. (Eds.). (2002). *Acculturation: Advances in theory, measurement, and applied research* (pp. 122–133). Washington, DC: American Psychological Association.

Constantine, M. G., Erickson, C. D., Banks, R. W., & Timberlake, T. L. (1998). Challenges to the career development of urban racial and ethnic minority youth: Implications for career counseling. *Journal of Multicultural Counseling and Development, 26,* 82–95.

Cross, W. E. (1971). Negro-to-black conversion experience. *Black World, 20*, 13–27.

Duncan, L. E. (2003). Black male college students' attitudes toward seeking psychological help. *Journal of Black Psychology, 29*, 68–86.

Durodoye, G., & Bodley, G. (1997). Career development issues for ethnic minority college students. *College Student Journal, 31*, 27–33.

Evans, K. M., & Larrabee, M. J. (2002). Teaching the multicultural counseling competencies and revised career counseling competencies simultaneously. *Journal of Multicultural Counseling and Development, 30*, 21–39.

Gomez, M. J., Fassinger, R. E., Prosser, J., Cooke, K., Mejia, B. & Luna, J. (2001). Voces abriendo caminos (Voices forging paths): A qualitative study of the career development of notable Latinas. *Journal of Counseling Psychology, 48*, 286–300.

Gross, L. (2004). Creating meaning from intersections of career and cultural identity. *New Directions for Student Services, 105*, 63–78.

Helms, J. (1990). *Black and white racial identity: Theory and research.* New York: Greenwood Press.

Helms, J. E., & Piper, R. E. (1994). Implications of racial identity theory for vocational psychology. *Journal of Vocational Behavior, 44*, 124–138.

Juntunen, C. L., Barraclough, D. J., Broneck, C. L., Seibel, G. A., Winrow, S. A., & Morin, P. M. (2001). American Indian perspectives on the career journey. *Journal of Counseling Psychology, 48*, 274–285.

Leong, F. T. L. (1995). *Career development and vocational behavior of racial and ethnic minorities.* Mahwah, NJ: Erlbaum.

Leong, F. T. L., & Chou, E. L. (1994). The role of identity and acculturation in the vocational behavior of Asian Americans: An integrative review. *Journal of Vocational Behavior, 44*, 155–172.

Leong, F. T. L., & Hartung, P. J. (2003). Cross-cultural career counseling. In G. Bernal, J. E. Trimble, A. K. Burlew, & F. T. L. Leong (Eds.), *Handbook of racial and ethnic minority psychology* (pp. 504–520).Thousand Oaks, CA: Sage.

Lucero-Miller, D., & Newman, J. L. (1999). Predicting acculturation using career, family, and demographic variables in a sample of Mexican American students. *Journal of Multicultural Counseling and Development, 27*, 75–93.

Luzzo, D. A, & McWhirter, E. H. (2001). Sex and ethnic differences in the perception of educational and career-related barriers and levels of coping efficacy. *Journal of Counseling and Development, 79*, 61–67.

Miranda, A. O., & Umhoefer, D. L. (1998). Acculturation, language use, and demographic variables as predictors of the career self-efficacy of Latino career counseling clients. *Journal of Multicultural Counseling and Development, 26*, 39–52.

National Career Development Association. (n.d.). *Career counseling competencies.* Retrieved January 7, 2004, from http://ncda.org

Parham, T. A., & Austin, N. L. (1994). Career development and African Americans: A contextual reappraisal using the Nigrescence construct. *Journal of Vocational Behavior, 44*, 139–154.

Pedersen, P. B. (1991). Multiculturalism as a generic approach in counseling. *Journal of Counseling and Development, 70*(1), 6–12.

Pedersen, P. B. (2003). Cross-cultural counseling: Developing culture-centered interactions. In G. Bernal, J. E. Trimble, A. K. Turner, & F. T. L. Leong (Eds.), *Handbook of racial and ethnic minority psychology* (pp. 487–503). Thousand Oaks, CA: Sage.

Richie, B. S., Fassinger, R. E., Linn, S. G., Johnson, J., Robinson, S., & Prosser, J. (1997). Persistence, connection, and passion: A qualitative study of the career development of highly achieving African American-black and white women. *Journal of Counseling Psychology, 44*, 133–148.

Spokane, A. R., Fouad, N. A., & Swanson, J. L. (2003), Culture-centered intervention. *Journal of Vocational Behavior, 62,* 453–458.

Sue, D. W., & Sue, D. (2003). *Counseling the culturally diverse: Theory and practice* (4th ed.). New York: John Wiley & Sons.

Sundberg, N. D. (1981). Cross-cultural counseling and psychotherapy: A research overview. In A. J. Mansella & P. B. Pedersen (Eds.), *Cross-cultural counseling and psychotherapy* (pp. 29–38). New York: Pergamon.

Swanson, J. A., & Fouad, N. A. (1999). Career theory and practice: Learning through case studies. Thousand Oaks, CA: Sage.

Swim, J. K., Hyers, L. L., Cohen, L. L., Fitzgerald, D. C., & Bylsma, W. H. (2003). African American college students' experiences with everyday racism: Characteristics of and responses to these incidents. *Journal of Black Psychology, 29,* 38–67.

Vontress, C. E. (1969). Cultural barriers in the counseling relationship. *Personnel and Guidance Journal, 48,* 11–17.

Walsh, W. B., & Srsic, C. (1996). Annual review: Vocational behavior and career development—1994. *Career Development Quarterly, 44,* 98–145.

Wear, D. (2000). Asian/Pacific Islander women in medical education: Personal and professional challenges. *Teaching and Learning in Medicine, 12,* 156–184.

Wechsler, D. (2003). Wechsler Intelligence Scale for Children, Fourth Edition: Administration and scoring manual. San Antonio, TX: The Psychological Corporation.

Westwood, M. J., & Ishiyama, F. I. (1991). Challenges in counseling immigrant clients: Understanding intercultural barriers to career adjustment. *Journal of Employment Counseling, 28,* 130–141.

Yancy, A. L. (1984). Crossing the barrier of counseling minority students. *Journal of College Student Personnel, 25,* 172–173.

CHAPTER 17

CAREER COUNSELING FOR CLIENTS WITH ADDICTIVE BEHAVIORS

CHRIS WOOD

The Ohio State University

From 1995 to 2002 there appear to have been moderate increases in the annual prevalence of illicit drug use overall for adults 18 to 40 years old (Johnston, O'Malley, & Bachman, 2003). From 2.3 to 6 percent of adults ages 18–40 indicate they use marijuana daily, while 24.9 to 40.7 percent report they consume five or more drinks in a row across a two-week time period (Johnston et al., 2003). "On the basis of the Regier et al. (1990) study, it would appear that at any given time, about 7.4 million Americans would meet the diagnostic criteria for alcohol abuse or dependency. Another 3.4 million Americans would qualify for a diagnosis of drug abuse or dependency" (Doweiko, 2002, p. 5). Research from the U.S. Substance Abuse and Mental Health Services Administration (SAMHSA) National Survey on Drug Use and Health indicated that of the 16.7 million illicit drug users, 74.3 percent were employed full or part time, as were 79.9 percent of all adult heavy drinkers (five or more drinks on the same occasion five or more times in the past month; SAMHSA, 2004). With this level of prevalence, the chances of providing career counseling to a client with addictive behaviors appear highly likely. Counselors in agencies, college-counseling centers, Employee Assistance Programs, and even schools need to be prepared to help clients struggling with both their career development and addictive behaviors.

Counseling individuals with career concerns and addictive behaviors involves dealing with two "problems." While at one time the predominant thinking was to treat addictions separately from other client problems, current professional literature encourages addressing such issues together (Miller, 1994). Moreover, as there is likely to be an inherent relationship between a client's career concerns and his or her addictive behaviors, it seems only logical that these respective issues be dealt with concurrently.

To counsel clients with addictive behaviors, it is first necessary to have an understanding of both (1) how addictions develop and (2) how people change behaviors. The process of developing addictions and the process of changing addictive behaviors involves essentially the same stages of change. Since changing careers also necessitates behavioral change, this process, too, follows the same stages of change.

CASE EXAMPLE

John is a 29-year-old, white male who has come to see you for career counseling. He is currently employed full time as a tester for a computer company. Additionally, he works part time as a disc jockey (DJ) for weddings and other social events on evenings and weekends. After high school, John started college at a local community college, taking primarily general courses in math, English, and computer technology to complete the requirements for an associate's or bachelor's degree. However, he quickly became disinterested in classes and left to go to work full time.

For the past several years John has been steadily employed in several different dot-com and web-based companies, moving from one company to the next when each company subsequently went out of business. In general he has been satisfied with the standard of living his vocation has provided him, but he finds the nature of his work at his current company "stifling." The part-time job as a DJ has given him a more creative outlet and provided him with a needed social context outside work.

John is currently very dissatisfied with the "rut" he has found himself in and feels he needs to make some changes in his life. While he likes the financial rewards of his tester position, he cannot imagine himself staying in that vocation for the rest of his life. John finds his work an increasing drudgery and is concerned about the lack of long-term stability in the industry. While he finds his work as a DJ much more interesting, his employment there is sporadic at best, and he believes the hectic "party" pace and atmosphere would wear on him if he were to try doing it full time.

John has also revealed to you that he currently copes with his job stress and dissatisfaction through recreational drug use. He has been an infrequent marijuana user for years and has recently started using cocaine regularly after being introduced to it through his work as a DJ. He says that marijuana helps him escape the intense pressure of his work as a tester and cocaine helps him become energized for his work as a DJ. While he is aware of an increase in his drug usage in recent months, his primary anxiety involves his current job situation.

STAGES OF CHANGE

Prochaska and DiClemente (1982) developed a transtheoretical model (TTM) of behavioral change. This model posits six segments in the process of intentional behavior change that can be described as the stages of change (DiClemente, 2003). These stages are precontemplation, contemplation, preparation, action, maintenance, and termination. Movement through these stages of change is generally recursive and cyclical (see Figure 17.1). Each of these stages has a unique character. There is an identifiable goal to be achieved in each specific stage. Similarly, the individual engaged in the process of change must successfully complete the necessary tasks of the subsequent stage in order to successfully progress in the change process. Counselors assisting individuals with the process of change can benefit from being aware of the stages of change, the goals for each stage, and the necessary tasks for each of the six stages.

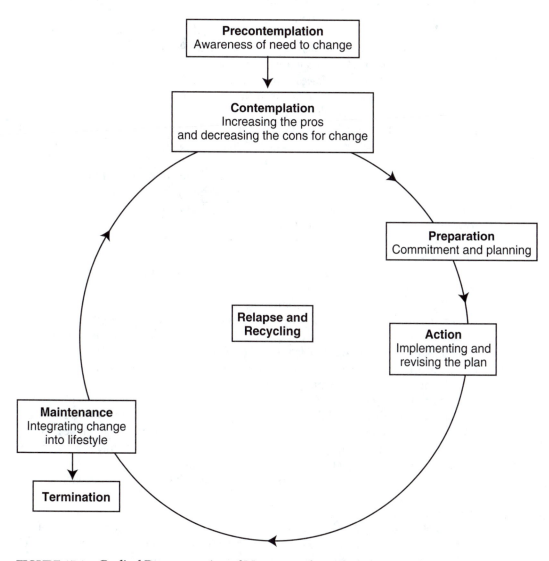

FIGURE 17.1 Cyclical Representation of Movement through the Stages of Changes

Precontemplation

As Figure 17.1 illustrates, precontemplation is the stage prior to entering the "wheel of change." The precontemplation stage is characterized by a lack of consideration of change. Individuals in the precontemplation stage do not feel the need to change current patterns of behavior or see no convincing reasons to consider behavioral change. Clients in this stage do not believe that the negative aspects of the current behavior outweigh the costs of actively engaging in behavior change. "As long as the current pattern of behavior seems functional for the individual or no compelling reason arises to disrupt this pattern, an individual can remain in precontemplation for extended periods of time, even a lifetime" (DiClemente, 2003, p. 26).

There are four categories of individuals in the precontemplation stage: reluctant, rebellious, resigned, and rationalizing (DiClemente, 1991; DiClemente & Velasquez, 2002). Individuals in the precontemplation stage are sometimes labeled "resistant." Understanding the four categories of precontemplators, however, can allow a counselor to use specific strategies to assist clients in changing problematic behavior.

Reluctant precontemplators are individuals who lack full awareness of their problematic addictive behavior and are therefore passively resistant. They do not wish to risk change as they do not see any potential benefits to changing their current status quo.

Rebellious precontemplators are actively resistant to change. They often have strong feelings against change and may have a heavy investment in their current addictive behavior. They do not like being told what to do and may even be hostile toward the proposal of a specific strategy for change.

The resigned precontemplator lacks the energy to invest in change and is prepared to accept that her or his current behavior is inevitable. The problem seems overwhelming, and the barriers to change are too great to warrant an investment of time or energy into the change process.

The fourth category of precontemplators is the rationalizing precontemplators. "These clients are not considering change because they have figured out the odds of personal risk, or they have plenty of reasons why the problem is not a problem or is a problem for others but not for them" (DiClemente, 1991, p. 193). Rationalizing contemplators sometimes like to debate their rationale for their current behavior, thus reinforcing their position against change.

The primary goal for the precontemplation stage is for the individual to begin to seriously consider the possibility of change. Since there has been little or no consideration of change of behavior in the foreseeable future, reaching this goal can be a formidable achievement. For the precontemplating client to envision change as a possibility requires successful completion of the major tasks in this stage.

The necessary tasks in the precontemplation stage include increasing client awareness of the need to change. There are multiple internal and environmental influences that impact the individual reasoning for considering change: social pressure, human development, relationships, values, economic pressure, and so on. Consideration of the current behavior within the context of these influences can compel an individual to explore the possibility of changing current patterns of behavior.

Increasing concern about the current pattern of behavior is another task for the precontemplation stage. Again this involves gaining an awareness of potential reasons for change as well as those factors that may positively or negatively impact the client's ability to even begin to consider change.

Instilling hope is perhaps the most profound task for the precontemplation stage. Generally, this initially involves exploring the barriers to change and generating productive strategies for overcoming such obstacles. Clients in the precontemplation stage may lack hope due to previously unsuccessful change attempts in the current or alternate patterns of behavior. It is important for the client in this stage to realize that setbacks in the change process are expected and are inherently different than a complete failure.

Contemplation

In the contemplation stage the client is engaged in a cost-benefit analysis. The client is weighing the risks associated with change against the potential benefits. This analysis becomes a period of instability for the client. Individuals may struggle with ambivalent or confusing thoughts and feelings about a given behavior pattern as they consider the possibility of change. "The contemplation stage involves a process of evaluating risks and benefits, the pros and cons of both the current behavior pattern and the potential new behavior pattern" (DiClemente, 2003, p. 28).

Contemplators are not yet ready to actively commit to the process of change. They are still gathering information and considering options. "Contemplation is the stage when clients are quite open to information and decisional balance considerations. Yet it is also the stage where many clients are waiting for the one final piece of information that will compel them to change" (DiClemente, 1991, p. 195). The goal for this stage, then, is a thoroughly reasoned evaluation that reinforces a client's decision to change. This evaluation should be composed of the carefully considered risks and benefits of change.

The task for the contemplation stage is to conduct a thorough analysis of the advantages and disadvantages of the current behavior. This analysis needs to include both the affective and cognitive rewards of the current behavior and the stake involved in change. At the same time, the client needs to fully realize the costs of continuing the current behavior and the potential return on the investment in an endeavor to change.

Preparation

Clients in the preparation stage are ready to make a change in the near future. "Preparation takes you from the decisions you make in the contemplation stage to the specific steps you take to solve the problem during the action stage" (Prochaska, Norcross, & DiClemente, 1994, p. 146). The decisional balance in the contemplation stage has been tipped in favor of change, and it is time to get ready. In the preparation stage, clients must solidify a commitment to change and operationalize their energy through developing a plan of action.

The primary goal for the preparation stage is to formalize a plan of action. The plan of action needs to be a specific, detailed list of the steps necessary to engage in active change. The plan of action must include those crucial elements necessary to mobilize client energy through initiating action. Inherent in a plan of action are several critical elements. Clients must believe in the feasibility of the plan. They need to see the plan as possessing a strong likelihood for bringing about the desired outcome (the new behavior). Moreover, clients need to believe in their own ability to successfully engage in the steps necessary to complete their plan of action. The tasks of the preparation stage involve reinforcing the client's commitment to change and determining the best plan of action.

Reinforcing the commitment to change is an important task in the preparation stage. In the preparation stage, clients will still be resolving feelings of ambiguity about change. The client is still engaged in the decision-making process in consideration of the current behavior and other alternatives. A commitment to change is crucial to mobilizing energy and formulating a plan for action.

As part of the task of developing a plan of action, there are several important considerations. The previous experiences with change should be considered in order to construct a plan that has optimal potential for success. Similarly, considering the potential difficulties in a plan is also useful to prepare for action. Finally, the client's courage and competency to be successful in the plan are key components of his or her potential to implement any plan of action.

Action

The action stage is the implementation of the plan of action. In this stage, most people make the move toward altering their behavior. This stage of change requires the greatest commitment of time and energy. For these reasons, it is also characterized by an attraction to the old patterns of behavior. It is often easier to return to the previous behavior than to follow through on the plan and begin to sustain a new behavior.

The goal for this stage is to establish a new pattern of behavior. In addition to the major task of implementing the plan of action, additional tasks include sustaining commitment in the face of obstacles to the plan and revising the plan as necessary in order to maintain the enterprise of change.

Maintenance

As Figure 17.1 represents, maintenance is the final stage before exiting the wheel of change. In this stage, "the new behavior must become integrated into the lifestyle of the individual" (DiClemente, 2003, p. 29).

The maintenance stage is distinguished by the clear absence of the previous behavior and the sustained presence of the new behavior. Still present, however, may be the urges and temptation to return to the previous behavior. "In the maintenance stage the person works to consolidate the gains made during the action stage and struggles to prevent relapse" (DiClemente & Velasquez, 2002, p. 212). It is important to note that relapse is not a collapse of the change process. People often "recycle" through one or more stages in the wheel of change before successfully negotiating the maintenance stage and exiting the wheel of change into termination.

Success in the maintenance stage allows the new behavior to become automatic and the new status quo (DiClemente, 2003). Ultimately, then, the client is able to exit the wheel of change (termination), with the new behavior as an integral part of a new lifestyle.

Termination

Termination is characterized by the final exit from the cycle of change. This is not so much a stage as such, but rather a new state of being, where a new behavior has replaced the old behavior and it would, in fact, take a substantial amount of effort to go back to it. In reference to addictive behaviors, this state is sometimes referred to as recovery. The goals and tasks of termination focus on the new way of being, which does not include the previous behavior. "The entire gestalt of life now supports a new lifestyle committed to not engaging in the addictive behavior" (DiClemente, 2003, p. 201).

The preceding discussion of the stages of change addresses primarily the change process for addictive behaviors. As may already be apparent, however, the stages are indicative of any behavioral change. This process also applies to those behaviors that comprise career change.

Case Example and the Stages of Change

The case example introduced at the beginning of the chapter demonstrates how career and lifestyle planning for clients with addictive behaviors can be conceptualized using the TTM stages of change. John is discerning two simultaneous and interrelated processes of change. In one respect he is exploring a career change, but there are also interconnected issues of drug use worthy of consideration in career and lifestyle planning.

In the case example, both John's career concerns and the addictive behaviors can be conceptualized within the TTM stages of change framework. This conceptualization can help a counselor understand John's situation and develop a strategy to help him. What stages of change is John negotiating?

John has come to see the counselor voluntarily. He was not mandated to see a counselor for a drug or alcohol "problem," nor has he sought career assistance as part of a severance package from a job loss. He is seeking career counseling and seems open to exploring different options. Clearly he is not in the precontemplation stage regarding his career concerns.

Although he has in one sense taken some action by seeking career counseling, he has no substantial plan beyond that initial step. Moreover he has no definite commitment to change beyond just the initial counseling session. Perhaps the following exchange between John and his counselor will help illuminate his stage of change regarding his career behavior.

> **Counselor:**   You wish you had greater opportunity for creativity at work and you're wondering if it is time for a career change.
>
> **John:**   Yes, but I make pretty good money, especially for someone my age. I do much better financially than most of my friends. I'd be stupid to give up a sweet deal like this.
>
> **Counselor:**   You like the financial rewards your job offers and you're thinking it might be a mistake to leave your present position.
>
> **John:**   Yeah, but I don't know how long this company's even going to last, I mean I've already been at two different places that went under, and each time it was really tough finding a new position.

Note that while the counselor is accurately paraphrasing the different messages from the client, each time John takes an opposing perspective. This exchange is indicative of the ambiguity present in the contemplation stage. John sees certain advantages to his present position and specific risks to change. At the same time he is cognizant of the drawbacks of remaining in his current situation and is considering the potential benefits of devoting energy to change. Clearly John is in the contemplation stage regarding his career behavior.

What about John's drug behavior? The following statement may make John's stage of change clearer.

> **John:**   When we have a product launch deadline, everyone gets really stressed. We put in 10- or 12-hour days. Sometimes I smoke some pot after I get home so that I can unwind before going to bed. And then sometimes I just don't have the energy to get geared up for work. I might do a line of coke as a pick-me-up. I don't drink coffee, so for me it's just a quick, albeit expensive, pick-me-up.

John does not appear to be overly concerned about his drug use. He states that his use of marijuana and cocaine currently serve a useful purpose in his life. For the most part, John does not seem to be interested in changing his behavior in this area of his life. These characteristics suggest that John is in the precontemplation stage. Although John does mention the "expensive" nature of his behavior, he has convinced himself of the necessity of his current behavior. For these reasons, John would most aptly be categorized as a rationalizing precontemplator.

Understanding the stage of change for John's career concern and his drug behaviors allows a counselor to select a strategy and specific techniques. The general principles of Motivational Interviewing (Miller & Rollnick, 1991, 2002) provide a guiding character as well as specific strategies for counselors to use in helping clients with addictive behaviors in the different stages of change. Following these principles and the specific strategies for the stages of change can assist counselors in helping clients with both their addictive behaviors as well as their career development.

MOTIVATIONAL INTERVIEWING

Motivational Interviewing (MI) is a counseling approach developed by Miller and Rollnick (1991, 2002) to assist individuals with the process of change. While originally conceptualized as an approach for working with clients with addictive behaviors, the approach has been used successfully with a range of behavioral changes, including physical exercise (Harland et al., 1999), weight reduction (Smith, Heckemeyer, Kratt, & Mason, 1997), bulimia (Treasure et al., 1999), marijuana use (Stephens, Roffman, & Curtin, 2000), and alcoholism (Project MATCH Research Group, 1997, 1998). Burke, Arkowitz, and Menchola (2003) conducted a meta-analysis of 30 controlled clinical research trials that investigated MI or adaptations of motivational interviewing (AMI). They determined that the research supported the efficacy of AMIs for problems involving alcohol and drugs as well as diet and exercise.

MI posits four principles to guide the counselor orientation toward the client. These four principles underscore the character of the MI approach and the subsequent strategies for each stage of behavioral change. The principles are (1) express empathy, (2) develop discrepancy, (3) roll with resistance, and (4) support self-efficacy.

Express Empathy

The first principle is to consistently express empathy, both immediately and throughout the change process. The emphasis should be on understanding the client's perspective, without blame or judgment. While a counselor may not agree with the client's behavior or approve of the client's choices, it is still possible to maintain a climate of acceptance. A climate of acceptance facilitates change. Conversely, judgment and blame tend to immobilize the change process. One way to conceptualize this process is that a climate of acceptance frees people to change rather than forcing them to devote energy toward resisting judgment.

Related to the notion of acceptance is the understanding that ambivalence is normal, and even a healthy, part of the change process. "Ambivalence is accepted as a normal part of human experience and change, rather than seen as pathology or pernicious defensiveness" (Miller & Rollnick, 2002, p. 37). Often we have a tendency to see ambivalent feelings and thoughts as unhealthy manifestations of an unwillingness to engage in positive change—as denial or resistance. An important element of the principals of MI, however, is to view ambivalence as a normal part of the change process—to be honored with empathy, as with all client experiences and perspectives. Understanding and accepting a client's ambivalence about change, then, becomes an essential component of being an empathic counselor.

The principle of expressing empathy is demonstrated through the use of counseling skills. Counseling skills are used to develop an awareness and understanding of client experiences. Through skillful reflective listening, the counselor is able to step into the client's phenomenal space, and thus empathically share his or her perspective. Moreover, counseling skills are also used to express the empathic understanding of client perspective through paraphrasing of messages and feelings.

Consider the opportunities for expressing empathy with John, the client described in the case example. Recall that John is expressing ambivalence over his current job. His last statement was the following.

John:	Yeah, but I don't know how long this company's even going to last, I mean I've already been at two different places that went under and each time it was really tough finding a new position.
Counselor:	You feel exhausted by the thought of having to search for a new vocation and at the same time you are frightened that your current position may be eliminated.

While other empathic statements are certainly possible, the counselor's response provides an example of skillful reflective listening that expresses understanding of the client's perspective. The same empathy could be expressed for John relating to his other behaviors.

John:	. . . And then sometimes I just don't have the energy to get geared up for work. I might do a line of coke as a pick-me-up. I don't drink coffee, so for me it's just a quick, albeit expensive, pick-me-up.
Counselor:	Your job is extremely stressful and leaves you physically and mentally drained. Sometimes you use cocaine to rejuvenate. While part of you feels this is a quick energizer, another part of you is concerned about the exp.ense involved with the use of cocaine.

Again, while there may be alternate ways of reflecting the client's thoughts and feeling, the counselor's statement demonstrates a specific counselor response expressing empathy for the client.

Develop Discrepancy

The second principle that underlies MI is to develop discrepancy between a client's present behavior and his or her goals and values. It is important to note that the counselor is to develop or amplify this discrepancy as initiated by the client and within the context of the client's perspective—and not to artificially create the discrepancy by imposing the counselor's perspective or value system. In one sense, the counselor is helping the client to identify and clarify personal goals and values. Concurrently, the counselor is helping to bring to the client's awareness the conflict between his or her current behavior and preferred state of being.

This discrepancy is, of course, the motivation for change. In order for change to occur, clients must be aware of the discrepancy between their current behavior and their desired self. Moreover it is the awareness of this discrepancy and the belief in their ability to successfully bring about change that fuels client energy to actively continue the process of change.

In utilizing the principal of developing discrepancy, the counselor places the responsibility for change on the client. "When motivational interviewing is done well, it is not the counselor but the client who gives voice to concerns, reasons for change, self-efficacy, and intentions to change" (Miller & Rollnick, 2002, p. 39).

In the case example, the counselor's last paraphrase to the client is an example of beginning to develop discrepancy.

Counselor: . . . While part of you feels this is a quick energizer, another part of you is concerned about the expense involved with the use of cocaine.

Here the counselor is using a paraphrase of message from the client and structuring the paraphrase so as to highlight the client's concerns about his present behavior. It is important to note the nonconfrontational style of the counselor's response.

The interrelationship of career or lifestyle planning and addictive behaviors presents unique opportunities to develop discrepancy within a client. Consider the following exchange between counselor and client.

John: I don't want to feel so exhausted all the time. I want to have the kind of job that is both fun and creative. My job is so stressful that I really need to go out and cut loose once in a while. Sometimes after I am a DJ for a wedding I'll still be pumped up and need to go out with coworkers to clubs or a party. When I have to work at my regular job the next day though, I'm usually exhausted and pretty hungover. It's tough to just get through the workday. I can't imagine trying to find the time to look for a new job, take classes, or go out and interview for a job or anything like that. Still I can't see myself staying a tester for the rest of my life either.

Counselor: You'd like to see yourself making a move toward finding a career that is more enjoyable than your present job. Right now the cycle of two jobs and partying with coworkers keeps you exhausted most of the time.

John: Exactly! I feel like all my energy is being sucked away, and while I can get it back for a while when I go out, the next day it's gone again.

Counselor: You would like to get out of this pattern of being drained at work, and feeling exhausted and hungover so that you can begin to start on changes you want to make in your lifestyle. However, something keeps you stuck in this present pattern . . .

The counselor is developing the discrepancy between the client's current addictive behavior and goal for changing careers. Similarly, the counselor is developing discrepancy between the client's current vocational behavior and wish to explore vocational options. In the broader sense, each of these changes involves altering the client's lifestyle.

Developing discrepancy when providing career counseling for clients with addictive behaviors, then, means developing discrepancy between their current behaviors (that keep them trapped in an undesirable lifestyle) and their goals for developing the lifestyle they would like to have.

It is important to remember that ultimately, the reasons for change come from the client, not the counselor. The counselor is helping the client see the discrepancies between the client's present behavior and the client's goals or values. "When motivational interviewing is done well, it is not the counselor but the client who gives voice to concerns, reasons for change, self-efficacy, and intentions to change" (Miller & Rollnick, 2002, p. 39).

Roll with Resistance

The third foundational principle of MI is to roll with resistance. Counselors sometimes conceptualize resistance as an attribute of the client—an unwillingness to engage in positive growth. In motivational interviewing, however, resistance is more appropriately conceptualized as a function of the counselor-client dynamics. In one sense, resistance is created by confrontational encounter with another person or an interaction that engenders defensiveness on the part of the client.

One way to deal with resistance or defensiveness is to try to overpower it with convincing arguments. This approach may just cause the client to become increasingly entrenched in his or her present position. Another approach, however, is to avoid arguing or trying to convince the client of the need to change, but rather to "roll with it" and allow the client to be the primary impetus for change.

Rolling with resistance calls for a counselor to take several stances with a client. One is that the counselor should not argue for specified change or try to convince the client of the need to change. Similarly, the counselor should not directly oppose resistance or defensiveness when presented by the client. Rather, the counselor should interpret the presence of resistance as a directive to change approaches. Consistently, the counselor must maintain the attitude that the client is the primary resource for generating solutions to the current situation. It is not the counselor's responsibility to find all the answers—and attempting to do so may simply cause a client to find fault in each suggestion proposed. Ultimately, it is the client who will be living with the new lifestyle, so it only makes sense that the changes are built on the strategies determined by the client.

Counselor:	. . . While part of you feels this is a quick energizer, another part of you is concerned about the expense involved with the use of cocaine [develop discrepancy].
John:	I don't think I'm an addict or anything. I mean, I've never hurt anybody else or myself, and I've never had any legal trouble or anything like that.
Counselor:	I'm not here to label you as addict, diagnose any problem, or convince you to do anything you don't want to do. I'm just here to help

you take a look at your current situation and how you'd like things to be. One thing you feel proud about is that your cocaine use has never hurt anyone [express empathy]. Tell me more about the things you feel good about in your current lifestyle [roll with resistance].

Support Self-Efficacy

Perhaps the most important guiding principle undergirding the MI approach is the conviction to support self-efficacy. "Perceived self-efficacy refers to beliefs in one's capabilities to organize and execute the courses of action required to produce given attainments" (Bandura, 1997, p. 3). Obviously, the belief in one's ability to successfully bring about change is a key motivator. Individuals who do not believe they are able to go through the process of change and successfully achieve a new lifestyle are less likely to even attempt change. Thus a counselor must consistently support the self-efficacy of clients throughout the change process.

The following dialogue highlights supporting self-efficacy in the process of career change.

John: I don't know, I've never really been good at job interviews.

Counselor: You mentioned before that you see communication as one of your strengths.

John: That's true, I'm as good or better than anyone at any of the places I've worked.

Counselor: And you've certainly been very articulate at describing your strengths to me.

John: Yeah, that's true too. I'm just so used to having my pot as a way to deal with stress and a little coke to get energized that it scares me to go into a job interview straight.

Counselor: It really frightens you to think about having to deal with stressful situations without marijuana or cocaine [express empathy].

John: When I flew home for Christmas to visit my folks I was too scared to take pot or coke with me through security. It was tough for a while, but I did okay without it. I even started jogging again, and sleeping better.

Counselor: While it was tough, you were able to go an entire week without using drugs. The Christmas holidays can be a very stressful time and you were able to deal with them drug free.

John: Yeah, that's true, my parents were just about enough to drive me over the brink but I made it through the visit.

Counselor: And even started yourself on an exercise regimen.

John: Yeah, now that I think about it I'm pretty proud at not letting everything get to me.

Following the previously described guiding principles of Motivational Interviewing, there are additional strategies that can assist a client with change. Facilitating "change-talk," responding appropriately to resistance, and strengthening the commitment to change are motivational interviewing strategies that utilize specific counseling techniques to assist clients.

Change-Talk

Change-talk is dialogue between counselor and client that is oriented toward the advantages of behavioral change. This dialogue tends to fall into four categories: (1) disadvantages of the status quo, (2) advantages of change, (3) optimism about change, (4) intention to change (Miller & Rollnick, 2002). To facilitate change-talk, a counselor will want to ask specific, open-ended questions in the subsequent order of the four given categories.

Consider how these open-ended questions can be used with the case example:

DISADVANTAGES OF THE STATUS QUO

Counselor: What worries you about your current situation—both your career and your drug use?

John: I don't see myself lasting long-term in either of my jobs. The DJ job is fun and it gave me some friends but I wouldn't want to do it full time and it's too expensive to party all the time. My tester job pays well but I don't think it will be stable in the long run and it's not really me. The drug use is really just an offshoot of two jobs—if I had a job that I really loved, I wouldn't need to party so much for relief.

Counselor: You like the friends you have made through your DJ job and the money you make as a tester. You don't want to be a DJ full time and the tester job doesn't suit you. You'd like to find a career you enjoy more. You'd like to have a lifestyle where you don't party to deal with stress.

John: Yeah.

The counselor used an open-ended question to elicit the client's perspective on the disadvantages of the status quo. Then the counselor carefully paraphrased the disadvantages expressed by the client.

Counselor: Why do you think you need to do something about your job situation and your drug use?

John: I guess I think working two jobs and my partying are really starting to wear me out.

Counselor: In what ways does this concern you?

John:	Well, I'm really tired a lot of the time. And . . . the partying is really getting expensive. I can afford it because I make pretty good money but I could be putting that money away to help with a job change.
Counselor:	What do you think will happen if you don't change anything?
John:	I'm either going to be let go at my tester job and have no savings to fall back on—or I'll just quit some day down the line because I can't take it anymore!

The preceding discussion between client and counselor illustrates how the example open-ended questions can be used to evoke a discussion of the disadvantages of the status quo. The dialogue presented here is an accelerated example of a discussion that likely needs to be conducted in much greater depth with the client. It is important to note that in this example, as with discussions in greater detail, the disadvantages of the status quo are those described by the client, not points argued by the counselor.

ADVANTAGES OF CHANGE

Counselor:	How would you like things to be different?
John:	I wish I had a better job. I wish I wasn't so tired all the time.
Counselor:	Describe how your job could be "better."
John:	Well, I'd like a job where I can brainstorm a little . . . be creative. Whenever I have an idea about something now it doesn't really matter because that's not my role. I have to put all my time and energy into just making sure things work as they're supposed to—and it doesn't really matter if I have ideas on how to improve features of the products. And, I'd like to have more positive contact with customers. Instead of just troubleshooting things for problems, I'd like to talk with people about the possibilities of products.
Counselor:	Describe how you'd like to be less "tired all the time."
John:	Well if my work were more stimulating, I'd be more energized. I wouldn't spend most of my day thinking about how I can't wait to get out and party or how I just wish I were at home trying to forget about work . . . And if I weren't so tired at work all the time, then the day wouldn't drag so much—then maybe I'd have some energy to change careers.
Counselor:	What would be the advantages of making a lifestyle change?
John:	I think I'd be happier if I weren't in this cycle of too much stressful work and then too much wild party. I'd bet I could get through tough days at work much easier, even if I just knew there were some change in sight.

OPTIMISM ABOUT CHANGE

Counselor: What makes you think that if you decide to make a change you could do it?

John: Well, I'm not that sure I can really. But, I've lost my job twice before and been able to find a new one in the same area pretty quickly. It's just that switching to a different area could be pretty tough, I don't know. . . . And with the partying, well I've cut back on that off and on at different times. I think it would be even easier to cut back on that stuff if my job situation were better.

Counselor: How confident are you—say on a scale from zero to 10, where zero is not at all confident and 10 is extremely confident—regarding this lifestyle change?

John: Probably a 5 for changing my partying and a 4 for changing my career . . . maybe a 4.5 overall.

Counselor: Why a 4.5 and not a zero?

John: Well I know I need to do something. I've changed jobs before and I have cut back on partying before. I think working on each will help the other.

Counselor: You think working toward a career change will help you cut back on your partying and you also believe that cutting back on your drug use will help your efforts toward changing careers.

Here the counselor has used an open-ended question to explore the client's optimism toward change. To further this understanding, the counselor asks the client to rate his confidence on a scale of 1 to 10. This is another motivational interviewing technique (sometimes called a ruler) designed to assess the client's confidence and to further elicit change-talk. It is interesting to note that in the case example above, the ruler technique elicited the client's first expression of a perceived connection between addictive behaviors and career concerns. Also, notice that the counselor asked why the client's assessment was not lower (and not the opposite). This encourages the client to express strengths toward change. Asking the client, "Why is it 4.5 and not 10?" would force the client to argue against change. The ruler technique can be used further as described below.

INTENTION TO CHANGE

Counselor: What would it take for you to go from 4.5 to a 5 or a 6?

John: If I had some sort of plan, I mean, if I knew what sort of steps I was going to take . . . and if, if I'd started the steps . . . then I'd feel more like an 8 or a 9, maybe even a 10 if I'd already started initiating the plan.

Counselor: What do you think you might do?

John: Well I could look through the want ads for a different job, but I've done that before and nothing there interested me much . . . and

> I could try to quit smoking dope, drinking, and coke total cold turkey, but then I wouldn't know what to do when I go out with friends . . . I guess I can't really think of any other ways.

Here the counselor builds on the ruler technique by asking the client to describe how he or she might further progress toward change. Moreover, the counselor is tapping into the client's current change strategies and estimated probability of success for those strategies. In this respect, the counselor has determined what the client believes is necessary to move toward change and has ascertained that the client lacks constructive strategies for effecting a change of lifestyle.

The case example illustrates some strategies for eliciting change-talk. Equally important is how the counselor responds to change talk. Miller and Rollnick (2002) encourage the use of specific counseling skills as a means of furthering change-talk and enhancing intrinsic motivation. These skills include: (1) elaborating change-talk, (2) summarizing change-talk, (3) affirming change-talk, (4) clarifying ambivalence, and (5) clarifying values.

Elaborating change-talk is accomplished when a counselor encourages a client to expound on statements of change. The counselor helps the client explore change-talk by using furthering responses such as, "Tell me more about [client's change statement]," "What are some other reasons you might want to make a change?" or "Give me an example of . . ." (Miller & Rollnick, 2002, p. 87). The intent of these directive counseling responses is to help the client to explore their intentions toward change.

Equally important in responding to client statements of change is reflecting change-talk. This counseling skill can help clients clarify ambivalence around change and continue exploration of client intentions toward change. Recall the previous counselor responses in the case example:

Counselor: You'd like to see yourself making a move toward finding a career that is more enjoyable than your present job. Right now the cycle of two jobs and partying with coworkers keeps you exhausted most of the time.

The counselor response reflects client change-talk concerning both the career and addictive behaviors. It is important for counselors to be aware that reflecting client statements of change can sometimes engender psychological reaction in a client and elicit client statements against change.

Counselor: You'd like to end your pattern of partying and being exhausted or feeling hungover at work.

John: Well, going out with friends gives me relief from the stresses of work.

In such cases it is necessary to use what Miller & Rollnick (2002) refer to as "double-sided reflection." Double-sided reflection can help a counselor avoid being caught in the position of arguing for change while the client argues against it.

> **Counselor:** You like the stress relief you feel from going out with friends and you hate feeling physically bad the next day after having been out partying with drugs and alcohol.

Summarizing change-talk is also another way for counselors to assist clients in exploring their feelings and thoughts about change. "In general, summaries are collections of change statements the person has made: disadvantages of the status quo, reasons for change, optimism about change, and desire to change" (Miller & Rollnick, 2002, p. 90). As with double-sided reflection, when reflecting change-talk, including both sides of ambivalence can be an effective tool in facilitating client movement toward change.

Affirming change-talk is also an important counselor response to client self-motivational change statements. Selective counselor responses such as, "That sounds like a good idea" and "That's a good point" (Miller & Rollnick, 2002, p. 91) can serve to reinforce a client's commitment to change and facilitate client movement through the stages of change.

Clarifying ambivalence involves helping a client to examine each side of the conflict surrounding change. This might mean the counselor and client evaluate separately the pros and cons for each of the change alternatives as well as the status quo. It is important that the counselor and client complete this process for each alternative separately as well as the current behavior and status quo.

Clarifying values is equally important and intrinsically related to clarifying ambivalence. Clients must be aware of their personal values in order to evaluate the advantages and disadvantages of change. Helping to discern what is truly important can help a client resolve ambivalence around change. Consider the following discussion:

> **Counselor:** Let's talk about some of the options you have been considering regarding changing your lifestyle. We can evaluate the advantages and drawbacks of each. Let's start with your current lifestyle.
>
> **John:** Okay, I make good money. I can afford to go out when I want.
>
> **Counselor:** You like the salary of your current job and having money for social activities. What else?
>
> **John:** I get along well with my boss. She trusts me to work independently, I mean; I don't have to report in on how I'm going to do everything.
>
> **Counselor:** You like to work independently and autonomy is important to you.
>
> **John:** Yes, exactly. I don't like it when someone is overseeing you all the time. I just wish I had more room to be creative in my work.
>
> **Counselor:** So the ability to express creativity is important to you too. What else do you like about your present lifestyle?
>
> **John:** Well, in my other job I like interacting with people—the people who hire me as DJ. And I like going out with coworkers after work, my second job has helped me make friends.

Counselor: An advantage of your job as a DJ is that it allows you to interact more with people—which you enjoy. Okay, what else?

John: That's all that I can think of. I think that if I had more opportunity for creativity and more autonomy I'd be much happier. My sister is a teacher and she is in total control of her classroom on a daily basis with a lot of ways to be creative. I have no desire to be a teacher but I think if I had that kind of situation—the money and the social extras would matter a lot less to me.

Counselor: So creativity and autonomy are more important to you than financial rewards.

John: I believe so, yes.

Counselor: What are some of the disadvantages of your current lifestyle?

John: Well I'm exhausted all the time. I'm either so wound up I can't relax or so drained I can barely function, but either way I feel totally empty on steady energy.

Counselor: What about your current lifestyle exhausts you?

John: Well, the stress when we have a deadline—say a product launch. Then there's a lot of pressure on everyone. And when I work pretty hard then I tend to party pretty hard too. I'd like to have time and energy to do some of the things I used to do like hobbies. (Laughs) Some more clean living type things like golf, and taking my sister's kids out for pizza.

Counselor: So feeling physically good is important to you. You also value family and having time to pursue personal interests.

John: Yes, I do value family, in fact I'd like to get married and have kids of my own someday. I just can't seem to meet anyone really nice. Most of the women I meet are at bars. That's one of the reasons I was thinking about going back to college, I mean it could be a way to meet new people.

Counselor: Okay, so one of the changes you're considering is going back to school. Let's talk about some of the advantages and disadvantages of that . . .

In the previous discussion, the client and counselor are exploring some of the pros and cons of the client's current lifestyle. Moreover, they are discerning the client's values and how those values relate to the client's current lifestyle and potential changes. Clearly, values play a central role in career development and lifestyle planning. Similarly, values are imperative to the change process for clients with addictive behaviors. As with other facets of career counseling, it is important that counselors explore with their clients the relevancy of their personal values to their career and lifestyle choices.

Dealing with Resistance

Some counselors find the most challenging aspect of counseling clients with addictive behaviors is encountering resistance. As mentioned previously, the MI approach takes a somewhat nontraditional view of resistance in the counseling relationship. Rather than interpreting resistance as a client trait that needs to be defeated, MI views resistance as a function of the counseling relationship. More specifically, resistance is, in a sense, psychologically engendered reactions from the counselor and a signal to defer the current tactic in favor of another approach. While this view of resistance is, in and of itself, a strategy for working with resistance in the process of change, there are additional strategies that a counselor might employ when encountering resistance. Simple reflection, double-sided reflection, reframing, and agreeing "with a twist" are four techniques posited by MI to diminish resistance and foster progress through the stages of change (Miller & Rollnick, 2002).

Simple Reflection.   One response to resistance is a reflective listening statement (Miller & Rollnick, 2002). By acknowledging the client's disagreement, disbelief, doubts about change, or differing perception, a counselor can avoid fostering increased defensiveness.

> **ADDICTIVE BEHAVIORS**
> **John:**   Who are you to be pointing out how I'm doing drugs? You've probably never had to put up with the kind of stress I'm dealing with. You've probably never even tried pot.
>
> **Counselor:**   It's hard for you to imagine that I could possibly understand what you're dealing with [or] You're very angry at me for asking about your drug use.

> **CAREER BEHAVIORS**
> **John:**   I don't know—if I went back to community college or technical college I'd probably just blow it.
>
> **Counselor:**   You don't see yourself being successful in community college or technical college.
>
> **Counselor:**   You feel frightened, then disheartened, when you think of not being successful in school.

The principles of MI continue to apply when dealing with resistance and giving simple reflection. It is imperative that the counselor continues to express empathy and to also support self-efficacy in subsequent work with the client. Similarly, a counselor may see an opportunity to deal with resistance and continue to develop discrepancy through double-sided reflection.

Double-Sided Reflection.   Sometimes resistance may manifest itself in the counseling relationship through a client's continued exploration of only the one side of the change argument. In response to this type of resistance it is helpful to use the previously discussed technique of double-sided reflection. Double-sided reflection is a technique that can assist counselor and client in exploring various sides of the ambivalence that can block change (Miller & Rollnick, 2002).

John:	Yes, I use a lot more than I used to, but it's not like I'm getting stoned or jacked up on coke all the time, I mean, I've only used it a few times at work and no one really sees me as an addict.
Counselor:	Part of you is concerned about your increased drug use and it's also important to you that people don't view you as an "addict."

When career counseling clients with addictive behaviors, double-sided reflection might also incorporate the facets of ambivalence that relate to career and lifestyle planning.

John:	I know it makes sense to cut back on my partying and the drugs if I'm going to start saving money and look at going back to school, but I don't think you realize how much stress I'm under at work, it's like a vise squeezing all the life out of me!
Counselor:	You'd really like to decrease your drug use, and you are afraid of how you'll cope without drugs to help you deal with stress.

As with other strategies suggested throughout this chapter, double-sided reflection has potential application for both career and lifestyle planning with clients and for counseling clients struggling with addictive behaviors. Just as client choices and behaviors in the career and lifestyle realm are inherently connected with client addictive behaviors, counseling interventions in one area can be used to assist in facilitating change in the other area as well.

Amplified Reflection.   Another potentially effective method for responding to resistance is amplified reflection. "A related and quite useful response is to reflect back what the person has said in an amplified or exaggerated form—to state it in an even more extreme fashion" (Miller & Rollnick, 2002, p. 101). It is important to note that this be done in a serious, straightforward tone that does not suggest sarcasm on the part of the counselor. Such a negative reflection from the counselor would likely only elicit greater resistance.

John:	I couldn't give up my partying with friends, I mean, what would they think—that I'm some kind of loser?
Counselor:	You can't even imagine not doing drugs with your friends. You couldn't handle their reaction if you quit. [or]
John:	You make it sound like I'm a raging alcoholic or a total drug addict! I didn't even come here to talk with you about that stuff!

Counselor:	You don't see any negative consequences from your drug and alcohol use—and you resent that I brought it up. In fact, you really see no connection at all between your drug and alcohol use and your career choices.
John:	Well, I know I need to take a look at how that stuff is impacting where I want to go . . . I mean, the drugs and partying aren't making it any easier to get out of my present job situation.

In each of the two previous examples, the counselor used amplified reflection to respond to resistance in the counseling relationship. In the second example, the counselor responded specifically to the issue of exploring addictive behaviors simultaneously with career concerns. The counselor's response using amplified reflection elicited the client arguments for exploring the relationship between addictive behaviors and career and lifestyle planning.

Reframing.   Sometimes clients express resistance through a self-defeating, problematic or counterproductive view of a situation. "A persistent use of a false or problematic perceptual frame indicates that the client is 'stuck' and likely to continue unless a change in perception can be engineered" (Gerber, 2003, p. 144). Reframing is the process of helping a client to alter the maladaptive frame into a new perceptual frame. More specifically, reframing in motivational interviewing may mean helping to generate a more adaptive perception of the process of change.

REFRAMING, ANOTHER USEFUL RESPONSE TO RESISTANCE

John:	I've tried to cut back on doing coke before, but I always get back into it.
Counselor:	You're very persistent. You're not afraid to try again when you aren't successful initially! [or]
John:	I don't know why I should bother trying to build a new lifestyle. I clearly blew it when I chose this career.
Counselor:	You've done a great job noticing some of the mistakes you've made in developing your current lifestyle—now you'll be able to avoid a lot of problems as we go through the process together.

Agreeing with a Twist.   Miller and Rollnick (2002) propose another technique for "rolling with resistance," which they call "agreeing with a twist." This technique involves initially concurring with a client by reflecting their message coupled with a slight twist or modification of resistant momentum. "Agreement with a twist is basically a reflection followed by a reframe" (Miller & Rollnick, 2002, p. 105).

John:	You're probably going to tell me I need to do some AA program or something and that I need to go back to school and get some exercise. It wears me out just thinking about it.

Counselor: You're exactly right—if I were to make out a giant "to do" list for you it would likely just disable you. It's paradoxical isn't it—when you're told what you "have to do," it can actually prevent you from doing the very things you want to do.

These strategies may provide some useful techniques for career counseling clients with addictive behaviors. When coupled with the philosophical perspective that resistance is an indicator for a counselor to change approaches rather than a client's pure rejection of positive change, these techniques can assist counselors in helping their clients avoid the detrimental consequences of addictive behaviors.

Consequences of Addictive Behaviors

It may be useful for career counselors who are counseling clients with addictive behaviors to have knowledge about some of the problems associated with addictive behaviors. In particular, counselors can benefit from an awareness of the negative consequences addiction may create in a person's career and workplace.

Smith (1993) conducted a literature review of research on workplace substance abuse and found that the most likely drug users in the workplace were white males ages 18 to 34 who have not completed high school. His review determined that the majority of studies in the area indicate that substance-abusing employees have higher rates of absenteeism and tardiness, higher turnover rates (jobs per year), and appear to be more likely to have an on-the-job accident.

Similarly, Mangione and colleagues (1999) found a positive linear relationship between self-reported work performance problems and drinking behavior. The researchers investigated work performance problems such as missed work, arrived late/left early, poor quality work, an argument with a coworker, or been hurt on the job. When career counseling clients with addictive behaviors, it might be beneficial to explore the potential existence of such work performance problems.

Kandel, Davies, Karus, and Yamaguchi (1986) conducted an eight-year follow-up of 1,004 young men and women starting at ages 15–16. They discovered that continued substance use was related to increased delinquency, unemployment, and divorce, among other negative outcomes.

In a similar study, Kandel and Davies (1990) investigated a subsample of males from the National Longitudinal Survey of Youth to explore the influence of drug use on the labor force. When controlling for factors such as educational level and prior employment, the researchers determined that illicit drug use has an impact on job mobility, durations of unemployment, and, in particular, employment gaps in the previous year.

Friedman, Granick, Bransfield, Kreisher, and Schwartz (1996) conducted a longitudinal study on the relationship between substance use and abuse by African American males in early adulthood and vocational career performance. The researchers found that the severity of substance use negatively affects vocational career performance (measured as an index of amount of time employed, vocational prestige, and level of education or vocational training).

Some research points to the potential connection between positive career development and decreasing substance abuse in the workplace. Garcia (1996) found that workers in high-paying industries are less likely to use drugs in the workplace. Similarly, Gleason, Veum, and Pergamit (1991) discovered that for young workers, drug or alcohol use at work was more common among blue-collar jobs such as craftworkers, operatives, and laborers than white-collar jobs such as professional workers and managers. A career counselor who is helping a client negotiate the contemplation stage in favor of positive change regarding addictive behaviors and career concerns may be not only helping a client grapple with current struggles but also helping to prevent future negative consequences.

Selecting a Treatment Program

Once a client has successfully negotiated the contemplation stage and determined that the negative consequences of the addictive behaviors warrant a behavioral change, a career counselor can be central in helping develop an action plan as part of the preparation stage. In assisting the client with developing an action plan, the process may benefit from the career counselor developing a treatment plan that considers the unique characteristics of the client and then matching a treatment program with those attributes.

Doweiko (2002) maintains that all treatment plans should include the following five components: (1) a description of the problem, (2) long-term goals, (3) short-term objectives (very specific, measurable behavior), (4) evaluation criteria, and (5) a target date for the goal. Perkinson and Jongsma (2001) outline similar steps in treatment plan formulation and describe multiple examples in their book, *The Addiction Treatment Planner*. Again, it is imperative to remember to utilize the principles of MI and to mobilize the client's energy and investment in plan development.

There is some evidence to suggest that matching client attributes to the specifically selected treatment when selecting treatment programs will increase the likelihood of treatment efficacy (Brown, Seraganian, Tremblay, & Annis, 2002; Mattson, 1994; Project MATCH Research (Group, 1997). In the broadest sense, this means considering factors such as client age, gender, severity of substance abuse, level of social support, and financial resources. On another level counselors might consider client preferences and cognitive, affective, or behavioral style in addition to cultural worldview in helping clients to select a treatment approach.

There are no shortages of assessments to assist counselors in determining the severity of client substance abuse (the Addiction Research Institute at the University of Texas provides a list of different assessments via their Website, which is listed at the end of this chapter). Counselors can use assessments to assist clients in determining suitable treatment.

Magura, Schildhaus, Rosenblum, and Gastfriend (2002) discuss using the American Society of Addiction Medicine (ASAM) Patient Placement Criteria in determining the appropriate level of treatment. The criteria outline four levels of care: (1) standard outpatient, (2) intensive outpatient, (3) residential, and (4) hospital. Moreover, these authors suggest using the following variables to determine the appropriate treatment level: acute detoxification and/or withdrawal, biomedical conditions, emotional/behavioral conditions, treatment acceptance/resistance, relapse potential, and recovery environment. Considering these variables can help counselors in finding appropriate treatment programs and making referrals.

The Substance Abuse and Mental Health Services Administration provides a Website service that locates substance abuse treatment facilities nationally (see Web address at the end of this chapter). Counselors can use this service as a starting point in an investigation of available referrals for their area.

McNeece and DiNitto (2005) make an excellent point regarding the importance of making referrals. "Making a referral on which the client follows through can involve more than writing a name and a phone number on a piece of paper" (p. 124). The authors maintain that counselors need to consider issues such as child care, language barriers, mental/physical disabilities, and level of social comfort and should consider accompanying clients to referral agencies.

A career counselor may need to help a client negotiate a balance between treatment and work requirements. This may require a career counselor to advocate on behalf of a client with an employer or assist a client by serving as a liaison helping a client communicate with treatment facilities or an employer.

It is important to note that in working with a client to determine treatment as part of the preparation stage, the process and outcome are contingent on the continued involvement and engagement of the client. They are, obviously, the most important factors in any treatment formula.

CONCLUSION

So what has become of the case client in the example, John? The counselor has developed discrepancy between his current addictive behaviors and his lifestyle objectives. John has moved from precontemplation to contemplation. He is ready to explore further his ambivalence concerning his use of drugs and alcohol. As he has already noted several disparaging aspects of his current behavior, he is already beginning to tip the scale in favor of positive change. Soon he will be ready to explore options for beginning to alter his addictive behaviors and develop a plan of action, as the preparation stage necessitates.

Regarding his career concerns, John seems ready to access career and educational planning information in an effort to develop an action plan for a career change. It may be logical for the counselor and John to formulate a plan for his career development and altering his addictive behaviors concurrently, as both involve a similar commitment of time and energy. Additionally the resources obtained for one may be relevant to the other. There may be intervention programs that John can access as a returning student that he may want to take advantage of—and John's investment in education and retraining will likely have financial implications for his use of drugs and alcohol in his current lifestyle.

It is imperative that the counselor and John consider all potential implications of his plan of action. It may be useful for the counselor and John to generate a menu of options as various potential plans and then evaluate each for the advantages or disadvantages and the probability of success. As always, the counselor will continue to foster John's sense of self-efficacy by continuing to review the substantial progress he continues to make in improving his lifestyle by changing his addictive behaviors and cultivating his career development.

Career development has been most profoundly defined as the "total constellation of psychological, sociological, educational, physical, economic, and chance factors that combine to shape the career of any given individual over the life span" (Sears, 1982, p. 139). Career counseling, then, should take into account those salient factors that impact a client's career development—including a client's addictive behaviors.

Understanding the stages of change for behaviors can assist counselors in working with clients struggling with addiction. Knowledge of a client's current stage of change can help a counselor conceptualize the necessary tasks to help him or her to continue on the path toward positive change. Moreover, the four guiding principles of motivational interviewing—express empathy, develop discrepancy, roll with resistance, and support self-efficacy—can provide a solid foundation for providing career counseling to clients with addictive behaviors. The specific MI counseling techniques introduced in this chapter provide counselors with a repertoire of tools to help them further positive change in clients and avoid the potential pitfalls posed by resistance.

Finally, while the case example demonstrates the stages of change and the use of specific counseling techniques, it is, of course, a parsimonious example. The process of change is often long, arduous, and riddled with frequent setbacks. It is important that counselors not give up on the process of change, just as they ask clients to continue to be motivated toward positive growth. Similarly, realizing the importance of addressing substance use and career development together may require a substantial change in practice for individual counselors, and even the profession as a whole.

We must become the change we want to see.
—Mohandas Karamchand Gandhi

USEFUL WEBSITES

Addiction Technology Transfer Center: http://www.nattc.org/

Motivational Interviewing Website: http://www.motivationalinterview.org/

National Clearinghouse for Drug and Alcohol Information (NCDAI): http://www.health.org/

National Institute on Drug Abuse: http://www.nida.nih.gov/ & http://www.drugabuse.gov

National Institute on Alcohol Abuse and Alcoholism: http://www.niaaa.nih.gov/

Practitioner Resources on Substance Abuse: http://www.athealth.com/Practitioner/particles/FR_SubstanceAbuse.html

National Institute of Mental Health: http://www.nimh.nih.gov/

The United States Department of Labor—Working Partners for a Drug Free Workplace: http://www.dol.gov/workingpartners/ & Substance Abuse Information Database (SAID): http://www.dol. gov/asp/programs/drugs/said/default.asp

American Council for Drug Education: http://www.acde.org/

Join Together Online—Boston University School of Health project to reduce substance abuse and violence: http://www.jointogether.org/home/

Journal of Occupational Health Psychology: http://www.apa.org/journals/ocp.html

Psychology of Addictive Behaviors: http://www.apa.org/journals/adb/description.html

Addictive Behaviors Research Center at University of Washington: http://depts.washington.edu/abrc/

National Center on Addiction and Substance Abuse at Columbia University: http://www.casacolumbia.org

Substance Abuse and Mental Health Services Administration (SAMHSA) http://www.samhsa.gov/ & SAMHSA Treatment Facility Locator: http://findtreatment.samhsa.gov/facilitylocatordoc.htm

Employee Assistance Professionals Association: http://www.eapassn.org

The Addiction Research Institute, Center for Social Work Research, University of Texas: http://www. utexas.edu/research/cswr/nida/index.html

American Society of Addiction Medicine (ASAM): http://www.asam.org/

REFERENCES

Bandura, A. (1997). *Self-efficacy: The exercise of control.* New York: W. H. Freeman.

Burke, B. L., Arkowitz, H., & Menchola, M. (2003). The efficacy of motivational interviewing: A meta-analysis of controlled clinical trials. *Journal of Consulting and Clinical Psychology, 71,* 843–861.

Brown, T. G., Seraganian, P., Tremblay, J., & Annis, H. (2002). Matching substance abuse aftercare treatments to client characteristics. *Addictive Behaviors, 27,* 585–604.

DiClemente, C. C. (1991). Motivational interviewing and the stages of change. In W. R. Miller & S. Rollnick, *Motivational interviewing: Preparing people to change addictive behaviors* (pp. 191–202). New York: Guilford Press.

DiClemente, C. C. (2003). *Addiction and change: How addictions develop and addicted people recover.* New York: Guilford Press.

DiClemente, C. C., & Velasquez, M. M. (2002). Motivational interviewing and the stages of change. In W. R. Miller & S. Rollnick, *Motivational interviewing: Preparing people for change* (pp. 201–216). New York/London: Guilford Press.

Doweiko, H. E. (2002). *Concepts of chemical dependency* (5th ed.). Pacific Grove, CA: Brooks/Cole.

Friedman, A. S., Granick, S., Bransfield, S., Kreisher, C., & Schwartz, A. (1996). The consequences of drug use/abuse for vocational career: A longitudinal study of a male African-American sample. *American Journal of Drug and Alcohol Abuse, 22,* 57–64.

Garcia, F. E. (1996). The determinants of substance abuse in the workplace. *Social Science Journal, 33,* 55–68.

Gerber, S. K. (2003). *Responsive therapy: A systematic approach to counseling skills* (2nd ed.). New York: Houghton Mifflin College/Lahaska Press.

Gleason, P. M., Veum, J. R., & Pergamit, M. R. (1991). Drug and alcohol use at work: A survey of young workers. *Monthly Labor Review, 114,* 3–7.

Harland, J., White, M., Drinkwater, C., Chin, D. Farr, L., & Howel, D. (1999) The Newcastle exercise project: A randomized controlled trial of methods to promote physical activity in primary care. *British Medical Journal, 319,* 828–831.

Johnston, L. D., O'Malley, P. M., & Bachman, J. G. (2003). *Monitoring the future, national survey results on drug use, 1975–2002. Volume II. College students and adults ages 19-40* (NIH Publication No. 03-5376). Bethesda, MD: National Institute on Drug Abuse.

Kandel, D. B., & Davies, M. (1990). Labor force experiences of a national sample of young men: The role of drug involvement. *Youth & Society, 21*, 411–445.

Kandel, D. B., Davies, M., Karus, D., & Yamaguchi, K. (1986). The consequences in young adulthood of adolescent drug involvement: An overview. *Archives of General Psychiatry, 43*, 746–754.

Magura, S., Schildhaus, S., Rosenblum, A., & Gastfriend, D. (2002). Substance user treatment program quality: Selected topics. *Substance Use and Misuse, 37*, 1185–1214.

Mangione, T. W., Howland, J., Amick, B., Cote, J., Lee, M., Bell, N., & Levine, S. (1999). Employee drinking practices and work performance. *Journal of Studies on Alcohol, 60*, 261–275.

Mattson, M. E. (1994). Patient-treatment matching: Rationale and results. *Alcohol Health and Research World, 18*, 287–296.

McNeece, C. A., & DiNitto, D. M. (2005). *Chemical dependency: A systems approach.* Boston, MA: Allyn & Bacon.

Miller, N. S. (1994). Psychiatric comorbidity: Occurrence and treatment. *Alcohol Health and Research World, 18*, 261–264.

Miller, W. R., & Rollnick, S. (1991). *Motivational interviewing: Preparing people to change addictive behavior.* New York: Guilford Press.

Miller, W. R. & Rollnick, S. (2002). *Motivational interviewing: Preparing people for change.* New York/London: Guilford Press.

Perkinson, R. R., & Jongsma, A. E., Jr. (2001). *The addiction treatment planner* (2nd ed.). New York: John Wiley & Sons.

Prochaska, J. O., & DiClemente, C. C. (1982). Transtheoretical therapy: Towards a more integrative model of change. *Psychotherapy, 19*, 276–278.

Prochaska, J. O., Norcross, J. C., & DiClemente, C. C. (1994). *Changing for good: The revolutionary program that explains the six stages of change and teaches you how to free yourself from bad habits.* New York: Morrow.

Project MATCH Research Group. (1997). Matching alcoholism treatments to client heterogeneity: Project MATCH posttreatment drinking outcomes. *Journal of Studies on Alcohol, 58*, 7–29.

Project MATCH Research Group. (1998). Matching alcoholism treatments to client heterogeneity: Project MATCH three-year drinking outcomes. *Alcoholism: Clinical and Experimental Research, 23*, 1300–1311.

Regier, D. A., Farmer, M. E. Rae, D. S., Locke, B. Z. Kieth, S. J., Judd, L. L., & Goodwin, F. K. (1990). Comorbidity of mental disorders with alcohol and other drug abuse. *Journal of the American Medical Association, 264*, 2511–2518.

Sears, S. (1982). A definition of career guidance terms: A national vocational guidance association perspective. *Vocational Guidance Quarterly, 31*, 137–143.

Smith, D. A. (1993). *A cross-disciplinary integrative summary of research on workplace substance abuse.* (ERIC Document Reproduction Service No. ED 366870)

Smith, D. E., Heckemeyer, C. M., Kratt, P. P., & Mason, D. A. (1997). Motivational interviewing to improve adherence to a behavioral weight control program for older obese women with NIDDM: A pilot study. *Diabetes Care, 20*, 53–54.

Stephens, R. S., Roffman, R. A., & Curtin, L. (2000). Comparison of extended versus brief treatments for marijuana use. *Journal of Consulting and Clinical Psychology, 68*, 898–908.

Treasure, J. L., Katzman, M., Schmidt, U., Troop, N., Todd, G., & de Silva, P. (1999). Engagement and outcome in the treatment of bulimia nervosa: First phase of a sequential design comparing motivation enhancement therapy and cognitive-behavioural therapy. *Behavioural Research and Therapy, 37*, 405–418.

U. S. Substance Abuse and Mental Health Services Administration. (2004). *Results of the 2003 national survey on drug use and health.* Available online at http://www.oas.samhsa.gov/nhsda.htm Retrived Oct. 9, 2004.

EPILOGUE

Career and lifestyle planning for counselors and other members of the helping professions is a topic that has not been traditionally included in textbooks of this kind; yet career and lifestyle planning for the helping professional is critical to career satisfaction and identity development across the career span. Chapter 18, "On Being a Career Counselor: Increasing Personal and Professional Effectiveness," fills this void. The chapter begins with a critique of current societal and organizational issues affecting human-services and mental-health professionals that are vital to the dialogue of cultivating career longevity and satisfaction. The general goal of the chapter is to inspire the reader to ask reflective questions on a deeper level and rethink the definitions and notions about a "career" in a helping profession. The concepts of growth, expansion and development, stimulation and vitality, usefulness, action, and sustainability are useful parameters for considering career development and its relationship to the personhood and lifestyle of people entering, or immersed in, the profession.

CHAPTER 18

ON BEING
A CAREER COUNSELOR

Increasing Personal
and Professional Effectiveness

SUZANNE R. S. SIMON
Portland State University

I am learning that even after all the mistakes I made—with all the damage I've done to others and myself—I am still alive. It is not too late for me to take stock of who I am and move on to something different and better. I'm learning there is always going to be something changing. When things change on the outside, I've got to start changing on the inside.

Struggling to fight back tears, a client tells her counselor about her history of substance abuse, depression, and homelessness over the last 60 years. She discloses that she has been clean for 2 years, after having had a major stroke that left her with limited use of her right arm and leg. While working with this client, the counselor begins to consider the notion of *viability*. He starts to think more reflectively about possible meanings and wonders how viability applies to him, as a member of the helping profession. He has felt increased pressure to limit his time with clients and shift his focus from application to measured outcomes, which are currently determined by insurance providers. As a result, an ongoing reconfiguration of his role as a mental health worker continues to occur. What implication does this hold for other counselors who aim to facilitate a sense of efficacy not only with clients, but also in themselves professionally? What might a sense of viability mean for today's practitioner? In his book, *On Being a Therapist*, Jeffrey Kottler (2003) elaborated on this idea and suggested that: "If we accept our responsibility as therapist models and agree to use our influence for the good of our clients, we are then committed to increasing our personal and professional effectiveness" (p. 41).

In the following pages, we will explore issues related to career and lifestyle planning for counselors within a conceptualization of *viability* as a framework for professional growth and development. The goal of this chapter is to inspire the reader to ask reflective questions on a deeper level and rethink definitions and notions of career itself (Richmond, 1997). Sources reviewed for this chapter range from works written by recent graduates to those by seasoned practitioners who have explored many aspects of career development. Fundamentally, this author intends to make explicit the grounding of this chapter in two beliefs: work in the helping professions is one of service, and practitioners should only ask of clients what they expect of themselves. As Kottler authentically claimed, "If we are not hypocrites, then we are models of change-in-action for our clients" (2003, p. 24).

The chapter will be divided into six general sections that parallel the popular definitions and uses of the term *viability*: "Growth," "Expansion and Development," "Stimulation and Vitality," "Usefulness," "Action," and "Sustainability." We will first begin with a critique and overview of current societal and organizational issues affecting human-services and mental-health professionals that are vital to the dialogue of cultivating career longevity and satisfaction. Themes such as creativity, resilience, self-awareness, and self-evaluation will be explored, along with a discussion about the concepts of talent, knowledge, and skills. An inquiry into the meanings of values and vocation, and their relation to career identity, will be followed by a consideration of the merit of assessment and skill transfer in times of transition. Specific suggestions for professional development will also be outlined. Additionally, this chapter will include a brief inquiry into life work and related themes of diversity, advocacy, and life satisfaction.

OVERVIEW: SOCIETAL AND ORGANIZATIONAL ISSUES IMPACTING MENTAL-HEALTH AND HUMAN-SERVICE PROFESSIONALS

In exploring the pressures and stressors that impact the work and roles of mental health clinicians, a number of career-counseling professionals have described high turnover and burnout rates, power struggles, feelings of fatigue and futility, role confusion, and organizational politics (Boyatzis, McKee, & Goleman, 2002; Buckingham & Clifton, 2001; Komisar, 2002; Kottler, 2003). Kottler asserted that practitioners are "spending almost as much time dealing with bureaucratic obstacles as with clinical responsibilities" (p. 86). Bernstein (1999) compiled a list of commonly expressed problems of health-service workers such as time constraints, strong emotional reactions, little money, and programs that "work against social values instead of promoting them" (pp. 14–17). Buckingham & Clifton (2001) claimed that only "20% of employees working in the large organizations feel that their strengths are in use every day" (p. 6).

In a more overarching consideration of work stress across disciplines, Gardner, Csikszentmihalyi, and Damon (2001) claimed that there is a "built-in tension" between practitioners, clients, and organizations which can "either result in fruitful synergy or degenerate into conflict" (p. 17). In their book, *Good Work: When Excellence and Ethics Meet*, Gardner et al. considered broader social contexts related to capitalism and the concept of "alignment," which can either result in power struggles or authentic modes for individual practitioners to "operate at their best" and function within a "thriving professional realm" (p. 27). Moreover, while the authors admitted that "not all spheres of life are best run on a market model" (p. 14), they also asserted that our market society, at its best, produces positive social influences from a variety of contributions by ethical "creator-leaders" (see pp. 17–20). Professionalism exists, in their model, in three overlapping realms, which include the individual pursuit of professional goals; domains of knowledge made up of cultural and ethical dimensions; and the larger society, which is made up of institutions housing individuals who seek out innovation and new tools.

Figler and Bolles (1999) emphasized that fluctuation is normal in our economy and that the "country thrives by having thousands compete with each other" (p. 217). As a result, the authors argued that it might not be desirable for any individual to use a lifetime of talents with only one employer. In this ongoing tension between professional and organization, the career journey must include a multiple awareness, involving individual experience, interactions within and between organizations, and the larger societal context. Boldt (1996) illuminated this point as he noted "to the extent that your work takes into account the needs of the world, it will be meaningful; to the extent that through it you express your unique talents, it will be joyful" (p. 9).

Work choices emerge from a convergence of both complementary and competing needs, perspectives, meanings, and goals. While it may be true that "career choice is a mystery because human beings are mysteries" (Figler & Bolles, 1999, p. 39), practical career choices cannot be separated from philosophical underpinnings (see Bloch, 1997; Boldt, 1996; Gardner et al., 2001; Melcher, 2002). Currently, individuals need to be career self-reliant (Brown, 1996); jointly balance their needs with those of the organization in pursuit of professional goals (Dubois, 2000); and begin to engender a new understanding of what career means (Dedominic, 2001). Gini (2000), in *My Job Myself: Work and the Creation of the Modern Individual*, explored the meaning of work through a combination of philosophical and sociological ruminations about how "what we do is what we become" (p. 12). And though many relevant themes arise for workers across disciplines to consider in Gini's work, the most vital assertion he made relevant to this chapter's discussion is the point that: "At its worst, work is a burden and a necessity. At its best, work can be an act of personal freedom and self-realization . . . work is a necessary and defining ingredient in our lives" (p. 12).

GROWTH

Creativity and Resilience

Creation, production, imagination, invention, and vision are all necessary components of both humane treatment and the pursuit of a career identity for the helping professional. A practitioner's self-awareness of ingenuity and resourcefulness engender a keen sensitivity to seek out and bring forth what is imaginative during times of career stagnation and growth. Hallmarks of creativity include openness and a willingness to seek out new patterns and ways of doing, being, or coping in order to *grow*. In evaluating the relationship between the personal and the professional life of a practitioner,

Kottler (2003) emphasized that the most important benefit beyond money or prestige this career provides for a practitioner is the opportunity for growth (p. 53). He asserted that any practitioner who "plays it safe" would not do "enough to ever produce dramatic results" (p. 156). Moreover, he added:

> Creativity also plays a role in the ways we maintain a freshness in our perspective, in the ways we stay energized and continue growing, learning, and improving our effectiveness. Finally, we are creative in the sometimes ingenious ways we help clients break loose from their rigid, self-defeating patterns, to think, feel, and act differently. (p. 242)

Additionally, Kottler (2003) believed that resilience emerging from a sense of creativity will help to navigate the ebb and flow of work challenges and that "creativity is the essence of what makes each one of us uniquely powerful and influential" (p. 242). He reiterated the point that improvisation within the therapeutic relationship is mirrored by the ability to be spontaneous as a professional. "Personal growth and creativity," he claimed, "are synonymous in the life of a therapist" (p. 243).

Many others support Kottler's emphasis on creativity as a vital strategy for renewal. Boyatzis et al. (2002) recommended actively calling a "time out" from a position—ranging from a sabbatical to stepping down—or seeking a new position while attempting to find unique understandings in familiar settings through utilization of educational resources and direction from a mentor (see pp. 10–19). Drucker (2002) believed that growth through stretching oneself for meaningful, yet reachable goals with measurable results keeps one motivated. Ibarra (2002) advocated for taking on projects outside of work, moonlighting, temping, and going back to school to build longevity through continuous experience and reflecting on past successes and defining moments. Ibarra grounded her book, *Working Identity: Unconventional Strategies for Reinventing Your Career*, in the concept of "communities of practice" (as conceptualized by Wenger, 1998, and Lave & Wenger, 1991) and "unfamiliar spheres," which include social networks and peer groups that inspire, support, and contribute to growth into contexts of "new selves" during transitions and career shifts (see pp. 120–129).

Depending upon culture, generation, and many other frames of reference, the concept of creativity is misunderstood (Kerka, 1999). Many researchers have defined and measured creativity across a broad spectrum which includes genius and artistic expression (Root-Bernstein & Root-Bernstein, 2001), traits and skills (Amabile, 1996), and prelinguistic impulse (Wiebusch, 2000), as well as calling it a sociobiological adaptation that "allows for the production of new or unusual associations among known ideas or concepts" (Preti & Miotto, 1997, para. 1). Dictionary definitions include such descriptions as resourcefulness, talent, ingenuity, originality, and cleverness. Most relevant to this exploration of creativity, however, was Powell's (1994) assertion that creativity is about finding and shaping one's life perception and telling this through creative expression (see also Kerka, 1999).

Environmental factors affect creativity both explicitly and implicitly, and the current climate of socioeconomic pressures continues to inform policy and decision making. We cannot hope to offer humane, productive, and appropriate therapeutic interventions if we do not become creative agents of change within ourselves and through our professional relationships. If during the process of becoming informed and knowledgeable practitioners we do not seek out the innovative and inventive, what can be expected of our ingenuity as helping professionals and mental health workers? Mihaly Csikszentmihalyi's (1996) words illuminate the infinitely broader social impact of creativity: "Unless humanists find new values, new ideals to direct our energies, a sense of hopelessness might well keep us from going on with the enthusiasm necessary to overcome the obstacles along the way. Whether we like it or not, our species has become dependent on creativity" (p. 318).

The hopelessness he ponders has profound global implications. Nonetheless, beneficial results often begin with individual potentialities. In many organizational settings, manifestations can occur that discourage unique approaches, new methods, or change as a result of economic pressures. However, the irony of this realization is that it takes a creative, inspired, and innovative person to ask and act on the question, *How can we do things better, or differently?* Current career trends reflect the transitory nature of jobs and the need for practitioners to redefine their career goals with resilience (Brown, 1996). Paradoxically, challenge and creativity are always inter-linked. A change—as a turning point, juncture, or condition of instability—*informs and is informed by* creativity that springs from reflection and honest evaluation of the self.

Application of Growth and Resilience Concepts

Kottler (2003) identified useful strategies for both the practice and the practitioner. Exploring each concept in detail is beyond the scope of this chapter, and readers are encouraged to review Kottler's original suggestions (pp. 223–226). For the purposes of enhancing our discussion, we will consider some of his ideas as we ask the question: *What is the best way to face a challenge as an opportunity for growth?*

Early identification and definition of a problem is vital. Rather than immediately reacting, it is important to clearly outline facts, assumptions, and beliefs, and explicitly define the challenge in order to evaluate options and cultivate resources. For example, a counselor may discover that he feels overwhelmed with the administrative responsi-bilities for his case management. The counselor can begin to constructively think about his own organizational skills and how he might work to better align them with administrative expectations. Just as this counselor might ask a client to reframe defeat-ing thoughts and seek solution-focused techniques, he should do the same for himself. The creative counselor who proactively faces such an impasse would seek out and inte-grate knowledge from a variety of other sources, observe colleagues familiar with administrative tasks, review literature or attend workshops designed to enhance orga-nizational skills, and evaluate what systems (i.e., filing or databases) are in place that could be modified to better facilitate productive administration.

EXPANSION AND DEVELOPMENT

Self-Awareness and Self-Evaluation

Boyatzis et al. (2002) found that there exists a need to frequently reflect on issues of bore-dom, confinement, and potential ethical conflicts as we explore *who we are* as individual professionals. Drucker (2002) emphasized that "self-management—knowing how to stay mentally alert and knowing how and when to change work—is vital" (pp. 74–75). He also argued that ongoing evaluation of strengths in order to understand our place within our career identity arises from discovering answers to such questions as *How do I perform? How do I learn? What are my values? And where do I (not) belong?* (pp. 78–87). Ibarra (2002) asserted that "we are made up of many selves and identities which impact our present work experience and future possibilities" (p. 37) and that many "assumptions we hold are hidden from our conscious awareness" (p. 82). However, even though maintaining objectivity may be difficult, "intentionally stepping back makes room for insights we have been incubating but cannot yet articulate" (p. 151). Like Boldt (1996), Richmond (1997), and Savickas (1997), Ibarra suggested purposeful time-out for reflective and mindful examination of where and who one is within a work context.

Specific to self-evaluation, Bernstein (1999) encouraged counselors to:

- Identify reasons for selecting such a career;
- Compile a list describing strengths brought to the particular discipline and population;
- Recognize characteristics that limit professional performance within this context; and
- Distinguish perceived external constraints that may impede performance.

Bernstein also considered the notion of *resources* a practitioner might consider relevant to career enhancement, both as an individual and as a member of an organization. Table 18.1 elaborates on Bernstein's perspectives (p. 56) as a tool for current job enhancement or for the professional preparing to seek work with a different organization.

Resources within Bernstein's framework are limited to conceptualizations of goals and values, responsibilities, methods, skills, materials, feedback, and rewards, though other variables unique to each individual do exist. The reader is encouraged, with the use of the chart, to reflect on each of these notions from a personal perspective, consider how the resources manifest in a particular organization, and evaluate the interaction of the two perspectives.

In addition, Gardner et al. (2001) suggest, "thoughtful practitioners should consider three basic issues" (pp. 10–11), defined as:

Mission	Defining features of a profession that sustains a person during a challenge
Standards	Established "best practices" often found in mentors and model leaders
Identity	Personal integrity and "deeply felt" values, which include personality traits, motivation, and intellect

The basic act of reflecting on one's personal definitions for these terms and how they relate to broader social meanings can have profound implications in terms of career-role exploration. Additionally, Gardner et al. (2001) offered a simple but relevant test for "contemporary professionals" to utilize, especially during periods of

TABLE 18.1   Bernstein's Framework

INFORMATION	SELF	REFLECTION	ORGANIZATION	INTERACTION
Goals and Values	What are mine?	Complete an inventory.	What are the organization's?	Do mine align with theirs?
Responsibilities	How do my personal goals relate to my career goals?	What are my short- and long-term goals?	How is the job conceptualized, described, and evaluated?	What does the organization expect *me* to accomplish?
Methods	What are my approaches to learning?	What can I do to align competing techniques?	How does the organization achieve results?	Are accepted frameworks outlined?
RESOURCES				
Skills	What are my strengths?	What can I *do* to hone and develop my skills?	What skills does the organization require?	What does the organization offer to improve skills?
Materials	Where are materials available?	Educational and professional support	What are the workplace resources?	What resources are provided to enhance work?
CONSEQUENCES				
Feedback	Do I actively reflect and seek feedback within and outside the organization?	What professional groups do I belong to? Do I participate in workshops?	Does the organization offer clear, frequent, and specific feedback?	Do I seek out formal and informal evaluations from colleagues?
Rewards	Do I use personal rewards to keep myself motivated?	Do I keep a record of accomplishments and achieved goals?	Are evaluations timely and proactive?	Are there recognition programs?

self-awareness and lifestyle planning that they call the "mirror test." The mirror test occurs when a person asks, *How do I feel about myself when I look in the mirror?* (p. 210). Like Gardner et al., other career specialists reviewed for this chapter suggest cultivating frequent reflections about the meanings and philosophies professionals hold about themselves as individuals and how they are enmeshed with work roles and identities (Bloch, 1997; Figler & Bolles, 1999; Richmond, 1997). Richmond also asserted that, fundamental to any exploration about the work a person does is the need to first ask

Who am I? (Richmond, 1997, p. 220). Following that, the recommendation is made to be mindful of how we find meaning in what we do through such techniques as meditation and visualization (Bloch, 1997, pp. 195–201).

Another emergent theme repeated throughout the literature emphasizes a strengths-based approach to self-evaluation. While it is important to recognize weaknesses, "strengths have their own patterns" (Buckingham & Clifton, 2001, p. 3). Drucker (2002) asserted that focusing on, and improving, strengths through feedback analysis is needed, *along with* "disabling intellectual arrogance," which prevents both skill acquisition and the awareness needed to eliminate bad habits (see pp. 76–78). Boldt (1996) claimed that "many people spend their whole lives working *against* their strengths" which leads to "obstacles to hearing [our] own calling" (pp. 8–9). He proposes the use of an acronym "I SEE" in the pursuit of "genuine life's work" (pp. 26–27):

I	Integrity	What speaks to my conscience?
S	Service	What touches my compassion?
E	Enjoyment	What uses my talents?
E	Excellence	What inspires me to do my best?

Figler and Bolles (1999) believed that most of us live in one of four "mental landscapes" of asking ourselves: *What is happening? Can I survive? What am I trying to accomplish? How am I doing?* (p. 190). Within the context of strengths-based perspectives, they recommend focusing "on what you know more than what you don't" (p. 194). Though they offered some suggestions to facilitate productive self-evaluation that are not groundbreaking, it is sometimes fruitful to state the obvious in times of needed critical self-reflection (pp. 206–211):

- Believe in yourself and challenge negative thoughts.
- Define immediately attainable tasks to gain inertia.
- Create a support group.
- Recognize intermediate successes.
- Acknowledge any sense of futility and reexamine it.
- Recognize language and cultural barriers.
- Address emotional and psychological issues.

Additionally, other relevant self-evaluative tools have been proposed for career and lifestyle planning. Here are three good examples:

1. Buckingham and Clifton (2001) suggested that the obstacles to building strengths often emerge as fears and need to be challenged. These may include the fear of being weak, the fear of failure, and the fear of discovering a true self due to "overtaking by the ego and overemphasis on externals instead of inner strength" (pp. 121–130).

2. Hansen (2001) encouraged seeking out the big picture and cultivating holistic (versus reductionist) thinking to better understand the changes going on around us; recognizing the importance of cultural themes as they impact society; and committing to the need for change throughout life (p. 3).
3. Zampetti (2000) developed the "3-6-9" test: "Have you learned anything new or taken on a challenge in the last three, six, or nine months? Why or why not?" (p. 4).

These are all productive questions for practitioners to consider in their ongoing career journey. Getting at individual meanings better prepares professionals to separate underlying assumptions from knowledge bases to productively evaluate talents and skill transference for their occupational pursuits.

STIMULATION AND VITALITY

Talent, Knowledge, and Skill Transference

In *Now, Discover Your Strengths*, Buckingham and Clifton (2001) claimed that most of us function from misplaced expectations. They noted that most people mistakenly believe that anyone can "learn to be competent in anything" (p. 7) and that efforts usually target improving weak skill areas. Rather, they suggest that instead of focusing on skill development, talents that will endure should be honed. Buckingham and Clifton differentiate between the concepts of talent, knowledge, and skills (p. 29) and propose that these *combine* to form our strengths. They define the three components as:

> *Talents* are naturally recurring patterns of thoughts, feelings, and behavior.
> *Knowledge* consists of facts and lessons learned.
> *Skills* are steps of an activity.

Additionally, Buckingham and Clifton (2001) believed that knowledge is composed of both facts (content) and experience (concepts). Richmond (1997) elaborated on this theme and claimed that abilities are unique and can change over time and are made up of knowledge gained through a combination of experience, skills use, and values, which anchor and filter abilities (pp. 225–227). *But how does one assess skills and consider abilities during times of career transition?* Specific to being a counselor, theoretical application boundaries are ever shifting within managed care contexts and economic pressures to produce "results." Kottler (2003) maintained that "everyone is eclectic and pragmatic, or at least integrative" (p. ix) which he claimed is "humbling and endlessly fascinating . . . [and] virtually impossible for us to reach a place where we can even think we really know what we are doing" (p. 14). He also suggested that it is vital to distinguish between being "burnt out" and "impaired" (p. 179). Additionally, Kottler reminds therapists to continually reflect on their own emotional and psychological frameworks that impact their abilities.

A critique related to the value of using personality and psychological tests for career planning and the application of common techniques for self-motivation is threaded throughout recent inquiry into career planning (Bloch, 1997; Figler & Bolles, 1999; Ibarra, 2002). Ibarra asserted that career advice linked to such tests produces a limiting definition of an inner self. Moreover, while she claimed that such personality-based and developmental approaches have merit, she also believes that "looking inward . . . often paralyzes us" and results in "missed opportunities" and inhibited growth into ongoing professional life phases (p. 37). She continued by noting that "our customary mind-set about who we are and what others expect undermines us in a myriad of subtle ways" (p. 87). Additionally, Ibarra captured the fleeting and shifting qualities of opportunity for skill acquisition and transfer with her assertion that "windows of opportunity open and close" (p. 155), and as a result, it is important to coexist in a seeming "incompatibility of old and new" (p. 152). She suggested applying "unconventional" strategies (pp. 167–170) that bridge old and new skills such as:

- Take action before introspection—change what you do *before* you think about it.
- Be open to many selves, not just one "true" self.
- Coexist willingly within the transition of holding on and letting go.
- Resist big changes and value small gains.
- Experiment with projects outside of work.
- Seek out new peers.
- Be aware of everyday meanings instead of waiting for epiphanies.
- Take breaks from habit for reflection.
- Be prepared for change at any time.

Bloch (1997) adds to this discussion with the point that "formal career counseling is not equal to finding meaning" and "instruments purporting to help in self-description to assist in finding meaning don't work" (pp. 191–192). Seasoned contributors to career theory and application Figler and Bolles (1999) believed the traditional approach of assessments preceding career choice is wrong and that "skills and interests cannot be 'added up' to suggest career options" (p. 42). They offered additional insight into the social and historical evolution of career placement and job hunting since the early 1900s with Parson's trait factor approach to a review of the current advances in career-counseling technology. They described the emphasis on psychological and vocational testing in the 1950s as being reconceptualized in the 1970s in a more holistic and proactive approach to career evaluation and attainment. The authors also described a time of expansive media and marketing during the late 1980s and early 1990s that resulted in larger forums for career strategizing and development. For example, membership in professional organizations increased along with the establishment of outplacement firms targeting high-level executives. The overview, however, culminates with a cautionary warning that we are experiencing a "trend toward a faster, more impersonal way of life" (p. 84).

Figler and Bolles argued for a "broader view of assessment" and critique of testing (pp. 119–124). They claimed:

- The whole cannot be predicted from sum of the parts.
- There is an overemphasis on initial career choice.

- Assessment should be future oriented rather than "stuck" in the present.
- Tests have low predictive value and offer false authority.
- Tests encourage dependence and limit options.

Ultimately, the combined messages of these authors convey the point that a balance must be struck with assessing, understanding, planning, and transitioning. As Brown (1996) stated: "Adaptability to change, positive and flexible attitudes, continuous learning, self-confidence, willingness to take risks, and a commitment to personal excellence are all characteristics identified with employability" (p. 1).

USEFULNESS

Values, Vocation, and Career Identity

An exploration into notions about values, altruism, and service is fundamental to this chapter's discussion. Such a journey must capture what is subjectively perceived as a career identity, and also professionally (externally) defined as a role in terms of educational guidelines or standards of practice. The sense of duality for a practitioner as being both called to serve and functioning as a professional model in an economically challenged arena is evident in the comments of newly graduated counselors and senior practitioners alike. In his book, *Becoming a Social Worker: Reflections on a Clinician's Transformative Journey*, Melcher (2002) poignantly noted that "part of becoming a clinical social worker is becoming comfortable with ambiguity" (p. 113). He believed social work is a "delicate balance of intellect and heart" (p. 33) and is actually a "way of *being* rather than just thinking or doing" (p. 43). He grounded his perspective in reference to the Buddhist tradition of "right vocation," which aims to work in genuine service to others and in a way best suited to the individual. Melcher noted:

> I still know of few professions that ask for more conscience, integrity, creativity, flexibility, and sense of purpose from their members than social work does. I believe that few other professions offer life-long opportunities to change, grow, and develop as a person and to continue to strive for being in the world in a compassionate and caring way. (pp. 114–115)

Specific to working in human services, Bernstein (1999) claimed that there are underlying values enmeshed with motives for such work, which include being proactive, focusing on results, empowering others, avoiding coercion, and being sensitive to diversity. However, she illuminated the same sense of dichotomy with the point that: "There is a myth that human services workers do not, and perhaps should not, think of themselves and their careers because they should be selfless people who dedicate their lives to others" (p. 166).

Corey and Corey (1989) examined possible motives for being a helper, which they frame as "needs" to make an impact, care for others, find self-help, be needed, or attain money and prestige. They also compiled a list of attitudes (pp. 14–15) they believe are representative of an "ideal helper," which speak both to in-practice skills and tools for career resilience:

- Commitment to honest assessment of strengths and weaknesses
- Open to getting any needed self-help
- Open to learning and curiosity
- Willing to take steps to fill knowledge gaps
- Acknowledge that education is never finished
- Patient and tenacious
- Seek inspiration, stimulation, and facilitation in self and others
- Draw on multiple resources
- Adapt to needs secondary to diversity, marginalization, and trauma
- Take care of self physically, psychologically, socially, mentally, and spiritually

The concept of mutuality is further illuminated by Gini (2000) with the claims that "work is both a necessary and defining ingredient in our lives" (p. 12), "the work ethic has elements of both myth and reality" (p. 27), and "Work fulfills a dual function in the development of the human psyche and character. It is both a response to the necessities of the existence and the means by which we come to know who we are and how and where we belong" (p. 43).

Additionally, an enhanced understanding of competing needs is put forth through suggestions such as finding balance of perceived lack of something (need), with an ongoing commitment to a way of life (values), and linking needs and goals (interests) as they relate to aspects of motivation (Savickas, 1997). Figler and Bolles (1999) believed that "purpose and meaning are at the center of most satisfying careers" (p. 24) while acknowledging that "there are always competing forces" when "giving yourself permission to be who you are" with a career choice (p. 39). They encouraged professionals to reflect on how they define success and what values of success they hold, and to frame the duality threaded throughout this discussion as compatibility of "doing well and doing good" as "the best road to success for both the individual and the organization" (p. 255). They explicitly argued, "altruism versus profit is a false controversy" (p. 252). The challenge for counselors is to find a balance between service and salary and experience this paradoxical position as symbiotic rather than as a polarity.

ACTION

Through a review of some current career-development literature, an attempt has been made to help counselors conceptualize this exploration into career and lifestyle planning through the notion of viability. The position of this author has been that attempts to facilitate growth and a sense of efficacy in mental health clients is mirrored by an *implicit* need to seek out, personally and professionally, what will sustain practitioners themselves. In addition, an *explicit* argument is being made that whether or not one's current work identity is satisfied, efforts to improve career satisfaction and resilience must be ongoing and emerge from reflective intention. Career viability consists of cultivating a continuous discovery of inner resources and value systems, along with taking actions that best utilize the combination of needs, goals, and skills that emerge at any given time for a professional.

In the previous sections, a brief inquiry into more personal themes of self-evaluation, skill exploration, and value systems was presented in order to encourage a more contemplative foundation for the remaining chapter discussion. After considering personal meanings as they relate to career goals and identity, it is time to consider how these interplay with ideas about professional development, career sustenance, diversity, advocacy, and lifestyle planning. Counselors, clinicians, and case managers must consider *how they act on who they are* within their career roles as they serve clients, organizations, and society. A variety of opportunities exist for enhancement of skills and professional image through the cultivation of an entrepreneurial spirit to do and be more than one job description can capture. Kottler (2003) illuminates the potential for a multifaceted and dynamic career identity for a counselor as he states:

> Clinicians who do research, give public lectures, publish articles, and write books report similar peak experiences. To teach is to continually evaluate what we do from the perspective of an innocent. We feel greater meaning not only in the single life that we help improve but also in how that life helps us understand and improve the process of change. (p. 176)

Bloch (1997) believed that the potential trajectory of successful lifework begins with three key interrelated and foundational "bases," which include utilizing techniques to be reflective, finding a sense of connectedness, and intentionally making things happen. In the following section, ideas about how to proactively pursue career development will be considered.

Suggestions for Professional Development

Many themes explored in the previous sections targeted the individual practitioner as the source of career impetus. However, our interactions with others who are clients, colleagues, peers, or employers are vital to various aspects of our work experiences and professional growth. Such important considerations as taking responsibility for relationships through establishing trust, fostering communication, setting appropriate boundaries, using time effectively, and understanding larger social contexts were noted throughout the literature reviewed for this chapter (see Bernstein, 1999; Brown, 1996; Drucker, 2002; Figler & Bolles, 1999; Gardner et al., 2001; Miller & Katz, 2002). Career resilience necessitates recognition of what is both unique and universal within and among professionals. Gardner et al. (2001) illuminated the convergence of person and society as they suggested that individuals, especially during challenging economic times, need to merge the Western sense of independent character development with Eastern perspectives of connectivity and mutual responsibility.

Additionally, the concept of community is an important component shared by both seasoned and newly entering mental-health workers. For example, Ibarra (2002) made an interesting case for seeking out new and different mentors and communities of learning and support. She argued that "long-standing social networks can inhibit us" and we "need contacts in unfamiliar spheres of interactions" (pp. 120–121). The idea of transitioning to "new" communities is an empowering consideration for both intentional choice of, for example, joining a professional group, and for coping with an unintended loss of membership as a result of job displacement. Ibarra believed: "Communities of practice are an integral part of the test-and-learn method because we need a context in which to learn both the substance and style of the new self we are trying to become" (p. 127).

The issue of identity conflict was noted for counseling professions as a result of being composed of "members [who] cannot decide whether they are scientists, philosophers, technicians, or artists" (Kottler, 2003, p. 147). Echoes of career identity dissonance also emerge in related themes of "murky business identity" (Komisar, 2002, p. 46) and perceived competition between work as a calling and larger contexts (Bernstein, 1999; Gardner et al., 2001; Melcher, 2002; Rayburn, 1997; Remen, 2000; Richmond, 1997). "Many professionals find it difficult to objectively review their own skills and identify their own deficiencies" (Bernstein, 1999, p. 123) and therefore benefit from group interactions such as classes, workshops, and membership in professional organizations. Learning from colleagues through establishing networks, actively using the library, and volunteering are just a few ways to create opportunities for professional development. Paralleling the concept of learning for skill development is the vital awareness of the interconnectivity of both gaining and giving through teaching. Kottler (2003) believed that "when you explain to others what you do, how you do it, and why you do it in a particular way, you are forced to think through the rationale for every intervention" (p. 176).

Additionally, professional development through the cultivation of new peer groups takes many forms through a variety of actions as suggested by Bernstein (1999), Boldt (1996), Figler and Bolles (1999), and Whiteside (2002):

- Move into policy design at the organizational, county, state, or federal level.
- Combine current expertise with related fields (e.g., law or education).
- Create low-cost community support through partnerships with other organizations such as establishing hotlines or public access radio or television shows.
- Cohost job fairs, workshops, and conferences.
- Participate in research or advancement of theory.

Fostering such networks begins with individual action grounded in self-promotion. Such entrepreneurial initiative, however, should not be viewed as a negative (see Figler and Bolles, 1999; Gardner et al., 2001). "Professional life without self-promotion is not possible," argued Figler and Bolles (p. 95). They believed that advocating for ourselves and being accessible to opportunities for growth are important to career sustainability. Further, Figler and Bolles grounded their suggestions for career development in a three-part skill base (pp. 95–96):

1. Be able to speak comfortably and succinctly about the work you do in 30 to 60 seconds—in any setting.
2. Put yourself in as many situations as possible to do item (1).
3. Write articles—for local papers or peer-reviewed journals.

They go on to suggest that entrepreneurial spirit is often stereotypically conceptualized and frowned upon by academicians or clinicians and should instead be viewed as a means of "American enterprise reasserting itself for the everyday person" (p. 214). Moreover, professional survival hinges (pp. 256–258) on being able to:

- Attract new clients.
- Sustain present clients.
- Reduce costs while adding value.
- Earn the regard of peers.
- Enhance the work of others.

In terms of professional development techniques, three overlapping areas of focus emerged and could be thematically grouped within the categories of thought-centered efforts, sustainability tools, and transition facilitation (Bernstein, 1999; Boldt, 1996; Figler & Bolles, 1999; Whiteside, 2002):

THOUGHT-CENTERED EFFORTS: REFLECT, EVALUATE, PLAN
- Complete an inventory of existing skills and transfer options.
- Do detailed research about career options.
- Commit to lifelong learning.
- Welcome change.
- Know when to expand your view or narrow your focus.
- Develop a career plan with goals and target dates.
- Take a risk with a new idea every year.
- Excel at your current job.
- Look beyond economics.
- Cultivate perseverance and patience.

SUSTAINABILITY TOOLS: ACTION AND EFFORT WITHIN CURRENT WORK CONTEXT
- Attend training programs, both external and organization sponsored.
- Meet with three supportive peer professionals once a month.
- Demonstrate qualifications and establish creditability.
- Learn market sense.
- Stay aware of larger societal influences through a variety of sources.
- Become an advocate.
- Earn income from several sources.
- Write and give public presentations in a variety of forums.
- Encourage others to observe your work and give feedback.

TRANSITION FACILITATION: CHANGING AND MOVING ON
- Aggressively market yourself with courage, skill, and integrity.
- Become an administrator or manager.
- Change the population you serve.

- Create a market niche.
- Simplify your life.

In their work, *On Becoming a Psychotherapist*, Dryden and Spurling (1989) compiled an exploration into the personal experiences of 10 therapists from a broad spectrum of practice. While each section was uniquely written, the editors organized the work by asking individual authors specific questions in the hope of facilitating the contributors (and readers) to "reflect on the personal dimensions of their decisions" related to entering the profession of psychotherapy (p. x). While reduction can lead to decontextualization of important notions, limits of scope and space in this discussion preclude a detailed overview of Dryden and Spurling's work. However, inquiry into the personal views of seasoned practitioners may hold meaning and relevance for career development and lifestyle issues. Readers are encouraged to review the original and complete work, but a synthesis is offered in Table 18.2, with two categories highlighted related to the themes of *sustenance* and *implications for other practitioners*, as noted by some of the contributors.

Internal tension exists as we endeavor to conceptualize who we are and the work we do. External tensions from larger social contexts for career expectations and work identity also impact the meanings we hold for ourselves. Kottler (2003) poignantly reminds us that it is the "ultimate hypocrisy of our profession that we do not or cannot do the same things we ask of our students and clients" (p. 57). However, he offers an optimistic view of an evolution in a counselor's vocation with the observation that initial idealism shifts from cynicism to pragmatism, which results in an integrated sense of flexibility. Gini (2000) adds to this with the point that: "By our work we acquire knowledge, meaning, relationships, and a general philosophy or attitude toward life. Any job, every job, gives us these 'skills' and no matter how high or low the task, for some workers, genuine satisfaction can be found" (p. 195).

We can therefore perceive work pathways as both intra- and interdependent in our pursuit of satisfying, meaningful, and economically sustaining work. Savickas (1997) believed that envisioning "work as a quest for self and a place to nourish one's spirit" (p. 3) can engender a context for self-development. Moreover, finding meaning through the unification of the *internal* feeling of being called to work with the *external* experience of being committed to and engrossed in work can enhance a sense of balance (Bloch, 1997). Cultivating a spectrum of options in order to be knowledgeable and mobile workers (Drucker, 2002), risk taking (Ibarra, 2002), managing stress through self-care (Bernstein, 1999), and challenging your own assumptions (Corey & Corey, 1989) are additional notions offered by career theorists to consider in lifework planning.

On a more transcendent level, Richmond (1997) claimed "if one accepts the definition of career as a journey that one feels called or commissioned to take . . . one cannot escape the fact that spirituality permeates work" (p. 212). Considered within such an intimate perspective, existence then becomes more about doing than about merely being (Register, 1987). Kottler (2003), Gini (2000), Rayburn (1997), Remen (2000), Richmond (1997), and Savickas (1997) all made clear in their research and writings that most who work in the helping professions feel compelled to do such work in order to be useful and with the belief that work defines us. What, then, are some considerations for issues of career diversity, advocacy, and longevity?

TABLE 18.2 Personal Views of Practitioners

CONTRIBUTOR(S)	WHAT SUSTAINS ME PROFESSIONALLY?	WHAT ARE MY SUGGESTIONS FOR OTHER PRACTITIONERS?
Mahoney & Eiseman (1989)	• Creative synergy as writer, therapist, researcher • Dialogue with colleagues • Guide others through teaching • Bearing witness	• Value and legitimate subjective experience • Examine quality of training and education
Bloomfield (1989)	• Diversity • Valuing subjectivity • Bearing witness	• Reflect on, be aware of, and note own words and actions
Thorne (1989)	• Being a member of a team • Access to resources • Valued supervision	• Maintain self-care • Beware of therapeutic philosophy overtaking life
Heppner (1989)	• Work with colleagues • Satisfaction in giving • Broad client spectrum	• Regular separation of self from role
Karp (1989)	• Work with colleagues • Enriched by client growth • Work as process of change	• Seek and find balance
Fransella (1989)	• More than a therapist • Helping others face challenges	• Commit to theory • Be reflexive
Street (1989)	• Less agency and colleague attachment • Focus on craft and basics	• Maintain awareness of self as therapist and person • Teach and train others
Rowan (1989)	• Viewing client change • International memberships • Participating in politics	• Vary work contexts • Learn across the life span
Chaplin (1989)	• Privilege to work with others • Deep, yet limited, intimacy • Vulnerabilities are strengths	• Establish a lifetime of work • Discover unique • Be humble

SUSTAINABILITY

Diversity and Advocacy

In her book, *Living with Chronic Illness: Days of Patience and Passion*, Cheri Register (1987) illuminated the myriad of ways illness impacts individuals, especially in the context of work. Through a detailed narrative of her own experience, along with interviews from a variety of people living with debilitating medical conditions, Register captured the integral theme of career viability we are attempting to explore. She made clear that as a society and as individuals, we are defined—and often measured—by the work we do. She called out to "disentangle the economic issues from the questions of identity and human worth" (p. 104). She noted: "For the chronically ill, the force of the work ethic is compounded by the stigma associated with being different . . . the standard against which we measure our performance is perfection, and any deviation from that norm is a source of embarrassment" (p. 88).

Ultimately, however, Register framed the challenges faced by people with a chronic illness with an encouraging recommendation to the patients themselves and for those around them to rethink work identity through resourceful actions to redefine job descriptions through the pursuit of nontraditional approaches such as consulting or project-oriented work, which can flex with shifting physical needs. Countless examples of loss turned to creation through skill development and resourceful career planning, which capitalize on the strengths of those who might initially be perceived as frail, have led to policy change, research advances, and social activism in such areas as cancer research, AIDS education, or substance abuse treatment. Register made more vivid her optimism with her statement that "in the end, [my] book may be the most concrete example I can offer of illness providing a vocation" (p. 105).

"There is a greater need for private practitioners who are prepared to work in minority and marginalized communities" (Kottler, 2003, p. 77). Melcher (2002) claimed that being a counselor "will entail becoming a political advocate, even more so than historically" (p. 114). Bureaucracies and policy debates converge on all arenas for helping professionals. Gardner et al. (2001) asked professionals to consider the impact of powerful societal trends through a combination of clarifying values (both personal and organizational), facilitating new perspectives, and ultimately, taking a personal stand when competing core values collide. Gini (2000) reiterated the duality of self and society by strongly advocating for individual pursuit of work that is "good for us" and by supporting as a society member the creation of work "that is good for individuals" (p. 57). In addition, Gini believed that work "must do two things—maintain life and add to it" (p. 221). Clearly, the thread of viability continues to weave through this exploration of diversity.

Miller and Katz (2002) outlined an effective and empowering paradigm for career enhancing perspectives within their construct of a "paradox of diversity" (p. 3), which holds that:

We are like *all* people because we share human needs for love, joy, and safety.
We are like *some* people because we share culture and experience.
We are like *no other* people because we are each unique unto ourselves.

They recast the strengths-based perspectives referred to earlier in this chapter by advocating for valuing individual and group differences as resources that need not be silenced or marginalized. Moreover, they called out for professionals not only to seek inclusionary groups (e.g., peer circles, departments, larger organizations), but also to model and engender such attributes (pp. 109–113) as:

- Leadership worthy of respect
- Support of work, life, and family integration
- Ample opportunity for continuous growth and development
- Environments that promote physical and emotional safety
- People treated as partners
- Communication that flows freely and clearly
- Roles and expectations being clearly stated

Within a broader context, Figler and Bolles (1999) cautioned that freedom, including freedom of work pursuit, should not be taken for granted. They advocated for encouraging passion in career choice, embracing risk taking, viewing all jobs as temporary in order to create new opportunities, seeking occasions to redefine career plans, and supporting the endeavors of others. They also suggested that social consciousness needs to be cultivated on two levels: service to the client and service to the community. Hansen (2001) suggested identifying multiple possibilities to achieving individual, personal, and social change through career contexts. She recommended conceiving of life planning in a more holistic view, rather than the traditional idea of matching the job with the person, and instead becoming increasingly more communitarian and global in terms of our career pursuits.

Explicit in the career paths of counselors is the intention to help others. However, the current economic pressures—along with ongoing personal challenges to navigate multiple roles held in our accelerated society—obscure *and* necessitate ongoing critical reflection about professional pursuits. Pettiford and Clarke (2001) compiled a list of 10 strategies to help cope with potential career setbacks:

1. Cultivate the ability to change perspectives without personalizing setbacks.
2. Reframe negatives as learning opportunities.
3. Keep the passion of your pursuit at the forefront, no matter how idealistic.
4. Learn from others about their successes and challenges.
5. Do not let pride keep you from making necessary changes or rethinking goals.
6. Disregard self-imposed limits arising from self-defeating thoughts.
7. Focus on the lessons learned rather than on a wounded ego.
8. Face adversity directly after contemplation.
9. Become fearless by focusing potential successes.
10. Stay motivated through techniques you find sustaining such as meditation, writing, peer support, or community work.

No matter what our belief systems, Figler and Bolles (1999) argued that we need to think about both our philosophy of work (nature and meaning), along with honestly exploring what they call our "theology of work" in terms of the *values* we hold about our work (p. 269). Dubois (2000) encouraged heightened awareness of gaps that exist with respect to culture, economics, age, or gender. Ultimately, a paradigm of career sustenance grounds us, not only in the ability to *survive*, but also in the ability to *thrive*.

Career-Life Satisfaction

The personal and professional roles of a mental-health worker are linked and, with heightened awareness and reflective action, can complement each other (see Kottler, 2003). Kottler speaks of "elation" at bearing "witness to another person's transformation—just as we are the catalyst of our own" (p. 257). Melcher (2002) suggested that practitioners explore influences that affect work choice, such as family history, role as caregiver, personal motives, and life experiences to better understand the interplay of the personal and professional. Gardner et al. (2001) offered the observation that lifestyle planning and satisfaction are affected by the convergence of achievement and values and noted, "If the fundamentals of good work—excellence and ethics—are in harmony, we lead a personally fulfilling and socially rewarded life. If they are not, either the individual or the community, or both, will suffer" (p. 16).

Remen (2000) elaborated on the theme of service by first considering the notion of integrity and the belief that "vitality is rooted in integrity," which springs from a life source grounded in "our authentic values" (p. 47). She differentiated between the empowering concept of service that she believes is life sustaining versus a draining context of fixing, and while she acknowledged that "caring can make us vulnerable" (p. 136), she added that, "seeing yourself as a fixer may cause you to see brokenness everywhere, to sit in judgment of life itself" (p. 199).

This seemingly subtle implication offers profound potential for practitioner resilience, with a shift in perspective of a therapeutic relationship that is fully equal and of shared responsibility. Such a conceptualization resonates longevity for the practitioner who then works from a place of energy rather than one of potential depletion. In a larger context, it also reflects paradigmatic potential for organizations and communities to ground in partnerships rather than in power relationships. Finally, Remen (2000) links themes of service, work roles, and career identity outlined in this chapter with reflective awareness about how we perceive of ourselves within such contexts:

> To recognize your capacity to affect life is to know yourself most intimately and deeply, to recognize your real value and power, independent of any role that you have been given to play or expertise you may have acquired. . . . There is no role that absolves us of the responsibility to listen, to be mindful that life is all around us, touching us. (p. 196)

SUMMARY

The primary goal of this chapter has been to awaken in the readers a desire to seek out the underlying and vital meanings we hold of our career identities and ourselves. Though various suggestions have been included to assist in a reflective pursuit, the author hesitates to encourage any formulaic approach to achieving life-work satisfaction. The literature reviewed offers a springboard for insight into the multilayered roles and experiences of health service and mental health professionals and is a catalyst for the readers to continue ongoing pursuit into both philosophical and technical inquiry into career planning and development.

The challenge of career self-reliance and career resilience can be frightening . . . however, many of these fears may be allayed as workers see evidence of their own progress toward career independence. Through continuous learning, individuals can gain a new sense of control, a new confidence in the timeliness and utility of their newly acquired knowledge and skills. . . . continuous learning is the path to job security and career health. (Brown, 1996, p. 2)

"Can you hear your own voice?" asked Figler and Bolles (1999, p. 146). This exploration began with a client's initial awareness of transformation and movement forward through a sense of self-efficacy. However, the therapeutic relationship is reflective and parallels what is both individual and shared between practitioner and client. Being fully present for the client and able to genuinely facilitate growth—no matter what the therapeutic approach or the context of the larger organization—can only arise from a practitioner who also works to cultivate imagination, expansion, activity, and creativity. Every professional's relationships, contexts, goals, and needs are constantly in flux. The vitality needed to navigate through challenges, setbacks, and successes emerges from, and is sustained by, an ongoing sense of viability—for self, other, and the community.

The following Websites provide additional information relating to the chapter topics.

USEFUL WEBSITES

American Counseling Association
http://www.counseling.org
American Mental Health Counselors Association
http://www.pie.org/amhca
American Psychological Association
www.apa.org
National Association of Counselors
www.naswdc.org

REFERENCES

Amabile, T. M. (1996). *Creativity in context.* Boulder, CO: Westview Press.

Bernstein, G. S. (1999). *Human services? . . . That must be so rewarding: A practical guide for professional development* (2nd ed.). Baltimore, MD: Paul H. Brookes.

Bloch, D. P. (1997). Spirituality, intentionality, and career success: The quest for meaning. In D. P. Bloch & L. J. Richmond (Eds.), *Connections between spirit and work in career development: New approaches and practical perspectives* (pp. 185–208). Palo Alto, CA: Davies-Black.

Bloomfield, I. (1989). Through therapy to self. In W. Dryden & L. Spurling (Eds.), *On becoming a psychotherapist* (pp. 33–52). London: Rutledge.

Boldt, L. G. (1996). *How to find the work you love.* New York: Penguin.

Boyatzis, R., McKee, A., & Goleman, D. (2002). Reawakening your passion for work. In *Harvard Business Review's On managing your career* (pp. 1–22). Boston: Harvard Business School.

Brown, B. L. (1996). *Career resilience* (ERIC Digest No. 178). Columbus, OH: Clearinghouse on Adult Career and Vocational Education. (ERIC Document Reproduction Service No. ED402474).

Buckingham, M., & Clifton, D. O. (2001). *Now, discover your strengths*. New York: Free Press.

Chaplin, J. (1989). Rhythm and blues. In W. Dryden & L. Spurling (Eds.), *On becoming a psychotherapist* (pp. 169–188). London: Rutledge.

Corey, M. S., & Corey, G. (1989). *Becoming a helper*. Pacific Grove, CA: Brooks/Cole.

Csikszentmihalyi, M. (1996). *Creativity: Flow and the psychology of discovery and invention*. New York: HarperCollins.

Dedominic, P. (2001, December, 10). Steering your career through troubled waters. *Los Angeles Business Journal*. Retrieved October 31, 2003, from www.findarticles.com

Drucker, P. F. (2002). Managing oneself. In *Harvard Business Review's On managing your career* (pp. 73–97). Boston: Harvard Business School.

Dryden, W., & Spurling, L. (Eds.). (1989). *On becoming a psychotherapist*. London: Routledge.

Dubois, D. (2000, December). The 7 stages of one's career. *Training and Development, 54*, 45–50.

Figler, H., & Bolles, R. N. (1999). *The career counselor's handbook*. Berkeley, CA: Ten Speed Press.

Fransella, F. (1989). A fight for freedom. In W. Dryden & L. Spurling (Eds.), *On becoming a psychotherapist* (pp. 116–133). London: Rutledge.

Gardner, H., Csikszentmihalyi, M., & Damon, W. (2001). *Good work: When excellence and ethics meet*. New York: Basic Books.

Gini, A. (2000). *My job myself: Work and the creation of the modern individual*. New York: Routledge.

Hansen, L. S. (2001, March). Integrating work, family, and community through holistic life planning. *Career Development Quarterly, 49*, 261–274.

Heppner, P. P. (1989). Chance and choices in becoming a therapist. In W. Dryden & L. Spurling (Eds.), *On becoming a psychotherapist* (pp. 69–86). London: Rutledge.

Ibarra, H. (2002). *Working identity: Unconventional strategies for reinventing your career*. Boston: Harvard Business School Press.

Karp, M. (1989). Living vs. survival: A psychotherapist's journey. In W. Dryden & L. Spurling (Eds.), *On becoming a psychotherapist* (pp. 87–100). London: Rutledge.

Kerka, S. (1999). *Creativity in adulthood* (ERIC Digest No. 204). Retrieved February 28, 2003, from http://www.adulted.augusta.k12.me.us/zCreativity%20in%20Adulthood.html

Komisar, R. (2002). Goodbye career, hello success. In *Harvard Business Review's On managing your career* (pp. 23–47). Boston: Harvard Business School.

Kottler, J. A. (2003). *On being a therapist* (3rd ed.). San Francisco: Jossey-Bass.

Lave, J., & Wenger, E. (1991). *Situated learning: Legitimate peripheral participation*. Cambridge, Cambridge University Press.

Mahoney, M. J., & Eiseman, S. C. (1989). The object of the dance. In W. Dryden & L. Spurling (Eds.), *On becoming a psychotherapist* (pp. 17–32). London: Rutledge.

Melcher, M. J. (2002). *Becoming a social worker: Reflections on a clinician's transformative journey*. Harrisburg, PA: White Hat Communications.

Miller, F. A., & Katz, J. H. (2002). *The inclusion breakthrough: Unleashing the real power of diversity*. San Francisco: Berrett-Koehler.

Pettiford, H., & Clarke, R. D. (2001, September). Caution: Stumbling blocks ahead: Coping with setbacks in one's professional life. *Black Enterprise*. Retrieved October 31, 2003, from www.blackenterprise.com

Powell, M. C. (1994). On creativity and social change. *Journal of Creative Behavior, 28,* 21–32.

Preti, A., & Miotto, P. (1997). *The contribution of psychiatry to the study of creativity: Implications for AI research.* CMG Psychiatry Branch, Cagliari, Italy. Retrieved February 28, 2003, from http://www.compapp.dcu.ie/~tonyv/MIND/antonio.html

Rayburn, C. A. (1997). Vocation as calling: Affirming response or "wrong number." In D. P. Bloch & L. J. Richmond (Eds.), *Connections between spirit and work in career development: New approaches and practical perspectives* (pp. 163–183). Palo Alto, CA: Davies-Black.

Register, C. (1987). *Living with chronic illness: Days of patience and passion.* New York: Bantam.

Remen, R. N. (2000). *My grandfather's blessings: Stories of strength, refuge, and belonging.* New York: Riverhead Books.

Richmond, L. J. (1997). Spirituality and career assessment: Metaphors and measurement. In D. P. Bloch & L. J. Richmond (Eds.), *Connections between spirit and work in career development: New approaches and practical perspectives* (pp. 209–236). Palo Alto, CA: Davies-Black.

Root-Bernstein, R. S., & Root-Bernstein, M. M. (2001). *Sparks of genius: The thirteen thinking tools of the world's most creative people.* New York: Mariner Books.

Rowan, J. (1989). A late developer. In W. Dryden & L. Spurling (Eds.), *On becoming a psychotherapist* (pp. 148–168). London: Rutledge.

Savickas, M. L. (1997). The spirit in career counseling: Fostering self-completion through work. In D. P. Bloch & L. J. Richmond (Eds.), *Connections between spirit and work in career development: New approaches and practical perspectives* (pp. 3–25). Palo Alto, CA: Davies-Black.

Street, E. (1989). Challenging the "White Knight." In W. Dryden & L. Spurling (Eds.), *On becoming a psychotherapist* (pp. 134–147). London: Rutledge.

Thorne, B. (1989). The blessing and the curse of empathy. In W. Dryden & L. Spurling (Eds.), *On becoming a psychotherapist* (pp. 53–68). London: Rutledge.

Wenger, E. (1998). *Communities of practice: Meaning, and identity.* Cambridge: Cambridge University Press.

Wiebusch, B. (2000, March 6). Creativity report (Brief article). *Design News.* Retrieved February 28, 2003, from http://www.findarticles.com/cf_0/m1068/5_55/59843342/p1/article.jhtml?term=creativity

Whiteside, D. (2002, July). Aim for success with a career action plan. *Healthcare Financial Management,* 70–71.

Zampetti, L. J. (2000, November). Moving up and out. *Information Outlook, 4*(11), 24–29.

Italicized page locators denote figures; italicized *t* denotes a table.